PALAEOLITHIC ART

PAOLO GRAZIOSI

PALAEOLITHIC ART

McGRAW-HILL BOOK COMPANY, INC.

NEW YORK   TORONTO   LONDON

1960

Published in Italy as L'ARTE DELL'ANTICA ETÀ DELLA PIETRA
by Casa Editrice G. C. Sansoni, Florence, 1956.

Printed in Italy
24332

CONTENTS

PART THREE

CAVE ART

FOREWORD

This book is not intended as a treatise, nor does it purport to be a corpus of the artistic achievements of the Old Stone Age — the Palaeolithic. It was written with the intention of presenting the reader with a panoramic view of that prodigious phenomenon which is the birth and development of the most ancient art in the history of man, and of showing him, in one richly illustrated volume, the principal " documents " of that art, both of the so-called mobiliary art (sculptures and engravings on functional objects ; engravings on fragments of bone, ivory and stone ; and statuettes) and of cave art (figures painted, engraved or carved in low relief on the walls of caves and rock shelters).

These two categories have never before been presented together in a single publication exclusively dedicated to European Palaeolithic art and illustrated with such a remarkably complete iconography. Various monographs on single caves have been published, some of them excellent, such as the classic, sumptuous publications of Capitan, Breuil, Peyrony, Alcalde del Rio, Obermaier, Verner and Sierra. Others have been devoted to particular aspects of Palaeolithic art, such as the early monumental collection of splendid reproductions of mobiliary art from a limited group of French deposits by Piette or, more recently, Breuil's magnificent work " Four Hundred Centuries of Cave Art ", fundamental in its particular field, which deals with cave art in its entirety.

Finally we have some textbooks of a general character on Palaeolithic art, of no great calibre if sometimes of considerable interest, and also books covering a wider field such as " Kunst und Kultur der Vorzeit " by H. Kühn, published about thirty years ago and only in part related to European Palaeolithic art.

I have attempted here to maintain the strictest objectivity with regard to the much debated questions of chronology, development and evolution in Palaeolithic art, and to avoid formulating hypotheses or pronouncing categorical opinions where the basis of a conclusive documentation is lacking. I believe it is preferable to accept the inevitable gaps in the evolution of Palaeolithic art rather than be obliged, sooner or later, to reconsider one's previous statements in the light of further research and discovery. Nevertheless the reader will find in this book some of the author's personal viewpoints on certain problems of a general nature concerning the phenomenon of evolution and diffusion in Palaeolithic art, and on more specific matters related to the interpretation of certain works, their chronology, etc.

The subject embraces an extremely long period in the last glacial epoch, extending from the appearance of man's first artistic efforts to the end of the glacial epoch itself — to the time that is, when, due to change of climate and natural habitat, a fundamental transformation occurred in human civilization which passed, after a phase of transition, from the purely hunting stage to agriculture and herding. During the period of transition included in the so-called Mesolithic, coming at the end of the last glacial epoch between the Old Stone Age (Palaeolithic) and the New Stone Age (Neolithic), European man still adhered to his purely hunting culture. Nevertheless, great cultural and ethnic changes were already beginning and strikingly different regional va-

riants appear, showing essential deviations from the Palaeolithic. We shall therefore conclude our survey at the threshold of Mesolithic art. The various artistic expressions of this Mesolithic period show such distinctive characteristics that they can be dealt with as a separate subject, independently from those of the preceding epoch.

It was no easy task to collect the data and iconography relative to the vast documentation on Palaeolithic art that has accumulated after more than a century of discovery and research. Works of mobiliary art, for instance, are to be found in some of the principal European museums; on the other hand, many of them belong to private collectors or to minor local museums and are not always accessible; furthermore, in several cases the stratigraphical data relating to them are uncertain, contradictory or nonexistent. I must therefore claim the indulgence of the reader for such omissions or errors of detail as he may encounter in this work.

Wherever possible I have examined the material at first hand, both in the case of mobiliary art and of cave art, and photographed it myself or had it photographed; in this I have been greatly helped by the good-will and effective assistance of my colleagues, the directors of museums, as well as private collectors and owners of decorated caves.

In this connection I extend the warmest thanks to Prof. Raymond Lantier, curator of the Musée des Antiquités Nationales de Saint-Germain-en-Laye, who opened the cases containing the Museum's precious collections and allowed me to photograph many items, or furnished me with copies of the Museum's photographs.

I also wish to acknowledge the kindness of the Comisarie General de Excavaciones Arqueologicas of Spain, who allowed me to photograph the Cantabrian caves, of Dr. Jesus Carballo, Director of the Prehistoric Museum of Santander, and of Professors Kimmig, Filip and Vogt, Directors respectively of the Museums of Tübingen, Prague and Zürich, as of many other foreign colleagues who generously furnished me with iconographical and bibliographical material, such as Professors M. R. Sauter of Geneva; H. G. Bandi of Berne; Herbert Kühn of Mainz; Lothar Zotz of Erlangen; Professor Garrod and M. C. Burkitt of Cambridge; Professor Boriskovskii of Leningrad; my French colleagues Colonel Louis, Commander Octobon, Messrs. Bétirac, Mandement, Simonnet, Mlle S. de Saint-Mathurin and the brothers Laborie, specialists in prehistoric art photography; my Spanish colleagues Professors Martin Almagro and Luis Pericot of Barcelona and Fletcher-Valls of Valencia. My thanks also go to my Italian colleagues Signora Jole Bovio Marconi, Superintendent of Antiquities in Palermo, to whom I owe the fine photographs of engravings from that city, and Prof. Antonio Radmilli of the Prehistoric Museum in Rome, who disclosed to me the first fruits of his very interesting recent discoveries in Tivoli.

And how can I adequately acknowledge the friendly collaboration of my colleagues Romain Robert, President of the Société Préhistorique de l'Ariège and Georges Malvesin-Fabre of the University of Bordeaux (whose premature death left his scientific work unfinished), both so generous with their help and advice? Many of the photographs published here were taken by me during the long hikes and explorative trips Robert and I undertook in the caves of Ariège and Cantabria, and most of the fine colour reproductions are his work, generously turned over to me. I recall with great pleasure the work I did in the Franco-Cantabrian caves with him, with the late Malvesin-Fabre and my colleague and dear friend R. Nougier of the University of Toulouse. My grateful thanks are also due to the late Maître, Comte Henri Begouen, never to be forgotten friend and teacher, and to his son Louis, who allowed me to examine their collections and made possible my frequent visits to the treasures of the Tuc d'Audoubert and Trois Frères caves. Finally, my heartfelt thanks to my assistant, Dr. Alda Vigliardi Micheli, for the willing and valuable help she gave me with the bibliographical research, the tedious labour of proof-reading and the execution of many of the drawings that illustrate this book.

I trust that the publication of this iconographical collection may be of use to those who, outside the specific field of palaethnology, are interested in other aspects of art: critical, historical, philosophical or creative.

Outside a limited circle of specialists, in fact, the amazing corpus of Palaeolithic art — of which the most significant and important works are shown here — is very little known, or, rather, practically ignored. Extremely vague ideas, approximations, inexactitudes and even errors are frequent with reference to the early expressions of art, and many people are far from suspecting that many thousands of years before the creation of the most ancient sculptures of dynastic Egypt (often described in textbooks and treatises as marking the furthermost limit of man's artistic achievement), an entire world of shapes, rhythms and colours opened up and flowered luxuriantly among the primitive inhabitants of Europe in the glacial epoch.

And yet I believe that through the study and knowledge of the most ancient sculptural and pictorial achievements of the human race, by reaching back to the primeval sources of art, we may penetrate the mysterious essence of this magnificent and deathless expression of the human spirit and understand better its multiform aspects — even though they may sometimes appear disconcerting and enigmatic — throughout the evolution of time. In other words, we may reach the solution to many worrying problems that can only be solved through a unified vision of the artistic phenomenon, particularly if based on concrete knowledge of its earliest origins. Finally, even today — why not? — we may find in the genuine masterpieces of our remote ancestors a source of meditation and inspiration and, as I believe, a new and sincere creative impulse.

And now a few words about this English-language edition. Six plates have been added since the Italian edition was published, and there are some changes in the distribution maps. In fact, in the years since the Italian edition new items of Palaeolithic art have come to light, some of them of exceptional importance, such as the superb cave of Rouffignac in the Dordogne. Although their own findings have not yet been published, René Nougier and Romain Robert, the discoverers of Rouffignac, have allowed me to reproduce four photographs of works in the cave. I sincerely appreciate their generous and liberal spirit of scientific collaboration.

At this point I wish to address the most heartfelt thanks to our great and most eminent teacher Henri Breuil, not only because we are indebted to him for the tracing, study and illustration of practically all the main specimens of Palaeolithic art and the establishment of their chronology and evolution — a debt of gratitude shared by all students of prehistory — but also because in this particular case he allowed me to publish a considerable number of his classic mobiliary and cave-art reproductions. Furthermore, his enlightened advice helped me to correct a few inaccuracies that appeared in the Italian edition, and to fill some gaps.

It would be impossible to tackle the subject of Palaeolithic art without basing one's research upon Breuil's unrivalled achievements in this field; in the study of man's most ancient art one encounters at every step the results of his long years of painstaking and devoted labour. I trust he will excuse me if I have found it impossible to quote him every time I refer to his work in the following pages; the list of acknowledgements to him would be interminable.

PART ONE

INTRODUCTION TO THE STUDY OF PALAEOLITHIC ART

PALAEOLITHIC ART

In the present state of our knowledge of this subject it is no easy matter to write a book on the most ancient art in the history of the human race; the author can hardly hope to complete his task to the entire satisfaction of his readers, particularly if they are at all inclined to be systematic and are moved by a desire for coherence and order, for they will expect an answer to many queries and would like to see the subject developed and resolved according to an organic plan — logically and completely.

Unfortunately, however, the aesthetic world of the stone age which at some moments achieved heights rarely surpassed in subsequent epochs can only be recalled out of the shadows of the past by attempts, frequently unsuccessful, to reconstruct remnants — often fragmentary and indeterminate — salvaged from the implacable demolition of time.

The available works are few, very few, although when assembled in a *corpus* they may appear quite impressive. Separated from the whole of which they were once a part, divided from each other by enormous gaps, by voids in time and in space which are sometimes impossible to fill, they survive as isolated and often uninterpretable pieces in a great mosaic, spread over thousands of years, which gives a striking picture of the birth, development, evolution, final decadence and conclusion of the art of ancient man in Europe.

The efforts of many researchers and scholars, directed for almost a century towards collecting, selecting, comparing and classifying in a chronological sequence the remains of this most ancient art, allow us today to realize some fundamental facts; one of these — a very important one in my opinion — is that art in its earliest known expressions is fully worthy of the name.

Secondly, we have some knowledge today of the more or less definite distribution in time and in space of determinate art forms, and from a general point of view we can follow — if incompletely and disjointedly — the process of transformation that assumes different characteristics according to the location of individual artistic expressions.

This great cycle was completed within a well-defined chronological period, distinguished by particular aspects of human civilization and by a succession of prodigious natural events — climatic, geological and biological — as a result of which the ecology and appearance of our regions were very different then from what they are today.

With the conclusion of this period — the geological era known as Pleistocene — and the end of the Upper Palaeolithic hunting culture there is a temporary ending of the great art phase which, throughout many thousands of years, even though showing variations of form and content, had maintained a fundamentally homogeneous character over a large part of Europe.

This, as we mentioned in the foreword, is the subject of this book; we shall try to reconstruct the " art " phenomenon from its birth to its conclusion within the boundaries we have traced; to follow, as far as possible, its various transformations, and to present its principal " documents ", following a logical sequence and attempting, as we go along, to interpret their significance and their genesis.

NATURAL ENVIRONMENT

First of all, we believe it necessary, for the benefit of those who are not particularly specialized in the field of prehistory, to present a brief, synthetic picture of the environment in which man lived from the moment the earliest art appears until the close of the Palaeolithic era, and of the culture of that very ancient humanity whose somatic characteristics we shall also briefly describe.

Decisive evidence of Man's presence on earth, in the shape of human skeletons and industry (worked stone objects), is met for the first time in the geological era known as Quaternary, in which our planet is at present. Man, one of the latest arrivals in the evolution of animal species, makes his appearance near the beginning of the Quaternary era, in the earliest, or Pleistocene, period, whose duration is estimated in hundreds of thousands of years — somewhere between 500,000 and 1,000,000 according to different authors. The second, or Holocene, period in which we are living today, is still very recent — only a few thousand years old.

THE GLACIATIONS.

The Pleistocene was a time of impressive climatic phenomena during which the climate changed repeatedly from temperate to arctic; these changes are connected with the four great glaciations known as Günz, Mindel, Riss and Würm, separated by three so-called "interglacial" periods. During the glaciations the glaciers of Northern Europe, of the Alps and of other mountain groups pushed outward, covering far more space than they do today, whereas in the intermediate periods they retreated. This was due to the displacement of the "snow-line", or limit reached by permanent snowfields, which was much lower during the periods of glaciation than at the present time; it is estimated that during the Würm glaciation the line descended, in the Alps, about 1100 metres. Evidence of this encroachment is found in obvious traces left by Quaternary glaciers, such as moraine deposits, and in the whole glacial morphology of zones that were intermittently icebound. During the Würm glaciation a blanket of ice over 1000 metres thick covered part of Northern and Central Europe, while small glaciers were formed in the Apennines, in Southern Spain and in the Atlas mountains of North Africa.

The expansion of glaciers in our continent resulted in a complete transformation of the botanical scene, so that tundra prevailed over a large part of Central Europe whereas the boreal conifer forest thrust down into Southern Europe, reaching well into the Italian peninsula. The forests existing today in the Apennines extended down to the sea.

During the interglacial periods, when glaciers retreated to their present limits and even further, the climate improved considerably and became similar to — sometimes even better than — the climate we now enjoy.

The phenomenon of glaciation had other far-reaching effects. The sheet that covered a large part of Europe and, during the Würm glaciation, reached, as we have said, an average thickness of 1000 metres, consisted of an immense mass of water withdrawn from the oceans. Its volume has been estimated at 33,837,000 cubic kilometres, and its retention on land caused a drop of about 90 metres in the level of the oceans and seas. It is obvious, therefore, that during the glaciations the configuration of continents and islands was entirely different from what it is today: for instance, all parts of the sea-bed, at present less than 90 metres below sea level, emerged above the surface during the Würm glaciation.

Fig. 1. Europe, during the maximum advance of the last glaciation (*modified from* DUBOIS, 1930).

As shown in Fig. 1, the Adriatic Sea was considerably reduced in area, the British Isles and the Scandinavian peninsula were joined to the continent, Corsica and Sardinia were united, the Black Sea was much smaller and the Straits of Messina much narrower than they are today.

This " eustatic " phenomenon, as it is called, was reversed during interglacial periods, when the glaciers withdrew within their present limits and the sea level was consequently raised; on the shores of the Mediterranean, for instance, about 20 or 30 metres above sea level there are still some stretches of Pleistocene beach, such as the " Tyrrhenian " beaches of the Riss-Würm interglacial period, containing shells from tropical seas (*Strombus*) that have completely disappeared from the Mediterranean today.

FAUNA.

The repercussions of climatic fluctuation were widely felt in the European zoological field. The " temperate " fauna that lived in Europe during the first part of the Pleistocene epoch, such as the *Machairodus*, a kind of tiger with enormous sabre teeth, the southern elephant (*Elephas meridionalis*), the hippopotamus (*Hippopotamus amphibius*), the " ancient elephant " (*Elephas antiquus*), Merk's rhinoceros (*Rhinoceros Merkii*) (the last three remaining longest in Southern Europe), was succeeded, with the advent of glaciers, by a " cold " fauna that remained until the end of the Pleistocene epoch. This, together with animals described by early palaeontologists as " indifferent to climate ", constitutes the zoological scene in the period during which Palaeolithic man expressed himself in art.

The great pachyderms with long hair or thick fur that lived in the tundra, spreading over the part of Central and Northern Europe that was free from ice, were the Mammoth (*Elephas primigenius*), a hairy elephant with enormous curved tusks that lived as far south as Italy and Northern Spain, and the woolly rhinoceros (*Rhinoceros tichorhinus*). Fossilized remains of mammoths were discovered in enormous quantities all over Europe and especially in Russia and in Siberia, where entire carcasses, complete with soft parts and fur, were found preserved in the frozen earth. These animals became extinct at the end of the Pleistocene epoch, but their image was fixed by Palaeolithic artists on the walls of caves or on objects of mobiliary art, so that it is possible today to study their morphological characteristics independently from the discovery of frozen carcasses.

Fauna of the " cold " species living today in arctic regions emigrated from our countries at the end of the Pleistocene epoch; among these are the reindeer, which overran the plains of France and other European countries in countless herds during the Würm glaciation, leaving fossilized remains as far down as Liguria (Balzi Rossi) and the Carso hills near Trieste (Pocala Cave), the southernmost points of their diffusion that have yet been brought to light.

Another boreal species deserving special mention is the arctic penguin (*Alca impennis*), extinct since the last century, whose remains were found in the deposit of Grotta Romanelli in Apulia and in Gibraltar.

Among the " temperate " animals which became adapted to the glacial climate of the late Palaeolithic period are the cave bear (*Ursus spelaeus*), the cave lion (*Felis spelaea*), the cave hyena (*Hyaena spelaea*), the deer, the horse, a small type of donkey (*Equus asinus hydruntinus*) that lived in great herds on the steppes of Southern Italy, other steppe animals pertaining to more Northern European regions, such as the Saiga antelope, and, finally, animals now living on the summits of European mountains such as the ibex, the chamois, etc.

The animal world of that remote era had a decisive influence on the evolution and development of Palaeolithic art : artists of the Old Stone Age were inspired by animals far more than by human beings. We shall see that the reproduction of the animals upon which man's livelihood depended was an act of hunting magic, whereby Palaeolithic man intended to favour the capture of those species.

ABSOLUTE CHRONOLOGY OF THE PLEISTOCENE.

The occurrence and succession of the natural phenomena — climatic, geological and biological — that were witnessed by prehistoric man embrace a period that seems inordinately long if compared with the historical period, or very short if compared with the combined length of the geological eras preceding the present one.

Absolute chronology is far from definitely established in the entire Pleistocene era. If we compare the evaluation in years of Quaternary periods according to different scholars, it is obvious that in most cases they are in complete disagreement. Nevertheless, in recent times new methods based on geological research and on nuclear physics are obtaining positive results, particularly with regard to the later Quaternary period, and an approximate estimate in years is now possible.

Among such methods we will mention that applied by the Swede de Geer, which consists in counting the number of annual sheets of deposit left, as they retreated, by the Scandinavian glaciers of the latest glaciation. Each one of these thin layers or varves consists of two parts of different nature : one part was formed at the height of the annual thaw, the other at a subsequent period, when finer materials were deposited; together they correspond to one solar year [1]. On the basis of this method a detailed chronology of the last 13,000 years was established for the Scandinavian region, and comparatively sure figures reached for previous periods; thus it is estimated that the maximum of the last expansion of the Würm glaciation occurred 18,000 years ago (W. III, Brandenburg moraines).

---

[1] GEER (DE), 1940.

A still more promising method, which has already produced the most interesting chronological estimates, is that invented by Libby and his colleagues of the Institute for Nuclear Studies in Chicago; it consists in the analysis of radioactive carbon contained in fossil organic remains [1]. It is based on the fact that living beings contain, besides normal carbon of atomic weight 12, a radioactive carbon of atomic weight 14 that disintegrates after the death of living matter at a rate determined by the well-known law of radioactive decomposition. Thus by analysing the C14 of organic animal or vegetable remains found in a deposit one can estimate its age and, therefore, by implication, the age of the objects found within the same layer. So far it has not been possible to calculate beyond a 50,000 year limit, because in that length of time radioactive carbon is reduced to a quantity that is not practically measurable.

As regards the Palaeolithic era, it seems that the Perigordian IV of Les Eyzies dates back to 24,000 years ago [2], the Holstein Magdalenian near Hamburg to 15,000 [3]; as yet, however, very few estimates have been attempted in the Palaeolithic field.

Some methods have also been proposed for estimating the absolute age of prehistoric times in their entirety. A system for establishing the chronology of the Pleistocene epoch, much favoured some time ago, was created by Milankovitch on an astronomical basis. He calculated the different degree of annual distribution of sun rays to which the earth was exposed during the Quaternary period. The varying intensity of solar radiation on our planet is due to fluctuations in the movement of the earth itself, causing a variation of the inclination of the terrestrial axis on the ecliptic (over a period of about 40,000 years), a variation of the precession of equinoxes (21,000 years), a variation of the eccentricity of the orbit (92,000 years) [4]. On such a basis a correlation can be established between the moments of minimum insolation and the glaciations. One of the suggested chronologies places the Günz glaciation at 600-550,000 years ago, the Mindel glaciation between 480 and 380, Riss between 240 and 180; the latest, or Würm, glaciation would have started 120,000 years ago. Milankovitch's system was much criticized and the chronological validity of this curve of solar radiation considered doubtful; recently, however, Brouwer and van Woerkom's new calculations have largely confirmed the theories of the Serbian scholar [5].

Finally, the chronological estimates of the last part of the Quaternary epoch appear susceptible of greater precision, particularly through the study of varves, but especially on the basis of the discoveries in the field of radioactive carbon that really appear to open new horizons to the absolute chronology of the prehistoric ages. This method, and the preceding one, are by and large confirmed by astronomical calculations.

The period that we are interested in — the Upper Palaeolithic — during which the human race first revealed its artistic gifts and which brought with its close the end of that great art, would therefore be situated, more or less, between 28,000 and 12,000 years ago.

---

[1] LIBBY, 1955.
[2] RUBIN, SUESS, 1955, p. 487.
[3] *Ibidem.*
[4] MILANKOVITCH, 1938.
[5] WOERKOM (VAN), 1953.

HUMAN TYPES AND UPPER PALAEOLITHIC CULTURES

During the entire Pleistocene epoch man lived exclusively on game and on the natural fruits of the earth, fashioned weapons and implements out of stone, bone, antler and, no doubt, wood, and knew nothing of either agriculture or herding. This, the Old Stone Age, is called " Palaeolithic ". It was followed by a period of transition known as " Mesolithic " or Middle Stone Age, situated in the Holocene epoch, during which man's economy was largely based on hunting. We then enter the " Neolithic ", or New Stone Age, (or " Polished Stone Age " as it was once called), which opens with a radical change in human economy based — although hunting was still practised — upon two new activities : agriculture and herding. New handicrafts also appear, such as the fashioning of fireproof pottery, weaving, stone polishing, etc.

We finally come to the age of metal, during which civilization assumed varied aspects according to its location, and increasingly complex forms of life made their appearance. Having left the cave that had been his dwelling throughout the Palaeolithic, man turned, in the Neolithic, to building hut-villages on dry land and also on stilts in swamps and lakes.

At the beginning of the Holocene — the Mesolithic — period, the climate assumed its present characteristics and consequently the flora and fauna became such as they are today. The great wild animals that had prevailed during the ice age emigrated northward or became extinct.

According to most authors the Palaeolithic is divided into three successive periods : Lower, Middle and Upper; some, however, merely divide it into Lower and Upper. The Upper Palaeolithic, situated in the second part of the Würm glaciation, is the one we are particularly interested in, because at the beginning of this period the earliest known artistic expressions appear, as well as human types whose somatic traits show a degree of evolution comparable with that of the human race today.

Prior to the Upper Palaeolithic the human form in Europe was distinguished by extremely primitive features, such as those of Neanderthal man in the Middle Palaeolithic. However, some European deposits of the Lower Palaeolithic yielded small quantities of human remains which, in some respects, anticipate the *sapiens* type and therefore belong to a strain other than that of Neanderthal.

HUMAN TYPES.

With the advent of the Upper Palaeolithic the European anthropological scene undergoes a definite change; from the beginning of that period all traces of the primitive Neanderthal stock, which had lived in Europe for many thousands of years and spread in Africa and Asia, disappear completely. We do not intend here to delve into the intrinsic or extrinsic causes

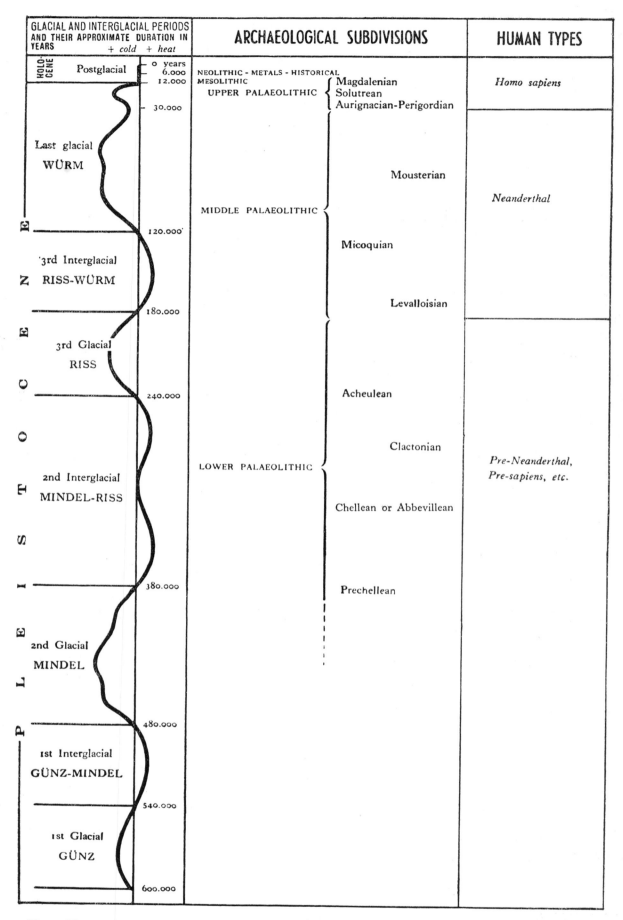

Fig. 2. The succession of human industries and their probable correlation with glacial and interglacial periods.

The vertical straight line in the centre of the left hand column represents the climate and limits of present-day glaciers, the curved line shows the alternation of glacial and interglacial periods. Beside them are the approximate ages, in years, deduced from Milankovitch's curve of solar radiation and de Geer's chronology of " varves ". The succession of Prehistoric cultures is indicated in parallel columns. This table of the Quaternary period shows the natural, archaeological and human phenomena in relation to the total chronology. It gives some idea of the enormous duration of the Lower and Middle Palaeolithic compared with the Upper Palaeolithic, at the beginning of which the first expressions of art appear.

of its disappearance; the fact is that from the inception of the Upper Palaeolithic human types appear whose characteristics place them in the same category as the races peopling the earth today : the *sapiens* type, or " Faneranthropus " as Sergi calls it, replaces the ancient " Palaeanthropus " (Neanderthal), and the even more ancient " Protoanthropus ".

This new man, with highly evolved somatic characteristics, appears in Europe already subdivided into different races, some of which may in certain respects be considered the prototypes of specific present-day groups.

The *Cro-Magnon* type, very tall and athletic, which is found in its most typical form in the Dordogne deposit of the same name and in the famous Balzi Rossi and Grimaldi caves in Liguria, appears in Aurignacian layers and continues through successive periods.

The *Combe-Capelle* type, regarded by some as proto-Mediterranean, is a small man; a single specimen was found in France, but it shows considerable affinity with the fossil specimens discovered in Moravia.

The *Grimaldi* type, of which only two specimens were found in the more ancient Upper Palaeolithic layers of the Fanciulli cave or " Grotte des Enfants " at Balzi Rossi (Liguria) shows possible negroid characteristics.

The *Chancelade* man, found in the Magdalenian layers of the deposit of the same name in the Dordogne, was believed at one time to be proto-Eskimo; later, however, this attribution was denied.

Other human types, with characteristics more or less related to one or another of the forms mentioned above, were found in various European locations. Some individuals of the Mediterranean type were discovered in the Upper Palaeolithic layers of the S. Teodoro cave in Sicily.

The ethnical panorama, as one can see, is already very complex and not always clearly defined from a chronological point of view, in the sense of a selection of types through the succession of various periods of the Upper Palaeolithic; it is therefore evident that different races coexisted during that period in Europe. So far it is obviously impossible to establish an exclusive connection between any particular form of culture and a specific human type.

In any case, it is undeniable that art in Europe appeared with *Homo sapiens*, whereas Palaeanthropus immediately preceding him left not the slightest trace of any form of art whatsoever.

* * *

Human artifacts, the so-called " industries " of weapons and stone implements produced in the Lower and Middle Palaeolithic, are technically quite simple and limited to a small number of types: implements obtained from pebbles flaked on all sides, usually oval (" coups-de-poing "), or from flakes of various dimensions chipped into shape. The former are typical of the Lower Palaeolithic, whereas objects fashioned from flakes are overwhelmingly predominant in the Middle Palaeolithic.

The industries of the Upper Palaeolithic, the period which interests us particularly, are fundamentally represented by tools fashioned in the so-called " blade " technique, in which a core of flint is struck into thin blades which are then worked into various shapes. With this technique — which is very different from the preceding ones — the men of the Upper Palaeolithic produced many different kinds of implements : these differentiations identify the various subdivisions of the period.

During this period, moreover, bone and antler implements that did not previously exist in a well-defined form, became increasingly elaborate.

INDUSTRIES.

The subdivisions of the Palaeolithic, established on the basis of the various forms of human industry, derive their names from localities in which such industries were found for the first time or in their most characteristic form.

Not only does each of these periods possess individual typological elements, but various kinds of artifact appear in different proportions from those of other periods; thus a particular industrial " atmosphere " prevails in each phase, arising from the combination of separate factors.

We should not expect the succession of Palaeolithic cultures to appear always and everywhere in a clear, definite and regular form; some of them are contemporary — that is, they

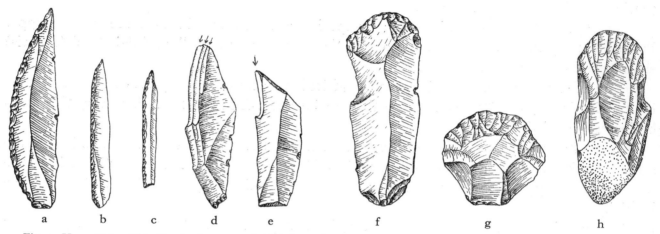

Fig. 3. Upper Palaeolithic flint implements : a)-c) blades with worked edges (" Châtelperron " and " La Gravette " type); d)-e) gravers; f)-h) scrapers on the end of a blade or " tarté ". (Actual size).

develop simultaneously even in relatively restricted areas. In some localities a single *facies* prevails for a long period, although replaced by later forms elsewhere. Passing, for instance, from France to Italy, we observe that, as far as our present knowledge goes, there is nothing comparable with the Solutrean and Magdalenian cultures; in Italy during the entire Upper Palaeolithic period, industries do not resemble those in France.

All this makes it rather difficult, and in some cases quite impossible, to establish a unified chronology for the various human industries as well as for the various phases of Palaeolithic art considered in the light of their geographical distribution. The subdivisions established in France, of which we give a diagram, apply also, in their more typical aspects, to large portions of Northern and Eastern Spain, parts of Switzerland, Germany and other neighbouring countries; but the further we move from this focal centre the more variations appear in this classic pattern.

Nevertheless we may give a brief description of the fundamental features of the various periods of the Upper Palaeolithic according to the accepted French classification. The *Aurignacian* [1]) was once divided into Lower, Middle and Upper. Following the identification by Peyrony of a " Perigordian " *facies* which he considered to have developed simultaneously with the Aurignacian, the latter term was restricted to its most characteristic phase — Middle, or Typical Aurignacian — while the Lower and the Upper were identified as different stages of the Perigordian. In other words, it is suggested that in some localities two cultures with different characteristics, the Aurignacian and the Perigordian, existed at the same time.

The Typical *Aurignacian* culture is distinguished by artifacts called burins, small stone implements, with a very strong point, used for carving hard materials such as ivory and stone;

---

[1]) From the deposit of Aurignac, Haute-Garonne.

by keeled scrapers; by simple blades and by a particular bone instrument, the "Aurignac" point, a flattened point of oval shape with split base (Figs. 3, 4).

The Lower *Perigordian* is particularly distinguished by flint blades with one retouched edge curved toward the extremity, known as "Châtelperronian" blades; the Middle Perigordian by the same blades in a more elaborate form, by truncated blades, etc.; the Upper Perigordian by points and blades with a retouched edge, called "Gravettian", and by stemmed points known as "Font Robert" points, after the site of that name (Fig. 3).

The *Solutrean* culture represents a sort of typological intrusion, or superimposition, in the evolution of French blade industries of the Upper Palaeolithic, and is characterized by flint points of a regular oval shape called "laurel leaves", carefully retouched on one side in the Lower, on both sides in the Middle Solutrean period, and by single-shouldered points ("à cran") in the Upper Solutrean (Fig. 5).

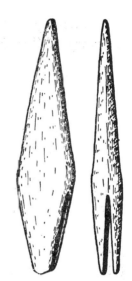

Fig. 4. Bone implements, Upper Palaeolithic: split-base point, Typical Aurignacian (actual size).

Besides an abundance of flint implements — large and small blades, burins called "parrotbeaks" ("becs de perroquet"), microlithic implements, etc. — the Magdalenian culture witnessed the great development of bone and antler working upon which the many subdivisions of this period are particularly based. In the Lower Magdalenian — Breuil's Magdalenian I, II, III [1]), also referred to as Early Magdalenian — we have bone and antler spearheads (which already appeared in the preceding period), plain with a single, or sometimes with a double bevelled base. The Upper Magdalenian or Late Magdalenian, divided into Magdalenian IV, V and VI, produced, in its first period (Magdalenian IV) bone harpoons with rudimentary, faint indentations; then, in Magdalenian V, single barbed harpoons, followed by double barbed harpoons in Magdalenian VI.

Other bone instruments, very interesting also from an artistic point of view because they are often beautifully decorated with sculptures in the round, bas-reliefs and engravings, are the spear-throwers, fashioned out of reindeer antlers; they are shaped like sticks with a hook at one end; some have a groove along their entire length. These were weapons used to extend the range of throwing spears or darts; they exist in a more or less identical form among primitive peoples of the present day. The pierced stick, or "bâton de commandement" as the early palaethnologists called it, is also fashioned from the antler of a reindeer, or, less frequently, of a deer; it is pierced at one end at a fork of the antler itself, and its use is somewhat mysterious: many contradictory explanations have been put forward; it has been called an arrow straightener, a buckle, and an instrument for tightening knots. In the past it was believed to be the sceptre of a tribal chief, and even part of a horse's bit; this last interpretation is completely fanciful, since it is certainly known that no animals were domesticated in the Palaeolithic era.

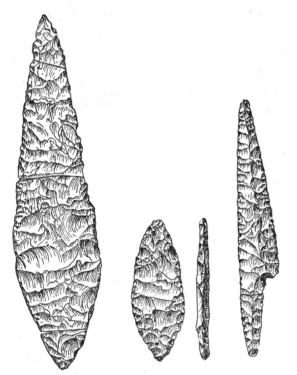

Fig. 5. Flint implements, Upper Palaeolithic: "laurel leaves" and "à cran" points, Solutrean (from CHEYNIER, 1949, pp. 65, 68, 75).

We shall see later that the artifacts described above, when they are skilfully decorated, should by

[1]) BREUIL, 1937a.

and large be considered ritual objects, and therefore non-functional, because the delicate workmanship would soon have deteriorated if the weapon had actually been put to use.

* * *

These palaethnological and palaeoanthropological documents, together with the entire category of " mobiliary art ", so called because it consists of portable items, were preserved in a particular environment — that of the deposits which accumulated inside caves or in the open country outside them. These are the two fundamental types of deposit formed throughout thousands of years as a consequence of various natural accidents.

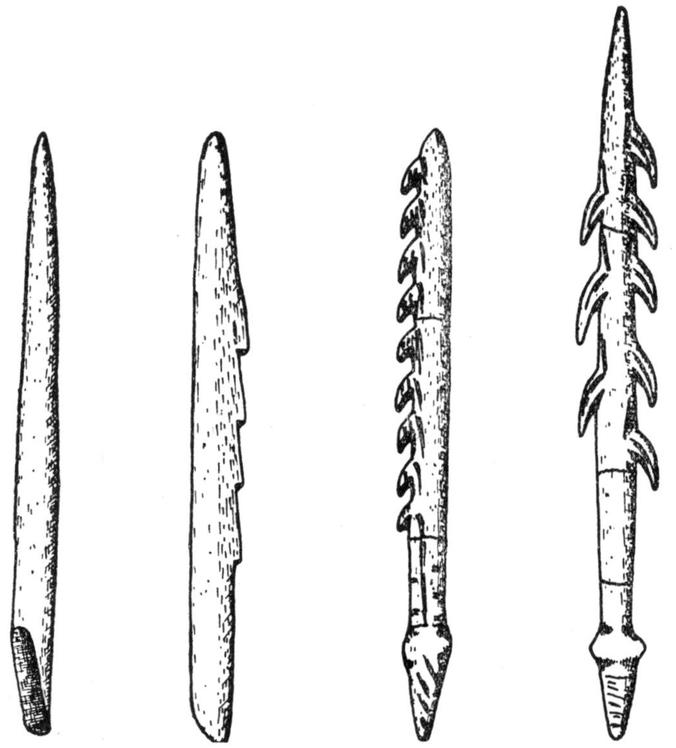

The formation of deposits in caves, which contain human artifacts and palaeontological remains, may have occurred in one of several ways : through the disintegration of the ceiling and walls of the cave itself, the accumulation of dust blown in from outside or ashes and charcoal from fires lit by the inhabitants, and above all through the formation of slope deposit at the entrance.

The layers outside are formed by alluvial deposits due to the fluctuation of rivers, to lake deposits, etc., and may also contain human artifacts and skeletal remains of the men who dwelt on these sites.

It is obvious, however, that the deposits in the caves or at their entrances are of greater interest to the palaethnologist, because they were formed in the protective environment of the caves by a regular, undisturbed accumulation of material. The excavation of these deposits may bring to light a perfect sequence of layers making it possible to establish an analogous chronology for the documents they contain.

Fig. 6. Bone implements, Upper Palaeolithic: a) spearhead; b) harpoon with rudimentary barbs, Magdalenian IV; c) single barbed harpoon, Magdalenian V; d) double barbed harpoon, Magdalenian VI.

Fig. 7. Action of the Australian spear-thrower (from BROUGH SMYTH, 1878, fig. 94).

The majority of mobiliary objects were taken from deposits in caves : small sculptures in the round, engravings on pebbles and on bone, implements fashioned out of reindeer antler and admirably decorated with carvings and engravings. And it is the direct relation, unfortunately quite rare, between these deposits and cave-wall pictures that has made possible the establishment of a relatively reliable chronology for the latter form of art.

THE DISCOVERY OF PALAEOLITHIC ART

The history of discovery in the field of Palaeolithic art covers almost a century, starting with the first really important discoveries made by Edouard Lartet in the Ariège district, and later, together with Christy, in the Vézère valley in the Dordogne, between 1860 and 1865. Previously, however — around 1840 — a bone engraved with figures of deer (Pl. 71, *c*) was picked up by Brouillet, a notary, in the Chaffaud cave near Savigné (Vienne); it was thought to be the work of ancient Celts, and in 1851 was given to the Cluny Museum. In 1887 it was passed on to the Museum of Saint-Germain-en-Laye near Paris. At about the same time as the Chaffaud discovery, a " bâton de commandement " engraved with an ibex and a leafy twig was found by Taillefer and Mayor in the cave of Le Veyrier at Salève in Savoy on the Swiss border (Pl. 91, *b*).

Lartet's discoveries date from 1860; shortly afterwards they were followed by other discoveries that led to the collection of the first important group of works of mobiliary art. In that year Lartet found a fragment of a " bâton de commandement ", fashioned from the antler of a deer and engraved with the figure of a bear, in the Massat cave in Ariège (Pl. 64, *c*), and continued his research in the Vézère valley. A little later Viscount de Lastic-Saint-Jal excavated the Bruniquel cave (Tarn-et-Garonne) and found several pieces of mobiliary art which he sold in the following year to the British Museum. Between 1866 and 1867 Peccadeau de l'Isle found, in the same cave, two of the most famous Magdalenian sculptures : the mammoth fashioned out of reindeer antler and the two reindeer following each other, in ivory (Pl. 34, *a*). These pieces, together with Peccadeau de l'Isle's entire Palaeolithic collection, were turned over to the British Museum in 1887.

That was indeed a fruitful period in the discovery of mobiliary art which enriched many French Museums and built up the core of the great Quaternary art collections of the Musée des Antiquités Nationales de Saint-Germain, inaugurated in 1867. We may mention some of the most interesting discoveries of this period : those made by Lartet together with the English archaeologist Christy in the cave of Les Eyzies and in other caves of the Vézère valley in the Dordogne; by the Marquis de Vibraye in Laugerie-Basse, also in the Vézère valley (1863), and by Elie Massenat in the same cave (1867). And so the importance of the Vézère valley as the centre of ancient Stone Age civilization became a recognized fact.

These amazing discoveries were received with a certain amount of scepticism, with regard to their antiquity. But the discovery of a fragment of mammoth tusk engraved with the figure of a mammoth, made by Lartet in 1864 in the cave of La Madeleine (Vézère) in a layer of the " reindeer age ", furnished what was considered conclusive evidence of the existence of Palaeolithic art, based on two fundamental facts : first of all, the engraving had clear-cut margins, such as would be produced by carving a tusk that was fresh, and not jagged as they would have been had the figure been engraved on fossilized ivory; this proved that the engraving was contemporary with the Pleistocene pachyderm itself. In the second place, the engraving portrayed an animal which is typical of the glacial era, proving that the artist had direct knowledge of the species.

Discoveries in the field of mobiliary art multiplied not only in the Dordogne but in other regions of France as well, particularly in the Pyrenees; further works of great interest were brought to light at Massat, at Mas d'Azil, at Lourdes, at Lorthet, etc., and even outside Europe. One of the finest works of Magdalenian art — a grazing reindeer engraved on a " bâton de commandement " — was discovered in 1874 in Switzerland, at Kesslerloch near Thayngen; in 1876 a horse of a distinctly Magdalenian type, engraved on bone, was found at Creswell Crags in England; in 1885 Jullien extracted from the Barma Grande cave at Balzi Rossi near Ventimiglia the first Palaeolithic anthropomorphic statuettes; other discoveries followed, in Germany and in Eastern Europe.

Edouard Piette's discoveries in the Pyrenees were exceptionally important. His excavations, started in 1871 at Gourdan, brought to light, during a long period of hard work (until 1897), admirable works of mobiliary art executed in sculpture in the round, engraving, low relief, on stone, bone and ivory, found in the caves of Lorthet, Arudy, Mas d'Azil and, finally, Brassempouy in the Department of Les Landes.

Although Piette's chronology of Quaternary art is absolutely unreliable because it is based upon incorrect stratigraphical interpretations, his work as an excavator was not wasted, for it produced the elements of an exceptionally interesting collection of Palaeolithic art objects, which, in their specific field, even today constitute the fundamental core of the Saint-Germain Museum.

Up to this time, that is to say until the closing years of the last century, discoveries in the field of Palaeolithic art were limited to mobiliary items and therefore revealed only a few aspects of the extraordinary talents possessed by the artists of the Old Stone Age; no specimens of painting and sculpture on cave walls in which their artistic faculties appear in all their beauty, had yet been brought to light, nor was there any indication that one day a series of prodigious masterpieces would spring forth from the shadowy depths of the French and Spanish caverns.

An unexpected event occurred one day in the summer of 1879. In that year a Spanish nobleman of Santander in Cantabria, Marcelino de Sautuola, was led by his twelve-year-old daughter to the discovery of the beautiful paintings in the Altamira cave; despite universal scepticism, he was the first to affirm their authenticity and great antiquity, but it took more than fifteen years for the exceptional importance of his great discovery to be accepted and acknowledged.

The circumstances that surrounded the finding of the Altamira paintings have been related in many treatises and textbooks on prehistory; nevertheless we shall repeat them briefly here, for they concern an important event in the history of great discoveries, whose purely historical connotations should not be overlooked.

About ten years prior to the discovery a sportsman, while searching the thickets on the gentle slopes on which Santillana del Mar is built, noticed that his dog, who was pursuing a fox, had disappeared among the bushes, and that the sound of its barking seemed to be coming from a great way away. He immediately realized that the animal had crawled into a hole in the earth, and searched the scrub until he found a narrow opening. That was how the Altamira cave was discovered. It is a very large cave, burrowing for hundreds of metres into the bowels of the hill. Seventy years later a dog once more touched off a discovery of the same kind — equally sensational : the Lascaux cave in France.

Nothing of particular interest was found at the time in the Altamira cave, and it was forgotten until six years later when Marcelino de Sautuola, who used to spend the summer months on his property near Altamira, was told by a labourer of the discovery of the cave;

he decided to excavate the deposits that had accumulated in several parts of it as he was interested in prehistory.

His research continued intermittently for four years, and finally one day in the summer of 1879, while rummaging in the blackish earth of a large trench the sensational discovery was made. On that day, as on many others, de Sautuola had taken his little daughter Maria with him; suddenly the child, who had wandered off into the cave to where light filtered in, raised her eyes to the ceiling and exclaimed : " Papá, mira toros pintados! " Her father rushed in, shone his lamp to where the child was pointing and in the uncertain glimmer saw the outline of a great bison, vigorously painted on the uneven rock surface; then he saw another, and yet another, all painted in vivid colour, fresh and clear as though they had been finished that very day.

After initial doubts de Sautuola recognized that the painted figures represented animals that had long been extinct in those regions, but had lived there in the remote ages which were the object of his studies and research in the same cave; they also showed analogies in style with the small sculptures fashioned out of reindeer antler and engravings on fragments of bone or stone that the Palaeolithic caves of France were yielding in increasing numbers. Furthermore, who could have executed those great paintings, requiring such hard work as well as exceptional skill and artistry, when the cave, until a few years before, was inaccessible to man and completely unknown to the local population? De Sautuola's conviction that the Altamira paintings were the work of Palaeolithic troglodytes was quite unshakable, and Villanova, another Spanish scholar, to whom Don Marcelino appealed for advice and collaboration, was equally certain. In 1880 de Sautuola published a monograph describing the discovery of the paintings and establishing their origin and age.

Truth often encounters apparently insurmountable obstacles before it is universally recognized as such; after a short period of intense interest in the cave, during which the King of Spain himself visited it, the Altamira paintings gave rise to widespread scepticism, de Sautuola's affirmations were refuted by " official " prehistorians as fantastic, and even the authenticity of his discovery was uncompromisingly denied.

Fifteen years of bitterness and disappointment followed for de Sautuola, during which he never tired of reaffirming vigorously what he believed to be the truth. But finally his faith and his scholarship met with complete, well deserved recognition.

In 1895 a French prehistorian, Emile Rivière, decided to visit Altamira personally and examine the paintings. He studied the walls and the deposits and was amazed and perplexed. He returned to France, engaged in a thorough examination of the walls of the deep, dark caverns of his own region — the Dordogne — and that same year, following indications furnished by the brothers Berthoumeyron, discovered the paintings and the engravings of La Mouthe cave which had been sealed, until then, by a large deposit, guaranteeing the authenticity of the pictures it contained. Further doubts and scepticism followed but at last the discoveries made shortly thereafter by Capitan, Breuil and Peyrony of caves decorated with engravings and paintings in Les Combarelles and Font-de-Gaume in the Dordogne, and the visit made in 1902 to those caves and to the cave of La Mouthe by the members of the Congress of the " Association Française pour l'Avancement des Sciences ", brought these scientific debates to an end.

It was the triumph of de Sautuola's ideas, but unfortunately he was not able to enjoy it because he had died a few years earlier. Here, at last, was irrefutable proof of the authenticity and Palaeolithic age of the Altamira paintings. Science was beginning to blaze a trail in the direction of a hitherto completely unknown branch of the most ancient art in the history of the human race.

From this moment discoveries in the field of cave art increased steadily. Everywhere in South-west France, and later in Spain, walls and ceilings of caverns were examined and new figures brought to light. After the engravings of La Mouthe, those of the Pair-non-Pair cave were discovered in 1896, as a natural consequence of the preceding discovery, by Daleau who, ever since 1883, had known of them without realizing their importance; it was only following the La Mouthe findings that he realized their value — which was magnified by the fact that those particular engravings were partly covered by *in situ* Palaeolithic deposits.

In 1901, as we have seen already, Capitan, Breuil and Peyrony discovered the engravings of Les Combarelles and the paintings and engravings of Font-de-Gaume, two of the most important monuments of Palaeolithic art, located at a short distance from each other in the Vézère territory. The next year Breuil discovered the engravings of Mas d'Azil in Ariège, and together with Cartailhac examined the paintings at Altamira. In 1903 Peyrony discovered the engravings on the walls of the Bernifal and La Calévie caves, also in the Vézère valley, and finally the first painted caves — after Altamira — were found in Spain : Alcalde del Rio discovered the cave of Hornos de la Peña and of Castillo, and, together with P. Sierra, those of Covalanas and of La Haza; P. Sierra discovered the Salitré paintings. All these caves are located in Cantabria.

The discoveries followed each other closely in France and in Spain; in Italy, too, the first Palaeolithic engravings came to light in 1905, found by P. E. Stasi and Ettore Regalia in the Romanelli cave near Otranto.

The names of some eminent French and Spanish scholars are connected, from this moment on, with the most important Palaeolithic art discoveries and studies; L. Capitan, H. Breuil, D. Peyrony, H. Obermaier, Comte Begouen, Alcalde del Rio, J. Cabré — just to mention a few of the principal ones. Among the most sensational discoveries were the splendid paintings of the Niaux and Portel caves in Ariège, found, respectively, by Mollard in 1906 and by R. Jeannel in 1908; the bison modelled in clay of Tuc d'Audoubert; the engravings found in 1912 in the Trois Frères cave (Ariège) by Comte Begouen and his sons; the headless bear and other clay figures of the Montespan cave (1923) discovered by N. Casteret and F. Trombe; the magnificent frieze of horses of Cap Blanc (Vézère) discovered by Lalanne in 1909, and later, the same Lalanne's discovery of bas-reliefs representing female figures in the Laussel rock shelter. Also in the field of bas-relief is the beautiful frieze of bison, horses and musk-ox found by Henri Martin in Roc de Sers (Charente) in 1927, and the frieze of animals and female figures of Angles-sur-Anglin discovered by Miss Garrod, Mlle Martin and Mlle Saint-Mathurin since 1948. But the most spectacular findings of these past few years are certainly the magnificent paintings and engravings in the Lascaux cave in the Dordogne, discovered in 1940 by some boys from Montignac-sur-Vézère, and the paintings and engravings in the Rouffignac cave (Dordogne) found by Nougier and Robert in 1956. Finally, we recall the first Italian Palaeolithic engravings of a strictly naturalistic order found in 1950 in a cave on the island of Levanzo (Egadi) by the author, together with A. Micheli and F. Minellono and followed, a couple of years later, by G. Meli's discovery of the engravings of Monte Pellegrino near Palermo.

At the same time as cave figures were being discovered, Palaeolithic deposits in France, Spain, Germany, Austria, Czechoslovakia, Russia and Italy were yielding countless pieces of mobiliary art : small sculptures on bone, stone and ivory; engravings, etc. The French caves contributed the largest number; for instance, the Isturitz cave (Basses-Pyrénées), excavated by Passemard and Saint-Périer between 1913 and 1936, produced large quantities of sculptures and engravings on bone, stone and even amber.

While it was not too difficult to establish the chronology of objects of mobiliary art (particularly if their stratigraphy had been ascertained and correctly interpreted) the same cannot be said of examples of cave art that usually lacked the stratigraphical data required for this purpose. As we shall see later, cave-wall figures are rarely found covered by deposits *in situ*, which would make it possible to date them on the basis of their relation to culturally and chronologically defined horizons. Therefore all attempts to establish a chronological and evolutional system for cave art were based, by and large, upon an examination of the superimposition of figures and a determination of other elements, such as affinity and progression in style, technique, etc., all of which unavoidably reflect the personal bias of the observer.

The early years of this century witnessed the birth of a new phase in the study of cave art; the creation by the Abbé Breuil of the outline of the evolution of paintings and engravings in the French and Spanish caves. He dedicated many years to this branch of research, working on actual material in the dark depths of many caves. The number of tracings he has made is prodigious : practically all the Palaeolithic caves of France and Spain were closely studied by this great French prehistorian, and countless works of art were traced and published by him.

Breuil presented the Congrès d'Anthropologie et d'Archéologie Préhistorique, held in Monaco in 1906, with the first outline of the evolution of cave art [1]); other, more perfected and complex outlines followed in 1912 [2]) and at the Congrès Préhistorique de France in 1934 [3]). These outlines constituted the basis of cave-art research.

Breuil classified the paintings and engravings of French and Spanish caves in two great cycles : Aurignacian-Perigordian and Solutrean-Magdalenian. Here, in brief, are the principal characteristics of each cycle : *Aurignacian-Perigordian* — The earliest artistic expressions in painting consist of stencils of hands in red or in black, meander paintings with the finger in red or in yellow that may develop into rudimentary figures, and " club-signs ", such as those of the Santian cave in Cantabria and of other Spanish caves. As to engravings, meanders were traced on clay, at first with the fingers and later with toothed instruments. Later still we have line drawings, then figures sketched in thick outline, sometimes dotted like the ones in the La Pasiega and Covalanas caves in Spain and the more ancient ones in Altamira and Castillo. Figures in monochrome silhouette then make their appearance, as in Altamira, La Pasiega, Portel, Lascaux, etc. Bichromatic figures are contemporary with these; there are a large number of both categories in the Lascaux cave in the Dordogne. Engravings derive from the meandering-line figures, and already tend to naturalism, although the legs of the animals are nonexistent or rigid, and the horns usually viewed from the front. Later these figures evolve : at first the engraving is light, but it becomes progressively deeper until it resembles low relief (Labatut, Laussel). *Solutrean-Magdalenian* — There are no certainly Solutrean paintings. During the earliest Magdalenian period we have a return to black line drawing, highly simplified. This is followed by drawings in thick black smudgy lines, then by flat black wash and finally — presumably with the advent of Magdalenian IV — well-designed figures appear in the Pyrenees, outlined in black and shaded with closely repeated lines. Following these are black figures modelled in chiaroscuro, and others, in a fine style, painted brown; finally we have the polychrome figures of Altamira, Font-de-Gaume, Bédeilhac, etc. Simultaneously with the progress of painting, increasingly skilful figures were produced in engraving and low relief; the twisted perspective of the first cycle disappears completely. The beautiful, delicate engravings of the Les Trois Frères cave belong to Magdalenian IV.

---

[1]) BREUIL, 1906b.
[2]) BREUIL, 1912.
[3]) BREUIL, 1934.

GEOGRAPHICAL DISTRIBUTION, APPEARANCE, DEVELOPMENT AND AESTHETICS OF PALAEOLITHIC ART

AREAS OF DISTRIBUTION.

Documents of Palaeolithic art are distributed over a vast area in Europe, but outside the boundaries of the continent they are represented by a few poor specimens in North Africa (Capsian engravings) and in Siberia (anthropomorphic statuettes of Maltà). A glance at the chart showing their distribution clearly proves that the focal centre of this art is located in France and in Cantabria. Although possibly this perspective may, at some future time, be found partially incorrect because it is in those countries that the most intensive research has been carried out, it is obvious that even in other parts of Europe — such as Germany where research in the Palaeolithic field is and has been considerable — works of art are fewer in number and inferior in quality to those in the French and Cantabrian regions.

While the distribution of objects of mobiliary art, found in exceptional quantities in France, extends in an easterly direction, deep into Russia (where anthropomorphic statuettes were found) and to England in the North, cave art is circumscribed within narrower boundaries, reaching to the Rhone valley in the East and to the southern districts of the Spanish peninsula and of Italy in the South [1]).

In France, the deposits that yielded the most important mobiliary art are mainly concentrated in the Dordogne and in the Pyrenees, including the entire zone south of the Garonne.

Outside France discoveries in the field of mobiliary art are fewer and less important. Towards the East there are some in Switzerland — such as the specimens of Schweizersbild and of Kesslerloch; in Belgium (Sy-Verlaine, Juzaine, Furfooz, Marche-les-Dames, etc.) and in Germany (Oberkassel, Balver, Klause, Vogelherd, Petersfels, Andernach, Hohlenstein, etc., and the far more northerly ones of Ahrensburg near Hamburg). Then we have the documents of Willendorf in Austria, of Pörgelberghöle in Hungary, and the Czech ones of Dolní Věstonice, Paulov, Předmostí, Brno and Pekarna.

After crossing a vast area in which nothing at all comes to light we reach Russia where curious geometrical figures were discovered in Mézine near Kiev, and naturalistic animal and female statuettes in the Don region (Gagarino, Kostienki) and at Jelisejeviči near Brjansk and elsewhere; finally, outside Europe, beyond the Ural mountains, we have the discoveries of Maltà on Lake Baikal. The northernmost European discoveries — apart from the above-

---

[1]) At Migrimeni on the river Kvirila near Ciaturi (Eastern Georgia) Zamiatnin found, in 1934, some more or les straight lines, occasionally intersecting each other, engraved without order on the surface of a rock shelter and covered by stalagmitic concretions incorporating Palaeolithic artifacts. It is impossible to attribute any figurative purpose whatsoever to these few scratches, even if they are of human origin. They are the only Palaeolithic graphic expressions found, up to the present, outside Europe, but by no stretch of the imagination can they be considered expressions of art.

mentioned ones near Hamburg — are from Central England, at Creswell Crags in Derby-shire, and elsewhere.

Specimens of Palaeolithic mobiliary art are also found in the South, although here, up to the present, they are widely spaced. The Spanish ones all come from a few localities in Cantabria such as El Pendo, El Rascaño, El Valle, and in Valencia, such as the Parpallò cave which contained countless engraved figures, and Tarragona (S. Gregori).

In Italy a group of anthropomorphic statuettes was discovered in Balzi Rossi near Ven-timiglia, and some geometrical figures engraved on bone and on stone in the same caves and in the Arene Candide cave near Finale Ligure. Female statuettes in Palaeolithic style, whose true chronology, however, is somewhat uncertain, were found in Emilia — in Savi-gnano on the Panaro (Modena) and in Chiozza (Reggio Emilia) — and in Tuscany on Lake Trasimeno. There are also the recent discoveries in Tivoli of naturalistic and geometrical art; the semi-naturalistic and geometrical engravings of Romanelli (Otranto); the discoveries of Monopoli in Apulia and of Levanzo in the Egadi islands, certainly date from the Upper Palaeolithic.

As we have said above, examples of cave art are distributed over a much more limited area : Southern France, with its many painted and engraved caves, is undoubtedly the richest territory; the northernmost expressions of cave art are also located in France — in Arcy (Yonne) and in Angles-sur-Anglin (Vienne). An area rich in material is Cantabria, from Biscay to the Oviedo region, with the maximum concentration in Santander; other, less fruitful areas are the southern regions of Castille (Los Casares near Guadalajara, Atapuerca near Burgos, etc.) and of Andalusia (three in the Malaga province, one in the province of Cadiz).

Up to the present, only engravings have been found in Italy : in Grotta Romanelli (Apulia), in the island of Levanzo (Egadi) and in the caves of Monte Pellegrino near Palermo.

No cave art has been discovered outside these three European regions; the date of the engraved deer found in Schulerloch near Neuessing in Bavaria is extremely dubious [1]).

As we shall show later, Palaeolithic mobiliary and cave art assume diverse aspects ac-cording to their geographical distribution. The term " Franco-Cantabrian ", in common use for a long time, applies to those particular expressions of art that reach their highest develop-ment in France and in Northern Spain [2]); they are related by an undeniable affinity of style and taste, and reveal the same mental outlook and the same artistic inspiration which is deeply realistic and impressionist. Rare, if typical, specimens of mobiliary art constitute the offshoots of Franco-Cantabrian art extending as far as Moravia and the Ukraine.

In the Franco-Cantabrian province, which extends far beyond the territory in which its art reaches the peak of development, the output of a type of mentality that we have defined as geometrical and abstract exists alongside those realistic expressions which are its dominant characteristic. We shall see that in the southernmost European territories — that is, in the Mediterranean area — these particular schematic and geometrical forms prevail in various localities; even when associated with realist art they lend an individual character to the centres of mobiliary or cave art in that region. Nevertheless here, too, the naturalistic figures of the Mediterranean area share some peculiar stylistic and technical elements.

In order to understand clearly the development and diffusion of Palaeolithic art we should examine separately the cave art and the mobiliary art of these two major " provinces": the Franco-Cantabrian and the Mediterranean, which extends from Sicily to Southern and Central Spain and includes the Rhone valley in France. We do not intend, however, to establish definite boundaries between these provinces, for such boundaries do not in fact

---

[1]) BREUIL, 1952, p. 24.
[2]) Other terms have been suggested, such as " Hispano-Aquitanian " or " Aquitanian-Cantabrian ", but we find it more convenient, in deference to a system of priority, to use the term " Franco-Cantabrian " which has long been accepted and the replacement of which would contribute nothing to the clarity of the exposition.

exist; on the contrary, we must always be aware of the fact that their definition is valid only in so far as it is meant to indicate the predominance in each province of one of the two styles, realist or abstract-geometrical, without the exclusion of the other.

Finally we shall examine a particular group, existing in Eastern Europe (Moravia and the Ukraine), of works of mobiliary art of a definitely geometrical order — complex geometry expressed in patterns which seem very different from the non-representation of the Franco-Cantabrian and Mediterranean areas.

We shall deal separately with this small group which seems, from an aesthetic point of view, completely extraneous to the panorama of Palaeolithic art, whereas chronologically it undoubtedly dates from the Upper Palaeolithic and is occasionally encountered in Moravia —where Franco-Cantabrian naturalism usually prevails.

EARLY SPECIMENS.

From the Aurignacian-Perigordian onwards all the different techniques employed in successive periods — sculpture, bas-relief, engraving and painting — existed contemporaneously; the earliest graphic and sculptural expressions appear to develop on the aesthetic lines that were to characterize art in the successive phases of the Upper Palaeolithic.

In other words, in certain essential respects Franco-Cantabrian Palaeolithic art has a fundamental unity from its inception to its conclusion, notwithstanding the changes in subject matter, technique, conception and, probably, purpose, that it underwent in the course of time. We can therefore speak, in a general sense, of a definite aesthetic concept in Franco-Cantabrian art as a whole, when we wish to follow its main lines of development.

But, as we have already noted, two distinct — even opposite — trends can be detected in Palaeolithic art from the beginning, one or the other predominating according to the province : the one definitely realistic, the other abstract-geometrical.

Undoubtedly the most perplexing aspect of the art phenomenon when it appears to us for the first time, is the high degree of maturity shown in the earliest expressions. The sudden appearance of stylistically evolved works of art takes us completely by surprise, with a marvellous eruption of aesthetic values, for there appears to be no hint of what was to come in the hundreds of thousands of years of human civilization which preceded it. It seems to contradict certain patterns into which the art factor has been moulded — based on " logical " criteria and facile comparisons with the art of children or present-day primitive peoples; consequently some authors believe that a long artistic experience, undergone in a part of the world as yet unidentified, must have led to the sculptural and graphic works of the Upper Palaeolithic, and that art, in its mature Palaeolithic form, was brought to Europe by new races of *Homo sapiens* which allegedly replaced the ancient Neanderthal and are supposed — but have not been proved — to have originated outside Europe. This is a mere hypothesis, unsupported, so far, by proven fact. On the contrary, the evidence at present confirms that prehistoric art in Europe is of greater antiquity than that of any other continent.

We have seen that outside Europe Palaeolithic art has been found, so far, in only two places : the Maltà excavations in Siberia, where some rather rudimentary anthropomorphic statuettes were discovered, culturally and chronologically related, in a general sense, to a period that produced far better sculpture of the same type in Europe (Pl. 12, *d, e, f, g*); and North Africa, with its " Capsian " sites belonging to a rather advanced Upper Palaeolithic period, that yielded a few geometrical and schematic figures engraved on ostrich eggs, slabs of stone and (rarely) the walls of caves (Fig. 13).

Two facts then emerge, on a strictly documentary level, with regard to this most ancient art : first, that with the exception of a few, negligible specimens (mentioned above) all works of Palaeolithic art — the oldest known to us so far — have been found in Europe, where this period is represented by an impressive flowering of fine works; second, that even the examples which belong unquestionably to the earliest phase — such as the small anthropomorphic Aurignacian-Perigordian sculptures — are works of amazing artistic maturity.

To explain this apparent anachronism attempts have been made to arrange the works, as they gradually come to light, in ready-made systems based on logical criteria (as mentioned above). As a result of such purely inductive " systems " conclusions have been reached which at first sight appear plausible but do not stand up to dispassionate examination, since they lack a real basis of observation and evidence.

With regard to figurative art in general, Luquet, referring to what apparently occurs in child art, believes that it must have reached its original form through several phases, the first of which he calls " fortuitous realism ". In this phase images are reproduced not intentionally but by chance : by trailing a finger in wet clay for instance, as children, imitating their elders, scribble with a pencil on a piece of paper; the movement would thus have been repeated for the satisfaction of leaving permanent marks. At a certain point primitive man, just like a child, would notice that some of his meaningless scrawls formed a pattern, suggesting to his rich but unbridled imagination a vague similarity with some concrete object. He would then try to repeat the image, bringing it closer and closer to reality; at this point we have what Luquet calls " intentional realism ".

" Figurative art " he says " consisting of the voluntary reproduction of an image with the intention of creating a resemblance, can be defined as intentional realism. This implies as a necessary condition on the part of the artist, the awareness of his faculty to create images and the desire to exert this faculty. These two psychological factors cannot originate elsewhere than in fortuitous realism. Consequently the genesis of figurative art consists in the passage from fortuitous to intentional realism " [1]).

All this is most suggestive, but as far as the genesis of art is concerned it adds up to a purely theoretical enunciation — a hypothesis lacking real documentary foundation. As we will have occasion to repeat later, the scrawls traced with fingers in the clay of European caves or painted on the cave walls might be of any age; so far no substantial stratigraphical element has proved beyond a doubt that they preceded the definitely figurative representations, and therefore constitute the only graphic expression of European Palaeolithic man at the start of his artistic evolution. And if, in the iconography that illustrates this book, the part relating to cave art shows, at the beginning, some roughly executed figures traced on clay, this is not in deference to any particular chronological system but following a principle of broad selection based on the degree of technical and stylistic development shown in the work. This principle has, in fact, dictated the order of presentation of cave art, except for some, unfortunately rare, cases in which incontrovertible proof of stratigraphy has enabled us to define the chronology with absolute certainty.

THE UTILIZATION OF NATURAL ACCIDENTS.

Nothing so far proves that fortuitous realism acted as a dominant creative impulse in the earliest forms of art; that the sight of natural formations, or other forms unconsciously created in the course of some entirely mechanical activity by early Upper Palaeolithic man, stimulated in him the desire and the capacity to imitate or, rather, to complete and make use of those forms in figurative works of art. On the contrary, this phenomenon occurs with greatest frequency at the peak of Franco-Cantabrian art; the artist avails himself with taste

---

[1]) LUQUET, 1930, p. 32.

and skill of natural accidents in the execution of graphic designs on rock surfaces and clay floors in the caves. Some of these works are shown on Pls. 273-279; they give the impression that artists of the more evolved phases were particularly sensitive to the stimulating effect of images in the evocative atmosphere of the caves, with their complicated stalagmitic decorations, their smooth rocky protuberances and their winding fissures. And the partiality shown by the creators of some of the most complex and mature works of Palaeolithic art for the subtle language of fortuitous realism leads us to think that it flourished especially in those who had attained a high degree of sensitivity in form and volume, and a remarkable mastery of technical skills.

Among the illustrations published here to show the exploitation of natural accidents is the classic one — which is certainly among the best — of the ceiling of the Great Hall in Altamira (Pl. 273); here, in exploiting their original shape, the rounded protuberances of the rock surface were not only covered with paint and transformed by the artist's brush into bison shown in various postures; they were also worked here and there with a graver to obtain a more realistic effect.

In the Castillo cave near Santander in Spain a stalagmitic formation suggested to the Palaeolithic artist the figure of a bison rearing up on its hindquarters. The formation calls to mind the animal's massive shape with heavy flesh and bulging muscles. The sinews of the hind leg are distinctly visible, and a long tail continues the humped outline of the back. The artist added a few bold black strokes emphasizing some further details and turned the natural resemblance into a piece of synthetic description, so that the animal appears against a background lighter than the remaining stalagmite.

There are many more instances of the same kind.

Pl. 276, a, b shows a stalagmitic formation in the Font-de-Gaume cave shaped like a horse in bas-relief; the Palaeolithic artist was struck by the resemblance and completed it with a few lines, creating the figure of a mare. Behind the mare is the finely drawn outline of a horse about to leap on her; at least, such is the most probable interpretation of the composition (Pls. 216; 276, a, b). And again in Pl. 276, c, d we reproduce a bison, also from Font-de-Gaume, obtained by making use of a large bulge in the rock surface. Similar cases were noted by Mandement in the cave of Mas d'Azil (Ariège), where the uneven surface of the cliff was transformed, with a few strokes of coloured paint, into synthetic portraits of animals (Pl. 276, e). In a deep branch of the Niaux cave, clefts in the rock wall suggested to the Palaeolithic artist the shape of a bull's head, which he completed by painting the nostrils in black and outlining other parts (Pl. 275, b). In the Portel cave (Ariège), stalagmitic formations were used to indicate anatomical details in painted figures: a small, roundish calcite concretion represents a horse's eye painted in red (Pl. 276, f) and the figure of a man is outlined round a phallic conical stalagmite (Pl. 257, c) [1].

One of the most evocative known specimens of " utilization " is the bison engraved on the clay floor of the Niaux cave [2]. Undoubtedly the entire figure was suggested by small cavities produced by water dripping on the clay from the ceiling.

This interesting work is reproduced in Pl. 277. There are about 10 round cavities, one of which was used to indicate the pupil of the animal's eye which was carefully traced around it; three more cavities represent, in the artist's intention, wounds in the body, each one with an arrow engraved in a kind of intellectual realism showing at the same time both the weapon and the wound inflicted by it.

We shall end this brief review with a mention of the mammoth figure in the Pech-Merle cave near Cabrerets (Lot) where a stalagmitic formation is made use of for the head and the trunk; the body is merely suggested by a few schematic black strokes (Pl. 279).

[1] NOUGIER, ROBERT, 1955; VÉZIAN, 1956.
[2] ROBERT, MALVESIN, NOUGIER, 1953.

4. — P. GRAZIOSI, Palaeolithic Art.

The same Pech-Merle cave contains evidence of the degree of suggestion exerted by the fantastic shapes of natural formations upon the imagination of Palaeolithic artists, who already possessed great experience in the field of figurative art. This cave, in fact, is famous for its many fine schematic representations of mammoths painted in black; the number of these animals is probably due to the presence in the cave of large stalagmitic formations which, in some cases, with their massive volumes, curved outlines and curious fringed excrescences reaching to the ground, suggest the shape of a great pachyderm. The style of these paintings in Pech-Merle is distinguished, in fact, by the summary portrayal of the animal's long fur as it appears in the evocative concretions of the cave itself. On Pl. 278 we show two of these strange natural stalagmite " statues ".

DEVELOPMENT, DISTINGUISHING CHARACTERISTICS, SUBJECT MATTER.

To return to the origin of the earliest expressions of Palaeolithic art, it is necessary for the moment to proceed very cautiously with the formulation of hypotheses and theories lacking, as we have seen, a basis of proven fact.

In the case of mobiliary art, a great number of examples of which can be dated with certainty from their stratigraphical position in a chronological sequence, it is undeniable that even in the earliest phases of the Upper Palaeolithic this branch produced works which represent a considerable artistic achievement, such as for instance the " Venus " statuettes, some engravings on stone slabs, etc.

We shall not go into the question of whether the appearance of sculpture in the round preceded or followed that of drawing and painting, since this is a very difficult one to solve on the basis of the evidence so far available. Piette and Luquet hold opposite opinions on the subject. Let us therefore simply acknowledge the fact that the first known expressions of art are far from primitive and infantile; on the contrary, they reveal an extraordinary mastery of technical means.

Furthermore, if we look at the entire artistic panorama of the Palaeolithic, we will immediately perceive that throughout the various periods, both mobiliary art and cave art underwent many changes of specific stylistic elements, while remaining constant in fundamental character; in the later phases, as opposed to the earlier ones, there is evidence of a greater attention to detail, the appearance of certain mannerisms, a more subtle technique and even what we might define as a kind of academic style evolved through the accumulated experience of successive generations of artists.

All this leads us to assume the existence, at that time, of proper art schools which led to the creation and improvement of techniques, and handed down to subsequent generations the knowledge and skill achieved through the centuries.

The discovery in some deposits — such as that of Limeuil, for instance (Pls. 79, c, e; 80) — of countless pebbles engraved with figures, often superimposed upon each other in a chaotic manner, has led to the belief — unsupported, however, by actual proof — that they were the work of art students, sketches executed in preparation for great cave paintings, or graphic notes — like pages from a sketchbook.

* * *

As we said above, during its entire evolution Palaeolithic art shows two trends; one realistic, the other schematic — both developing along completely separate lines according to the region and period.

In the Franco-Cantabrian province the dominant trend is realistic; however, as Castillo says in his recent excellent work on the aesthetics of Quaternary art [1], " the images are not an exact replica of nature; they are, rather, suggested by reality and follow more or less the shape of real things. Truth is artistic, not optical or sensory ". Castillo therefore suggests that Palaeolithic art should be termed representational rather than realistic. In this he agrees with Luquet, according to whom the Palaeolithic artist was not concerned with what he saw but rather with what he knew about his subject [2].

In fact, in cave art particularly, certain conventions are often used for parts of the animals' bodies and to suggest specific postures; stylizations also appear, gradually becoming more frequent and definite without detracting from the spontaneity and realism of the artist's work. This might be a consequence of the fact that the creator had to reproduce reality without having the living model before his eyes. It seems probable, therefore, that the Palaeolithic artist established some " somatic canons " for certain species of animal in which he was particularly interested, and these canons he elaborated through a daily, direct experience of forms and postures, so as to be able to reproduce them at any moment in the dark depths of the caves — not as the image of a particular individual but as a synthesis of the species itself.

With this process a kind of hyper-realism or hyper-naturalism is reached, on the basis of which the Palaeolithic troglodytes were able to express absolute reality — nature, in its deep, unchanging essence, the universal aspect of a species in its outward form and in its very life. In these works it is movement in particular which is seized not with the cold realism of the camera but rather, as in Greek art, as a synthesis of the vast visual experience acquired by the artist through the contemplation of nature. This, no doubt, explains the appeal and emotional character maintained by Palaeolithic art throughout the phases in which an excess of technical skill tempered its primitive spontaneity and suggestive dynamism, bringing it to the verge of academic convention.

Franco-Cantabrian art, thanks to this outburst of life and movement in the form of a synthesis free from excessive pictorial conformism, has been labelled " expressionistic " — because of its being unencumbered by superstructure, and reduced to the essential elements that evoke reality. It has also been called " impressionistic ", but the term, in this case, is used simply to indicate an immediate, spontaneous reaction to the visual and intellectual impressions created in the artist's mind by the world surrounding him; it does not imply a reference to the significance of colour and light, for, as we shall see, colour and light are unknown, in Franco-Cantabrian art, as dominant, concrete pictorial values.

Colour, in fact, is but an accessory in the creation of an art based exclusively on graphic values and chiaroscuro. As Castillo rightly states, " the Palaeolithic artist is not concerned with colour; to him the concept of colour is practically nonexistent; .... painting never abstracts from line — never dominates or destroys it " [3]. All this clearly applies also to the creations of the great polychromatic phase, as in Altamira and Font-de-Gaume, but we are inclined to disagree with Castillo when he says that these creations lack chromatic harmony; in our opinion such harmony does exist — even though in an instinctive, muted form — in the choice and combination of some of the colours of the limited Franco-Cantabrian palette.

However, it is certain that polychromatic painting is either extremely simple and flat, as in Lascaux, or was used, as in Font-de-Gaume and Altamira, as a device to stress the modelling or accentuate the relief of a figure by displaying it against a background of a different colour. Finally, the caves that contain polychrome paintings are extremely few compared with those in which the Palaeolithic artist used a single colour to outline his animal figures and extend his research into the field of chiaroscuro.

---

[1] Castillo, 1953-54, p. 25.
[2] Luquet, 1923, p. 17.
[3] Castillo, 1953-54, p. 10.

* * *

We have already referred to the consistent character of Palaeolithic art, which is apparent, if only on general lines, throughout its entire development. Such consistency applies not only to its aesthetic orientation, but also to the subject matter with which it is concerned. Subjects stem from two fundamental themes: the human figure, prevailing in the earlier phases (Aurignacian-Perigordian), and the animal figures that flourish throughout the entire Upper Palaeolithic, reaching their highest peak and completely overshadowing anthropomorphic representations during the Solutrean and Magdalenian periods. Apart from these two subjects a third, consisting of geometrical and abstract designs, forms a separate category of slighter interest; we shall deal with it later.

The human form is mainly exploited in mobiliary art, although in cave art as well, of the Aurignacian-Perigordian period and the first part of the Magdalenian, there are fine specimens of a naturalistic order executed in low relief, as in Laussel, Angles-sur-Anglin and the recent discoveries of La Magdeleine.

Cave painting and engraving, on the other hand, with their monstrous representations, treat the human figure in a grotesque and fantastic manner totally lacking reality. It is a fact that Magdalenian cave art tends fundamentally towards a representation of the animal world, with the human form gravitating around it as an accessory element.

Whether the dominant subject is anthropomorphic or zoomorphic, the Palaeolithic artist's interest is almost exclusively concentrated on the portrayal of single beings. Isolated figures appear far more frequently than groups in the art of the period: the relation of one figure to another is rare and fails to achieve particularly striking results.

In other words, deliberate scenic creation is rare and mediocre. With very few exceptions such compositions in cave art are extremely simple and elementary, consisting usually of a couple of animals opposite each other or following one another, generally a male and a female seen in profile; the intention in relating the two figures is obvious. In other cases the sequences of figures (or parts of figures) are more numerous, giving the impression that the artist wished to represent a herd. It is not always certain, however, that the sequence was planned as a composition; rather it may be unintentional and answer an instinctive rhythmic feeling that comes very close to decoration.

The best specimens of this style are found in the Lascaux cave, which also contains what is certainly the most complex and suggestive known "scene" in the whole of Palaeolithic cave art. This scene is distinguished by considerable dramatic sense, and consists of a wounded bison attacking a hunter (Pl. 283, *b*). An analogous — if somewhat less striking — composition consists of a musk ox pursuing a man, and is part of the famous frieze, executed in high and low relief, of Le Roc (Charente) (Pl. 155, *a*).

A sense of composition is more frequently apparent in mobiliary art, as we can judge from the illustrations in this book: couples or groups of interrelated animals; strange compositions of animal and human figures, possibly with mythical or magical connotations (Pl. 87); some rare hunting scenes (Pl. 86, *a*), and still others, all generally of obscure significance. We must therefore acknowledge the fact that Palaeolithic artists were concerned with the creation of "scenes" more often and with more satisfactory results in mobiliary than in cave art.

Another noteworthy fact is that these artists, in relating two or more figures, abstract them completely from the surrounding landscape; each figure is placed in a void, without the slightest indication of background. There are some rare specimens of mobiliary art in which a few horizontal lines at the level of the animals' feet are possibly meant to represent the ground line. In the case of cave art such indications are practically nonexistent: a few may be detected, as we shall later show, in Lascaux.

Attempts at perspective and foreshortening are found in mobiliary art : animal figures are placed on different planes and partly conceal each other, or are viewed from the front or from the rear. Finally, in a few cases the Palaeolithic artist successfully, if unconsciously, reached the boundary beyond which lay the conquest of perspective. This great late-comer among the inventions of the artistic mind was anticipated, as we will see later, by two very early and rudimentary specimens of Upper Magdalenian mobiliary art (Pl. 89, b, c). No such traces appear in cave art — at least so far as present-day discoveries are concerned.

With regard to decoration, it is practically nonexistent in cave art. Only in the Lascaux cave might it be said to appear, although opinions on this point differ considerably. I think nobody, upon entering the Pech-Merle and Font-de-Gaume caves, or even the great hall in Altamira, could detect an intention to create something that may be called decoration — in the accepted sense of the word — in the disorderly distribution and superimposition of magnificent animal figures over the ceilings and walls. On the other hand, in the great Hall of Bulls at Lascaux and its axial corridor we are agreeably struck by the rhythmic distribution of masses of colour that turn out to be splendid animal figures. The great black bulls, for instance, are deployed in an impressive semi-circular sequence, and on the ceiling, where the axial corridor starts, three cows, painted in red, are placed in three corners with their heads towards the centre; together with the figure of a small horse they form a symmetrical pattern, to delimit the vault.

We cannot affirm that the intention of the Lascaux artists was to decorate the great cave; it is permissible to suppose, however, that an instinctive taste for symmetry inspired them to distribute their paintings so as to achieve a sense of harmonious decoration.

The intention to decorate, on the other hand, is evident in many works of mobiliary art, particularly where the sculpture or engraving is executed on a fashioned object such as a weapon or a tool; this subject is exhaustively treated in another chapter, and we shall therefore only mention here that the figures reproduced on these objects are often adapted to the shape of the object itself, and are sometimes repeated rhythmically and symmetrically. A concrete figure is occasionally broken up and schematized with a definitely decorative intention, and many purely ornamental designs, no matter what their origin — spirals, gratings, wavy lines, etc. — appear to have no other purpose than that of embellishing an object.

End of Palaeolithic art and its hypothetical descendants.

An overall look at Palaeolithic art as a whole and at its various manifestations from their inception down to the moment, marked by the division between Pleistocene and Holocene, when they disappear — in the form of mobiliary art — from European prehistoric deposits, proves, particularly in the case of mobiliary objects and the few cave specimens whose chronology is certain, that during the Palaeolithic each manifestation displayed, at one time or another and on general lines, its own special characteristics. We shall see in the course of this book what went into creating the distinction, which is usually more a matter of form and style than of quality; we shall also see — in mobiliary art — that some techniques were particularly developed in certain periods of the Palaeolithic; e. g., sculpture in the round on carved objects, and cut-out silhouettes (" contours découpés ") appeared almost exclusively in Upper Magdalenian IV.

Although during the Upper Magdalenian period Franco-Cantabrian mobiliary art showed a tendency to decline (the figures are cruder, more stylized and degenerate : see Pls. 72, f ; 88, h), on the other hand there are some fine engravings of animals with firm, pure outlines from the end of this period (Pl. 71, e).

Furthermore, it is certain that stylized, geometrical and schematic figures made their appearance early in the Magdalenian, and also in the Aurignacian-Perigordian (Pls. 31, *a*; 97, *b, c*; 92, *a-c*).

However, when the ecological conditions of Europe underwent a radical change at the advent of the Holocene era and the Pleistocene fauna disappeared, the Mesolithic communities of Europe where the great Palaeolithic art had flourished no longer produced works of art comparable with those of the great Palaeolithic era. The deposits of Mas d'Azil, Tardenois, Sauveterre and other Western European excavations have produced only miserable signs and vague representations, among which are the famous pebbles painted in ochre from the Mesolithic layers of Mas d'Azil (Ariège) and of other contemporary sites, with incomprehensible schematic signs that generally have nothing in common with the abstract and geometrical figures of the Palaeolithic.

The great realistic art seems to have disappeared completely, or at least to have survived only in a few summarily executed, semi-naturalistic engravings. Cave art in the Franco-Cantabrian province (its most productive area) seems to have died out altogether, after the flourishing output which can safely be attributed to the Palaeolithic on account of the portrayal of Pleistocene animals.

All the specimens of Holocene cave art found in Europe are the result of a concept, a trend and a technique differing in every respect from those of the preceding period. Yet there are a few exceptions : in two regions widely separated from each other — Scandinavia and Eastern Spain — some examples of cave art, some engraved on large rock surfaces in the open, others painted under overhanging cliffs, can definitely be termed naturalistic; they are attributable to post-Pleistocene, Mesolithic, or even, in the case of a few specimens, later periods [1]).

The Scandinavian engravings are surprisingly similar to some Franco-Cantabrian ones, particularly in their precise way of reproducing animal figures which approximates to the more archaic phases of Franco-Cantabrian art — both cave and mobiliary.

The painting of Eastern Spain (the "levantine" style of the Spanish authors) differs from the Franco-Cantabrian particularly in the manner of treating the human form, which is reproduced countless times in extraordinarily dynamic postures and with a certain tendency to stylization of a particular kind.

On the opposite shore of the Mediterranean, in North Africa and especially in the Saharan region, a type of rock art with strong naturalistic tendencies flourished; it dates probably from the Neolithic period surviving through proto-historic and even historic times (the period of the dynastic Egyptian civilizations). This art can be subdivided into many chronological and cultural phases; it left a great number of animal and human figures engraved on rocks in the open or in shelters under cliffs. These figures show a noticeable affinity, so far as painting is concerned, with the paintings of Eastern Spain, while some phases of engraving resemble works that are believed to be Palaeolithic, and appear in other Mediterranean areas (the Rhone valley, Sicily). On the other hand they are also undeniably related to the Franco-Cantabrian province.

The affinities between the Mediterranean province, the realistic Mesolithic art of Eastern Spain, and the Neolithic and more recent art of North Africa will be discussed in a later chapter.

To conclude, it is clear that in the post-glacial Mesolithic period, the engraving and painting which flourished in Europe differed entirely from Franco-Cantabrian art, being definitely schematic; on the other hand some cave art in certain localities inside and outside Europe appears to have inherited Franco-Cantabrian realism — in what ways and through what channels we do not know. This is the case in Scandinavia and in Spain with regard to Mesolithic art, and in the later, multiform, luxuriant production of North Africa.

---

[1]) Breuil and Obermaier, on the other hand, consider the greater part of the paintings in Eastern Spain to be Palaeolithic.

SIGNIFICANCE AND PURPOSE
OF PALAEOLITHIC ART

Even from a very brief preliminary survey of the various aspects of Palaeolithic art and related problems it can be seen that this wonderful expression of human intelligence was undoubtedly an important, complex, even essential part of the life of those ancient people.

We are justified in assuming that the men of the Old Stone Age devoted themselves intensely and continuously to the creation of pictorial, graphic and sculptural works, for notwithstanding the inexorable destructiveness of time over many thousands of years, such works have survived in considerable numbers.

So prodigious an activity could not have been dictated by creative impulse for its own sake, nor can we consider it an expression of the aesthetic sense and taste of single individuals possessed of unusual gifts. Something essential to the very life of those people, stemming from a deeply felt need, must have been at the root of Palaeolithic man's artistic activity. This has become more and more evident with the progress of discovery in the fields of mobiliary and cave art.

Two theories of the meaning of Palaeolithic art are well known : one of these, in contradiction to what we have just said, holds that the artistic achievements of Palaeolithic man were a purely aesthetic expression stemming from a natural impulse free from all practical concern. This theory was adopted by the supporters of " art for art's sake ".

The other sees in the products of Palaeolithic art, particularly of cave art, a strictly utilitarian activity connected with the magic of hunting and of reproduction among animals.

Comte Begouen, one of the liveliest supporters of the latter concept, demonstrated in convincing fashion the existence of " Quaternary magic " with such famous discoveries in the field of Palaeolithic art as, for instance, the clay bison of Tuc d'Audoubert.

We do not wish to return to a question which was exhaustively debated and which has now been superseded. Neither of the hypotheses is acceptable in an extreme form : obviously Palaeolithic works of art would not have existed without the appearance — we cannot tell whether sudden or gradual — of man's ability to reproduce the reality surrounding him; and without the purely aesthetic desire, born from his awareness of this ability to produce such works, there would have been no Palaeolithic art. But it is equally true — as irrefutable evidence has confirmed — that Palaeolithic man was urged to exteriorize his artistic gifts through the reproduction of visual reality by the need to attain practical ends : the capture of prey, for instance, was for him the indispensable condition of life itself.

It is known that present ethnography (we shall not restate here the evidence often repeated in publications on this subject) offers countless instances of magic practices related to hunting, effected by reproducing the animals singled out for capture, not only in graphic and pictorial images but also by camouflage, or by imitating their postures in pantomime and dance.

Once again, the entire output of Palaeolithic cave art appears to be more or less tied to this essential purpose. But even so we cannot be absolutely exclusive : it is possible that in some cases the Palaeolithic artist sought to fulfil an instinctive desire for pure artistic creation, apart from all material considerations. Practical purpose and aesthetic aspiration are not incompatible, and even if we should conclude that cave art hinged on the creation of images almost exclusively connected with magic, the same cannot be said of mobiliary art, where a fundamentally decorative intention is often obvious in the engraved or sculptured object.

In the same way that art at all times and in every country was — and is — to a great extent tied to aims and ideals of a religious order, which were and are still a source of inspiration and creative impulse for the artist, a " religious " attitude provided a basis for the marvellous artistic production of Palaeolithic man.

Disregarding for the present the obvious ornamental element in mobiliary art (with which we shall deal later), let us briefly examine some of the clearer signs of magic in many specimens of Palaeolithic art, particularly cave art from which, as we have seen, all decorative or purely aesthetic intention, as well as all intention to commemorate events, is absent.

One of the facts that constitute fundamental proof of the lack of decorative intent in this art is the placing of cave paintings and engravings which, with very few exceptions such as the Lascaux cave, are scattered without order or sequence on the walls and on the ceilings, often superimposed and cancelling each other out. Sometimes they are found in almost inaccessible recesses and narrow clefts inside the caves, where it is impossible to see them except with difficulty and from a distorted angle.

It is certain that works so placed were not meant to be admired or to produce a decorative effect. One gets the feeling that the artist's aim was the execution of the subject for its own sake without relation to surrounding figures and background. When two figures form a scene they are almost invariably male and female animals, a very simple composition connected with the propitiatory magic of animal reproduction.

Such compositions appear in various localities spread over the area of distribution of Palaeolithic art, even outside the Franco-Cantabrian province. Pl. 284 shows some in which a deliberate intention to relate animals of opposite sexes is obvious. This is the case in La Mairie, where we see a bull pursuing a cow, and in Le Portel, where two bison face each other, or in Les Combarelles, where two reindeer are shown approaching each other — a combination identically repeated in Font-de-Gaume (Pl. 217), in one of the most famous of Palaeolithic paintings. Again in the cave on the little island of Levanzo in the Egadi archipelago there is a composition identical in spirit and construction to that of La Mairie, consisting of a bull following a cow (Pl. 297, c). At La Chaire à Calvin we have a real scene of copulation in the bas-relief frieze of horses (Pl. 164, c) and a similar meaning can probably be read into the two horses painted in Font-de-Gaume (Pls. 276, a, b; 216). Finally we should mention the celebrated clay statues of Tuc d'Audoubert in Ariège, reproducing two bison, male and female, following each other; the male is in the act of rearing up on the other's hindquarters for the purpose of copulation (Pl. 165, b). On the subject of this most interesting sculptured group and of the suggestive traces of magic rites accomplished in proximity to it, see the paragraph on p. 149 and foll.

Besides taking the form of approaches and copulation between animals, the magic of reproduction is represented by pregnant females, such as the mares painted in Lascaux (Pl. 282, b), those sculptured in low relief in Le Roc (Pls. 154, 155), and others.

But the kind of magic specifically concerned with the capture and slaughter of game is more often found and more clearly illustrated. It applies far more frequently to " useful " animals such as the reindeer, the bison and the horse, which Palaeolithic man hunted for food; but it is also found in connection with dangerous species, such as the bear and the lion, which had to be destroyed.

Countless bison, horses, oxen, ibexes, deer, reindeer, etc., are engraved or painted with weapons transfixing their bodies. In Lascaux, feathered objects — surely arrows and javelins — are seen flying around animal figures (Pls. 182; 183; 274,a,b). In Niaux we have clear pictures of animals struck by pointed, feathered arrows; the points probably consisted of two flint blades inserted obliquely at the end of the shaft (Pls. 205,b; 207). Also in Niaux, within the outline of a bison carved on the clay floor, arrows of the same kind are engraved next to cavities produced by dripping water and used by the Palaeolithic artist as representations of the animal's wounds : we have already discussed this figure in a previous chapter (p. 25 and Pl. 277).

We will not enumerate all the examples of this sort, for they are plentiful and obvious not only in cave art but also in mobiliary art. Let us mention instead what can be considered direct and tangible evidence of magic rites accomplished by acting out the kill on an imitation of the animal itself. The figure of a horse engraved on clay in the Montespan cave (Pl. 280, c) is pockmarked with holes produced — or so it appears — by spear thrusts; the famous headless bear in the same cave also has holes, probably caused in the same manner, in its massive, crouching body (Pl. 168). This large and rudimentary clay statue, which is hidden in the deepest recess of the cave, has given rise to an imaginative theory; it is supposed to have been used as a sort of dummy figure — over which the pelt of a real bear was thrown to make it more lifelike — afterwards being attacked with spears. This subject is fully treated in the paragraph concerning this cave on p. 151 and foll.

Figures of wounded animals are also plentiful; on Pl. 280, d there is a bear engraved in the Les Trois Frères cave, with circular marks on its body indicating wounds, and blood pouring from its open mouth; the crouching bison on the ceiling in Altamira are surely intended as dying animals with buckling legs (Pls. 246, 248).

Finally another aspect of magic practices related to the capture of prey is revealed in Palaeolithic art : the reproduction of designs meant to represent traps, nets, etc., in association with animal figures. Here, too, evidence is varied and plentiful; mainly tectiform signs such as those engraved on the mammoths in the Bernifal cave in the Dordogne (Fig. 17) or painted next to horses, oxen and deer in the Lascaux cave (Pls. 189, 190), checkered oblongs, among which are the so-called " escutcheons ". These figures will be dealt with in a special chapter (p. 187).

The meaning sometimes given to handprints found in connection with animal representations, like those at Pech-Merle, is that of taking possession of the prey.

All the examples mentioned above — portrayals of coupled animals, pregnant females, animals struck by weapons, wounded, or shown in connection with traps, etc. — are clear and well-defined instances of a certain kind of magic; no elaborate interpretation is needed to understand it. But in Palaeolithic cave art, as well as in mobiliary art, curious figures are sometimes related to each other to form compositions apparently born, in view of their strangeness and incomprehensibility, of an esoteric vision; these, too, probably have magic connotations whose nature, however, is somewhat obscure. They belong to a fantastic, unreal, possibly mythical world which has no apparent connection with the clear, elementary and practical world of hunting magic, in its simplest expressions.

Pl. 283, a, for instance, shows the strange composite animals of the Les Trois Frères cave : bears with the heads of wolves and the tails of bison, and reindeer with webbed feet (Pl. 282, c), followed by another animal with the body of a reindeer and the head of a bison.

It would be useless to try to interpret these absurd compounds; we may be sure, however, that the Palaeolithic artist created them with a deliberate purpose originating in an imaginary world beyond the bounds of concrete reality.

Other evidence speaks of an unreal, magical atmosphere in which the Palaeolithic mind roamed : among the most suggestive is the so-called " sorcerer " at Les Trois Frères — half human and half animal; we shall describe him in detail later (p. 137). This figure is engraved and painted in the Sanctuary — the innermost recess of that complex and impenetrable Ariège cave (Pl. 281).

Below this strange being there are numerous small animal figures perfectly executed; they are so finely engraved that the utmost attention and a slanting light are needed to examine them. Among these figures are the hybrid ones described above. They represent animals of the Pleistocene superimposed upon each other so as to be practically indistinguishable (Pl. 145); the Abbé Breuil worked long and painstakingly to decipher and trace them.

These splendid figures were found in a group on a relatively small surface, dominated by the sorcerer above, who is much larger and perfectly isolated and visible. It is undeniable that this figure is closely related to the others, and one also gets the impression that the artist, in working on the small animal figures which are superimposed and carelessly distributed, was more concerned with the careful reproduction of each separate animal than with the artistic effect of the whole. The sorcerer — or mythical being — was perhaps supposed to dominate and preside over the creation of the animal representations on the rock surface below him, as though the hunter wished to propitiate him with the execution of those engravings.

There are further specimens of hybrid figures hovering in that unreal territory separating the animal from the human world which we can quote for example (Pls. 87, f; 259); they do not always lend themselves — as some would have it — to such rational interpretations as that they are reproductions of sorcerers or hunters camouflaged in animal hides for magic purposes, or in order to approach the hunted prey unseen. They can be explained, rather, as the expression of a primitive mentality which failed to establish definite boundaries between humans and animals but saw in all the creatures surrounding it a vital expression of nature, of which it felt itself to be an integral part, therefore establishing with those creatures deep and indissoluble ties. The spiritual world of Palaeolithic man must have been imbued with all this, and surely his imagination, when exteriorizing itself in expressions of figurative art, was deeply influenced by it.

Mobiliary art also furnishes instances of these strange expressions of the Palaeolithic mentality, with figures whose meaning it is quite impossible to penetrate. Such, for example, are the processions of anthropomorphic figures surrounding a great bison whose head, backbone and hoofs alone are traced (Pl. 87, c, d); or the curious composition repeated three times in three widely separated localities — two in France and one in Spain — representing a deer seen from the back, together with the large head of a carnivorous animal (Pl. 90, a, c). There are many similar instances.

It is obvious that cave art in particular was tied both to propitiatory hunting magic — in which case it should be considered as definitely practical — and to expressions of a mythical, or at least esoteric character pervading the primitive mind, and of which very little is known.

We should keep in mind, however, that in order to achieve his aims Palaeolithic man not only reproduced the animal world or the semi-human world examined above; he also often portrayed the human form, realistically executed in its anatomical details, especially in the earlier — or Aurignacian-Perigordian — period. We shall discuss fully later on the female statuettes which stress the attributes of femininity and fertility, and which really seem dedicated to a different cult — the cult of maternity, of the perpetuation of the human species.

A last word about mobiliary art : often engraved or sculptured figures are found mutilated or broken into fragments; in some deposits the number of mutilated figures is such that one is led to believe they were damaged intentionally. Convincing instances of this practice are found in the Isturitz cave, with its numerous small stone statues and engraved figures. This iconoclasm was also interpreted as part of the hunting magic ritual intended to favour the capture of game. Recently Radmilli extracted from the Upper Palaeolithic deposit of Polesini, near Tivoli, a pebble bearing the engraving of a carnivorous animal; this figure shows several circular cavities, obviously produced by striking it with a blunt instrument (Pl. 107, a).

PART TWO

MOBILIARY ART

TECHNIQUE, SUBJECT MATTER, CHRONOLOGY

The amazing phenomenon of Palaeolithic art can be better understood if we examine "mobiliary art" separately from cave art. First of all because only in the case of the former, where the condition of the deposits allows it, can we establish a chronology which is reliable because based on stratigraphy, and thus follow the evolution of that form of art on a firm basis. In the case of cave art, with rare exceptions where the figures were covered by dateable deposits, or where fragments of rock bearing engraved or painted figures, detached from the wall, had fallen into the deposit itself, a chronological order can only be determined — even so with a large margin of doubt — by patiently comparing the style, subject matter and technique with specimens of mobiliary art. In the second place a large part of mobiliary art was born of a spirit and a purpose different from that which engendered cave art. Although the magical connotations of a great number of these works are certainly predominant, there also appears a decorative intention which is completely lacking in cave art. The wish to decorate is sometimes so strong that not only is reality highly distorted to adapt the design to the function of the implement or weapon, but figurative elements are broken up by progressive schematization into shapes not immediately recognizable, whose probable origin can only be detected by studying the various phases leading up to their final form.

In the works of mobiliary art that have reached us, the Palaeolithic artist made use, with remarkable skill, of materials such as stone (calcite, schist, sandstone, serpentine, etc.), bone, the antlers of reindeer and sometimes of deer and, more rarely, mammoth tusks; in a few cases he also used amber or lignitic coal. Statuettes found in a Moravian deposit (Dolní Věstonice) were moulded from a mixture of a clayey substance and powdered bone, but this technique was very exceptional in the Palaeolithic; some statues and bas-reliefs were executed in pure clay — the clay from the caves in which they were made. They were modelled directly on the ground, or against the rocky surface of the deep caverns where they were discovered, and it is owing to the complete isolation in which they remained after their creation that they were able to survive down to the present.

Clay modelling apparently preceded a technique that was to flourish and develop in a more perfected form, also in the field of statuary, many thousands of years later as pottery, whose first appearance, as we have said, is exclusively Neolithic and begins with the agricultural and pastoral cultures [1]).

With these materials (stone, ivory, bone) the Palaeolithic people executed works of mobiliary art in the round, in low relief — sometimes highly accentuated, at other times so shallow as to approximate to "champlevé" (a technique that consists in hollowing out the

---

[1]) It is not improbable that the Palaeolithic people carved, engraved and painted also on wood, particularly in those European countries where adequate material was plentiful; naturally, however, none of these works survived. This hypothesis is supported by modern ethnographical research which confirms the fact that primitive peoples use wood as well as stone, bone, ivory or pottery in making works of art.

area surrounding the figure's outline) — in engraving, in painting and " contour découpé ",
a special process in which flat figures were cut out of thin pieces of bone, with the details
engraved but with no relief.

As we have said before, the different techniques used in mobiliary art did not develop
to the same extent in all phases of the Upper Palaeolithic; nor were they all made equal use of.
Painting, for instance, which reached such a high point of development in cave art left practically no trace in mobiliary art, if we except — apart from traces of colour on some sculptured
figures — a series of simple figures painted on slabs found in the Parpallò cave in southern
Spain and a few sporadic painted signs, also on stone slabs, found in Germany and Italy. It
is hard to say whether this is due, at least in part, to the fact that paint deteriorated in the
deposits inside the caves; undoubtedly, however, Palaeolithic painting was more often carried
out on large surfaces, and reached its peak in cave art.

Sculpture in the round, in the form of individual statuettes, appears to have flourished
particularly in the early Upper Palaeolithic — or Aurignacian-Perigordian — period; whereas
there are no objects sculptured with a decorative intention from this period. Ornamental
sculpture, on the other hand, predominates during the last phase of Upper Palaeolithic — the
Magdalenian — when sculpture in the round is less frequent.

Engraving on fragments of stone and bone not shaped into implements appears —
although in small quantities — even in the Aurignacian-Perigordian period, together with
statuettes sculptured in the round; this technique continued in the Solutrean period and was
highly developed in the Lower Magdalenian. Engraving on manufactured objects — weapons
and implements — is practically unknown in the Aurignacian-Perigordian while it flourished
in the Magdalenian, producing some of the finest and most elaborate works of art.

To conclude, mobiliary art reached the peak of its development in the late Upper Palaeolithic period, and more specifically in Upper Magdalenian (IV-VI), with sculpture and
engraved objects and with engravings on chance objects. Non-decorative sculpture, in the
sense of sculpture not bound to the functional object, is present in the Aurignacian-Perigordian in mature forms that spread all over Europe, reaching as far as Siberia; in later periods these forms, with their specific style and particular technique, disappear from the picture
of Palaeolithic art.

Palaeolithic mobiliary art thus thrusts out offshoots in many directions from the great
Franco-Cantabrian centre; it transcends the boundaries of Aquitania and reaches localities
far removed from the centre of major development, sometimes with its fundamental stylistic
and technical characteristics practically intact, in other cases slightly altered, but not enough
to prevent recognition of its origin. We have already alluded to the wide diffusion of Aurignacian-Perigordian sculpture in the round, but in the light of our present knowledge we
cannot confidently and unequivocally place its original centre in Aquitania (Cantabria seems
so far to be excluded, since no specimens have been found there) rather than elsewhere
within its vast area of distribution.

Real masterpieces of Magdalenian engraving on bone have also been found in Switzerland
(Thayngen), and others, of a true Aquitanian type, deep into Moravia (Pekarna), where
they appear related to local art markedly schematic in style (Předmostí) whose area of diffusion reaches as far as the Ukraine (Mézine). Centres of Palaeolithic mobiliary art also exist in
Italy : they have yielded specimens of an art that can be considered an offshoot of the great
Hispano-Aquitanian focal centre; in some localities, however, such as Grotta Romanelli,
schematic and abstract expressions of a very special character were found.

In Southern Spain, near Valencia (Parpallò cave), there is a deposit rich in mobiliary
art, engravings and paintings with naturalistic patterns, clearly revealing their connection
with the Franco-Cantabrian centre, and expressions of definite schematism similar to those
found in Italy, mentioned above.

This cursory glance at the geographical distribution of Franco-Cantabrian mobiliary art proves that the focal area of this particular form of art was located in Aquitania, whence it reached out in various directions, probably creating new centres of artistic genesis in widespread and distant localities.

We must also add that if the term " Franco-Cantabrian " clearly defines the geographical distribution of cave art, it is less accurate in the case of mobiliary art; as we leave the French Pyrenees and penetrate into Cantabria the latter form, while showing undeniable characteristics proper to Franco-Cantabrian art, is represented by works of small artistic merit and relatively few in number, little more than a peripheral reflection of the potent Aquitanian centre.

We shall now briefly list the subjects treated by this art in its various phases, and, in the case of sculpture and engraving on fashioned objects such as weapons and implements, the criteria that guided the Palaeolithic artist in decorating them.

It is certain, as noted before, that widely diversified intentions inspired the artists of the Upper Palaeolithic period — the Aurignacian-Perigordian and the Solutrean-Magdalenian — in the execution of their work. The former were mainly concerned with the reproduction of the human form, specifically of the female figure, in which they excelled; whereas the Solutrean-Magdalenian artists seldom portrayed human beings : on the rare occasions on which they did they tended to express them in primitive, clumsy forms, rather dedicating their amazing creative power and their skilful and subtle technique to the portrayal of the multifarious animal life around them. From this they gathered inspiration for certain decorative forms which reveal their origin through the gradual schematization of parts of animal bodies.

Innumerable reproductions of the fauna that lived in Europe at that time, particularly the animals that were essential to the life of those hunting peoples, are therefore encountered in the Magdalenian layers.

According to the different periods and localities, some species were pictured in greater numbers than others; this applies also to cave art. But if we consider Upper Palaeolithic mobiliary art as a whole we shall see that the species portrayed most frequently and in greatest detail are the horse, the bison and the reindeer; after these come the deer, the ox (Bos primigenius), the ibex, the fish and the snake; then the great feline animals, the bear, the fox, perhaps the hyena, the chamois, and other species still, down to the amphibians (very rare) and the insects. But the Magdalenian artist — like the Aurignacian-Perigordian — chose his material not in the animal world alone; many objects are decorated with ornamental patterns, such as barbed harpoons, or ropes twined around bone rods, or, very occasionally, leafy twigs and even small plants with their roots. From these subjects, as from the animal world, the Palaeolithic artist evolved, through a gradual elimination of concrete expressions, to a level of true abstraction, creating purely decorative geometrical patterns, engraved or sculptured.

The fragment of stone, or pebble, upon which the Palaeolithic artist executed his work may have been submitted to a preliminary process that involved smoothing its surface or trimming its edges; more frequently, however, it was left in a rough state. In some cases a pebble was used as a pendant, and pierced with a hole for hanging; in others, the natural resemblance between a piece of stone and a specific subject was stressed by flaking or carving. Here we are already in the realm of rudimentary sculpture. It is highly probable that in the case of mobiliary art — as in cave art — the execution of such images was dictated by the original shape of the rough material. It is also possible that the shape and size of a fragment limited the artist's field in choosing his subject, which consequently acquired a sort of rigidity and distortion.

Functional, manufactured objects that the Palaeolithic craftsman embellished with his great art generally belong to precise categories; these we mentioned when giving a summary of the succession of Palaeolithic cultures and industries (pp. 12-14).

The artifacts most often carved or decorated with engravings are the " bâtons de commandement ". One of these appears already in the Perigordian period, at Laugerie Haute; it is deeply engraved with a double outline of mammoths (Pl. 24, c, d). Some date from the Lower Magdalenian and are crowned with curious, synthetic animal heads (Placard) (Pls. 29, 30). They develop and multiply, with an extraordinary variety of decorative patterns, throughout the entire Upper Magdalenian period. Sometimes they are fashioned out of deer antlers, as in the case of the Teyjat and El Pendo " bâtons "; reindeer antlers were more generally used. The " bâtons de commandement " of Arene Candide (Finale Ligure) are made of elk antler. Stumps of the antler's branches, left at the level of the hole, are often decorated with figures engraved or carved into the shape of animal heads turned in opposite directions, as, for instance, at Laugerie Basse; or into phallic shapes, as at Gorge d'Enfer (Pls. 45, a; 96, g).

We shall not discuss again here the use to which these mysterious " bâtons de commandement " were put, for we have already mentioned the various hypotheses existing on this subject; we will only repeat that often the fragility, delicacy and beauty of the decorations seem hardly compatible with practical and frequent use. Where this kind of decoration exists the round hole may have been pierced to suspend an object invested with purely magical or ornamental qualities.

The practical purpose of another object — often masterfully carved — the " spear-thrower ", is also perplexing, especially because in many cases the twisted or arched shaft is hardly adapted to the requirements of its use as a weapon. Undoubtedly, however, these hooked artifacts are structurally spear-throwers; they possess the simple morphological elements that distinguish the spear-thrower known to present-day ethnographers. This contradiction between the fragility of these decorated Magdalenian weapons and the practical function that they were intended to fulfil might be solved by considering them not as weapons to be used as such, but as ritual objects, copied from real weapons and manufactured for magical or ornamental purposes.

Spear-throwers are decorated in one of two different manners : one consists of ornamenting the shaft — among these is the famous specimen decorated with an ibex that was found in Mas d'Azil (Pl. 32); the other crowns the end with a small carving — like the spear-thrower of Gourdan which is decorated with a diminutive human (or ibex?) head (Pl. 81, a, b). The hooked extremity of others is carved with more or less massive figures (possibly intended to balance the weapon), often animals with feet planted on the edge of the stick opposite the hook. In such cases the broad part of the antler was used (Pls. 35, a; 37, etc.).

" Bâtons de commandement " and spear-throwers are not the only bone artifacts that were decorated. Some javelin-heads have also been found, with ornaments — schematic or semi-realistic — engraved or carved in low relief; serpentine figures, zig-zag lines, etc. Cylindrical " rods " or semi-cylindrical " half-rods " were decorated with complex scrolls and other purely ornamental figures. Harpoons with one or two series of barbs were embellished with simple lines which followed the shaft and branched out into the barbs, or developed into even more complex patterns. All this constitutes the realm of geometrical and stylized figures with which we shall deal extensively in another chapter.

Finally we should mention, outside the frame of functional objects and imitations of functional objects, the engraved or carved bone pendants (one of which, found in Mas d'Azil (Pl. 42, a) is carved with two ivory ibexes) and the perforated bone disks engraved with simple ornamental patterns, and also, in some cases, with realistic figures (Pls. 96, c, d; 63, a).

We may now proceed to an examination of the more important works of mobiliary art in order throughout the Upper Palaeolithic period, attempting to reconstruct, on broad lines, the evolution of this art in the territory of its maximum development and its diffusion outside that territory. It is not as difficult or uncertain to establish the succession of the various phases of mobiliary art in the Palaeolithic as it is to determine a chronological sequence in the case of cave art; a large number of mobiliary art specimens were found *in situ*, in an unequivocal stratigraphical position, so that it was easy to determine their chronology. By means of stylistic comparison it has also been possible to define chronologically many works of great artistic importance concerning which stratigraphical data were unavailable, insufficient or dubious, because they came from early excavations or robbed sites, or were found in the refuse from previous excavations.

THE FRANCO-CANTABRIAN PROVINCE
AND ITS OFFSHOOTS

AURIGNACIAN-PERIGORDIAN

SCULPTURE

On several occasions we have mentioned, in previous pages, that Aurignacian-Perigordian deposits all over Europe have yielded a considerable quantity of sculpture on stone, bone and ivory; in the whole of the period, however, there are very few known specimens of bone implements and weapons decorated with the kind of naturalistic designs that are plentiful in the Magdalenian period.

This would seem to indicate that an entirely different mentality prevailed in the two periods : the later witnessed the birth of particular aesthetic intentions, whereas in the earlier sculpture was an end in itself — the statuette was created as such, with no ornamental intention.

Small pieces of sculpture (at that time they were always small) were often executed with great care, and the artist, as we shall see, emphasized certain details — always the same ones — neglecting others.

The subject matter of Aurignacian-Perigordian sculpture also included the animal world; but the human form was generally treated with greater skill and attention. In this connection we should keep in mind that whereas anthropomorphic statuettes occur from France to Siberia, zoomorphic Aurignacian-Perigordian sculpture, as far as we know, was confined to a much more limited area, an area unrelated to the territory in which Franco-Cantabrian art reached the peak of its development — Aquitania. The documents found so far have come from Germany (Vogelherd), Moravia (Věstonice, Předmostí) and Russia.

Zoomorphic sculpture therefore appears for the moment to have had its origin and earliest diffusion outside the geographical area of Franco-Cantabria; should we then conclude that the same applies to anthropomorphic sculpture? Although female statuettes, dated as far back as the Aurignacian-Perigordian, were found in Aquitania (proving that they were widely diffused in the extreme West of Europe), we are not justified in assuming that Aquitania was their centre of origin.

ANTHROPOMORPHIC STATUETTES.

All the pieces of anthropomorphic Aurignacian-Perigordian sculpture so far brought to light have some morphological details in common; in each specimen the same taste, the same aesthetic sense are evident. In other words, the statuettes we are dealing with here have a well-defined, unmistakable " style ". And this style spread, during the early part of the Upper Palaeolithic era, over an astonishingly vast area — particularly for that time.

Anthropomorphic Aurignacian-Perigordian statuettes are almost exclusively female; only very exceptionally do they portray a male. A synthesis of their fundamental characteristics shows that heights vary between 3,5 cm. (Trasimeno) and 22 cm. (Savignano); the same materials mentioned in connection with Palaeolithic sculpture of all periods in general were used in their execution (stone, ivory, bone, etc.). Approximately sixty statuettes or fragments of statuettes have so far been brought to light; of these, however, only a few are in a condition which allows us to distinguish clearly the stylistic characteristics we are about to discuss. In many cases the fragments are so small and in so poor a state of preservation, or the pieces of sculpture at so early a stage of elaboration, that it is impossible to establish their morphology. The illustrations show the most interesting, complete pieces (Pls. 1-12).

As we examine the best specimens of early sculpture we are immediately struck by the exuberant forms carefully stressed by the primitive artist; the statuettes — almost invariably nude — generally have voluminous breasts, an adipose stomach and thighs, with hips and buttocks cushioned in fat. A proper " polysarcia " localized in specific parts of the body or, in some cases, affecting it all, together with an accentuation of the pubic region, is the dominant note in these sculptures; notwithstanding such exaggeration — which in some cases is quite monstrous — the final result is often amazingly well-balanced, showing taste and a lively sense of reality.

All the known statuettes are lacking feet; the legs are almost invariably fused together, ending in a point a little below the knees. Arms are often missing, and where they exist they are undersized, bent inwards and resting on the enormous breasts. The head does not always take the same shape : it may be roundish, oval, oblong or even replaced by a kind of conical appendage. The features are hardly ever formed (except in the case of a few, isolated statuettes), whereas the hair is sometimes treated with great attention to detail : it may be divided into many little braids reaching the shoulders (Brassempouy, Pl. 1, a) or disposed in symmetrical circles around the head (Willendorf, Pl. 9).

By and large the Palaeolithic artist scrupulously emphasized certain parts of the body, particularly the parts relating to femininity, neglecting or barely suggesting others that did not interest him inasmuch as they were not directly related to the aim of his work.

The exuberant fleshiness, full of life and feeling; the sense of female fulfilment radiating from the little masterpieces, unequivocally reveals that the end sought by the artist was an expression of fertile femininity — maternity in its fullest, most absolute sense.

Some of these statuettes are executed with such a feeling of reality, the plastic values are accentuated with such artistry, the interplay of volumes shows such consummate skill and the work as a whole such taste, that even where figures are treated with paradoxical exaggeration or startling distortion the effect, far from being grotesque and unpleasant, is humorous — as in the case of the Willendorf statuette — or almost surrealistic as in the case of Lespugue (Pl. 3).

This is the period in which the female body in all its vibrant realism triumphs in Palaeolithic art : during the entire prehistoric period, only in the Aurignacian-Perigordian statuettes and in the bas-reliefs of the same period (of which we shall speak later) was the image of womanhood permeated with so potent a breath of life. Later, with the advent of the Solutrean period, the tradition of fine female representation was lost, and in the subsequent Magdalenian period the female form was treated in a crude, rudimentary fashion or else — as recent discoveries have disclosed — in a fashion which, while adhering to realistic traditions, approaches what we might call a kind of composite academism. The religious mentality of the new Palaeolithic generations turns towards other interests.

Successively, in the prehistoric period of agricultural and pastoral peoples and in the protohistoric period, a rigid, shapeless schematization of the female form widens the gap between those early works, saturated with emotion and instinctive beauty, and the later ones. Only here and there — in Neolithic Malta, for instance — a glimmer of the earlier fire reappears in some graceful terracotta statuettes from the prehistoric past of that island.

We should keep in mind, however, that not all the Aurignacian-Perigordian statuettes reveal the skill of a master or appear to have been the object of careful, painstaking work. Some of them — such as the statuettes of Trou Margrite in Belgium, of Kostienki in Russia (Pl. 11, c) and of Předmostí in Moravia — are summarily and roughly carved. Others are rigid, rudimentary, and tend towards a sort of schematization; such are the Siberian statuettes of Maltà, which differ considerably, with regard to modelling, from the majority of Western statuettes; among these, too, very poor specimens are sometimes found in the same deposits as the fine works described above (Brassempouy, Balzi Rossi).

The Palaeolithic statuettes were called " Venuses " by early palaethnologists, as though they represented the personification of feminine charms in those remote times. The term is still in use today.

Up to the present they have been found in France, Belgium, Germany, Italy, Moravia, Austria, European Russia and Siberia.

BRASSEMPOUY (Pls. 1; 2, a, b). The first female statuette in Aurignacian-Perigordian style was found in France, in 1892, in the " Grotte du Pape " at Brassempouy (Landes) by P. E. Dubalen who unearthed a torso, unfortunately incomplete, carved from a mammoth tusk; this piece became famous and can be considered one of the finest known specimens. The subsequent excavations of Edouard Piette and Joseph de la Porterie, carried out in that rich deposit up to 1897, brought to light more female sculptures and fragments of carved ivory; half a dozen of these are very interesting; among them is a beautiful small head with long hair [1].

In deference to historical exactitude we should mention that about thirty years before, in 1861, E. Dupont had found a human figure roughly carved on bone in the Trou Margrite cave near Dinant (Belgium) in a layer of that deposit which, on the strength of the description left by the discoverer of the artifacts, can be attributed today, approximately, to the Perigordian period [2].

To return to Brassempouy; the pieces of sculpture that are finished and whose state of preservation allows us to evaluate their characteristics are the fragment mentioned above, consisting of the right thigh and part of the stomach of a female figure; two fragments of torsos, and a female head.

The first is the most famous, and it truly deserves its reputation. Unfortunately only a fragment has survived, but it is sufficient to reveal the artist's technical skill and acute sensitivity (Pl. 1, b). We are struck by the manner in which the swelling thigh is joined to the convex, fleshy pubis, by the softness expressed in the treatment of the stomach and hips, and the round masses above them. Only an examination of the original can do justice to the artistry with which the material was treated in its polished surfaces.

And what can we say of the torso — unfortunately eroded and fractured in several places — shown in Pl. 2, a? Seen from the back this statuette of modest dimensions offers an extraordinary wealth of detail and forceful plastic effects.

The small head (we cannot rule out the possibility that it may have been part of a complete statue) is undoubtedly one of the most curious products of Palaeolithic sculpture, with its long, slender neck framed in thick hair effectively rendered by deeply engraved lines, and its pointed face with finely modelled planes (Pl. 1, a). Viewed in profile, the line of the cheek is lifelike; the features are somewhat stylised : the mouth is not traced, nor are the eyes under the forcefully designed arched brows. A vigorous use of the engraving tool, which is particularly evident from the front, gives the Brassempouy head a flavour of immediacy and sincerity, coupled with a certain archaism, that make it a specimen of the highest interest.

---

[1] PIETTE, 1895; PIETTE, LA PORTERIE, 1897.
[2] DUPONT, 1872, p. 87 and foll.

We have described the hair : Piette called this figure " la tête à la capuche ". But it is simply a coiffure divided into slender braids, and the small horizontal parallel lines engraved on each braid are apparently intended to represent transverse binding of the braid itself. This type of head-dress curiously recalls to mind that of present-day African tribes — the Ethiopians, for instance.

Other fragments of lesser importance were found in Brassempouy. Pl. 2, *b* shows a female torso, very much deteriorated; the lower half of a male statuette, and the fragmentary legs of a third. Another fragment of torso also exists (the " figurine à la pèlerine ") and, finally, two small, sketchy figures outlined on an ivory stick by a few cracks and engraved lines.

The Brassempouy statuettes are now in the Musée des Antiquités Nationales of Saint-Germain-en-Laye near Paris.

Regarding the exact stratigraphical position of these pieces of sculpture nothing very definite is known. Data published by La Porterie and Piette, and particularly the conclusions reached by the latter — who was determined to group the entire output of Palaeolithic sculpture into a single period — is not such as to enlighten us concerning the true chronology of the statuettes. The Abbé Breuil [1]), who re-examined the question and attempted to interpret Piette's findings, came to the conclusion that they belong to the Middle Aurignacian period [2]).

LESPUGUE (Pl. 3). The next of the Palaeolithic statuettes, taken in the geographical order, is the famous, highly interesting " Venus " of Lespugue. It was found by Saint-Périer in 1922 in the Rideaux cave of Lespugue (Haute-Garonne), in an intact deposit labelled Upper Aurignacian by the discoverer [3]).

This statuette, carved from a fragment of mammoth tusk, is 147 mm. high; the breasts, stomach and left side (forearm and thigh) are considerably damaged, but the abrasions are not such as to prevent a perfect reconstruction of the sculpture; the opposite, or right side being intact, Saint-Périer's work of reconstruction was reduced to a purely mechanical task, and the resulting figure can be studied almost as though it were the complete original.

Viewed from the front it has the outline of a lozenge — as first Saint-Périer and later Passemard [4]) pointed out. We are struck at once by the three-dimensional composition of this curious piece of sculpture, based on the superimposition of spheroid masses rhythmically related : a composition that greatly transcends the accepted limits of anatomical realism, clearly showing a tendency towards stereometric abstraction; yet the monstrous female figure, enormously bloated in its lower half and exceedingly slender from the waist up, has great expressiveness and perfect balance. The Lespugue statuette offers a suggestive interplay of volumes, with its inclined head and expressionless face, its meagre torso — slightly curved inward as though to create, together with the inclined head, a concave space opposed to the excessive convexity of the lower part — and its thin arms resting lightly and meekly on the enormous breasts that cover, like over-ripe gourds, the stomach protruding over the pubic triangle : they seem intended to relate the fragility of the upper half to the crude materialism of the lower. The adipose thighs continue the rounded line of the hips bulging out exaggeratedly to the sides, and a definite narrowing separates them from the legs which, following the style of all Aurignacian-Perigordian statuettes, are short, joined together and end in a point.

---

[1]) BREUIL, 1909.
[2]) He explicitly affirms (BREUIL, 1937a, p. 17) : " A la base de ce niveau (*Middle Aurignac.*) appartient certainement l'assise à statuettes de Brassempouy ". Recently (BREUIL, LANTIER, 1951, p. 183 and foll.) he repeated that the statuettes were of the Aurignacian period — actually attributing them to the earlier part of Typical Aurignacian : " elles ont été bien trouvées *sous* l'Aurignacian typique, à sa base ".
[3]) SAINT-PÉRIER, 1922; *idem*, 1924.
[4]) PASSEMARD L., 1938, p. 107.

SIREUIL (Pl. 2, c). This statuette was discovered quite accidentally in 1900 on the path that leads to the entrance of a small stone quarry in the commune of Sireuil near Les Eyzies in the Dordogne. Breuil and Peyrony [1]), who visited the place after the discovery, believe that it comes from the deposit of a cave that was destroyed by stone quarrying. The few pieces of flint found on the ground in the neighbourhood are of the Middle Aurignacian type. Though there are no certain data on the stratigraphy and chronology of this statuette, it was classified with the Aurignacian-Perigordian " Venuses " because of its particular characteristics.

In fact, while differing somewhat from the specimens attributed to that period, it reveals the plastic sensitivity found in many of the famous statuettes, and, as in some of these, a certain sense of humour. The shape is somewhat flattened and was obviously meant to be viewed in profile; the relation between the body and legs is disproportionate, and the outline distorted. The head is missing — probably broken off — and so are the hands [2]). The arms are short and rigid, the breasts far less developed than is usual in Palaeolithic Venuses. The stomach protrudes, the legs are exceedingly short; the buttocks are highly developed and project backwards; they would suggest steatopygia were not their shape due to the above-mentioned distortion of the body. The lower part is treated very realistically, and the whole suggests, rather than a normal individual, a deformed being or one afflicted by acondroplastic dwarfishness. The legs are joined together by the feet, which are reduced to a small protuberance through which a conical hole was bored — used, according to Breuil, for suspending the figure.

Breuil believes that the sculpture as a whole suggests a woman lying on her stomach with her bust raised and resting on her arms; Regnault [3]), on the other hand, thinks the woman is kneeling.

Undoubtedly the Sireuil statuette, while showing some of the characteristics of the Aurignacian-Perigordian female statuettes — particularly in the lower part of the body — should be considered a rather dubious work, for it differs in many ways from the others; moreover the date, in this case, is most uncertain — one might say totally unknown.

THE ITALIAN VENUSES. The area of distribution of statuettes of the Aurignacian-Perigordian type extends well into the Italian peninsula.

The first discoveries in Italy date from a rather early period in the history of palaethnological research : in fact, the Italian statuettes were the first to be found in Europe, and even preceded the discoveries on French territory.

As we saw above, the first Brassempouy statuette was brought to light in 1892, whereas the Balzi Rossi discoveries in Liguria took place between 1883 and 1895 : the first was published fifteen years later by Reinach (1898). But these findings, as we shall see, are surrounded by much stratigraphical uncertainty — an uncertainty which unfortunately surrounds all the discoveries made in this field in Italy, causing years of bitter controversy.

None of the Italian discoveries can be defined with certainty from a chronological point of view, because they were dug up accidentally by novices or by simple labourers, and stratigraphical re-examination subsequently carried out on the spot threw no positive light on their chronology, which therefore has always been based on a simple stylistic diagnosis and on a few dubious and inconclusive observations.

However, the form and character of these statuettes is such that they can only be placed in the same group as the Aurignacian-Perigordian ones. We may therefore call them " statuettes of the Aurignacian-Perigordian *type* ", but it would be daring to attribute them all, in an

---

[1]) BREUIL, PEYRONY, 1930.
[2]) The head must have originally possessed long hair, traces of which still adhere to the shoulders.
[3]) REGNAULT, 1931, p. 262.

absolute way, to that period; in fact no stratigraphical evidence disproves the execution in Italy of an archaic sculptural style at a later date. In mentioning this possibility we do not intend at present to put forward a positive suggestion to this effect.

Statuettes of this type have been found in four localities in Italy : Balzi Rossi di Grimaldi near Ventimiglia, where a considerable number came to light; Savignano on the Panaro near Modena, where the famous Savignano " Venus " was found; Chiozza di Scandiano near Reggio Emilia, and, finally, an unidentified place on Lake Trasimeno.

A) *Grimaldi* (Pl. 4). The discovery of the Grimaldi statuettes in Balzi Rossi is due to Jullien, an antique dealer who carried out excavations — or rather, disorderly dangerous rummagings — in this cave with the sole purpose of selling the objects he thus collected. These statuettes were concealed by the discoverer for many years, so that information concerning them is highly dubious and contradictory, not only with regard to their stratigraphical position but also to their site. According to the data published in 1898 by Reinach — on the strength of Jullien's statements — the objects were found in the Barma Grande cave, a cave which is known to have contained a vast deposit, many metres thick, of Mousterian and Upper Palaeolithic date. According to information obtained by Breuil [1]), on the other hand, some at least of the statuettes would have been extracted from another of the Balzi Rossi caves, not clearly identified; it might be the Grotte du Prince, which does not seem to contain a deposit more recent than the Middle Palaeolithic. As one can judge from these remarks great uncertainty surrounds the provenance of these objects, and hence their stratigraphy and age.

Many doubts were also raised as to their authenticity, and Jullien was even accused at the time of having faked them; these doubts are no longer justified, at least as far as most of the more important statuettes are concerned.

In fact, subsequent study seems to prove quite clearly that some of them came from the Barma Grande deposit and therefore (since at that time the Mousterian layers had not been reached) from Upper Palaeolithic layers.

The Balzi Rossi statuettes number about fifteen in all. Eight are now in the Musée des Antiquités Nationales of Saint-Germain, and the others are dispersed among private collections; one of them is an isolated head. One is bone and the rest are steatite; they are of small dimensions, even the largest is less than 7 cm. high.

We show here (Pl. 4, *b*) seven of the more important ones, among which is the so-called " negroid head ". The small size of these pieces did not always allow the artist to elaborate them very much : in fact they are rather summarily executed, roughly carved and often asymmetrical — mere sketches. Some, however, notwithstanding their diminutive proportions, show a considerably advanced technique and a carefully polished surface (Pl. 4, *a*).

Among the better specimens is the one first described by Reinach (Pl. 4, *a*). It is carved out of yellow steatite and possesses, to a great extent, the characteristics of many Aurignacian-Perigordian statuettes : featureless head, barely sketched arms, over-developed adipose masses. Here, too, the rotundity of stomach and breasts is schematically accentuated, harmonizing with and balancing that of the head which is bent forward with long hair following the neckline — as in the Lespugue " Venus ". Seen from the front, as from the side and from the back, this statuette shows purity of line and rhythmic balancing of masses; it expresses, in the perfect smoothness of its planes, a lively sense of plastic values.

The second figure in Pl. 4, *b*, slender and more roughly made than the first, is excessively narrow seen from the front, probably due to the insufficient dimensions of the fragment of stone used in its execution, so that the traditional development of adipose masses — particularly on the breast and stomach — is present only when the statuette is viewed in

---

[1]) BREUIL, 1928.

profile; the stomach and buttocks are of an extraordinary shape and size, the latter assuming a positively steatopygic aspect.

This Ligurian statuette is one of the instances adduced in proof of the presence of steatopygia in the Grimaldi sculptures. But it is possible that such an abnormal development, only exceptionally encountered in Aurignacian-Perigordian sculpture, is due, in this case, to the shape of the raw material used.

In a word this statuette displays the usual characteristics of the other Aurignacian-Perigordian sculptures : the absence of features, the typical shape of the head, the pointed legs and missing feet.

The first statuette of Pl. 4, b, while showing a horizontal spread, particularly in the region of the stomach and hips, that gives it from the front the appearance of a lozenge, nevertheless, in profile resembles the build of the preceding one; in this case, however, the buttocks do not assume a steatopygic aspect, but develop, more or less, like the buttocks of the statuette on Pl. 4, a.

We shall pass over the other more or less fragmentary and incomplete figures and describe, instead, the so-called " negroid " head (Pl. 4, b). However small and rudimentary it may be, this piece undoubtedly displays somatic characters that partly recall the features of a negro; the resemblance is accentuated by the headdress, divided into squares, and by the shape of the head, similar to that of the ulotrichia of negroes. But it would be rash to insist upon such an affinity, and even more, in the light of our present knowledge, to draw conclusions based upon ethnic similarities.

B) *Savignano* (Pls. 5-7). The discovery of the famous Savignano " Venus " dates from 1925; at that time the repertory of European female statuettes of the Aurignacian-Perigordian type was large enough to enable us to classify the new find in that group, on the mere basis of its morphological characteristics.

In fact the Savignano Venus was immediately attributed to the Upper Palaeolithic period, although no stratigraphical evidence was available to establish its chronology. For this reason the attribution was not unanimously accepted at first : on the contrary, it touched off a lively controversy which subsided with the universal recognition of the statuette's undeniable Palaeolithic characteristics [1].

The circumstances surrounding this discovery are well known, and so we shall only summarize them here. While digging the foundations of a farmhouse in a locality, about 1200 metres from the Panaro river, called Ca' di Prà Martin near Savignano (Modena), workmen unearthed the statuette lying about one metre below ground level. They showed their discovery, by chance, to the writer's father, Giuseppe Graziosi, a sculptor, who immediately realized its artistic and archaeological importance and bought it as a gift for the Italian State; the State assigned it to the Prehistoric Museum L. Pigorini in Rome, where it is still to be found. Excavations were carried out on the spot shortly afterwards by order of the Superintendent of Antiquities of Emilia, but no archaeological or geological evidence emerged to clarify the problem of the statuette's chronology.

---

[1] Immediately following the discovery of the statuette, this controversy centred upon the respective merits of an attribution to the Upper Palaeolithic or the Neolithic. The writer, in an essay published immediately after the discovery (Graziosi, 1924; idem, 1925) maintained, on the basis of certain stylistic characteristics, that the sculpture dated from the Aurignacian period. ANTONIELLI, on the other hand, published some articles (1925; idem, 1926) affirming its Neolithic age, on the basis of his personal opinion regarding the careful polishing of the surfaces — which reminded him of the skill of " polished stone " craftsmen — and of the Venus's resemblance to the Grimaldi Venus which, as a pupil of Pigorini's school, he considered Neolithic; finally, on account of his negative stand with regard to the presence of Upper Palaeolithic in Italy — a position that the followers of the above-mentioned school still maintained at that time. But, as we have already said, the controversy came to a natural conclusion with the acknowledgement of the Palaeolithic age of the Venus on the part of many scholars, such as BATTAGLIA (1926), PATRONI (1937, p. 137) and VAUFREY (1926), who took part in the debates and expressed their agreement on the subject.

The deposit was found to consist of clayey alluvial soil, in the higher part, with layers of large river pebbles deeper down, forming part of the second terrace of the Panaro river. The deposit immediately under the humus topsoil is Pleistocene, but the shallow depth at which the Venus was found, in an area that had probably been cultivated, does not allow us to affirm categorically that it originally lay in the Pleistocene deposit itself; on the other hand, no archaeological material was found in that deposit. Only on the surface of the series of terraces surrounding the locality some Neolithic artifacts of Mousterian-like form, and implements fashioned out of blades of Palaeolithic type, were found. This kind of mixture often occurs in surface deposits. However, the absence of data attesting the Palaeolithic origin of the Savignano statuette does not prove the contrary; that is, it does not allow us to exclude the possibility of its belonging to this period.

The Savignano Venus is 22 cm. high; it is carved in serpentine stone, of a greenish-yellow hue with darker streaks — a stone that is common in that part of the Apennines. We cannot rule out the possibility that it may have been carved on a stone carried down to the valley by a stream or a river. It is the largest statuette of the type known to us so far, and certainly one of the finest, although here, too, the artist developed the figure exuberantly, while remaining within the boundaries of absolute anatomical normality : a fat woman, yes, but not a polysarcic one; if we were to complete it, in our imagination, by adding the parts that the artist, as usual, neglected to carve — particularly the legs — the resulting figure would be more slenderly proportioned than most Aurignacian-Perigordian statuettes, especially the squat Venus of Willendorf (Pl. 9).

Let us now enumerate the principal characteristics of the Savignano Venus, that are in agreement with the canons of anthropomorphic Aurignacian-Perigordian sculpture : — legs joined together, ending in a point with no feet; puny arms, in this case barely indicated in the forearms which fold over the breasts; featureless face — the head is actually replaced by a conical appendage that counterbalances, in the upper part of the statuette, the tapering legs.

This is, so far, the only known case among the Palaeolithic Venuses in which the head has such a curious shape; even when it tends to be conical, it is always formed and isolated from the rest of the body. Perhaps this peculiar shape was dictated by the outline of the stone, but more probably it was intentional.

As Antonielli observes, this supposition seems to be supported by the presence of " a blunt ridge running longitudinally down the middle of the pointed end . . . almost as if to suggest the bilaterality of the face ". In the eyes of the same author, the " conical point assumes almost the aspect of a hood " [1]). A ritual mask, therefore, or a simple appendage, to which the head, modelled in clay or some other substance, was originally attached; or merely the stylization of a part of the female body that aroused little interest in the artist. It is difficult to reach a positive conclusion in the matter.

Among the sculptures of this type the Savignano Venus, perhaps more than any other, speaks a fundamentally realistic language. The anatomical construction of this vigorous fleshy body is expressed in a fully mature art form that might even be termed classical. The various anatomical details are acutely analysed, captured and reproduced with deep realism and fused into a perfectly balanced, harmonious whole. Note, for example, that the back of the figure is treated with astonishing force and plastic sensitivity (Pl. 7). Below the armpits the waist tapers and the hips swell in a harmonious curve, and a realistic roll of fat is placed at the lower extremity of the back, above the vigorously modelled buttocks which, with their dividing cleft, are an admirable piece of anatomical realism. We do not hesitate to describe this piece of sculpture as masterly.

---

[1]) ANTONIELLI, 1926, p. 290.

Seen in profile, the statuette loses none of its admirable realism, splendidly effective in the fleshiness of the thighs, the sustained volume of the stomach and the exuberant breasts. The gluteus region protrudes in such a manner as to suggest the steatopygia of the Hottentots; we shall discuss this later.

Seen from the front the pubic triangle is well defined and rounded; protruding above the breasts the clavicle is marked as a wide ridge. A certain asymmetry can be detected in the thighs and in the breasts, probably due to the shape and quality of the stone from which the figure was carved.

The exceptional artistic merit of this piece of work becomes increasingly evident as we study the statuette in all its details and realize the technical subtlety, the taste and the consummate sensitivity that went into its making.

C) *Chiozza* (Pl. 8, *a*, *b*). In September 1940 Dr. De Buoi, of Scandiano near Reggio Emilia, was fortunate enough to discover, in a pile of stones that had been removed from a brick-pit near Chiozza (Scandiano), a female statuette of stone with the typical morphological characteristics of Palaeolithic sculpture [1]).

Unfortunately the discovery lacked stratigraphical evidence of any kind. Its characteristics, however, are such as to attach the statuette, from a stylistic point of view, to the great family of anthropomorphic sculptures of the Aurignacian-Perigordian class.

Subsequent examination of the locality where the discovery was made threw no light on the statuette's stratigraphical origin; on the contrary, it actually added to the uncertainty about the chronological attribution that the figure's style suggests to us.

Nevertheless, it seems logical to include this work in the group of " Venuses ", with due reserve regarding its chronology, for we do not know where else it could belong.

The Chiozza Venus measures 20,5 cm. high, and is carved from a block of felsitic-micaceous sandstone, the so-called " macigno " of the Modenese Apennines.

With regard to volume it appears to be inscribed in a parallelepiped; this is probably due to the stone's original shape and to the artist's intention to exploit volume to the greatest possible extent.

It is not only the general appearance of this figure and the taste distinguishing it that immediately call to mind the Palaeolithic Venuses; the resemblance is also confirmed by a more careful analysis of some of its particular features.

The head is bulbous, shaped like a mushroom, featureless, and tilted forward slightly; it recalls the Grimaldi, Lespugue, Willendorf and Gagarino Venuses. The rounded shoulders are reminiscent of Willendorf, and the great, pendulous breasts resting on the stomach resemble all the more corpulent Aurignacian-Perigordian Venuses. The stomach, not quite so bulky as in some analogous statuettes, is particularly realistic, with a fold dividing it transversally. Its very slight — nearly flat — protuberance may be a direct consequence of the stone's original shape, to which we can also attribute the flatness of the hips, buttocks and thighs.

Here, too, the arms were neglected to an extreme degree, for the upper arm, nearly always indicated — even if only in a rudimentary manner — in the other statuettes, is completely lacking.

The legs are massive, divided by a deep cleft, and end — as almost invariably — in a point, with no feet whatsoever. The knees are marked by a deep indentation right around the legs and might suggest an incision made for the purpose of hanging the figure by a thong. The buttocks, as we have said, are laterally compressed and particularly developed lengthwise.

---

[1]) DEGANI, 1940; GRAZIOSI, 1943.

Although by and large the Chiozza Venus is somewhat rigidly and summarily executed, it reveals, in many details, a considerable plastic sense, particularly in the stomach and the thighs, which start from a fold separating them from the adipose mass of the buttocks, and the firmly marked pubic triangle.

To conclude, the Chiozza Venus, while revealing, in comparison with its more famous sisters, a certain divergence from the more lively expressions of Palaeolithic realism, is without doubt one of the more characteristic and remarkable specimens of this particular type.

A few words about its probable origin : when Dr. De Buoi discovered it the statuette was lying, as we have already said, in a pile of stones undoubtedly extracted from the brick-pit. This pit — which furnished material for a neighbouring brick factory — was opened in the more recent alluvial deposits of the Secchia river and its tributaries, deposits which, according to the present writer's personal examination, proved to be Holocene. The stones were scattered around inside the pit, whence they were regularly removed and collected in a heap during the extraction of the clay. The statuette, therefore, like the stones, was lying in the pit.

Furthermore, when the pit was excavated the remains of Late Neolithic (Eneolithic) — or more recent — dwellings, remains of huts and tombs, were revealed; these were thoroughly excavated by Laviosa Zambotti [1]) shortly after the discovery of the Venus.

The stones removed from the group of huts, and particularly the hearthstones, are of a purplish hue — the same as that which streaks some parts of the statuette. All this appears to support the theory that the Venus lay originally in the Late Neolithic deposit.

To conclude, as the situation stands today we can formulate the following hypotheses around the stratigraphical origin of the Chiozza Venus :

a) it comes from a Pleistocene deposit, underlying the Holocene layer, which was no longer visible when we examined the locality.

b) it comes from the Holocene deposit.

c) it comes from the Late Neolithic dwellings.

The first hypothesis is the least convincing : examinations by the writer and others in the Chiozza pit failed to bring to light Pleistocene deposits, that must lie far below the more recent layers and were never reached, at least in recent times, by digging operations.

Even if we assume that the Venus came from the Late Neolithic deposit, this does not authorize us, if we wish to maintain a scrupulous scientific objectivity, to draw conclusions about chronology and assign the statuette to the same age as the layers from which it came. In fact, we cannot exclude the possibility that it may have entered the deposit at a later period; thus it may be a Palaeolithic statuette discovered elsewhere by Late Neolithic man and brought home by him as a curiosity or an object of veneration. Other instances are known of objects (stone artifacts, tertiary fossils, etc.) originally from earlier deposits, that were found, kept and perhaps used by men of later periods.

The typically Palaeolithic character of the Chiozza Venus counsels us not to rule out this hypothesis " a priori "; however, we cannot entirely exclude the possibility of further research revealing, in other deposits, the same phenomenon as in Chiozza, thereby causing us to revise, on the basis of more numerous instances, our views on the chronological value of the Aurignacian-Perigordian style in the field of anthropomorphic sculpture, with extremely important consequences in Palaethnology.

D) *Trasimeno* (Pl. 8, *c*, Fig. 8). The so-called " Trasimeno Venus " was discovered in circumstances even more uncertain than the preceding ones. In 1938 Count Palma di Cesnola and L. Cardini saw it in a palaethnological collection of flint artifacts that an early researcher,

---

[1]) Laviosa Zambotti, 1943, p. 75 and foll.

Funghini, had gathered in various localities on Lake Trasimeno towards the end of the nineteenth century [1]).

The small figure lay among these artifacts, whose original location it was impossible to ascertain but which were probably found in surface layers and could be typologically referred to the Mousterian, Neolithic and even, perhaps, Upper Palaeolithic periods.

It is clear that no archaeological or stratigraphical evidence accompanied the statuette; its attribution to the family of anthropomorphic sculptures of the Aurignacian-Perigordian type can be on morphological grounds alone.

The figure, carved in soft soapstone, is fragmentary and small — only 3,7 cm. high. A curious problem arises over its description, for it can be interpreted in two different ways, or, rather, viewed with either end uppermost.

The Abbé Breuil believed that it was possibly meant as a kind of " calembour ", made purposely to be seen in both positions [2]).

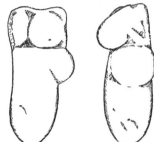

Fig. 8. The Trasimeno statuette viewed according to the second interpretation.

According to the position given in the sketch reproduced on this page the legs consist of a conical-cylindrical appendage, the breasts protrude and hang down, while slight relief forming a broken line on the intact side seems to indicate a slender arm folded across the chest. The buttocks, in this position, are displaced to the sides, and the head is missing — probably broken off. Seen upside down the head consists of a large conical-cylindrical appendage — the same constituting the legs in the first position; the breasts are displaced to the sides and the buttocks are well-defined, prominent and separated by a deep cleavage; part of the stomach and the legs are missing (Pl. 8, c).

There are elements of probability in both interpretations, but also anatomical incongruities, more evident, perhaps, in the second position on account of the slight ridge which in the first would represent the arm.

According to the Abbé Breuil it should not be ruled out, however, that the statuette might also have phallic connotations. In this respect we recall the presence, in Palaeolithic art as well, of figures lending themselves to more than one interpretation; among them is the Magdalenian statuette of Mauern (Pl. 82, h) which, according to its illustrator Zotz, represents another incomplete female figure and, at the same time, has phallic connotations when viewed from another angle (so as to form a second plastic " calembour " in the Abbé Breuil's sense) : according to the same German scholar it is an androgynous being, which he compares to the Trasimeno Venus (p. 97) [3]).

MAINZ. In a deposit of recent loess in Linsenberg near Mainz, Neeb found, between 1922 and 1924 [4]), some fragments of a statuette of greenish sandstone, very incomplete and possibly of Aurignacian type. These fragments, roughly and summarily carved, reveal nothing, from an artistic point of view, corresponding to Aurignacian anthropomorphic sculpture.

WILLENDORF (Pl. 9). The figure of an obese woman, discovered by Szombathy in 1908 in a loess deposit near Willendorf — 20 km. from Krems in Lower Austria — is certainly one of the masterpieces of Palaeolithic sculpture [5]).

The Willendorf deposit consists of 9 superimposed archaeological layers, and the statuette came from a layer containing artifacts believed by Breuil to be Perigordian. It is carved in

[1]) PALMA DI CESNOLA, 1938.
[2]) GRAZIOSI, 1939, p. 161.
[3]) ZOTZ, 1951, p. 336.
[4]) NEEB, 1924.
[5]) SZOMBATHY, 1909.

calcareous stone, measures 11 cm. in height, is perfectly preserved in all its parts and at the time of its discovery showed traces of red-ochre paint. The main characteristics common to all Aurignacian-Perigordian sculpture are present, and can be summarized as follows : featureless face, missing feet, enormous development of adipose masses. Nevertheless the Willendorf statuette has its own individual character distinguishing it from all the others; if anything, it is closer to the Russian statuettes of Gagarino than to the Western European ones, while sharing in the style and taste of Aurignacian-Perigordian female sculptures.

Its singularity consists in an exaggerated — but nonetheless lively — reproduction of reality : what we might define as a " borderline case " of prosperous feminine adiposity. Unlike Lespugue, the Willendorf Venus does not tend towards a kind of sublimation of the human body which, while inspiring the creation of works of great aesthetic taste, yet abstracts from reality by blatantly distorting it; we are here on a plane of concrete realism, while all that is paradoxical and grotesque in the obese human form is emphasized in a manner that might almost be called humorous.

From a plastic point of view the Willendorf Venus shows an extraordinary artistic maturity; the volumes are treated perfectly, and from whichever angle it is viewed the whole sculpture is always circumscribed within a well-balanced outline.

The squat, thick-set figure is topped by a large, roundish head covered with thick hair that has been compared to the woolly hair of negroes — although this appearance is given by a complicated headdress of long braids wound in spirals around the head and divided by transverse bindings similar to the bindings on the small head in Brassempouy. The puny arms are folded over the breasts in the usual position, but they differ from the majority in that they are well modelled and joined to the shoulders with perfect anatomical realism.

Small markings at the wrists seem to indicate the presence of bracelets, and the hands are clearly, if summarily, divided into fingers. The huge breasts, shaped like gourds, rest on the bloated stomach, pressing into it with their weight. Enormous hips protrude at the sides, and at the back the gluteus region, which is rather flat, is divided from the fat, rounded back by a deep, very realistic cleavage. The legs, with voluminous thighs partly covered by the pendulous stomach, are divided below the knees and end in stumps, without feet.

The most striking feature of this admirable statuette is the accurate realistic description of anatomical details, particularly of the actual morphology found only — or mainly — in a female body deformed by excessive adipose tissue : for instance, rolls of fat, dimples above the breast near the armpit, at both sides of the back near the articulation of the arms and under the buttocks, etc.

All this gives the impression, or even confirms, that the Palaeolithic artist executed his work from a living model who stood before him.

The knees are perfectly rendered from a plastic point of view, nor is the realistic representation of the navel or the pubic region neglected. This statuette more than any other denotes the lively, urgent necessity felt by the artist to express the attributes of triumphant female flesh and extol potential maternity. Before a work of art like the Willendorf Venus (photographs cannot do justice to its quality) we are inclined to wonder whether, in that remote prehistoric moment, the Aurignacian-Perigordian sculptors had not already refined their artistic talent through a long technical experience and in accordance with definite aesthetic canons; in short, through a proper school of art.

DOLNÍ VĚSTONICE, BŘNO, PŘEDMOSTÍ (Pl. 10). Czechoslovakia has produced some anthropomorphic sculptures from deposits containing artifacts of the Perigordian type.

The celebrated " Venus ", modelled in a clayey substance mixed with pulverized bone (Pl. 10, b) was discovered in 1925 by Absolon in the Věstonice deposit [1]). It possesses the

---

[1]) ABSOLON K., 1929.

essential characteristics of the other European Aurignacian-Perigordian statuettes to which it is related stylistically; however, it reveals a lesser degree of plastic sensitivity — having somewhat rigid, angular lines — and seems to have lost the softness and tasteful realism that distinguish the better works of Aurignacian-Perigordian anthropomorphic sculpture. Five more fragmentary female statuettes of the same type were later found in the same deposit[1].

The ivory object shown on Pl. 10, c was also found in Věstonice; it has been interpreted as an exaggerated stylization of the female body. It consists of a simple, shuttle-shaped object, crossed by a few parallel lines and furnished with two oval appendages that are supposed to represent the breasts. A similar interpretation was given to another, fork-shaped object found in the same deposit. Also from Věstonice is a small ivory human head which, though treated rather summarily, is remarkable from a stylistic wiewpoint (Pl. 10, a); the principal features are, exceptionally, carved with skill. It is hard to say whether this head is male or female; it is crowned with a voluminous coiffure or headdress.

Finally we should mention a masculine ivory torso, also from Czechoslovakia, with one fragmentary arm and an apparently unfinished head. This fragment, which is meaningless from a stylistic point of view owing to its poor state of preservation, was found in the Brno deposit (P. 10, d)[2].

Four mammoth metacarpals, roughly carved into vaguely human forms, were found in the Předmostí deposit in Moravia. Breuil and Lantier believe that they are cores of statuettes modelled in some plastic material such as clay or wax[3].

KOSTIENKI (Pl. 11). More female statuettes were discovered in a Pleistocene deposit at Kostienki in Russia, 35 km. south of Voronezh on the right bank of the Don.

In 1923 and in the following years P. P. Ephimenko found some figures carved from mammoth tusks and stone[4]: one of the most important of these, discovered in 1923, is an ivory statuette of Perigordian age (Aurignaco-Solutrean according to Ephimenko), about 12 cm. high (P. 11, a). The head is missing, probably broken off in antiquity; the legs are joined and severed below the knee, the shoulders are broad and the large breasts rest on the stomach; the arms are slender, barely suggested and, as in the case of the other statuettes, it is impossible to be certain of the position of the forearm, which appears, however, to lie on the breast.

All in all this is a fine piece of work in which, as in many others previously described, the typical luxuriant femininity of the Palaeolithic is apparent.

Another statuette in ivory, discovered in 1936, shows the same characteristics, but the legs and feet have survived whole : this is exceptional for female statuettes of the Palaeolithic era. The position of the head is the same as in the Willendorf and Gagarino statuettes. It is the most beautiful and the best preserved piece of sculpture at Kostienki[5].

A similar statuette, carved from a mammoth's tusk, was unearthed in 1931 at the same site; it is a little over 11 cm high and in a bad state of preservation, but it shows a structural affinity with its predecessors, including the typical separation of the legs from the knee down, noticeable in the case of the Venus at Willendorf (Plate 11, b). All three have, behind, an ornamental motif at the waist; the first has one at the shoulders also.

Besides these three ivory statuettes there are many others in stone at Kostienki : one, discovered by Ephimenko in 1931, is a rough, unfinished figure about 15 cm high, but showing undeniable traces of the characteristic shape of the Russian statuettes (Plate 11, c); another discovered in 1936, is 4 cm high, rather crude and with the arms folded on the swollen stomach[6]. There are over 60 further fragments of human figures in stone discovered at

[1]) ABSOLON V., 1939, fig. 1.
[2]) MAKOWSKY, 1892.
[3]) BREUIL, LANTIER, 1951, p. 186.
[4]) EPHIMENKO, 1926; idem, 1936; idem, 1958; GOLOMSHTOK, 1938, pp. 322, 323.
[5]) EPHIMENKO, 1958, fig. 142.
[6]) EPHIMENKO, fig. 144.

Kostienki, as well as numerous animal heads and figures (mammoths, lions, wolves, etc.). All these works are mentioned and described in Ephimenko's fundamental work on Kostienki I, recently published [1].

Finally, an even more sketchy and diminutive human figure, in bone, was discovered at Kostienki II by Boriskovskii in 1953 [2].

GAGARINO (Pl. 12, a-c). There is an undeniable resemblance between the Willendorf Venus and some of the Russian ivory statuettes found in the Gagarino deposit near Tambov on the upper course of the Don [3]. This resemblance, in some cases quite striking as can be judged from the illustrations, is surprising if we consider the great distance that separates Willendorf from Gagarino — about 2000 km. in a straight line.

The statuettes were discovered in 1928 by S. N. Zamiatnin while excavating a deposit that consisted of the foundations of a sort of subterranean Palaeolithic dwelling. This pit dwelling was found in a layer of clay similar to loess, at a depth of 1,5 m. below ground level; it was about 40-60 cm. deep, oval-shaped with a maximum diameter of 5,50 metres. The bones of great animals (mammoth, with 20 whole tusks, *Rhinoceros tichorinus*, ox, etc.) were placed in a circle around this area : according to Zamiatnin they formed the walls of the hut. The flint artifacts are Perigordian.

The statuettes were found along the periphery of the hut; they are 7 in number : two are intact, one has broken legs, three are in fragments and one is unfinished.

Pl. 12, *b* shows the figure that most closely resembles the Willendorf Venus : it is 6 cm. high and has the same overdeveloped breasts, hips and stomach, grouped to form the maximum volume in the centre of the figure. The head shows the peculiar rounded outline of the Willendorf Venus, with hair summarily suggested by dotted lines following the same pattern as that which takes a more realistic and accurate form in the Austrian Venus. The arms are rudimentary, but according to Zamiatnin the position of the forearms indicates that they cross over the breasts like the arms of the Willendorf and Lespugue statuettes. The legs are broken off, so we cannot tell what their original position was. This, on the other hand, is clearly discernible in the statuette measuring 5,5 cm. in height on Pl. 12, *a*; it is yet another element of surprising similarity with the Willendorf Venus, for here too the legs separate under the level of the knees and end in unfinished stumps. Like the preceding one, this second Gagarino figure, although somewhat less thickset, recalls, structurally, the Willendorf Venus; it differs, however, in the position of the arms which, with elbows resting on the chest, are lifted towards the chin in a position unusual in Palaeolithic statuettes.

The third figure (Pl. 12, *c*) measures little more than 7 cm., and although it possesses the same morphological characteristics as the other two in many details — thereby suggesting that it was created following analogous stylistic principles — it is much more slender and develops in a vertical instead of a transverse sense. The legs, which are long and slender, are executed with vivid realism : they too seem to be joined at the knee and divided immediately beneath it, ending in stumps with no feet.

In all these figures the roundish head leans forward, in the same position as the Venuses of Willendorf, Lespugue, Grimaldi, etc. All have sloping shoulders and adipose masses treated with the same realism. Undoubtedly the Gagarino statuettes are part of the great family of Aurignacian-Perigordian female sculptures, even through they are treated in a more summary manner than most masterpieces of this form of art.

AVDEJEVO. Four female ivory statuettes were found by Vojevodoski in the Avdejevo deposit on the river Seïm near Kursk. The deposit consists of hut floors similar to the Kostienki

[1] EPHIMENKO, ch. VIII, figs. 342-409.
[2] BORISKOVSKII, 1956, fig. 10.
[3] GOLOMSHTOK, 1938, p. 325; *idem*, 1933.

ones and believed by Russian scholars to be synchronous with them. Together with the statuettes were several bones engraved with geometrical figures and a small mammoth roughly carved from a mammoth's vertebra; the summary execution of the latter recalls the ivory mammoth of Předmostí that we shall discuss further on (Pl. 16, *e*). All these objects were recently published by Gvosdover [1]).

Two of the statuettes are merely roughed out, another is in a fairly advanced stage of elaboration and the fourth is even more finished. There is an obvious affinity between these figures and the classical Aurignacian-Perigordian European ones, particularly the Russian statuettes of Kostienki and Gagarino.

The most complete figure, which is reproduced here (Fig. 9) is slender and flattened, with a rather small, bulbous head, large breasts and barely indicated arms folded over the breasts in the usual position. The legs, like the legs of other Russian statuettes and of the Willendorf Venus, do not end in a point according to the rule prevailing among western statuettes, but tend to separate below the knee. A comparison of the Avdejevo statuette with those found in Kostienki and Gagarino, particularly with the figures in Pls. 11, *g* and 12, *c*, points out the almost complete identity between them.

Most Russian authors attribute the hut floors of Avdejevo, like those of Kostienki, to the Middle Solutrean. However, Gvosdover admits [2]) that both the Avdejevo and the Kostienki statuettes conform with the Aurignacian tradition, and should therefore be considered together with the other European female sculptures of the same type.

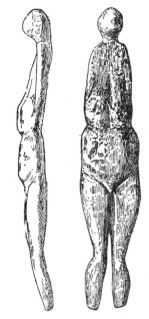

Fig. 9. Ivory statuette from Avdejevo, near Kursk, half natural size (from Gvosdover, 1953, fig. 21).

MALTÀ (Pl. 12, *d-g*). Although the documents we are about to discuss were found outside Europe, it is fitting to mention them briefly here because they show some connection with the works of art described above; furthermore, together with the mediocre Capsian works of North Africa, they are the only undeniably Palaeolithic works outside Europe.

These specimens consist of a series of 11 anthropomorphic female statuettes and of 5 others, considered by some as representing birds with long necks and by others as stylizations of human figures. They were found by Gerasimov in a deposit of the alluvial terraces of the Balaia river in the village of Maltà near Lake Baikal (Siberia) [3]). The archaeological strata of this deposit yielded artifacts that, by and large, can be defined as belonging to the Perigordian type, although the chronological value of this attribution is dubious and it is specifically denied by many specialists [4]).

The statuettes are carved of bone and represent women. They are long, rigid and crude, far more rudimentary and mediocre than most European statuettes. The features are more or less clearly indicated. The hair is suggested by lines and dots. Some of them are reminiscent of the small ivory sketches of Brassempouy (Pl. 2, *b*). A family likeness with the European statuettes is undeniable.

In another Siberian station — Bureti on the right bank of the Angara — not far from Maltà and with a similar production to that of Maltà, Okladnikov, in the course of excavations carried out between 1936 and 1940, found five female statuettes [5]). One of them is particularly interesting: it is ivory, 9,5 cm. high, strewn with small incisions in the shape of half-moons

---

[1]) GVOSDOVER, 1952; *idem*, 1953.
[2]) GVOSDOVER, 1953, p. 218.
[3]) GERASIMOV 1931; *idem*, 1935. Gerasimov continued his excavations at Maltà in 1956-57 finding many other statuettes of women and birds (information kindly given to the author by Professor Boriskovskii).
[4]) GOLOMSHTOK, 1933.
[5]) OKLADNIKOV, 1941.

which, according to its discoverer, might represent a fur garment. The head is covered by a hood, also dotted with half-moons. The body is elongated and rigid, and recalls, in structure, the statuettes of Maltà.

The enormous distance that separates the Maltà deposit from the westernmost limit of the European area of diffusion for Aurignacian-Perigordian anthropomorphic sculpture — about 4500-5000 kilometres — is certainly a curious fact and should be taken into account in studying the origin and diffusion of Quaternary art.

*   *   *

And now, after reviewing the documents of Aurignacian-Perigordian anthropomorphic sculpture — which confer so definite a character upon this ancient phase of Palaeolithic art — we shall mention briefly, before passing on to other subjects, some questions relative to the interpretation and significance of these female statuettes.

One of the most debated questions raised by Piette as soon as the first discoveries were made regards an anatomical peculiarity attributed to them by this author and considered by him to have special ethnic connotations : namely, steatopygia [1].

It is known that steatopygia — an exaggerated corpulence, posteriorly developed, in the region of the buttocks — is one of the curious racial characteristics of the Bushmen and Hottentots, peoples that inhabit Southern Africa and today — particularly the former — are on the way to extinction.

Understandably, the presence of such a singular ethnic feature in statuettes that were believed to portray faithfully the somatic character of their living models raised the question of the possible presence in Europe, during the Upper Palaeolithic period, of people of the Bushman-Hottentot type. Furthermore, the discovery of negroid skeletons in Balzi Rossi seemed to confirm this hypothesis — although those remains did not belong to men of the Bushman race.

But even a superficial — if objective — examination of the various " Venuses " of the European Aurignacian-Perigordian type clearly proves that none of those statuettes — with the exception perhaps of two very dubious instances (the " Savignano Venus " and one of the Grimaldi ones; Pls. 5; 4, b) — is steatopygic; on the contrary, as Passemard pointed out [2], they nearly always show a sort of " platypygia ", or flattening of the buttocks, whereas the hips bulge out inordinately to the sides. The generic qualification of " steatopygic ", for many years attributed to female statuettes of the Aurignacian-Perigordian type has therefore had to be completely discarded, at least with regard to the majority of them.

As to the most likely interpretation of the vast geographical diffusion of small anthropomorphic sculptures and their significance, we can only formulate hypotheses. It seems probable that these sculptures were invested with religious or magical powers; many authors — among them Begouen and Mainage [3] — believed them to be idols connected with the cult of fecundity and maternity. Undoubtedly the people of this ancient phase of the Upper Palaeolithic were interested in the reproduction of the female form and emphasized the features specifically connected with sexuality and procreation; in every part of Europe, and even outside it, this interest is always encountered, and always displayed in accordance with almost identical aesthetic canons, leading us to believe that so widespread a phenomenon must have had its roots in a deep reason, in a potent impulse, such as the diffusion of certain magical or religious beliefs.

---

[1] PIETTE, 1894.
[2] PASSEMARD L., 1938, p. 132.
[3] BEGOUEN H., 1935, p. 7; MAINAGE, 1921, p. 286.

ZOOMORPHIC STATUETTES

Up to the present no zoomorphic sculptures have been found in the Aurignacian-Perigordian deposits of France. Animal statuettes in deposits definitely belonging to this period have been discovered, so far, further east, and particularly in the Middle and Evolved Aurignacian deposit of the Vogelherd cave in Württemberg [1]); in two others, considered Perigordian, in Moravia, namely: Předmostí [2]) and Věstonice [3]); in a deposit in Hungary at Pörgölhegy, which is believed to belong to the end of the Aurignacian [4]); and in several Russian sites including Kostienki [5]). We might also add the remote station of Maltà near the Baikal Lake in Siberia, to which we referred in connection with the anthropomorphic statuettes; this deposit yielded some strange bone sculptures, probably schematizations of birds (Pl. 12, g) and a naturalistic engraving of a mammoth, etc.

The Vogelherd statuettes, of modest dimensions, carved in ivory, are little masterpieces (Pls. 13, 14). Among the more interesting and better preserved ones are a mammoth, a horse with long, arched neck, a large feline animal — probably a leopard — and still others, usually feline, and considerably deteriorated.

In this archaic phase of zoomorphic sculpture a certain stylization is already evident in the rendering of some morphological details (dotted and parallel lines to indicate feline fur, cruciform markings on the mammoths (Pl. 13, b), etc.). The elegant curve of the little horse's neck (Pl. 13, a) prolongs the no less expressive line of its back and the perfect representation of its head. This style constitutes something different from that which led to the realism of zoomorphic Magdalenian sculpture.

A further limestone statuette, representing a horse, lacking legs and head but appearing, notwithstanding its fragmentary state, well modelled and proportioned, comes from the Pörgölhegy cave, near Bakonybel (Veszprém), in Hungary.

The deposit of Předmostí (Moravia) produced the schematic figure of a mammoth, also on ivory (Pl. 16, e). Rather than a proper three-dimensional piece of sculpture, this Předmostí statuette might be considered a sort of " silhouette ", summarily cut out of a thick ivory fragment and marked by a few lines engraved on both sides. But notwithstanding this rudimentary technique the subject's realism erupts, in the eyes of the observer, from the apparently shapeless fragment, with its protuberant head and hide barely suggested by summary parallel lines.

Finally, still in Moravia, we have the Dolní Věstonice deposit which, besides the female statuettes mentioned before, produced many animal sculptures (Pls. 15, 16), made with a mixture of loess and powdered, burnt bone mentioned in a previous chapter (p. 56). None of these animals is over 8 cm. high; among them are a bear (Pl. 15, b), a mammoth, a horse, a rhinoceros (Pl. 16, a), a lion, two owls (Pl. 16, b), etc.; 116 pieces, whole statuettes and fragments including human figurines, were discovered at various times by Absolon in the Věstonice deposit; in addition, 474 fragments of the curious mixture of which they are made were also found [6]). The Věstonice statuettes are distinguished by the same sharp realism that is generally, to a greater or lesser extent, a feature of all Palaeolithic works of art. However, they do not yet show the consummate technique and elaborate attention to detail that flourished in the more advanced phases of Upper Palaeolithic. The modelling is crude, but the character of the different species is always successfully stressed in the balanced

[1]) RIEK, 1932-33.
[2]) MASKA, OBERMAIER, BREUIL, 1912.
[3]) ABSOLON V., 1939.
[4]) ROSKA, 1956.
[5]) EPHIMENKO, 1926; idem, 1936; idem, 1958.
[6]) ABSOLON V., 1939, p. 251.

proportions, even where morphological details are reduced to essentials in the roughly sketched masses.

The fundamental characteristic of the Věstonice sculptures is therefore a lively realism, together with a synthesis sometimes deeply stressed, as for instance in the owls on Pl. 16, *b*.

Comparing them with the small ivory sculptures of Vogelherd we are struck by the resemblance between the two groups in the general plastic construction of the figures, some of which tend, in both cases, to be elongated. Nevertheless, a greater attention to detail is evident in the German statuettes; this may be partly due to the different materials employed, and consequently to different techniques; the use of a graver in the second group made it possible for the artist to bring out a greater wealth of detail.

Notwithstanding the restricted number of pieces brought to light up to the present, this rapid survey enables us to realize that at its earliest appearance in Europe zoomorphic Aurignacian-Perigordian sculpture was also possessed of its own definite style. It is useless to search for the origin of that style — or for any precedent whatsoever; for, so far, we know of no examples of zoomorphic sculpture which preceded, in time, those described above. In the light of our present knowledge, therefore, these are to be considered the most ancient documents of their kind produced by Man.

ENGRAVING

The range of figures, engraved upon objects datable, by stratigraphy, to the Aurignacian-Perigordian period is not large; on the contrary, it is very limited if we compare it with the impressive flowering of mobiliary engravings in the Magdalenian period. Furthermore, while some works show a hesitant style and a crude technique which place them in the realm of the primitive, others possess a definitely personal style and great expressiveness which while remaining within boundaries of simplicity and purity of line, might be termed archaic.

But all this cannot, for the present at least, be considered particularly significant, because the specimens of this period — particularly the Aurignacian ones — are too few to allow us to decide whether their degree of artistic merit should be attributed to different stages of evolution or simply to the degree of skill of the craftsmen who produced them. In Western Europe, about fifteen or a few more deposits altogether have yielded engravings of the Aurignacian-Perigordian period on stones and pebbles, whereas the Typical Aurignacian examples can be counted on the fingers of one hand.

To this ancient phase belongs the celebrated fragmentary figure of a horse, of which only the hindquarters survive, engraved on the frontal bone of a horse and discovered in the Typical Aurignacian layer of Hornos de la Peña in Cantabria (Pl. 17, *a*). It is an inconspicuous fragment, yet it reveals the firm hand and scrupulous realism employed by the artist in the execution of his work. This engraving has been compared, for its style, to the horse engraved on the rock wall near the entrance to the same cave, and has therefore been used as a " zone fossil " in determining the age of the latter, and consequently of other Franco-Cantabrian works of parietal art which appear to follow the same style.

Pl. 18, *a* and *b* shows some engravings on stone from Rebières and Laugerie Haute in the Dordogne; the latter belong to Perigordian III. The figures in this case are executed somewhat clumsily. The same may be said of the Gargas engravings, and of those of the Saut-du-Perron (Loire) Perigordian, reproduced in the same plate (*d, e*). Also the engravings found in Isturitz (Pl. 17, *b-d*), in the strata of the famous cave in the Pyrenees that Saint-Périer calls Upper Aurignacian or Gravettian [1]), show the same irresolution and clumsiness.

---

[1]) SAINT-PÉRIER, 1952.

These works, therefore, seem to belong to a chronologically advanced phase of Aurignacian-Perigordian, but a phase in which the design was still indeterminate and primitive.

A bone pendant found by Saint-Périer in the Perigordian layers of the cave of Les Rideaux in Lespugue (Haute-Garonne) is engraved in a rather evolved style with a design of two vipers (Pl. 25, a).

On a " bâton de commandement " in Laugerie Haute (Dordogne) — an exceptional specimen of an Aurignacian-Perigordian decorated implement — two mammoths, facing each other, are deeply engraved (Pl. 24, c, d). The figures are well proportioned and vigorously traced; at first they were attributed by Peyrony to the " proto-Magdalenian " period [1]), but recently Peyrony himself revised his opinion after an examination of the materials found in the deposit, and assigned them to the evolved Perigordian period [2]).

With the engraved pebbles of " Grotte du Trilobite " and of Abri Labatut, which are considered Perigordian, we reach a definite form of art that finds expression in forceful realism and a clearly defined style.

The pebble of Le Trilobite (Yonne) (Pl. 19, a) is lightly engraved with the superimposed outlines of several woolly rhinoceroses. The hide of the animals is barely suggested by a brief row of hairs on the head and under the jaw. These are synthetic figures, crude and barely outlined, but they describe perfectly the massive structure of the pachyderm and seize, with a great sense of life, certain details and postures, such as the shape of the hoof, the movement of the legs and the distinctive bearing of the tail.

It is interesting to note that here, as in other Perigordian figures, all four, and not only two hoofs are visible, and in motion.

A masterpiece of the graphic art of this period is one of the two horses engraved on a pebble in Abri Labatut, near Sergeac in the Dordogne (Pl. 19, b, c). This stone was in a Perigordian layer; on both sides are horses, so finely engraved that they have to be searched for closely under a slanting light. One of them is barely sketched, the other, the better one, is complete and shown in the act of rearing up on its hind legs. The animal's savage impetus is admirably expressed in the thick, flowing mane and the intense motion of the front legs. Careful attention to detail is evident in this figure, in which the artist accurately described the limbs, the muscles of the neck, the hairy jaw, the eye and the nostril. It reveals a style that we shall encounter later in other works of mobiliary and cave art.

The pebble of Laraux (Pl. 18, c), also Perigordian, is engraved with an incomplete horse that has some points of resemblance with the horse of Abri Labatut in the detail of the head, the manner of suggesting the coat, etc., although it is a work of lesser importance. We shall encounter this style again in a later period; for instance in the horse's head of Klause in Bavaria (Pl. 77, b), in Laugerie Basse, and elsewhere.

Pl. 24, a, b shows a curious series of figures engraved on a fragment of slate found in the Péchialat cave in the Dordogne. Unfortunately the stratigraphical position of this piece is very dubious. The Abbé Arlie found it on the surface, together with other objects, among the refuse of previous excavations. Owing to the fact that previously the cave had yielded Aurignacian (or Perigordian) artifacts, Breuil assigned the piece to that period [3]). We are therefore not absolutely sure of the chronological attribution of the Péchialat engraving. However, the originality of the subject and the fact that it is one of the rare specimens of composition in Franco-Cantabrian art persuaded us to reproduce it here. The scene is rather childish from the point of view of composition; the single figures are somewhat irresolute and primitive in design though the outline of a bear standing on its hindquarters is rather good. This curious composition has been interpreted as a fight between a bear and two

---

[1]) Peyrony D., Peyrony E., 1938, p. 30.
[2]) Peyrony, 1952.
[3]) Breuil, 1927.

men : we must point out, however, that the figure on the right — judging from the tracing Breuil made of it — suggests a quadruped or a human figure in disguise, for one can detect a tail, and perhaps horns.

Finally, we shall close the list of Aurignacian-Perigordian engravings on stone — not a very long list, it is true — with a series of fine figures lightly engraved on the surface of pebbles gathered on different occasions in the French deposit of La Colombière (Aïn) (Pls. 20-23). The first group of these pebbles came from excavations carried out by Mayet and Pissot before the first World War [1]); subsequently, in 1948, Bryan and Movius, two members of the Harvard University expedition, reopened the excavation and found another engraved stone [2]).

These stones, belonging to the Perigordian period, have as many as 5 or 6 outlines of animals engraved on each side, some complete and others unfinished. It is not easy to distinguish one from the other, because the surfaces are covered with a tangled mass of fine lines, undecipherable at first sight. In Pl. 23 we reproduce a selection made by Movius of the various superimposed figures on the two sides of the pebble discovered by the American expedition.

In order to understand how the Palaeolithic artist was able to design this intricate mass of superimposed outlines while adhering to reality in each separate figure, we must assume that before starting on a new figure he obliterated the pre-existing ones with ochre, mud or some other substance, and engraved the new outline on this fresh surface. The chaotic disposition of the various figures, some upside-down in relation to others, leads us to believe that each one was executed separately while the others were hidden from the artist's eyes.

The animals represented are as usual varied : the horse, ox, wild goat, bear, a feline of some kind, and a reindeer and woolly rhinoceros. The last two animals are drawn with plumed arrows piercing the belly.

The style of the La Colombière engravings is excellent : some of them accurately give such details as the eyes and hide of the rhinoceros, the horse's mane, etc. They are distinguished by the same forceful realism we shall later encounter in the most successful works of Magdalenian art, but they also maintain a specific character in the linear simplicity of design, the flowing profile, closed and very often absolute — that is, with only one of each pair of limbs showing. Absolute profiles are not the rule, however, for in a few specimens four or three legs are visible (Pls. 20, a; 23). In the case of La Colombière, therefore, the absolute profile is not due to an immature technique but rather to a specific aesthetic taste.

Beside the figures engraved on stones there are some, in La Colombière, on bone. Pl. 25, b shows a fragment of mammoth bone bearing the outline of a bearded man, with hairy body and well-defined features — a rare occurrence, as we know, in Palaeolithic anthropomorphic engraving. The incomplete outline of another body, possibly female, is also visible, as well as the figure of a bear and the antler of a reindeer, all superimposed upon each other. Yet another bone is engraved with a reindeer (Pl. 25, c).

To conclude; towards the end of the Perigordian period art such as that at La Colombière appears already well defined from a stylistic point of view — one could almost say mature; it shows some distinctive characteristics which differentiate it from the art preceding it, and also from the contemporaneous Aurignacian-Perigordian works, as well as from the art that is to follow in the Magdalenian period; while as a whole it takes its place in the great course of Franco-Cantabrian art, in which it is a definite stage, or at least a distinct local expression.

The functional interpretation of the La Colombière palimpsests is that the pebbles were, so to speak, pages from a sketchbook upon which the Palaeolithic artist tried out designs that he would later use as models for great mural engravings. Another hypothesis, according to which the La Colombière engravings had an essentially magical purpose, seems more acceptable.

---

[1]) MAYET, PISSOT, 1915.
[2]) MOVIUS, 1949; idem, 1952.

SOLUTREAN

Solutrean examples of mobiliary art are few, and the deposits that have produced them so far are almost exclusively limited to Aquitania, with a few exceptions such as the Parpallò cave near Valencia and the Klause cave in Bavaria. This type of work appears to decline during the Solutrean period, both in quantity and, to some extent, quality. For instance, sculpture in the round, with the exception of a few rudimentary specimens in Isturitz, is completely lacking [1]). Some fragments of sculpture in low and high relief were found in the Middle Solutrean layers of Solutré and Isturitz. In the first case, a few small limestone pebbles are carved with incomplete, fragmentary animal figures in high relief : a bison and some deer; a certain skill is shown in their execution. On Pl. 26, *a* we reproduce one of the Solutré deer, which is headless. A fragmentary horse, in Isturitz (Pl. 26, *b*) is a far better piece of work and shows a certain analogy, in its vigorous technique and style, with some bas-reliefs found in the Magdalenian layer of the same cave.

Engravings on stone fragments are more numerous and represent the prevailing technique in Solutrean mobiliary art. Here too, as in the Aurignacian-Perigordian products, artistic value fluctuates considerably; however, by and large a more mature artistic capacity appears in some engravings of the later Solutrean, where precocious Magdalenian influences are already sensed. Such, for instance, are the engraved slabs of Badégoule that come from Middle Solutrean layers : about fifty of them, engraved with figures that are easily identifiable : they have been published in part by Cheynier [2]). They are the product of a somewhat rudimentary art in which subjects were often expressed in an uncertain, confused manner, and the same can be said of the engravings on stone of Abri Lachaud, of the Upper Solutrean, published by the same author [3]) (Pl. 26, *e, f, g*). Furthermore, the stones are engraved with so dense a superimposition of outlines that at first sight they appear indecipherable. The same can be said of the Isturitz engraved slabs from Typical (Middle) Solutrean levels; here too we have summary, somewhat rigid outlines or inextricable tangles of superimposed signs (Pl. 26, *c, d*).

On the other hand at the shelter of Le Roc (Charente), a deposit containing Solutrean artifacts including " pointes à cran ", and famous for its frieze in low and high relief (pp. 143-144), a fine outline of a bison was discovered — together with other figures, more archaic in style but expressing the zoological characteristics of the species they represent. The unmistakable maturity of its style and its vigorous technique herald the appearance of the great production of Magdalenian art (Pl. 28, *c*).

The Upper Solutrean of Le Fourneau du Diable in the Dordogne again yielded, besides the great bas-relief of whi chwe shall speak later, some figures engraved on limestone and one

---

[1]) This applies of course only to the decorative sculpture on tools, etc., or on a truly miniature scale with which this section is concerned : larger scale sculpture, as will be shown later, flourished during the Solutrean.

[2]) CHEYNIER, 1949.

[3]) CHEYNIER, 1953.

on a graphite pendant, which reveal an expressiveness close to that of the Magdalenian while yet retaining the unfinished aspect and the chaotically tangled lines mentioned in connection with Badégoule and Isturitz (Pl. 27, *b*, *c*).

The somewhat rigid outline of the front part of the ibex is engraved on an Upper Solutrean limestone fragment at Jean-Blancs (Pl. 27, *d*) : it does not yet show the distinctly Magdalenian traits that we have noted, for instance, in the bison of Le Roc.

A few limestone pebbles engraved with intricate lines and indecipherable signs were found in the Final Solutrean layers of the Lachaud shelter in Tarrassou (Dordogne); one of them, however, bears an interesting figure of a rather evolved type representing a reindeer apparently licking its young [1]).

Finally, the Lower and Middle Solutrean levels of the Parpalló cave near Valencia produced countless fragments, both engraved and painted. These are, in part, realistic animals, and in part geometrical figures — zig-zag lines, serpentine designs, etc., of obscure significance, with which we shall deal extensively later when discussing the Mediterranean " province " (Pls. 102, 103). The animal figures show obvious Franco-Cantabrian derivation, while showing the graphic synthesis and restraint of a distinctively archaic style when compared with the great Magdalenian art.

Outside France, we recall the figure of a mammoth from the Solutrean level of Klause in Bavaria, lightly engraved on a piece of ivory : this figure is rather rigid, but nevertheless quite expressive (Pl. 27, *a*).

To conclude, the finds of Solutrean mobiliary art so far are few and do not show particular characteristics. This art is represented by mediocre and rather indeterminate specimens, from a stylistic point of view, except for those phases in which the first symptoms of Magdalenian influence appear. Scanty documentation does not permit us to make positive statements about its effective position in the general development of Franco-Cantabrian Palaeolithic art. We shall only mention that it was preceded, in the Perigordian period, by works of art that were undoubtedly superior, such as those of Abri Labatut and La Colombière. In this respect we should not lose sight of the possibility that some cultural expressions lingered on beyond their time, or that two different cultures developed on parallel, independent lines.

However, on the basis of the material now available, the Solutrean, as far as mobiliary art is concerned, appears to be a phase of pause, if not actually of retrogression, in the development of Palaeolithic art which had achieved, in the Aurignacian-Perigordian, a high degree of technical maturity in engraving and sculpture in the round — the latter is indeed almost unknown so far in Solutrean deposits.

Instead, high and low relief predominate in impressiveness if not in quantity in Solutrean art; with the superb specimens of Charente and Dordogne, a forcefulness and distinctive style are achieved which make this period particularly important in the picture of the development of Palaeolithic art. It is almost as though the creative impulse of the Solutrean artist was concentrated on the execution of great sculptured friezes to the detriment of smaller, less important works of art.

---

[1]) CHEYNIER, 1953, figs. 5, 6.

LOWER MAGDALENIAN

Mobiliary art flourishes in its finest and most complex forms in the Magdalenian period. Besides the engravings on fragments of stone and bone which might be said to be the only products of this art in the Solutrean and, with the addition of statuettes sculptured in the round, in the Aurignacian-Perigordian also, a distinctly ornamental form of art grows and dominates in the Magdalenian : engravings, shallow bas-relief sculpture, decorated weapons and implements made of bone and, more rarely, of ivory. We can say definitely that we are confronted here for the first time (if we except the very rare instances noted in the preceding paragraphs) with decorated implements (Pls. 24, c, d; 25, a), and with the efforts of Palaeo-lithic artists to adapt their art to the shape and function of different objects. During the long pre-Magdalenian period, the artist expressed himself freely in engravings and sculptures, without being particularly influenced by the shape of the object he was working on : in the Magdalenian, on the other hand, the work is often subordinated to the object which must be decorated and consequently technical devices are used in its creation that sometimes lead to true stylization of the design.

Engraving, sculpture and bas-relief do not appear to have developed concurrently in all the phases of Magdalenian art; these techniques are present in turn according to the different periods, some of them disappearing almost completely at determinate stages in the develop-ment of mobiliary art.

Let us consider the Magdalenian period subdivided, according to Breuil's classification, into 6 horizons (Magdalenian I-VI) and grouped successively into Lower (I, II and III) and Upper, or Typical Magdalenian (IV, V and VI). We shall see that each one of these subdivisions is distinguished by specific forms of mobiliary art.

Sculpture in the round, almost nonexistent, as we have seen, in the Solutrean period, remains, during the entire Lower Magdalenian — with the exception of rare, ill-defined cases — circumscribed within forms that might be termed rudimentary. In Magdalenian IV it suddenly erupts in works that are far superior to anything produced before in this field by prehistoric man, and also to anything produced by primitive man today. It can be said that apart from the Aurignacian-Perigordian anthropomorphic statuettes, only in Magdalenian IV does sculpture in the round live and find expression in real works of art. In fact, in Mag-dalenian V and VI we pass from an extraordinary flowering of figures carved on bone, ivory and stone during the preceding phase to a poorer production, very limited in number : a few animal heads, very simply sketched on the ends of " bâtons de commandement " dis-covered in some Aquitanian and Cantabrian deposits (La Vache, El Pendo, etc.).

This also applies to the small bas-relief which is quite rare in the Lower Magdalenian (Magd. III) and develops, with a number of fine works, in Magdalenian IV, to disappear in V and reappear, in a very crude form, in Magdalenian VI, within a rather limited area of distribution.

" Contours découpés " also reach the peak of their development in Magdalenian IV, whereas previously they were nonexistent, at least in their most typical forms (with the exception of the Aurignacian-Perigordian Lespugue fish shown on Pl. 31, g); on the rare occasions when this technique made its appearance in the successive stages of Upper Magdalenian, the figures were cut out of thick pieces of material (Magdalenian V fish in the El Pendo cave in Cantabria).

Engraving, on the other hand, whether on manufactured objects or on fragments of bone or stone, is present during the entire Magdalenian, though in forms and percentages that vary according to the different phases of the period. Lower Magdalenian also produced, together with figures of small artistic merit, some pure outlines of animals, executed with great skill.

Following the great epoch of Palaeolithic mobiliary art — Magdalenian IV — we still find, in Magdalenian V and VI, superb figures engraved on bone and stone, on fashioned objects and on fragments; the deposits of Magdalenian V in particular yielded some of the most famous masterpieces of Palaeolithic engraving (Pls. 64, 65, 66, etc.). In Magdalenian VI, next to very fine specimens of engraving, others are undeniably decadent : summary figures of animals, roughly executed and anatomically disproportionate herald the imminent disappearance of an art that had already reached and passed the peak of its vitality (Pl. 72).

Sculpture in the round did not produce any very important specimens of mobiliary art in the initial phases of the Magdalenian. In fact, in Magdalenian I and II it is restricted, in its best known examples, to rough, summary animal heads sculpted at the end of " bâtons de commandement ". See, for example, the probable representation of a fox's head (Pl. 29); of a rabbit's head (Pl. 30, b) and of other ill-defined animal heads (Pl. 30, a, d) at Placard (Charente) and at Laugerie Basse (Dordogne). Furthermore, the figure of a fish in a more realistic style, attributed by Breuil and Saint-Périer [1]) to a very early Magdalenian level, was found at Gourdan (Haute-Garonne) (Pl. 30, c). An ornamental intention begins to appear : sculpture on manufactured objects, nonexistent in preceding periods, is evident here. It would therefore seem that the decoration of objects — not only with sculptures but also with engravings — is to be detected for the first time in the Lower Magdalenian period.

Mobiliary engraving in this period (specifically in Magdalenian III) already reveals an artistic maturity evidently connected with past Perigordian experience — in the decoration both of fashioned objects and of fragments of bone. Nevertheless, more primitive, inferior designs such as those executed on stone in La Marche (Dordogne) (Pl. 30, f, g) are contemporary with fine engravings on objects or on bone fragments : for instance, the sequence of deer heads in simple, pure outline engraved upon a " bâton de commandement " at Laugerie Haute (Dordogne), attributed to Magdalenian III (Pl. 31, b). We should also note in this connection the fine, masterfully executed figures representing deer heads, found in Magdalenian layers of the Spanish cave of Castillo (Pl. 31, f) and in layers still containing Solutrean artifacts, according to Alcalde del Rio [2]), in the cave of Altamira (Santander) (Pl. 31, c, d), shown together with the preceding ones to illustrate the great affinity existing between them.

As young deer heads, exactly similar to those of Castillo and Altamira, also appear engraved on the walls in the same caves, they provide a relevant datum point in the relative chronology of Palaeolithic Cantabrian cave art.

On Pl. 31, a we see other ruminants' heads engraved on bone spearheads found in the Lower Magdalenian layers (I-II) of Placard; these figures are reduced to their essential graphic elements. Also the ibex head engraved on a pebble in Pech de la Boissière (Dordogne) is very elementary in style (Pl. 30, e).

---

[1]) BREUIL, SAINT-PÉRIER, 1927, p. 11.
[2]) ALCALDE DEL RIO, in : CARTAILHAC, BREUIL, 1906, p. 274.

Numerous stones engraved with tangles of animal figures come from the Madgalenian III of Angles-sur-Anglin (Vienne) [1].

During the Lower Magdalenian human figures were already engraved on stone (La Marche, Vienne) (Pls. 82, *i-k*; 83, *a-d*), on bone (Marcamps, Gironde) (Pl. 81, *e*), or carved on the extremity of " bâtons de commandement " (Placard) (Pl. 81, *c*). We shall deal later with Magdalenian anthropomorphic representations (p. 85 and foll.). It is enough here to recall that the human figure is clearly, if infrequently, represented in the ancient Magdalenian, both in more or less monstrous forms as in Placard, and with careful realism as in the cave of La Marche, which yielded an exceptional series of true portraits from Magdalenian III.

We should mention, finally, that primitive schematizations, generally engraved on bone objects, appear during the Lower Magdalenian; these schematizations sometimes reveal their derivation from realist subjects, but they are often reduced to incomprehensible abstractions, tending towards purely geometrical expressions, and may be said to constitute a special group of more or less complex, essentially decorative designs. But of this, too, we shall speak later, in connection with schematic stylized art and purely ornamental design (p. 93 and foll.).

To conclude : the Lower Magdalenian witnessed the establishment, and a considerable artistic production, of engraving not only on stone or bone fragments, as in the preceding period, but also on manufactured objects, weapons and implements; sculpture, in mobiliary art, on the other hand, is still limited to poor, infrequent works on manufactured objects. But low and high relief on cave walls reached an impressive development in this earlier Magdalenian, connected in some way with the preceding Solutrean expressions in this particular technique.

---

[1] SAINT-MATHURIN (GARROD), 1951, p. 415.

UPPER MAGDALENIAN

We now reach the golden age of Palaeolithic mobiliary art. In Upper Magdalenian, and specifically in Magdalenian IV, all techniques from engraving to sculpture are simultaneously employed, and certain special processes — such as " contours découpés " — appear, to disappear with the end of Magdalenian IV, leaving but few traces in later periods. At this time the Palaeolithic artist expressed himself in astonishing works whose able realism and distinctive style suggest the existence of a real Franco-Cantabrian " school ". The multiplicity of subjects, mainly selected from the animal world, the suppleness and variety of their postures, their suggestion of movement, etc., make this imposing array of little masterpieces a unique element in the history of primitive art.

SCULPTURE

During Magdalenian IV countless statuettes were carved in the round, either singly or, in many cases, upon manufactured objects; stone, bone, reindeer antler and, more rarely, ivory, were the materials used. The subject matter of Magdalenian sculpture is almost exclusively drawn from the animal world; representations of the human figure are limited to a very restricted number of examples. Countless animal species are represented : mammals, birds, amphibians, fish, insects, etc. The mammals naturally predominate, particularly the species that provided the Palaeolithic hunter's sustenance.

A large number of fragmentary stone sculptures were found in the Isturitz cave (Basses-Pyrénées); a superb horse's head and a bear's head are reproduced on Pls. 46, *b* and 47, *b*. The former, treated with great style, is full of life and strength; the latter is sharply realistic, and even though executed with the simplest technical means, seizes successfully the animal's sly expression and fleshy, sniffing nose. On Pl. 47, *c* the hindquarters of a crouching ruminant are beautifully carved. This piece is fragmentary, like many other statuettes and small bas-reliefs from the Isturitz cave that were obviously broken deliberately; at Isturitz, as in other Palaeolithic deposits, such systematic destruction seems to reveal a sort of ritual iconoclasm, probably as part of magic practices. Sculpture on stone at Isturitz has its own individual character : the technique is simple, but the result is often more forceful and expressive than in many other works of the same period.

Another famous piece of sculpture was found in the Magdalenian layers of Isturitz : not stone, this time, but reindeer antler; it represents a feline animal with slender body and rather rudimentary head; it is a fine, realistic piece of work, although it somehow fails to respect the animal's true proportions. The sculpture is linear and simple, carefully polished on all its surfaces (Pl. 46, *a*).

There are some interesting details on this statuette : on the flank near the chest and on the thigh two barbed spearheads are engraved, probably connected with propitiatory hunting magic, and five holes are bored in the head, chest, stomach and legs. These were probably for suspending the object or for sewing it to the owner's clothing, but they might also be wounds, in which case their presence should be considered in the same light as the presence of the two spearheads.

Independent sculptures such as those found at Isturitz are infrequent in the Magdalenian period: many isolated statuettes give the impression that they were originally carved on implements from which they later became detached. This might be true of the magnificent ivory horse from Lourdes (Hautes-Pyrénées) (Pl. 42, b), whose hindquarters, by which it was probably attached to a spear-thrower, are missing; also of the headless bison of Mas d'Azil (Ariège) (Pl. 40, c) and of another masterpiece of Magdalenian art — the small head of a neighing horse, carved in bone, also from Mas d'Azil (Pl. 43, a) — as of many other isolated heads and bodies of animals found in various French deposits. Some implements were found still attached to the fractured extremities of animals that had originally decorated them (Pl. 36, d).

To return to independent sculpture, we should mention the ivory block of Mas d'Azil (Pl. 42, a), with two ibexes in high relief placed crosswise on its two sides. This fine piece must have been intended as a kind of pendant, judging from the holes obviously made for hanging or sewing it to clothing. Its surfaces are polished maybe by use, so that the details of the carving are somewhat indistinct.

We remarked above that Magdalenian ivory sculptures are quite rare: besides the Lourdes horse just mentioned, two of the most important ones are the reindeer pursuing each other from Bruniquel (Tarn-et-Garonne) (Pl. 34, a, b) and the equally famous " hyena " on a spear-thrower from La Madeleine (Dordogne) (Pl. 41, b).

Figures on spear-throwers are sometimes carved along the shaft, or at the end, using the broad part of the antler. Among the former is the interesting ibex of Mas d'Azil (Pl. 32); part of the shaft consists of the animal's hindquarters, elongated and distorted to fit the cylindrical space; this shows the extent to which the Palaeolithic artist could transform reality by altering the true proportions of an animal's body without impairing the realistic effect of his work.

The necessity of adapting visual reality to the implement's function was a decisive factor in the creation and systematic repetition of certain plastic distortions that subsequently crystallized into stylistic patterns. We have an example of this in the arbitrary position of the reindeer's antlers: to avoid the insurmountable difficulty of representing them in their natural position, raised upright above the body, without exposing them to eventual damage or destruction, in the beautiful ivory group of Bruniquel mentioned above they were extended along the animal's back.

Another example of this unreal position of the reindeer's antlers is the fine sculpture decorating the so-called " dagger " of Laugerie Basse (Pl. 33, b): here too the animal's posture was adapted according to the shape of the object upon which it was carved; the reindeer is placed at the extremity of the long shaft and shown in the act of jumping; with neck and head held incredibly erect and antlers flattened out along its nape and back, it appears to stretch upwards, prolonging in a sinuous elegant line the normal shape of the implement with its pointed muzzle forming the extremity.

Further instances of spear-throwers with figures adapted to the cylindrical shape of the shaft were found at Bruniquel decorated with horses' heads; another, shown on Pl. 33, a, was found at Laugerie Basse.

To this brief list of carved spear-throwers we may add the fragmentary spear-thrower of the Les Trois Frères cave (Ariège) (Pl. 35, b), of small artistic merit, whose extremity is summarily carved into the shape of a bird; the hook forms the animal's beak. To the side and lower down, the neck and head of another bird appear; the eye is represented by a hole that must originally have contained a different substance, as in the small ibex head from the same deposit, the possibly anthropomorphic head on the Gourdan spear-thrower (Haute-Garonne) (Pl. 81, *a*, *b*) and the ibex of Bédeilhac (Ariège) (Pl. 37, *c*).

Finally, another clear example of this particular practice is the superb jumping horse discovered in 1948 by Bétirac (Pl. 38) in the Abri Montastruc in Bruniquel. The spear-thrower in this case has no hook — it is known as a female spear-thrower [1]); a partial groove along the shaft ends between the animal's feet. Like the others, it has a suspension hole at the lower end, while the upper is decorated with the carving of the horse. The animal's position, with hindquarters extended along the shaft and forelegs folded and joined to fit the shape and size of the instrument, can be compared to the position of the Laugerie Basse reindeer mentioned above (Pl. 33, *b*); the Bruniquel sculpture, however, is far superior in taste and in technical proficiency. The small figure is lifelike, admirably balanced on the end of the slender shaft; the artist's daring in undertaking so difficult a task and the skill with which he fulfilled it make of this object one of the most remarkable works of Palaeolithic mobiliary art. It is complete in all its parts, and was found practically intact in the deposit, broken into two fragments that still held together at the time of its discovery. This was undoubtedly a ceremonial spear-thrower, for it lacks the requisites of a functional weapon : it is too small, the groove is incomplete and the shaft is curved.

A clever device was used by the Palaeolithic artist to render the particularly static quality of the animal sculpted at the end of spear-throwers : he carved it with feet joined together on the top of the instrument — a formula often repeated in the repertory of Magdalenian mobiliary art.

The animal most frequently shown in this position is the ibex, because it is a habit of this particular species to gather its feet together when standing on a narrow peak. The Palaeolithic artist seems to have borrowed from nature a pose that gives a static, robust quality to the figures decorating the extremity of spear-throwers.

The headless ibexes of Arudy and Isturitz (Basses-Pyrénées) (Pl. 36, *a*, *b*) are among the finest specimens of figures with joined feet planted on the weapon's shaft. The Arudy specimen is vigorously sculpted; it denotes a style that is already quite definite, distinguished by a certain hardness of line and conventionality that we shall encounter, in a more or less similar form, in other Magdalenian works, especially in the description of muscles and fur on the limbs, the profile in slight relief and the deliberate disproportion of certain parts, due to the structural relation between sculpture and implement. The short, arched tail harmoniously prolongs the deeply concave line of the back. Underneath, part of the spear-thrower's hook is visible. According to Breuil and Lantier, originally the heads of these two ibexes were probably carved in wood or antler and attached to the figures [2]).

Another masterpiece of Magdalenian art should be listed among the sculptures of the kind already described (Pl. 37, *a*, *b*). It was discovered by Marthe and Saint Just Péquart in 1940 [3]) while digging tunnels in the Mas d'Azil cave. It reached us miraculously intact, and at the time of its discovery it was truly unique of its kind. At the top of the shaft of a long spear-thrower a small animal is balanced, solidly planted on feet which are joined together; it is probably a young ibex. The forehead is prominent and the empty eye sockets must have originally contained some plastic substance. The limbs are lifelike, and as a whole the figure is far more dynamic than the two incomplete ibexes of Isturitz and Arudy, although the posture and style show obvious points of contact with the latter. But we are here on a different artistic level : this vivacious little work is full of liveliness and humour and reveals the artist's consummate technique and singular sensitivity. Furthermore, instead of simply

[1]) BÉTIRAC, 1952.
[2]) BREUIL, LANTIER, 1951, p. 190.
[3]) PÉQUART, 1942.

reproducing an animal — as do most of the Franco-Cantabrian mobiliary sculptures — it reproduces a rather complex, curious scene, a scene that might even seem vulgar but whose significance undeniably transcends what it actually represents. The young ibex turns its head round in astonishment to observe a kind of cylindrical object which it is expelling from behind; upon this object two little birds are perched, whose tails form the spear-thrower's hook. A puzzling scene, and one whose remote significance or purpose we are unable to grasp. Is it simply absurd fantasy or, more probably, the expression of a magic or religious mentality? Whatever the origin of this extraordinary work it is certain that the Magdalenian artist succeeded admirably in giving it an expression of innocence and alarmed surprise. The anatomical detail is astonishingly realistic, particularly in the muscles tensed in effort, the position of the short tail curled over the back — which is typical of the species — and many other details.

Surely so delicate and elaborate a piece of work (the limbs, for instance, are " à jour ") was not intended for use. The spear-thrower of Mas d'Azil must also have been a symbolic or ceremonial object, like many others, variously decorated, of the Magdalenian period.

An object of great interest because of its relation to Péquart's above-mentioned discoveries was brought to light in 1950 by Romain Robert in Bédeilhac [1]). In a narrow gallery of that famous cave, which produced Magdalenian artifacts and art-works of the same period, he found the sculptured end of an antler spear-thrower whose shaft, broken off in antiquity, could not be located (Pl. 37, c). The surprising fact about this little sculpture is that it is almost identical to the one from Mas d'Azil. Here too, a young ibex turns its head to observe an appendage expelled from under its tail, upon which a small, rather schematic bird is poised. Unlike the ibex of Mas d'Azil the Bédeilhac one has folded legs and rests its stomach on the end of the spear-thrower instead of standing on it. The effect, as a result, is more compact, for there is no open space between the legs. The head, with prominent forehead, lively, realistic features and small erect ears shows traces of a dark resinous substance adhering to the eye sockets. Another small cavity, empty now but which surely, at one time, contained the same substance, marks each of the animal's hoofs. Although very similar, the two sculptures are not equally finished. The scrupulous rendering of detail and the plastic elaboration of the Mas d'Azil sculpture is more advanced, whereas the Bédeilhac figure is rather crude. The style, however, is the same, the inspiration identical in both works, and so is the manner of dealing with the morphological characteristics of the species. Not only do the two little ibexes appear to stem from the same " school "; they seem to show the same hand in their execution. Here too, as in Mas d'Azil and in other Magdalenian sculptures, the representation of the muscles is somewhat stylized.

The distance between Mas d'Azil and Bédeilhac is approximately 30 km. in a straight line; this might explain the presence in both caves of works by the same craftsman. According to Robert the Bédeilhac sculpture is the artist's first attempt to realize his original idea, whereas the Mas d'Azil ibex is the more mature, complete rendering of the same subject; unless we should consider the first a copy of the second by another artist.

Another surprising parallel with the above mentioned works is worth noting. The headless ibex of Arudy (Pl. 36, a) shows not only the same pose, but also a rather voluminous appendix under the tail capped by a protuberance with parallel engravings, which appears to be the same as the corresponding feature with the small schematic bird similarly placed on the ibexes of Mas d'Azil and Bédeilhac. This third example, found at a considerable distance from the others appears to confirm the existence of a common figurative formula of magico-religious significance, widely current in Aquitania during the Magdalenian.

The formula employed in the carving of the ibexes on the spear-throwers of Arudy, Isturitz, Mas d'Azil and Bédeilhac, which consists of joining the animals' feet, is repeated

---

[1]) ROBERT, 1951; idem, 1953.

on some other Magdalenian sculptures, even where the figure is in a different relation to the object — that is, where it is not attached to it by the feet. Such is the famous mammoth carved from a reindeer antler that was brought to light during the excavations started by Peccadeau de l'Isle in 1866 in the Abri Montastruc deposit of Bruniquel (Pl. 34, c), the deposit in which Bétirac unearthed the magnificent spear-thrower decorated with a horse which we have mentioned above (Pl. 38).

Like the previously mentioned instances of Mas d'Azil and Abri Montastruc this is an extreme example of adapting the sculpture to the function of the implement, where the shaft is formed by the figure or by part of it. In this case it is formed by the mammoth's trunk; unfortunately, only part of the broken shaft remains, the part adjoining the trunk. This work shows a strong trend towards stylization, in the trunk, the head and the tusks (which are parallel to the trunk and joined to it). As a whole the figure is rather harsh and angular : the legs converge, at the extremity, in straight lines. Although more rigid and, we might say, more geometrical, the Bruniquel mammoth in its general configuration has points of contact with the Arudy ibex. Both sculptures are flattened and restricted within triangular outlines whose sides are formed by the lines of the back and of the straight, converging limbs.

The Bruniquel mammoth, finally, is an interesting example of restoration : its tail — forming the hook of the spear-thrower — was broken, and another tail was grafted on to the back, a little higher up than the original stump.

Fish were often used in the decoration of implements of elongated shape such as spear-throwers, obviously because of their long, narrow form. In this connection we might mention the spear-thrower of Mas d'Azil shaped like an eel (Pl. 49, b), on which the hook, according to Breuil [1]) is the tail of another little fish whose body was destroyed. The design of the side fins — two lines indicating their movement perfectly — is realistic, though simplified.

Another fine sculptured fish is the trout of Lourdes; originally it probably decorated a spear-thrower (Pl. 49, c) : it is carved on bone and was found in the " Grotte des Espélugues ".

The series of sculptures on spear-throwers, both complete and fragmentary, continues with specimens often of rare beauty; from figures adapted to the shape of cylindrical shafts — such as the ibex of Mas d'Azil (Pl. 32) — we pass to figures carved from the broad part of the antler at the end of the spear-thrower; in this case, too, as we have seen, the small figure was adapted as far as possible to the shape of the weapon. But some sculptures are simply attached to the shaft without actually conforming to its shape : they stand out from it, and are structurally independent.

There is a considerable number of these sculptures, both complete and fragmentary, detached from the weapon of which only the extremity with the hook remains.

Some of them show that the primitive artist, when no longer restricted to a particular shape, gave free outlet to his imagination and to his creative spirit. For instance, this is evident in the splendid group of two headless fighting ibexes discovered by Comte Begouen [2]) in the Les Trois Frères cave (Pl. 35, a); we do not know which to admire the most : the masterful technique, the perfection of form or the surging vitality. The maturity of Magdalenian art is here revealed in one of its most felicitous expressions characterized by lively realism but clearly possessing those elements of stylization already observed in other works; e. g., the limbs' profiles are indicated by means of a slight ridge, and the fur is suggested by regular dotted lines.

The same elements of stylization appear in another sculpture, also discovered by Comte Begouen — the fragmentary deer of Enlène (Pl. 35, c). An equally outstanding piece of work is the headless bison of Mas d'Azil (Pl. 40, c); the volumes are skilfully treated, the details

[1]) BREUIL, SAINT-PÉRIER, 1927, p. 11.
[2]) BEGOUEN L., 1931; BEGOUEN H., 1936.

are stressed with care and the whole design is excellent. Here, too, the hide is stylized in the usual manner.

The bison turning its head from La Madeleine (Pl. 41, *a*) is a harsher, more linear work in which the volumes are very much flattened. But the movement of the head — although the latter is out of proportion — is lifelike and forceful: a device used here to solve the technical problem inherent in the reproduction of a difficult pose has achieved its purpose perfectly, adding a flavour of ingenuity that in no way disturbs the sculpture's balance and expressiveness. This formula, in which the head is shown twisted back, is encountered in other works of art such as, for instance, the admirable group of deer engraved on bone in Lorthet, from a later Magdalenian phase (Pl. 64, *b*).

The so-called " hyena " found in the same deposit of La Madeleine is one of the few known Palaeolithic sculptures on ivory (Pl. 41, *b*). It is not sufficiently realistic to allow us to determine the species with certainty, but nevertheless it is a most interesting piece of work. This statuette shows evident traces of the instrument used in carving the hard material: firm, vigorous cuts furrow the ivory surface.

Three fine horses' heads, two of which are sculpted in the round and the third in bas-relief, are grouped together at the end of a possible fragmentary spear-thrower found in Mas d'Azil (Pl. 40, *a*, *b*) to form an extremely decorative composition. Like several other horses' heads in mobiliary Magdalenian art, the head in low relief seems to be partly skinned revealing the subcutaneous anatomy; we shall go into this later.

Various other pieces, more or less fragmentary, are reproduced in the illustrations; all share some fundamental stylistic characteristics. There are many animal heads, all of them executed with the usual realism.

One of the masterpieces of Palaeolithic mobiliary art is the famous head of a neighing horse carved from a reindeer antler in Mas d'Azil, reproduced in every textbook on prehistory. The life that emanates from this little sculpture, and its technical perfection, leave us spellbound (Pl. 43, *a*). Here, too, the stylization mentioned on previous occasions is evident in the representation of the coat. Some authors have felt justified in comparing this piece of work to Greek sculpture.

Finally we shall mention the " skinned " and " flayed " horses' heads in the same deposit, curious representations of real " pièces de boucherie " — as Piette called them [1]). The head in Pl. 43, *b* is extremely realistic: the anatomy of the muscles and ligaments is emphasized, the eye sockets are empty and a few cervical vertebrae are still attached to the skull. The equine head in Pl. 43, *c* has been completely stripped of its skin and reduced to a skeleton. Also the jawbone shows deeply stressed anatomical details. Horses' heads treated anatomically appear in other sculptures as well, and also in cut-out profiles or " contours découpés " and engravings. One of the three carved on a reindeer antler in Mas d'Azil (Pl. 40, *a*) — the one in bas-relief — clearly shows parts of the muscular system and all the teeth, just as they would appear if the lips were removed. The muscular system is also apparent in a more or less stylized form, almost as though by transparency, in several horses' heads in " contours découpés " from Mas d'Azil and other deposits.

This stylization of subcutaneous anatomy, erroneously interpreted in some instances as representing a harness, gave rise, in Piette's time, to the unfounded hypothesis of the domestication of horses during the Palaeolithic.

It is hard to explain the significance of these strange portrayals of animal anatomy; we shall see later that they are not limited to horses alone. In view of the hunting activity of Magdalenian peoples, it seems probable that they are also related to special practices in hunting magic.

---

[1]) PIETTE, 1906, p. 42 and foll.

Sculpture on " bâtons de commandement " exploits the stumps of the tines of reindeer antlers where they fork out close to the usual site of the perforation. We have seen before, in the Lower Magdalenian, primitive sculpture executed on " bâtons de commandement " according to this system; many instances are found in Upper Magdalenian as well, most of them fragmentary.

Usually they are animal heads in relief, whereas the bodies are carved in low relief along the shaft. Volumes are often flattened in the sculptural decoration of " bâtons de commandement ".

At times the stumps of the two tines were carved with two figures symmetrically arranged, such as the stylized heads of bison from Laugerie Basse (Pl. 45, a, b) or the phallic figures from Gorge d'Enfer (Dordogne) (Pl. 96, g). Here, too, the work of art was subordinated to the material used, creating a tasteful decorative pattern that we shall find repeated several times.

Having reviewed some of the principal sculptures of Magdalenian IV and considered their decorative function, we reach the conclusion that it is in this phase of the Magdalenian that mobiliary sculpture in the round attains its highest expression; we might almost say that it develops and comes to a close during this phase. Let us, for instance, consider the expressions of mobiliary art of the latest Magdalenian phase; Magdalenian VI. Here sculpture in the round is represented by very few specimens, so crudely executed that we hesitate to call them sculpture at all. From Magdalenian V or early VI is a fragment of a " bâton de commandement " discovered by Robert in the cave of La Vache (Ariège) (Pl. 48, a), representing a curious ruminant's head. This piece of work is on a level much inferior, from a plastic point of view, to that reached in the Magdalenian IV. See, moreover, some " bâtons de commandement " from the Cantabrian caves : the cave of El Pendo near Santander produced one whose extremity, opposite the hole, was roughly shaped like a fish's head — a very decadent piece of work (Pl. 48, c). In the Magdalenian VI layers of Cueva del Rascaño (Santander) a fragment of " bâton " was found, decorated at the top with a roughly sketched head which has been interpreted as that of an ibex, childishly rendered (Pl. 48, b).

Finally, a famous piece from the Magdalenian VI layer of El Pendo reveals — as we shall shortly see — a certain skill in the execution of some deer's heads engraved upon it; but the main intention, which had small success, was to give the object as a whole the form of a horse's head, with a hole representing the eye, and the mouth roughly indicated by a few deeply engraved lines (Pl. 73, a, b).

By and large these extreme sculptural expressions of the Upper Magdalenian can be compared, in their simplicity and crudeness, to the first sculptures of the earlier Magdalenian; these also were executed on " bâtons de commandement ", and an attempt was made to transform the ends into animal heads, as at Placard.

Thus, as a whole, this cycle in the realm of sculpture seems to show an analogous aesthetic and technique at its beginning and its end.

" CONTOURS DÉCOUPÉS "

We must now discuss the technique known as " contours découpés " in which a thin sliver of bone (often the hyoid) is cut into the outline of a figure and embellished with engraved details.

This particular process appears to be a simplification of three-dimensional sculpture — a sort of intermediate stage between sculpture and drawing. Fine specimens of this type of work were produced in the Magdalenian period.

The figures — usually of small dimension and representing parts of animals, particularly the head — are often pierced with a suspension hole.

There are countless horses' heads from various deposits such as Arudy, Mas d'Azil, etc. Ibex and chamois heads are less numerous. A fine series of the latter (or perhaps they are ibexes), all identical, was found by Simonnet [1]) in the Labastide cave (Hautes-Pyrénées) (Pl. 53, a). Their uniformity leads us to believe that they were elements in a necklace or some other ornament.

The same technique was used in the execution of all the horses' heads in Pl. 52, found at Mas d'Azil.

We remarked earlier (p. 76) that the halter-like markings around the necks of the horses in Arudy, Brassempouy and other deposits led Piette to suppose [2]) that these animals were already domesticated in Magdalenian times. The Arudy head shown here, in particular, seems, to judge by the strange signs engraved on it, to have a sort of rope tied round it. However, on careful examination of this specimen, and especially comparison of its markings with the markings on other horses' heads, we come to the conclusion that by these strange designs the Palaeolithic artist wished to define, more or less schematically, the different parts of the head — muscles, ligaments, hair etc. This procedure reveals the same curious mentality as that which caused the primitive artist to depict the internal parts of an animal's body with intellectual realism, by a kind of " transparency ".

Fish were often reproduced in " contours découpés ". In the Lower Magdalenian deposit of " Grotte des Boeufs " near Lespugue, Saint-Périer [3]) found a sole with a wide, leaf-shaped body through which the backbone shows up in transparency (Pl. 31); the eyes, as in real soles, are both on the same side of the head. This is one of the most ancient specimens of " contours découpés ", a technique that reached its peak in Magdalenian IV.

The fine fragmentary trout in Pl. 50, e was found in Lorthet (Hautes-Pyrénées) : it has the characteristic spots of the species, and shows, by transparency, its digestive tube.

A real masterpiece of Magdalenian art is the partly silhouetted figure of a fish, in the cave of Rey near Les Eyzies in the Dordogne, that forms the handle of a curved spatula fashioned out of a thin piece of bone (Pl. 50, d). We are confronted here again by an instance in which a subject is adapted to the function of the implement it decorates — a technique that as we have seen so often resulted in very fine works of art and achieved its ornamental purpose.

This subject is repeated, in a simplified form, in the decoration of other implements of the same type, reduced, however, to the fish's caudal, dorsal and anal fins, which in some cases are highly schematized; see, for instance, the objects found in the same deposit at Rey, and in other deposits both near and far (Bout du Monde near Les Eyzies, Mas d'Azil, etc.) (Pl. 50, b, c).

Speaking of fish, we also recall a figure that is rather crude and simplified — although there is an attempt to reproduce the scales by cross-hatching — cut out in the shape of a fish on a thick piece of bone from the Magdalenian VI layers of El Pendo (Santander) (Pl. 53, d) : it may be considered as exceptional, for the technique of " contours découpés " is restricted to Magdalenian IV.

Two serpents from Lorthet (Pl. 53, b, c) are engraved and carved in shallow relief on oval slivers of bone slightly wider at the head. On one of them an interesting geometrical decoration runs along the reptile's sides (Pl. 53, c).

We must also mention a feline animal found in Arudy (Pl. 51, b), cut out of a thin sliver of bone, and, finally, the largest known figure in " contours découpés ", a fragmentary bison, found in Isturitz (Pl. 51, a). The pieces were picked up on separate occasions over a period of years; they lay in different parts of the cave, more than 150 metres apart. The complete figure is 22 cm. long. The details are accurately engraved with obvious stylization; the beard

---

[1]) SIMONNET, 1950.
[2]) PIETTE, 1906.
[3]) SAINT-PÉRIER, 1925, p. 34.

area is represented by parallel lines surrounded by a strip forming a right angle and filled with V-shaped signs that are repeated on the animal's back. The outline is treated in a supple, vigorous manner.

To conclude, " contours découpés " make their first appearance, exceptionally, in the Lower Magdalenian, and develop with countless specimens portraying a great variety of animal subjects during Magdalenian IV, after which they disappear, leaving only an occasional glimmer in Magdalenian VI, such as the El Pendo fish.

There are intermediate forms between real sculpture and " contours découpés "; we have an example in the lizard of Laugerie Basse (Pl. 49, a). Often, in the case of sculpture in the round, figures tend to diminish in thickness as they increase in size, probably because of the actual shape of the antler, as in the case of the Bruniquel mammoth (Pl. 34, c), the Madeleine bison (Pl. 41, c), etc. Perhaps it was this necessity to adapt the proportions of the figures to the dimensions of the material used that gave birth to a " taste " for " contours découpés "; the bones used in their execution (the hyoid, for instance) were too thin to allow the creation of anything but two-dimensional images.

" CHAMPLEVÉ " AND " BAS-RELIEF " FIGURES

The processes known as " champlevé " and " bas-relief ", evidently related to sculpture in the round, were highly developed during Magdalenian IV. Sometimes a figure in which the head, for instance, was modelled in the round has a body in bas-relief; at other times — as in the object fashioned from a reindeer antler and decorated with horses' heads in Mas d'Azil (Pl. 40, a) — two heads are sculptured in the round and a third in shallow relief. The technique used in this case can be explained, where it is a matter of decorating artifacts, by the necessity to adapt the figure to the shape and proportions of the implement. Here, too, we can but repeat what we said in connection with sculpture : the Magdalenian craftsman restricted his figures within the limits imposed by the shape of the object, adapting, and in some cases distorting his work without betraying the refined taste and technical skill that characterize these great achievements of the Old Stone Age.

We have magnificent specimens in the ruminant figures engraved on " bâtons de commandement " in Mas d'Azil (Pl. 56, a) and Arudy (Pl. 54). Also from Arudy is a fine sculptured horse's head that follows the roundish surface of the object without losing its proportions (Pl. 55, a). From Laugerie Basse we reproduce, on Pl. 56, b, c, a " bâton de commandement " with on one side a superb reindeer head, and on the other a whole reindeer, with turned head. The latter covers the entire surface of the object with its long, slender body and with antlers elegantly branching towards the pointed extremity in a harmoniously planned decoration.

Finally, there is the " bâton de commandement " from the Chancelade cave in Raymonden (Dordogne) with the figure of a great bird, probably a bird of prey, sculptured in shallow relief, flattened out, enveloping with its body and wings the curved surface of the cylindrical shaft (Pl. 55, b). Simple lines portray schematically the wings and merely suggest some details of the plumage, offering an interesting example of stylization and making of the bird itself a particularly curious and decorative work.

Bas-relief was used not only on manufactured objects — where the image often had to be adapted to the shape of the object itself, as in the case of sculpture — but also on fragments of stone and bone that left the artist wider scope. Among the shallow bas-reliefs of this kind are a large number of specimens from the Magdalenian IV layers of the Isturitz cave, the famous cave in the Pyrenees which produced such a rich harvest of reliably dated art from the Aurignacian-Perigordian to the Magdalenian periods.

Most of these specimens are fragmentary, and many works of art from this deposit appear to have suffered deliberate destruction in Palaeolithic times. Nevertheless the fragments help us to appreciate the technique of the ancient sculptors, who worked their material with firm, deep strokes and showed the skill of great masters. The rude simplicity with which the rock was cut to obtain the effect of relief, with no subsequent finishing off once the image was realized, confers an immediacy upon these works which increases their expressiveness and emotional power. In fact, a large part of the sculptured surface was not even hollowed out : the relief was obtained by deep incision which created, around the outline of the figure, a clearly delimited area of depression. Among the figures of bison, horses and reindeer (Pls. 58; 59, a, b) are a few wounded or dying animals, as in Pls. 59, a and 58, a.

A more uniform manner of hollowing the background to obtain a greater degree of relief is observed in the fine, accurate sculpture on stone of a bison's head at Laugerie Basse (Pl. 59, c). Also from Laugerie Basse is the superb fragmentary horse on a bone sliver, whose pure outline is carved in shallow relief (Pl. 57, e) : here, too, the details of the head are stressed with care; the eye, the nostrils, the thick mane and, as if transparently, some of the teeth.

On the opposite side of this same bone fragment is the strange scene of a woman and a reindeer (Pl. 58, c) which we shall discuss when speaking of the human figure.

Also from Laugerie Basse is a beautiful ibex in shallow relief on a reindeer antler — a fine piece of carving.

ENGRAVING ON MANUFACTURED OBJECTS

There are no well-defined boundaries between relief and engraving. The sculptures in shallow relief at Isturitz, for instance, were not created by hollowing out the whole area around the figures, but by making a broad, deep incision. Between this technique and that of engraving is a very short step : however, we do not intend to establish derivation, still less precedence, on the basis of this observation.

Engraved manufactured objects are innumerable in Magdalenian IV, and the figures that decorate them are often incomparably beautiful; but Magdalenian V also left a number of fine works. The objects most frequently decorated were " bâtons de commandement "; there are also many interesting perforated bone disks that must have been used as buttons or as elements in necklaces or other ornaments — decorated with fine, delicate engravings — all from Magdalenian IV.

Some objects, as we have seen, when carved in relief or in the round involved a distortion of the figures; engraving, on the other hand, required no such distortion, because the Palaeolithic artist made free use of the entire curved surface, as in the case of " bâtons de commandement ", to execute in its natural proportions the subject of his choice.

In executing a design on a cylindrical object the artist was never hindered in the reproduction of reality by the form of the surface at his disposal. In fact, if we transferred the design to a flat surface, the figure obtained would be perfect and show none of the disproportions and uncertainty that one would logically expect to find in a pattern — sometimes a very complex one — engraved upon a curved surface.

Let us consider, for instance, the deer of Lorthet (Pl. 64, a, b) : in the original design going right round the cylindrical " bâton " the deer's antlers almost join up with their feet. The development of these engravings on a flat surface shows us images in which reality is perfectly respected and not only are proportions and forms faithfully reproduced, but the resulting composition achieves a balance and a decorative quality that make the object one of the masterpieces of Quaternary art.

This group (one of the rare instances of composition in Palaeolithic art) probably represents a herd of deer crossing a stream, suggested here by four superbly executed salmon leaping realistically among the deer's legs; the movements are represented so exactly as to convince us once more of the power of observation of the Palaeolithic artist, not only with regard to the shape, but also to the life of the animals surrounding him.

The last deer of the herd turns its head round with a timorous expression that is perfectly rendered; above it two lozenge-shaped figures, crossed by a vertical line, are impossible to interpret.

Unfortunately this beautiful composition, revealing such extraordinary technical maturity, is fragmentary.

The " bâton de commandement " of Teyjat (Dordogne) (Pl. 66, a, b), decorated with figures of horses, birds and vaguely anthropomorphic beings, is another interesting example of designs executed on cylindrical objects; several more are shown in the illustrations (Pls. 65-68).

This exceptional skill of the Magdalenian artist is a peculiarity of the period, and seems to tell of a long, consummate graphic experience, acquired in the decoration of curved objects such as reindeer antlers in general and " bâtons de commandement " in particular.

In this connection, too, the Magdalenian artist's ability reaches a very high standard; outlines are freely and firmly drawn without hesitation or retouching. This also applies to engravings on unshaped objects such as chance pieces of bone, ivory or stone. The realism of these works of art is astounding.

Among the most famous is the grazing reindeer of Thayngen in Switzerland (Pl. 67, a); here we are at a loss to know which is more admirable : the purity of design or the lifelike representation of the animal.

The deer of Les Hoteaux (Aïn) (Pl. 65, a) is a more impressionistic vision of nature, expressed with great simplicity by a master.

The Montgaudier (Charente) seals (Pl. 65, b) are extremely realistic and show the most careful analysis in reproducing the morphological characteristics of the species : note, for instance, how faithfully the folds of skin at the throat are observed. The " bâton de command-ment " of Montgaudier shows on its opposite side a complicated design of eels or snakes unrolling along the entire length of the object.

The " bâton de commandement " of Teyjat, to which we alluded above (Pl. 66, a, b), bears a series of figures distributed over its entire surface, some superimposed upon each other with no logical connection. On one side is a fine horse, with its hide characteristically stylized in a manner that is seen on other Magdalenian equine figures; it is followed by a smaller, incomplete horse. Before and behind the large horse and on the opposite side of the object are three curious anthropomorphic figures masked with animal heads — the so-called " diablo-tins " or imps (see also Pl. 87, f) — and the fine head of a deer delicately engraved, with its ears superimposed upon three serpentine, dotted figures. Finally, on the opposite side, there are three, incomplete figures of swans with long, sinuous necks.

The " bâton de commandement " of Gourdan (Pl. 66, c) is engraved with a series of four chamois' heads on one side and three on the other; there can be no doubt as to their attribution : they are flanked by the head of a deer and the head of what is probably a marmot. The succession of these figures has a rhythmical quality that is found in other works of mobiliary art, where a sequence of animal heads creates a decorative pattern, for example at Laugerie Basse, Mas d'Azil (Pl. 57, a) and elsewhere. We have noted the same thing in the sculptured reindeer of Bruniquel (Pl. 34) and will encounter it again in cave art — for instance at Lascaux.

The decoration of manufactured objects with engraved designs produced works of great artistic merit during the Magdalenian period; even the last phase of this period left, besides figures that already reveal obvious symptoms of decline, some designs that fully maintain the tradition of refined, accurate and lifelike representation which distinguishes the most flourishing moments of Magdalenian graphic art. A magnificent specimen is the group of five does' heads delicately engraved upon a " bâton de commandement " at El Pendo (Santander) that dates from Magdalenian VI and of which we have spoken before (p. 77) (Pl. 73, *a*, *b*). This is a very fine piece of work, exactly similar to another version of the same subject from Magdalenian VI in the Cueva del Valle, also in the neighbourhood of Santander (Pl. 73, *c*). This formula, consisting of the exquisite graphic description of the animal heads, is also found in other works of Magdalenian art. It is to be seen for instance in the bison's head engraved on a spatula discovered by Robert [1]) at La Vache, dating from the end of Magdalenian V or the beginning of Magdalenian VI (Pl. 71, *a*). This fine engraving is accompanied by small tree figures and others of a decorative nature, difficult to interpret. We also recall the fine deer engraved on a " bâton de commandement " from the Magdalenian VI layer of the cave of Castillo near Santander (Pl. 72, *d*). This figure, like the two Spanish ones mentioned above, is carved from deer antler in the best Franco-Cantabrian tradition; it shows, however, some resemblance with works of the later phase of Magdalenian VI, engraved or partly sculptured in shallow relief, which are quite crude both in technique and execution. We refer to the herds of horses executed on " bâtons de commandement " of La Madeleine (Pl. 72, *c*, *e*), in which head and body are out of proportion and poorly executed. Here we enter a phase of undeniable decadence.

ENGRAVINGS ON CHANCE FRAGMENTS OF STONE AND BONE

To return to the best manifestations in the field of engraving technique, we must consider the enormous production of figures that are not engraved on objects such as weapons and implements (and therefore, from a certain point of view, tied to a decorative purpose) but on fragments of stone and bone and consequently uninfluenced by the original shape of the object. Several authors have said that we are here sometimes dealing with " pages from a sketchbook " [2]).

In this kind of work the Magdalenian artist was undoubtedly able to express himself with greater freedom and forceful realism; this applies to cave art as well. Magdalenian IV left splendid animal figures, often shown in motion; here too the entire Pleistocene fauna, from its humblest representatives — insects — to huge pachyderms, is portrayed. We shall not linger over what we have already noted in connection with other manifestations of Magdalenian art : the realistic expression of animal life and the profound anatomical research that went into each portrait. We shall restrict our comments to the finest pieces of work here reproduced : the Isturitz hare (Pl. 74) is certainly one of the most interesting specimens of the entire Palaeolithic, a pure, essential vision of reality in which life and form are fused in perfect harmony.

A particularly important piece, not only for its intrinsic value but also for what might be called its historical interest, is the fragment of mammoth tusk from La Madeleine (Pl. 60, *a*) vigorously engraved with a charging pachyderm; this fine piece of work was among the first to be discovered; and it furnished irrefutable proof of the existence of Palaeolithic art (p. 15).

---

[1]) ROBERT, KÜHN, 1952.
[2]) Several such engravings have been considered as exercises or sketches for the execution of works of greater importance. The figure of a bison engraved upon a stone fragment in Abri de la Genière near Serrières-sur-Aïn, absolutely identical with one of the great bisons painted in the cave at Font-de-Gaume, is often mentioned in this connection (KOPPERS, 1950). Its authenticity, however, is very dubious.

The quail of Isturitz, engraved on a reindeer antler (Pl. 62, *d*) expresses unmistakably, with exceptionally simple means, the reality of the species; also from Isturitz is the fine horse's head on stone (Pl. 75, *a*) which, though very lightly engraved, is a work of undeniable merit.

A very important series of engraved stones from Laugerie Basse contains some figures executed in a more elaborate style; among them we reproduce, on Pl. 76, *b*, a superb bison, perfectly proportioned and accurately described in its somatic details, that recalls the monumental works of cave art of the greatest Franco-Cantabrian period; a walking deer (Pl. 76, *a*), turning its head with the lifelike gesture observed in other specimens of mobiliary art of this period (such as the Lorthet deer mentioned above; Pl. 64, *b*); a bear, admirable for the realism of its slow, undulating movement, which we shall also see effectively portrayed in cave art.

Two birds, probably herons, on a fragment of stone in Labastide are also exquisitely engraved (Pl. 75, *b*). A curious composition, lightly engraved upon a bone fragment in Les Trois Frères was discovered by Comte Begouen [1]) (Pl. 60, *b*) : among other figures there are three fragmentary birds, a grasshopper observed with such care and precision in morphological detail that it can be identified as " Troglophilus " [2]); and two other unidentifiable figures.

The bear engraved on a pebble in the cave of Massat (Ariège) is famous (Pl. 77, *c*).

Engravings of considerable importance were still produced in Magdalenian V : the beautiful young deer on stone of Bout du Monde (Dordogne) (Pl. 78, *c*); the fine group of bisons' heads and the bird of Puy de Lacan (Corrèze) (Pl. 78, *a*, *b*), also engraved on fragments of stone; the two wolves facing each other on a piece of bone in the cave of La Vache (Pl. 70, *b*) from late Magdalenian V or early Magdalenian VI — a piece of work whose forceful realism brings it close to another group of two animals, also on bone, from Brassempouy (Pl. 70, *a*).

We have mentioned the horses from Magdalenian VI, ill-proportioned and crude in outline, that were found in the cave of La Madeleine and reproduced, in more or less similar forms, in other caves of the late Magdalenian period such as the remote Cova del Valle (Santander) (Pl. 72, *b*), Laugerie Basse, and elsewhere.

A typical example of decadent art is the " bâton de commandement " of Magdalenian VI from the French cave of Loubressac (Vienne) (Pl. 72, *f*); the bison are summary and rigid, lacking true inspiration. Many similar specimens could be listed.

---

[1]) BEGOUEN H., BEGOUEN L., 1928.
[2]) VIDAL Y LOPEZ, 1937, p. 9.

THE HUMAN FORM
IN MAGDALENIAN MOBILIARY ART

The human form in Magdalenian art requires a chapter to itself. Anthropomorphic representation in this period, in fact, is based on an aesthetic conception which seems very different from that which characterizes the representation of animals. Many of the works that have survived reveal a certain difficulty in reproducing the subject, both in engraving and in sculpture; childish design, summary technique and, often, neglect of details place these works in a different category altogether from the fine female statuettes by Aurignacian-Perigordian artists. We should add that with a few exceptions the Magdalenian deposits have produced a relatively small number of human figures compared with the large number of animals.

An over-all glance at Magdalenian mobiliary art reveals without doubt that from an artistic point of view Palaeolithic man was far more interested in the animal world. This, as we shall later see, is even more obvious in cave art.

Realistic human figures, in which the artist appears to portray a specific person, are very rare. As examples there are the figures engraved on stone at La Marche. Often, in fact, individual personalities are concealed beneath strange masks that draw their origin from the animal world : men with theriomorphic heads, with tails or with long fur covering their bodies, etc., real anthropoid monsters of a hybrid nature.

Both in Lower Magdalenian and in its later phases the same sense of being a " minor art " is given by these anthropomorphic figures, in contrast to the fundamental importance of zoomorphic figures. The discoveries made so far lead us to believe that the human figure was treated with greater interest and realism in the Lower Magdalenian. If this were to be ultimately confirmed, we might see in it a continuation of the taste and interest that distinguish the Aurignacian-Perigordian reproduction of the human form.

The most important cache both in the number of specimens and in artistic merit, was found in the Lower Magdalenian layers of the above-mentioned cave of La Marche at Lussac-les-Châteaux (Vienne). There were some complete human figures on fragments of stone, but the majority of the representations are of heads which, with the careful emphasis on certain facial details, give the impression that they were intended as real portraits (Pl. 83, a-d).

The discovery of the La Marche figures between 1937 and 1938 was published in 1940 [1]); at the time, the authenticity of these figures gave rise to lively controversy in scholarly circles. The authoritative intervention of the Abbé Breuil, who investigated the matter exhaustively, finally put an end to all doubt, and today the authenticity of the engravings is generally accepted [2]), although there is some doubt as to the correctness of the reproductions of some of those previously published.

---

[1]) PÉRICARD, LWOFF, 1940; LWOFF, 1941; *idem*, 1942; *idem*, 1943.
[2]) GRAZIOSI, 1946.

Undoubtedly their strange, unusual character justifies, at first sight, a certain scepticism, due also to the difference between most of them and all that we know of Franco-Cantabrian art.

The engraved stones — about 200 of them — were found at a distance of 5 or 6 metres from the entrance of the cave, lying directly in an archaeological stratum that could be assigned to Magdalenian III. Many were lightly engraved, others executed with deeper incisions : among them there were also some animal figures (Pl. 30, *f*, *g*).

Among the human figures published by Lwoff at different times are some obese women, probably pregnant, treated in a different spirit from the majority of the other female figures, and recalling the nude female statuettes of the Aurignacian-Perigordian period. These apparently come from the lower archaeological stratum of La Marche (Pl. 82, *i-k*).

But outside this small group we enter a world that differs noticeably from the taste and the formulae encountered so far in Franco-Cantabrian art. For instance, some erect male figures, curiously garbed, with beards and strange head-dresses, are shown in various postures, designed in a clumsy, hesitant manner that is nevertheless lively and realistic; these figures do not follow any of the known canons of Palaeolithic art (Pl. 83, *c*); these are the figures that arouse the greatest diffidence with regard to their graphical interpretation, and should therefore be considered with all due reservation. However, it is highly probable that a further careful examination will reveal errors of interpretation, for it is extremely difficult to decipher the very faint tracery : we may find that the figures are quite different from the interpretations so far published.

The series of " portraits " — male and female heads in which the details of head-dress and physiognomy are carefully stressed — finds an echo in other Palaeolithic anthropomorphic figures.

They are seen in profile, and almost invariably show — sometimes to a very high degree — a curious prognathism (Pl. 83, *a-c*) that may reproduce to an exaggerated extent a somatic, and therefore racial, trait in the model; it appears more logical, however, to assume that it is due to a simple artistic convention or — in Breuil and Lantier's opinion [1] — to the Palaeolithic artist's habit of portraying animals. To a lesser degree also the little Aurignacian-Perigordian ivory head of Brassempouy (Pl. 1, *a*), like the heads of La Marche, shows a tendency towards a forward projection of the face. The human head in bas-relief of Angles-sur-Anglin (Pl. 160) has the same morphological traits as those which distinguish the engravings of La Marche.

Besides these realistic human representations, in the Lower Magdalenian period we have figures of a stylized kind such as the human faces of " Grotte des Fées " (Marcamps, Gironde) (Pl. 81, *e*) and Placard (Pl. 81, *d*).

Anthropomorphic sculpture in the round already makes an appearance at the end of Magdalenian III or the beginning of Magdalenian IV, though it differs considerably in form, and especially in artistic merit, from the Aurignacian-Perigordian sculpture : a series of curious little lignite figures from the Magdalenian deposit of Petersfels (Baden) (Pl. 82, *e*, *f*) are highly stylized, flattened and pierced with a hole — probably to be used as pendants. A fragment of limestone from the Magdalenian layers of Hohlenstein in Bavaria is lightly engraved with three strange figures, interpreted as schematizations of female bodies [2]; similar designs appear on another piece of limestone (Fig. 10) found in 1950 by Darasse at the bottom of the Magdalenian IV layer of the Fontalès shelter near Saint-Antonin (Tarn-et-Garonne) [3]. These simple outlines recall the small lignite sculptures of Petersfels described above. Female figures of the same type are engraved on rock fragments found in the Magda-

---

[1] BREUIL, LANTIER, 1952, p. 198.
[2] BIRKNER, 1928.
[3] DARASSE, 1956.

lenian III or IV layers of the cave of La Roche (Dordogne); we shall return to them later (p. 182).

A recent discovery in Germany introduced a special feature into the modest panorama of anthropomorphic Magdalenian sculpture. In 1948 Lothar Zotz [1]) found in a Magdalenian deposit of the Mauern cave near Neuburg (Bavaria) a limestone statuette, rather summarily executed (Pl. 82, *h*), of a female figure reduced almost exclusively to the gluteus region. This is enormously emphasized as in other statuettes — for instance in that of Pekarna (Pl. 82, *g*) [2]).

In the Mauern sculpture, which is a little over 7 cm. high, all details of the body were omitted, including the head, chest, arms, etc. Nevertheless the realism of the gluteus region

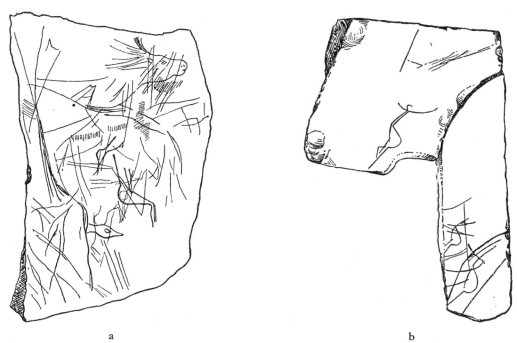

a   b

Fig. 10. Schematizations of female bodies, engraved on stone: a) Fontalès (Tarn-et-Garonne), one sixth natural size; b) Hohlenstein (Bavaria), one half natural size (from DARASSE, 1956, figs. 1, 2).

places this work closer to the more ancient female statuettes than to the impersonal, mediocre ones of the Magdalenian period. It particularly resembles the " Trasimeno Venus " described above (Pl. 8, *c*), as seen according to the first interpretation, in which the very summary execution of the rest of the body is reduced to two conical appendages : one, the larger, representing the torso, and the lower, smaller and more pointed one, the legs. The German statuette was painted with ochre.

Zotz points out that it might be interpreted as having two distinct meanings : female, if the rounded parts are considered as buttocks; male, if they are considered as phallic representations. Something of the kind was already suggested in the case of the Trasimeno Venus, and we agree with Zotz that other statuettes may also have been intended to represent androgynous beings : on this subject the German scholar recalls that the concept of the androgynous being spread, in ancient times, from India to Babylon, Greece, etc. [3]).

If the Neuburg statuette had not been found in an unmistakably Magdalenian layer, we would be inclined to place it in the great family of Aurignacian-Perigordian Venuses [4]). It can therefore be considered a continuation of the taste and style of that more ancient phase of anthropomorphic sculpture. In any case we should not forget the problems raised by the

[1]) Zotz, 1951.
[2]) Absolon, 1932, Pl. XXII, 9; this author, unlike others, appears to consider it Aurignacian.
[3]) Zotz, 1951, p. 339.
[4]) It is definitely assigned by Zotz in his recent monograph to the Perigordian horizon which he subsequently identified at Mauern. Zotz, 1955, p. 25, footnote 1.

female statuettes of Perigordian type found in Italy, with their undetermined stratigraphy and chronological uncertainty.

From the Jelisejeviči deposit near Bryansk in Russia, believed to be Lower Magdalenian, we have a statuette in mammoth ivory, 15,5 cm. high, representing a woman; although somewhat rigid, especially in the upper half, and rather disproportionate, it shows undeniable stylistic affinity with the Aurignacian-Perigordian anthropomorphic sculptures. F. Hančar, in fact, considers it of Aurignacian tradition [1]).

Also from Russia, Molodova near Stai Usciza on the Dniester, is an ugly little human figure, very summary and without arms, seen from the front, carved on a reindeer antler " bâton de commandement " [2]).

Among other statuettes an ugly female figure, carved on a horse's tooth, was found in Mas d'Azil (Pl. 82, d); we are here very far indeed from the tasteful, intelligent realism of Aurignacian-Perigordian sculpture.

From Laugerie Basse came the shapeless sketch in Pl. 82, b, as well as the so-called " Vénus impudique " (Pl. 82, a), an ivory statuette, harsh and rigid, that has nothing in common with the exuberant adipose Venuses of an earlier period. It is incomplete; the arms and head are missing, and it ends at the top, in a chisel-shaped appendage; possibly the missing parts were originally modelled in some plastic material and attached to the statuette.

The reindeer antler spear-thrower of Gourdan (Pl. 81, a, b) is crowned, at the top, with a head that has been interpreted as human, though showing very few human characteristics : the great round, deep sockets must have originally contained eyes of a different substance, as we have seen before in Bédeilhac, Les Trois Frères, etc. The hook is formed by a kind of braid, or lock of hair starting at the nape. This little head recalls those of the young ibexes on the spear-throwers of Mas d'Azil (Pl. 37, a, b), Bédeilhac (Pl. 37, c), etc.; the so-called braid could then be interpreted as stylized horns. We might also consider this strange being as a humanized animal or theriomorphic being. We enter here a realm of Magdalenian aesthetics, which hovered between fantastic artistic creations — neither human nor animal — perhaps expressing thereby the sense of communion with other living beings that frequently appears to characterize the spirituality of primitive peoples.

Anthropomorphic iconography in the Magdalenian period produced countless similar specimens; in some cases, however, we get the definite feeling that the animal aspect of the human beings simply represents material camouflage. The two figures, male and female, engraved upon a pebble in La Madeleine, prove that this is in fact the case (Pl. 86, b) : the body of one is complete and treated realistically; both wear obvious animal features or masks on their heads. The same deposit produced another similar figure, less realistic, engraved on bone (Pl. 86, c).

The fragmentary bone disk of Mas d'Azil (Pl. 85, a) has an ithyphallic figure, seen in profile, engraved on one side, and another, seen from the front, on the other side.

Some human figures engraved on stone were found in Isturitz. In Pl. 84, a is a strange character, probably seated, with thin body bent forward and a grotesque, long-nosed face; it is probably wearing a mask. The drawing of this figure is crude. The head in Pl. 84, c is more realistic; perhaps it, too, wears a mask that shows, as though transparently, the underlying features. A bearded head with thick hair, realistically engraved on stone, is shown in Pl. 84, b.

A human figure vigorously and freely outlined on a tablet of schist was found in Lourdes (Pl. 85, b). It is the figure of a man with a long beard, apparently bald and wearing a long horse's tail — obviously a disguise. On a " bâton de commandement " in Gourdan (Pl. 84, e) another human being with long hair is engraved in a stylized but skilful fashion.

---

[1]) Hančar, 1949-53, p. 5.
[2]) Schokvkoplias, 1957a, p. 29.

Still in the field of masked figures are the "diablotins" mentioned above, engraved on a "bâton de commandement" found in the Abri Mège at Teyjat (Pl. 87, *f*) : these are probably men camouflaged with chamois' heads and hides, shown in the act of dancing.

Among the more realistic figures not wearing masks is the bearded man pursuing a bison engraved on a "bâton de commandement" at Laugerie Basse; it is one of the rare "scenes" in Franco-Cantabrian art (Pl. 86, *a*). This composition provides further proof of the fact that Magdalenian artists were less skilful in executing human figures than in executing animals : the bearded man is far more clumsily drawn than the bison, although there is no doubt that they are both produced by the same hand.

Another composition of obscure significance, engraved on bone, was found in the Magdalenian IV layers of Isturitz (Pl. 84, *d*) and it shows a man following a woman. Although quite realistic, these two figures illustrate, to a certain extent, the structural uncertainty characteristic of most Magdalenian anthropomorphic figures. The woman is naked, and there are clear indications of hairiness in places on her body. The man is also hairy, especially about the head and face. Both are wearing ornaments : the woman has anklets and a kind of necklace prolonged by a strip down her back, and the man a triple collar with indications of a similar strip down the back, and a triple bracelet. The outline of the man is somewhat indefinite, and Saint-Périer does not exclude the possibility that he might be wearing a mask. An interesting detail is the spearhead with double row of barbs engraved on the woman's thigh; according to Saint-Périer it symbolizes the victory of man over woman [1]).

Both sides of a bone fragment in Laugerie Basse are engraved, one with the fine horse's head in low relief already mentioned (Pl. 57, *e*), and the other with a fragmentary composition (Pl. 85, *c*) consisting of a reindeer, only the hind legs of which remain, and a woman, apparently lying on her back and obviously pregnant, with her head missing at a break in the specimen. This woman, too, wears similar bracelets and a necklace, and the hairy parts of her body are suggested by small parallel lines as in the Isturitz woman (Pl. 84, *d*) whom she resembles also from a stylistic point of view.

Finally, we reproduce the curious processions of men already referred to. Pl. 86, *e* shows a succession of nine individuals, one of which is fragmentary, engraved on bone in Gourdan; they should undoubtedly be considered human figures, crudely represented and all alike. In the cave of Les Eyzies another group of nine individuals was found (Pl. 87, *a*, *b*), stylized in practically the same manner; they appear to be carrying sticks on their shoulders and are moving towards a bison which dominates the group. Four curious fringed figures, not easy to interpret, complete the picture.

Nine individuals, similar to the preceding ones, engraved upon a sliver of bone pierced with a suspension hole were found in the Raymonden deposit (Pl. 87, *c*, *d*) : one of them is carrying something that looks like a leafy bough on his shoulder. They are deployed in two lines, mirroring each other with heads towards the centre where the partial figure of a bison, which looks dissected, is engraved; only the large head and front legs of the animal are outlined, while the rest is completed merely by a suggestion of the backbone.

Emphasis on the anatomical details of animals is, as we have seen before, a feature of other Magdalenian figures (see the skinned horses' heads in Pl. 43, *b*, *c*). The significance of these, as of the scene just described, is not easy to determine : here, too, we are undoubtedly in the presence of magic, esoteric things.

---

[1]) SAINT-PÉRIER, 1936, p. 115.

COMPOSITION AND PERSPECTIVE
IN FRANCO-CANTABRIAN MOBILIARY ART

We have said before, and confirmed by a description of various works of mobiliary art, that the Palaeolithic artist infrequently placed figures in relation to each other with the intention of creating a scene. In the Magdalenian, as in the periods that preceded it, a sense of composition appears to some extent, both in mobiliary art and in cave art as well.

Animal, and sometimes human figures that are, or appear to be, drawn in intentional proximity to each other to form a real scene are extremely few, in sculpture or engraving. Occasionally two animals, male and female, are shown together : among these are the reindeer carved in ivory at Bruniquel (Pl. 34, a) and engraved at Petersfels (Baden) (Pl. 68, b). The sexual significance of such compositions is obvious.

Among these specimens are the deer engraved on a tine in Lorthet (Pl. 64, b); the scenic intention is obvious here : to show a herd crossing a brook. The same may be said of the engraving on bone from Pekarna (Moravia) (Pl. 69, e), representing a fight between two bison.

The sequence of horses from La Madeleine and El Valle (Pl. 72, b, c, e), the chamois' heads of Gourdan (Pl. 66, c) and the two young deer from Chaffaud (Vienne) (Pl. 71, c); the reindeer of Massat (Pl. 71, b) and La Madeleine (Pl. 71, d); the cow with a calf from Mas d'Azil (Pl. 70, c) and other analogous figures, may be confidently recognized as compositions or scenes. However, a simple sequence of figures does not always denote a definite intention on the part of the artist to represent herds of animals; such sequences can also be interpreted as the expressions of a particular taste for rhythm in decoration.

We have already mentioned the engraved stone at Péchialet (Pl. 24, a, b), attributed to the Perigordian period, in which three figures seem to compose a picture of a fight between a bear and two human beings — one of them at least, appearing human. Human figures provide some other instances of composition, among them the hunting scene of Laugerie Basse (Pl. 86, a), the man following a woman from Isturitz (Pl. 84, d), the processions of Gourdan, Les Eyzies and Raymonden (Pls. 86, e; 87, a-d), and others.

Three small compositions engraved on bone from Mas d'Azil, Lorthet and El Pendo are particularly interesting (Pl. 90, a, b, c). Although they were found in widely separated localities (Lorthet and Mas d'Azil are in the Pyrenees, El Pendo in Cantabria), they are almost identical; in fact, one is inclined to believe that they are the work of the same artist, or, at least, copies of each other. They show a stag, seen from the back and foreshortened, flanked by another animal — probably carnivorous — of which only the head is visible; in the El Pendo specimen the characteristics of the carnivore are sufficiently suggested by clearly visible sharp teeth. The fact that this curious composition should be repeated with the same details proves its illustrative purpose; its significance is impossible to explain.

These compositions have another interesting aspect : they constitute some of the few known instances of foreshortening in the reproduction of animal figures. Animals, as we have seen, are usually shown in profile — the most simple and, we might say, instinctive manner of portrayal. Furthermore, they reveal an attempt to achieve perspective — an even more rare occurrence in Franco-Cantabrian art. In the Mas d'Azil specimen, in fact, the deer seems to be placed in the foreground with respect to the other animal.

Among figures in frontal perspective we recall the engraving on bone from Gourdan (Pl. 88, a), of an elk with great antlers rendered with perfect realism. Also seen from the front is the ibex engraved upon a bone in Laugerie Basse (Pl. 88, d), a stylized figure with globular body and atrophied limbs, probably squatting. And again, an ox head engraved on a stone in Limeuil is viewed from above (Pl. 88, g). Finally, the head of a bear, seen directly from the front, is engraved on bone at Massat (Pl. 88, f) and, also engraved on bone, a succession of deer heads in Teyjat (Pl. 88, b) are superimposed in a vertical line; the rhythmical repetition of these figures gives them an exquisitely decorative flavour, and finally the bear, part of a small group of bears engraved on bone recently discovered by Robert in the Upper Magdalenian layer of the cave of La Vache (Ariège) (Pl. 89, d).

But are these few, simple compositions sufficient to justify us in speaking of perspective in Franco-Cantabrian art? In very few cases is the attempt successful. Others, such as the figures engraved on the previously-mentioned stones of Limeuil, leave us somewhat perplexed and hesitant. Pl. 90, g shows one of these stones, where the Palaeolithic artist attempted to represent a herd of deer : the intention is perfectly evident in the lively, diversified postures of the figures and their distribution on the stone's surface. The artist, here, really appears to have tried to draw the animals on receding planes. The same applies — if less obviously — to the herds of horses from the same deposit in Pl. 90, e and f. Note, also, in these three compositions, what is probably a rudimentary attempt to represent the " landscape " with more or less horizontal signs indicating the ground.

A deliberate intention on the part of the Magdalenian artist to show various elements of a composition on different planes is clearly evident in the engraved bone of Teyjat (Pl. 89, c), and especially in the pebble, also engraved, of Chaffaud (Pl. 89, b). The first of these two singular works shows a herd of reindeer, in which a simple but effective device creates the impression of a long procession of animals. It consists in representing the whole of the first three and the last animals in the herd, but only the branches of the antlers and, with a few vertical strokes, the feet of the others. This is a successful impressionistic convention for suggesting reality and movement. In the case of the Chaffaud pebble, perspective is even more clearly achieved : two herds of horses — independent of each other — are represented by the same method as that adopted for the reindeer of Teyjat : the whole of the first and last animals are given but only the heads and hoofs of the others. The animals are galloping in line abreast. They are placed close to each other on different planes, and diminish in size as they retreat into perspective. The heads partially conceal each other, and in accordance with a perfectly understood rule of perspective there is no superimposition or crossing of the outlines.

This is perhaps the only instance in Franco-Cantabrian art to suggest that the Palaeolithic artist, towards the end of the period, had begun to conquer — perhaps unconsciously — those elementary principles which rediscovered, developed and codified, were to produce, many thousands of years later, the boundless world of perspective in figurative art.

Undoubtedly perspective, even in the most flourishing period of Palaeolithic art, was a sporadic, almost accidental phenomenon. Our evidence at present suggests that it had no influence on the development of the great Franco-Cantabrian mobiliary and cave art, for this art failed completely to create a landscape background for its figures.

STYLIZATION, SCHEMATIZATION, GEOMETRICAL AND ABSTRACT PATTERNS IN FRANCO-CANTABRIAN MOBILIARY ART

The realistic figures, that increased especially during the Magdalenian period, either as independent forms or with definite decorative intention, so dominate the scene in Franco-Cantabrian mobiliary art that it may be described as fundamentally realistic. But together with these fine works of a strictly realistic order, other figures, in far smaller numbers, came to light in the same deposits. These figures transcend the boundaries of so-called " visual " realism and tend towards schematic, and stylized forms, until they become expressions of an intellectual and definitely abstract art in which decoration, increasingly stressed, leads to the creation of purely ornamental patterns, geometrical, or at least lacking any apparent significance.

However, such stylized patterns do not always seem to serve exclusively for decorating the object, either because of their simplicity and mediocrity, or because of the nature of the object decorated, which may not have been manufactured. In this case the schematic figures are isolated, extreme simplifications of realistic prototypes, probably symbolical expressions of ideas or subjects that interested the artist for specific reasons of his own. We seem to be here in a field of true abstraction.

However this may be, in the Aurignacian-Perigordian period we can already see the establishment of schematizations, stylizations and ornamental patterns of different derivation, at different stages of their development towards pure geometrical or abstract forms.

Expressions of decorative art exist, as we know, in all present-day primitive peoples. According to current opinion [1]), they are not purely and intentionally ornamental or geometric : they derive from the simplification of actual objects and are inspired by the animal world, the human figure and, very rarely, according to Haddon [2]), by vegetable forms.

In Franco-Cantabrian art, too, there are cases we can follow of this transformation of concrete objects into purely ornamental forms, lacking all apparent significance, and it is probable that, as among primitive peoples, so also in Palaeolithic art all, or almost all geometric decorative and abstract patterns derive from the world of concrete reality. These derivations can be reached by tracing back the gradual replacement of certain designs of a strictly naturalistic order by purely ornamental forms; the progression is particularly convincing when it appears on the same object or on objects found in the same layer of a given deposit.

More than half a century ago Breuil began a study of these variations and started to collect evidence relating to them; he has continued to do this in the succeeding years. Up to the present only a few have been published in some preliminary notes of about 50 years ago [3])

[1]) DENIKER, 1926, p. 247 and foll.
[2]) HADDON, 1895.
[3]) BREUIL, 1905; idem, 1906.

and, twenty years later, in a work written in collaboration with Saint-Périer, exclusively devoted to the representation of fish, amphibians and reptiles in Quaternary art [1]). As he himself has said [2]), Breuil was inspired to study the distortion of realistic Palaeolithic figures into ornamental patterns by Balfour's book on the origins of decorative art in presentday primitive peoples, and by Haddon's book on the evolution of art [3]).

Since then the material assembled by the eminent prehistorian has undoubtedly increased very greatly, and we trust he will soon issue the promised book on this subject.

In the recent book on men of the Old Stone Age which he published in collaboration with Lantier [4]) he devotes a few paragraphs to Palaeolithic decorative art, dividing it into two groups — one with a figurative origin, the other with a technical origin. In the first group he distinguishes primitive " schemata " consisting of highly simplified images which follow the abstract representation of intellectual realism which existed before the Magdalenian period, alongside naturalistic art. In this group also he places the ornamental and stylized art that began to develop in Magdalenian IV and found full expression in the extraordinary proliferation of ornament in Magdalenian V and VI.

In the case of ornamental art with a technical origin, decoration is directly inspired by the actual fashioning of the bone (reproduction of suspension holes, cuts, transversal grooves, etc.), or by the graphic imitation of various processes (probably plaited straw or the binding on the shafts of certain instruments) and also by copies of artifacts such as barbed harpoons, etc. All this, naturally, is simplified, schematized and reduced to geometric figures.

Breuil's analysis, though brief, is convincing and will be all the more so when supported, in his future work, by all the evidence as yet unpublished.

Even a brief examination of a single part of the enormous range of stylized, geometrical and decorative figures in Franco-Cantabrian art shows clearly that the earliest expressions of mobiliary art are associated with purely ornamental patterns.

Among the objects shown in Pl. 92, *a, b, c* are a pendant and an ivory plug, found in the Aurignacian layer of Brassempouy, the same deposit as that which gave us the famous female ivory statuettes. They are decorated with zig-zag lines or with a sort of network, derived, perhaps, from the imitation of plaited straw, and they convincingly prove the ancient origin of geometrical Palaeolithic decoration. Parallel rows of V-shaped signs of obscure significance (Pl. 92, *f*) are also found in Typical Solutrean, for instance in Isturitz. Lower Magdalenian also produced specimens of this kind, as in La Marche [5]) or in the Angles-sur-Anglin rock shelter [6]) where triangular or trapezoid figures filled with criss-cross lines of no apparent significance are engraved upon horse incisors (Pl. 92, *k*).

Also in this Lower Magdalenian we witness the appearance of apparently meaningless designs that nevertheless reveal their derivation from real subjects whose schematization, upon closer examination, is quite obvious. In Pl. 97, *b, c* we reproduce simple figures engraved on spearheads from the Lower Magdalenian layers of the Maszycka cave in Ojkow (Poland) and from approximately the same period at Placard, that seem to be derived from the eye and the horn of a bison. It is interesting to find this kind of stylization, so early, turn towards the creation of a purely ornamental element; we shall encounter it in later periods when the Magdalenian artist produces his impressive works of cave art and repeats the curious formula of the eye joined to the horn in realistic representations of bison.

But it is especially in Upper Magdalenian — and particularly its later phases — that ornamental elements of all sorts and origins appear on bone and antler artifacts; in some cases

---

[1]) BREUIL, SAINT-PÉRIER, 1927.
[2]) BREUIL, 1937, p. 56.
[3]) BALFOUR, 1893; HADDON, 1895.
[4]) BREUIL, LANTIER, 1951.
[5]) PÉRICARD, LWOFF, 1940, figs. 7, 8.
[6]) ROUSSEAU, 1933, fig. 4.

the origin of these designs is unmistakable, in others it can only be presumed. An original figure may be broken up into its component parts, some of which are isolated and used as decorative elements, or brought together in an arbitrary manner in no way betraying their original relation. The break-down of a realistic subject — human or animal — and its decomposition into several parts that become independent decorative elements is a common feature of present-day ethnography.

It is well known that among primitive peoples today ornamental designs derive from real objects, and their origin can usually be deduced even through the complex process of transformation and dislocation to which they are submitted. The patterns most frequently encountered are drawn from the animal world and the human figure — very rarely from the vegetable

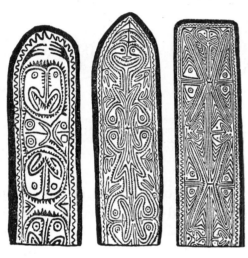

Fig. 11. Stylization and disintegration of the human face into ornamental elements, on belts from British New Guinea (from HADDON, 1894, figs. 43, 41, 39).

Fig. 12. Ornamental patterns derived from a bird's head and neck, on wood, from British New Guinea (from HADDON, 1894, figs. 74, 73).

world. Sometimes they arise from industrial techniques: typical examples of this are ceramics decorated with patterns derived from plaited straw or rope.

As we shall see, in Franco-Cantabrian mobiliary art decoration by and large follows the same rules, except that the human figure, so predominant in the creation of primitive ornamental patterns today, does not seem to have inspired the Paleolithic artists to the same extent.

Distortion and the breaking up of concrete objects with the intention of creating ornamental elements is practiced everywhere today — from Oceania to America. New Guinea gives us countless interesting examples, assembled and examined by Haddon more than half a century ago [1]. Human features appear transformed into spirals, zig-zag or Greek key patterns that completely fill the decorated space and among which eyes are still discernible in the form of dotted circles or lozenges; mouths appear as strips folded at one end, etc. [2] (Fig. 11). In some extreme cases a bird's head is reduced to multiple serpentine, spiralling or meandering lines disposed with perfect symmetry in the decorated space [3] (Fig. 12).

The decoration of pre-Columbian pottery shows many instances of distortion and dismemberment, and further instances are found here and there among present-day primitive peoples. We must beware, however, as Haddon says [4], of facile comparisons in the reconstruction of the *origin* of an ornamental pattern; simple patterns may appear in similar forms in several countries, yet have different origins and, of course, different meanings.

[1] HADDON, 1894.
[2] HADDON, 1894, pp. 26-45.
[3] HADDON, 1894, pp. 51-80.
[4] HADDON, 1894, p. 249.

Instances of the break-up of concrete and naturalistic subjects into abstract elements
— the change from an organic-naturalistic conception to an inorganic-abstract one — were
pointed out by Bianchi-Bandinelli in the case of Celtic coins of the first century B. C. He gives
some clear, instructive examples [1]).

On the obverse of a coin from Gaul is an apparently incomprehensible decoration consisting
of squares, circles and half-moons. It derives from the head of Apollo engraved on the obverse
of a gold coin from the reign of Philip of Macedonia in 336 B. C., imitated by the Gallic people
as far back as the third century. The figure of a chariot on the reverse of the original coin
appears on the Celtic coin dissociated, as volutes and spirals. Between the realistic prototype
and the extreme abstraction, intermediate stages allow us to follow the transformation of

a   b   c   d

Fig. 13. Gradual disintegration of the head of Apollo into inorganic elements: Celtic coins of the III
and I centuries B. C. – a) Avernii, III or late IV cent. B. C. (from BLANCHET, 1905, fig. 54); b), c) Atre-
bates, I cent. B. C. (from BLANCHET, 1905, figs. 294, 295); d) Nervii, 90 B. C. (from BLANCHET, 1905,
fig. 305).

the original subject : thus the forehead, cheeks, chin and lips of the head of Apollo are used
as separate elements; the nose and chin are taken apart and then joined together again [2])
(Fig. 13).

To return to Palaeolithic schematization, in Pl. 99, d-g is a series of engravings on bone,
related to an ibex seen from the front; all these figures were found in the same Upper Magdalenian
deposit of El Pendo (Santander) and their common origin makes them particularly instructive.
The first piece (Pl. 99, d) is a crude sculpture, in very shallow relief, outlined by a deep incision.
It represents an ibex seen from the front, in which the muzzle, horns, ears and trunk are
clearly visible, whereas the hindquarters are barely suggested. This figure, though inspired
by reality, already shows a definite trend towards schematization.

In Pl. 99, e schematization is carried further : the animal, again viewed from the front,
is reduced to horns, ears and a vertical line representing the entire body. Pl. 99, f shows these
elements in an even more geometrized form, reduced to comma-shaped signs while maintaining their original positions, so that the horns and the ears are still recognizable. In Pl. 99, g
only the horns are represented, by V-shaped signs placed one above the other in what has
become a purely decorative pattern. This progression can be used as a key to the original
significance of other V-shaped signs in Palaeolithic ornamental art.

A series of figures engraved upon a single bone fragment from Massat (Pl. 97, m) shows
the progressive transformation of a wild goat into a geometrical design whose significance would
be impenetrable if considered in isolation.

One of the subjects that is found at the origin of a great number of purely geometric
decorative figures and signs is the fish. It is transformed and decomposed into countless different elements often joined together to form complex figures of a variously ornamental nature.

We refer, for instance, to an interesting series of engravings on bone fragments all from
the same deposit of La Madeleine and specifically from Upper Magdalenian; this series,
because it was assembled in the same layer of the same deposit, furnishes most suggestive
evidence for the transformation of realistic figures into schematic ornamental elements.

[1]) BIANCHI-BANDINELLI, 1952, pp. 77-84.
[2]) BIANCHI-BANDINELLI, 1952, p. 82.

Pl. 98, *a* shows a group of such figures, the last few of which would have no meaning at all if we were unable to interpret their origin through other, more realistic figures.

The first is a fish, whose characteristics are summarily but clearly traced; the following figure shows a higher degree of stylization, and the third consists of a shuttle-shaped design that suggests the outline of a fish but lacks details such as eyes, mouth, etc. From the fourth, even more simplified figure we pass on to the fifth, in which the animal is reduced to a simple shuttle divided into parallel segments. The last figures of the series explain the decorative elements derived from the fish, in the form of a chain, also found on other Magdalenian objects; at Lorthet, for instance, where ample, sinuous indentations develop along a bone staff (Pl. 98, *b*).

A rhythmical disposition in series of figures probably derived from fish is found on bone staffs in the La Madeleine deposit (Pl. 98, *c, d*) and elsewhere.

Isolated parts of animals, in which stylization has not yet reached a degree sufficient to conceal their origin, are sometimes used separately as elements of decoration. Thus in Pl. 99, *b* three fish tails follow each other vertically on a bone staff, also from La Madeleine. A " bâton de commandement " from Laugerie Basse has two fish tails, quite recognizable, at its extremity (Pl. 99, *c*); and in Pl. 50, *c* the same pattern of a stylized fish tail crowns the top of a bone spatula from Mas d'Azil. We can clearly establish the significance and origin of this decoration through a series of similar objects from the caves of Rey and Bout du Monde in Les Eyzies, reproduced in Pl. 50, *b, d*.

Finally, we introduce another instance of the progressive stylization of a fish carried out on the same object, this time on a Magdalenian bone rod in the Petersfels cave. The first figure, in which the fish's head is clearly recognizable, is followed by other, simplified shuttle-shaped figures crossed by parallel lines, oblique or converging to a " V " (Pl. 99, *a*).

Pl. 96, *f, g* shows two phallic sculptures decorated by zig-zag signs, circles and dotted lines, that have also been interpreted as conventionalized representations of fish.

We have already alluded to the presence, even in Lower Magdalenian, of figures derived from the simplified eye and horn of a bison. In Pl. 97, *a-e* is a series of such elements that appears to show a progressive stylization towards a very curious spiral decoration on half-rods, found in large quantities in the Magdalenian IV layers of some caves in the Pyrenees. The patterns on these objects are so complex that in some cases they approach the baroque (Pls. 94, 95).

The Abbé Breuil, in the brief notes mentioned before, gives series of figures derived from heads of horses viewed from the front and others from goat or deer heads [1]).

Pl. 97, *f-i* shows rods and half-rods with roundish figures, sometimes joined to other signs, that might also derive from an animal's eye. On the same plate, Figs. *j-l*, are wavy strips formed by many little parallel lines, possibly representing the pelt of horses or other mammals. This is a recurrent formula in Franco-Cantabrian art — for instance on a horse at Isturitz (Pl. 45, *f*) and on the superb sculpture from Lourdes (Pl. 97, *e*), etc.

Instances of decoration obtained with the disconnected elements of animal figures are found also in the more ancient Magdalenian phases, as in Placard where the branched figure in Pl. 92, *g* clearly derives from the antler of a deer. Also in Placard there are many designs of no apparent significance such as those shown in Pl. 92, *g-j*, some of which might be intended as schematizations of fish.

In the Marsoulas cave geometrical patterns assume more complex, definitely decorative forms (Pl. 93, *a-d*): lozenges, series of dots, cruciform figures, ovals, networks, disposed with a particular rhythm and alternation. Each of these signs suggests all sorts of possible derivations: by and large, however, they are impossible to interpret. These decorations, so

---

[1]) BREUIL, 1906.

differentiated and definite, floating in the realm of abstraction, begin in the Lower Magdalenian and show clearly that pure ornament, as an end in itself, was already established in the earliest phases of Magdalenian art, at the same time as representational art.

Some bands of wavy lines engraved on bone at Isturitz (Pl. 93, *h-j*) may be inspired by the vegetable world; the presence of a more realistically executed plant on one of these frag-

Fig. 14. Australian churinga, or whirring tablet (National Museum of Anthropology and Ethnology, Florence).

ments appears to support this theory. These Isturitz decorations have a curious flavour of modern floral design.

Unmistakable vegetable forms, somewhat stylized, are also found, if rarely, in Franco-Cantabrian mobiliary art.

The twigs of the Trilobite cave (Arcy-sur-Cure) (Pl. 91, *a*) are distinguished by a greater realism, and so is the twig engraved on a "bâton de commandement" from Le Veyrier (Haute-Savoie) (Pl. 91, *b*), one of the first objects of Palaeolithic art to be discovered. The engraved bone of Mas d'Azil is decorated with a little plant with its roots (Pl. 91, *e*). The figure in Pl. 91, *d*, from Laugerie Basse is more highly schematized: Fig. *c*, also from Mas d'Azil, seems to represent a transition towards the arrows or harpoons of Isturitz, Duruthy (Landes) and La Vache (Pl. 91, *f*, *g*, *h*).

The exclusively decorative purpose of some figures in Franco-Cantabrian art is clearly discernible, for instance, in objects that must also have had ornamental functions : pendants, pierced buttons, etc. One of these, shown in Pl. 96, *b*, is an elliptical bone pendant from Saint-Marcel with saw-toothed edges, decorated with engraved concentric circles.

An ivory disk from Petersfels (Pl. 96, *d*) is decorated with lines radiating from the central hole, and with zig-zag segments. Parallel lines decorate another bone disk from Mas d'Azil (Pl. 96, *c*). In Pl. 63, *a*, *b* some bone disks from Laugerie Basse are engraved not with geometrical ornaments but with realistic animals, a young deer and an ox. The bear-tooth pendants of Duruthy are decorated with a fish and a seal (Pl. 63, *c*). We mention these realistic designs here, although it is not their place, because they are carried out on objects belonging in the same category as those referred to above.

Highly stylized figures of insects, also on pendants, are reproduced in Pl. 96, *l*, *m*; they were found in Le Trilobite and Laugerie Basse.

One could give many other examples of geometrical patterns with exclusively decorative functions, such as those reproduced in Pl. 93, *a-f*, *h-j*. Finally, a curious object is shown in Pl. 96, *a* : an elongated oval with a hole at one extremity, which has been compared to the " churinga " or bull-roarers of the Australian aborigines. These are primitive musical instruments used in sacred ceremonies in Australia, Papua and elsewhere and which issue a sound when swung round and round on the end of a long string. This object, found at Lalinde (Dordogne), bears a remarkable resemblance to such instruments; it is decorated with strips of parallel lines, placed horizontally and vertically and interlaced.

But decoration does not appear to be the exclusive function of geometrical and abstract art in the Magdalenian period. In fact, some complicated signs of obscure significance are found traced upon shapeless fragments. For instance, Pl. 96, *e* shows a " tectiform " from Isturitz (so defined by Passemard)[1] which bears an obvious relation to analogous painted or engraved figures in cave art which we shall discuss later. This tangle of impenetrable meanings is engraved upon a pebble, which in itself would seem to exclude a decorative purpose.

---

[1] PASSEMARD, 1935.

Finally, there are the strange signs at one time engraved upon bone fragments. They are possibly meant as property marks or they might be mnemonic signs (Pl. 96, *h-m*).

The stone fragment reproduced in Pl. 96, *n*, with three double series of parallel dotted lines traced across it, was found in Upper Magdalenian layers of the Klause cave in Bavaria. These very simple signs foreshadow the Azilian conventional signs that replaced, with their very mediocre production, the great art of Franco-Cantabria and elsewhere. The same schematic tendency distinguishes Palaeolithic art in some Mediterranean regions as well.

SCHEMATIC ART
IN EASTERN EUROPE

A separate place in Palaeolithic art must be reserved for a small group of engraved and sculptured figures found in East European deposits; here the art is highly stylized or reduced to pure geometrical ornament. The group is outside the range of the schematic decorative art of Franco-Cantabria, and has its own particular character.

A series of curious ivory objects, sculptured and engraved, were discovered by Volkov and Ephimenko [1]) and recently, between 1954 and 1956, by Schovkoplias, in the Upper Palaeolithic deposit of Mézine in the Ukraine, excavated between 1907 and 1909; opinions are sharply divided as to their possible significance.

One group consists of sculptures that are generally broad and rounded at the base, narrower and tapering towards the top; seen in profile some of them resemble a flask with a long neck and a small stand at the base; others are elongated, pointed at one end, with a slight swelling at the bottom. Their surface is decorated with V-signs and zig-zag lines disposed in perfect symmetry, with parallel lines and complex rhomboid patterns. Near the base, on the flattened surface opposite the round protuberance, there is usually a triangular mark (Pl. 101).

These curious objects have been interpreted as phalli, as birds, and also as schematized female figures; the latter interpretation is the most generally accepted [1]).

Another singular object, also found at Mézine, is probably a bracelet fashioned from a mammoth tusk; it consists of a curved rectangular plaque with three holes pierced at each end as if for lacing it round the wrist. It is covered with a symmetrical pattern of rhomboids and zig-zag lines, similar to the decorations on the objects mentioned above. Analogous patterns are found on other ivory plaques. Another ivory bracelet of the same kind, with engraved herring-bone geometrical decorations, was very recently discovered at Mézine by Schovkoplias during excavations carried out in 1954-56. He also found some other objects of an exceptional order; two mammoth jaw-bones and a scapula with geometrical designs, zig-zag lines, painted in red [2]).

In Mézine we witness the establishment of geometrical ornaments in a clearly defined form, following a fundamental pattern of broken lines which develops into perfect " Greek key " and rhomboid designs; the flavour is very different from the Franco-Cantabrian, and anticipates the ornament of a much later period.

With regard to the age and industrial *facies* of the Mézine deposit opinions differ : Obermaier considers that it belongs to the end of the Aurignacian (that is to say, to the Perigordian), but calls it " prolonged and degenerate Aurignacian " [3]), thereby implying that it might synchronize with later Eastern European periods. Burkitt also assumes an extension of this " Upper Aurignacian " [4]). The Russian authors attribute Mézine to the Magdalenian or to the period of transition between Solutrean and Magdalenian, and so does Menghin [5]). To conclude, notwithstanding the difficulty of establishing references to the classic French schema, it seems

[1]) VOLKOV, 1912; EPHIMENKO, 1913.
[2]) SCHOVKOPLIAS, 1957, figs. 5-8; *idem*, 1957a, p. 25 and plate p. 23.
[3]) OBERMAIER, 1925, p. 130.
[4]) BURKITT, 1925, p. 130.
[5]) MENGHIN, 1931, p. 163.

evident that Mézine should be considered as belonging to the last phase of Upper Palaeolithic and more or less corresponding to the Magdalenian of Eastern Europe.

Some schematic designs of obscure significance are engraved on fragments of mammoth tusk found in the St. Cyril Street deposit in Kiev. According to Ephimenko they are Lower Magdalenian [1]). But there are various opinions about the chronology of this deposit.

A couple of fragments are decorated with very simple patterns, one of which consists of a segment bearing twenty-three small perpendicular, equidistant lines — a kind of " pectiform " — and the other of two parallel segments joined by nine little perpendicular lines. A third fragment of mammoth tusk is covered with a series of complicated and incomprehensible figures : zig-zag lines, curved parallel lines with short vertical strokes, ladder-shaped figures, strange outlines that somewhat recall animal heads and suggest, to some authors, a bird and a turtle (Pl. 101, *l*). All in all these are highly schematized signs strongly resembling the Mézine ones.

Finally, some other geometrical designs consisting of zig-zag lines, herring-bone and diamond-shaped patterns, criss-cross lines, etc., were found in the deposits of Avdejevo near Kursk and Jelisejeviči, mentioned before in connection with the female statuettes [2]).

In more westerly locations in Central Europe, and specifically in Czechoslovakia, we have products of a schematic art that is much further removed from the Franco-Cantabrian and closer to the Ukrainian forms. In the famous deposit of Předmostí, excavated in 1880 (the same year as that which produced, from Perigordian layers, the ivory statuette mentioned in an earlier chapter; Pl. 16, *e*) fragments of ivory and bone were found engraved with geometrical patterns of a purely ornamental nature; also one very stylized female figure engraved on a piece of mammoth tusk (Pl. 100, *a*). This figure (interpreted as female by Obermaier) [3]), consists fundamentally of bands of concentric lines forming ellipsoidal patterns, with which the breasts, stomach (with clearly marked navel) and pelvis are represented; a variously decorated triangle indicates the head, a ladder-shaped band, narrow and curved, the right arm, and another of vertical lines the right leg. The left arm and leg are missing due to an abrasion of the ivory. Geometrical designs on bone are generally quite simple (Pl. 100, *c*, *d*) : perfectly regular series of V-signs, vertically or horizontally aligned; festooned lines, strips of " plaited " segments, etc. On an oval ivory pendant, pinched in at one end, groups of parallel concentric lines are engraved in a " finger-print " pattern (Pl. 100, *b*).

These objects are considered by Czech authors to be Solutrean, whereas Obermaier refers them to the Upper Aurignacian (or Perigordian) period [4]).

Předmostí appears to mark the westernmost boundary of the diffusion of the schematic art which is well established in the Ukraine. Essentially it is very different from Franco-Cantabrian art. Realistic art also is present in Moravia, with the Magdalenian engravings of Pekarna (Pl. 69); furthermore, the mammoth from the Předmostí deposit and the statuettes found in Věstonice — more ancient than the Pekarna material — are of an undeniably realistic order, very far from any form of schematization. The schematic art of Předmostí, therefore, is unique and should be considered separately from the other art expressions that followed it or appeared simultaneously in the same territory; if anything it is closer to Ukrainian art.

At Mézine schematic art is even more highly developed in its sense of geometry; it creates and repeats complex, definite motifs such as the perfect Greek key patterns. If the chronology of these Central and Eastern European discoveries is more or less exact, the higher degree of geometrical specialization in Ukrainian art would confirm its more recent origin in relation to the art of Předmostí. We would therefore see at Mézine, firmly established and perfected, the patterns that we shall later see employed in Carpathian-Danubian Neo-Eneolithic art.

[1]) EPHIMENKO, 1936, p. 437.
[2]) GVOZDOVER, 1953, fig. 10 *et passim*; HANČAR, 1956, pl. I, figs. 2-4; POLICARPOVIC, 1940, figs. 1, 2.
[3]) OBERMAIER, 1925, p. 256.
[4]) OBERMAIER, 1925, p. 125.

THE MEDITERRANEAN PROVINCE

We have alluded before to the reasons why it is possible to assemble in a separate group (with the exception of the Italian anthropomorphic statuettes of strictly Aurignacian-Perigordian type, examined with similar sculptures from other parts of Europe) the graphic works of Palaeolithic mobiliary art and cave art distributed over the Mediterranean area, appearing in some places with a prevalence of schematic and geometric figures, many of them with no ornamental purpose. In fact, with very few exceptions, all ornamental patterns are engraved on pebbles or on shapeless rock fragments.

Realistic, naturalistic or semi-naturalistic figures are also present in this " Mediterranean province ", the numbers varying according to the locality. However, while showing in many cases obvious stylistic ties with Franco-Cantabrian art, they are almost invariably treated very simply and usually indicate, compared with the mature realism of Aquitanian art, a stage that might at times be regarded as somewhat primitive. This, we must remember, applies to known works of mobiliary art; cave art occasionally reaches a stage of high artistic evolution.

But, we repeat, it is the abstract element that gives, because of the high percentage of finds, a special character to the mobiliary art of the Mediterranean province. And this element is in general totally different from the elements we have seen, both in decorative and in non-decorative forms, in Franco-Cantabrian mobiliary art.

In Franco-Cantabrian art, in fact, geometrical or apparently abstract patterns often stem from the stylization of naturalistic elements that can be traced, as explained above, through successive stages. The interpretation of patterns in Mediterranean art, on the other hand, is often impossible; sometimes they are obviously inspired by concrete objects, such as ribbons and knots, whose remote significance, however, is not suggested at first sight by their shape.

A kind of obscure symbolism prevails in this art, together with figures of a naturalistic order inspired — except on rare occasions — by the animal world.

We have noted something of the sort in the mobiliary art of Eastern Europe, but in that case — apart from the character of the schematized or stylized figures which differs, as we shall see, from that of the Mediterranean ones — the ornamental intention is often quite obvious.

The principal centres of Palaeolithic mobiliary art in the Mediterranean province are the Parpallò cave near Valencia and the Romanelli cave near Otranto. Other, less

Fig. 15. Engravings on fragments of ostrich eggs, Capsian (from VAUFREY, 1955, fig. 85).

important, centres are the Ligurian cave of Balzi Rossi near Ventimiglia (which produced a very limited number of geometrical designs on stone and a couple of fragmentary naturalistic figures) and the cave of Arene Candide near Finale Ligure, with its exceedingly simple patterns, consisting of radiating lines, engraved upon " bâtons de commandement ". Furthermore, very recently various specimens of naturalistic and geometrical art have been found in the deposit of Grotta Polesini near Tivoli, in the Monopoli cave in Apulia and in the cave on the little island of Levanzo.

On the opposite shore of the Mediterranean — the African shore — the only examples of mobiliary art, unmistakably belonging to the pre-Neolithic period, consist of Capsian engravings on the shells of ostrich eggs (Fig. 15). An undeniable affinity exists between these and some engravings on stone of the above-mentioned Mediterranean centres.

But, as we shall see later, this kind of art appears not only in mobiliary form; in Romanelli and in a cave in Southern Spain — La Pileta, near Malaga — as in other French Mediterranean localities, it appears also in the form of cave art.

PARPALLÒ.

The cave of Parpallò near Valencia contains one of the most important Upper Palaeolithic deposits known in Europe today. In the course of several excavations, beginning in 1929, Luis Pericot found an astonishing quantity of engraved and painted rock fragments (approx. 5000).

His excavations penetrated nine metres of deposit and brought to light a complex series of horizons : a basic Gravettian, four Solutrean (Lower, Middle, Upper and Final) and four Magdalenian. The latest Magdalenian horizon is Magdalenian IV, also identified by the typical primitive barbed harpoons that it contained.

The Solutrean of Parpallò shows very special characteristics : an industry in which, besides the typical artifacts, countless very evolved elements appear, such as pedicled arrowheads, with and without wings, which were considered to belong exclusively to the Neolithic or to a later period until they were found in this Spanish cave.

The industrial horizons of Parpallò refer chronologically — and, except for the abovementioned particularity of the Solutrean layer, typologically as well — to analogous horizons in the Franco-Cantabrian region.

Pericot clearly demonstrated all this in his exhaustive work on the subject [1]).

The artistic evidence at Parpallò was found at every level from the earliest, Gravettian, layer to the latest, which was labelled by Pericot Magdalenian IV. It appears in the form of engravings on stone and bone — the latter much less plentiful — and of paintings on stone, which are not as common as engravings.

Engravings on bone are characteristic of Magdalenian layers and appear most often in Magdalenian III. They are rare in the Aurignacian-Solutrean layers — in fact there is only one specimen, with a rather elaborate design.

Engraving on bone at Parpallò is exclusively geometrical; a few figures approach realistic forms, but they are very dubious.

The geometrical patterns consist of zig-zag, wavy or crossed lines, etc. [2]).

Engraving and painting on stone are the most important forms of expression at Parpallò. The engravings — far more numerous, as we have said, than the paintings — range from Gravettian to Magdalenian, whereas the paintings are almost without exception Solutrean.

---

[1]) PERICOT, 1942.
[2]) PERICOT, 1942, figs. 77-79.

By and large this art shows, with regard to zoomorphic representation, an evolution from lower to higher levels. In fact, as Pericot points out [1]), in the older layers the figures are crude and incorrectly proportioned; they improve in the Solutrean, and some are even composed as scenes (deer suckling a fawn in Pl. 102, *f*). In the Magdalenian layers they become progressively more elaborate until towards the end some of the best specimens of that art are produced. But as noted above, at the same time as realistic pictures of animals, obscure geometrical and abstract designs develop freely in some layers : strips of parallel lines — straight, wavy, serpentine, zig-zagging; reticulate figures, radiating lines, rectangular or tree-shaped figures; ribbons unrolling sinuously or tied in knots, sometimes with a loop, or noose, at one end.

Occasionally geometrical and realistic figures appear on the same object, and it is impossible to say whether and to what extent they relate to each other (Pl. 103, *c*) [2]). Geometrical signs are sometimes painted, but far more often engraved.

Geometrical figures are already present in the Solutrean layers (Pl. 103, *a*, *b*), but they reach full development in the higher Magdalenian layers, of which they are the most characteristic feature (Pl. 104, *b-n*).

Though it may be possible to trace a certain affinity between the geometrical patterns of Parpallò and the repertory of schematic-geometrical Franco-Cantabrian art, it is in another Mediterranean Palaeolithic deposit — Grotta Romanelli in Apulia — that we find instances of resemblance with the Spanish cave engravings. We shall discuss this later.

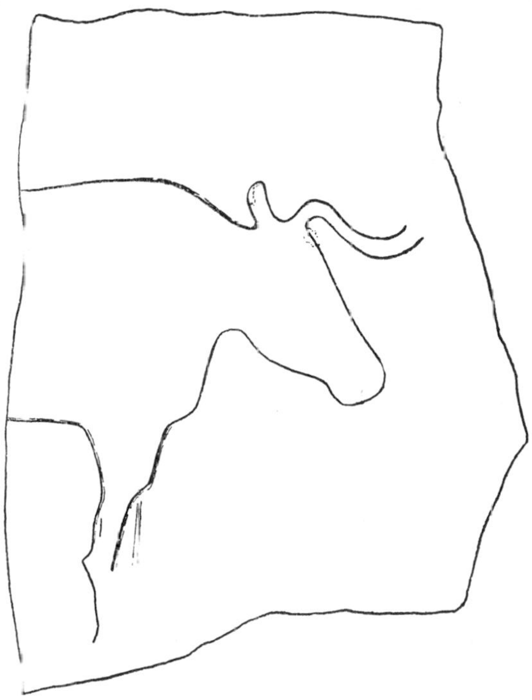

There is no point in lingering over the subject of Parpallò; Luis Pericot dealt with it exhaustively in his great work, where the most interesting and significant engraved and painted figures are reproduced.

Fig. 16. Cave of Parpallò. Ox engraved on stone; the horns are drawn with open outlines (from PERICOT, 1942, fig. 510).

To conclude, we shall summarize a few essential points connected with interesting and curious expressions of Palaeolithic art.

As a whole, the realistic art of Parpallò is undoubtedly related, stylistically, to Franco-Cantabrian art, while remaining, even in its most evolved phases, on a level of much greater technical simplicity. In most instances, to the elaborate execution of the Magdalenian engraving in Aquitania and to the firm, continuous line that generally encloses the entire figure, Parpallò opposes a hurried — one might almost say nervous — outline, often partial or achieved after several tentative attempts. The absence of descriptive details within the outline, the occasional faulty drawing and the lack of proportion between different parts of the various animals make the Parpallò engravings a crude and mediocre artistic achievement compared with Franco-Cantabrian mobiliary art; nevertheless they display some of the immediacy and lively realism that are a feature of the Franco-Cantabrian material. Some particular stylistic features at Parpallò are also found in works of cave art discovered recently in another part of the Mediterranean area; for example the outline is often interrupted at the tip of the horns (p. 198, Fig. 16).

The art discovered at Parpallò is therefore a peripheral, one might almost say provincial, expression of the great Aquitanian art. At a certain moment, however, it acquires its own

[1]) PERICOT, 1950, pp. 82, 83.
[2]) PERICOT, 1942, figs. 195, 215, 360.

striking individuality in the many curious geometrical figures that dominate the last two Magdalenian phases; at the very moment, in fact, when the opposite style of great realism triumphs in Aquitania.

One cannot compare painting in Parpalló, which asserts itself in the Solutrean layers of the cave, with Franco-Cantabrian painting, for painted figures are almost nonexistent in Palaeolithic Franco-Cantabrian mobiliary art (Pls. 102, *d*, *e*, *h*, *i*; 103, *e*, *f*). Nevertheless, a certain affinity with the most primitive cave painting gives the Parpalló paintings an archaic flavour, in the characteristic arched shape of the horses' necks, for instance, their elongated jaws and thick manes. Undoubtedly, in some specimens such as the ruminant, painted and engraved, in Pl. 102, *e*, painting in Parpalló seems to show high technical possibilities. It is therefore in the more recent phases of its development that the Parpalló art, through its schematic figures, assumes the particular character that appears to relate it to the graphic expressions of other centres of Palaeolithic art in the Mediterranean province.

LIGURIA.

Geometrical art appears in other localities along the shores of Mediterranean. In Liguria it is present in a few mediocre works, so far the only Palaeolithic graphic material from this region — with a couple of fragmentary or rudimentary realistic figures. These are the fragmentary head of a horse, engraved on stone, and the rudimentary head of an ox engraved, with other signs, on a pebble, found by Octobon among the material excavated by Bonfils in Barma Grande [1]).

Other engraved stone objects also come from Barma Grande. The exact stratigraphical position of these objects is unknown, for they are the result of old excavations carried out without method. One can only say that they come from Upper Palaeolithic layers. In Pl. 106, *b*, *c* are photographs and tracings of two pebbles bearing zig-zag lines and networks that may be compared with analogous geometrical expressions in the cave of Parpalló.

Groups of parallel lines radiate from the hole on a " bâton de commandement " found in the Upper Palaeolithic layers of Arene Candide, near Finale Ligure. This very important deposit revealed to its excavators — L. Bernabò Brea and L. Cardini — an impressive sequence of strata ranging from the Upper Palaeolithic to the time of metal, and contained in the lower level a Palaeolithic grave of the greatest interest for the inhumation rites that it revealed [2]). The skeleton of a young man, stretched out and lying on its left side, was embedded in a layer of red ochre and surrounded by a large number of funeral objects (*Nassa* shell headdress, sea urchin shells, deer teeth, *Nassa* bracelets, bone pendants, a great flint blade held in the right fist, etc.). Four " bâtons " are of particular interest : they were carved from a piece of elk antler, very broad at the pierced end, and are the only implements of their kind found so far in Italy. Their position in relation to the skeleton implies that they were attached to a thong or rope which passed over the man's shoulders.

Three of these objects are decorated at the broad end with parallel lines disposed without order or in groups of three, radiating from the margin of the hole to the outer edge, and on the shaft with transverse lines like " marques de chasse " — as one can see, a very rudimentary decorative theme. This is all that Arene Candide has produced, up to the present, in the field of graphic art (Pl. 106, *a*).

---

[1]) OCTOBON, 1952, figs. 1, 6.
[2]) CARDINI, 1942.

ROMANELLI.

We shall leave the recent discoveries in Lazio to a later chapter and descend into Apulia.
If we except the rudimentary Ligurian engravings just mentioned, Grotta Romanelli, until
a few years ago, was the only locality in Italy with Palaeolithic engravings on cave walls and
stones.

The mobiliary art of Romanelli includes some specimens that have much in common
with those from Parpallò. In Romanelli, however, the engraved stones were all found in one
part of the deposit — in the upper, brown-earth part — and realistic designs are extremely
rare, the great majority consisting of more or less geometrical figures with an indefinable
significance — expressions of a fundamentally abstract art.

The figures are almost invariably engraved with a very fine line, so fine that careful examination under a magnifying glass and a slanting light is required to distinguish them. They
are generally executed on limestone fragments fallen from the ceiling and the walls of the
cave. The stratigraphical position of the works of mobiliary art in Romanelli is reliable, for
they were gathered *in situ* by Baron G. A. Blanc while excavating the famous deposit in 1914
and in the following years. They were found, as noted above, in the upper, brown-earth part
of the deposit, and specifically in levels B, C and D, most frequently of all in the latter [1].
Although it is impossible to establish typological relations between artifacts from these strata
— they are, in a broad sense, Gravettian — and those of the classic Franch succession, nevertheless they are probably referable to the last Würmian oscillation and to an advanced phase
of Upper Palaeolithic — corresponding, perhaps, to the Magdalenian.

The realistic figures known, up to the present, through the publications of Stella and
Blanc [2] are four in number : to these we should add a crude figure, interpreted by L. A. Stella
as the sculptural representation of a human head [3]. Pl. 109, *a-d* shows the artistic mediocrity
and rudimentary technique of these figures. The most important is perhaps the fragmentary
feline figure in which the hindquarters, one of the forelegs, the line of the back and stomach,
and the tail, are clearly distinguishable. The childish but efficient manner of representing
the claws is interesting. The back half of the figure is filled with parallel lines. This design
is superimposed upon another, consisting of a sort of rectangle longitudinally crossed by
a few parallel lines; many lines radiating from both sides almost cover the pebble's surface.
According to Blanc it might be the representation of a trap, executed previously.

The probable representation of a wild boar, also engraved with fine, incomplete strokes
is of a naturalistic order, even if extremely simple. Finally we have two rather summary outlines, portraying two mammals, probably ruminants, one of which is galloping or jumping.
According to Stella the head of the latter animal — which might be an ox — is " drawn in
perspective, within the outline of the body, as though bent down " [4] : the front part is crossed
by parallel vertical lines.

But as we have said, most of the engravings on stone in Romanelli are schematic or abstract. We enter here an artistic world that has notable points of contact with Parpallò, and in
particular with the Magdalenian layers of that Spanish cave.

The predominant pattern of this series consists of strips of lines; single, multiple, parallel,
interwoven, straight or curved. Usually they unroll like sinuous ribbons. The engraving reproduced in Pl. 109 is very interesting; two such ribbons are wrapped round the pebble and
crossed as though to tie it up. The realism of these figures is increased by the presence, half-

[1] BLANC G. A., 1928, p. 398.
[2] STELLA, 1935; BLANC A. C., 1938; *idem*, 1940.
[3] STELLA, 1935, pl. II.
[4] STELLA, 1935, p. 7.

way up one of the ribbons, of a sort of swelling that probably represents a knot, and on the other by the presence of a noose at one end, whereas the other end of both ribbons widens into a sort of fringe. It is useless to venture an explanation of this or that curious figure in Romanelli; sometimes, as in these last instances, patterns may appear to be concrete in form but are undoubtedly abstract in significance.

Figures similar to these are also found in Parpallò (Pl. 104, *g*, *l*), and this fact, because of the singularity of the subject, undoubtedly indicates a more or less direct relation between the two Mediterranean centres of Palaeolithic art.

We recall the reader's attention to the tree-shaped figures in Pl. 110, *c*, whose outlines are entirely filled in with zig-zag lines, very carefully traced. This pattern is found, as we have seen, in Parpallò, as well as on the Capsian engraved ostrich egg-shells, and in Balzi Rossi.

The pattern that consists of strips of parallel lines crossed at right angles like plaited straw is also of a geometrical order, like the engravings on stone in Pl. 110, or the engraving on a piece of horse metacarpal found at the beginning of the century by P. E. Stasi, the discoverer of the Romanelli cave [1]).

Finally, we should mention the only undoubtedly Palaeolithic painting found to date in Italy, on a block of limestone from the B-C layer of Romanelli.

Here, too, we are in the presence of complete schematization, similar to that which characterizes prehistoric painting of a much later date : so-called " pectiforms ", identical to those that appear so plentifully in schematic Spanish cave art of Neolithic and later periods, also found, in more or less similar forms, on pebbles in Mas d'Azil. The Romanelli stone has five superimposed rows of such pectiform figures (Pl. 109, *f*) : each one of them, according to Blanc [2]), the combination of several distinct figures rather than a single pectiform. Thus there are pectiforms with two or three teeth (interpreted as female or male schematizations), or with several teeth (interpreted as zoomorphic schematizations). Whatever the correct interpretation of these signs may be — and it is not easy to decide—in the case of the Romanelli painting we are undeniably faced with the precocious appearance of a schematic pictorial element that is to reach full development in the post-Pleistocene, and particularly in the art of the new cultures of herding and farming peoples, where schematism definitely replaces Palaeolithic realism.

The Romanelli evidence therefore represents a sort of link between two artistic realms that appear to be fundamentally opposed; on the other hand we should keep in mind that in this same deposit those particular microlithic artifacts (geometrical tools, micro-gravers, etc.) that form the industrial basis of subsequent Neolithic cultures, are present in large quantities.

TIVOLI, MONOPOLI, LEVANZO.

Between 1951 and 1954 Antonio Radmilli discovered in the layers with Gravettian artifacts in the cave of Polesini, near Tivoli (Lazio), together with some pebbles decorated with little vertical parallel lines variously arranged or with V-signs, two pebbles with engraved designs [3]). One is engraved with a strange figure shaped like a fish tail and closely filled with crossed lines (Pl. 108, *a*); the other bears the figure of a mammal, probably carnivorous (Pl. 107, *a*). It is impossible to judge clearly the significance of the former : Radmilli quotes Breuil, to whom he submitted his find, as saying that it might be " the schematization of a human

---

[1]) REGALIA, STASI, 1904, pl. III, fig. 4.
[2]) BLANC, 1938.
[3]) RADMILLI, 1954; *idem*, 1954a.

figure, or else, if you turn the pebble over, of an animal's head " [1]). In any case it is a schematic design that can be included in the Mediterranean repertoire of stylized and abstract art.

Other geometrical designs, engraved upon bone or stone, were found by Radmilli in his latest excavation of 1955 [2]). In Pl. 108, *d*, *e* we reproduce two zig-zag figures engraved on bone, which are not the only ones in the layer, and another similar one (*b*). The same plate (*i*) shows a curious Greek key design recalling the ornamental patterns found on the ceramics of the Apennines, and a group of strange leaf-shaped figures that suggest barbed missiles (fig. *l* of the same plate). There is also a shuttle-shaped figure engraved on a pebble, crossed by transverse, parallel lines, perhaps the schematization of a fish (*c*); a whole repertory of abstract-geometrical art, as one can see, related to other specimens of the same Mediterranean type. But expressions of an essentially realistic art are also found, as in Parpalló, next to the above-mentioned figures : some are rather mediocre; others, of fine workmanship, discovered during the 1955 excavation, recall the typical forms of Franco-Cantabrian art.

On the pebble reproduced in Pl. 107, *a*, a finely engraved figure is undeniably realistic, if somewhat incorrect and crude. It may represent a wolf, and from a stylistic point of view can be placed among the few semi-naturalistic engravings on stone from Grotta Romanelli (Pl. 109, *a-c*). The eye and mouth of the animal are indicated, and, with dotted lines, the fur also. The upper edge of the pebble is decorated with three groups of little parallel lines, symmetrically disposed.

An interesting fact stressed by Radmilli [3]) is the presence on the pebble's surface of various small cavities produced by striking the object — probably in connection with destructive magic practices.

The hindquarters of a deer are engraved on a large stone; the design of this figure is pure and the proportions perfect (Pl. 107, *d*). Also on a stone is the lightly engraved head of an ox, with horns in perfect perspective and an appendage that is probably an ear (Pl. 107, *e*). The head of a horse on stone and the head of a deer on bone have a distinctly Franco-Cantabrian flavour; although traced rather lightly and retouched, so that it is hard to interpret them, many details are visible, such as the nostrils, eyes, etc. (Pl. 107, *b*, *c*). To conclude, therefore, in Tivoli we have in the same Upper Palaeolithic layer geometrical and schematic figures, together with other contemporary figures of a strictly naturalistic order.

On a pebble found by F. Anelli [4]) in the Upper Palaeolithic deposit of Monopoli (Apulia) in 1952, the outline of an ox's head with a long, sinuous horn turned forwards is very faintly engraved (Pl. 106, *d*). Its simplicity and posture recall the treatment of the bovine heads on the wall engravings of the Levanzo cave (Sicily), even though in the latter the outline of the horns is not closed.

This cave is on the little island of Levanzo in the Egadi archipelago, opposite Trapani. It not only contains the famous cave-wall engravings, which will be discussed exhaustively further on, but a recently discovered work of mobiliary art.

While excavating there in 1953 the present writer found, in the Upper Palaeolithic deposit, a stone engraved with the figure of an ox. The forequarters and part of the hindquarters were missing, not because they had been broken off but for lack of space [5]). The photograph published here (Pl. 111) clearly shows that the animal's outline is perfectly closed, in front, at the edge of the stone, with no trace of its forequarters showing; the hindquarters continue on the other side of the stone beyond the front margin, as one can see by examining the original. This proves that the figure was executed on an isolated piece of rock that was

[1]) RADMILLI, 1954, p. 16.
[2]) RADMILLI, 1956.
[3]) RADMILLI, 1954a, pp. 53, 54.
[4]) ANELLI, 1952.
[5]) GRAZIOSI, 1954.

15. — P. GRAZIOSI, *Palaeolithic Art*.

not attached to the cave wall. It can therefore be included in the category of mobiliary works of art.

The engraving is vigorous and naturalistic, though imperfectly executed; artistically it is inferior to the majority of engravings on the walls of the same cave. The figure is shown in absolute profile, and has a somewhat primitive flavour, harsh and lacking in detail; the rendering of the horns — which appear to be double, unless this is due to retouching — denotes a certain hesitancy : their outline is not open as in the horns of the oxen engraved on the walls; however, the animal shows some affinity with the latter engravings in the direction and movement of the horns themselves, in the shape of the pointed muzzle and in the lack of detail in the body. As a whole this figure is undoubtedly cruder than the others, a fact that might be attributed to the artist's inferior ability or to the greater difficulty inherent in the execution of a design on an isolated stone that offers a restricted surface compared with the space on the cavern walls.

On the other hand we cannot establish absolute synchronism between this work and the cave-wall engravings, and it is therefore possible that the chronological factor has something to do with the fact that the two examples are of unequal merit, though belonging to the same art cycle.

To conclude, we would draw attention to a straight segment, parallel with the ox's horns, which might be interpreted as a weapon piercing the animal's forehead. On the surface of the stone, both inside and outside the principal figure, numerous lightly engraved signs cross each other in various directions, outlining a mammal's head level with the front part of the ox, as can be seen in the sketch published with Pl. 111.

* * *

What conclusions are to be drawn from the study of these examples of " Mediterranean " art ? The material at our disposal is still not sufficient for us to formulate hypotheses clarifying the possible connections and derivations of this particular expression with others in European Palaeolithic art.

We shall discuss more extensively later the comparatively small number of geometrical elements and abstract schematic figures which appear also in Franco-Cantabrian cave art. These are the so-called tectiforms, shield-signs, club-signs, serpent-signs, etc., that in some cases seem to attempt to reproduce the shape of real objects and are therefore open to interpretation, while in other cases they appear to have no concrete significance whatsoever. Radiating lines or serpentine lines, like the ones that are engraved on pebbles in Romanelli and in Parpallò, are also found on the walls of the Altamira cave. And we have seen all sorts of schematic signs in considerable numbers in Franco-Cantabrian mobiliary art, especially in the Upper Magdalenian.

Nevertheless, the Franco-Cantabrian province is dominated by naturalism, both in cave art and in mobiliary art, at every stage of its evolution.

The Mediterranean group, on the other hand, shows the establishment of the most advanced schematism : both in the Magdalenian layers of Parpallò and especially in the Upper Palaeolithic layers of Romanelli and the Ligurian caves it is the distinguishing, and in a certain sense the dominating feature. Realistic art is also found in these two localities, but in a modest form in the former, and hardly at all in the latter. It appears, however, in a typical form in some works at Tivoli, and a few mediocre ones in the caves of Monopoli and Levanzo. But as we shall see later, a profoundly realistic form of cave art existed even in the Mediterranean province; furthermore, it flourished luxuriantly in the Sicilian caves of Levanzo and Addaura from which schematism is totally absent. All this suggests the existence in France, in the

Pyrenees, and in the entire Mediterranean basin, of an ancient store of artistic ideas held in common, in which two trends, naturalistic and abstract (or schematic), coexisted from the beginning. They assert themselves differently according to locality : the naturalistic trend in the Franco-Cantabrian region, the schematic trend on the two opposite shores of the Mediterranean, in Spain and in Italy.

Contemporaneously in the Mediterranean basin the naturalistic trend, which appears in some caves in a rather poor form and even, as at Romanelli, in an almost embryonic form, developed and flourished in other localities, spreading to Sicily with the cave art found there and, in post-Palaeolithic times, to Eastern Spain and North Africa, of which we shall speak in another chapter. The schematic trend continued to develop into increasingly definite forms, and in much later periods became established and diffused over a large part of the European continent, leading to the abstract and schematic art of Mesolithic and later times.

PART THREE

CAVE ART

CHARACTERISTICS AND CHRONOLOGY

Palaeolithic cave art takes the form of engraving, low or high relief, and painting, and our examples of it have survived up to the present thanks to the protective environment in which they were executed. It is probable that at least some categories — low and high relief, for instance — were also executed on rocks in the open, but none of these have reached us, owing to the destructive effects of external agents.

Inside the caves, too, many destructive factors undoubtedly acted upon painted and engraved figures: this is proved by the coloured stains and fragments of engraving that occasionally recall the existence, in earlier times, of figures that have since disappeared.

The disappearance of paintings and engravings is generally due to the action of water or humidity, altering the rock surface and destroying whatever was on it; or to the crumbling of the rock face for various reasons inherent in the nature of the rock itself. In fact the Palaeolithic cave figures that have survived are almost exclusively found on particularly resistant calcareous rocks.

An example of the different behaviour of rock surfaces with regard to the preservation of figures is found in Lascaux; here the paintings are perfectly preserved in a part of the cave where the walls are covered by a hard, resistant calcareous layer, whereas they are completely or almost completely erased, as proved by the complete or fragmentary engraved outlines that have survived, in another part in which no solid protective layer exists and where the rock has undergone a process of disintegration over many thousands of years.

The disappearance of paintings and engravings is also due to the formation of stalagmitic layers which gradually increase in thickness until they cover them completely. In some cases, however, when the process stopped at an early phase, leaving the figures visible or only partially obliterating them, it created a protective layer and furthermore furnished conclusive proof of authenticity. In Pl. 114 Palaeolithic paintings and engravings are reproduced, from two widely separated caves — Le Portel in Ariège and Levanzo in Sicily — and both are covered by a stalagmitic veil. A long time was necessary for the veil to form, probably several centuries, and this excludes any possibility of the works being modern forgeries.

In a great majority of cases, particularly in the Franco-Cantabrian province, engravings and paintings are found in the deep recesses of the caves where daylight does not penetrate or penetrates only very faintly. And often painted or engraved caves are difficult of access. There is no doubt that Palaeolithic man voluntarily sought out dark, remote places in which to execute his work.

Figures are very rarely found in parts of caves open to daylight. One of the few exceptions is a horse engraved at the entrance to Hornos de la Peña in Spain. Outside the Franco-Cantabrian province some engravings were found in the same position in the Sicilian caves of Monte Pellegrino.

It is interesting to note, on the other hand, that the great friezes sculptured in low and high relief during the Upper Palaeolithic are never situated in the depths of the caves, but — at least on present evidence — only in shelters with good natural light, as in Le Roc, Le Cap Blanc, Angles-sur-Anglin, etc., or close to the cave entrance, as in La Magdeleine.

In fact it is because of the protective environment of the caves that so many engravings, and particularly paintings, survived despite the ravages of thousands of years. Although, as we have seen, even in the remotest corners cave figures are subject to damage and destruction, it is obvious that none at all would have reached us had they been exposed to the effects of the weather.

Paintings and engravings are spread without apparent order on the walls and ceilings of caves, often superimposed and cancelling each other out.

The dimensions of works of cave art vary considerably, from small figures barely a few inches high, to colossal painted images five and a half metres long, like the black bulls of Lascaux. Such large dimensions are exceptional, though Franco-Cantabrian paintings over a metre long are frequent, particularly in the polychromatic phase.

It is impossible to explain the impressive results achieved by Palaeolithic artists in the execution of important works such as the paintings of Lascaux and Altamira — covering, in a marvellous display of colours, many square metres of rock surface — without presuming a close collaboration between several well-organized and disciplined artists. It has even been suggested, as we shall shortly see, that proper art schools existed at the time. One cannot believe, in fact, that such works of art could be the result of the momentary whim of single individuals : on the contrary, they denote, on the part of their creators, vast experience acquired both in the aesthetic and in the technical field through long, assiduous practice and a truly professional selectivity.

The technique used in painting, for instance, was certainly very complex. It involved searching for colouring substances — which were sometimes needed in very large quantities; blending these with other elements to render them fluid; applying them to the rock surface with appropriate tools to make them adhere permanently — all processes requiring long practice and expert craftsmanship, indispensable to the Palaeolithic artist in the preparatory phase before the actual execution of the creation in which his talent finally had free rein.

The chromatic scale of the colouring materials used was very limited : from black to light yellow, through various shades of brown and red. Black was probably obtained from vegetable or animal carbon and manganese; various kinds of ochre, found in nature, furnished the other colours. White, probably obtained with calcium carbonate, is extremely rare.

The colours were applied either dry by means of fragments of ochre (found in some deposits in the form of crayons : Pl. 113, c) or sprayed on to the wall in a powdered form — a system mainly used to obtain handprints. But often the powdered substance must have been mixed in a semi-fluid medium such as fat, white of egg, vegetable juice, blood serum or simply water. However, despite extensive research, considerable doubt remains on this point : according to Herberts the colouring substances were just mixed with water, or even applied dry on a previously dampened surface. Whatever the system used in preparing and applying colour, it has in many places defied the centuries, reaching us brilliant and intact.

It is hard to tell what tools the artists used. Undoubtedly the painting was sometimes done simply with the fingers but in other cases a kind of brush must have been employed, though it would be useless to try to guess its shape and quality. Finally we find a sort of " blown technique ", as at Lascaux, where colour in dry or liquid form seems to have been applied through a tube.

Some deposits, such as Abri Casserole in the Dordogne [1]), produced stone cups containing

[1]) KELLEY, 1939, fig. 3.

traces of ochre; in La Madeleine [1]) fragments of stone were found impregnated with ochre, suggesting a kind of palette or mortar for grinding the colours.

Among the implements used by Palaeolithic artists in the execution of engravings and bas-reliefs are gravers, sometimes found in obvious relation to the works in the caves. Gravers of exceptional dimensions were found in the Solutrean deposit of Le Roc in Charente which produced the famous blocks carved in low relief. Martin believes these to have served as sculptor's tools (Pl. 113, *d*).

Among the objects that were essential for the creation of works of cave art were the lamps, some of which have been found in French Upper Palaeolithic deposits : the stone lamps of Lespugue, of La Madeleine, and the famous lamp of La Mouthe, decorated with the engraved figure of an ibex and containing a residue of charred fatty substance (Pl. 113, *a, b*) [2]). Furthermore, some caves produced charred remains of torches, probably made of resinous wood.

Finally, Palaeolithic man left a suggestive trace of his passage in the footprints on the mud floors of some painted or engraved caves, such as Pech-Merle, Tuc d'Audoubert, Niaux, Aldène, etc. (Pl. 112).

* * *

Since the time when Marcelino de Sautuola revealed to the world the first prehistoric wall paintings, the range of pictorial and sculptural evidence from the walls and ceilings of Palaeolithic caves in the Franco-Cantabrian region has greatly increased. This is the result of an intense, almost feverish search on the part of scholars and amateurs alike for these amazing products of the human mind and spirit. Even today in the deep dark caves of France, Spain and Italy admirable works are brought to light. At present the amount of Palaeolithic painting and engraving known is really most impressive; but many examples have not yet been published and are therefore still unknown even to specialists.

Despite such plentiful material, the chronology of a great many works has not yet been satisfactorily established or unanimously accepted; this is essentially due to the almost total lack of stratigraphical data relating to cave art.

In fact, only in rare instances have cave paintings or engravings been found in relation to *in situ* deposits containing human implements, or covered by such deposits, or buried in them in the form of rock fragments fallen from the walls of the caves themselves; and it is only in such favourable circumstances that the *ante quem* chronology of these figures can be established beyond doubt.

The discovery *in situ* of painted or engraved mobiliary art identical in style with figures on the walls of the caves containing the deposits, or of nearby caves, constitutes the most reliable element for dating works of cave art, in that it allows us to establish their precise chronology, and not just an *ante quem* limit.

But these conditions are very rare. Nevertheless, after long and patient analysis, comparison and synthesis, and by making use of the limited stratigraphical data, the Abbé Breuil created a chronological system for Franco-Cantabria that is still used today to determine the age of works of Palaeolithic cave art as they are brought to light.

If we were to consider all the cases in which it has been possible to establish correspondences between the cave-wall figures — even if mere fragments fallen into the deposits — and *in situ* deposits themselves, we would realize that these cases are extremely few.

One of the most interesting and important instances is undoubtedly the cave of Pair-non-Pair in Gironde.

---

[1]) CAPITAN, PEYRONY, 1928, fig. 65.
[2]) SAINT PÉRIER, 1906, fig. 9; CAPITAN, PEYRONY, 1928, fig. 14; RIVIÈRE, 1899.

This cave was discovered by F. Daleau [1]) in 1881; he found it filled by a deposit that reached as high as 70 cm. from the ceiling. This deposit, over 7 metres deep, revealed a succession of Mousterian layers in its lower section, and, above, strata of Upper Palaeolithic. The latter contained Typical Aurignacian layers at the bottom, followed by Perigordian layers described, at the time of their discovery, as Magdalenian.

In 1896, his interest aroused by the finding of engravings in the cave of La Mouthe, Daleau started to examine the walls of Pair-non-Pair and to scrape off the earthy residue of the deposit that adhered to them. His research was crowned by success, and on the 31st of August of that year he discovered the first engravings in the cave; others subsequently came to light.

It was possible to ascertain that the engravings were covered by Perigordian strata and were situated above the Typical Aurignacian strata. There was no doubt, therefore, that they could be considered earlier than the Solutrean and Magdalenian periods, and consequently assigned to one of the Perigordian phases or to the end of the Aurignacian.

For this reason the cave of Pair-non-Pair provides a basis for the chronological determination of cave engravings of pre-Solutrean periods on the strength of their stylistic characteristics, where these are comparable with those of the works found in this cave.

An analogous instance on a more limited scale is furnished by the small cave of La Grèze, near Les Eyzies in the Dordogne. Here, a few years after the discovery of Pair-non-Pair, Dr. Ampoulange [2]) found the figure of a bison deeply engraved on the rock wall. It came to light as he removed the deposit, containing human implements, that covered the engravings. At first it was labelled Solutrean, in accordance with the knowledge possessed at that time, but subsequently, with the definition of the Aurignacian culture, the deposit was attributed to the Aurignacian and is still considered so by Breuil today.

The cave of La Mouthe, in the same locality, is undoubtedly less important than the two previously mentioned, because the situation of the Magdalenian deposit that obstructed the entrance right up to the ceiling, while proving that the figures on the walls could not be of a later date, does not admit a more precise chronology.

Further instances of correspondence between wall figures and *in situ* deposits exist in the case of sculpture in low and high relief. The bas-reliefs of Laussel, representing human figures, lay in the Aurignacian deposit; the impressive frieze of bison, horses and ibexes of Le Roc was found beneath Upper Solutrean layers; the beautiful sequence of horses in Le Cap Blanc was apparently related to a Lower Magdalenian deposit. The great block sculptured with figures of oxen in Le Fourneau du Diable was covered by Upper Solutrean strata, and the horses in low relief in La Chaire à Calvin were buried in Lower Magdalenian strata. Layers of Magdalenian III covered the bas-reliefs of Angles-sur-Anglin and contained fragments of the frieze itself.

Painted or engraved rock fragments fallen from the walls of caves and shelters were found in the Aurignacian strata of La Ferrassie, Belcayre, Abri Labatut, Abri Blanchard and in the Upper Magdalenian deposits of La Mairie à Teyjat, etc.

As regards *in situ* discoveries of mobiliary art with designs identical in style to the figures traced on the walls of caves containing the deposits — discoveries that have played a particularly decisive part in the establishment of precise chronologies — we recall the caves of Castillo and Altamira, in whose Magdalenian III or Upper Solutrean deposits some young deer heads were found engraved on fragments of bone, similar in every way to those engraved on the cave walls; also the case of Hornos de la Peña, from whose Typical Aurignacian deposit a bone fragment came to light, engraved with the hindquarters of a horse very much resembling the horse engraved on one of the walls in the same cave.

---

[1]) DALEAU, 1902.
[2]) CAPITAN, BREUIL, AMPOULANGE, 1904.

This is the only material whose comparative study might enable us to attempt the chronological classification of cave art. As we have seen, at present it is very scarce and fragmentary and if based on this alone our picture of the chronological sequence and evolution of Quaternary cave art would be incomplete and uncertain. In fact definition of age in the case of a great deal of cave art is approximate or impossible. But a " stratigraphical " succession of paintings or engravings is often discernible in the great palimpsests on the walls of certain caves, and the Abbé Breuil is a master in this field.

His unrivalled experience after more than half a century enables him to distinguish the various strata of wall figures with an assurance that is unique.

" If an engraving cuts across the colour or encroaches on it " he writes " the engraving is more recent than the painting; if the engraved line is wholly or partially filled with paint, the engraving is the older. "

" Another problem is when the engravings cut across each other : it may happen that the most recent line encroaches on or partly destroys the oldest, but it may also happen that the first tool slipped from one side to the other of the old incision without going inside it, so that the order of superimposition remains uncertain and should be established by comparison. If we examine the superimposition of the painted figures of different colour and style, we are once more up against causes of error making conclusions uncertain... The surfaces painted successively with different colours have neither the same intensity nor the same perpetuity; red is a richer colour tending to come through black and come out above it; a line painted in deep colour does the same, if a light colour-wash be superimposed. "

" On the contrary it may happen that the most recent application of colour adheres badly on a pre-existing tint, thus inverting the appearance of the actual succession of the paintings. There are therefore doubtful cases, in which personal opinion plays a part and, in spite of my long training in this exercise, I am not sure that I have never been mistaken " [1]).

As one can see, the reading of wall palimpsests in Franco-Cantabrian caves — as also the later ones in other parts of the world — can sometimes lead to interesting results, but it can be very difficult and misleading. The superimposition of cave-wall figures has a strictly local value, and should be used with great caution in determinations of a general character. We should keep in mind that superimpositions may have occurred within a very brief span of time, and could even be the work of the same artist. Their importance, therefore, should not be overestimated : their study can lead to useful results only if integrated with a study of the style of the figures themselves and accompanied by an exhaustive comparative examination.

To attempt the classification of the various phases of Palaeolithic art on a documentary basis, we believe it necessary to start from works that are accompanied by the stratigraphical data mentioned above; once the stylistic characteristics are established we should try to assemble and subdivide, wherever possible, on the strength of these characteristics, the impressive range of cave art known to us today.

We shall start by considering the figures which, because of their stratigraphical characteristics, undoubtedly belong to the more ancient phases of the Upper Palaeolithic, the Aurignacian-Perigordian.

---

[1]) BREUIL, 1952, p. 38.

THE FRANCO-CANTABRIAN PROVINCE

ENGRAVINGS

The rock fragments that Peyrony found in the Aurignacian deposit of LA FERRASSIE in the Dordogne are very crudely engraved (Pl. 118, *a*, *c*); in the lower strata they portray ruminant heads and vulvar figures, and in the upper (Aurignacian IV) a roughly sketched head, probably feline, and a painted rhinoceros's head, which is extremely primitive.

Vulvar figures of the same kind, engraved on blocks fallen into the deposit, were found in the Aurignacian strata of ABRI BLANCHARD (Pl. 118, *b*), and in the same deposit, but in slightly higher strata, a block with two oxen painted in black against a red background (Pl. 169, *a*).

Finally, at BELCAYRE, also in the Dordogne, in the valley of the Vézère, the Typical Aurignacian deposit produced another large block with a very rudimentary, if better proportioned, figure of a ruminant, probably an ibex, represented by a simple closed outline and sculptured with uniform hammering (Pl. 118, *e*).

From the Perigordian layers engravings, bas-reliefs and paintings were brought to light in considerable quantities. These, like the foregoing ones, are all expressions of cave art executed on fragments that flaked off the cave walls, or on large isolated blocks on the spot; this gives them all the same " functional " significance.

The figure of a horse in bas-relief, found in ABRI LABATUT between two Perigordian layers, cannot be of a later period on account of its stratigraphical position; we have here a form of art that is far removed from anything we might call " a primitive sketch ". The outline is vigorously engraved and characterized by lively realism (even if lacking the free style of similar works of a more evolved period) although the limbs are rather stiff, lending a certain awkwardness to the whole figure (Pl. 153, *b*). Note the characteristically elongated nose that the animal shows in an already stylized form often to be encountered in other works of the same period.

From the same layers of the same deposit are a rock fragment with the print of a hand against a coloured background and another, of the same age, bearing traces of black figures filled with red. These figures are similar in technique to the pictorial fragments of Abri Blanchard referred to above : superimposed upon them are other figures among which is a fragmentary deer painted in black, consisting of a mere outline but already showing some details, such as the eye and nostrils, and an attempt to achieve relief in the description of the neck (Pl. 169, *b*). Here too, as in Pl. 153, *b*, the nose is elongated and pointed. The antlers, though erased at the base, are branched and drawn in what the French call " perspective tordue ", that is, from the front and on the same plane, whereas the body is shown in profile [1]).

These few paintings are mentioned here, although we are now dealing specifically with engraving, because they are the only specimens of painted cave-wall figures found *in situ*

---

[1]) BREUIL, 1927.

in Aurignacian-Perigordian deposits and we have therefore thought fit to examine them together with the rare engravings that were found in the same conditions.

Finally we reach the engravings of the famous cave of PAIR-NON-PAIR, whose discovery was related above. Undoubtedly these figures precede the end of the Perigordian period, for they were completely covered by Perigordian strata. It is indeed amazing, in so ancient a phase of art — a phase that we would logically expect to produce the first hesitant attempts, the first expressions of the creative labour that was to give birth to art in the full sense of the term — it is amazing, we repeat, that the figures of Pair-non-Pair already show true artistic maturity, proving the existence of a style already established in its essential elements and with well-defined characteristics.

Fig. 17. Cave of Pair-non-Pair. Group of engravings reproduced in Pls. 119, 120 (from BREUIL, 1952, fig. 383).

The figures of Pair-non-Pair, of which the most interesting are reproduced in Fig. 17 and Pls. 119 and 120, represent horses, oxen and ibexes; also bears, mammoths and stags.

That the style of Pair-non-Pair is anything but primitive is also proved by the frequent and skilful foreshortening of the animals' legs, all four often being shown in perfect perspective, and the liveliness with which movement is seized.

In some places the engravings are superimposed in an inextricable tangle that has led writers to disagree in their interpretations. We note G. Malvesin-Fabre's interpretation of one of the best-known figures at Pair-non-Pair which is reproduced in every textbook on the subject. This is the horse turning its head and compared by Daleau, on account of its position, to the *Agnus Dei*. In a recent article [1]) Malvesin-Fabre and David relate that following careful examination of the figures at Pair-non-Pair in different lighting conditions they came to the conclusion that the *Agnus Dei* was a composite figure resulting from the superimposition of an ibex with lowered head and a horse, facing in opposite directions. The photograph reproduced here (Pl. 119, *a*) which, together with the other photographs of Pair-non-Pair, we owe to the courtesy of Professor Malvesin-Fabre, is quite convincing in this respect: Daleau's early interpretation on the other hand presents a figure whose extreme disproportion and faulty design has nothing in common with the poise that usually distinguishes Palaeolithic figures — including those of Pair-non-Pair.

If we examine the engravings of Pair-non-Pair in detail we find that oxen horns, for instance, are not shown in " perspective tordue ", but according to principles of perspective that characterize the more evolved phases of Palaeolithic art. Furthermore, the limbs are often designed with care, and the feet are hoofed or cloven according to the species. These very ancient works of graphic art are distinguished by their power of observation, adherence to nature, liveliness and technical skill. We also recall the typical shape of the horses' heads, with elongated noses, described above; we shall encounter this particular shape in other works with an archaic flavour in Franco-Cantabrian art.

To continue this rapid survey of examples of cave art whose Aurignacian-Perigordian age is proved by their relation to *in situ* deposits, we return to the bison in the little cave of LA GRÈZE near Les Eyzies in the Vézère valley (Pl. 121). This figure, as we noted above,

---

[1]) DAVID, MALVESIN-FABRE, 1950.

was covered by a deposit that Breuil considers Aurignacian; it is very realistically and boldly traced, but a certain rigidity in the limbs, of which only two — one for each pair — are visible, gives it a particularly harsh quality. The horns are viewed from the front, although the animal is drawn in profile; this detail, as we have seen, appears to distinguish the works of a more archaic style.

Further examples of cave art which belong unmistakably to the Aurignacian-Perigordian period, because of their position in the deposits, are found in the field of bas-relief. A considerable number of blocks sculpted in low relief were found in the Perigordian layer of the LAUSSEL shelter in the Dordogne : five human figures, three female, one male and a couple probably representing a scene of childbirth, as well as a few incomplete animal figures (Pls. 150-152). This important group will be discussed later in connection with bas-relief. We shall only mention here that the female figures have a stylistic affinity with the more Typical Aurignacian-Perigordian statuettes, indicating that, at least in bas-relief, th eAurignacian-Perigordian artists used the same style whether they were executing works of cave art or mobiliary art.

* * *

Thus some works of cave art, unmistakably shown by stratigraphy to belong to the Aurignacian-Perigordian period, allow us to establish some elements of stylistic distinction for this period, e. g., the elongated shape of horses' heads (as in the bas-relief of Abri Labatut and the engravings of Pair-non-Pair) or the " perspective tordue " of ruminants' horns (such as the bison of La Grèze and the painted stag of Abri Labatut).

But other elements as important as the stratigraphical ones allow us to establish a chronology for some examples of Palaeolithic cave art, thus defining certain stylistic characteristics tied to the period; we allude to possible stylistic affinities between the rare Aurignacian-Perigordian objects of mobiliary art and the cave-art figures.

Let us examine the famous pebble, engraved on both sides, from Abri Labatut (Pl. 19, c), to which we may add the mediocre Perigordian figure of Laraux (Pl. 18, c). The extremely fine rearing horse of Labatut, with minutely described coat, has a special character of its own which we shall encounter in a very similar form in some cave-art figures. Among the engravings of the Gargas cave in the French Pyrenees, for instance, see the horse's head in Pl. 129, a, which shows the same delicacy and firmness of line, the same sure, expressive analysis of details such as the coat, eye, nostril, etc., and the same vigorous, lifelike movement of the neck.

Other equine heads in the same unmistakable style and figures of horses are published in Breuil's recent volume [1]). Finally analogous characteristics appear in the fine mare painted in black in the Spanish cave of La Peña de Candamo (Pl. 233, b). Here, therefore, is another definite style in Perigordian cave art — in our opinion, one of its most felicitous expressions.

We have already mentioned the bone fragment engraved with the hindquarters of a horse that was found in the Typical Aurignacian deposit of Hornos de la Peña in Cantabria (Pl. 17, a); it has usually been considered identical with another, more complete figure engraved on the wall of the same cave (Pl. 126, a). Although the resemblance does not appear to us to be particularly striking, there is undoubtedly a certain affinity between the two, even if the cave-wall figure is more supple and dynamic and denotes, perhaps, a more evolved artistic level. If we relate the Hornos de la Peña figure to the Aurignacian (or Perigordian) period, it becomes a further point of stylistic reference to be used in the chronological determination of other works of cave art for which we lack stratigraphical data. The same movement in the outline of the back and thigh and the same manner of joining the tail to the body are found, for in-

---

[1]) BREUIL, 1952, figs. 283-285, 287.

stance, in one of the fragmentary engravings from the Barabao cave (Pl. 125, *c*), and the same simplicity of construction of the figure, the same lively motion, in some engravings from the cave of La Mouthe (Pl. 124).

Also in connection with the few works of Perigordian mobiliary art so far discovered, we note that the fine engravings on pebbles from La Colombière (Pls. 20-23), with their characteristic manner of showing, usually, only two of the animal's limbs, have interesting points of comparison with expressions of cave art — for instance with some Spanish engravings in the Los Casares cave (Guadalajara) (Pl. 127), where the same primitive system of representing only one limb for each pair is followed; these engravings, on the other hand, are distinguished, as in La Colombière, by an excellent realism showing an obvious artistic maturity. See, particularly, the woolly rhinoceros in Pl. 127, *a*.

The morphological examination, therefore, of mural figures definitely assigned to the Aurignacian-Perigordian period (because of their direct association with *in situ* deposits and because of a stylistic affinity with figures of mobiliary art unmistakably dated to this period) points to some characteristics that appear to be tied to this early phase of Upper Palaeolithic and are found more or less frequently — if not exclusively — in it. We shall summarize them briefly : the elongated shape of the horses' heads; frontal perspective of antlers in the figures of deer viewed in profile (Abri Labatut) and of bison (La Grèze), whereas ibexes' antlers are viewed, as in Pair-non-Pair, either from the front or from the side. The limbs are sometimes drawn so that each one in a pair conceals the other, as in La Grèze and Los Casares, or the probable Aurignacian ibex of Belcayre (the latter excessively rigid and summary); but in other examples from the same period, e. g., Pair-non-Pair, all four limbs are visible.

Even the small amount of material examined already is sufficient to show that at least by the Perigordian period works of art of considerable aesthetic value were created, inspired by a profound naturalism, alive and dynamic both in zoomorphic and anthropomorphic representations — as we have already seen in mobiliary art. We have to turn to some Aurignacian deposits in the Vézère valley to find awkwardly executed, childish figures such as the Belcayre ibex or the crude animal figures of La Ferrassie where, as in Abri Blanchard, primitive vulvar figures are also present. But the Typical Aurignacian layer of the same Abri Blanchard produced the painting shown in Pl. 169, *a* which, even though reduced to a mere fragment, reveals a rather advanced colour scheme, for it is painted in black against a red background.

To conclude, even the more ancient works of cave art (confidently assigned to the Aurignacian-Perigordian because found in direct or indirect association with *in situ* deposits) show the precocious appearance in Franco-Cantabria, together with some very primitive expressions, of highly evolved art forms possessing technical and stylistic characteristics of their own. In certain cases these may constitute useful comparisons in determining the chronology of examples of cave art where stratigraphical data is lacking.

*   *   *

On the basis of the " key works " mentioned above we shall briefly review those examples of cave art attributable, on the strength of a more or less direct affinity with the works mentioned above, to the more archaic phases of Upper Palaeolithic art.

The cave of LA MOUTHE has produced many engravings and some paintings unmistakably belonging to various phases of Upper Palaeolithic — from Aurignacian-Perigordian to Magdalenian.

In 1895, following the excavation by the owner of the cave of part of the filling deposit, access was obtained for the first time to a corridor that until then had been completely blocked.

The Magdalenian layers of the deposit reached the ceiling. When this deep corridor was cleared figures were discovered on its walls and such convincing evidence won, for the first time, definitive recognition from official science for the existence of cave art in the Early Stone Age.

Of particular interest in the La Mouthe cave is a large group of deeply engraved figures that obviously resemble some of the above-mentioned Aurignacian-Perigordian works. The fine bison in Pl. 123, a (the first figure discovered in 1895) shows an affinity, in the shape of its horns and the outline of its back, with the bison of La Grèze which is incontrovertibly dated through its relation to the *in situ* deposit. The latter figure, however, is somewhat harsher in design and shows only two legs — rigid and rather crudely executed — whereas the bison of La Mouthe is more supple and lively, and the perspective of all four legs shown in motion is good. Artistically it is a more mature work than the former, and can be compared, from this point of view, with the engravings in Pair-non-Pair.

The bull in Pl. 124, though more simple in style, is also full of life and motion; it, too, belongs to an archaic phase and recalls, in the characteristic line of the neck and back, some of the Pair-non-Pair figures. The same deep, firm incision and the same simplicity of outline appear in the large ox in Pl. 123, b which is truly majestic in its linear sobriety.

A bison, with horns seen in characteristic frontal perspective, was found in 1941 by Chamarty and Truffier [1]) in the cave of LE GABILLOU near Mussidan in the commune of Sourzac (Dordogne) (Pl. 122, b). This cave contains a fine series of engravings of animals in motion, very expressive and skilfully treated, even if showing some harshness and hesitancy. They were probably not all executed at the same time. In Pl. 122, besides the bison that underlies a small horse, we reproduce the head of a bull (a), carelessly done but very lifelike with its great oval eye; a curious hare (d), deeply engraved, equally lively and expressive although summary and disproportionate; and a fine reindeer (c), drawn with firm lines. The reindeer, too, is incomplete and like the hare has roughly sketched legs and no feet.

This group, to which we should add some other animals and a crudely sketched anthropomorphic figure (Pl. 258, b) has a distinctly archaic flavour that in no way detracts from the dynamism and life of the interesting figures.

Also in the Dordogne, in the Vézère valley, half a kilometre from the little town of Le Bugue, is the cave of BARABAO where in 1951 Norbert Casteret [2]) discovered some figures engraved on the ceiling and on the walls, whose surface, owing to an advanced process of disintegration, has today become very plastic while keeping its original appearance. The incision is generally deep and was made, it seems, when the rock still retained its original hardness. The figures are up to two metres long, and can usually be seen only in special lighting conditions; they are simple and not always easy to interpret, owing to their poor state of preservation. Most of them are horses and oxen, handsomely executed; the figure of a man is also discernible. The outline of the animal in Pl. 125, c recalls other Aurignacian-Perigordian figures such as, for instance, the horse of Hornos de la Peña. The ox's head in Pl. 125, a is very primitive. All in all this group is definitely archaic, and appears to belong to the Aurignacian-Perigordian period.

The outline of the simple but excellent engravings of Pair-non-Pair is repeated in some engraved figures in France and in Spain where the sloping line of the neck and back also shows, at times, a more or less accentuated depression.

In the Spanish cave of CASTILLO near Puente Viesgo in Cantabria, for instance, there is a group of figures in the same style (Pl. 128, a, c). The rigid drawing of the legs and the economy of detail accentuates their archaic character. Because of such characteristics these and other

---

[1]) CHAMARTY, TRUFFIER, 1941.
[2]) BREUIL, 1952, pp. 308-309.

analogous — if more elaborate — figures (such as those at Hornos de la Peña) relate to the Aurignacian-Perigordian period.

The same stark but vigorous style is encountered in the French cave of EBBOU in Ardèche, where, a year after the end of the last war, the Abbé Glory [1]) discovered numerous series of engraved horses, oxen, ibexes, deer and a mammoth (Pl. 288). The horses' heads are characteristically elongated as in Pair-non-Pair, and the outline of the back is equally harsh; the oxen show only one horn of each pair, viewed in profile and turned forwards. But we shall return to the Ebbou engravings when discussing the Mediterranean province; we shall see, in fact, that certain features invite stylistic comparisons between the figures of Ebbou and the recent discoveries in the little island of Levanzo (Sicily).

Further points of comparison exist with figures engraved in Cantabrian and Aquitanian caves, and further works could be added to the group of engravings in Aurignacian-Perigordian style.

* * *

To proceed with the examination of later works of art we may now consider those which, because they were found in unmistakable direct or indirect association with later Aurignacian-Perigordian deposits, provide basic evidence for the chronological attribution to the second part of the Upper Palaeolithic of certain styles, processes and techniques.

The majority of the many splendid specimens of post-Perigordian bas-relief known at present were found associated with *in situ* deposits; on the strength of this stratigraphical evidence they were assigned to the Solutrean or the Magdalenian. Surveying this production of cave art as a whole (with which we shall deal extensively later) we get the impression that a common taste and certain common stylistic elements distinguish many of the works of art of both periods: the Final Solutrean zoomorphic figures, vigorously carved on great blocks of stone at Le Roc de Sers (Charente) (Pls. 154-156) and Le Fourneau du Diable (Dordogne) (Pl. 157, *a*) are not very far, in style and conception, from the Lower Magdalenian figures of Angles-sur-Anglin. In fact, as we shall see later, they actually share some identical features.

The Solutrean layers of LAUGERIE HAUTE produced some large blocks of stone crudely engraved with animal figures that conflict with the fine, more or less contemporary figures of Le Roc de Sers [2]). Also in Laugerie Haute, in the higher, Early Magdalenian, levels rock fragments were found with deeply engraved figures of oxen, simply but firmly outlined and well proportioned (Pl. 130).

To conclude, if we compare these works of sculpture, belonging to cultures ranging from Upper Solutrean to Lower Magdalenian, we realize that it is far from easy, on the basis of the documentation at present available, to establish the succession and transformation of style and technique. In this connection we should not discount the possibility of the existence and development of parallel industries at certain stages of the Magdalenian and Solutrean cultures.

The fine engravings on stalagmites in the cave of LA MAIRIE À TEYJAT (Dordogne) (Pls. 146; 284, *a*) were discovered *in situ*. Fragments of engraved stalagmite were unearthed in an Upper Magdalenian stratum (Magd. V). It seems certain that the engravings were executed after the fragments had fallen from the stalagmite, because only on these fragments are there figures turned in every direction, proving that their creator was free to move around the blocks, whereas on the walls figures are traced in a normal position. The fact that the blocks fell in the Magdalenian V layer of the deposit before they were engraved proves that the figures were executed in that period and no later, because the Magdalenian V layer underlay one of Magdalenian VI which must therefore have been formed subsequently.

---

[1]) GLORY, 1947.
[2]) PEYRONY D., PEYRONY E., 1938, pl. IV.

The engraved figures of La Mairie à Teyjat show a high degree of artistic development. As opposed to the other examples examined previously they belong to a closing phase in the evolution of Palaeolithic art; this is confirmed, moreover, by the fact that they can be assigned to the Upper Magdalenian.

These cave-art figures, on the other hand, are in perfect harmony with the mobiliary art of the same period, which also reached the peak of its evolution in the Upper Magdalenian. Among the outstanding features are the care with which the feet of animals are represented and the manner of drawing the base of the bison's horn — in direct continuation of the eye — a manner also employed in the evolved phases of mobiliary art.

And so we come to the end of the list, unfortunately a short one, of the more important examples of cave art that it is possible to situate with certainty both stratigraphically and chronologically. On the one hand the Palaeolithic mural engravings clearly develop from simple — though excellent — forms to the elaborate expressions of a later age in which a technical virtuosity is achieved which marks the peak of this type of art, as in La Mairie. On the other hand it is not possible, in the present state of our knowledge, to follow this evolution through the successive stages of different cultures and periods because we lack intermediate stratigraphical data between the extreme forms, and because where such data exist (as in the case of Aurignacian-Perigordian engraving and of Solutrean and Magdalenian bas-relief) the specimens may show the same artistic level in different periods, or, on the contrary, various degrees of artistic maturity in contemporary deposits.

Finally, keeping of course to works which can be chronologically dated from their stratigraphy, we must restrict ourselves for the present, in the matter of the evolution of Palaeolithic cave sculpture, to definite facts; it is particularly important to note, towards the end of the Magdalenian, the appearance of elaborate forms that seem to bear no relation to works of an earlier period.

A comparison with the engravings of La Mairie à Teyjat will also help us to distinguish the later, more evolved expressions in the great mass of Franco-Cantabrian cave art.

* * *

We shall now briefly review some of the more important groups of cave engravings of the Franco-Cantabrian region, attempting as we go along to point out the stylistic relationship between them and the engraved or sculptured figures we have dealt with already. This review will follow, broadly speaking, the geographical order.

We have already mentioned the cave of HORNOS DE LA PEÑA, in the neighbourhood of Torrelavega near Santander, in connection with the engraved horse resembling the figure carved on bone which was discovered in the Aurignacian deposit of the same cave by Alcalde del Rio in 1903. With the exception of this horse, which is situated in the well-lighted front part of the cave, the engravings are dispersed in deep, dark corridors difficult of access. Many meandering figures and some crude, summary animals are traced on the damp clay; other engravings show different styles. Pl. 126, b shows an incomplete horse with long neck and thick mane, of a rather archaic sort, that somewhat recalls the horses of Pair-non-Pair; it probably belongs to the Aurignacian-Perigordian period, as do some other figures in the same cave. Some more elaborate horses, and especially some firmly and skilfully traced bison, should undoubtedly be placed at a higher level of technical evolution, such as that of the Magdalenian figures : for instance, we see the same manner of representing the base of the bison's horn as directly touching the eye in the engravings, dated with certainty, at La Mairie, and in works of mobiliary art of the Upper Magdalenian.

Some horses in a rather advanced style, finely engraved, were found in the narrow corridors of the EL BUXU cave near Cardes (Oviedo) (Pl. 131); Obermaier, La Vega del Sella and Breuil assign them to Lower Magdalenian [1]). Other figures portray stags, ibexes and a bison. The engraved and painted figure in Pl. 131, c represents a deer with antlers viewed in profile. Some tectiforms are also interesting; we shall deal with them later (Pl. 271, a).

A fine horse, delicately engraved in an advanced style, with accurately stressed morphological details, was found with other figures in the cave of PINDAL near the village of Unquera (Oviedo); we shall return to this cave in connection with painting. The animal's coat is minutely described and the figure is complete in every detail. The skill and precision of this piece of work place it with the best and most evolved specimens of Magdalenian art. A fine fish engraved in the same Pindal cave (Pl. 134, a) is also of a high artistic level : its small head is full of movement and the large tail fins give it a particular liveliness. This is one of the few fish found in Franco-Cantabrian cave art; in mobiliary art, on the other hand, fish were thoroughly exploited as a subject and schematized and broken down into their constituent elements until they assumed a definitely ornamental function.

Among the other Spanish caves with more or less evolved engraved figures is LA LOJA near Oviedo; in a deep gallery, about 46 metres from the entrance, are half a dozen figures of oxen, attributed by Breuil to Upper Perigordian or Lower Magdalenian [2]); fine works, if somewhat rigidly executed.

Pl. 133, d shows an ibex, finely engraved, quite elaborate and rich in detail, from the cave of Castillo mentioned in connection whith engravings attributed, on stylistic grounds, to the Aurignacian-Perigordian; it is an excellent piece of work, and so is the beautiful stag, equally rich in detail and perfectly executed both as to chiaroscuro and volume, engraved in the cave of Altamira (Pl. 133, a).

Finally, before leaving Spain we should mention the fine engravings, chaotically superimposed, of LA PEÑA DE CANDAMO in the neighbourhood of S. Roman de Candamo (Oviedo). Walls dripping with moisture are densely covered with lightly engraved figures mixed with paintings in various styles; it is often difficult to distinguish them without the help of a special light from the side. We publish here a beautiful stag turning its head, struck by darts, very delicately executed, well balanced and carefully observed in details such as the hoofs (Pl. 135, a). An equal degree of skill and artistic evolution is revealed by the fine bison in Pl. 135, b and by the two bulls in Pl. 136. Perspective in these figures is treated with great skill, both with regard to the position of the horns (not shown in " perspective tordue " in the sense of the term as applied to some Aurignacian-Perigordian figures) and in the construction of the animals' bodies, particularly the two bulls and the bison — very realistic, with ample folds of skin on neck and chest. In Pl. 137, a is a fine ruminant's head, probably an ibex, with horns distorted in an extravagant form of stylization.

LES COMBARELLES.

The most impressive group of engravings found so far in the Franco-Cantabrian province is undoubtedly the group at Les Combarelles in the Vézère valley (Dordogne). This cave consists of two corridors, one of which — the left one — is 237 metres long and penetrates the flank of the mountain like a long, narrow tunnel. On its walls, starting at 160 metres from the entrance, are approximately 300 engraved figures, the first of which were discovered in 1901. According to Breuil's list [3]) there are 116 horses, 37 bison,

---

[1]) OBERMAIER, LA VEGA DEL SELLA, 1918; BREUIL, 1952, p. 383.
[2]) BREUIL, 1952, p. 377.
[3]) CAPITAN, BREUIL, PEYRONY, 1924, p. 21.

19 bears, 14 reindeer, 9 other deer, 13 mammoths, 9 ibexes, 7 oxen, 5 lions, 5 wolves, a rhinoceros, and other more or less recognizable animals; also 39 human or semi-human beings. The size of these figures varies between 10 cm. and one metre long. Some are lightly, others deeply engraved.

The figures can hardly be distinguished unless they are lighted from the side; in fact, they are often superimposed or interlaced, and made all the more indecipherable by the roughness of the rock surface and the fissures and cracks that furrow it; isolated from each other and clearly distinguished they are striking expressions of an art that has reached an exceptional degree of maturity. They can be likened to the fine engravings in the Spanish caves mentioned above: perfect proportions, nimbleness of movement, lively naturalism, skilful description of detail and definite sense of volume. The numerous horses are elaborately executed in their various parts, their noses well described, their manes and tails scrupulously represented, their hoofs perfectly shaped and proportioned. See, for instance, Figs. d, c of Pl. 139 and Fig. b of Pl. 140.

Among the various engravings of Les Combarelles a beautiful cave lion deserves particular attention (Pl. 141); we are at a loss to know which to admire more: the realism of the animal's actual appearance or the mastery with which its vigorous nature is expressed.

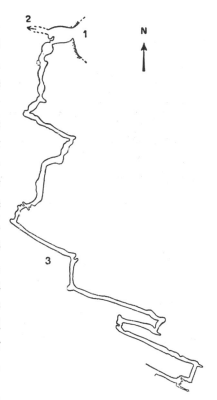

Fig. 18. Les Combarelles. 1. Entrance to the cave. 2. Side gallery. 3. Beginning of engravings in principal corridor.

The bear in Pl. 142 can also be considered one of the finest works of Palaeolithic art, especially on account of the remarkable accuracy with which its slow and heavy gait is rendered.

Fig. 19. Engravings in the cave of Bernifal (Dordogne). Mammoth with superimposed tectiforms, bison, deer, horses (from BREUIL, 1952, fig. 328).

Breuil situates the Les Combarelles engravings between Lower and Middle Magdalenian. They undoubtedly belong to the phase marking the highest peak in the evolution of Franco-Cantabrian art, for their faithful reproduction of reality and the high standard of their technique.

Figures of the same type, but in far smaller numbers, were subsequently discovered in the right-hand gallery of Les Combarelles.

BERNIFAL.

Not very far from Les Combarelles, in the Beune valley, another cave with engraved figures was discovered by Peyrony in 1902. Most of the figures are mammoths; some, very lightly engraved, recall the mammoths of Font-de-Gaume that we shall discuss later; others underlie tectiform figures — very numerous in this cave — and form a kind of frieze. There are also bison, horses and other animals (Fig. 19). One of the mammoths is shown struck by arrows. According to Breuil these engravings are by and large comparable with those of Les Combarelles.

LES TROIS FRÈRES.

Les Trois Frères near Montesquieu-Avantès (Basses-Pyrénées), already mentioned in previous pages, is of exceptional interest in the study of Palaeolithic art. It was discovered in 1914 by the three Begouen brothers, sons of the eminent prehistorian of Toulouse, Comte Begouen,

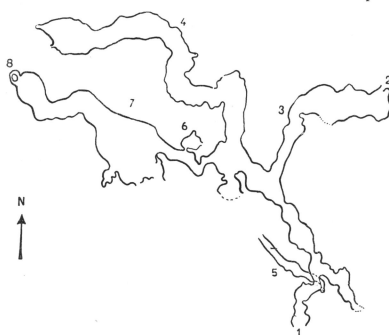

and is named after them [1]). It consists of a complex of winding corridors on different levels, with wells, halls, etc., difficult and often impossible to penetrate. Its outstanding importance is due first of all to the quantity and magnificence of the engravings, which undoubtedly belong to more than one period; in the second place, to the fine, plentiful examples of the technique known as " cameo ". Finally this cave, and particularly its deepest section (the so-called Sanctuary) furnishes, by means of its impressive images, one of the most convincing proofs of the magical purpose of Palaeolithic art.

Fig. 20. Cave of Les Trois Frères. 1. Old entrance. 2. New entrance. 3. Corridor with painted hands. 4. Gallery with dotted lines. 5. Dots and painted figures. 6, 7. Engraved feline animals. 8. The Sanctuary.

The cameo technique in Les Trois Frères exploits the peculiar conditions of the rock surface. A thin coating of yellowish clay covers the walls; this was engraved so that the rock, which is blue-black, shows through. But the rock surface also has a superficial white skin, providing the artist with three different shades with which to play by carving the rock or simply scraping away the clayey film. This allowed him to achieve, at times, a real chromatic effect (Pl. 145, a).

The figures in the Sanctuary are so finely engraved that generally oblique lighting is needed to distinguish them. Here is one of the finest moments in Franco-Cantabrian realism: the engravings can really be called exceptional, for the masterly assurance of their execution, their unsurpassable realism and the subtle technique that skilfully expresses chiaroscuro and volume by means of fine, firm, closely repeated lines. Furthermore, a particular character is given to the Sanctuary of Les Trois Frères by the tangle of figures and signs that overlap and encroach upon each other. Nevertheless, once each figure is distinguished it appears an

[1]) BEGOUEN H., 1936, p. 16.

undeniable masterpiece. This tangle of engraved figures is unmatched — in the same fashion and with the same magnificence — by any other group of Franco-Cantabrian engravings. The tracings that Breuil made of them [1]) convince one of their exceptional quality (Pl. 145). One really gets the impression that the Magdalenian artist did not attach particular importance to the result of his work as a whole, but rather to the specific act of creating this or that figure.

The marvellous engraved figures of the Sanctuary are small; they represent bison, horses, oxen, rhinoceros, reindeer, mammoths and also fantastic beings, half human and half animal. By and large they are of a very advanced style (referred by Breuil to Magdalenian IV), but some underlying figures (according to Breuil's observations) are more archaic; among the latter are a few bison with horns in frontal perspective, executed in the particular manner that we noted in some engravings attributed to the Aurignacian-Perigordian period (La Grèze, La Mouthe, etc.).

A mammoth and an ibex are more deeply engraved than the others; two curious owls, traced in another part of the cave, are considered by Breuil to be Aurignacian.

To return to the Sanctuary, we should add that it looks like a rough chapel, with walls and ceiling broken up by recesses with rounded, polished surfaces. The back of this shadowy chapel is covered with fine engravings of animals, but a particularly suggestive character is conferred upon the impressive conglomeration of figures by a strange anthropomorphic being, 75 cm. tall, engraved and painted in black. This is the only painting in the Sanctuary and from a height of 4 metres it dominates the animal figures traced below it. It can be reached by means of a narrow natural gallery that opens on the same level but is invisible as one observes the figure from the centre of the Sanctuary (Pl. 281).

This curious personage, reproduced in all the textbooks as the " sorcerer of Les Trois Frères ", is shown in the act of dancing, with body flexed forward and legs bent in movement. The head is crowned with two large stag antlers, and the ears are also the ears of a stag. The face is turned towards the observer; the eyes, with their round pupils, are set very close together. The nose is thin and pointed like a beak, and underneath it is a downturned, brief half-circle. A large striped segment, probably a beard, hangs over the chest: the toes and fingers are clearly traced. The sorcerer also has a large tail that might be a horse's tail and beneath it the genitals are accurately shown.

This figure is completely and carefully engraved: the outline of the back, shoulders, chest, abdomen, legs and tail is traced with a thick black line. Traces of paint also adhere to the forehead, nose and eyes. It is probably the representation of a masked man or mythical being.

Another strange little hybrid figure, half animal and half human, similar to the sorcerer, is lightly engraved in the Sanctuary, hidden among the fine figures mentioned above (Pl. 282, c).

These two, and other figures, appear to be connected with the mysterious, complex world of Quaternary magic.

In concluding this brief review of the more interesting aspects of Les Trois Frères we should mention the figure of a lioness with the head many times retouched and therefore confused in design, of an advanced style, though somewhat harsh and clumsy, engraved and partly painted in a small recess.

There are two other lions, considerably deteriorated, their heads viewed from the front and with large round eyes, fine examples of the same perspective as that which distinguishes the sorcerer (Pl. 144, b).

---

[1]) BREUIL, 1952, figs. 125-129.

18. — P. GRAZIOSI, Palaeolithic Art.

FONT-DE-GAUME.

As specimens of the most advanced Magdalenian graphic art we illustrate the small mammoths finely engraved in the cave of Font-de-Gaume (Pl. 149). Their relative chronological position seems unmistakable, according to Breuil's observations [1]. In fact they are superimposed upon polychromatic figures which, as we shall see later, represent the most advanced phase — at least from the point of view of technique — in Magdalenian painting.

This stratigraphical superimposition is confirmed by the nature of the figures, which transcend the accurate realism of Palaeolithic art, as shown by their specific mannerisms. These mannerisms, tasteful on the whole, by distorting reality create conventional patterns — such as, for instance, the representation of the pachyderms' feet as semi-circles, or the simplification of their large bodies — which are far removed from the concrete naturalism of the best Magdalenian specimens and appear to be firmly established here.

ROUFFIGNAC.

On 26th June 1956 an exceptionally interesting discovery — undoubtedly one of the most important in the field of Palaeolithic art since Lascaux — was made in the Dordogne, in the Vézère valley, by René Nougier and Romain Robert.

Le Cro du Cluzeau, a vast cave near the village of Rouffignac, consisting of 8 or 10 kilometres of winding corridors, revealed to the two French scholars one of the most magnificent collections of engraved and painted figures known to us today. Immediately following the discovery Henri Breuil visited the spot and confirmed the exceptional importance of this new monument of Palaeolithic cave art, and on 20th July Nougier and Robert announced their discovery at the closing session of the XVth "Congrès Préhistorique de France" in Poitiers.

Up to the present approximately 1000 mammoths, 17 bison, 11 ibexes, 9 horses, 10 rhinoceroses, 2 felines and 4 human figures have been found, but the list will probably lengthen as previously unexplored parts of the immense cave are examined [2].

The paintings, with which we shall deal later, are exclusively carried out in black, and most of the engravings are traced on rock surfaces that had acquired a clayey consistency; in some cases meandering fingerprints were impressed on the plastic coating. Plates 147 and 148 show a series of engraved mammoths — the animal most frequently portrayed in Rouffignac, both in engraving and in painting — and one rhinoceros. The figures are generally carefully drawn, with details such as the fur and the eyes often recalling in style and technique — in some cases almost identically — the small engraved mammoths of Font-de-Gaume, superimposed on the polychromatic paintings and consequently attributed to the most advanced phase of Franco-Cantabrian art (Pl. 149). We therefore believe that the mammoths engraved in Rouffignac can also be considered as belonging to a late phase in the evolution of Palaeolithic cave-wall art.

Note the mammoths in Pl. 148, *a*, *b*. One of them is scored by a series of vertical parallel

---

[1] CAPITAN, BREUIL, PEYRONY, 1910, p. 117.
[2] The events that followed the discovery are well known, particularly the absurd controversy over the authenticity of the figures, started by the French press and reported all over the world. The discussions dragged on for many months until groups of scholars from France (Breuil, Casteret, etc.) and other countries (Graziosi, Almagro) confirmed the authenticity of the Rouffignac figures, both individually and collectively, and the French Ministry of Education finally "classified" the cave. (For the Rouffignac controversy, see NOUGIER, ROBERT, 1957; GRAZIOSI, 1957a; *idem*, 1959; GARROD, 1958; SAINT-MATHURIN, 1958; *idem*, 1959; BREUIL, 1959).

lines, the other by a serpentine line. The former curiously resembles the *megaceros* engraved on clay in Pech-Merle (Pl. 117, *a*), different in style from the Rouffignac figures but also scored by parallel lines.

* * *

Before leaving the subject of Palaeolithic engraving, we have a word to say about the other engravings on clay that are often found on the ground, or on the surface of cave walls made plastic by decalcification, as in Rouffignac, or covered by a layer of clayey substance.

From the point of view of material execution, engraving on clay is different from engraving on rock in that it can be done with the fingers alone or with any pointed object; apart from this technical difference, however, engravings on clay should be considered together with the other examples of cave art, with regard to style and purpose; nothing, so far, indicates that this process was more prevalent in one period than another. It is true, as we have said before, that on the basis of a purely theoretical reconstruction of the evolution of Palaeolithic art some authors have thought it logical to conclude that the earliest graphic works of Man, because of the greater simplicity and immediacy, were executed in clay, particularly in the form of meandering lines and serpentine signs made by casually trailing fingers on the soft substance. Without denying *a priori* that this may have been the case, in the present writer's opinion insufficient material has emerged to confirm it or to justify us in building hypotheses and theories about the origin and evolution of art upon such a presupposition; much less can we consider the meanders and doodles encountered in the caves of France and Spain as necessarily belonging to the earliest artistic expressions of the human race and to no other. Nothing prevents us from supposing that these extremely simple graphic expressions, requiring no expert hand, may have been traced at any period, from the most remote Prehistory to our own times. The same applies to painting — as we shall later explain.

If, in the case of engraving on rock, the possibility exists of a direct relationship to *in situ* deposits (and therefore of a direct chronological determination), obviously the same does not obtain in the case of engraving on clay, unless the engraved surface was well covered by a stalagmitic crust before the deposit was formed. Therefore, in the case of engraving on clay we must restrict ourselves, as regards possible chronology, to purely stylistic factors.

In Pls. 115-117 we have assembled reproductions of some engravings on clay, grouping them according to artistic accomplishment, without, of course, attributing to such an order the significance of a chronological succession.

Pl. 115, *a* shows meandering lines found in the cave of Altamira, traced with fingers and representing a crude ox head, hardly recognizable in the photograph. Figs. *b-d* of the same plate show outlines of animals in the cave of La Clotilde de Santa Isabel in Cantabria : they are crude, primitive, awkward figures.

An almost indecipherable tangle of figures and lines is traced on the clayey surface of the ceiling in Pech-Merle (Pl. 116). The head of a mammoth with a long trunk is discernible, also some naked female figures, one of which is illustrated in the same Pl. 116, *c* and sketched, together with another, in Pl. 257, *a*, *b* : with their pendulous breasts and voluminous structure they recall the Aurignacian-Perigordian female statuettes and also the Lower Magdalenian women engraved on stones in the cave of La Marche (Pl. 82, *i-m*).

Also in the category of crude, primitive figures is a stag with enormous antlers, traced in Pl. 117, *a*, probably a *megaceros*, also from Pech-Merle. The drawing is childish and hard to decipher on account of the many vertical signs that are superimposed upon it, recalling, as we have seen, the signs covering one of the mammoths in Rouffignac.

The horse of Gargas reproduced in Pl. 117, *b*, though summarily executed, is of a better style. Its nose is elongated in a form (called by the French '' duck's bill '') encountered, as we have pointed out before, in rather archaic expressions of Franco-Cantabrian art. In Pl. 117, *c* another animal, probably a deer, is rapidly sketched on the clay floor of the cave of Niaux, Ariège; this figure is graphically more refined, as shown in well-outlined details such as the eye and ear.

Finally we illustrate a series of engravings on clay denoting a stage of complete artistic maturity. They include the beautiful fish of Niaux (Pl. 138, *a*), the bison and the horse's head of Bédeilhac (Pl. 138, *b*, *d*) (not quite as pure and skilful in line as the preceding figure but still to be classified among the works of the finest Magdalenian period) and, lastly, the magnificent horse of Montespan, executed with the most subtle, mature technique (Pl. 138, *c*).

BAS-RELIEF

Most of the bas-relief sculpture was found in direct association with *in situ* deposits, either because it consisted of fragments which had fallen from the walls into the deposit or because the deposit itself, as we have seen, had previously covered the carved walls. This has made it possible to date the figures, at least *ante quem*.

A fact that should be emphasized with regard to bas-relief, surely a fact of some significance though we are not yet prepared to offer explanations or hypotheses, is the constant presence of stone sculpture in low and high relief in recesses or caves exposed to daylight, as opposed to engravings and paintings which are generally found in the deeper and darker parts of the caves. Only very rarely have Palaeolithic bas-reliefs been located in those shadowy depths and they have invariably been modelled in clay. It is because of their location in caves open to daylight and therefore inhabited by man, where deposits containing human implements were consequently formed, that it has been possible to date the Palaeolithic bas-reliefs through their relation to the deposits themselves.

Some reason must have induced Palaeolithic artists to use low-relief technique only in works that were to be exposed to the light and looked upon by all. The fine bas-reliefs of Le Roc and Le Cap Blanc, with their friezes of bison and horses, suggest that the artist, in carrying out his work, was guided by the intention of creating a harmonious sequence of figures. With very few exceptions (such as Lascaux) this is not apparent in the disorderly juxtaposition and mutual obliteration of the figures engraved or painted in the gloomy depths of many Franco-Cantabrian caves. It should furthermore be noted that realistic human figures appear in the low-relief friezes, both in those attributed to the Perigordian, as at Laussel, and in the Magdalenian friezes, as at Angles-sur-Anglin. In low relief, moreover, the features of the human face were reproduced (Pl. 160), whereas cave engravings and paintings confine themselves to deformed human figures, semi-animal in appearance and completely depersonalized, with features concealed behind monstrous animal masks.

In the description of Palaeolithic bas-reliefs below, we follow an established — in some cases, presumed — chronological order, which shows that, as in the case of sculpture in the round, the human figure prevails in earlier periods (e. g., Perigordian bas-reliefs at Laussel) whereas zoomorphic representation is predominant later.

THE SHELTER OF LAUSSEL.

The very important series of sculpted blocks discovered by Dr. Lalanne in 1911 in the Upper Aurignacian (or Perigordian) deposit of the Laussel shelter in the Dordogne was found in one small area; the main figure was carved on a large block that dominated the others and was later sectioned so as to enable the sculptures to be removed from the cave [1].

---

[1] LALANNE, 1911; *idem*, 1912; LALANNE, BOUYSSONIE, 1941-47.

Besides a number of fragmentary animal figures of slight interest, the Laussel deposit produced five blocks with human figures : three female, one male, and a fifth representing a scene of childbirth or copulation (Pls. 150-152).

The most important complete human figure, which was sculpted on the large block, represents a naked woman with adipose hips and large pendulous breasts (Pl. 150). Thick hair falls to the shoulders, the face is featureless. The right arm is bent outward, the hand grasping a horn-shaped object, while the left arm lies along the body with hand resting on the abdomen. A glance at the plates reproducing the anthropomorphic Aurignacian-Perigordian sculptures will convince us of the close analogy between the Laussel Venus and many of those female statuettes. The same exuberant fleshiness, the same disposition and interpretation of masses and volumes, the same rudimentary modelling of the head and the same way of treating the hair; in short, the same spirit animates these and the other anthropomorphic Aurignacian-Perigordian representations, and all show, by and large, the same degree of technical and artistic maturity. Some traces of ochre adhering to these bas-reliefs lead one to suppose that they were originally coloured red.

In the fragment of a female figure reproduced in Pl. 151, *b*, voluminous breasts rest on the rounded stomach, at the centre of which the deeply marked umbilical depression adds a note of vivid realism. The hair is stylized in a squared pattern similar to that of some Aurignacian-Perigordian Venuses. The figure is sculpted in a careful and precise technique, with smooth, well-polished surfaces.

Equally marked by vivid realism is the sculpture reproduced in Pl. 151, *a*; it, too, represents a woman, in approximately the same pose as the preceding figure. The right arm is extended horizontally, the hand grasps a curved object — probably a horn or a jar. Although the details of this figure may seem less accomplished, perhaps because of its deteriorated condition, it appears to be a work of greater artistic merit than the celebrated Venus mentioned above. The well-balanced volumes, bold lines and supple movement of the arm and of the slightly inclined head give it a particular feeling of life. As a matter of interest, this bas-relief was subjected to many adventures at the time of its discovery : it was stolen one night from Dr. Lalanne by one of his workmen, smuggled into Germany and sold to the Berlin Museum.

The fourth fragment shows a small figure (21 cm. long), roughly hammered out; a deeply-cut engraving rather than a proper bas-relief (Pl. 151, *c*). It shows the figure of a woman viewed from the front, very sketchily and incorrectly done. She appears to be holding her legs in her hands, bending them sharply backwards with feet touching the hips. At the lower extremity the head and shoulders of another human being are lightly engraved. This group has been interpreted as a scene of copulation or childbirth; the second figure may, however, be independent from the first, and if so it might be simply a separate sketch, unfinished or subsequently destroyed in the execution of the larger figure.

The last of this series of bas-reliefs deserves particular attention. It represents a very slender male figure (Pl. 152), well proportioned and revealing, as do all the others, the firm hand and fine artistic sense of its creator. It wears a sort of belt around its waist, and has no head or feet due to the fracturing of the stone. The arms must have been held horizontally out from the shoulders, but only part of the left arm remains. This particular stance led to the conclusion that the man was holding a bow : he is consequently known as the " archer of Laussel ". It seems more likely, however, that he was about to throw a javelin or use a spear-thrower.

Terme Pialat.

Another example of anthropomorphic art showing some interesting affinities with the Laussel figure is the bas-relief found in 1913 at Terme Pialat, between Couze and Belvez in the Dordogne valley, in a deposit attributed to the Middle Aurignacian. Two figures in light low relief represent women, both very crudely executed. This is a mediocre piece of work, archaically treated; from a technical point of view it has some affinity with the Laussel " childbirth " scene (Pl. 153, a). One of the figures, seen in profile, has prominent breasts, abdomen and buttocks, a bulbous, featureless head and no arms. Although its artistic merit is negligible it resembles in style the Aurignacian-Perigordian figures.

ABRI DU POISSON (GORGE D'ENFER).

On the ceiling of Abri du Poisson, Gorge d'Enfer, near Les Eyzies, the figure of a fish, probably a salmon, is sculpted in shallow low relief which one could almost call " champlevé " (Pl. 153, c). It is simple but lifelike in design; some of the morphological details, such as the mouth, the eye, etc., are sketched in profile. It is one metre long. In 1932 Peyrony attributed it to the Upper Aurignacian (Breuil today confirms this by defining it " Perigordian ") because he considered it probably belonged to the upper level of the cave's deposit, which dates, in fact, from that period. This is not definitive, even though the level referred to is the top layer of the deposit and only 1,30 m. from the ceiling; the engraving might have been added later. Nevertheless, a certain technical affinity with the horse of Abri Labatut, which was found in Perigordian layers and is also sculpted in shallow low relief (Pl. 153, b), supports this chronological attribution.

THE SHELTER OF LE ROC DE SERS.

The great sculptured frieze of Le Roc de Sers in the Charente valley is unquestionably one of the most important monuments of Palaeolithic art, and constitutes, together with the sculptures of Angles-sur-Anglin and Le Cap Blanc, the most impressive and complex expression of Franco-Cantabrian high and low relief.

It was discovered between 1927 and 1929 by Henri Martin in the course of excavations carried out in the deposit extending under the rocky cliff which forms the large Le Roc shelter [1]. According to the discoverer, the blocks, face down, were situated in the middle of the Upper Solutrean deposit. This stratigraphical position was confirmed by the recent excavations of Lantier and Mlle Martin. The blocks must originally have formed a continuous frieze against the wall, but for natural reasons according to Lantier (and not iconoclasm as Martin would have it) they fell on to a platform, about 5 metres wide, that ran round the base of the walls.

During the 1951 excavations [2] Lantier discovered two more sculpted blocks, still in their original position against the rock ledge (Pl. 156, a). He was also able to ascertain that this ledge must have continued, with its frieze, in a more or less straight line beyond the limits assumed by Martin when he attempted to reconstruct the " sanctuary ", giving it a semi-circular shape. The sculpted blocks of Le Roc are shown in Pl. 154, a in what Martin assumed to be their original position.

The subjects represented in Le Roc are largely zoomorphic, but there are two human figures as well. In order of frequency we have horses, bison, oxen, ibexes, deer and a bird. It is interesting to note that many of the animals portrayed were, at a later period, transformed into others, often zoologically absurd. Many of the horses, for instance, seem to have been obtained by elaborating pre-existing bison, and the head of a bison (Pl. 154, b) has been curiously transformed into what appears to be the head of a wild boar. This reveals the workings of the Palaeolithic artist's mind : he obliterated the original figures of his engravings, and especially of his wall paintings, by superimposing new figures; elsewhere he modified them or used

---

[1] MARTIN, 1928; idem, 1932.
[2] LANTIER, 1952.

them in the execution of new subjects, almost as though he was obliged to create all his works in the same place or on the same rock surface.

On the whole the Le Roc sculptures show a certain unity, both stylistic and technical, although, as Lantier observed, they are not contemporary even though they all belong to the Solutrean age. This is proved by the re-workings mentioned above, which are probably due to the Palaeolithic artist's changing interest in different species of animals.

Dimensions vary, the smaller figures being slightly less than 40 cm. and the larger ones close to 70 cm. long. Although they usually appear isolated and independent, in some cases they are related to one another and form a composition or scene.

The technique displayed in the large blocks is often vigorous; the artist carved the stone forcefully, obtaining powerful lights and shadows in high relief that in some cases approaches sculpture in the round, and has an extremely suggestive plastic effect.

The animals reproduced in Pl. 154, b are among the most complete fragments in Le Roc. A small horse follows a bison, whose head has been transformed into that of a wild boar; the original curve of the bison's back, still discernible in the outline of the shoulders, was hollowed out for the purposes of transformation. The bodies of both animals are well constructed, the volumes are full and the polished surface shows careful finish. The two figures, in their respective positions, form a curved line that stresses the movement of the marching couple; their hoofs are finely sculptured and their limbs are sinuous. Both are pregnant females, as are most of the animals found in Le Roc.

The figures on this block are sculpted with great care; the background is regularly hollowed out but the margins do not appear to have been trimmed at all: in fact, at the extreme left a piece of the original surface remains as it was before carving, contributing to the feeling of immediacy and vigour that distinguishes this fine piece of work.

One of the most suggestive fragments in Le Roc is reproduced in Pl. 155, a. Though not as clearly as those mentioned above, several figures are more or less distinctly visible on this great block which measures 1,52 m. by 50 cm. From left to right are the outline of a naked man, probably wearing a mask; a horse; some other animal, identified by Martin as a badger; another horse; finally, a superb group consisting of a large ox with head threateningly lowered, charging a fleeing man with a sort of pole on his shoulder. The running movement is convincingly expressed in the flexing of the man's knees. The large ox head is sculpted in the round and juts out from the plane of the bas-relief, giving an effect of great forcefulness. Some very difficult plastic problems have been successfully tackled here, as is proved, among other things, by the perfect perspective of the animal, which appears almost to spring out from the massive stone block.

We are faced, in Le Roc, with an art so mature as to place these works among the highest sculptural and pictorial achievements of the Magdalenian age. It might even be said that in some respects, and particularly with regard to the solution of the specific technical problems mentioned above, art rises here to heights never surpassed, or even equalled. For instance; the two ibexes facing each other in the superb composition of Pl. 156, b, creating, with the balance of their volumes and of their outlines, a well-defined geometrical space, are of a high order of pure rhythmic design presaging a deliberately decorative monumental art, an art never before so clearly announced by any known specimen of Palaeolithic cave painting or sculpture.

LE FOURNEAU DU DIABLE, LAUGERIE BASSE, LA CHAIRE À CALVIN, ISTURITZ, BÉDEILHAC.

From another Upper Solutrean deposit in the Dordogne, Le Fourneau du Diable near Bourdeilles, Peyrony extracted in 1924 a large block bearing about 10 figures sculpted in low relief and engraved [1]. Pl. 157, a shows the fragment which contains the finest sculptures,

---

[1] PEYRONY, 1932a.

among them a superb bovine, probably a cow, in forceful relief, perfectly executed in its anatomical details. Two other bovines stand close to it, one of which is considerably deteriorated and the other, probably a bull judging by its massive proportions, is set further back from the first, which covers its lower half in accordance with a correctly observed perspective.

These sculptures, particularly the principal one, are undoubtedly comparable to the Le Roc frieze where the rock is treated in the same manner and the figures reveal the same plastic sensitivity, the same technique in dealing with sinews, limbs, etc.

From the Laugerie Basse deposit near Les Eyzies, probably from the Magdalenian levels, we have a fragment in high relief portraying the head of a musk ox, summarily executed but nevertheless recalling, by its forceful structure, the figures of Le Roc (Pl. 157, c).

Three horses and what looks like an ox, sculpted on the walls of the cave of La Chaire à Calvin near Le Mouthiers (Charente), resemble, in their figuration, the Le Roc animals, and more closely still some of the animals of Angles-sur-Anglin, particularly the ibex. These sculptures were discovered in 1926 by David while removing the Lower Magdalenian layers and some elements of Solutrean industry below them (Pl. 164, c). According to David, these are Solutrean sculptures [1]).

A dozen animals carved in rather flat low relief were discovered by Passemard on a wall of the Isturitz cave (Basses-Pyrénées). They portray reindeer, deer, horses and a bear, partly superimposed upon one another. Pl. 164, a shows a reindeer partially covered by two deer.

Passemard found these sculptures covered by strata of Magdalenian IV, immediately above layers containing Solutrean implements that did not, however, reach the level of the figures [2]).

Palaeolithic artists also modelled clay in low relief. Four small bison, poorly made, are attached to a clay ledge in the Bédeilhac cave (Ariège). The larger and more visible one, reproduced in Pl. 164, b, measures 29 cm.; it is a rough statuette shaped in clay and, according to Begouen, subsequently attached to the ledge where it was found. Though difficult to date, Begouen believes that the Bédeilhac statuettes belong to the advanced Magdalenian period [3]).

Clay sculptures in low and high relief, representing animals and usually very poorly executed, were also found in the Montespan cave (Haute-Garonne); we shall come back to them later (p. 151 and foll.).

THE SHELTER OF LE CAP BLANC.

The style of the famous horses sculpted in high relief in the shelter of Le Cap Blanc, on on the right bank of the Beune near Les Eyzies in the Dordogne, may well be termed classical. They form a long row on the wall of the cave, and though rather deteriorated are clearly visible, standing out forcefully against the uneven rock surface. They are eight in number, including a head that later became detached from the wall.

Besides the horses other more or less recognizable and interpretable figures also exist: two probable oxen and two small bison, one of which is almost completely destroyed and the other carved in very shallow relief; we should add a third, found in the shape of a fragment in the Magdalenian layer of the deposit in front of the cave. Peyrille excavated this deposit in 1911 and unearthed some implements belonging to the Lower Magdalenian period (Magd. III); in the same year he discovered the sculptures, also attributed, by Lalanne and Breuil, to Lower Magdalenian [4]).

[1]) DAVID, 1929; idem, 1947.
[2]) PASSEMARD H., 1944.
[3]) BEGOUEN, 1931.
[4]) LALANNE, BREUIL, 1911.

Upon entering the shelter — which is 4 metres deep and is now enclosed with a pro-tective wall — one is truly impressed by the great frieze although it is heavily damaged. Pls. 158 and 159 show the principal figures among the horses : two of them are turned towards the right, and one, certainly the most beautiful of all, towards the left. Unfortunately the poor state of preservation of these sculptures prevents us from enjoying them in all their original beauty and harmony : from the badly damaged surface many details that undoubtedly lent additional value to the work have disappeared, leaving only a few traces. At the time of its discovery the largest of the horses showed some traces of red ochre.

The horses of Le Cap Blanc are carved in high relief reaching a depth of 30 cm. in some places. To obtain this relief the rock was vigorously hewn, only, however, within the limits of the surface strictly necessary for the execution of the figures, so that they seem to be en-closed in a rough niche. The legs of the two animals on the left, though much deteriorated, are visible, whereas those of the horse on the right were completely destroyed because, accord-ing to Lalanne and Breuil, they were carved " below the more resistent calcareous zone that entirely circumscribes the two preceding figures " [1]).

The modelling is vigorous, the volumes perfect and the few details that are still discernible — such as the nostril and mouth of the first horse on the left — show great sensitivity (Pl. 158, c). Before it was damaged the third horse must have been amazingly impressive : it measures 2,15 m. and is constructed with such skill and such a true sense of volume, chiaroscuro and anatomy that even though fragmentary (a fact that, on the other hand, only adds to its charm) it strikes us as one of the finest works of animal sculpture produced at any period, from pre-history onwards. Note the artist's mastery in attaching the strong neck to the rounded jaw, the harmony with which the sinuous outline joins the hollow of the ear to the convex fore-head, the soft treatment of the planes that extend, smooth and sensitive, over the vigorous muscles and strong frame of the animal's body; and how expressive the head, despite the injury of time and the lack of detail. The entire figure, in strong relief, springs from its rocky niche clearly outlined against the hollowed background, revealing the artist's perfect sculptural technique, and particularly his consummate experience of dealing with the difficult art of high and low relief.

All in all we do not entirely condemn the enthusiasm of some admirers who, at the time of their discovery, compared the Le Cap Blanc horses with the horses of the Parthenon.

* * *

There are other caves in the Beune valley with figures in high relief, badly deteriorated and generally indecipherable, that from a stylistic point of view seem to approach the figures of Le Cap Blanc. In the COMMARQUE cave opposite Le Cap Blanc, horses, ruminants and ibexes are carved or engraved; other figures, among which a horse is recognizable, were found in the cave of NANCY, but these were all more or less reduced to vestiges.

Glancing at the various works that we have examined so far — the most accomplished and important in the field of Franco-Cantabrian low and high relief — we realize that the horses of Le Cap Blanc, more slender and morphologically quite different from the horses of Le Roc are, by comparison with the other works previously examined, treated in a more mature style revealing greater assurance and balance, and denoting, perhaps, greater technical experience. They already show, one might say, a sort of academism that makes them technically more perfect than the others, while attenuating, in a certain sense, the liveliness and immediacy of the sculptured figures of Le Roc.

---

[1]) LALANNE, BREUIL, 1911, p. 393.

If the attribution to the Magdalenian period of the Le Cap Blanc horses is, as it appears to be, correct, it perfectly explains their higher degree of technical evolution compared with the other sculptures mentioned above.

ANGLES-SUR-ANGLIN.

Among the discoveries of the past few years in the field of Palaeolithic art a particularly important one has been the finding, by three ladies — Mlle Susanne Saint-Mathurin, Dr. Dorothy Garrod and Mlle Germaine Martin — of a series of bas-reliefs in a large shelter under a cliff near the village of Angles-sur-Anglin (Vienne).

This shelter, known locally as Roc aux Sorciers, is quite shallow, but it extends over almost 50 metres at the foot of a great cliff overhanging the river Anglin.

The excavations were carried out intermittently by Rousseau from 1927, and regularly, from 1948, by the above-mentioned ladies, in two different parts of the deposit: Rousseau worked the higher part, known as Cave Taillebourg, and the three ladies the same part and the lower one known as Abri Bourdois.

In the first part, the lower strata of the deposit revealed some Magdalenian III products underlying a pile of stone blocks and sterile material produced by the flaking of the overhanging rock; among these products were a few fragments with bas-relief carvings that had fallen from the walls and the ceiling. Only one sculpted figure — a rather deteriorated bison — was still in place on the wall itself (Pl. 162, c).

In the other part of the cliff, above a basic stratum also belonging to Magdalenian III, a layer of Magdalenian VI was found which, on removal, revealed a superb series of figures carved upon the wall [1]).

The distance between these figures and the bison of Cave Taillebourg is 35 metres, and it is probable that if this vast zone too were freed from the deposit, the rock wall would reveal further sculpted figures, forming a truly magnificent bas-relief frieze.

The figures so far found on the walls include bison, ibexes, horses, and three curious nude women (Pl. 162, a). The low ceiling prevented the completion of the upper parts of the bodies of these female figures. Only one of them seems to have a head, traced on the ceiling itself.

Among the figures carved on blocks found in Cave Taillebourg is the splendid head of a young ibex (Pl. 161), some beautiful horses' heads (Pl. 162, b), bison, chamois, and a very curious bearded human head seen in profile, carved in bas-relief, engraved, and also painted (Pl. 160): its somatic features recall those of the heads engraved on stone fragments in the cave of La Marche (Pl. 83, a-d).

The group of ibexes in Abri Bourdois [2]) is lively and original; the ibex head found in the deposit is very lifelike and expressive. The horse's head reproduced in Pl. 162, b is of an extreme elegance, with dilated nostrils, lips drawn back from teeth, and ears erect.

The female figures, particularly the middle one, though reduced (as Pl. 162, a shows) to the abdomen, pubes and part of the thighs, are treated with a fine sense of volume and anatomy. At first sight they appear to be far from the conventional scheme of female figures in the Aurignacian-Perigordian period, for they are much more slender. They are not so different, however, as to prevent us from comparing them, for instance, with the realistic plasticity of the Brassempouy Venus (Pl. 1, b).

Breuil [3]) sees affinities between these figures and the ivory Venus of Laugerie Basse (Pl. 82, a), probably on account of the emphasized sex — a trait that is shared by them all.

[1]) GARROD, 1949; GARROD, SAINT-MATHURIN, 1952; SAINT-MATHURIN, GARROD, 1951.
[2]) GARROD, SAINT-MATHURIN, 1952, figs. 2, 5.
[3]) BREUIL, 1952, p. 335.

But the rigidity, one might almost say the " wooden " quality of the Laugerie Basse statuette is very different from the rounded softness of the women of Angles-sur-Anglin.

In Pl. 162, *a*, beneath the women, is the rear end of a bison with characteristically shaped tail, identical with the tail of one of the Le Roc bison [1]).

In connection with this relation to Le Roc de Sers, we should mention the existence in Angles-sur-Anglin of bored attachments carved out of the rock, whose significance or function is unexplained but which appear to have been used to attach a rope or cable (Pl. 162, *c*); they are similar to the attachments found by Lantier on one of the carved blocks in Le Roc [2]). This detail and other undeniable stylistic affinities create a close tie between these two monuments of Palaeolithic art; a tie, on the other hand, that would be denied by their presumed difference in age — Magdalenian in one case, Solutrean in the other. Nevertheless we cannot exclude the possibility that the difference in cultural character of the horizons from which the two monuments come may be due to a phenomenon of industrial protraction.

LA MAGDELEINE.

We shall conclude this brief review of Palaeolithic bas-relief with a recent discovery — certainly one of the most unexpected and amazing discoveries of the past few years — the female figures in the cave of La Magdeleine near Penne (Tarn), found by Bessac in 1952 and, up to the present time, only very briefly reported by Bétirac and Breuil [3]).

About 6 metres from the entrance to the cave, in full daylight, two female figures and two animals are symmetrically arranged : on the left is a horse, on the right a bison. As can be seen in Pl. 163, *c* (courtesy of Vergnes, the photographer) the horse, in shallow bas-relief, is in a fine natural style and the same state of preservation as the two female figures.

According to Breuil the animals and the female figures are unquestionably contemporary; this refers the female bas-reliefs to the Palaeolithic period, despite the great difference in style between them and the other works of Franco-Cantabrian anthropomorphism.

The two female figures are without doubt the most unbelievable find in the vast repertory of Franco-Cantabrian art. They are something absolutely new and cannot be likened to Aurignacian-Perigordian sculpture, with its adipose female statuettes, or to anthropomorphic Magdalenian mobiliary or cave art which is generally monstrous, or at least, with few exceptions, poorly executed.

The two women of La Magdeleine are placed at a height of approximately 3 or 3,50 m. on the wall; they are half reclining, with torsos slightly raised; one of them (Pl. 163, *a*) is leaning on her right side with right leg outstretched and left leg flexed. The breasts are clearly discernible.

The other figure (Pl. 163, *b*) appears to be leaning on her left arm, with the other horizontally extended. The legs are flexed as though the figure were seated and leaning back against a support.

These sculptures are much deteriorated and have so far been photographed in very difficult conditions owing to their position on the cave walls. For this reason the reproductions are distorted and hard to interpret but nevertheless one can appreciate the realism, skill and freedom of execution of the sculptures. Here is something new that has no equal in Franco-Cantabrian anthropomorphic art, especially on account of the relaxed position of the female bodies and the spirit — which we might term extraordinarily modern — animating them.

---

[1]) BREUIL, 1952, fig. 402.
[2]) LANTIER, 1952, p. 331.
[3]) BÉTIRAC, 1954; BREUIL, 1954.

CLAY STATUES

Tuc d'Audoubert.

" Les Magdaléniens modelaient aussi l'argile " : with this laconic telegram Count Begouen announced, in 1912, to Prof. Cartailhac in Toulouse, the sensational discovery of the clay statues of Tuc d'Audoubert. They confirmed in a decisive and spectacular manner the hypotheses formulated with regard to the significance of Franco-Cantabrian art, and threw light upon a new aspect of that art itself, proving that it also existed in the form of statuary. As Begouen relates it, the eminent palaethnologist answered from Toulouse with an even pithier message : " J'arrive ". Two days later, together with Breuil and under the guidance of Begouen, he penetrated the depths of Tuc d'Audoubert [1]).

Up to that time Palaeolithic sculpture was known in the form of objects of mobiliary art, such as the female statuettes sculpted in the round and figures carved on implements, or in the form of cave art such as the bas-reliefs of Le Cap Blanc and Laussel.

Figures modelled in the round and destined to remain in the environment in which they were executed were unknown at the time, nor did a single clue suggest that they might exist. The repertory of such statues was never very much enlarged even after the discoveries of Tuc d'Audoubert; in fact only one other cave — Montespan in Haute-Garonne — produced a really significant specimen. Nevertheless the existence of real " statuary " in the Upper Palaeolithic is now, on the evidence of these few examples of it, an acknowledged fact.

The statues of Tuc d'Audoubert are modelled in clay from the cave itself, and a careful examination of them and of their environment allows us to reconstruct decisively the system employed by Palaeolithic artists in making them.

The discovery was made by Comte Begouen's sons. Through passages which were extremely difficult of access, and by removing some stalagmitic formations that blocked the narrow corridors, about 700 metres from the entrance they reached the terminal recess of that complicated cavern and found two bison modelled in clay on the floor, leaning against a large fragment of stalagmite.

Fortunately the Begouens always scrupulously avoided taking any measure to make the cavern easier of access, so that with the exception of a few minor alterations this marvellous Palaeolithic shrine has remained — and will, we trust, remain in future — almost inviolate, protected from any and every kind of vandalism or degradation, by the enormous difficulty of penetrating it and the impossibility of entering even the forepart of the cave without adequate preliminary organization and expert guides.

Tuc d'Audoubert, in its general configuration, consists of a long tunnel, so narrow at certain points as to oblige the visitor to crawl on his stomach, sometimes up steep slopes, for

[1]) Begouen H., 1926, p. 10.

long distances, scraping his shoulders against the rock. Before starting on this exhausting expedition one has to cross by boat part of the cave that is flooded by an underground stream, the Volp, which is quite impracticable in rainy weather. The stream leaves the cave through a picturesque arch (Pl. 165, *a*), and one must navigate upstream for about 80 metres through a dark tunnel in order to reach a small platform from which the difficult passage starts.

Scattered here and there on the walls of Tuc d'Audoubert are engraved figures, some of them very fine (Pl. 143), but a really breathtaking sight greets the visitor in the terminal hall, at the end of his long trip through the dark bowels of the cave. This hall is pervaded by an atmosphere of mystery that is almost tangible, and joins the remote world, of which traces are still alive and intact, to the reality of the present.

The past comes alive in the so-called " Salle des Talons", a small, low chamber on whose clayey floor about fifty fresh and unmistakably human footprints — or rather, heelprints — are clearly visible (Pl. 167, *c*). They are divided, so it appears, into five tracks, as though young individuals (judging from the small size of the prints) had crossed the floor walking on their heels — according to Begouen, in order to reach five clay cones placed in a corner of the chamber. Whatever interpretation is given to these footprints, they are undoubtedly one of the most suggestive sights in the whole cave.

A few metres further on is the terminal hall containing the famous clay bison. These two statues, a male and a female, are respectively 63 and 61 cm. long, and are in the middle of the chamber, leaning obliquely against a large fragment of stalagmite. They are practically intact except for a few cracks, and look exactly as they did when the Palaeolithic men who accomplished magic rites in the cave saw them for the last time (Pls. 165, *b*; 166; 167, *a*, *b*). The primitive sculptor's work looks as if it were just finished, and some fragments of clay, manipulated and fallen from his hands to the floor during the execution of the statues, are still lying around. On the clayey substance, soft even today, fresh traces of the spatula or fingers that shaped it are still visible. These traces are so evident that it is perfectly clear how the statues were made.

The two animals, well proportioned and shaped in the fine, linear style of Magdalenian art, are considerably flattened seen from the front and the back, although in profile the volumes are perfectly rendered. In fact, the opposite

Fig. 21. Tuc d'Au- side was left unfinished because the figures are leaning against a rocky spur.
doubert. 1. Entrance. Rather than real sculpture in the round this, one might say, is very accen-
2. Underground
course of the Volp. tuated high relief; the statues seem therefore to derive, technically, from the
3. Passage to upper
gallery. 4. "Chatiè- bas-reliefs that are so plentiful in Franco-Cantabrian art.
re". 5. Prints of
human heels. 6. It is possible, as we said, to understand the technique of the sculptors.
Clay bison.

The animal's outline was deeply engraved on the clay floor; the block of clay, circumscribed by the engraved line and resembling a " contour découpé ", was then extracted, propped against the support and modelled, gradually acquiring relief and detail. About 80 cm. from the two statues the outline of a bison, 60 cm. long, is actually engraved on the clay floor; obviously it was to have been used to create a statue but for some reason was discarded.

Furthermore, in the Salle des Talons there is a large hole from which a block of clay was taken; this block lies nearby in fragments, and must have been dropped accidentally by whoever was removing it (Pl. 167, *c*).

Finally, the " contour découpé " of a small bison, of which the modelling had just been started, lay, at the time of the discovery, next to one of the large bison, on the same stalagmitic formation. This little "plastic sketch" is now at the Musée des Antiquités Nationales in Saint-Germain [1]).

To return to the principal group, we can also observe some other technical devices used by the Palaeolithic artists in fixing the statues. Pl. 167, *b* shows the male bison seen from the back: it is obvious that in order to create an impression of greater verticality and stability, large and small stones were inserted between it and the rock against which it leans. In Pl. 167, *a*, marks left by a spatula and fingers are clearly visible, for instance at the extremity of the hind leg; the care with which the entire surface of the statue was polished is also evident.

Pls. 165, *b* and 166 underline, with different lighting effects, various carefully rendered details such as the eye and nostril; the mane and beard are indicated by short parallel lines, in the manner that we have observed in many Magdalenian figures. The horns are intact — short and curved at the extremity.

These works of art, remarkable for fine style, forceful, lively realism and accurate modelling, reveal the great love and interest that the artist brought to the accomplishment of his task.

According to Begouen this composition is connected with propitiatory rites of animal reproduction, like all the others in which a male and a female are shown together. Begouen also believes that the footprints were left on the clay floor by young men and are traces of a ritual dance or march connected with rites of sexual initiation or procreation.

We do not think it an exaggeration to say that the Hall of the Bison in Tuc d'Audoubert is more deeply impressive than any other monument of the past, however splendid.

MONTESPAN.

Palaeolithic statuary is not limited to the examples from Tuc d'Audoubert, although these are certainly the finest and most important pieces known to us at present. In the Montespan cave in Haute-Garonne, Casteret and Godin discovered in 1923 some other clay statues, crude and fragmentary but even so of great interest in the study of Palaeolithic magic. As Casteret picturesquely describes it, the conquest of the gallery containing the statues was truly a bold and brave enterprise [2]).

The cave of Montespan consists of a complex series of galleries and halls traversing the hills between the villages of Ganties and Montespan for a distance of 1200 metres, as the crow flies. A little stream runs through the complex, filling it, in some places, up to the ceiling. As far back as could be remembered it had remained inaccessible except for one occasion during a few days in 1881, after an unusually long period of drought. In 1911 the eminent speleologist Norbert Casteret succeeded, by diving into the water, to climb over a siphon and penetrate the inner recesses of the cave. Shortly afterwards the passage was drained and in August 1923 the statues, and subsequently the engravings that we mentioned previously, were discovered.

In the part of the cave nearest the village of Montespan a long, narrow gallery known as the Great Gallery, or Casteret-Godin Gallery (penetrated by Casteret in 1923) produced the most interesting works. A crude clay figure leans against the wall; it is a fragmentary quadruped interpreted by Begouen and Casteret as a feline [3]). Only parts of the animal survive : the chest, forelegs and neck, one hind leg and the extremity of the tail (Pl. 168, *d*).

Rather than a piece of sculpture in high relief this is to be regarded as a real statue, even if somewhat flattened. Some holes in the chest were probably made with a pointed instrument. According to Trombe and Dubuc, the illustrators of Montespan, it must have been inten-

[1]) REINACH, 1913, p. 185, fig. 5.
[2]) CASTERET, 1937.
[3]) BEGOUEN, CASTERET, 1923, p. 536.

tionally destroyed by the Magdalenian hunters themselves during the performance of rites
in the remote " sanctuary " : some shapeless pieces of clay, found on the floor next to the
statue, appear to be fragments detached from it [1]).

About 30 metres away is a large, bulky clay figure (Pl. 168, *a*, *b*, *c*) completely isolated
from the wall; it is about one metre long and 60 cm. high. It is the rough sketch of a headless
crouching bear, whose front left leg is complete with paw and clearly distinguishable, whereas
the right leg is fragmentary. The accurate proportions and well-rounded volumes of this large
figure express the animal's general structure with a certain degree of realism : however, from
a plastic point of view it is somewhat elementary, particularly if compared with the elaborate
bison of Tuc d'Audoubert. The crude, incomplete nature of this figure could be explained,
according to the hypothesis of Begouen and Casteret, by the fact that it was a sort of model
figure over which the hide and head of a real bear were draped; magic hunting practices
would have been performed upon this dummy — rendered lifelike with the animal hide
covering it — by the Palaeolithic hunters who struck it with arrows, as deduced from the
many holes that pierce it. In fact, at the time of his discovery Casteret found fragments of
a bear's skull between the paws. This, added to the fact that the bear is headless, supports
the hypothesis.

Furthermore, according to Begouen and Casteret, " the section of the neck, smooth
and polished like the rest of the body, is marked by a triangular hole ". This hole, they believe, was made to insert a wooden peg upon which the real bear's head rested. This interpretation, as the reader can judge, is most suggestive [2]).

The present writer visited the cave of Montespan in the summer of 1950, with his friend
Romain Robert, and they examined the clay statues — reached after an exhausting trip through
low-roofed corridors with water up to the waist. All the statues seemed poorly preserved
and the bear, placed a few centimetres from the wall and about half a metre from the ceiling
gave one the impression that it was about to fall apart. The side that is against the wall (invisible
in the photographs) is better executed than the other and shows a well modelled thigh. We do
not know whether it was due to further deterioration of the statue since its discovery, but
the present writer could see no trace of some of the details described by Begouen and Casteret.
The section of the neck did not appear to be polished at all : on the contrary, it was rather
rough. The hole that is presumed to have contained a peg to support the head does not exist
— at least, it is not large enough for its alleged purpose. There are several little holes here and
there on the neck and chest, many of which, however, appear to be due to natural causes —
the sort of small cavities in the clay that can be seen all over the cave. The largest hole, which
appears to be artificial, is on a level with the chest, but (as can be seen in the photograph in
Pl. 168, *b*) it is also small and so shallow as to exclude the possibility of its having contained
a wooden peg destined to support the heavy head of a bear.

It is a pity that no photographs were published of the bear seen from the front at the
time of its discovery; they might have been very useful for the purpose of comparison with
the present condition of the statue. No photographs, as far as we know, show the fragments
of the bear's skull in their original position between the paws. Therefore photographs taken
before the eventual deterioration of the statue would have been extremely useful. Certainly,
if it were not for the testimony of its discoverers, the fact that the bear of Montespan — such
as it appears today — is headless, might be explained simply by the fracturing *ab antiquo*
of the head, or by its destruction by the Palaeolithic men themselves, as was suggested by

---

[1]) TROMBE, DUBUC, 1947, p. 75.
[2]) Begouen and Casteret's hypothesis is effectively upheld by Frobenius's reference to analogous rites practised by some
African tribes. The Senegambia Mandé and the Volta Bambara fashion a headless clay statue that is draped in a leopard, or lion,
skin, with head intact. This dummy is placed in the middle of a circular area surrounded by a thorny hedge, within which the
hunter performs a ritual dance. Frobenius does not hesitate to establish analogies between all this and what presumably happened
before the statue of the bear in the Montespan cave (FROBENIUS, 1933, pp. 80-83).

some authors in the case of the other broken statues. On the other hand the simplicity of the modelling, the scarcity of detail and the physical condition of the surfaces recall the feline animal in the same cave, which was never believed to have been used as a dummy.

The statues in the Montespan cave cannot be considered outstanding specimens of Palaeolithic art; nevertheless they are of extreme interest for investigating the nature and rites of Palaeolithic magic.

Other works of Palaeolithic magic are found in the Montespan cave, some in the form of engravings on clay. We shall mention here, to conclude, the so-called " hunting scene ". It consists, according to Begouen's interpretation, of a row of horses of varying degrees of artistic merit [1]. The head and neck of the last horse of the series is well designed in the best Franco-Cantabrian tradition, with accurately executed details such as the mane, ears, nostrils, mouth, beard, etc. (Pl. 138, c). The other parts of the body are partially covered by stalagmitic concretions and appear to be more roughly executed. The animal is shown as if falling down, with its back to the ground. Other " silhouettes " follow, cruder than the previous one, all marked with holes. The first is clearly discernible (Pl. 280, c), the others are less distinct because they are covered with vertical parallel lines. Finally, at the end of this series, a hole in the clay, 15 cm. wide, is also surrounded by engraved lines. According to Begouen this represents a real hunting scene, executed for magical purposes, in which horses are being driven into a corral (vertical lines) towards a sort of trap or trench represented by the cavity in the clay that concludes the series.

----

[1] TROMBE, DUBUC, 1947, p. 51; BEGOUEN H., in " Journal des Débats " (October 10th, 1926), quoted by Trombe and Dubuc.

PAINTING

The paintings in Franco-Cantabrian cave art are even more difficult to date than the engravings.

While in the case of engraving we have seen some very significant instances of association between engraved figures and *in situ* deposits, none exist in the case of painting, with the rare exceptions mentioned above (p. 127). Thus a chronology of the various phases of painting was established on the basis of a study of the superimposition of figures, their stylistic affinities with engravings and, occasionally, with mobiliary art. Account was also taken of the sometimes excessively subjective judgments of various scholars — judgments that might be defined as logical and which are somewhat untrustworthy because unsupported by concrete evidence.

An overall glance at the enormous quantity of painted figures in the caves of France and Cantabria immediately shows that they can be assembled in a few groups characterized by specific styles, mannerisms, colour schemes, etc. Some figures, for example, consist of a simple outline while in others technically more advanced volume is admirably rendered and polychromatism achieves with a limited range amazing effects of chiaroscuro. This polychromatic phase is present in several localities in the vast Franco-Cantabrian territory, from Biscay to the Dordogne, always with special characteristics by which it is easy to distinguish it.

It is also true that monochrome painting is present in a notable series of very elaborate works of art that share the manner and expression of polychromatic works, and are related to them even though they lack colour.

Besides figures consisting of a mere outline there are outlines filled in with a single colour or crudely multicoloured, different in form and style from the figures of the previous group, but so well defined that we can place them in other groups with their own specific characteristics.

Some figures are more difficult to place in one or other of these groups because they have affinities with both. It is clear that a generic selection of Franco-Cantabrian paintings on the basis of their style and technique is possible, though not in all cases. A plan showing the succession in some of these groups, particularly if based on a comparison with wall engravings and objects of mobiliary art, might be accepted as a working hypothesis, but it is clear that we are still far from possessing sufficient elements to establish the precise chronology of each document or stylistic group, much less to create a sound, definitive system for the evolution of Franco-Cantabrian painting.

We have already alluded to the rare cave paintings found *in situ* in deposits; among the more important ones are two quadrupeds, probably oxen, painted on large stones from the Aurignacian strata of Abri Blanchard (Pl. 169, *a*) and the incomplete stag, painted in black on a stone, from the Perigordian strata of Abri Labatut (Pl. 169, *b*). It is interesting to note that the paintings of Abri Blanchard, which are among the earliest paintings for which a chronology has been established, show an advanced technique — a black outline against a red background — the opposite of what one might have expected.

We shall now briefly review some of the most important examples of pictorial art, attempting to group them according to style and technique, without of course attributing precise chronological value to the various groups. In the course of this review we shall dwell at length on some of the more important cave-wall paintings of France and Spain.

CAVES WITH FIGURES IN SIMPLE TECHNIQUE.

The Perigordian strata of ABRI LABATUT produced, among other things, a block with the negative imprint of a hand outlined in black. As stated by the Abbé Breuil in his celebrated chronology of Palaeolithic pictorial art [1]) this discovery proves that the shape of a hand was reproduced, even in the more ancient strata, by a method that could be called mechanical. The practice of making handprints was widely diffused in the Palaeolithic and is also found among the primitive peoples of the present day.

In a great majority of cases the handprints of the Palaeolithic caves are negative; that is to say they were obtained by placing the open hand against the rock wall and spraying colour round it, outlining its shape against a black or red background. The colour was applied with something resembling what is known in some countries today as an " aerograph ". It was skilfully employed also in the execution of some of the animal figures in the Lascaux cave, for instance. Less frequently hands were reproduced as positive impressions, by dipping them in paint and pressing them on the rock (Pl. 260, c).

The cave of Gargas has almost 150 handprints, in black and in ochre, the great majority of which are left hands spread more or less chaotically on the walls (Pls. 260, b, d; 263).

It is interesting to see that in many of the Gargas hands the joints of one or more fingers are missing (Pl. 260, b, d), and that the same mutilated hands were reproduced several times. Ritual mutilation of finger joints, as we all know, is also frequent among present-day primitive peoples in Oceania, Africa and America [2]).

Handprints are also found in about fifteen other caves in France and Spain. We recall the numerous prints at Altamira, Pech-Merle (Pl. 260, a) and especially at Castillo, also predominantly made with left hands. In Pls. 260, 262 and 263 we reproduce various handprints which, though among the simplest and most primitive artistic expressions, are very suggestive when they appear in the shadows of the deep recesses of the caves.

The hands that surround the curious horses of Pech-Merle shown in Pl. 196 lend the strange composition an atmosphere of mystery.

With regard to chronology, that handprints already appear in the Aurignacian-Perigordian period is sufficiently proved by their presence in the Perigordian deposit of Abri Labatut. But we cannot rule out for certain the possibility that so simple and spontaneous a method of reproducing part of the human body (a part which in every age, prehistoric and historic alike, has been considered extremely important from a magic and esoteric point of view) was also used in later periods, particularly as it is so common among primitive peoples today. It is therefore very likely that some of the handprints in other Franco-Cantabrian caves are of a much later date. Referring to ancient and modern ethnography, outside Europe there are the positive and negative hands, also showing various mutilations, painted in shelters under cliffs in Australia and North America, and those found in Patagonia and recently published by Menghin [3]).

On the basis of the Perigordian painting at Abri Labatut (of a stag with antlers viewed from the front in " perspective tordue " (Pl. 169, b)), we can select similar figures and refer

---

[1]) BREUIL, 1912; *idem*, 1934.
[2]) MALVESIN-FABRE, NOUGIER, ROBERT, 1954, p. 12 and foll.; CADEO, 1954, p. 98 and foll.
[3]) MENGHIN, 1952.

them, by analogy, to an equally archaic phase of pictorial art. For instance, the antlers of the deer sketched in the cave of Le Portel (Pl. 172, *a*, *b*), the deer of the Lascaux cave (with which we shall deal later) (Pl. 174) and those of the cave of La Pasiega in Monte Castillo (Santander) (Pl. 223, *a*, *d*).

The cave of LE PORTEL in Ariège is undoubtedly one of the most interesting caves containing Palaeolithic paintings, both for the quantity and quality of the paintings themselves and because they seem to be clearly referable to various phases of Palaeolithic art. One group, containing the above-mentioned figures, is of an archaic flavour and shows an affinity of style with some engraved figures of the Aurignacian-Perigordian period. Other figures are much more evolved and show a higher degree of artistic maturity. A notable series of horses shown in Pls. 172 and 173 belongs to the first group; the heads have the characteristic elongated jaw and neckline mentioned in connection with Pair-non-Pair, the bas-relief of Abri Labatut and other works of unmistakable Aurignacian-Perigordian date. The shape of the galloping legs is also remarkable; the swollen joints and round hoofs are drawn according to a process which is essentially different from that employed in more advanced pictorial expressions. The majority of the Lascaux horses are treated in an analogous manner.

Although often barely sketched or badly preserved, the outlines of these archaic horses of Le Portel confirm the existence, even in artists of the more archaic phases of Franco-Cantabrian art, of great gifts of immediacy and sensitivity. I shall mention below the more evolved paintings found in the same cave.

The characteristic perspective of the bison's horns, seen in the engraved figure of La Grèze (Pl. 121) (which is certainly pre-Solutrean), and in the bison of La Mouthe (Pl. 123, *a*) (an obviously archaic work) is very clear in the painted bison of MARCENAC, an incomplete figure but one in which firmness of line and incisive adherence to nature are quite remarkable (Pl. 169, *c*).

The figure of a stag in the cave of PECH-MERLE is also archaic, incomplete and reduced to a simply traced outline of the back and chest, and a synthetic description of the branching antlers (Pl. 170, *b*). From the same cave comes the figure of a bull with horns viewed in the usual perspective (Pl. 170, *a*), clearly recalling, in the steep profile of neck and back and the prominent chest, analogous figures engraved in Pair-non-Pair, La Mouthe and Castillo — all belonging to the archaic phase of Franco-Cantabrian art. The paintings of oxen in the cave of LA PEÑA DE CANDAMO in Spain (Pl. 219) belong to the same group.

An elephant painted in red in a very simple synthetic manner with only two legs showing (in accordance with the system used in Aurignacian-Perigordian art) and suggesting a rather archaic style, was found in the cave of CASTILLO near Santander (Pl. 220, *b*). This suggestion of great antiquity is supported by the figure's poor state of preservation; it is more faded than the majority of paintings in the same cave.

This also applies to a red elephant in another Cantabrian cave, that of PINDAL near Oviedo (Pl. 220, *a*). Here, too, the colour is faded and the painting, executed with the same economy as the Castillo elephant, has partly disappeared. At the centre of the outline a large irregular stain of the same colour was interpreted by some scholars as the representation of the animal's heart. This interpretation, in our opinion, is unfounded.

This and the preceding figure are always referred to as representations of the hairless elephant, or *Elephas antiquus*[1]. This identification, if correct, would obviously give a well-defined climatic significance to the period in which the painting was executed; but we are not prepared to accept it. The outline of the Pindal elephant might well be that of a mammoth, especially on account of its dome-shaped head. The fact that hair was not shown does not exclude this possibility, since the synthetic character of the drawing may well explain

[1] BREUIL, 1952, pp. 368, 379.

its lack of detail. On the other hand such details as were shown originally may have disappeared owing to the painting's advanced state of deterioration. With regard to the elephant of Castillo, even though the back and head are not as typical of the mammoth as the back and head of the Pindal figure, the present writer also denies that it is necessarily the reproduction of a hairless elephant, because the extreme summariness of the figure does not admit of a specific identification. We would be inclined to agree with Leonardi, who sees in the Castillo elephant the possible reproduction of a new-born, or very young mammoth [1]).

We should bear in mind, when interpreting these figures, that no remains of *Elephas antiquus* have yet been found in the Upper Palaeolithic deposits of Cantabria which did, however, contain remains of mammoths.

In November 1952 the discovery of the paintings in the cave of COUGNAC near Gourdon (Lot) further documented the study of the more simple and primitive forms of Franco-Cantabrian cave art. About twenty animal figures and a few signs, including some tectiforms, are painted in bistre-red and black. Méroc and Mazet have recently published them, stressing their archaic character and the superimpositions that justify certain chronological subdivisions [2]). There are 5 deer (two of which have palmate antlers and are probably *megaceros* or elks: Pl. 171, *c*), 7 ibexes (4 of which are fragmentary), 5 elephants and 3 anthropomorphic beings.

These figures are viewed in absolute profile, simply and without detail. In some cases, such as the ibex in Pl. 171, *b*, we have some chiaroscuro and closely drawn lines. Sometimes, as in the little deer in Pl. 171, *c*, the antlers are shown in " perspective tordue ". The elephants, so far as we can judge from the reproductions published to date, are rather clumsy and rigid; the animal in Pl. 171, *a* resembles a mammoth on account of its dome-shaped head, like the elephant of Pindal. The fact that no hair is visible on these figures does not strike us as being sufficient reason for considering them portrayals of hairless elephants. In the more archaic forms of cave art which are distinguished, among other things, by a lack of detail, it is easy to understand that the artist usually restricted himself to sketching the animal's bare outline.

The ibexes are finer and more balanced. Among the human figures, two, shown in the act of running, and one in an upside-down position, are curious; all have arrows piercing their bodies.

This is the first obvious case in Franco-Cantabrian cave art in which a probable representation of " killing magic " appears in connection with human beings, unless the figures are to be considered as commemorative. We shall return later to the anthropomorphic representations of Cougnac (p. 182).

Finally we should mention the paintings in the cave of VILLARS (Périgord), very recently discovered by Pierre Vidal and the Abbé Glory; up to the present only a few illustrated papers (" Radar ", Paris, 16/2/58; " L'Europeo ", Milan, 20/4/58) have published them. The few photographs that have been published show a bison, a galloping horse and a human figure, all rather simple from a technical point of view. The man somewhat recalls the anthropomorphic figures of Cougnac mentioned above.

LASCAUX.

At this point we should consider one of the most outstanding monuments of prehistoric art known to us, the famous cave of Lascaux, near Montignac-sur-Vézère in the Dordogne.

It was discovered by chance on the 11th of September 1940 by four local boys : Ravidat, Marsal, Agnel and Coencas. Until that day its existence was totally unknown for it had been

[1]) LEONARDI, 1955.
[2]) MÉROC, MAZET, 1953; *idem*, 1956.

inaccessible since prehistoric times on account of the complete obstruction of the original entrance, which even today has not been discovered. The boys penetrated the cave by enlarging a small opening in the ceiling, through which they had seen their dog disappear.

The first report of the discovery was made exactly one month later by the Abbé Breuil to the Académie des Inscriptions et Belles Lettres [1], and the first publication on Lascaux as a whole, containing a considerable collection of photographs, was issued by Windels, in collaboration with Annette Laming, in 1948 [2].

Countless articles and illustrations have made the world aware of the marvels of Lascaux. Seventy fine colour photographs of the more important paintings have been published in a volume with a commentary by G. Bataille [3]. Consequently today the amazing figures of painted and engraved animals are universally known. There are so many of these animals that they cover dozens of square metres of rock wall and ceiling; most of them are admirably preserved and some attain dimensions that are exceptional in Palaeolithic cave art. Nevertheless an exhaustive study of the Lascaux paintings has not yet been undertaken, nor has a *corpus* of the figures been published. The work of classifying the paintings into their various pictorial and graphic groups is far from complete. Both *The Lascaux Cave Paintings* by Windels, so far the most complete book on the subject, and the chapter that Breuil devotes to it in his *Four Hundred Centuries of Cave Art* [4] are informative rather than definitive stylistic and chronological studies of these extraordinary works of Palaeolithic art.

Glancing through the ample bibliography on this cave we see that the various scholars are not at all in agreement concerning the age to which the art of Lascaux should be attributed, as a whole or in part: for instance, Breuil places it in the Aurignacian-Perigordian cycle [5], while Kühn [6] differs considerably in assigning it to the Upper Magdalenian.

Such widely varying points of view are due, as usual, to the perpetual uncertainty that prevails over determining the chronology of cave paintings without the support of stratigraphical data. However, in the case of Lascaux there is a general tendency to consider the paintings and engravings, taken as a whole, as belonging to a rather archaic phase in the evolution of Franco-Cantabrian cave art. Furthermore, no matter how many different styles and techniques are unmistakably recognizable among the various figures, the great majority give an impression of homogeneity which is strengthened by their powerful dynamism, a particular feature for which we look in vain, in so exuberant and constant a form, in the figures of the other decorated caves of France and Spain.

The term "archaic" applied to Lascaux, however, is based upon a generic impression rather than on a sufficient number of concrete elements. Lascaux, in fact, is entirely different from the elaborate expressions of polychromatic art at Altamira and Font-de-Gaume, which were situated at the peak and end of the evolution of Franco-Cantabrian painting. Its bold spontaneity, its expressiveness, its strength and a certain ingenuousness that belongs to some works, place the art of Lascaux, logically, at an earlier stage than the composed and skilful polychromatic paintings of the other two caves. Even a more minute analysis of the anatomical details of the painted animals shows that the representation of some of them was not achieved in the correct, mature style of Altamira, Font-de-Gaume and Niaux, but was arrived at in a more hesitant, unreal manner, evident, for instance, in the hoofs of the bison, bulls and horses.

On the other hand there are noticeable affinities with mobiliary figures that are undeniably Aurignacian-Perigordian. For instance, the fine horse engraved on a pebble from Abri La-

---

[1] Reproduced in "Atlantis", Madrid, vol. XVI (1941), pp. 349-355.
[2] WINDELS, 1948.
[3] BATAILLE, 1955.
[4] BREUIL, 1952, pp. 106-151.
[5] BREUIL, 1952, pp. 149 and foll., 407.
[6] KÜHN, 1952.

batut (Pl. 19, c) undeniably resembles its Lascaux counterparts in the manner in which the hoofs are represented, among other things.

Nevertheless we cannot ignore the fact that trial excavations in the cave deposit brought to light some bone artifacts of a very evolved type and fragments of charcoal which, according to the C 14 analysis performed by Libby, revealed an age of approximately 15,516 years (± 900) [1]. If these remains of human habitation were really to be related to the figures in the cave, the figures, or part of them at least, would occupy a much later position in the chronology than their characteristics lead us to suppose : they would belong to the Magdalenian period. In that case we should consider the art of Lascaux as an instance of stylistic conservatism. This would apply in many other cases too, and would prove once more that the creation of a system of evolution and chronology for Franco-Cantabrian art is anything but simple, owing to the complexity of the phenomenon and the scarcity of the evidence at our disposal.

The cave of Lascaux consists of a great hall about 30 metres long by 10 metres wide, a corridor 18 metres long that prolongs the hall in an axial direction, and another narrow corridor 15 metres long, branching out from the west side of the hall and opening into another vast hall known as the Nave. At the bottom of a well, 7 metres deep, at one end of the " Apse " there is an interesting little group of painted figures.

In the corridor, Nave and Apse there are painted and engraved figures, whereas the great hall and the narrow corridor contain only paintings.

Like the majority of painted Palaeolithic caves in France and Spain, Lascaux today is equipped for tourists. A great entrance has been opened, with a bronze door reached by a flight of steps. Beyond the door is a waiting-room : a second door opens onto a steep stairway that descends to yet another door beyond which is the Great Hall of Bulls. Concrete walks, handrails, etc. make the visit to Lascaux most convenient, and a well-engineered lighting system renders the paintings clearly visible.

The figures are painted, or painted and engraved; some figures are only engraved, but probably most of these at one time were also painted; the paint would have disappeared following the disintegration of the calcareous surface. On the walls of the main hall and of the axial corridor (covered by a hard coating of calcite that has remained intact) the paintings are admirably preserved and maintain a surprising freshness and intensity of colour.

However peculiar it may seem — we might even say exceptional in Franco-Cantabrian cave art — many of the Lascaux figures give the definite impression of having been distributed around the walls and on the ceiling in accordance with a decorative plan, or rather (if one wishes to avoid an expression that is too binding), with the intention of filling the great empty spaces with a harmonious interplay of forms. In the rhythmic sequence of enormous black bulls around the walls of the Great Hall one cannot fail to detect an intentional symmetry; the pattern of the two bulls facing one another in this group seems to have been created purposely, and so does the combination of three red cows on the ceiling of the little corridor.

In Lascaux, as in all Franco-Cantabrian caves, animal art predominates : one solitary painted human figure exists, camouflaged as an animal and rather schematic in design.

The subject most frequently repeated is the horse, of which there are about sixty well-preserved specimens, including two donkeys or hemiones, and many other fragmentary figures; the ox follows with 20 figures, some of them colossal — up to five and a half metres long (Pl. 176). Next in order of frequency come the deer and the ibex. There are 7 bison; 6 feline animals, all engraved; a rhinoceros, a wolf, a bear and a strange, undefinable animal that has been much discussed (Pl. 180, b). Furthermore, some geometrical figures called " blazons ",

---

[1] PEYRONY, 1950; JOHNSON, 1951, p. 11; LIBBY, 1955, p. 85.

divided into squares and rectangles like checkerboards, are filled with different colours and engraved, or consist of a simple grid (Pl. 269).

All the horses of Lascaux have more or less the same character. Besides the dynamism that they share with all the other paintings in the cave, they all have legs of the same shape and with the same characteristic hoofs : the legs are rather short, the hoofs rounded and usually well detached from the narrow ankles. The mane is short, thick, often painted in a different colour from the body. Some of the horses are more slender and have longer legs, but we would not venture to say that they belong to another zoological variety or attempt to establish a chronological selection on the strength of their stylistic differences.

These horses are often polychrome : simple polychromy that consists of outlining the animal in black and accentuating the mane, also in black; the body is filled in with ochre, creating an effect of chiaroscuro and volume. In some cases the entire head and neck are painted in black, as in Pl. 175; but in this particular case, according to Breuil, it is due to subsequent retouching.

The head is often small, elongated as in the figures that we have defined as archaic (p. 128); sometimes the nose is considerably drawn-out. In other cases the head is shorter and more massive. The forehead can be concave or straight : we do not think, however, that it is possible to group the Lascaux horses into straight, convex and concave anatomical forms on the strength of these slight variations.

Horses, in some instances, are intentionally grouped together to represent herds running or on the move, as for instance the horses in

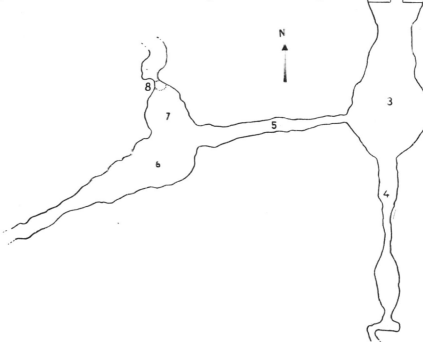

Fig. 22. Cave of Lascaux. 1, 2. Entrance, visitors' waiting-room and staircase leading to depths of cave. 3. Great Hall of Bulls. 4. Axial corridor. 5. Corridor with engravings. 6. Nave. 7. Apse. 8. Well.

Pl. 175; note the marvellous impressionism characterizing them. The movement of the running herd was obtained by disposing the figures in different positions in relation to a hypothetical ground-line represented by the darker zone of the rock surface. Among the most remarkable of the Lascaux horses is the so-called "Chinese horse" in Pl. 186 whose outline, firmly and swiftly traced, describes an animal that is well-proportioned and full of life, if somewhat squat. The few yellow brush strokes that fill in the upper part of its body and the black indicating mane and nose are sufficient to lend relief and volume to this very fine, original piece of work.

The Lascaux oxen are about twenty in number, and according to Windels [1]) they should be divided into two types : the large *Bos primigenius*, with arched horns slightly turned outwards, reproduced in the great hall and in the axial corridor; and the more frail *Bos longifrons*, with shorter horns and straight back and nose. Also according to Windels the figures in Pls. 182, *a* and 179 belong to the latter type, and those in Pls. 182, *b*, 176 and 177 to the *primi-*

---

[1]) WINDELS, 1948, p. 118.

21. — P. GRAZIOSI, *Palaeolithic Art.*

genius type. But these distinctions are not specific, as proved convincingly by Koby [1]); they are due to sexual dimorphism. The two forms reproduced in Lascaux are simply male and female animals of the *Bos primigenius* species, a wild species that was common in the Palaeolithic era and became extinct in Europe in the 17th century. From the descriptions of contemporary authors we know that the bulls of this species were black, whereas the cows were of a reddish colour, exactly as the Lascaux artists represented them, accentuating moreover the robust quality of the former and the frailty of the latter. The *longifrons* species is none other than the *brachicera*, which was never found in Europe in a wild state and which makes its first appearance in the Neolithic era as a domesticated animal.

The bulls in the main hall are truly magnificent; although there is a certain imbalance between the different parts of their bodies (the head is too small, the legs too rigid, etc.), they are nevertheless powerfully expressive and, considered in detail, real masterpieces of Palaeolithic impressionism. A few strokes of colour lend relief and life to the head of the bull in Pl. 181, in a manner unsurpassed by the most elaborate chromatic technique. And if we examine the great black bull in the corridor (Pls. 182, *b*; 183), we are amazed by the realism of the head which, although completely filled in with black paint and treated without any particular attempt at chiaroscuro, is perfectly rendered with regard to volume. Although executed with a different technique, from the point of view of form and expression this painting seems to belong to the same group as the bulls of the Great Hall : compare, for instance, its hindquarters, and particularly the gluteus region, with the thighs of the other bulls.

Breuil places this superb figure [2]), together with the " jumping cow ", in the later pictorial series at Lascaux — the 14th. This " jumping cow " (Pl. 189) is one of the most beautiful and powerful figures in Lascaux, and, we might add, in all Franco-Cantabrian cave art. Livelier than the above-mentioned bull, it shows an admirable mastery of anatomy, particularly in the position of the limbs : considerable difficulties were brilliantly overcome by the artist in the reproduction of so unusual a movement. With skilful lighting the thigh of the left leg stands out from the black mass, and the figure acquires, with the contortion of the entire body, the quick lashing of the tail and the vehement forward tension of its front legs, a vitality and realism that are truly prodigious. Perhaps, as Breuil believes [3]), this dynamic posture is due to the presence, lower down, of a herd of little horses; the artist did not wish to obliterate them with the larger figure and was therefore obliged to raise the cow's hind legs.

The great bull facing the cow on the opposite wall covers several pre-existing figures : two bichromatic cows, one of which is almost completely obliterated, are visible.

The bulls in the main hall also are superimposed upon other figures, of red oxen, bear (Pl. 194, *c*) and deer (Pl. 174) : one of them (Pl. 180, *a*), the first on the left wall, underlies in its turn a series of small galloping horses (Pl. 175).

Thus superimpositions are numerous in Lascaux. In the Great Hall and the axial corridor Breuil distinguishes 14 " layers " of figures [4]) adding, however, that it is not without hesitation that he establishes a sequence of the various techniques; earlier figures were often retouched at a later period, " making any appreciation of their age a very difficult matter " [5]).

Breuil's sequence opens with the figure of the " small arm of a child stencilled in faded red ", the only instance in Lascaux of anything comparable with the handprints of other caves. Allied with this red outline are a few other small figures in simple outline. The series continues with the deer with stiff legs (Pl. 174), and closes with the large bull in Pl. 182, *b* and the jumping cow (Pl. 189). The other ten subdivisions are inserted between these extreme groups; among them are the bichromatic horse in Pl. 175 (series 8a), the horses with slender legs and small

---

[1]) KOBY, 1954.
[2]) BREUIL, 1952, p. 121.
[3]) BREUIL, 1952, p. 122.
[4]) BREUIL, 1952, pp. 111-122.
[5]) BREUIL, 1952, p. 114.

heads such as the one in Pl. 192 and the other one, shown upside-down (Pl. 185, *b*) (series 8b), the great bulls outlined in black in the main hall (series 9a), the red animals with black heads such as the cow in Pl. 182, *a* (series 11a), the herd of small horses in the same Great Hall (series 12) and the bulls in Pl. 182, *b*, obliterated by the black bull (series 13), the great black bull and the jumping cow in the corridor (Pl. 189) (series 14). Finally, Breuil considers the frieze of deer heads in Pl. 194, *a* as belonging to the latest phase of painting at Lascaux.

It is hard to say what chronological value can be attributed to these superimpositions. Between the red cows and the black bulls of the Great Hall, superimposed upon them, what period of time can have elapsed? Thousands, hundreds of years, or less? It is true that stylistic differences can often be detected between one figure and another, but generally they are not sufficient to justify clear-cut separations: on the whole (as we have said before) the whole art of Lascaux seems to be dominated by the same impulse, the same dynamic expressiveness; and some well-defined technical devices are shared by the majority of the paintings. An examination of the subjects represented in relation to the different styles mentioned above reveals no element in favour of a marked chronological diversity between the various groups of figures. The same animals were treated with all the stylistic variations present in Lascaux.

But let us continue our examination of the subjects reproduced here. The bison are seven in number. The two examples shown in Pl. 193 are black, but the one on the left also has a large reddish stain on its back. The drawing is forceful and well balanced, the figures are well built and full of life. Breuil believes this group to be the reproduction of a scene observed by the Palaeolithic hunter: stationed on the bison's path, he sees them advance towards him and then, becoming aware of his presence, swerve to escape in opposite directions [1]). The two animals are placed in perfect perspective with regard to each other, and their bulk is indicated in an efficient, lifelike manner.

The same cannot be said of the bison in Pl. 283, *b*, part of the famous " tragic hunting scene " painted in the well at Lascaux. This figure is barely outlined and slightly tinted in its lower part: it is clumsy, rigid, poorly executed with regard to proportion and volume. Although the scene as a whole does not lack drama and expressiveness, both the animal and the man are drawn in a stilted, naive manner, stylistically isolated from and opposed to the other art at Lascaux, in which the dominant note is a free line, well balanced design and mature analysis of reality.

The same difference is observed in the rhinoceros painted close to the scene on the same wall; although incomplete and rather summary (Pl. 195, *b*) this figure is treated with skill and with a fine sense of volume. We do not hesitate to rule out the possibility of its being part of the adjoining scene. If the diversity of style between the rhinoceros and the man-bison combination was not enough, the " blown technique " in which the rhinoceros is executed would prove it beyond a doubt.

The scene itself represents a wounded bison, with entrails hanging from its stomach, in the act of assaulting a man who is falling backwards. The latter figure is rather schematic; it has a bird's head, and a bird crowns the top of a hooked instrument, probably a spear-thrower, that is close to its right hand; both hands have only four fingers. Another hooked segment lies at the man's feet, and a third, longer one, is placed obliquely on a level with the bison. The shorter segment might be interpreted as a second spear-thrower, and the third as a spear or a hooked javelin; or they could both be fragments of a single object, such as a long barbed spear broken in half.

This composition might have had a commemorative purpose, but more probably it was linked with magic practices.

Among the deer, the one in Pl. 195, *a* has oddly-shaped antlers, exaggeratedly developed

---

[1]) BREUIL, 1952, p. 129.

and branched — probably a stylization of the antlers of an old male animal expressed in a dashing, exuberant manner. An analogous, if less exuberant example of stylized antlers is found in the group of small deer in Pl. 174: one of them has branches represented by two parallel, curved lines. This detail is sufficiently convincing of a direct relation between this and the preceding figure, even if the second is far better executed.

More synthetic but also more expressive are the deer in Pl. 194, a — the famous series of heads that have been interpreted as the representation of a herd crossing a stream. The five heads are actually placed as though the animals were immersed in the stream up to their necks. However, the existence in the Nave of a frieze of eight engraved and painted ibex heads disposed in a similar manner leaves us rather doubtful as to the interpretation suggested for the deer; we are more inclined to think that both cases are due to a particularly synthetic " manner " of representing a herd.

The four ibex heads shown in Pl. 194, b are black with red antlers; but the colour, which has partly disappeared, is barely visible in the photograph.

We shall conclude these brief remarks on some of the principal works at Lascaux by recalling the small bear that belongs, on account of the concave shape of its forehead, to the species of brown bear rather than cave bear (Pl. 194, c). It is covered by the outline of the stomach of one of the bulls on the north-east wall of the Great Hall and is a lively, well-designed little figure. Finally, in Pl. 180, b is the so-called unicorn, the first of the series of animals along the west wall of the main hall. It is a strange animal with a fantastic shape; its body might belong to a rhinoceros, dappled with roundish stains; its head, with a rectangular nose, is small, out of proportion to the body and surmounted by two long obliquely-angled antennae. This figure has been variously interpreted as a mythical animal, a demonic being, a sorcerer camouflaged with the hide of an animal, etc. Representations of fantastic composite animals are frequent in Franco-Cantabrian art (Pls. 282, c; 283, a) and they have usually been interpreted as expressions of a magical or religious nature.

PECH-MERLE.

One of the most singular and important monuments of cave art in France is undoubtedly that of Pech-Merle, near the village of Cabrerets (Lot), with its numerous painted and engraved works belonging to various phases. A visit to Pech-Merle is also very rewarding because of the atmosphere of mystery which, more than in any other Palaeolithic cave, reigns in these dark corridors, winding passages and vast halls where the visitor suddenly comes upon the black outlines of mammoths, oxen and horses against the white calcareous surface of the walls and ceilings. These ghostly figures, emerging from the shadows of thousands of years, with their special character, their peculiar disposition on the walls and their interrelations, more than anywhere else create the atmosphere of a really remote place, consecrated to the magic rites of our Palaeolithic ancestors.

The paintings of Pech-Merle were discovered in 1922 by a young man from Cabrerets, André David, and his family, and were examined and traced by the Abbé Lemozi who had followed immediately behind them into the cave [1]).

Access to Pech-Merle at the time of the discovery was very difficult: through a narrow subterranean way, slippery and completely obstructed in two places by stalagmitic formations that had to be demolished before proceeding further. Beyond this a descent, by means of a rope, led into a deep abyss that gave access to a vast system of underground caves, among which was an immense hall, 140 metres long and about 15 metres wide, where the principal paintings were found. Today access to Pech-Merle has been made practicable by the

[1]) LEMOZI, 1929.

creation of an artificial entrance at the end opposite the one through which David first entered. Like Lascaux, Pech-Merle is now provided with stairways, handrails, board-walks and lighting equipment.

We have mentioned above some paintings from this cave — an ox and a deer (Pl. 170) which, owing to their stylistic and technical characteristics, were considered archaic forms of Franco-Cantabrian art. The en-gravings on clay are also assigned to the archaic phase of Palaeolithic art and among them, in a compli-cated tangle of meandering signs, the figures of some mammoths, a deer (Pl. 117, *a*) and three women of the Aurignacian-Perigordian type (Pls. 116; 257, *a*, *b*) are distinguish-able. These figures — as well as another human figure painted in red and probably masked (Pl. 257, *e*) — will be discussed later. We should now describe some of the cave's more important pictorial compositions.

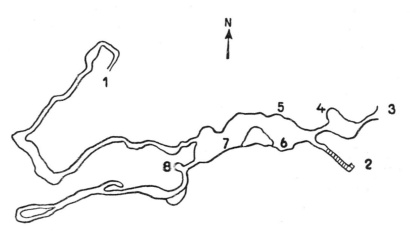

Fig. 23. Cave of Pech-Merle. 1. Natural entrance. 2. New artificial entrance and staircase. 3. Access to recently discovered galleries. 4. *Megaceros* engraved on clay. 5. Great frieze of horses. 6. Mammoth Chapel. 7. Hall with engravings on clay. 8. Human footprints.

The two horses with black heads in the great hall are famous (Pl. 196). The animals, probably pregnant mares, are turned in opposite directions, their hindquarters superimposed. Each one is 1,60 m. long and 90 cm. high. The outlines, painted in black, are pure, although the forelegs are somewhat rigid and too slender. The heads also are small in proportion to the bodies, and have the elongated shape that we have mentioned several times in the foregoing pages and termed archaic. In this respect they approach some of the horses in Le Portel and Lascaux, and they also share another characteristic: head and neck are painted in black, " hooded ", with flat, uniform colour, as we have seen in the horse in Pl. 175, and also in the cow in Pl. 182, *a* of Lascaux.

The mares of Pech-Merle are marked with black dots of various dimensions filling the entire outline of their bodies; they are also surrounded by dots, mostly black, with about a dozen red dots. Some are disposed in order around the neck of the animal on the right, as though following its profile and the outline of the rock surface. Note that at this point the extreme right margin of the great vertical rock panel that bears the painted figures seems naturally shaped so as to suggest a horse's head, a " chess horse " as Nougier and Robert rightly observed [1]. Within this natural figure, outlined by a thin red line, the head and neck of the horse on the right are inscribed.

Fig. 24. Cave of Pech-Merle. Pike outlined in red, much faded, superimposed on the black horses in Pl. 196.

Six negative handprints, four right and two left, complete this strange composition, disposed around the horses; two of these prints, high up on the wall, are perfectly clear. They seem to signify possession of the prey on the part of the Palaeolithic hunters.

Superimposed upon all this is a pike, outlined in red and much faded. It is hardly visible (Fig. 24).

On the opposite side of the great hall, in a recess approximately 7 metres long facing the panel with the horses, about twenty animals are traced in black. They are mostly mammoths,

[1] NOUGIER, ROBERT, 1954, p. 11.

superimposed upon each other but for the major part characterized by the same style and probably belonging to the same phase of art. In this " Mammoth Chapel ", besides the pachyderms are four oxen, a couple of bison and a horse, more or less completely represented. These figures, though simply outlined with no attempt at chiaroscuro, are nevertheless well rendered from the point of view of volume, stark in design but well balanced and lifelike. Generally no morphological detail is reproduced, except in the case of the mammoths whose long fur is indicated by rapid, firm perpendicular strokes. Notwithstanding the simple technique, some of the animals' anatomical characteristics are faithfully and acutely observed. Note, for instance, the mammoths' tails (Pl. 197) and the outline of their backs and dome-shaped heads. The mammoth in Pl. 198, *a*, although graphically very simple, is a powerful work masterfully synthesizing the essential features of the great inhabitant of the tundra of glacial Europe. The same applies to the mammoth in Pl. 197, *a* and *b* painted outside the Chapel, whose compact mass expresses in an unsurpassed manner the ponderous animal's blind strength.

The bison in Pl. 198, *b*, whose clean-cut outline emphasizes its curved, protuberant hindquarters (which struck the Palaeolithic hunter as especially dangerous) is a work of great merit in its simplicity; its line, as we shall shortly see, is similar to that of analogous figures in the cave of Castillo in Cantabria (Pl. 221, *c*). The oxen are also finely executed and full of life (Pls. 198, 199); while resembling some of the Lascaux cows in the shape of the head and horns, they are better balanced graphically, and the hoofs are drawn in a different manner, designed with care, in full profile, according to a convention also encountered in the hoofs of the bison mentioned above and of the fine horse in Pl. 198, *b*, a stylistically mature piece of work, if simple in structure and lacking the elaborate chiaroscuro and the morphological details that appear and develop in Niaux, Font-de-Gaume and Altamira. The cow in Pl. 199, *b*, is also remarkable, drawn with head downwards as though falling or slipping on a steep slope, a posture that we shall find repeated in the Spanish cave of La Pasiega (Pl. 228, *b*).

The works in the Mammoth Chapel are more advanced than the hooded horses of the same Pech-Merle cave and than other, technically complex works in Lascaux, while showing some resemblance with the latter as we have noted.

In 1949 a new gallery was discovered in Pech-Merle; it contains red dotted lines that lead through an oval opening, 50 by 30 cm. large, to a low chamber in which one can only remain in a crouching position. Strange figures of animals with voluminous bodies are traced in black and in red on the walls; they have tiny, horned heads that might be the heads of ibex (Pl. 199, *c*) and show some affinity with the hooded horses of the great hall.

MONTE CASTILLO.

La Cueva del Castillo. In this cave, opening into the mountain of the same name near Santander, simple outline figures were found. From a certain point of view they show an affinity with some of the figures of the Mammoth Chapel of Pech-Merle. We have already alluded to this famous Spanish cave when speaking of engravings and of a painted elephant (pp. 131-132, 157-158, Pl. 220, *b*). The forepart of the cave contained a very important deposit with human artifacts that produced, in stratigraphical succession, industries of the Tayacian and Micoquian, Mousterian, Aurignacian-Perigordian and Magdalenian periods, and finally of the Mesolithic. Excavations were carried out here by Alcalde del Rio first, and later, between 1909 and 1914 by Obermaier and Wernert [1]). In 1903 Alcalde del Rio discovered the paintings

---

[1]) OBERMAIER, 1925, pp. 175-180.

and engravings in the complex network of corridors, halls and passages that make up the deep cave.

The paintings of Castillo belong to various phases of Franco-Cantabrian cave art. Breuil, who studied them and published his findings in 1911 together with Alcalde del Rio and Lo-renzo Sierra[1]), divided them into various groups, from the Aurignacian to the Upper Mag-dalenian.

The bison in Pl. 221, c, although more rigid and prim-itive, shows some affinity with the bison of Pech-Merle, as does the ox head in Pl. 221, b and the ox in Pl. 222, b. The cave also contains some other bison, very much deteriorated, related to the polychrome fig-ures of Altamira; many handprints, dotted lines, and a great variety of tectiforms, " boat-signs ", etc.

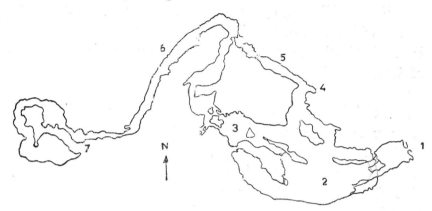

Fig. 25. Cave of Castillo. 1. Entrance. 2. Main hall. 3. Hall with stalagmite bison. 4. Recess with tectiforms. 5. Gallery with handprints. 6. Gallery with dots. 7. Painted elephant.

La Pasiega. Close to the opening of the Castillo cave, at about the same level and on the same steep flank of the mountain, is the entrance to the cave of La Pasiega, discovered in 1911 by Obermaier and Wernert[2]). On the walls of the corridors and in narrow clefts are paintings of various kinds; animal figures, tectiforms, and also a very few engravings that in our opinion all share stylistic and technical peculiarities. They are usually animal figures in simple outline with skilfully portrayed details such as the eyes, nostrils, mane and other parts of the coat. Chiaroscuro is also successfully attempted, and in some cases the entire figure is filled in with colour, deeper in some parts than in others to create an effect of shadowing. Deer are plentiful, as are young deer and horses, but there are also a few bison and oxen.

Undoubtedly some of the La Pasiega figures are rather archaic : we have already referred to the deer with antlers viewed in frontal perspective (Pl. 223, a, d). There are also some horses with elongated heads that recall the horses of Le Portel and Lascaux (Pl. 223, b, e, f). However, between these figures and the freer, stylistically more advanced ones, intermediate forms can be detected. Of the two very similar horses in Pl. 223, e, the lower, although incomplete, already shows the free outline of back, stomach and hips of the marvellous horse in Pl. 224, a, b, a masterpiece of Franco-Cantabrian art. The fine sober drawing, the reality and life that emanate from this graceful little figure reveal not only the artist's own particular gifts, but also, in the writer's opinion, the profound graphic experience that only comes with an established style. The head is no longer elongated. The young deer in Pl. 224, c, d can be placed in the same stylistic category, although it does not equal the horse in liveliness and delicacy.

Breuil divides the art of La Pasiega into seven successive series, plus three additional parallel series[3]); he considers it as belonging to the Aurignacian-Perigordian cycle. Very few figures, in his opinion, belong to the Magdalenian cycle.

We shall not deal here with questions of chronology, for our purpose at present is to review some of the principal works of Franco-Cantabrian cave art, following as far as possible a specific order dictated by the stylistic and technical characteristics of the works themselves.

[1]) ALCALDE DEL RIO, BREUIL, SIERRA, 1911, pp. 112-193.
[2]) BREUIL, OBERMAIER, ALCALDE DEL RIO, 1913.
[3]) BREUIL, 1952, p. 476.

Before leaving La Pasiega we should mention the ox in Pl. 228, *b*, shown with its head downwards (in the same position as the ox of Pech-Merle, Pl. 199, *b*); also one of the great bison in Castillo (Pl. 222, *c*) shown in an upside-down position, as are a few similar specimens which we shall discuss later.

Finally, Pl. 228, *a, e, f* shows three horses, of cruder workmanship than the ones described above, with heads of a different type from the so-called archaic ones; in some cases the outline is obtained with dotted lines, as in some drawings that we shall examine later, from the cave of Covalanas (Santander) (Pl. 230, *b*).

Las Monedas and *Las Chimeneas.* To round off the painted caves of Monte Castillo there are two caves that were recently discovered: Cueva de las Monedas [1]) in 1952, and Cueva de las Chimeneas [2]) in 1953. Here too the paintings are simple, outlined in black. About thirty figures were found in Las Monedas: horses, oxen, bison, deer, stags and some indecipherable signs. Usually the figures are well outlined, lifelike although sometimes lacking somewhat in suppleness, particularly in the legs. They are enriched with a few details such as the eye and some lines representing the fur. Occasionally there is a suggestion of chiaroscuro. Relief is obtained by the correct outlining of different parts of the body and by a fine sense of perspective in the drawing of the limbs. Among the better figures of Las Monedas is a stag, of which the front part alone has survived, and a horse with a hair-line dividing the coat from the stomach (Pl. 229, *e*). A wild goat (Pl. 229, *d*) and an ox also have lines dividing different parts of the body. By and large the figures in this cave, although technically austere, belong to a phase that is already quite advanced.

The paintings in Las Chimeneas are not so rich in detail and somewhat less supple — at least, judging from the photographs published to date. There are also some engraved figures. The same animals are represented here as in Las Monedas.

COVALANAS.

About 50 km. east of Monte Castillo near the village of Ramales, is the cave of Covalanas, where in 1903 Sierra and Alcalde del Rio [3]) discovered a series of red paintings all representing young deer (with the exception of a horse and an ox); Breuil believes these paintings to be Perigordian [4]). The outline is simple, linear, often dotted in the manner we have seen employed in La Pasiega; in fact the horse in Pls. 230, *b* and 231, *b* recalls the horse of La Pasiega in which this technique was used (Pl. 228, *a, f*). The style of the Covalanas paintings in many instances is clumsy; various figures, however, such as the group of deer in Pl. 231, *a, c*, one of which turns its head backwards, the young deer in Pl. 232, *a* and the walking ox (Pls. 232, *b*; 274), are lively, firmly and skilfully executed. The visitor to Covalanas is impressed, above all, by the intensity and extraordinary freshness of the colour.

LA PEÑA DE CANDAMO.

This cave, situated near San Roman de Candamo (Oviedo), is the most westerly of the Cantabrian caves. We have mentioned it several times (p. 134) in connection with its engravings (Pls. 135; 136; 137 *a, b*) and some primitive paintings (Pl. 219). But a group of painted

---

[1]) CARBALLO, 1953a; RIPOL PERELLÒ, 1953.
[2]) CARBALLO, 1954; ECHEGARAY, 1953.
[3]) ALCALDE DEL RIO, BREUIL, SIERRA, 1911, pp. 14-22.
[4]) BREUIL, 1952, p. 347.

figures in a more evolved technique is shown in Pl. 233. Among them is a horse whose pure outline is executed with a fine black line. It has slender legs and a small, rather elongated head; the thick mane is indicated by a single curve; the eye, nostrils, lips, and the hair on its jaw are carefully drawn. The fine linear technique and the manner in which the details are stressed recall the engraved horses of Perigordian mobiliary art in Laraux and Abri Labatut (Pls. 18, *c*; 19, *c*) and the horses engraved on the walls in Gargas (Pl. 129); the feet are treated in the same manner as the feet of the archaic horses in Franco-Cantabrian art.

An ox head, rather crude, with horns viewed from the front, is outlined in red above the horse; it should be referred to the same archaic phase as the oxen in Pl. 219 mentioned above. Below it is a horse's head sketched in red in some detail. Finally, clearly superimposed upon the legs and stomach of this horse is yet another horse, very fine, painted in sienna. This one is different from the others, both morphologically because it is squat, with short neck and legs, and technically because it is drawn with a thick line, slightly blurred here and there.

Also in Candamo are the interesting outlines of a deer (Pl. 234, *a*) and a horse with the front half painted in red and the rear half engraved, evolved stylistically if rather simple from a technical point of view (Pl. 234, *b*).

PINDAL.

The cave of Pindal, mentioned already in connection with its engravings (Pl. 134) and a painted mammoth (Pl. 220, *a*) is also located in Cantabria; it contains bison, partly engraved and partly painted. One of the bison in Pl. 235 is delicately engraved except for the backline, which is painted; another (upper right in Pl. 235, *a*) is engraved and partially painted in front. These figures already show the highest degree of artistic evolution, comparable with the works of the most advanced phase of Franco-Cantabrian art (see, for instance, the manner in which the horn and eye are represented, almost touching). Two other figures, far cruder and more carelessly executed, are painted in red close to the preceding ones : a horse's head and another bison; lower down, in the same Pl. 235, *a* and *b*, is a group of club-signs, and to the left many dotted lines, of which we shall speak later.

LE PORTEL.

Here we are again in France, where we shall briefly consider a series of works introducing us to a phase of art in which a degree of brilliance in style and technique is apparent, established and realized in accordance with definite manners and rules. We are back in the cave of Le Portel (Ariège) which we have already examined in connection with a group of archaic painted figures (Pls. 172, 173).

The first of the three bison in Pl. 200, *a*, *b*, *c* is mainly painted in black with an engraved outline; the other two are more summarily sketched. In Pl. 284, *c* the two bison facing each other are accurately described in all their details, such as the eyes, horns, beard, etc.; one of them is well shaded in the lower part of its body. They already show the clearly defined stylistic mannerisms of the more evolved expressions of Franco-Cantabrian cave art.

The reindeer in Pl. 200 is sketchily but masterfully done. The reproduction distorts it considerably, for it is hard to protograph because of its position on the ceiling of a corridor so low that one is obliged to crawl through it. The movement of the animal, appearing to writhe as if mortally wounded, and its general configuration, somewhat recall the ox of Pech-Merle in Pl. 199, *b*.

Also the horses in Pls. 200, *e* and 201, *a*, *b*, *c* show that a definition of aesthetic values is here achieved; they already appear to have crystallized into formulas and incline, in certain respects, towards mannerism. Note, for instance, the zig-zag line that divides the coat of the horse in Pl. 201, *a* into various zones — something we have already seen in Upper Magdalenian mobiliary art.

This horse in Pl. 201, *a* is an excellent piece of work, traced with firmness and a masterly sense of balance; unfortunately, because of the difficulty of photographing it, this picture too is considerably distorted and loses much of its character.

Many of the works of art in the cave of Le Portel mark the entrance into a phase of monochrome painting immediately preceding the great polychromatic art that reaches its peak in Altamira and Font-de-Gaume. (We do not wish, by this statement, to affirm a true chronological succession but rather a different degree of elaboration of technique).

This monochrome phase achieves the highest form of pictorial virtuosity with the marvellous figures of Niaux in Ariège.

ROUFFIGNAC.

We have mentioned the cave of Rouffignac previously, in connection with its countless engravings; we shall now briefly survey the paintings, equally interesting and plentiful, that are scattered all over the cave, mainly in the so-called "Voie Sacrée" and "Galerie Breuil" and on the "Grand Plafond".

Here too the animal most frequently portrayed is the mammoth, followed by the bison, the ibex, the horse and the rhinoceros.

All the figures are painted in black and the medium is manganese [1]).

They consist of mere outlines, rather bold and vigorous, with some details such as the eye and fur generally correctly represented, although the technique, by and large, is simple and there is no attempt at chiaroscuro. Where the figure is complete the feet are also accurately drawn. On the whole, art here has reached a high degree of technical development which is all the more striking in that the results are obtained with simple graphic means.

In several cases the intention to render a composition or scene is obvious in Rouffignac. Pl. 203 shows a detail of a long row of mammoths, and Pl. 202 of a series of woolly rhinoceroses. Pl. 203, *b* shows part of a fine, if simple, composition of two mammoths facing each other, and the same plate (*d*), two bison, one of which is partly engraved and partly painted — as we have seen elsewhere, for instance in the cave of Pindal (Pl. 235).

However, in other places, e. g., on the "Grand Plafond", fine figures of ibexes, horses, rhinoceroses and mammoths are casually distributed facing in every direction and occasionally overlapping.

The rhinoceroses somewhat recall those engraved on Perigordian pebbles from the cave of La Colombière (Pls. 21, 23) and Le Trilobite (Pl. 19); graphically, however, they are more complex and reveal a degree of suppleness and decision that places them on a higher artistic level. On the other hand, if only because of the way they are grouped, they appear to form a single unit with the mammoths and therefore should relate to the latter chronologically as well. The first impression one receives from an overall examination of the Rouffignac paintings is that most of them belong to the same stylistic phase. This impression comes from the fact that some details are often repeated; the eye, for example, is rendered with great liveliness in mammoths, ibexes, bison and horses as a more or less triangular shape, with the brow clearly suggested. The extremity of the nose is represented in the same manner in different species; see the rhinoceros and the horse in Pl. 202, *b, d*.

---

[1]) GRAZIOSI, 1956a; *idem*, 1957a.

By and large, then, the paintings are rather evolved despite their technical simplicity, and their style is identical with that of many engraved figures in the same cave (compare, for instance, the heads of the rhinoceroses in Pl. 147, *a* and 202, *b* with the mammoths in Pls. 148, *e*, and 203, *b*).

NIAUX.

The narrow, impractical entrance to the cave of Niaux opens about 4 km. from the little town of Tarascon-sur-Ariège, on a steep cliff 100 metres above the deep gorge of Vic-de-Sos, a tributary of the Ariège river, at a height of 668 metres. This is the northern side of the Pyrenees, a region which is among the richest in Palaeolithic cave art.

Although long known to the local people, the paintings of Niaux were first published in 1906 by Commandant Mollard, who informed Cartailhac and Breuil of their existence [1].

A complete *corpus* of these paintings does not exist, but we have descriptions of them and research by Cartailhac, Breuil, Nougier, Robert and others [2].

The painted figures are in the so-called Black Hall, a great circular chamber about 800 metres from the opening. On the wall opposite the entrance to the Black Hall where the rock surface recedes, forming a sort of niche, are many animals painted in deep black, apparently quite fresh. Most of them are bison — the animal most frequently portrayed in this cave (there are about 25) — but there are also a few splendid figures of horses and ibexes, and one deer. These paintings are linear in outline, executed with great care, masterfully,

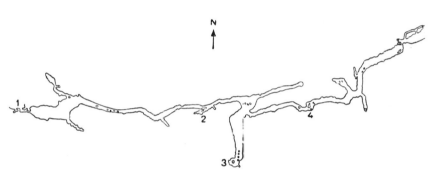

Fig. 26. Cave of Niaux. 1. Entrance. 2. First painted signs. 3. Black Hall containing the principal group of paintings. 4. Human footprints.

if soberly shaded and rich in detail. We do not have to point out the very high artistic level reached by the painters of Niaux: a glance at the plates published here is enough. The drawing is of great purity, realism and expressiveness.

The paintings of Niaux compare with the finest mobiliary figures of Upper Magdalenian — the most flourishing period of this particular form of art. Certain stylistic elements, already codified in this phase of Franco-Cantabrian art, are clearly apparent here; for instance, the shape of the bisons' horns, viewed in perfect perspective and in relation to the animals' eyes; the accurate representation of the hoofs; the manner of indicating the beard, the hairy back, etc.

Among the horses (see Pls. 210, *b*; 211, *a, b, c*) the squat type is frequent, with furry coat, carefully drawn nose, eyes and hoofs. These animals have blunt heads, very different from the horses of Lascaux and the archaic horses of Le Portel and other caves.

Pl. 212 shows a magnificent deer, with few details but perfectly executed relief.

In Niaux there are also some simple figures, such as the ox in Pl. 275, *b*, in which natural accidents were exploited; others are engraved on the clayey floor of the cave: superb representations of bison and fish to which we referred in an earlier chapter (Pls. 277; 138, *a*).

On the animals, and particularly on the bison, arrows are often painted in black and sometimes in red; they are obviously connected with propitiatory hunting magic

[1] CARTAILHAC, BREUIL, 1908.
[2] NOUGIER, ROBERT, 1954a.

(Pls. 205, 207, 209). The bison engraved on clay also has some darts leading to small natural cavities, produced by dripping water, that were used to represent wounds (Pl. 277).

Niaux also contains countless signs of various types — club-signs, dotted lines, etc., painted in red or in black, some of which are probably Mesolithic (Pl. 272, *d, e, f*).

The bison of the Spanish cave of Santimamiñe are very similar in style and technique to those at Niaux.

SANTIMAMIÑE.

This cave, consisting of a few rather small chambers, opens into the mountains of Cortezubi in the Guernica region (Biscay). It contains various bison outlined in black and summarily shaded, also a horse, a bear and a deer's head.

The bison, generally speaking, repeat the style of the bison in Niaux, which they also resemble in the manner of applying the paint and shading the figures. They are not as perfect as the paintings of the French cave, their outlines are not quite so firm and the colour is less skilfully applied.

Two bison face each other, placed vertically on the cave wall (Pl. 238, *b*). In the same vertical position, but back to back, are two more bison, partly obliterated, one of which is reduced to part of the outline of the back (Pl. 236, *c*).

The bear and the deer's head are much faded; they belong in a different category from the other figures (Pl. 232, *a*).

To conclude this brief survey of the more stylistically advanced monochrome paintings of Franco-Cantabrian art, we should mention two other bison that seem to belong in the same category as those just mentioned: one in LA PASIEGA, outstanding among the majority of the paintings in that cave, and one, in approximately the same style (although more summarily executed) in the cave of LA PEÑA DE CANDAMO; they are shown in Pl. 238, *c, d*.

* * *

We now come to the outstanding period in the evolution of Franco-Cantabrian art: the great polychromatic paintings. At this point it would seem that the Magdalenian artist, having acquired a refined taste, an almost perfect technique and some fundamental principles of style, achieved complete mastery of his craft and of his tools; he was equipped for and overcame the ultimate test — the conquest of polychromy.

The polychrome painting that we have seen appear at a flourishing moment in Franco-Cantabrian art, when the magnificent works of Lascaux were created, is still very far from the amazing combination of colours in Altamira and Font-de-Gaume. In Lascaux, in fact, an animal's body, outlined in black, was filled in with simple, flat colour; or some parts of the body, such as the head, feet, tail, etc., were painted in black — as in the reproduction of cows and horses; or again, black was used to emphasize certain details such as the mane, ears, nostrils, or to create an effect of chiaroscuro against a coloured background. We have also seen different shades of red, black and yellow juxtaposed in the checks of the so-called " blazons ".

The figures that we are about to examine, on the other hand, are of a far more complex polychromy — making use of certain graphic devices, the better to exploit the limited scale of colours found in mineral ochres. This polychromy confers greater strength and splendour upon expressions of very advanced Magdalenian art.

However, according to Castillo, the Palaeolithic artist was not really concerned with colour. " Polychromy " he says " with its graduated shades, was used to strengthen the illusion of form that started with line and continued with modelling " [1]). While acknowledging that colour had a largely subsidiary function, we believe that many of the paintings in Altamira also reveal a real, if simple, taste for the juxtaposition of tones and colours which create chromatic harmonies.

Very few caves contain polychrome figures of so advanced a phase. We have already mentioned the bison, very much faded, of CASTILLO. We should now mention the caves of LABASTIDE (Hautes-Pyrénées) with its great painted horse [2]), and MARSOULAS (Haute-Garonne) where Regnault discovered in 1897 some figures that were later examined by Cartailhac and Breuil [3]). This cave contains many engravings and paintings belonging to various phases. A great bison, 2,25 metres long, and a horse, also over 2 metres long (both, unfortunately, much deteriorated) are assigned to the polychrome phase.

A few bison in the cave of Marsoulas deserve special attention; they show only the front part, executed in a curious technique consisting of red dots covering the entire body except the head, shaded in brown and accurately engraved. On account of their curious technique these figures appear to belong to an advanced phase of cave art; if not later, they are probably contemporary with the great polychrome figures in the same cave.

Polychromy is present in a few other places, for instance in the cave of BÉDEILHAC in Ariège, but only in the form of vestiges of once important pictorial compositions (Pl. 213, a).

Tracings of the bison and horses made about thirty years ago when the paintings were in a better state of preservation were recently published by Breuil [4]). But the real monuments of polychromatic art are only two in number, one in Spain, the other in France: Altamira and Font-de-Gaume.

The former is of unparalleled splendour, particularly because of the perfect state of preservation of a great majority of the paintings, whose colours are extremely fresh. The latter cave is not as striking due to a considerable deterioration of the figures, many of which are barely distinguishable, and also to the technique which is less brilliant and not as effective as that of the artists of Altamira.

ALTAMIRA.

The romantic circumstances that led to the discovery of the Altamira paintings (the first discovery in the field of Palaeolithic cave art) have been related earlier.

When little Maria de Sautuola saw the first " toros " traced on the low ceiling the Altamira cave did not look anything like it does today: fallen rocks made access to it not only difficult but dangerous; the great painted ceiling at some points was little over a metre from the ground, and it was therefore somewhat difficult to examine the figures. Today Altamira is equipped for tourists and a visit to the principal hall — containing the polychrome paintings — and to other parts of the cave presents no difficulties: electric lighting, masonry and reinforcement of the imperilled ceiling and walls, board walks, isolation of the great hall by means of a partition, levelling of the ground, etc., have made this Cantabrian cave easily accessible.

Altamira opens into calcareous formations near the village of Santillana del Mar in the Cantabrian mountains, 30 km. west of Santander. It extends over 270 metres in the shape of a great zig-zagging gallery with lateral corridors, the first of which, 30 metres from the entrance, contains the famous paintings.

---

[1]) CASTILLO, 1953-54, p. 10.
[2]) BREUIL, 1952, p. 258.
[3]) CARTAILHAC, BREUIL, 1905.
[4]) BREUIL, 1949.

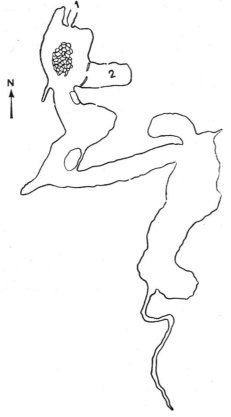

Fig. 27. Cave of Altamira. 1. Entrance.
2. Hall with polychrome paintings (from
BREUIL, OBERMAIER, 1935).

In this hall, 18 m. long and 9 m. wide, the polychrome figures are painted exclusively on the ceiling and are particularly dense to the left of the entrance.

Breuil discovered other strata of paintings and engravings underlying the polychrome ones. In fact there are some red figures painted in flat colour or merely outlined (Pl. 240), handprints, etc., traced on the ceiling, particularly to the right. To these we should add engravings representing masked men, some animals and some figures consisting of radiating lines that Breuil interpreted as huts. According to Breuil, all this should be referred to the Aurignacian-Perigordian period [1].

For our part we are content to acknowledge that paintings of a more primitive order, merely outlined or filled in with flat colour (and whose precise chronology we shall not now discuss) underlie, in Altamira, the marvellous polychrome paintings and some monochrome black paintings, rich in chiaroscuro, that share the stylistic characteristics of the polychrome ones.

The polychrome figures are 25 in number, some incomplete or interlaced with others but the majority accurately finished and independent, clearly visible in their brilliant colours. The freshness and brilliance of the colours is what strikes one first on entering the great hall. The reds, pinks and browns stand out vividly from the undulating surface of the ceiling, spreading over it like a great precious tapestry. But another thing strikes one also, crossing the threshold of this " Sistine Chapel " of prehistory — something no photograph can sufficiently convey — and that is the impression of relief given by the paintings. The Palaeolithic artist

Fig. 28. Cave of Altamira. Group of polychrome figures on ceiling of Great Hall
(from BREUIL, OBERMAIER, 1935, fig. 4).

actually made use of some natural formations of the rocky ceiling that recalled the shape of a bison's body, painting them accurately and completing the missing parts with colour, thus obtaining figures of admirable effectiveness (Pl. 273) which really appear to be detached from the ceiling.

---

[1] Breuil also attributes 5 drawings traced in black and some engraved heads of young deer to the end of the Solutrean period or the beginning of the Magdalenian; six black figures, modelled, to Magdalenian V, and finally all the polychromatic paintings to Magdalenian VI (BREUIL, 1952, p. 71).

The effect is most suggestive, above all on account of the dimensions of the bison, varying between 1,40 m. and 1,80 m. in length. A deer, the largest figure in the hall, measures 2,25 m.

But our wonder increases when, on examining these extraordinary works of art in detail, we realize the complex technique with which they were executed. Almost all the figures are engraved as well as painted. Engraving as a complement to painting is not a new process, for we have seen it used in Lascaux; but at Altamira some parts of the figures were also scraped so as to obtain special effects of light and shadow.

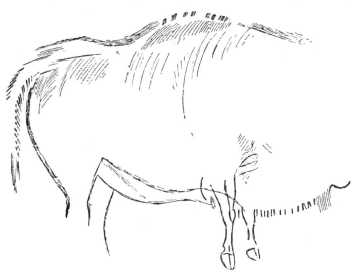

The work was started, according to Breuil, by tracing the outline of the figure, either painting or engraving it. It was then coloured, and finally the outline was stressed by engraving, and some details such as the eyes, ears and horns were emphasized, also with engraved lines. Some parts were then scraped and even washed to obtain shadings and blend the colours, with a resulting effect of light and shadow that renders the volumes more lifelike.

Fig. 29. Cave of Altamira. Engraved outline of the painting in Pl. 250, c (from BREUIL, OBERMAIER, 1935, fig. 7).

As we have said, when the polychrome figures of Altamira were executed there were already some other, more ancient figures, painted and engraved on the ceiling of the great hall; in some instances the pre-existing figures were at least partially erased, as proved by the traces that can still be detected, to make room for the later ones; at other times the pre-coloured surface was used, adapted to new figures and partially washed and scraped.

In some cases paintings of different periods are juxtaposed and superimposed, so that it is very difficult to distinguish them; for instance, in the group in Pl. 244 a bison or ox is discernible, interlaced with another animal, perhaps a horse, with various signs and with a large head that might belong to a horse, or to a wild boar — according to Cartailhac and Breuil [1]).

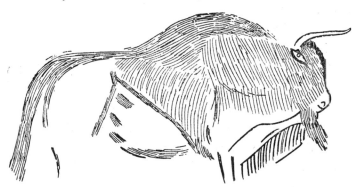

Fig. 30. Cave of Altamira. Engraved parts of a painted figure (from BREUIL, OBERMAIER, 1935, fig. 6).

But superimposition entailing the destruction or utilization of preceding figures is practised, in the case of polychrome paintings, not only to the detriment of more archaic ones; images of the polychromatic phase also cover each other, damaging other images of the same type and period. This iconoclasm was therefore practised within the frame of the same phase of cave art, at the same time, one might say; it is not merely the case of a new world destroying part of another, older and forgotten one with the intention of reworking the rock surface.

Undoubtedly the wild boar in Fig. 33 (of which only Breuil's tracing of the engraved parts is shown, as the original is difficult to identify in its different parts because of its very bad condition) overlies another figure of the same animal, obliterating it almost completely and leaving only the hoofs — identical to its own in style and technique — showing through.

[1]) CARTAILHAC, BREUIL, 1906.

Upon the fine polychrome bison in Pl. 250, *b* the incomplete figure of a wolf was partly superimposed after washing and scraping the figure of the bison. Again, the lowing bison in Pl. 242 was superimposed upon another bison, also polychrome, partly destroying it. A small deer, belonging to the polychrome group on account of its darker hoofs and shaded stomach, underlies, according to Breuil, an incomplete polychrome bison, and is superimposed in its turn upon another larger deer [1]).

These facts are certainly to be considered in the interpretation of the significance of Palaeolithic art; once again they appear to exclude all decorative intention in cave painting, and to prove that the images created by the artists of Altamira must have had, in their minds, more or less contingent values and functions. The animal that figures most frequently in the polychrome paintings of Altamira is the bison, of which 15 specimens exist; another (Pl. 244), according to Breuil, is rather more bovine. There are two unmistakable wild boars (Pls. 244, 254); three deer, one very fine and of large dimensions (2,20 m.) (Pl. 252), the other two more or less obliterated by superimposed figures; finally, an incomplete horse (Pl. 251) and what appears to be the head of another horse (Pl. 244).

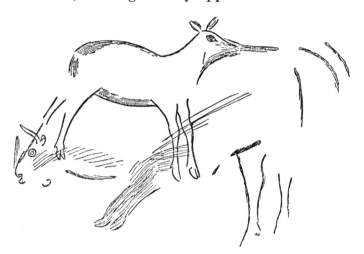

Fig. 31. Cave of Altamira. Engraved outlines of polychrome paintings (from BREUIL, OBERMAIER, 1935, fig. 17).

It would certainly be worth lingering over each one of these admirable figures if space would allow, but we shall have to be satisfied with pointing out, here and there, the more interesting details. Many descriptions exist in the bibliography of the subject; furthermore, from the photographs that we show here and from the vast iconography published by Cartailhac, Breuil and Obermaier [2]) we can get a more or less accurate idea of the beauty and skill of the polychromatic paintings in Altamira. However, no reproduction can give a really adequate idea of the originals, or evoke the attractiveness of these paintings seen in their natural environment: direct photography deprives us of the possibility of appreciating some parts of the paintings that are considerably faded; moreover, many details do not appear clearly on a photograph. Reproductions of Breuil's polychromatic tracings lead to the opposite extreme: the colours, intensified by printing, stand out too vividly against the absolutely white background of the paper; sometimes, owing to technical requirements, when tracing the figures it was necessary to complete and fill in the painted surface where it showed gaps in colours, as is obvious, for instance, if Pl. 254 is compared with the published tracing of this figure.

A glance at the plates is sufficient to convince one of the fact that in its polychrome phase Palaeolithic cave art really reaches a technical peak. The artist now applies with great assurance formulas and stylistic rules matured with the experience of centuries, already well-defined in the monochrome painting of Niaux but made even more effective in polychromy.

In some figures, for instance, through a subtle application of tones and shading and a skilful blending of colours, chiaroscuro reaches a perfection unequalled by any other primitive form of art: the volumes acquire extraordinary power and the figure develops with perfect balance and emerges, alive and concrete, from the rough surface of the rock. The hair, beard and fur of the bison have an almost tangible reality, now soft, now velvety, now rough. Details are emphasized carefully by means of engraved lines: sometimes, as in the horns of the animal

[1]) CARTAILHAC, BREUIL, 1906, pp. 86-88, 100.
[2]) CARTAILHAC, BREUIL, 1906; BREUIL, OBERMAIER, 1935.

in Pl. 245, they are only engraved. The bison's bulging muscles vibrate under their many-coloured coats, and great soft folds of skin hang from throat, breast and hips. The few colours that made up the palette of the artists of Altamira are combined with taste, and a full scale of shades, from the most delicate to the most vivid, was formed by blending them.

Certain stylistic conventions, already observed in the more evolved Magdalenian monochrome paintings, are present in Altamira; fresh ones emerge, to give unmistakable character to this peak of Palaeolithic art. The typical joining — more or less close — of eye and horn is present in most of the bison of Altamira, as in Niaux,

Fig. 32. Cave of Altamira. Engraved parts of the painting in Pl. 250, *b* (from BREUIL, OBERMAIER, 1935, fig. 15).

Le Portel, etc.; the cloven hoofs of the bison, deer and wild boars are shown in a strictly conventional manner that is uniform in Altamira but not, for instance, in Niaux. The stylization of the hoof is accompanied by a more or less accentuated stylization of the legs — slender, rather rigid and marked at the joints. Other similar stylizations are more or less evident.

Fig. 33. Cave of Altamira. Engraved outlines of two painted and superimposed wild boars (from BREUIL, OBERMAIER, 1935, fig. 20).

All this certainly does not detract from the perfection of the Altamira paintings, nor does it diminish their lively naturalism; we feel, however, that in this amazing display of volume, tone and skilful technique Palaeolithic art is exhausting the impulse, the dynamic sense of nature that aroused our admiration in the magnificent frescoes of Lascaux, for instance, and tends towards a conventionalism in which intellect and skill prevail over impulse and spontaneity.

It is now customary to say that Altamira represents the academic phase of Palaeolithic art, and to a certain extent this is indeed the impression we receive from those consummate polychrome paintings in which movement seems congealed within definite formulas, as for instance in the crouching bison or in the animals rearing up on their hind legs — hind legs that are rigidly designed, whether running or stationary.

FONT-DE-GAUME.

The cave of Font-de-Gaume, discovered in 1901 by Peyrony, was the object of careful research on the part of Capitan, Breuil and Peyrony himself and was published in 1910, together with a complete iconography traced by Breuil, in the fine series published under the patronage of the Prince of Monaco [1]).

This cave, opening on the steep flank of the valley of the Beune (a tributary of the Vézère), about 1 km. from the village of Les Eyzies in the Dordogne, consists of a narrow gallery, 124 metres long. The paintings start 65 metres from the entrance, beyond a very narrow passage known as the Rubicon; they are distributed along the walls of the main gallery, 48 metres long, a lateral gallery and a small vaulted chamber called the " Salle des Petits Bisons ".

[1]) CAPITAN, BREUIL, PEYRONY, 1910.

23. — P. GRAZIOSI, *Palaeolithic Art*.

A visitor to Font-de-Gaume, who has admired the magnificent paintings reproduced
in the fine volume by Capitan, Breuil and Peyrony, will no doubt be disappointed; in many
cases, instead of vigorous lifelike figures he will barely be able to detect a few traces of colour on the walls of the cave, and they will not always assume definite forms in his eyes.
Only after a careful examination of these vestiges in different lighting conditions, and par-
ticularly, where it exists, the engraved outline of the figure to which they belong, will he be able to reconstruct the original picture and understand its significance. In very few cases is the painted figure, if much deteriorated, clearly comprehensible at first sight.

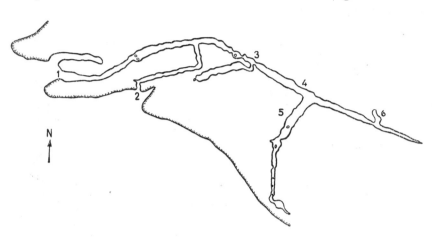

Fig. 34. Cave of Font-de-Gaume. 1. Main entrance. 2. Side entrance. 3. Passage
known as "the Rubicon". 4. Main painted gallery. 5. Painted side gallery. 6. Hall
with small bison.

The authors themselves warn their readers of the difference that exists between the paintings and the reproductions published in their work. "The colours were carefully studied"
they say " but it has been necessary, in order to trace them intelligibly, to reinforce them con-
siderably. Thus the majority of the figures are far less visible in the cave than in our plates.
The reddish colour and sometimes also the brown of the background, and the countless modern
inscriptions that soil the walls, completely alter the clarity and vigour of the shades that our
reproductions have of necessity assumed " [1]).

Polychrome paintings were not the only pictures found in Font-de-Gaume. As in Altamira, the investigators of the cave brought to light the existence of strata of paintings and
engravings of an earlier date than the polychrome figures.

They establish five series, the earliest of Perigordian age, the latest Magdalenian. Some
figures, less evolved than the polychromes and the monochrome modelled ones, are merely
traced in flat colour.

In Pl. 218, *a* we reproduce a fine rhinoceros painted in red, well built and firmly balanced,
in which the volumes and the perspective of the legs are perfectly rendered. Though simple
in technique, its style is very good and anything but primitive.

In the same plate (*b*) we reproduce another monochrome figure, an ox, already quite
complex in technique with chiaroscuro, excellent modelling, skilful shading. All in all it is
a lifelike piece of work in which details are carefully stressed, such as for instance the design
of the hoofs that already approaches the style of the polychrome figures.

Also in Font-de-Gaume the subject most frequently encountered in the polychrome
phase is the bison. There are about sixty of them, as opposed to a dozen reindeer, one wolf
and a few mammoths.

A magnificent horse outlined in black in a very advanced style, perfectly modelled and
certainly comparable, on an artistic level, with the polychrome figures, is painted in the lateral

[1]) CAPITAN, BREUIL, PEYRONY, 1910, p. 17. We should also keep in mind that very probably between the time when
Breuil made his tracings in the early years of this century and today, the paintings of Font-de-Gaume must unfortunately
have undergone progressive deterioration. The more or less continuous passage of visitors, whose numbers notably increased
when the cave was equipped, cannot fail to have had, in the course of half a century, a detrimental effect with regard to
the preservation of the paintings. The condensation of vapour, the effect of the very breath of such a large number of people,
of draughts caused by their passage as well as the direct, mechanical action of shoulders and arms unavoidably rubbing against
the walls of the narrow corridors, has led to a more or less rapid deterioration of the paintings in Palaeolithic caves. It would
really be worthwhile, in order to avoid an irreparable loss, for the owners to forgo the financial benefits deriving from entrance
fees and to close the caves to the public.

corridor (Pl. 216). This figure is preceded by another, probably a mare, obtained by completing with a few strokes a stalagmitic formation that naturally suggests the shape of a horse. It is partly visible in Pl. 216, and is reproduced entirely in Pl. 276, *a*, *b* : the same plate also shows a bison, where use was made of a natural accident in the Font-de-Gaume cave.

But it is with the polychrome painting of Font-de-Gaume that we are mainly concerned.

The artists of this cave when depicting bison sometimes surpassed, in strength and grandeur if not in technique, the analogous figures in Altamira. See, for instance, the animal in Pl. 215. This beautiful painting is executed in simple polychromy consisting of brick-red partly outlined in black, shaded with extreme skill and well high-lighted; its powerful relief is perhaps increased by the uniformity of its colouring. The force and majesty of this figure stem from the abnormal development of the animal's forepart : the nape rises, high and voluminous, above the head and the profile is abrupt, exaggerating the bison's true shape; the folds of skin on the throat and chest are paradoxically developed.

Fig. 35. Cave of Font-de-Gaume. Engraved outline of the painting in Pl. 215 (from CAPITAN, BREUIL, PEYRONY, 1910, fig. 72).

All this was treated by the artist with a sensitivity that in no way detracts from the harmony and balance of the figure, but expresses, in an almost dramatic way, the threatening aggressiveness of the wild beast as it must have appeared to Palaeolithic man in the course of his dangerous hunting expeditions.

The entire outline and the details of this painting are accurately engraved (Fig. 35). It is undeniably one of the liveliest and most impressive works of Palaeolithic art.

The bison of Font-de-Gaume are executed in various shapes and different degrees of polychromy; but despite the considerable difficulty involved in their interpretation (owing

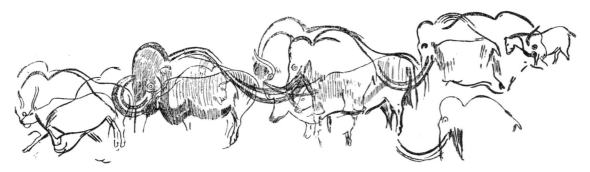

Fig. 36. Cave of Font-de-Gaume. Engraved outline of paintings in Pl. 218, *a* (from CAPITAN, BREUIL, PEYRONY, 1910, fig. 33).

to their poor state of preservation) they all show the technical ability and forceful expressiveness that made this cave — when the figures still had their original freshness — a gallery of unrivalled masterpieces.

Special consideration should be given to the two reindeer reproduced in Pl. 217 — and facing each other in the principal corridor — not only for their beauty but also because they represent a rare example of composition in Franco-Cantabrian cave art.

Of the female, on the right, only a few traces remain, whereas the male is still clearly visible. A minute analysis of various details, strong relief and perfect adherence to nature characterize these fine specimens of polychrome cave art.

Another reindeer is shown in Pl. 218, *d*; it is a reproduction of the tracing made by Breuil, in which both outline and colour were considerably heightened. Also in Pl. 218, *c* is the figure of a wolf, painted in black against a background previously coloured red; the details of the head and feet are carefully engraved. This, too, is the reproduction of a tracing by Breuil.

Finally, in Pl. 218, *e* we show Breuil's tracing of the great frieze in the main gallery, consisting of a series of polychrome bison superimposed upon figures of reindeer, above which some mammoths are painted and engraved. The outlines of the bison are also engraved (Fig. 36). This series is now barely discernible, but the faithful tracings guarantee the fact that each figure is engraved. Here too, as we pointed out on p. 138, the mammoths were executed at a later date than the polychrome figures.

ANTHROPOMORPHIC FIGURES IN CAVE ART

All we have said with regard to the anthropomorphic figures of Magdalenian mobiliary art applies in general to cave art as well. Here, too, the human figure appears infrequently, and its artistic merit is far inferior to that of the animal figures. There is a predominant tendency to represent man in more or less monstrous guises, often semi-animal or masked; in other words, to give an image of man as unrealistic and impersonal as possible.

Many of the guises and attitudes seen in mobiliary art are repeated in cave art, and some of the same kind of " masks " are to be found in both. Nevertheless, whereas in mobiliary art some representations tend towards definite realism — as, for instance, the La Marche engravings (Pl. 83) where human features are recognizable — this does not usually occur (so far as we know on the basis of present-day documentation) in cave paintings and engravings, with the exception of a few rather unsuccessful attempts such as those of the Marsoulas cave (Pl. 258, c, e).

Sculpture in low relief is a different matter altogether. At Angles-sur-Anglin, as we have mentioned before, the bearded head of a man has features resembling, to a certain extent, the features of some of the La Marche figures, and the three " Venuses " found in the same cave are of a thoroughly realistic order. The two naked women of La Magdeleine, lying in a relaxed pose, are so realistic and so polished in style as to seem positively unrelated to Palaeolithic art.

It would therefore appear that the representation of human beings in cave art answers different purposes or, at least, is linked to different artistic concepts, in the case of engraving and painting and in the case of bas-relief. On the other hand we should not forget that sculptures in low relief are found in different locations from engravings and paintings, the former being invariably situated in shelters formed by overhanging cliffs or in caves exposed to daylight, whereas the latter are generally concealed in the deep recesses of the caves.

A limited number of the human figures engraved or painted on cave walls in France and Spain are reproduced in Pls. 257-259; they were selected with the intention of presenting the more characteristic and interesting examples. These figures, however uncertain their chronological attribution, probably belong to different ages, from the Aurignacian-Perigordian to the Magdalenian; some distinctive traits nevertheless appear to relate them all.

Pl. 257, a, b shows synthetic female outlines traced on the clay surface of the Pech-Merle cave in the Lot valley (see also Pl. 116, b, c); these are said to belong to an early phase of Franco-Cantabrian art — probably to the Aurignacian-Perigordian; there is a marked analogy in style between the female statuettes and the bas-reliefs of that period.

The human figure in Pl. 257, c was found in Le Portel; its outline is roughly painted around a stalagmitic formation, used as a representation of the sex, which it no doubt evoked for the artist. The monstrous individual reproduced in the same Pl. 257, d is painted in La Peña de Candamo, near Oviedo; it is half human and half animal, and suggests a demonic being.

In the same plate, Fig. *e*, is the so-called "archer" of Pech-Merle, a figure with round, polished cranium and pointed face; Figs. *f* and *g*, as well as Pl. 258, *a* show a series of anthropomorphic monsters found in the cave of Los Casares near Guadalajara, on whose walls, beside the animals mentioned before (Pl. 127) some human figures are engraved. These too, probably Perigordian, show traits already noted in the other figures : rounded hairless head, pointed snout or beak (as in the individual in Pl. 257, *g*) or a dog's muzzle, such as that in Pl. 258, *a*. The latter figure, which is harsh and faulty in design, is pictured in the act of diving between two other figures somewhat resembling fish; Spanish authors therefore call this work the "fishing scene"[1]). There are several more anthropomorphic representations in Los Casares; some are ithyphallic, some have raised arms, others have enormous animal heads. All are more or less crude sketches.

Very roughly executed and lacking both head and feet are the three human figures of the Cougnac cave (p. 158, Pl. 171, *a*, *c*). One of these figures, whose face ends in a duck's bill, is sketched as though falling down head foremost; another flat-nosed creature is bowed forwards, shown in the act of walking. As we have said before, the bodies of all these figures are pierced with darts, which suggests magic death practices seen for the first time in Franco-Cantabrian cave art in connection with creatures of human form.

In Pl. 258, *b* the "woman" of Le Gabillou is reproduced; it is a very poorly executed piece of graphic art compared with the fine, vigorous zoomorphic representations found in the same cave (Pl. 122). And what of the strange human figures — approximately 40 of them — engraved on the walls of Les Combarelles, with simian features, bald, rounded heads, sketchy details, false and unreal postures (Pls. 258, *f*, *g*; 259, *a*)? They are contemporary with the admirable horses, reindeer, bears and mammoths found in the same cave, and are probably the work of the same artist. This, in a most productive and lavish phase of Magdalenian art.

In Pl. 258, *d* is a large rock fragment from the Magdalenian III or IV layers of the La Roche cave, near Lalinde in the Dordogne. It is inscribed with strange figures that might be interpreted as highly stylized outlines of steatopygous female bodies and bring to mind the small sculptures of Petersfels and Pekarna (Pl. 82, *e*, *f*, *g*), or even some of the light sketches engraved on stone in Hohlenstein (Bavaria) and Fontalès (Tarn-et-Garonne), believed to be schematic renderings of female bodies (p. 86)[2]). We are also reminded, by certain features, of outlines carved on the walls of Grotta Romanelli in Apulia — synthetic representations of female figures that we will discuss later (p. 196, Pl. 291, *c*)[3]).

Continuing the examination of human or semi-human figures in Franco-Cantabrian cave art, we see that both in the more ancient specimens, such as the anthropomorphic representations of Los Casares, Le Portel, Candamo, Pech-Merle and Cougnac mentioned above, and in the more recent ones such as those found in Les Combarelles, the same awkward childish drawing prevails, in sharp contrast to the mastery displayed in the animal figures of corresponding periods. The same details and postures are often repeated: the flat-nosed head of the Los Casares man in Pl. 258, *a* is very similar to the head of the Les Combarelles figure in Pl. 259, *a*; the posture of the "praying figure" of Altamira (Pl. 259, *b*) bears a close resemblance to that of the Hornos de la Peña figure in Pl. 259, *c*. They are all related through the same marked tendency to avoid defining the human form, leaving it as far as possible indeterminate, midway between man and beast; and, especially, to transform or conceal all human semblance in the features. One is inclined to conclude that the Palaeolithic artist, a master in the rendering of anatomical details from the animal world, lost all his power of observation and expression as soon as he was confronted with the portrayal of his own species; or perhaps

---

[1]) CABRÉ J., 1940, p. 85.
[2]) BIRKNER, 1928, pl. 2; DARASSE, 1955.
[3]) Battaglia pointed out at the time the affinities existing between the female outlines of Hohlenstein, La Roche, Pekarna, Petersfels and Romanelli (Battaglia, 1935).

he was affected by powerful inhibitions and taboos that stayed his hand from reproducing human beings in a form immediately recognizable or clearly differentiated from the animal world pictured in the sombre depths of the same caves.

In a very few cases, as in Marsoulas (Pl. 258, *c, e*), human features are outlined, but they are far from displaying the incisive, skilful realism that invariably distinguishes the animal figures.

It has been said that the constant tendency shown by the Palaeolithic artist to confer certain animal characteristics upon the human figure, both in engraving and in painting, is due to the inexperience of an artist devoted almost exclusively to the reproduction of the animal world; in his work the shape of the animals would therefore be reflected in the shape of the men. Although this hypothesis may contain an element of truth, it fails to explain why, contemporaneously with the engravings and paintings, some of which can be referred to the Upper Palaeolithic, the fine, realistic female statuettes and the Aurignacian-Perigordian bas-reliefs of Laussel were being executed and, at a later period, the bas-reliefs with female figures of Angles-sur-Anglin and La Magdeleine — proving that the Palaeolithic artist was perfectly capable of expressing the human form with perfect realism.

We must therefore consider that the artist intentionally portrayed the human form, on the walls of dark caves in France and Spain, in an imperfect manner — impersonally, with masked features or semi-animal traits. In certain cases the mask is obvious, as in the famous sorcerer of Les Trois Frères, a work which is far from carelessly executed and shows skill and attention in the fashioning of all its details (Pl. 281).

Preoccupation with religious or magical conventions is, as we have seen, undoubtedly responsible to a large extent for the specific manner in which the human figure is treated in the cave pictures of the entire Upper Palaeolithic. The fact that bas-relief, which invariably appears in naturally lighted shelters or at the entrance of caves, shows realistic reproductions of the human figure, must be taken into account in evaluating the facts mentioned above.

VARIOUS SIGNS

To conclude this overall survey of cave art in the Franco-Cantabrian province, something should be said about figures and signs whose significance is obscure and which often appear to float in an atmosphere of pure symbolism or abstraction; these have been called, more or less appropriately, " tectiforms ", " shield-signs ", " boat-signs ", " club-signs ", etc.

We enter here a totally different figurative field from that in which Franco-Cantabrian cave art, essentially realistic and naturalistic, expressed itself. Between these two expressions of the same art (their common origin is indisputable) there is a veritable chasm, a deep and definite gulf that makes it impossible to trace any apparent connection between the one and the other.

Pls. 264-272 show various signs found in the caves of Aquitania and Cantabria; they are of different types, most of them painted, some engraved.

Whereas in mobiliary art, as we have seen, it is possible to reconstruct the derivation of schematic or geometrical figures from those representing concrete subjects, in cave art the origin is rarely apparent and we must be content with supposing that some of these strange figures are a schematized, or at least conventional or symbolic, representation of objects the true nature of which is left to our imagination; such objects may have actually existed, but neither cave art nor mobiliary art have yielded realistic representations to provide a clue in seeking a progression or link between the successive figures.

In calling them " tectiforms " we assume that these figures were meant to represent huts, or tents, or maybe traps for animals, or even shelters for ghostly beings; these conclusions are dictated by the shape of the figures that suggest a closed space or hut covered by a roof. The number and variety of the tentative interpretations indicates that all are more or less unsubstantiated. And when we refer to certain odd signs as " shield-signs " we do not intend to suggest that they actually represent shields, but only that in shape they roughly resemble them; the term " shield-sign " is used to differentiate them from other signs. Nevertheless, in a certain number of cases these figures, however schematic they may be, reveal their significance clearly enough. In Pl. 270, *b*, for instance, there is a sign painted in the cave of Font-de-Gaume that in a simplified manner really does appear to represent a hut, with a roof, a supporting ridge-pole and two semi-circular openings. By analogy, the same interpretation may be given to the next sign, and consequently to the other schematized signs in the same cave (Pl. 270, *c*) and to the engravings, also in Font-de-Gaume, seen in Pl. 270, *d*, as well as to a number of similar signs engraved in Les Combarelles (Pl. 270, *e*). In the nearby cave of La Mouthe there is another of these supposed huts : it is engraved and painted in black, light and dark shades of red, and brown. As pointed out by Leonardi, its double-eaved roof recalls the very primitive huts in use even today in the neighbourhood of the cave [1]).

---

[1]) LEONARDI, 1955.

Capitan, Breuil, Peyrony and De Mortillet [1]) have drawn many ethnographical parallels with the huts, tents and other buildings of present-day primitive peoples, and they are certainly most convincing. Since these tectiforms in Font-de-Gaume, Bernifal [2]) and elsewhere are often found in conjunction with animal figures, French authors have raised the question of whether they were meant to be purely representative of human habitations or whether "their presence, in conjunction with animals, might not be interpreted as symbolizing some idea or some mysterious relationship " [3]).

The " hut " with double-eaved roof and ridge-pole is found, in such a realistic form, only in the Dordogne. The tectiforms of Altamira, for instance, are far less defined : even though some of the figures resemble the Dordogne hut, others that derive from them have an entirely different appearance. Alcalde del Rio and Breuil worked out a series for the figures of the same type in Altamira and in Castillo, starting with those which appear closer to the Dordogne tectiforms and ending with ladder-shaped and ribbon-shaped signs (Pl. 268) [4]). The Castillo tectiform illustrated in Pl. 265, *d* is one of the figures, among analogous Spanish ones, that more closely approximates to the Dordogne tectiforms, although it could be more accurately termed a boat-sign; but in the figures that apparently derive from it (Pl. 265, *b*), found in the same cave, the resemblance diminishes progressively, due to the vertical position in which they were drawn or to the fact that in some cases they overlap each other (Pl. 266, *a*). However, even if we were to agree that many strange figures found in Spanish caves might possibly derive, morphologically, from a tectiform prototype, it is unlikely that they maintained the same concrete significance throughout successive transformations and did not assume different, perhaps abstract meanings.

The same occurs in La Pasiega, where a few figures approach the tectiforms and others, probably derived from them, evolve towards shapes that bear little resemblance to a hut — also because they are drawn on the walls of the caves in many different positions. Breuil and Obermaier [5]) regroup the tectiforms of La Pasiega into three families : in the third group they see more points of analogy with the French tectiforms. The curious figure in Pl. 266, *e* is believed by these authors to be the representation of a roofless hut, with walls, doors and a central pole [6]). This figure is part of the mysterious " inscription " of La Pasiega which has been so widely discussed. It also contains two feet, probably human, an E-shaped sign and other signs and stains. It would be futile to attempt an explanation of this truly cabbalistic composition.

The so-called tectiforms and other derived figures in Altamira, Castillo and La Pasiega are considered by Breuil, Obermaier and Alcalde del Rio to be far more ancient than the figures of Font-de-Gaume which, according to them, are contemporaneous with the later polychrome figures.

Other rectangular figures are engraved in the Spanish caves. Pl. 271, *a* shows one of these in the cave of El Buxu in Asturias, where there are also many others, more or less alike and all engraved.

Fantasy has a free hand in the interpretation of these tectiforms, but the most rational explanation given so far is that they are in fact huts, particularly the Dordogne ones, or perhaps traps when, as in Bernifal and elsewhere, they are superimposed upon figures of animals. Obermaier offers another interpretation that is worth mentioning : he suggests that they may be traps for evil spirits; he was led to this conclusion by comparing them with devices constructed for that purpose by the primitive peoples of Celebes and Malacca. A parallel between

---

[1]) CAPITAN, BREUIL, PEYRONY, 1910, p. 227 and foll.; DE MORTILLET, 1903.
[2]) CAPITAN, BREUIL, PEYRONY, 1903; BREUIL, 1952, fig. 328.
[3]) CAPITAN, BREUIL, PEYRONY, 1910, p. 229.
[4]) ALCALDE DEL RIO, BREUIL, SIERRA, 1911, figs. 188, 189, 193.
[5]) BREUIL, OBERMAIER, ALCALDE DEL RIO, 1913, pp. 37-41.
[6]) BREUIL, OBERMAIER, ALCALDE DEL RIO, 1913, p. 37.

the reproduction of these traps, published by Obermaier, and the Spanish tectiforms — particularly the fringed ones of El Buxu and La Pileta [1]) — is certainly suggestive.

However, the fact that these strange drawings are often accumulated in isolated recesses of caves, as in Castillo and La Pasiega where they are painted inside a narrow cleft (Pl. 266, c) leads one to believe that Palaeolithic man considered them of a sacred nature or wished to enshroud them in a particular atmosphere of mystery.

Some curious rectangular figures engraved and painted in the cave of Lascaux have been called by French authors " blazons " and are also believed to be tribal signs. Usually the rectangle is divided into three equal parts breadthwise, and into two or three unequal parts lengthwise. In some cases the resulting checkerboard is painted in several colours : black, red, yellow, brown, mauve (Pl. 269). Others are more simple, crisscrossed such as those related to the cow in Pl. 189 or to the ibexes in Pl. 190. The hypothesis of a hunting instrument has also been advanced. Other categories of figures of obscure significance are also found in Franco-Cantabrian cave art : Pl. 266, b shows a series of figures that Alcalde del Rio and Breuil situate among the tectiforms [2]) but which have their own specific " bell " configuration, totally obscure as to interpretation.

The many club-signs found in almost identical form in France and in Spain are more open to interpretation. In the Pindal

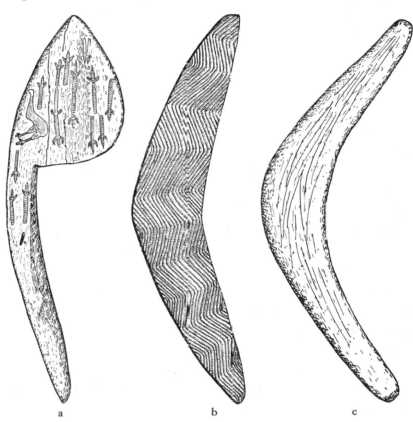

Fig. 37. Australian weapons. a) Lil-li, or pseudo-boomerang used both for striking and for throwing (Ethnographical Museum, Rome); b)-c) Boomerangs (National Museum of Anthropology and Ethnology, Florence).

cave near Oviedo, in that of Niaux and of Les Trois Frères (Pl. 271, d), they consist of a straight line with a thickening or swelling at the upper extremity, and appear to represent axes, maces or clubs. Closely resembling these but with the thickened part near the centre of the line, and in some cases more pointed, are the club-figures of Altamira (Pl. 272, a) and La Pasiega (Pl. 271, e); some of them are slightly curved, approximating to the shape of boomerangs and similar weapons. This type of weapon is as widely diffused in the world today — from Australia to Malaya, India, Africa and America — as it was in ancient times in pre-dynastic and dynastic Egypt, Mesopotamia and North Africa (where it occurs in the local cave engravings), in Scandinavian Prehistory, etc. All these club-signs seem to be highly schematized reproductions of weapons, but Palaeolithic deposits have yielded no trace of the weapons themselves.

Feathered missiles or darts appears to be the most obvious explanation of the " feather-signs " seen around the animals in Lascaux (Pls. 186-187).

---

[1]) OBERMAIER, 1918.
[2]) ALCALDE DEL RIO, BREUIL, SIERRA, 1911, p. 180.

Finally, Pl. 271, *b* shows a series of curious signs painted in red, following parallel lines, on a wall of the Santian cave near Santander; these figures — about 15 — are the only ones found in the cave; some of them resemble animal paws or stylized human arms whose hands, through successive transformations, have assumed the appearance of tridents. Some are fringed along one side. It is impossible to venture an interpretation : perhaps those strange, semi-realistic figures stand for an abstract concept rather than a concrete subject. The same applies to the dots that are disposed in strips to form the outline of tree-like figures, as in Castillo (Pl. 265, *a, b*), or in circles, as at Niaux (Pl. 272, *b*). In other cases dots forming long lines, single or multiple, or grouped in some parts of the cave, have been interpreted as indicating a route.

Of equally obscure significance are some long barbed lines (Pl. 272, *g, h*), painted in the Marsoulas cave (Haute-Garonne) and believed to be of a very late period, perhaps Mesolithic.

* * *

An overall survey of the tectiforms, club-signs and other figures of Franco-Cantabrian cave art in the light of their geographical distribution shows that, at least in so far as present knowledge allows us to assume, they increase in number and in variety as we proceed from North to South. The Dordogne, in fact, contains fewer specimens than the Pyrenees, and these are predominantly tectiforms. In the more southerly caves club-signs, barbed figures and dotted lines are plentiful; we find them in Niaux, Les Trois Frères, Marsoulas and other localities, whereas the same is not true of the tectiform of Périgord. As we reach Cantabria these signs multiply greatly with regard to number and variety. The tectiform is rarely seen in a form resembling the tectiforms of the Dordogne; it is usually quite different and appears in a variety of shapes that reveal their derivation from one another. The term " tectiform " loses its descriptive value and becomes a purely conventional expression. The club-signs, on the other hand, are identical with the club-signs of the Pyrenees.

At the southern extremity of Spain, in the cave of La Pileta which we shall discuss later, obscure signs, which it is practically impossible to interpret in realistic terms, form a large percentage of the figures painted on the walls.

It would seem therefore that in cave art figures of a symbolic or abstract nature become increasingly plentiful as one moves from the more northerly locations of Palaeolithic cave art towards the Mediterranean.

Finally, figures of this type exist, in the principal forms described above, only in cave art, whereas Franco-Cantabrian mobiliary art offers a repertory of geometrical and schematic figures not found on the walls of the caves.

THE MEDITERRANEAN PROVINCE

With cave art, as with mobiliary art, it is possible and fitting to consider separately the material discovered to date in caves distributed within that large area surrounding the Mediterranean basin from France to Southern Spain, and from Sicily to the Italian peninsula, which we have called the Mediterranean province.

This distinction, however, is not intended to be particularly binding from the point of view of chronology and style between the various works in question. For the present it should only be used as a basis for the comparative examination of some products of Palaeolithic cave art that were brought to light within this Mediterranean area and which seem to share certain peculiarities not found, or found in different proportions — in the art centres of the Franco-Cantabrian region — as we saw in the case of mobiliary art.

We have in fact observed that the works of mobiliary art reveal, at least at certain moments, converging trends with regard to form and content in the Mediterranean centres so far examined (such as Parpallò, Romanelli, Balzi Rossi, etc.). The most fundamental trend of all is towards geometrical and abstract forms.

The cave art of this province reveals these same forms — quite evident in some places — simultaneously with expressions of genuine naturalism.

However, in the latter case such expressions assume their own definite " personality " which creates a sort of common atmosphere and makes them, as a whole, something different from the figures of cave art in the Franco-Cantabrian province. Certain affinities between the works of both provinces nevertheless speak of a common origin or a more or less direct derivation from each other.

In the few centres so far discovered in the Mediterranean province there appear expressions that may show naturalistic or abstract tendencies, or even both together.

It is hardly necessary to repeat that owing to the scarcity of material all that we have said so far, with our conclusion, is no more than a simple working hypothesis.

The caves to be examined are La Pileta in the province of Malaga (Southern Spain), about 40 km. in a straight line from the Mediterranean coast; Grotta Romanelli on the Otranto canal (Southern Italy); Levanzo, on the little island of the same name off the western coast of Sicily; Monte Pellegrino near Palermo (Sicily) — also on the Mediterranean coast — and, finally, La Baume-Latrone near Nîmes, and Ebbou near Vallon (Ardèche), as well as a few other caves in the lower stretch of the Rhone valley, on the French shore of the Mediterranean.

LA PILETA.

The paintings in the cave of La Pileta, discovered by Verner in 1911 and subsequently published by Breuil, Obermaier and Verner [1]), are located in the deep part of the cave in

---

[1]) BREUIL, OBERMAIER, VERNER, 1915.

places difficult of access, and belong to different stylistic groups. According to the above-mentioned authors four pictorial phases are represented in La Pileta : a group of yellow figures, very primitive, consisting of serpentine and parallel lines, and also rough animal outlines; a group of red figures representing animals such as bulls, ibexes and deer; these, in turn, are obliterated by a third group of black ibexes, horses, deer, oxen and fish; finally there are some late, post-Palaeolithic drawings.

While some of the animals are in a good naturalistic style and show affinities with Franco-Cantabrian art (e. g., the animals in Pl. 286, *c, d*, red and yellow; and *f*, black) others, such as the ox in Pl. 285, *d*, painted in black, are much more rigid and schematic and constitute something quite individual, which is found in a similar form in Romanelli. The yellow serpentine figures, others in red or black and some curious black figures consisting of radiating lines (Pls. 285, *f*, 286, *a, b*) are of obscure significance and form part of the abstract expressions

Fig. 38. Fallow deer painted in black, from Ardales (Malaga).

to which we alluded above. They confer a particular character upon the art of La Pileta, a character apparent in all the different groups, even though they are all obviously influenced by the focal Franco-Cantabrian area.

In each of the three phases established in La Pileta by Breuil and Obermaier, figures of a naturalistic order exist, more or less finely executed, as well as many obscure figures, plentiful both in the cruder (and according to the two authors, more ancient) phase represented by yellow parallel lines, and in the later phase represented by red and black figures.

The serpentines — very simple, spontaneous graphic expressions — are identical, apart from the technique of parallel lines, whether traced in yellow or in black. All three colours were used to represent animals similar in style, possibly more rigid and archaic in the black phase, although Breuil and Obermaier consider it the latest Palaeolithic phase of this particular cave.

Among the animals are horses with the characteristically shaped heads that we have seen among the more archaic figures of Franco-Cantabrian art. Other black figures, such as the ibex in Pl. 286, *f*, are freely drawn and lifelike and can compare with the best line drawings of Franco-Cantabrian art.

Although the distinguishing of the various layers in La Pileta is certainly no easy task — judging from the writings of Breuil and Obermaier — and even if as a whole they appear somewhat chaotic, particularly in the published iconography, nevertheless an undeniable fact emerges : the coexistence in each one of these phases of naturalistic figures revealing Franco-Cantabrian influence, with a large repertory of schematic, geometrical and abstract figures among which the most characteristic is the serpentine, sinuous line, and, in the group of black paintings, the figures which consist of radiating lines.

The art of Southern Spain differs, as a whole, from the usual Franco-Cantabrian panorama; in certain respects it is related to the mobiliary art of Parpalló and Romanelli and, with the technique of sinuous parallel lines, to the cave art of another Mediterranean cave — La Baume-Latrone.

The cave of ARDALES (Malaga), is 45 km. in a straight line from La Pileta. In this cave were found yellow and reddish paintings (Fig. 38), and engravings on clay of a very primitive style resembling in their simple technique and elementary outline the figures of La Pileta, as well as a few figures of horses resembling the most archaic Franco-Cantabrian art.

LA BAUME-LATRONE.

The figures of La Baume-Latrone, discovered in 1940 by three boys from Nîmes, were published from 1941 onwards by Comte Begouen, Glory and Drouot [1]). The cave consists of a complex of corridors connecting it with other nearby caves; its principal entrance opens into a steep cliff on the left bank of the Gardon, 14 km. from Nîmes. About 80 m. from the entrance the gallery was completely sealed by a mound of clay that was removed by its discoverers. After a difficult passage and some steep descents, the hall that contains the figures — known as " Salle Begouen " — is reached 237 metres from the entrance. Here some markings

Fig. 39. La Baume-Latrone. Group of paintings reproduced in Pl. 287
(from BERGOUNIOUX, GLORY, 1952, fig. 113).

were made by drawing three or four fingers over the altered clayey surface of the wall : one wonders if these are simple meanders or crude zoomorphic figures (ox, horse?). There are also some engravings of uncertain significance, made with a flint instrument — perhaps a deer and a saiga antelope.

The paintings are more plentiful and definite; they consist, for the major part, of figures traced with several fingers — in the same technique as the engravings. According to Begouen they are contemporary with the latter, because some traces of red paint were found in the grooves, proving that the fingers that made them were stained with paint. There are also a few figures in simple outline.

The system of finger painting is extremely simple : the artist of the crude figures of La Baume-Latrone drew along the wall with several fingers dipped in the same reddish clay as that which forms the floor of the cave. The figures stand out clearly against the light surface of the ceiling, which they cover almost completely. Besides some positive handprints there

[1]) BEGOUEN H., 1941; DROUOT, 1953.

25. — P. GRAZIOSI, *Palaeolithic Art.*

are also a few curious figures traced with undulating lines, most of which are elephants — at least half a dozen — highly stylized, with trunks curiously prolonged in zig-zag bands (Pl. 287, *a*, *b*, *d*, *e*). They are probably mammoths, judging from their dome-shaped heads. According to Drouot, a strange spidery figure (Pl. 287, *a*, top) is the extreme stylization of an elephant, reduced to the head with raised trunk and tusks turned sideways, with a mere trace of the back and of the front leg.

In the middle of this tangle of figures, covering the principal panel of the hall, is a serpentine creature with a carnivore's head and wide-open jaws filled with teeth; it is probably a feline animal or bear with an extremely synthetized body represented by a sinuous line.

The few figures traced in outline (according to the French authors, of a later date than the finger paintings and engravings) are mere sketches. They include an animal — perhaps a bear —, the very crude head of an ibex, two simplified deer and a rhinoceros which is incomplete but better than the other figures (Pl. 287, *c*). They are all more realistic than the figures traced with fingers, and not quite as extravagantly shaped.

From a stylistic point of view the principal group of paintings in La Baume-Latrone does not appear to belong to any known group in the Franco-Cantabrian province, apart from the fact that doodles on clay may belong to any place and any time. The bizarre aspect of these figures gives a very singular character to the art of La Baume-Latrone. If anything, the use of several fingers and the tendency to trace undulating and serpentine lines recalls the technique of La Pileta.

EBBOU.

The cave of Ebbou is situated on the left side of the valley of the Ardèche — a tributary of the Rhone, in the neighbourhood of Vallon. It, too, is deep and conceals its treasures in a place difficult of access, far from the entrance. Here Glory discovered, in 1946, numerous engravings — about seventy — representing oxen, horses, deer, ibexes, a mammoth, two bison and other indeterminate animals [1].

Judging from the published reproductions the figures are drawn in simple outline, generally lacking details such as the eye, fur, etc. The legs are summarily sketched and always end without feet, in a point or with two crossed lines. Notwithstanding the simplicity — one might almost say the awkwardness — of their execution, these figures are traced freely

Fig. 40. Cave of Bayol. Ibex painted in red (from DROUOT, 1953, fig. 3).

in a continuous line, by a firm, skilful hand, and the proportions are usually respected. The horse in Pl. 288, *a* is similar, in the shape of its head and neck, to archaic figures in Franco-Cantabrian art. As a whole the works of Ebbou constitute something that recalls, on the one hand, Aquitanian and Cantabrian archaism, and yet shows, on the other, its own peculiar characteristics and individuality; for example in the manner of portraying the oxen's horns (generally only one horn, viewed in profile and turned forwards) and in the pointed feet, as well as in the general structure of the figures.

---

[1] GLORY, 1947.

Some of these stylistic elements exist in other Mediterranean graphic works that show obvious relationships with the material at Ebbou, and in particular with the examples of Sicilian Palaeolithic art that we shall shortly discuss.

The realistic art of the lower Rhone valley is therefore already somewhat detached from the focal centre of Aquitanian-Cantabrian art. This region, separated by the Cévennes from the more westerly areas of diffusion of Franco-Cantabrian art, appears in fact, from a geographical point of view as well, to be a northerly offshoot of the peripheral Mediterranean region.

On the evidence of the pictures that have been published, the other works of cave art found in this zone — in the caves of LE COLOMBIER, CHABOT and LE FIGUIER — as well as in the " Cañon " of the Ardèche and in OULLINS and BAYOL, do not appear to possess characteristics belonging to the Franco-Cantabrian style : the animals painted in the cave of Bayol in Collias show evident affinities, in the characteristic manner in which the legs are treated for instance, with the engravings of Ebbou [1] (Fig. 40).

ROMANELLI.

The first cave-wall engravings of Romanelli (Otranto) were discovered about 1905 by Paolo Emilio Stasi, and published by him in the same year in collaboration with Ettore Regalia [2]. The find consisted of only two figures, an ox and a geometrical pattern, both of considerable importance and the authors devoted to them several pages of acute observation (remarkably acute when we consider the period and the outlook prevailing at that time in the field of palaethnology).

Subsequently, on the occasion of his excavations in 1914 and 1921, Baron Blanc cleaned part of the ceiling by removing the lichen that covered it and brought to light, especially on the great cornice that traverses the ceiling itself in the form of a natural arch, various deeply engraved figures of uncertain significance, probably anthropomorphic, and some vulvar designs, of which he published tracings and photographs in 1927, accompanied by a page of comment [3].

Between 1929 and 1930 the present writer undertook an interpretative and comparative study of the Romanelli engravings, attempting to place them, together with the engravings on pebbles from the same cave, in the general frame of European Palaeolithic art [4].

On the basis of Blanc's observations the chronology of the wall engravings of Romanelli could be established by the existence, in the Upper Palaeolithic strata of the deposit, of some blocks detached from the ceiling that bear analogous engravings, as well as by the presence of engravings in parts of the ceiling where it would have been impossible to execute them after the formation of the deposit which almost fills the cave today. Furthermore, there are undeniable affinities between some of the wall engravings and engravings on pebbles found in the deposit — for instance, between the geometrical pattern in Pl. 290, b and that on the pebble in Pl. 110, e.

The most realistic figure (and, though rough and incomplete, the only one that is at least recognizable) is an ox (Pl. 290, a) on the right wall of the cave as one enters. We have said before that this, with the one next to it, was the first figure to be discovered. Although summary, the drawing is realistic and the animal's characteristics are quite effectively rendered. Its discoverers at first took it for a horse, but the line of the back and the way the head is joined

[1] DROUOT, 1953a, figs. 2, 3.
[2] REGALIA, STASI, 1905, pp. 133, 137, 164-165, 171-172.
[3] BLANC G. A., 1928, pp. 410-411, pls. XLV-LII.
[4] GRAZIOSI, 1929; idem, 1932-33.

to the body are typical of an ox. It is limited to the front part, and the outline of the back reaches about as far as the hips. The legs are missing, unless one considers a few vertical parallel lines engraved in front of the breast as representing the forelegs. The horn, viewed in profile, is very rudimentary. The animal's body is crossed by perpendicular lines that might represent darts.

A short distance from the ox, on the same wall and at the same height, is the geometrical design mentioned before, consisting of bands of vertical and oblique lines alternating with a certain regularity (Pl. 290, b)

In many parts of the ceiling are more or less deeply engraved lines, sometimes intersecting, with no apparent significance. But other lines are visible, especially on the great cornice, of which an interpretation might be attempted. They form roundish, oval and shuttle-shaped figures. Some of them, such as those in Pl. 291, a (left), b, c (right), resemble vulvar figures similar to those of La Ferrassie and Abri Blanchard (Pl. 118, a, b); others might represent fish (Pl. 291, e, extreme right). Certain shuttle-shaped figures, particularly those in Pl. 291, c (first on the left) and d, because of their resemblance to the outline of some Aurignacian-Perigordian female statuettes [1] are very probably anthropomorphic female representations, highly stylized. Affinities can also be traced in schematized, shuttle-shaped human figures in Franco-Cantabrian mobiliary art — for instance, the figures engraved on bone in Les Eyzies (Pl. 87, b), Raymonden (Pl. 87, c) and Gourdan (Pl. 86, e).

These possibly human figures are exceedingly schematized and (as seen in the sequence in Pl. 291, c) assume increasingly elongated forms until any eventual reference to the outline of a human body becomes highly improbable; they come progressively to resemble fish. If this were really the meaning of the " shuttle-shaped " figures, it would be an instance of the transformation of one subject into another, substantially different, one by means of gradual morphological distortion due perhaps to a sort of fortuitous realism — a fact that is not new in expressions of primitive art.

As one can see, the specimens of cave art in Romanelli are particularly poor and, with the exception of one definitely realistic, if very crude, ox they are all more or less schematic or abstract forms, like the examples of mobiliary art in this cave.

On another occasion we compared the cave figures of Romanelli with the expressions of Palaeolithic art in Southern Spain [2]); e. g., the ox recalls an analogous figure painted in the cave of La Pileta (Pl. 285, d). This comparison acquires validity if we take into account the affinities between the Spanish cave and the figures engraved on pebbles in Romanelli. The art of the latter cave must be considered as a whole — mobiliary and cave art together — if we would grasp its relation to the art of Southern Spain. Such a relation exists, perhaps, rather in the general sense of a particular aesthetic mentality (different in both cases from that which is fundamentally at work in Franco-Cantabrian art) than in actual stylistic points of reference.

Levanzo.

The Levanzo engravings were discovered in the summer of 1950 by Alda Micheli, Franca Minellono and the present writer, following a careful inspection of the rock walls of the cave in the course of excavations that we had undertaken in the deposit [3]).

The previous year Franca Minellono had notified the writer of her discovery of some paintings of Eneolithic date or later, in the same cave; it was as a result of that first discovery that we went to Levanzo for further research and excavation.

---

[1]) GRAZIOSI, 1932-33, pl. 5.
[2]) GRAZIOSI, 1932-33, pl. 5, pp. 28-29.
[3]) GRAZIOSI, 1950; idem, 1953.

Levanzo is a small island in the Egadi Archipelago, about 9 nautical miles from the west coast of Sicily, opposite the city of Trapani. It consists of a calcareous formation reaching a maximum height of 278 m. and a maximum length of 4 km.; it is 2 km. wide. The cave opens on the southern coast of the island, in a small cove known as " Cala Genovese ", about thirty metres above sea level, at the foot of a vertical cliff that can be reached from the beach by climbing a large cone-shaped mound of detritus.

It consists of a front chamber, open to daylight, about 12 metres deep, in which a deposit containing human artifacts was excavated, and an inner chamber about 35 metres long, absolutely dark, to which we gained access by crawling through a very narrow corridor about 3 metres long. The paintings of a later period and the engravings were found in the second, dark chamber.

The Palaeolithic age of the latter is attested by their particular style and by the fact that they represent animals typical of late Sicilian Pleistocene, such as *Bos primigenius*, *Cervus elaphus* and a small animal of the equine family, probably *Equus hydruntinus* — all species whose remains were found in the Quaternary deposit of the forepart of the cave. Furthermore, the most recent excavations brought to light, from the strata containing Palaeolithic fauna and industries, a rock fragment bearing the engraved figure of an ox with, more or less, the characteristics of the wall engravings.

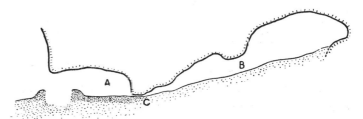

Fig. 41. Cave of Levanzo. Rough sketch showing section of forepart of cave (A) with deposit containing human artifacts, and rear of cave (B) which is accessible through a narrow underground passage (C).

These engravings indicate a very ancient physical state; their patina is the same as that of the rock surface, and their antiquity is confirmed, among other things, by the fact that one of the figures (Pl. 293) is engraved in a part of the cave where the whole rock wall underwent a process of decalcification which softened it, but which still had its normal consistency at the time the engraving was made, as proved unequivocally by the morphology of the engraving itself. The figures vary in dimension between a maximum of 53 and a minimum of 15 cm. One fragmentary figure is about 80 cm. high.

The subject matter in general is drawn from the animal world; 33 figures, including complete and incomplete ones, have been distinguished so far. They can be divided as follows : 12 horses, one of which is dubious; 10 oxen, 6 deer, one of which is dubious; one probably carnivorous animal and 4 human figures, one of which is reduced to the legs alone.

Although they are not all executed with the same skill, they show the same technical and stylistic characteristics and can therefore be considered as belonging to the same artistic phase and as being more or less contemporary.

The figures are engraved with uniform lines that vary somewhat in width and depth : in some cases where the rock is better preserved they are clearly visible; in others oblique light is needed because of the decay, at some points, of the surface — and consequently of the engravings themselves.

The style is definitely naturalistic, and in the better figures it reveals a profound sense of reality and a spirit of observation that are translated into harmonious forms; their balance recalls that of the finest works of Franco-Cantabrian art. Nevertheless, even though this vividly expressed sense of communion between the artist and nature is a characteristic shared by both forms of art, Levanzo possesses its own peculiar stylistic manner which in certain respects brings it close to the wall engravings of the Rhone valley and to some engravings in Mediterranean Spain.

In fact we might say that the outline, traced with mastery and assurance in a continuous line was the only means by which the artist could express volume; and the volume, even though lacking all elements of chiaroscuro, is generally perfectly rendered.

Most of these drawings are totally lacking in details such as the fur, eye, etc. In some figures these are suggested by lines, either on the nose or on some other part of the body, and in a couple of cases the eye is shown.

The feet are sometimes missing, and in other cases drawn in profile; ears are usually present, also tails, and in the case of two oxen the tongue protrudes (Pl. 297).

The majority of the figures are shown in profile, with all the legs visible, drawn in excellent perspective. In one instance (Pl. 298) the frontal perspective of the head and chest is successfully achieved. The horns of oxen are executed in a particularly stylized manner: invariably only one horn is visible, open at the tip, sometimes widely spread as in the animals in Pls. 297; 298, c.

Among the best engravings in Levanzo is the young deer turning its head in Pl. 293, a very lifelike figure with pure, firm outlines, comparable with the finest works of Franco-Cantabrian art.

In this connection we should point out that in works by other authors [1]), this animal has been called a horse or a donkey: it is really impossible to understand how the interpretation could be so confused, for the tail is no donkey's tail but the characteristic tail of a deer; and in addition to the ears both antlers are clearly visible on its head; moreover the head is identical, in form, with that of the young deer of Pl. 295 and very different from that of horses represented in the cave.

Another deer, also looking backwards, is very skilfully executed though somewhat harsher than the previous one (Pl. 295, a). Note here, too, the probable representation of a single antler and of an ear with open outline.

The group in Pl. 298, including a great bull with massive but agile body, is a superb piece of work. It is placed opposite the figure of another bovine, probably a cow, with head viewed in frontal perspective. Beneath the bull is a grazing horse.

Another noteworthy group is composed of a great bull with protruding tongue, of which only the forepart was executed, following a cow perfectly and soberly outlined (Pl. 297, c). This composition very much recalls, in spirit, an analogous one in the cave of La Mairie à Teyjat (Pl. 284, a).

The equines, shown in Pl. 296, a, with large head and slender legs, and Pl. 295, c with slender neck, are not horses but a species of donkey — probably *Equus asinus hydruntinus*, whose remains were found in the Quaternary deposit of the Levanzo cave. The equines in Pl. 296, c are of the same type: a mare and a foal, shown in perspective on two different planes. The animals in Pl. 297, b and in Pl. 299, a are probably horses.

We shall close these brief remarks on the Levanzo engravings by mentioning the human figures, one of which, as noted above, consists of legs shown in the act of running. Above them is the head of a great ox with protruding tongue (Pl. 297, a, b).

Three more figures are joined to form a little composition (Pl. 300): the incomplete figure on the left has raised arms and appears to possess a sort of beak. The central figure has no arms, its head is cone-shaped and a string-like appendage falling on to its breast is probably a beard. Along the outline of the head, shoulders and torso is a series of parallel lines; a sort of belt formed by five lines surrounds its waist. The third figure, too, has a cone-shaped head, and, like the others, no features; its arms are bent down in an arc and its legs are widespread. It appears to be dancing; some lines on its left arm are probably bracelets. Above this group is a band of parallel lines of obscure significance. Like the majority of anthropomorphic figures in Franco-Cantabrian art, the human figures of Levanzo are much more clumsy and less realistic than the animals.

A last word on the subject of anthropomorphic representation in Levanzo: besides the black paintings of a late period to which we have alluded above (p. 196) there is a human

---

[1]) BREUIL, 1952, fig. 524; KÜHN, 1952, pl. 31; BANDI, MARINGER, 1952, fig. 16.

figure painted in red, in a different style from the rather schematic black ones. This red figure tends towards realism. If we compare it with the figure on the right of the Palaeolithic engraved group, we note the same movement in one of the arms bent in an arc and in the entire body, the same characteristic cone-shaped head from which, in both cases, what is probably a beard hangs down; furthermore, both figures have one leg bent.

We do not attach undue importance to this resemblance, for as far as we know it might simply constitute an indication, to be ultimately confirmed, of the existence in Sicily of pictorial expressions simultaneously with Palaeolithic engravings.

It is worth noting that at the time when the engravings were executed and the strata containing Pleistocene fauna were formed, the island of Levanzo was joined to Sicily; it is impossible, in fact, that a rock 4 kilometres long at the most could have furnished subsistence for the wild animals portrayed on the walls of the cave and whose remains were found in the actual deposit. This is further confirmed by the fact that a wide shoal, whose deepest point today is but 40 metres, extends between Levanzo, the nearby island of Favignano and the Sicilian coast. Therefore, during the Würm glaciation (when the level of the sea was 90 metres lower than at present) a wide strip of land must have joined the two islands to Sicily. The Palaeolithic age of the Levanzo engravings is thus unquestionable.

This rapid overall view of the engraved figures in the Levanzo cave clearly indicates that a vividly naturalistic art, already considerably evolved if very simple in its graphic characteristics, flourished during the Upper Palaeolithic in this central area of the Mediterranean.

Undoubtedly it is very close to the classic art of the Franco-Cantabrian province; on the other hand, as we have seen, it shows some individual traits that are not found in Aquitania and Cantabria but relate, in certain respects, to other works of cave and mobiliary art in the province that we have called Mediterranean.

With regard to the former, we have already mentioned the engravings of Ebbou in the lower Rhone valley, which, while recalling some examples of Franco-Cantabrian art (like the Levanzo engravings), nevertheless have their own special characteristics that are repeated in the Sicilian cave: e. g., the sober design, consisting almost exclusively of an outline; the absence of detail; the manner of representing the horns of oxen, etc.

The mobiliary art of Parpallò shows even more definite affinities with Levanzo; for instance, the horns of oxen are sometimes represented in an identical manner, with open outline (Fig. 14); the shape often recalls, in its simplicity and elegance, the animal figures of Levanzo.

Romanelli, with its abstract and geometrical character, is certainly very different from the Sicilian cave. The only naturalistic wall figure, the ox in Pl. 29c, a, is particularly crude; nevertheless here too the horn is treated in the same way as the antlers of the young deer turning its head in Levanzo (Pl. 295, a).

To conclude, North African cave art — which, at least as far as present documentation is concerned, is later than Palaeolithic — shows points of comparison with Levanzo, particularly the engravings of Arréchin in Fezzan [1]), of Spanish Morocco [2]), and others.

We shall discuss later the position that Levanzo might assume within the frame of cave art in the Mediterranean province, and of Palaeolithic art in general.

MONTE PELLEGRINO.

Two years after the Levanzo engravings were discovered another very interesting group of engravings came to light in a Sicilian cave: Addaura near Palermo, one of a group of contiguous caves sheltered by an overhanging cliff on Monte Pellegrino. Giosuè Meli discovered

---

[1]) GRAZIOSI, 1942, pls. 120, 121 and *passim*.
[2]) ALMAGRO, 1944, *passim*.

them by following the directions of a local labourer whom he had questioned about the possible existence of cave figures in that area. A study of the Addaura figures made by Signora Bovio Marconi, Superintendent of Antiquities in Palermo, underlined their great importance from every point of view. These new documents of cave art were illustrated in various publications to which we refer the reader for further details [1]). We shall give a brief description of the figures accompanied by a few personal comments.

The little cave of Addaura, known as Addaura II, which opens under an overhanging cliff facing the sea on Monte Pellegrino, is of small dimensions (6,05 m. long by 5,28 m. wide, with an opening that widens to 6,35 metres) : it is therefore well lighted, as are also the figures engraved at the back of it, to the left.

At one time it must have been filled, to a height of between 1,80 and 3 metres from the actual ground level, by a deposit containing human artifacts, removed at an unascertained date; a small amount of concreted layer containing mollusc shells and fragments of flint still adheres to the walls.

The external talus, when excavated by Marconi and Bernabò Brea, produced some Upper Palaeolithic Sicilian industries in the deepest layer of the deposit, while the higher layers, which had been disturbed, " must have contained more evolved, perhaps Mesolithic artifacts " [2]).

The engravings, having the same patina as the rock surface, are situated at a height of 2,15 and 3 metres above the actual ground level; some of them are partially covered by concreted remains of the archaeological deposit. This proves that they are earlier than the higher layers of the deposit itself.

In another cavity of the great Addaura shelter known as cave B, opening to the east of Addaura II, two mediocre figures of oxen were later discovered (Pl. 305, b, c). Marconi distinguishes three different engraving processes in Addaura II : a) fine, rather superficial line; b) deep, wide incision with triangular section; c) deep incision, different from the preceding one. Human figures and animals were executed with the first process, human figures and one animal with the second, and only two animals with the third.

In Addaura, as opposed to all that we have seen in Palaeolithic art, the majority of figures are anthropomorphic — 17, against about 15 animals, including some fragmentary ones. The figures engraved with a deep incision are almost exclusively human beings — ten, against a single animal figure in the second group. In the first group, on the other hand, the majority consists of animal figures; about a dozen — most of them fragmentary — as against seven humans. Only two animals were found in the third group.

A very peculiar aspect of Addaura is therefore the predominance of human figures, not only numerical but also, one might say, topographical, where they all form a great central group on the wall, clearly visible, deeply engraved and accurately executed. The animals, on the contrary, are placed peripherally, and by and large are far less visible.

The human figures of Addaura are substantially different from the figures of Franco-Cantabrian art considered as a whole. Although the features, and in general the hands and feet, are not represented, and the heads are sometimes elongated into a kind of beak, the men of Addaura are nevertheless generally decidedly realistic. Although quite simple from a graphic point of view, they are executed with great mastery, anatomically well conceived and full of life and dynamism.

The arms and legs follow the movement of the flexible bodies with perfect rhythm and balance; foreshortening is freely treated, and frontal perspective brilliantly achieved — as in the man with raised arms at the upper centre of the group in Pl. 301. Here is a whole

---

[1]) MARCONI BOVIO, 1952-53; *idem*, 1953; *idem*, 1953a.
[2]) MARCONI BOVIO, 1952-53; p. 16.

world of forms and rhythms, very different from Franco-Cantabrian anthropomorphism if only because of the well-defined, clearly scenic intention evident in the suggestive grouping of the Addaura figures. In fact the principal group (Pl. 301) forms a scene whose significance, for the present, escapes us, although many interpretations have been offered, some of them quite extravagant [1]).

In fact, as Marconi points out, a connection undoubtedly exists between the various individuals, revealed by their postures and by their respective positions: they are turned towards a centre formed by two human beings, horizontally placed, around which others appear to be performing a dance or a ritual march. It is impossible to say how many figures belong to the principal scene: the three figures at the top and the ones to the left of the central group are unmistakably involved; the figure at the bottom centre, bent fowards as if dancing or marking time, is also probably included in the scene. The figure partly distinguishable on the left of the previous one, and the other two figures preceding it on the right, may be extraneous to the composition.

The significance of this group is very hard to explain; we believe that on the strength of a single work any hypothesis is open to criticism. Marconi's own theory (in which the entire composition should be considered as being connected with the representation of initiatory rites, perhaps involving virility) is the most convincing, if the accentuation of the sex in the central figures, whose slender bodies, as she says, could be the bodies of adolescents, is intended to express a particular sign of virility. In this connection, however, a doubt arises as to whether the emphasized sex might not be a phallic sheath, owing to its curious appearance, for it is scored by a longitudinal segment in the same manner as the beak-shaped appendage on the head of the man with raised arms to the right.

The postures of the two central figures are really hard to interpret. They are, first of all, emphatically alive and dynamic: the bodies are arched, the legs sharply bent — actually flexed so as to touch the gluteus region with their heels. The arms of the upper figure are stretched forwards, whereas in the lower they are bent at the elbows, with hand touching the shoulders or grasping the neck; or they might be holding a sort of rope, represented by a line drawn parallel to the body, tied around the feet at the other end. The constriction of this hypothetical rope would explain the sharply bent knees. Both arms are drawn in correct perspective, only the elbow of the right arm showing beyond the outline of the head. This figure seems to be leaning its elbows on the ground and arching its body upwards. The figure above it covers, for reasons of perspective, the knees of the former (which is represented as being the farther from the observer) and also shows a similar tension of the legs and trunk; here too a double line — perhaps representing one or two segments of rope — starts at the feet and reaches the shoulders. It seems slightly less taut than in the other figure. In this case the arms are not bent behind the back but stretched out and lightly flexed. A line crosses the torso obliquely; it might be interpreted as a prolongation of the rope (or of one of the two ropes) passed around the man's shoulders.

Assuming that Marconi's definition of the two figures as acrobats is correct, we might imagine, as a simple hypothesis, two phases of an acrobatic excercise: one during the tension of the rope, the other at an earlier or later stage when the end of the rope is not fixed but falls around the acrobat's shoulders.

Naturally these hypotheses have no value other than that of a simple " intellectual exercise "; one might even think, for instance, that if the ropes really represent shackles starting at the feet, the violently contorted legs could belong to prisoners; or suppose that the segments are not ropes binding the feet, but items of clothing — as Marconi also suggests.

Undoubtedly the two central figures of the composition appear powerfully to attract

---

[1]) MARCONI, 1953; idem, 1955; CHIAPPELLA, 1954; BLANC, 1954a.

the interest of the surrounding figures, judging from the attitude of apparent amazement or emotion expressed by their raised arms. The heads of some of these personages end, as we noted before, in a curious beak that also exists in other figures, such as the one below and to the right of the central ones (Pl. 301), those in Pl. 303 centre, and in Pl. 302 right. The human figures generally have what looks like thick hair; some, however, are completely bald — like one of the two figures with raised arms in Pl. 301. One of the individuals at the centre, in the dynamic posture described above, has a thick head of hair; the other has a smooth, roundish head.

To continue this brief examination of the engravings of Addaura, we call attention to a female figure, reproduced in Pls. 302 (upper right) and 303 (lower left). It carries a large bundle on its back and walks, like the others, with long strides. Above this woman (Pl. 303) a man with thick hair is carrying a pole; he may be related to the fine figure of a fallow deer below him.

Passing on to the animals, with the exception of the two schematic oxen that we shall shortly discuss, they are exclusively deer and equines. The magnificent fallow deer mentioned above is executed with great realism; form and volume are perfectly achieved without resorting to chiaroscuro; the outline is pure, linear and very lifelike. The head is identical to another, engraved with a very fine line under the legs of the individual to the right of the principal scene, shown in Pl. 301. Although this figure, as opposed to the other fallow deer, is very lightly engraved, it shows such affinity of style with the former as to be unhesitatingly placed in the same artistic phase (Pl. 305, a).

The equine figures, particularly the figure in Pl. 302, a, are very similar to the Levanzo equines: see, for instance, the hindquarters of the Addaura ones, represented in the same manner as the hindquarters of the Levanzo donkey in Pl. 296, a.

On the other hand the general characteristics of these zoomorphic engravings are shared by analogous figures in the Egadi cave: simple outlines, completely, or almost completely, lacking in detail. As in Levanzo, here too not all the animals are perfectly drawn, and not all reveal the same workmanship.

The human figure of Addaura, on the other hand, is completely different from the human figure of Levanzo: it is on another plane, and we seek in vain among the fine anthropomorphic figures of the Palermo cave for possible analogies with the three poorly executed little figures of the Egadi islands. The only affinity — not a stylistic one — is found in the beak-shaped head of one of the Levanzo figures.

It is very difficult to explain this great divergence in anthropomorphic representations where undeniable affinities exist among the zoomorphic pictures in the two caves; nor can it be justified, in this case, by the existence of different phases or strata, for the fine anthropomorphic figures of Addaura seem to be unmistakably related to some at least of the animal figures in the same cave, and we cannot, for the present, dissociate the three human beings of Levanzo from the animal figures, to which they are related by technique, physical condition, etc.

For the time being we prefer simply to note the facts stated above, without venturing any hypothesis whatsoever on the subject.

We have seen that Marconi divided the engravings of Addaura into three groups distinguished by different technical processes: figures engraved with a fine, superficial line; or engraved with a deep, wide, triangular incision, or thirdly with an incision equally deep but different from the preceding one. The present writer's brief visit to Addaura confirmed for him the existence of these distinctive processes. The examination — unfortunately very rapid — that he was able to make of the engraved wall left the following impressions: the style and character of the human figures, both deeply and lightly engraved, are practically identical; they show the same manner of dealing with anatomy, the same movement, the same characteristic garb. On the other hand, the only animal deeply engraved like the human figures of the principal group, the great fallow deer, is stylistically identical with the finely traced antelope's head underlying the man with raised arms (Pls. 303; 305, a). Undoubtedly the figures executed with a deeper incision — the ten men of the principal scene and the large animal — are partly superimposed upon lightly engraved figures and were therefore executed at a later date, but this does not seem to have any value with regard to a real succession of different phases of art : the same people, the same artists used the same surface within a very short period, to create new works, and the process of deeper incision may have been used to give greater relief to the new figures executed over the older ones. Rather than two distinct art phases, these different groups denote separate moments of creation : all the human beings of Addaura, and consequently a large number of the animals as well, must have belonged to the same art and the same culture.

The two oxen, on the other hand, show an unmistakable divergence in character and style from the other animals portrayed in Addaura. Also the technique, as Marconi observes, varies from that of the other figures : in the present writer's opinion the difference is inherent in the clumsy outline, which is here and there hesitant and retouched. This peculiarity is shared by both figures, although one (Pl. 304, c) is more deeply engraved than the other (Pl. 304, b). These oxen, therefore, should be placed on an artistic and technical level much inferior to that of the other figures in the Palermo cave; awkward and crude in style; lacking proportion; harsh in line; angular, casual drawing — particularly of the figure in Pl. 304, b, which is inferior in every way to the other and gives the impression of being of a later date. In one of the figures the limbs are barely suggested, in the other they end in a point, in a similar manner to that which we have noted in the figures of Ebbou (Ardèche) (Pl. 288).

The horns of both animals are characteristically turned forwards and open at the tip, as in Levanzo. With regard to their relative chronology, while considering them of a different age from the other engravings in the same cave, we would not venture to place them so far from the latter as to exclude the possibility that they might have been influenced by some elements of the dominant style of animal representation in Levanzo. The typical form of the horns, which is encountered both in Levanzo and in Addaura, speaks of obvious ties between the two caves.

Also the figures found in the nearby little cave B, to which we referred above, are very poorly executed; crude and faulty in design. The outline of one is more sinuous and recalls the ox mentioned in a previous chapter (pp. 113-114; Pl. 111), engraved on a stone in the Palaeolithic deposit of Levanzo; the other, harsher one, has three radiating lines on its head — probably the schematized representation of horns or ears, and perhaps even of a weapon.

To conclude these remarks on cave art in Sicily and in the Mediterranean province generally, we should mention the very recent discovery of animal figures engraved in a little cave on the south-west flank of the same Monte Pellegrino : the cave of NISCEMI, discovered in 1954 [1]).

Three bulls and two small horses are all executed in approximately the same style as the animals of Addaura and Levanzo (Pl. 306). The bulls, one of which is incomplete, are outlined with vigour and assurance; the bodies are massive and the heads small; two of them have a single horn showing, whereas the third has two horns, with open outlines, in correct perspective.

The horses are identically represented with forelegs rigidly extended, the left leg thrust forwards as in the horse of Addaura and the fawn of Levanzo in Pl. 295, b. The mane is

[1]) MARCONI BOVIO, 1954-55.

short and thick, roughly indicated by a series of short parallel lines, as in the Levanzo animal in Pl. 295, *c*.

The discovery of the Niscemi engravings further emphasized the stylistic links between the zoomorphic cave art of Monte Pellegrino and the little island of Levanzo.

* * *

A fundamental fact emerges from this examination of the engravings of Monte Pellegrino : the originality of this art, the very special place it undeniably occupies in the panorama of early and late prehistoric art. It is connected with Levanzo as we have seen by animal figures both of Addaura and Niscemi, and from this point of view it might be inserted in the rather hazy picture of the art of the Mediterranean province. But the extraordinary anthropomorphic representations of Addaura prevent us from making further comparisons and ties. Franco-Cantabrian art, of course, sometimes treats the human figure in a realistic manner; apart from the Aurignacian-Perigordian bas-reliefs and statuettes, even in the Magdalenian period we occasionally encounter nudes expressed in a well-balanced, realistic form, both in mobiliary art — as in La Madeleine (Pl. 86, *b*) — and in cave art, as in Angles-sur-Anglin (Pl. 162, *a*) and La Magdeleine (Pl. 163). These instances, however, are far from frequent, and they totally lack the spirit, dynamism and exuberant vitality that animate the Addaura figures and combine them into complex lifelike scenes. In order to establish comparisons we should find compositions of anthropomorphic figures possessing the three essential elements forming the fundamental character of Addaura — realism, dynamism and scenic intent. In Levanzo, the three little human figures do, in fact, appear to form a scene, and a certain rudimentary dynamism is apparent; but it is impossible to compare them, from the point of view of style and anatomical realism, with the superb, mature representations of Addaura.

Leaving Palaeolithic cave art our attention is attracted by the Mesolithic pictorial art of Eastern Spain, particularly for its dynamism and the scenic character of its pictures of men and animals. But if we proceed to analyse the morphology and style of those human figures, we shall see that while in Addaura they are expressed in realistic terms (although some elements of stylization begin to emerge) in the pictorial art of Eastern Spain they attain a sort of expressionism that distorts the human form, shaping it to suit specific expressive requirements and producing something very different from the well-constructed figures of the Palermo cave.

The art of Eastern Spain represents, compared with Addaura, a development of those dynamic tendencies firmly established in the Sicilian cave, a development leading in the extreme Spanish pictures to an increasingly exaggerated distortion of the realities of the human form in favour of greater expressiveness of movement.

Where else should we seek comparisons? Marconi rightly points out a possible affinity with North African cave art and particularly with Hoggar [1]). In fact, some elements of resemblance with the men of Addaura can be traced in the immense repertory of figures engraved and painted on the rocks of the Sahara desert. Here a sense of composition is particularly stressed at times, and the human figures occasionally show in the different phases of that art, a fine, exuberant dynamism; furthermore, the morphology of single figures is sometimes far more realistic than in the figures of Eastern Spain.

Besides the paintings of Wadi Mertutek in Hoggar [2]) to which Marconi refers, possible elements of comparison should be sought in the rich, inexhaustible galleries of cave art in the cliffs and caves of the Tasili region, in Southern Algeria on the Fezzan border : Wadi

[1]) MARCONI BOVIO, 1952-53, p. 13.
[2]) CHASSELOUP-LAUBAT, 1938.

Gerat produced engravings of masked, half-naked men in lively postures, anatomically correct, which in certain respects recall Addaura [1]). Among the many paintings discovered by Brenans and J. Tschudi, and recently among the extraordinary findings reproduced by H. Lhote, in other localities of the Tasili region, there are points of reference with the Sicilian cave [2]). Also in the Saharan Atlas — in Ksar el Ahmar for instance [3]) — we have figures of men in frontal perspective, of a fine naturalistic order, with arms raised as in Addaura. Finally, in the Sahara (Wadi Arréchin in Fezzan and elsewhere) a certain similarity can also be detected with the animals of Levanzo (and therefore also of Addaura).

To conclude, even if the anthropomorphic representations of Addaura fail to suggest convincing comparisons with Franco-Cantabrian Palaeolithic art, while keeping their sharp individuality they do sometimes recall the post-Palaeolithic art of Eastern Spain, and more definitely still, of the Sahara region.

Let us now summarize briefly some of our observations on the art of the Mediterranean region, taking into consideration also what we have said before on the subject of its mobiliary art.

First of all we should emphasize that the separation of this artistic centre from the great Franco-Cantabrian province does not amount, at present, to a definite stylistic selection, but should be regarded simply as a subdivision based primarily upon simple geographical criteria and used for the convenience of exposition.

However, an analysis of the material known from this vast Mediterranean area shows, as we have seen, that many of the works assume, in their various groupings, certain personal characteristics that distinguish them from the canon of Franco-Cantabrian art and show them as evolving along their own specific lines, while maintaining more or less close ties of relationship and origin according to their location.

These trends are towards schematic, abstract forms or naturalistic forms — where they do not exist together in the same place, as in the mobiliary art of Parpalló, the cave art of La Pileta or, especially, in the mobiliary art of Tivoli. The naturalistic trend, which undeniably reflects Franco-Cantabrian art, produced the engravings and paintings on pebbles of Parpalló, the engravings of Tivoli, a few other mediocre engravings — always in the realm of mobiliary art — in Italy (Monopoli, Romanelli), some of the cave paintings of La Pileta, the engravings of Ebbou and of other Languedoc caves, and those of Levanzo and Addaura. The abstract or geometrical trend appears exuberantly in the form of mobiliary art on the pebbles of Parpalló, particularly in the Upper Magdalenian layers of that cave, sometimes accompanied by realistic figures; on the stones of Romanelli — where it almost predominates — on a few pebbles in Barma Grande, on the " bâtons de commandement " of Arene Candide (in a very elementary form), on pebbles and bone fragments in Tivoli; it also appears in the form of cave art in La Pileta, simultaneously with naturalistic figures; in La Baume-Latrone and in Romanelli (in the two latter cases accompanied by rare attempts at realism).

There are two distinct forms of expression, therefore, that nevertheless seem to be closely linked with each other, at least at the point of origin. In fact even where realistic works are not accompanied — as in Levanzo — by schematic or geometrical works, they still show obvious affinities with other naturalistic representations in places such as Parpalló, where they appear next to figures of a schematic, abstract order. The two trends therefore coexist in the Mediterranean province, and according to the place and time of their appearance, they balance or prevail over one another. Unfortunately we do not yet possess sufficient material to establish the possible significance of all this from a chronological point of view; the determination of the age of Sicilian cave art is particularly uncertain, owing to the diffi-

---

[1]) PERRET, 1936, pls. VIII 1, IX 1; REYGASSE, 1935, fig. 11.
[2]) BREUIL, LHOTE, 1954, *passim*; TSCHUDI, 1952, *passim*; LHOTE, 1958, *passim*.
[3]) FLAMAND, 1921, pl. XI.

culty of situating Upper Palaeolithic Sicilian industries in the general framework of the development of Palaeolithic cultures in Europe.

With regard to the relationship of " Mediterranean " art to the art of Franco-Cantabria, many hypotheses might be ventured — but they would still be no more than hypotheses and, owing to the scarcity of material, very frail ones at that. We may at least observe that on the walls of Franco-Cantabrian caves, next to splendid realistic works, we have — if in a minor key — an entire range of signs and figures, more or less geometrical, whose significance is obscure and which appear to involve a sort of symbolism. These are signs known under such conventional and generic terms as tectiforms, pectiforms, club-signs, etc. We may therefore imagine that from France and the Pyrenees an ancient artistic substratum spread through the Mediterranean basin; the antiquity of this substratum would explain some of the archaic characteristics of the naturalistic animal figures of Parpallò, the Southern Spanish caves and the Ardèche region, for within it both trends existed at the start and developed, outside the Franco-Cantabrian region (where the realistic trend triumphed), with the ultimate predominance of the symbolical-schematic (Iberian peninsula, Apulia, North African Capsian) or the naturalistic trend (Sicily).

While we are still in the realm of the hypothetical, we may even suppose that these different trends clearly present in the Mediterranean province led, in post-Palaeolithic times, on the one hand (the schematic-symbolical) to the schematic art that was diffused over a great part of Europe, and on the other (the realistic) to the examples of dynamic, impressionistic art, in which the human figure plays so important a part, in Eastern Spain and the Sahara. This, moreover, might explain certain affinities between the animal figures of Ebbou or Levanzo and analogous engravings in Fezzan and other districts of North Africa.

DISTRIBUTION   MAPS

2. MAP SHOWING DISTRIBUTION OF CAVES AND ROCK SHELTERS CONTAINING WORKS

Inset map labels:
Périgueux
Vézère
39 40
38 41
Les Eyzies 37 43
36 Beune
34 42
35 Sarlat 44
33
32
Dordogne
Couze
Céou

Main map labels:
69 Nottingham
London
86 Hamburg
85
Brussels
Namur 74
70 71 72 73
Bonn 84
83 Coblenz
Mainz
82
Rhine
79
78 Ulm
Paris
Seine
75 77
76
62 Dijon
Bern
Loire
Poitiers 60
59 61
57 58
56
64 Bourg
63 Maçon 65
66 Geneva
67
55 54 Lyon
53 52
51 50 47
49 46 Rhône
31 48
Périgueux
Bordeaux
Dordogne Les Eyzies (32-45)
Genoa
94
93
30 68
29 Nîmes
Garonne
Montpellier
Santander
6 7 Bilbao
3 13
Oviedo 12 Pau 22 Toulouse
5 8 9 Tarbes
4 10 14 15 16 20 21 24 25
11 17 18 19 23 27
26 28
Burgos
Douro
2 Tarragona
Madrid
Tajo
Valencia
1
Lisbon
Málaga
Cádiz
Gibraltrar
0 80 160 200 km

1. MAP SHOWING DISTRIBUTION OF WORKS OF MOBILIARY ART MENTIONED

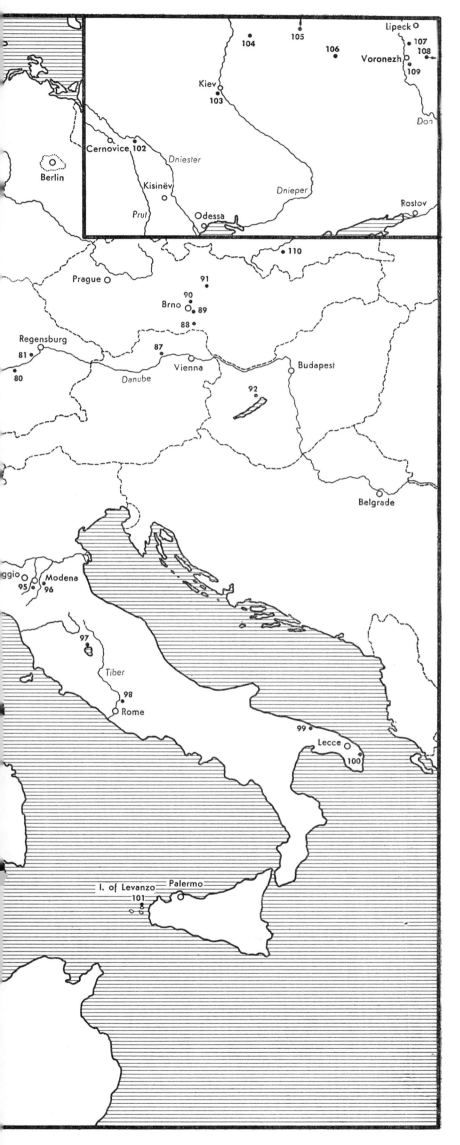

SPAIN

1. Parpalló (El).
2. Sant Gregori.
3. Cueto de la Mina (El).
4. Hornos de la Peña.
5. Castillo (El).
6. Altamira.
7. Pendo (El).
8. Rascaño (El).
9. Valle (El).
10. Santimamiñe.

FRANCE

11. Isturitz.
12. Duruthy.
13. Brassempouy.
14. Arudy.
15. Lourdes.
16. Lorthet.
17. Labastide.
18. Gourdan.
19. Gargas.
20. Lespugue.
21. Marsoulas.
22. Tuc d'Audoubert (Le).
23. Trois Frères (Les), En-lène.
24. Mas d'Azil (Le).
25. Portel (Le).
26. Massat.
27. Bédeilhac.
28. Vache (La).
29. Bruniquel.
30. Fontalés.
31. Fées (Les).
32. Jean-Blancs.
33. Lalinde (La Roche).
34. Limeuil.
35. Mouthe (La).
36. Gorge d'Enfer.
37. Laugerie Basse, Laugerie Haute.
38. Eyzies (Les), Bout-du-Monde (Le).
39. Villepin.
40. Madeleine (La).
41. Labatut.
42. Rey.
43. Sireuil.
44. Pech de la Boissière.
45. Péchialet.
46. Badégoule.
47. Puy-de-Lacan.
48. Lachaud.
49. Raymonden.
50. Rebières.
51. Fourneau du Diable (Le).
52. Teyjat : La Mairie, Abri Mège.
53. Roc de Sers (Le).
54. Montgaudier.
55. Placard (Le) (Roche-bertier).
56. Chaffaud.
57. Marche (La).
58. Loubressac.
59. Laraux.
60. Angles-sur-Anglin.
61. Saint-Marcel.
62. Trilobite (Le).
63. Saut-du-Perron.
64. Solutré.
65. Colombière (La).
66. Veyrier (Le).
67. Hoteaux (Les).
68. Pont-du-Gard.

ENGLAND

69. Creswell Crags.

BELGIUM

70. Trou Margrite, Trou de Chaleux.
71. Furfooz, (Trou du Frontal).
72. Sy-Verlaine.
73. Juzaine (Coléoptère).
74. Marche les Dames, Goyet.

SWITZERLAND

75. Kesslerloch.
76. Schweizersbild.

GERMANY

77. Petersfels.
78. Vogelherd.
79. Hohlenstein.
80. Neuburg.
81. Klause.
82. Mainz.
83. Andernach.
84. Oberkassel.
85. Balver Höhle.
86. Ahrensburg.

AUSTRIA

87. Willendorf.

CZECHOSLOVAKIA

88. Dolní Věstonice Pavlov.
89. Brno.
90. Pekarna.
91. Předmostí.

HUNGARY

92. Pörgölhegy.

ITALY

93. Balzi Rossi.
94. Arene Candide.
95. Chiozza.
96. Savignano.
97. Trasimeno.
98. Tivoli.
99. Monopoli.
100. Romanelli.
101. Levanzo.

RUSSIA

102. Molodova.
103. Kiev.
104. Mézine.
105. Jelisejeviči.
106. Avdejevo.
107. Gagarino.
108. Maltà, Burieti (Siberia).
109. Kostienki.

POLAND

110. Maszycka.

IN THE TEXT.

SPAIN

1. Palomas (Las).
2. Pileta (La).
3. Ardales.
4. Cala (La).
5. Reguerillo (El).
6. Hoz (La).
7. Casares (Los).
8. Atapuerca.
9. Penches.
10. Mestas (Las).
11. Peña de Candamo (La).
12. Buxu (El).
13. Pindal.
14. Loja (La).
15. Meaza (La).
16. Aguas de Novales (Las).
17. Clotilde de Santa Isabel (La).
18. Altamira.
19. Santian.
20. Pendo (El).
21. Monte Castillo : Pasiega (La), Castillo (El), Chimeneas (Las), Monedas (Las).
22. Hornos de la Peña.
23. Salitré.
24. Covalanas.
25. Venta de la Perra (La).
26. Haza (La).
27. Sotarriza.
28. Santimamiñe.
29. Berroberria.

FRANCE

30. Isturitz.
31. Etcheberri Sasiziloaga.
32. Labastide.
33. Gargas.
34. Tibiran.
35. Montespan.
36. Marsoulas.
37. Tuc d'Audoubert (Le).
38. Trois Frères (Les).
39. Mas d'Azil (Le).
40. Portel (Le).
41. Bédeilhac.
42. Niaux.
43. Ussat (Les Églises).
44. Sallèles - Cabardès (Gazel).
45. Aldène.
46. Magdeleine (La).
47. Pech-Merle.
48. Cantal.
49. Marcenac.
50. Sainte-Eulalie.

51. Cougnac.
52. Rocamadour : Les Merveilles, Abri Murat.
53. Terme Pialat.
54. Jean-Blancs.
55. Lalinde (La Roche).
56. Barabao.
57. Ferrassie (La).
58. Gorge d' Enfer, Oreille d' Enfer.
59. Laugerie Basse, Laugerie Haute.
60. Croze à Gontran (La).
61. Mouthe (La).
62. Font-de-Gaume.
63. Combarelles (Les).
64. Calévie (La).
65. Bernifal.
66. Beyssac, Nancy.
67. Commarque.
68. Grèze (La).
69. Cap Blanc.
70. Laussel.
71. Labatut.
72. Blanchard.
73. Castanet.
74. Reverdit.
75. Belcayre.
76. Rouffignac.
77. Lascaux.
78. Sudrie (La).
79. Pair-non-Pair.
80. Gabillou (Le).
81. Fourneau du Diable (Le).
82. Villars.
83. Mairie à Teyjat (La).
84. Chaire à Calvin (La).
85. Roc de Sers (Le).
86. Angles-sur-Anglin.
87. Arcy-sur-Cure (Grotte du Cheval).
88. Ebbou.
89. Colombier (Le).
90. Figuier (Le).
91. Ouillins.
92. Chabot.
93. Baume Latrone (La).
94. Bayol.

GERMANY

95. Schulerloch (?).

ITALY

96. Romanelli.
97. Monte Pellegrino (Addaura Niscemi).
98. Levanzo.

LOCATION OF WORKS OF MOBILIARY ART
SHOWN ON DISTRIBUTION MAP [1]

SPAIN

ALTAMIRA **6** (*Santillana, Santander*). Cartailhac, Breuil 1906, pp. 271-274; Breuil, Obermaier 1935, pp. 167-174.

CASTILLO (EL) **5** (*Puente Viesgo, Santander*). Breuil, Obermaier 1912, pp. 8-14; Id. 1913, pp. 3-5.

CUETO DE LA MINA **3** (*Llanes, Asturias*). Vega del Sella 1916.

HORNOS DE LA PEÑA **4** (*Torrelavega, Santander*). Breuil, Obermaier 1912, pp. 6-8.

PARPALLÒ (EL) **1** (*Gandia, Valencia*). Pericot 1942.

PENDO (EL) **7** (*Escobedo, Santander*). Carballo, Gonzales Echegaray 1952 ; Carballo, Larin 1932; Obermaier 1932.

RASCAÑO (EL) **8** (*Mirones, Santander*). Obermaier 1923.

SANT GREGORI **2** (*Falset, Valencia*). Vilaseca 1934.

SANTIMAMIÑE **10** (*Cortézubi, Vizcaya*). Aranzadi, Barandiaran 1935.

VALLE (EL) **9** (*Rasines, Santander*). Breuil, Obermaier 1912, p. 2; Id. 1913, pp. 2-3.

FRANCE

ANGLES-SUR-ANGLIN **60** (*Vienne*). Rousseau 1933; Garrod 1949; Saint-Mathurin, Garrod 1951.

ARUDY (Gr. des Espélugues) **14** (*Basses-Pyrénées*). Mascaraux 1910; Piette 1904; Id. 1907 *passim*.

BADÉGOULE **46** (*Bersac, Dordogne*). Cheynier 1949.

BÉDEILHAC **27** (*Tarascon, Ariège*). Begouen H. 1929; Id. 1949; Malvesin-Fabre, Nougier, Robert 1953; Octobon 1950; Robert 1943; Id. 1951; Id. 1953; Robert, Kühn 1952.

BOUT-DU-MONDE (LE) **38** (*Les Eyzies, Dordogne*). Alcalde del Rio, Breuil, Sierra 1911, pp. 222-225.

BRASSEMPOUY (Grotte du Pape) **13** (*Landes*). Piette 1895; Id. 1906; Id. 1907 *passim*; Piette, La Porterie 1897; Id. 1898.

BRUNIQUEL **29** (*Tarn-et-Garonne*). Cartailhac 1885; Breuil 1905 a; Bétirac 1952.

CHAFFAUD **56** (*Savigné, Vienne*). Bertrand 1887; Cartailhac 1903.

COLOMBIÈRE (LA) **65** (*Poncin, Aïn*). Mayet, Pissot 1915; Novius 1949; Id. 1952.

DURUTHY **12** (*Sordes, Landes*). Lartet, Chaplain Duparc 1874.

ENLÈNE, see TROIS FRÈRES (LES).

EYZIES (GR. DES) **38** (*Dordogne*). Capitan, Breuil, Peyrony 1906.

FÉES (LES) **31** (*Marcamps, Gironde*). Daleau 1875.

FONTALÉS **30** (*Saint-Antonin, Tarn et Garonne*). Darasse 1955.

FOURNEAU DU DIABLE (LE) **51** (*Bourdeilles, Dordogne*). Peyrony 1932 a.

GARGAS **19** (*Aventignan, Htes-Pyrénées*). Breuil 1952 a.

GORGE D'ENFER **36** (*Tayac, Dordogne*). Girod, Massenat 1900.

GOURDAN **18** (*Hte-Garonne*). Piette 1904; Id. 1907 *passim*.

HOTEAUX (LES) **67** (*Rossillon, Aïn*). Tournier, Guillon 1895; Boule 1895.

ISTURITZ **11** (*Hasparren, Basses-Pyrénées*). Passemard 1944; Saint Périer 1930; Id. 1936; Id. 1952.

JEAN-BLANCS **32** (*Bayac, Dordogne*). Peyrony D., Peyrony E. 1934.

LACHAUD **48** (*Terrasson, Dordogne*). Cheynier 1953.

LABASTIDE **17** (*Aventignan, Hautes-Pyrénées*). Begouen H. 1938; Simonnet 1947; Id. 1950.

LABATUT **41** (*Sergeac, Dordogne*). Breuil 1929.

LALINDE (Gr. de la Roche) **33** (*Dordogne*). Peyrony 1930.

LARAUX **59** (*Lussac-les-Châteaux, Vienne*). Pradel, Chollet 1950.

LAUGERIE BASSE, LAUGERIE HAUTE **37** (*Les Eyzies, Dordogne*). Bourlon 1916; Breuil 1934 a; Cartailhac, Breuil 1907; Girod, Massenat 1900; Maury 1924; Peyrony D., Peyrony E. 1938; Piette 1906 *passim*.

LESPUGUE (Grottes des Harpons, des Boeufs, des Rideaux) **20** (*Hte-Garonne*). Saint Périer 1922; Id. 1924; Id. 1925; Id. 1926.

---

[1] The localities are listed in alphabetical order, grouped under countries and accompanied by a few bibliographical notes. Each name is followed by a number that also marks its location on the distribution map.

ENGLAND

BELGIUM

SWITZERLAND

GERMANY

AUSTRIA

CZECHOSLOVAKIA

PAVLOV **88** (*Moravia*). Klima 1957.
PEKARNA **90** (*Brno, Moravia*). Absolon 1939; Absolon, Cziźek 1932.
PŘEDMOSTÍ **91** (*Přerov, Moravia*). Breuil 1924 a; Kříž 1903; Maska 1886; Maska, Obermaier, Breuil 1912.

HUNGARY

PÖRGÖLHEGY **92** (*Bakonybel, Veszprem*). Roska 1956.

ITALY

ARENE CANDIDE **94** (*Finale Ligure*). Cardini 1942.
BALZI ROSSI **93** (*Grimaldi di Ventimiglia*). Breuil 1928; Graziosi 1943; Octobon 1952; Passemard L. 1938; Piette 1902; Reinach 1898.
CHIOZZA **95** (*Scandiano, Reggio E.*). Degani 1940; Id. 1944-45. Graziosi 1943; Id. 1941-46.
LEVANZO **101** (*Egadi, Sicilia*). Graziosi 1954.
MONOPOLI **99** (*Apulia*). Anelli 1952; Graziosi, Cadeo, Brambilla 1958.
ROMANELLI **100** (*Otranto, Apulia*). Blanc G. A.1928; Blanc A. C. 1938-39; Id. 1940; Graziosi 1932; Id. 1932-33; Stella 1935.
SAVIGNANO **96** (*Modena*). Antonielli 1925; Id. 1926; Battaglia 1926; Graziosi 1924; Id. 1925; Vaufrey 1926.
TIVOLI **98** (*Lazio*). Radmilli 1954; Id. 1954 b; Id. 1956.

TRASIMENO **97.** Graziosi 1938; Id. 1939; Palma di Cesnola 1938.

RUSSIA

AVDEJEVO **106** (*Kursk*). Gvosdover 1953; Id. 1956.
BURIETI **108** (*Angara river, Siberia*). Okladnikov 1940.
GAGARINO **107** (*Tambov*). Golomshtok 1933; Id. 1938, pp. 324-327; Samiatnin 1935.
JELISEJEVIČI **105** (*Brjansk*). Hančar 1949-53; Policarpovic 1940.
KOSTIENKI **109** (*Voronež*). Boriskovskiï 1956; Ephimenko 1926; Id. 1953; Id. 1958; Golomshtok 1938, pp. 308-324; Reinach 1924.
KIEV **103.** Boriskovskiï 1953, pp. 160-175; Golomshtok 1938, pp. 386-393.
MALTÀ **108** (*Irkutsk, Lake Baikal, Siberia*). Gerasimov 1931; Id. 1935; Golomshtok 1933; Salmony 1931.
MÉZINE **104** (*Kroletz*). Ephimenko 1913; Boriskovskiï 1953, pp. 278-285; Golomshtok 1938; Schovkoplias 1957; Volkov 1912.
MOLODOVA **102** (*Stai Usciza, Kamenez Podolski*). Schovkoplias 1957 a, p. 29.

POLAND

MASZYCKA **110** (*Oikow, Krakow*). Hoernes 1903, pp. 175-178.

LOCATION OF WORKS OF CAVE ART
SHOWN ON DISTRIBUTION MAP

SPAIN

AGUAS DE NOVALES **16** (*Novales, Santander*). Alcalde del Rio, Breuil, Sierra 1911, pp. 46-49.

ALTAMIRA **18** (*Santillana, Santander*). Sautuola 1880; Cartailhac, Breuil 1906; Breuil, Obermaier 1935.

ARDALES **3** (*Alora, Malaga*). Breuil 1921.

ATAPUERCA **8** (*Ibeas, Burgos*). Breuil 1952, p. 391.

BERROBERRIA **29** (*Navarra*). Loriana 1940.

BUXU (EL) **12** (*Canga de Onís, Asturias*). Obermaier, La Vega del Sella 1918.

CALA (LA) **4** (*Malaga*). Breuil 1952, p. 295.

CASARES (LOS) **7** (*Ribas de Saelices, Guadalajara*). Cabré Aguiló 1934; Id. 1935; Id. 1940.

CASTILLO (GROTTA DEL), see CASTILLO (MONTE).

CASTILLO (MONTE) **21** (*Puente Viesgo, Santander*). Grotte di : *El Castillo*. Alcalde del Rio, Breuil, Sierra 1911, pp. 112-193 — *La Pasiega*. Breuil, Obermaier, Alcalde del Rio 1913; Gonzales, Ripoll Perelló 1953-54 — *Las Monedas*. Carballo 1953; Patronato Santander 1953; Ripoll Perelló 1953; Id. 1956. — *Las Chimeneas*. Gonzales 1953; Carballo 1954.

CHIMENEAS (LAS) see CASTILLO (MONTE).

CLOTILDE DE SANTA ISABEL (LA) **17** (*Torrelavega, Santander*). Alcalde del Rio, Breuil, Sierra 1911, pp. 40-46; Ripoll Perelló 1957.

COVALANAS **24** (*Ramales, Santander*). Alcalde del Rio, Breuil, Sierra 1911, pp. 40-46.

HAZA (LA) **26** (*Ramales, Santander*). Alcalde del Rio, Breuil, Sierra 1911, pp. 11-14.

HORNOS DE LA PEÑA **22** (*Torrelavega, Santander*). Alcalde del Rio, Breuil, Sierra 1911, pp. 85-111.

HOZ (LA) **6** (*Santa Maria de Espino, Guadalajara*). Cabré Aguiló 1934.

LOJA (LA) **14** (*El Maxo Panes, Santander*). Alcalde del Rio, Breuil, Sierra 1911, pp. 50-52.

MEAZA (LA) **15** (*Comillas, Santander*). Alcalde del Rio, Breuil, Sierra 1911, pp. 50-52.

MESTAS (LAS) **10** (*Las Regueras, Asturias*). Obermaier 1914.

MONEDAS (LAS), see CASTILLO (MONTE).

PALOMAS (LAS) **1** (*Tarifa, Cadiz*). Breuil, Burkitt 1929.

PASIEGA (LA), see CASTILLO (MONTE).

PEÑA DE CANDAMO (LA) **11** (*S. Roman de Candamo, Asturias*). Pacheco 1919.

PENCHES **9** (*Oña, Asturias*). Pacheco 1917.

PENDO (EL) **20** (*Escobedo, Santander*). Alcalde del Rio, Breuil, Sierra 1911, pp. 35-39.

PILETA (LA) **2** (*Benaoján, Malaga*). Breuil, Obermaier, Verner 1915; Jordà 1955.

PINDAL **13** (*Columbres, Asturias*). Alcalde del Rio, Breuil, Sierra 1911, pp. 59-81; Jordà, Berenguer 1954.

REGUERILLO (EL) **5** (*Torrelaguna, Madrid*). Maura 1952.

SALITRÉ **23** (*Miera, Santander*). Alcalde del Rio, Breuil, Sierra 1911, pp. 23-26.

SANTIAN **19** (*Puente Arce, Santander*). Alcalde del Rio, Breuil, Sierra 1911, pp. 26-35.

SANTIMAMIÑE **28** (*Cortézubi, Vizcaya*). Aranzadi, Barandiaran, Eguren 1925.

SOTARRIZA (LA) **27** (*Santander*). Alcalde del Rio, Breuil, Sierra 1911, pp. 8-9.

VENTA DE LA PERRA (LA) **25** (*Molinar de Carranza, Vizcaya*). Alcalde del Rio, Breuil, Sierra 1911, p. 2-8.

FRANCE

ALDÈNE **45** (*Cesseras, Hérault*). Guerret 1927; Glory 1956 a.

ANGLES-SUR-ANGLIN **86** (*Vienne*). Garrod 1949; Garrod, Saint-Mathurin 1952; Saint-Mathurin 1950 a; Saint-Mathurin, Garrod 1951.

ARCY-SUR-CURE (Grotte du Cheval) **87** (*Yonne*). Bailloud, Tendron 1946; Bailloud 1947.

BARABAO **56** (*Le Bugue, Dordogne*). Breuil 1952, pp. 308-309; Glory 1956.

BAUME-LATRONE (LA) **93** (*Nîmes, Gard*). Begouen 1941; Drouot 1953.

BAYOL **94** (*Collias, Gard*). Bayol 1935; Drouot 1953.

BÉDEILHAC **41** (*Tarascon, Ariège*). Cartailhac, Breuil 1910; Begouen H. 1931; Breuil, Vidal 1949.

BELCAYRE **75** (*Thonac, Dordogne*). Delage 1934.

BERNIFAL **65** (*Meyrals, Dordogne*). Capitan, Breuil, Peyrony 1903.

BEYSSAC, NANCY **66** (*Sireuil, Dordogne*). Capitan, Breuil, Peyrony 1915.

BLANCHARD **72** (*Sergeac, Dordogne*). Didon 1911.

CALÉVIE (LA) **64** (*Les Eyzies, Dordogne*). Capitan, Breuil, Peyrony 1904.

CANTAL **48** (*Cabrerets, Lot*). Lemozi 1937.

CAP BLANC (LE) **69** (*Meyrales, Dordogne*). Lalanne, Breuil 1911.

CASTANET **73** (*Sergeac, Dordogne*). Peyrony 1935.

CHABOT **92** (*Aiguèze, Gard*). Breuil 1952, pp. 207-209; Louis 1947; Raymond 1900, pp. 50-62.

CHAIRE À CALVIN (LA) **84** (*Le Mouthiers, Charente*). David 1929; Id. 1934; Id. 1947.

COLOMBIER (LE) **89** (*Virac, Ardèche*). Glory 1947 a.

COMBARELLES (LES) **63** (*Les Eyzies, Dordogne*). Capitan, Breuil, Peyrony 1924.

COMMARQUE (NANCY, BEYSSAC) **67** (*Sireuil, Dordogne*). Capitan, Breuil, Peyrony 1915.

CROZE À GONTRAN (LA) **60** (*Les Eyzies, Dordogne*). Capitan, Breuil, Peyrony 1914.

COUGNAC **51** (*Peyrignac, Lot*). Méroc, Mazet 1953; Id. 1956.

EBBOU **88** (*Vallon, Ardèche*). Glory 1947.

EGLISES (LES), see USSAT.

ETCHEBERRI **31** (*Cahoucihigue, Basses-Pyrénées*). Laplace-Jauretsche 1952.

FERRASSIE (LA) **57** (*Les Eyzies, Dordogne*). Peyrony 1934.

FIGUIER (LE) **90** (*Saint-Martin, Ardèche*). Breuil 1952, p. 209.

FONT-DE-GAUME **62** (*Les Eyzies, Dordogne*). Capitan, Breuil, Peyrony 1910.

FOURNEAU DU DIABLE (LE) **81** (*Bourdeilles, Dordogne*). Peyrony 1932 a.

GABILLOU (LE) **80** (*Sourzac, Dordogne*). Chamarty, Truffier 1941; Gautier, Hervé, Malvesin-Fabre 1952.

GARGAS **33** (*Aventignan, H^{tes}-Pyrénées*). Cartailhac, Breuil 1910 a ; Malvesin-Fabre, Nougier, Robert 1954; Regnault 1906.

GORGE D'ENFER, OREIL D'ENFER **58** (*Les Eyzies, Dordogne*). Peyrony 1932; Breuil 1952, p. 307.

GRÈZE (LA) **68** (*Marquay, Dordogne*). Ampoulange, Pintaud 1955; Capitan, Breuil, Ampoulange 1904.

ISTURITZ **30** (*Hasparren, Basses-Pyrénées*). Passemard 1944.

JEAN-BLANCS **54** (*Bayac, Dordogne*). Peyrony D. 1912; Peyrony D., Peyrony E. 1934.

LABASTIDE **32** (*Aventignan, H^{tes}-Pyrénées*). Breuil 1952, p. 258; Casteret 1932.

LABATUT **71** (*Sergeac, Dordogne*). Breuil 1927.

LALINDE (Gr. de la Roche) **55** (*Sergeac, Dordogne*). Peyrony 1930.

LASCAUX **77** (*Montignac-sur-Vézère, Dordogne*). Bataille 1955; Breuil 1952, pp. 106-151; Windels 1949.

LAUGERIE BASSE, LAUGERIE HAUTE **59** (*Les Eyzies, Dordogne*). Peyrony 1938; Breuil 1952, p. 305.

LAUSSEL **70** (*Marquay, Dordogne*). Lalanne, Bouyssonie 1941-46.

MAGDELEINE (LA) **46** (*Penne, Tarn*). Bétirac 1954; Breuil 1954.

MAIRIE À TEYJAT (LA) **83** (*Dordogne*). Capitan, Breuil, Peyrony, Bourrinet 1912.

MARCENAC **49** (*Cabrerets, Lot*). Lemozi 1936.

MARSOULAS **36** (*Salies-du-Salat, H^{te}-Garonne*). Cartailhac, Breuil 1904; Id. 1905; Méroc, Michaut, Ollé 1948.

MAS D'AZIL (LE) **39** (*Ariège*). Breuil, Begouen 1913; Nougier, Robert 1954 b.

MERVEILLES (LES), see ROCAMADOUR.

MONTESPAN **35** (*H^{te}-Garonne*). Trombe, Dubuc 1947.

MOUTHE (LA) **61** (*Les Eyzies, Dordogne*). Breuil 1952, pp. 292-303; Rivière 1901; Id. 1903.

MURAT, see ROCAMADOUR.

NANCY, see BEYSSAC.

NIAUX **42** (*Tarascon, Ariège*). Capitan, Breuil 1908; Begouen H. 1934; Breuil 1950; Id. 1952 a; Nougier, Robert 1954 a.

OREIL D'ENFER, see GORGE D'ENFER.

OULLINS **91** (*Garn, Ardèche*). Breuil 1952, p. 207.

PAIR-NON-PAIR **79** (*Marcamps, Gironde*). Breuil 1952, pp. 319-329; Daleau 1902; Malvesin-Fabre 1950.

PECH-MERLE **47** (*Cabrerets, Lot*). Breuil 1924; Lemozi 1929, Nougier, Robert 1954.

PORTEL (LE) **40** (*Loubens, Ariège*). Breuil, Jeannel 1955; Vézian 1945; Id. 1956.

ROCAMADOUR (Abri des Merveilles, Abri Murat) **52** (*Lot*). Lemozi 1936; Peyrony 1926.

REVERDIT **74** (*Sergeac, Dordogne*). Delage 1935.

ROC DE SERS (LE) **85** (*Sers, Charente*). Lantier 1952; Martin 1928; Id. 1932.

ROUFFIGNAC **76** (*Dordogne*). Nougier, Robert 1956; Id. 1957; Id. 1957 a; Id. 1959; Breuil 1959; Saint-Mathurin 1959; Garrod 1958; Graziosi 1956; Id. 1957 a; Id. 1959.

SAINTE-EULALIE **50** (*Cabrerets, Lot*). Lemozi 1920; Id. 1936.

SALLÈLES-CABARDÈS (Gr. de Gazel) **44** (*Aude*). Cannac 1948.

SASIZILOAGA **31** (*Cahoucihigue, Basses-Pyrénées*). Laplace-Jauretsche 1952 a.

SUDRIE (LA) **78** (*Villac, Dordogne*). Flory, Bay, Koby 1949.

TERME PIALAT **53** (*Saint-Avit-Sénieur, Dordogne*). Délugin 1914.

TIBIRAN **34** (*Aventignan, H^{tes}-Pyrénées*). Malvesin-Fabre, Nougier, Robert 1954.

TROIS FRÈRES (LES) **38** (*Montesquieu-Avantès, Ariège*). Begouen H. 1936; Begouen, Breuil 1930; Id. 1934; Id. 1958; Breuil, Begouen 1902, pp. 152-177.

TUC D'AUDOUBERT (LE) **37** (*Montesquieu-Avantès, Ariège*). Begouen H. 1912; Id. 1912 a; Id. 1926; Id. 1936; Begouen, Breuil 1958.

USSAT (Grotte des Eglises) **43** (*Ariège*). Breuil 1939.

VILLARS **82** (*Champagnac-de-Bélair, Dordogne*). « Radar » 1958; Roghi 1958.

GERMANY

SCHULERLOCH (?) **95** (*Neuessing, Bayern*). Zotz, Freund 1951.

ITALY

LEVANZO **98** (*Egadi, Sicily*). Graziosi 1950; Id. 1950 a; Id. 1950 b; Id. 1953.

MONTE PELLEGRINO (Addaura, Niscemi) **97** (*Palermo, Sicily*). Marconi Bovio 1952; Id. 1953; Id. 1953 b; Id. 1954-55.

ROMANELLI **96** (*Otranto, Apulia*). Blanc G. A. 1928; Graziosi 1932-33.

BIBLIOGRAPHY

ABSOLON K., *Une nouvelle et importante station aurignacienne en Moravie*, « Revue Anthropolog. »,
Année XXXVII, **1927**, pp. 75-88.
— *The Venus of Vestonice, faceless and visored*, « The Illustrated London News », 30 nov. **1929**, p. 936.
— *Représentations idéoplastiques anciennes et nouvelles de femmes du Paléolithique moravien*, « XVᵉ Congrès
Intern. d'Anthropol. et Archéol. Préhist. », Paris, **1931**, pp. 329-332.
— *Les nouvelles fouilles dans la grotte de Pekarna et les poignards faits en mâchoires de cheval*, « Mé-
langes de Préhist. et d'Anthrop. offerts au Prof. Comte H. Begouen », Toulouse, **1939**, pp. 257-262.

ABSOLON K., CZIŽEK R., *Die Palaeolithische Erforschung der Pekárna-Höhle in Mähren*, « Mitteilungen aus
der Palaeolithischen Abteil. am Mähr. Landesmuseum », N. 26, Brno, **1932**.

ABSOLON V., *Nouvelles découvertes de statuettes modelées dans l'Aurignacien de Moravie*, « Mélanges de
Préhist. et d'Anthrop. offerts au Prof. Comte H. Begouen », Toulouse, **1939**, pp. 249-255.

ALCALDE DEL RIO H., *Las pinturas y grabados de las Cavernas prehistóricas de la provincia de Santander.
Altamira, Covalanas, Hornos de la Peña, Castillo*, Santander, **1906**.

ALCALDE DEL RIO H., BREUIL H., SIERRA L., *Les cavernes de la région cantabrique*, Monaco, **1911**.

ALLAIN Y., *Un appeau magdalénien*, « Bull. Soc. Préhist. Française », T. XLVII, **1950**, pp. 181-192.
— *Nouvelles découvertes dans le gisement magdalénien de la Garenne (Com. de St-Marcel, Indre)* « Bull. Soc.
Préhist. Française », T. LIV, **1957**, pp. 223-227.

ALMAGRO M., *El arte prehistórico del Sahara español*, « Ampurias », VI, **1944**, pp. 273-284.
— *El Paleolitico Español*, in « Historia de España » di R. Menéndez Pidal, vol. I, parte III, Madrid
1947, pp. 243-485.
— *Arte prehistórico*, in « Ars Hispaniae », vol. I, Madrid, **1947 a**.

AMPOULANGE U., PINTAUD R. C., *Une nouvelle gravure de la grotte de la Grèze (Dordogne)*, « Bull. Soc.
Préhist. Française », T. LII, **1955**, pp. 249-251.

ANDREE J., *Die erste Aurignacien-Gravierung in Deutschland*, « Ipek », **1930**, pp. 109-110.

ANELLI F., *Scavi eseguiti nella Grotta Mura di Monopoli*, « Archivio Storico Pugliese », Organo Soc. Storia
Patria per la Puglia, Anno V, fasc. I, **1952**.

ANTONIELLI U., *Una statuetta femminile di Savignano sul Panaro e il problema delle statuette dette « stea-
topigi »*, « Bullettino di Paletnologia Italiana », Anno XLV, **1925** (pubblicato nel 1926), pp. 35-61.
— *La statuetta femminile steatopigica di Savignano sul Panaro*, « Rivista di Antropologia », vol. XXVII,
1926, pp. 283-299.
— *Savignano sul Panaro. Esame litologico di una statuetta femminile steatopigica e saggio di scavo nel sito
del rinvenimento*, « Atti Accad. Naz. Lincei », Notizie e Scavi di Antichità, vol. II, serie VI, fasc. 4,
5, 6, **1926 a**, pp. 149-162.

ARANZADI (DE) T., BARANDIARAN (DE) J., *Exploraciones en la Caverna de Santimamiñe (Basondo : Cortézubi)*, 3ª memoria, *Yacimientos azilienses y paleoliticos*, Bilbao, **1935**.

ARANZADI (DE) T., BARANDIARAN (DE) J. M., EGUREN (DE) E., *Exploraciones en la Caverna de Santimamiñe (Basondo : Cortézubi)*, 1ª memoria, *Figuras rupestres*, Bilbao, **1925**.

ARMSTRONG A. L., *Notes on four examples of palaeolithic art from Creswell Crags, Derbyshire*, « Ipek »,
1927, pp. 10-12.

AUSSELET-LAMBRECHTS C., *L'Art et la Parure en Belgique pendant le Paléolithique supérieur*, « Bull. Soc.
Préhist. Française », T. XXVII, **1930**, pp. 468-482.

BAILLOUD G., *Découvertes et travaux récents à la Grotte du Cheval à Arcy-sur-Cure (Yonne)*, « Bull. Soc.
Préhist. Française », T. XLIV, **1947**, pp. 97-105.

BAILLOUD G., TENDRON G., *Les gravures pariétales de la Grotte du Cheval à Arcy-sur-Cure (Yonne)*, « Bull.
Soc. Préhist. Française », T. XLIII, **1946**, pp. 155-160.

BALDWIN BROWN, G., *The Art of the Cave Dweller*, London, **1928**.

BALFOUR H., *The evolution of decorative art*, London, **1893**.

BANDI H. G., *Die Schweiz zur Rentierzeit*, Frauenfeld, **1947**.

BANDI H. G., MARINGER J., *Art in the Ice Age*, Basel-London, **1953**.

BATAILLE G., *Lascaux, ou la naissance de l'art*, Genève, **1955**.

BATTAGLIA R., *Qualche osservazione sulla « Venere del Panàro »*, « Rivista di Antropologia », vol. XXVII, **1926**, pp. 337-344.
— *I graffiti antropomorfi di Grotta Romanelli*, Pubblic. dell'Ist. Ital. di Paleont. Umana, Firenze, **1935**.

BAYER I., *Die falsche Venus von Wisternitz und ihre Geschichte*, Brünn-Prag-Leipzig-Wien, **1931**.

BAYOL J., *Mémoires d'un vieux fouilleur. III, Grotte à peintures de Collias*, Vienne, **1935**.

BEGOUEN H., *Une nouvelle grotte à gravures dans l'Ariège. La Caverne du Tuc d'Audoubert*, « Congrès Intern. d'Anthrop. et d'Archéol. Préhistoriques », Genève, **1912**, pp. 489-497.
— *Les statues d'argile de la Caverne du Tuc d'Audoubert (Ariège)*, « L'Anthropologie », T. XXIII, **1912 a**, pp. 657-665.
— *Sur une sculpture en bois de renne provenant de la Caverne d'Enlène*, « L'Anthropologie », T. XXIII, **1912 b**, pp. 287-305.
— *L'art mobilier dans la Caverne du Tuc d'Audoubert (Ariège)*, « Ipek », **1926**, pp. 219-228.
— *Nouvelles fouilles dans les grottes de Montesquieu-Avantès (Ariège)*, « Ipek », **1928**, pp. 98-99.
— *Les peintures et dessins de la grotte de Bédeilhac (Ariège)*, « Ipek », **1929**, pp. 1-5.
— *Nouvelles découvertes dans les Pyrénées*, « Ipek », **1930**, pp. 116-117.
— *Sur un os gravé de la grotte de Marsoulas*, « Revue Anthropologique », Année XL, **1930 a**, pp. 358-360.
— *Les modelages d'argile de la Caverne de Bédeilhac (Ariège)*, « Ipek », **1931**, pp. 7-8.
— *Dessins inédits de la Grotte de Niaux (Ariège)*, « Ipek », **1934**, pp. 1-3.
— *L'aspect de l'humanité préhistorique*, Toulouse, **1935**.
— *Les Grottes de Montesquieu-Avantès (Ariège), Tuc d'Audoubert, Enlène, Les Trois Frères. Le Musée de Pujol.* (Publié à l'occasion du XIIᵉ Congrès de la Soc. Préhist. Franç.), Toulouse, **1936**.
— *Les plaquettes de pierre gravées de la grotte de Labastide (Hautes-Pyrénées)*, « Ipek », **1938**, pp. 1-10.
— *La Grotte de La Baume Latrone à Russan (Sainte-Anastasie)*, with a note by G. ASTRE and A. GLORY, « Mémoires de la Soc. Archéol. du Midi de la France », T. XX, **1941**, pp. 101-130.
— *De la mentalité spiritualiste des premiers hommes*, « Académie des jeux floraux », Toulouse, **1943**.
— *Bédeilhac*, « Bulletin Soc. Préhist. de l'Ariège », T. IV, **1949**, pp. 25-28.
— *Un « Objet orné » en forme de tête d'ours provenant de la caverne des Trois-Frères*, « Bull. Soc. Préhist. de l'Ariège », T. VI, **1951**, pp. 31-32.

BEGOUEN H., BEGOUEN L., *Découvertes nouvelles dans la Caverne des Trois Frères à Montesquieu-Avantès (Ariège)*, « Revue Anthropologique », Année XXXVIII, **1928**, pp. 358-364.

BEGOUEN H., BREUIL H., *De quelques figures hybrides (mi-humaines et mi-animales) de la caverne des Trois Frères*, « Revue Anthropologique », Année XLIV, **1934**, pp. 115-119.
— *Les cavernes du Volp. Trois Frères-Tuc d'Audoubert.* Paris, **1958**.

BEGOUEN H., CASTERET N., *La Caverne de Montespan (Haute-Garonne)*, « Revue Anthropologique », Année XXXIII, **1923**, pp. 533-545.

BEGOUEN J., *De quelques signes gravés ou peints des grottes de Montesquieu-Avantès*, « Mélanges de Préhist. et d'Anthrop. offerts au Prof. Comte H. Begouen », Toulouse, **1939**, pp. 281-287.

BEGOUEN L., *Notre campagne de fouilles dans la caverne des Trois Frères (1930-1931) (Ariège)*, « XVᵉ Congrès Intern. d'Anthr. et Archéol. Préhist. », Paris, **1931**, pp. 333-340.
— *Pierres gravées et peintes de l'époque magdalénienne*, « Mélanges de Préhist. et d'Anthrop. offerts au Prof. Comte H. Begouen », Toulouse, **1939**, pp. 289-305.

BERGOUNIOUX F. M., GLORY A., *Les premiers hommes*, 4ᵉ édit., Paris, **1952**.

BERTRAND A., *L'os de renne gravé du musée de Cluny*, « C. R. Acad. Inscr. Belles Lettres », **1887**, p. 221.

BÉTIRAC B., *L'Abri Montastruc à Bruniquel (Tarn-et-Garonne)*, « L'Anthropologie », T. LVI, **1952**, pp. 213-231.
— *Les Vénus de La Magdeleine*, « Bull. Soc. Préhist. Française », T. LI, **1954**, pp. 125-126.

BIANCHI-BANDINELLI R., *Tarda antichità nella scultura romana*, Ed. Universitaria, Firenze, **1952**.

BIRKNER F., *Paläolithische Kunst aus dem Ries in Bayern*, « Ipek », **1928**, p. 97.
— *Eine altsteinzeitliche Felszeichnung im unteren Altmühltal in Bayern*, « Ipek », **1938**, pp. 157-158.

BLANC A. C., *Dipinto schematico rinvenuto nel Paleolitico Superiore della Grotta Romanelli in Terra d'Otranto*, « Rivista di Antropologia », vol. XXXII, **1938-39**, pp. 101-113.
— *Nuove manifestazioni di arte paleolitica superiore della Grotta Romanelli in Terra d'Otranto*, « Accademia d'Italia, Rendiconti Classe Scienze fisiche, matematiche e naturali », fasc. 8, serie VII, vol. I, **1940**.
— *Considerazioni su due figure dell'Addaura*, « Quaternaria », I, **1954**, pp. 176-180.
— *Il sacrificio dell'Addaura ed il nesso ideologico tra morte e generazione nella mentalità primitiva*, « Quaternaria », I, **1954 a**, pp. 184-186.

BLANC G. A., *Grotta Romanelli, II*, « Archivio per l'Antrop. e l'Etnol. », vol. LVIII, **1928**, pp. 365-411.

BLANCHET A., *Traité des monnaies gauloises*, Paris, **1905**.

BOAS F., *Primitive art*, new edition, New York, **1955.**

BORISKOVSKIĬ P. I., *Paleolit Ukraini*, « Materiali i issdelia avdeevskoi po archeologhii SSSR », n. 40, Akademija Nauk SSSR, Moskva, Leningrad, **1953.**
— *Raskopki paleoliticeskogo jilisctia i progrebenija v Kostenkach II V 1953 godu*, « Sovetskaja Archeologhia », XXV, **1956**, pp. 173-188.
— *Isucenie paleoliticeskich jilisct v sovetskom sojuse*, « Sovetskaja Archeologhia », **1958**, n. 1, pp. 3-19.

BOULE M., *Review of* : Tournier, Guillon C., *Les hommes préhistoriques dans l'Aïn*, 1895, « L'Anthropologie », T. VI, **1895**, pp. 314-317.
— *Travaux exécutés en 1913. Rapport général*, « L'Anthropologie », T. XXV, **1914**, pp. 225-232.
— *Review of* : Breuil, *Rapport sur les fouilles dans la Grotte du Mas d'Azil (Ariège)*, in « Bull. Archéol. »,
1902, « L'Anthropologie », T. XIV, **1903**, pp. 188-192.

BOURDELLE E., JEANNEL R., *Les dessins rupestres d'Equidés da la Grotte du Portel (Ariège)*, « C. R. Congrès
préhist. de France », XIᵉ sess., Périgueux, **1934**, pp. 304-311.

BOURLON (le Cap.), *Nouvelles découvertes à Laugerie Basse. Rabot, os outilisés, oeuvres d'art*, « L'Anthropologie », T. XXVII, **1916**, pp. 1-26.

BREUIL H., *Rapport sur les fouilles dans la grotte du Mas d'Azil (Ariège)*, « Bulletin Archéologique », **1902.**
— *Station de l'âge du renne de Saint-Marcel (Indre) d'après les fouilles de M. Benoist*, « L'Anthropo-
logie », T. XIII, **1902 a**, pp. 145-165.
— *La dégénérescence de figures d'animaux en motifs ornementaux à l'Epoque du Renne*, « Comptes Rendus
Acad. des Inscript. et Belles Lettres », **1905**, pp. 105-120.
— *Prétendus manches de poignard sculptés de l'âge du Renne*, « L'Anthropologie », T. XVI, **1905 a,**
pp. 630-632.
— *Exemples de figures dégénérés et stylisées à l'Epoque du Renne*, « Congrès Internat. d'Anthrop. et
d'Archéol. Préhist. », XIIIᵉ sess., vol. I, Monaco, **1906**, pp. 394-403.
— *Rhinocéros gravé sur schiste de la grotte du Trilobite, à Arcy-sur-Cure (Yonne)*, « Revue Ecole d'An-
throp. », Année XVI, **1906 a**, pp. 242-247.
— *L'évolution de l'art pariétal de l'âge du renne*, « Congrès Internat. d'Anthrop. et d'Archéol. Préhist. »,
XIIIᵉ sess., Monaco, **1906 b**, pp. 367-386.
— *L'évolution de l'art quaternaire et les travaux d'Edouard Piette*, « Revue Archéologique », 4ᵉ série,
T. XIII, **1909**, pp. 378-411.
— *L'âge des cavernes et roches ornées de France et d'Espagne*, « Revue Archéologique », T. XIX, **1912,**
pp. 193-234.
— *Nouvelles découvertes à Laugerie Basse : les oeuvres d'art*, « L'Anthropologie », T. XXVII, **1916,**
pp. 13-26.
— *Nouvelles cavernes ornées paléolithiques dans la province de Malaga*, « L'Anthropologie », T. XXXI,
1921, pp. 239-253.
— *Nouvelles figurations humaines de la Caverne David à Cabrerets (Lot)*, « Revue Anthropologique »,
Année XXIV, **1924**, pp. 165-171.
— *Notes de voyage paléolithique en Europe centrale. II, Les industries paléolithiques du loess de Moravie
et Bohème*, « L'Anthropologie », T. XXXIV, **1924 a**, pp. 515-552.
— *Les origines de l'art décoratif*, « Journ. de Psychologie normale et pathologique », XXIII, n. 1-3,
15. 1.-15, 3, **1926**, pp. 364-375.
— *Oeuvres d'art paléolithiques inédites du Périgord et art oriental d'Espagne*, « Revue Anthropologique »,
Année XXVII, **1927**, pp. 101-108.
— *Reinseignements inédits sur les circonstances de trouvaille des statuettes aurignaciennes des Baoussé Roussé*,
« Archivio per l'Antrop. e la Etnol. », vol. LVIII, **1928**, pp. 281-286.
— *Gravures aurignaciennes supérieures de l'Abri Labatut à Sergeac (Dordogne)*, « Revue Anthropolo-
gique », Année XXXIX, **1929**, pp. 147-151.
— *L'évolution de l'art pariétal dans les cavernes et abris ornées de France*, « Congrès Préhistorique de
France », XIᵉ sess., Périgueux, **1934**, pp. 102-118.
— *Les oeuvres d'art magdaléniennes des fouilles Le Bel-Maury à Laugerie Basse*, « C. R. Congrès Préhist.
de France », XIᵉ sess., Périgueux, **1934 a**, pp. 89-101.
— *Oeuvres d'art magdaléniennes de Laugerie Basse (Dordogne)*, « Actualités scientifiques et industriel-
les », Paris, **1936.**
— *De quelques oeuvres d'art magdaléniennes inédites ou peu connues*, « Ipek », **1936-37**, pp. 1-16.
— *Quarante ans de Préhistoire*, « Bull. Soc. Préhist. Française », T. XXXIV, **1937**, pp. 52-67.
— *Les subdivisions du Paléolithique supérieur et leur signification*, « Congrès Internat. d'Anthrop. et d'Ar-
chéol. Préhist. », C. R., XIVᵉ sess., Genève, **1912**, pp. 165-238 (2ᵉ édition, **1937 a**).
— *Peintures magdaléniennes de la grotte des Eglises à Ussat (Ariège)*, « Mélanges de Préhist. et d'An-
throp. offerts au Prof. Comte Begouen », Toulouse, **1939**, pp. 271-279.
— *Les peintures et gravures pariétales de la Caverne de Niaux (Ariège)*, « Bulletin de la Soc. Préhist.
de l'Ariège », T. V, **1950**, pp. 9-34.
— *Quatre cents siècles d'art pariétal*, Montignac, **1952.** [English text translated by Mary E. Boyle, 1952].
— *Gravures sur schiste Périgordiennes de la Caverne de Gargas*, « Mélanges en hommage du Professeur
Hamal Nandrin », Soc. Royal Belge d'Anthropologie et de Préhistoire, **1952 a**, pp. 42-50.
— *La Caverne de Niaux. Compléments inédits sur sa décoration*, « Bulletin de la Soc. Préhist. de
l'Ariège », T. VII, **1952 a**, pp. 11-35.

— *Bas-reliefs féminins de la Magdeleine (Penne, Tarn) près Montauban (Tarn-et-Garonne)*, « Quaternaria », I, **1954**, pp. 49-53.
— *Des preuves de l'authenticité de la Caverne de Rouffignac*, « Bull. Soc. Préhist. Française », T. LVI, **1959**, pp. 82-92.

BREUIL H., BEGOUEN H., *Peintures et gravures préhistoriques dans la grotte du Mas d'Azil*, « Bull. Soc. Archéol. du Midi de la France », **1913**.
— *Nouvelle gravure d'homme masqué de la caverne des Trois Frères (Montesquieu-Avantès, Ariège), associée avec des figures animales composites*, « C. R. Académie des Inscriptions et Belles Lettres », **1930**, pp. 261-264.
— *Quelques oiseaux inédits ou méconnus de l'art préhistorique*, « Congrès Préhist. de France », C. R., XIIᵉ sess., Toulouse-Foix, **1936**, pp. 475-488.
— *Les Trois Frères*, in : Breuil H., « Quatre cents siècles d'art pariétal », Montignac-sur-Vézère, **1952**, pp. 152-177.

BREUIL H., BURKITT M., *Rock Paintings of Southern Andalusia*, Oxford, **1929**.

BREUIL H., JEANNEL R., *La grotte ornée du Portel a Loubens (Ariège)*, « L'Anthropologie », T. LIX, **1955**, pp. 197-204.

BREUIL H., KÜHN H., *Die Magdalénien-Skulptur von Oberkassel*, « Ipek », **1927**, pp. 193-194.

BREUIL H., LANTIER R., *Les Hommes de la Pierre Ancienne*, Paris, **1951**.

BREUIL H., LHOTE H., *Les roches peintes du Tassili-n-Ajjèr*, « Actes du IIme Congrès Panafrican de Préhistoire », Alger, **1952**, pp. 65-219.

BREUIL H., NOUGIER R., ROBERT R., *Le « Lissoir aux ours » de la grotte de « La Vache », à Alliat, et l'ours dans l'art franco-cantabrique occidental*, « Bull. Soc. Préhist. de l'Ariège », T. XI, **1956**, pp. 15-78.

BREUIL H., OBERMAIER H., *Les premiers travaux de l'Institut de Paléontologie Humaine*, « L'Anthropologie », T. XXIII, **1912**, pp. 1-27.
— *Institut de Paléontologie Humaine. Travaux exécutés en 1912*, « L'Anthropologie », T. XXIV, **1913**, pp. 1-16.
— *Institut de Paléontologie Humaine. Travaux de l'année 1913. Travaux en Espagne*, « L'Anthropologie », T. XXV, **1914**, pp. 233-253.

BREUIL H., OBERMAIER H., *The Cave of Altamira at Santillana del Mar, Spain*, Madrid, **1935**.

BREUIL H., OBERMAIER H., ALCALDE DEL RIO H., *La Pasiega a Puente-Viesgo (Santander)*, Monaco, **1913**.

BREUIL H., OBERMAIER H., VERNER W., *La Pileta a Benaojan (Malaga)*, Monaco, **1915**.

BREUIL H., PEYRONY D., *Statuette féminine aurignacienne de Sireuil (Dordogne)*, « Revue Anthropologique », Année XL, **1930**, pp. 44-47.

BREUIL H., SAINT-PÉRIER (DE) R., *Les poissons, les batraciens et les reptiles dans l'art quaternaire*, « Archives de l'Inst. Pal. Hum. », Mém. n. 2, Paris, **1927**.

BREUIL H., VIDAL G., *Les fresques de la Galerie Vidal à la Caverne de Bédeilhac (Ariège)*, « Bull. Soc. Préhist. de l'Ariège », IV, **1949**, pp. 11-16.

BRITISH MUSEUM, *A Guide to the antiquities of the Stone Age in the department of British and Mediaeval antiquities*, London, **1902**.

BRODRICK A. M., *Lascaux, a commentary*, London, **1949**.

BROUGH SMYTH R., *The Aborigines of Victoria*, London, **1878**.

BURKITT M. C., *Prehistory*, Cambridge, **1925**.
— *Art in the old stone age*, « Eidos », n. 1, **1950**, pp. 4-10.
— *The Old Stone Age, a study of palaeolithic times*, Third edition, London, **1955**.

CABRÉ AGUILÓ J., *El Arte rupestre en España*, « Comisión de Investigaciones paleontológicas y prehistóricas », n. 1, Madrid, **1915**.
— *Las cuevas de los Casares y la Hoz*, « Archivo Español de Arqueología », **1934**, n. 30, p. 30.
— *Cave art of some 30.000 years ago : a wonderful discovery in Spain*, « The Illustrated London News », May 25, **1935**.
— *Figuras antropomorfas de la Cueva de los Casares (Guadalajara)*, « Archivo Español de Arqueología », **1940**, n. 41, pp. 81-96.

CABRÉ M. E., *Neu entdeckte Felsenmalereien aus der alten Steinzeit Mittelspaniens*, « Die Umschau in Wissenschaft und Technik », Frankfurt A. M., 29 sept., **1935**, pp. 797-799.

CADEO G. C., *Il contributo dell'etnografia all'interpretazione delle raffigurazioni di mani delle grotte paleolitiche franco-cantabriche*, « Natura », vol. XLV, **1954**, pp. 95-108.

CANNAC M., *Découvertes de poteries de l'âge du Bronze et de gravures paléolithiques sur parois dans la grotte de Gazel, près Sallèles-Cabardès (Aude)*, « Bull. Soc. Préhist. Française », T. XLV, **1948,** pp. 152-161.

CAPITAN L., *Les manifestations ethnographiques et magiques sur les parois de la Grotte de Montespan*, « Revue Anthropologique », T. XXXIII, **1923,** pp. 545-550.

CAPITAN L., BOUYSSONIE J., *Limeuil, son gisement à gravures sur pierres de l'age du renne*, « Publicat. de l'Inst. Intern. d'Anthropol. », n. 1, Paris, **1924.**

CAPITAN L., BREUIL H., AMPOULANGE U., *Une nouvelle Grotte préhistorique à parois gravée*, « Revue de l'Ecole d'Anthropologie », Année XIV, **1904,** pp. 320-325.

CAPITAN L., BREUIL H., BOURRINET P., PEYRONY D., *L'Abri Mêge. Une station magdalénienne à Teyjat (Dordogne)*, « Revue de l'Ecole d'Anthropol. », Année XIV, **1906,** pp. 198-212.

CAPITAN L., BREUIL H., BOURRINET P., PEYRONY D., *La Grotte de la Mairie à Teyjat (Dordogne)*, « Revue de l'Ecole d'Anthropol. », Année XVIII, **1908,** pp. 153-173 e 198-218.
— *Observations sur un bâton de commandement orné de figures animales et de personnages semi-humains*, « Revue de l'Ecole d'Anthropol. », Année XIX, **1909,** pp. 62-76.

CAPITAN L., BREUIL H., PEYRONY D., *Les figures gravées à l'époque paléolithique sur les parois de la Grotte de Bernifal (Dordogne)*, « Revue de l'Ecole d'Anthropol. », Année XIII, **1903,** pp. 202-209.
— *Une nouvelle grotte à parois gravées: La Calevie (Dordogne)*, « Revue de l'Ecole d'Anthropol. », Année XIV, **1904,** pp. 379-381.
— *Les gravures de la grotte des Eyzies*, « Revue de l'Ecole d'Anthrop. », Année XVI, **1906,** pp. 429-441.
— *La Caverne de Font-de-Gaume*, Monaco, **1910.**
— *La Croze à Gontran (Tayac), grotte à dessins aurignaciens*, « Revue Anthropologique », Année XXIV, **1914,** pp. 277-280.
— *Nouvelles grottes ornées de la Vallée de la Beune (Dordogne)*, « L'Anthropologie », T. XXVI, **1915,** pp. 505-518.
— *Les Combarelles aux Eyzies (Dordogne)*, Paris, **1924.**

CAPITAN L., BREUIL H., PEYRONY D., BOURRINET P., *Les gravures sur cascade stalagmitique de la grotte de la Mairie à Teyjat (Dordogne)*, « Congrès Internat. d'Anthrop. et d'Archéol. Préhist. », C. R. de la XVIᵉ sess., Genève, **1912,** pp. 498-514.

CAPITAN L., PEYRONY D., *Les origines de l'Art à l'Aurignacien moyen. Nouvelles découvertes. La Ferrassie*, « Revue Anthropologique », Année XXXI, **1921,** pp. 92-112.
— *La Madeleine: son gisement, son industrie, ses oeuvres d'art*, Paris, **1928.**

CARBALLO J., *Las cavernas con pinturas rupestres del Monte Castillo (Santander)*, « Archivo de Prehistoria Levantina », vol. IV, **1953,** pp. 67-73.
— *Caverne de « las Monedas » au Monte-Castillo (Puente Viesgo)*, « Bulletin de la Soc. Préhist. de l'Ariège », T. VIII, **1953 a,** pp. 69-74.
— *Las cuevas pintadas del Monte Castillo*, « Rivista di Scienze Preistoriche », vol. IX, **1954,** pp. 114-120.

CARBALLO J., GONZALES ECHEGARAY J., *Algunos objetos inéditos de la Cueva de El Pendo*, « Ampurias » XIV, **1952,** pp. 37-42.

CARBALLO J., LARIN B., *Exploración en la gruta de « El Pendo »*, « Junta superior de excavaciones y antigüedades », Madrid, n. 2, **1932.**

CARDINI L., *Nuovi documenti sull'antichità dell'Uomo in Italia. Reperto umano del Paleolitico Superiore nella Grotta delle Arene Candide*, « Razza e Civiltà », III, n. 1-4, **1942,** pp. 5-25.

CARTAILHAC E., *Oeuvres inédites des artistes chasseurs de rennes*, « Matériaux pour l'Hist. primit. et naturelle de l'Homme », Année XIX, **1885,** pp. 63-75.
— *La France Préhistorique*, Paris, **1889.**
— *Gravure inédite de l'âge du renne. Grotte du Chaffaud (Vienne), Collection Gaillard de la Dionnerie*, « L'Anthropologie », T. XIV, **1903,** pp. 179-182.
— *Les stations de Bruniquel sur le bord de l'Aveyron*, « L'Anthropologie », T. XIV, **1903 a,** pp. 129-150 and 295-315.

CARTAILHAC E., BREUIL H., *Les peintures et gravures murales des cavernes pyrénéennes. I, Altamira*, « L'Anthropologie », T. XV, **1904,** pp. 625-644.
— *Les peintures et gravures murales pyrénéennes. II, Marsoulas, près Salies du Salat (Haute-Garonne)*, « L'Anthropologie », T. XVI, **1905,** pp. 431-444.
— *La Caverne d'Altamira à Santillane près Santander (Espagne)*, Monaco, **1906.**
— *Les oeuvres d'art de la collection Vibraye au Musée National*, « L'Anthropologie », T. XVIII, **1907,** pp. 1-36.
— *Les peintures et gravures murales des cavernes pyrénéennes. III, Niaux (Ariège)*, « L'Anthropologie », T. XIX, **1908,** pp. 15-46.
— *Les peintures et gravures murales des cavernes pyrénéennes. IV, Gargas, C.ne Aventignan (Hautes-Pyrénées). V, Bédeilhac et Pradières, près Tarascon (Ariège)*, « L'Anthropologie », T. XXI, **1910,** pp. 129-150.

CASTERET N., *Dix ans sous terre*, Paris, **1937**.
— *La grotte de La Bastide*, « L'Illustration », 17 sept., **1932,** pp. 73-76.

CASTILLO (DEL) A., *Estética del Arte paleolitico*, « Ampurias », voll. XV-XVI, **1953-54,** pp. 1-41.

CAU-DURBAN D., *La grotte de Marsoulas*, « Matériaux pour l'Hist. primit. et nat. de l'Homme », T. XIX, **1885,** pp. 341-349.

CAZALIS DE FONTDOUCE P., *L'Age du Renne dans le Bas-Languedoc*, « Matériaux pour l'Hist. prim. et nat. de l'Homme », T. VII, **1872,** pp. 282-286.
— *L'homme dans la Vallée du Gardon*, Montpellier, **1872 a.**

CÉLÉBONOVIC S., SAUTER M. R., *Préhistoire* (Collection art et nature), Genève-Paris, **1957.**

CÉLÉBONOVIC S., GRIGSON G., *Old Stone Age*, London, **1957.**

CHAMARTY, TRUFFIER, *La Grotte du Gabillou*, « Bull. de la Soc. Histor. et Archéol. du Périgord », **1941,** pp. 107-113.

CHASSELOUP LAUBAT (DE) F., *Art rupestre au Hoggar (Haut Mertoutek)*, Paris, **1938.**

CHAUVET G., *Os, ivoires et bois de renne ouvrés de la Charente*, « Bull. de la Soc. Archéol. et Hist. de La Charente », VIII série, T. I, **1910,** pp. 1-191.

CHEYNIER A., *Badegoule, station solutréenne et proto-magdalénienne*, « Archives de l'Inst. de Paléont. Humaine », Mém. 23, **1949.**
— *Stratigraphie de l'abri Lachaud et les cultures des bords abattus*, « Archivo de Prehistoria Levantina », IV, **1953,** pp. 25-55.

CHIAPPELLA G., *Altre considerazioni sugli « acrobati » dell'Addaura*, « Quaternaria », I, **1954,** pp. 181-183.

DALEAU F., *Grottes des Fées (âge du renne) située au Roc, commune de Marcamps, Canton de Bourg (Gironde)*, « Mémoires de la Soc. Archéologique de Bordeaux », T. I, **1875,** pp. 109-119.
— *Les gravures sur rocher de Pair-non-Pair*, « Actes de la Société Archéologique de Bordeaux », T. 21, **1896,** p. 235.
— *Gravures paléolithiques de la Grotte de Pair-non-Pair, Commune de Marcamps (Gironde)*, « C. R. Assoc. française pour l'advanc. des Sciences », Montauban, **1902,** pp. 786-789.

DANIEL R., *Gravures sur pierre de la Grotte du Trilobite à Arcy-sur-Cure (Yonne)*, « Bulletin Soc. Préhist. Française », T. XXXIII, **1936,** pp. 675-678.

DARASSE P., *Deux oeuvres d'art magdaléniennes de l'abri de Fontalés, près Saint-Antonin (Tarn et Garonne)*, « Bull. Soc. Préhist. Française », T. LII, **1955,** pp. 715-718.
— *Dessins paléolithiques de la Vallée de l'Aveyron identiques à ceux de l'Hohlestein en Bavière*, « Quartär », 7/8 Band, **1956,** pp. 171-176.

DAVID P., *Frise de l'Abri sous roche de la Chaire à Calvin ou de « La Papeterie » commune de Mouthiers (Charente)*, « C. R. Assoc. Franc. pour l'advanc. des Sciences », **1929,** pp. 478-482.
— *Abri de la Chaire à Calvin, commune de Mouthiers (Charente)*, « C. R. Congrès préhist. de France », XIᵉ sess., Périgueux, **1934,** pp. 373-378.
— *La Chaire à Calvin (Commune de Mouthiers-Charente)*, « Bull. Soc. Préhist. Française », T. XLIV, **1947,** pp. 31-32.

DAVID P., GAUTIER J., HERVÉ M., MALVESIN-FABRE G., *Le Gabillou*, in : Breuil H., « Quatre cents siècles d'art pariétal », Montignac, **1952,** pp. 310-311.

DAVID P., MALVESIN-FABRE G., *Une interpretation nouvelle pour une gravure de Pair-non-Pair*, « Bull. Soc. Préhist. Française », T. XLVII, **1950,** pp. 139-141.

DÉCHELETTE J., *Manuel d'archéologie préhistorique, celtique et gallo-romaine. I, Archéologie préhistorique*, Paris, **1908.**

DEGANI M., *Una statuetta femminile preistorica e un sepolcreto neolitico scoperto a Chiozza di Scandiano (Reggio Emilia)*, « Atti della Società dei Naturalisti e Mat. di Modena », vol. LXXI, **1940,** pp. 11-22.
— *Sulla statuetta femminile scoperta a Chiozza di Scandiano (Reggio Emilia)*, « Bullettino di Paletnologia Italiana », N. S. anno VIII, **1944-45,** pp. 1-14.

DELAGE F., *Gravure aurignacienne de Belcayre (Dordogne)*, « Congrès Préhistorique de France », C. R. XIᵉ sess., Périgueux, **1934,** pp. 388-392.
— *Les roches de Sergeac (Dordogne)*, « L'Anthropologie », T. XLV, **1935,** pp. 281-317.

DÉLUGIN A., *Relief sur pierre aurignacien à représentation humaine découvert au Terme-Pialat, commune de Saint-Avit Seigneur (Dordogne)*, « Bull. Soc. Histor. et Archéol. du Périgord », **1914,** pp. 3-11.

DENIKER J., *Les races et les peuples de la Terre*, Paris, 2ᵉ édit., **1926.**

DIDON L., *L'Abri Blanchard des Roches*, « Bull. de la Soc. Hist. et Archéol. du Périgord », T. XXXVIII, **1911,** pp. 246-261 and 321-345.

DROUOT E., *L'Art paléolithique à la Baume Latrone*, « Cahiers Ligures de préhistoire et d'archéologie », 2, **1953**, pp. 11-46.
— *Les peintures de la Grotte Bayol à Collias (Gard) et l'Art pariétal en Languedoc méditerranéen*, « Bull. Soc. Préhist. Française », T. L, **1953 a**, pp. 392-405.

DUBOIS M. G., *Un tableau de l'Europe Flandrienne*, « Livre Jubilaire du Centenaire de la Soc. Géol. de France », **1930**, pp. 263-277.

DUCROST, ARCELIN A., *La stratigraphie de l'éboulis de Solutré*, « Matériaux pour l'hist. prim. et nat. de l'Homme », T. XI, **1876**, pp. 496-500.

DUPONT M. E., *L'homme pendant les âges de la pierre dans les environs de Dinant-sur-Meuse*, Paris, **1872**.

ELOY L., *Une gravure paléolithique sur plaquette d'ivoire de Marches-les-Dames (Province de Namur)*, « Bull. Soc. Préhist. Française », T. LIII, **1956**, pp. 769-722.

EPHIMENKO P. P., *Kamennije orudija paleoliticeskoi ctojanki v s. Mesine Cernigovskoï gub.*, « Ejegodnik Pysskogo Antropologhiceskogo obscestva nri S.-Peterburskom universitete », T. IV, SPB, **1913**, pp. 67-102.
— *Statuétka soliútreiskogo vremeni s beregov Dona* « Materiali po etnografii Russkii Musei », Tom. III, Vipusk I, Leningrad, **1926**, pp. 139-142.
— *Kostienki I*, Sovscenia « Gosudarstreennaja Akademja istorii materialnoï kulturj », no. 11-12, **1931**.
— *Pervobitnoje obscestvo*, Moskva-Leningrad, **1938**, Kiev, **1953**.
— *Kostienki I*, « Akademia Nauk SSSR Institut istorii materialnoï kultura », **1958**.

FERRY (DE) H., ARCELIN A., *Le Maçônnais préhistorique*, Paris, **1870**.

FILIP J., *Pravěké Československo*, Praha, **1948**.

FLAMAND G. B. M., *Les pierres écrites*, Paris, **1921**.

FRANZ L., *Alteuropäische Wurfhölzer*, « Festschrift, publication d'hommage offert au P. W. Schmidt », Wien, **1928**, pp. 800-808.

FROBENIUS L., *Kulturgeschichte Afrikas*, Zürich, **1933**.

GAILLARD C., *L'art préhistorique à La Genière, commun de Serrières-sur-Aïn*, « Ipek », **1928**, pp. 1-12.

GARRIGOU F., *Age du Renne dans la grotte de la Vache. Vallée de Niaux près de Tarascon-sur-Ariège*, « Bull. Soc. Hist. Nat. de Toulouse », T. I, **1867**, pp. 58-67.

GARROD D., *The upper palaeolithic age in Britain*, Oxford, **1926**.
— *Finding the earliest realistic portrait in the history of man*, « The Illustrated London News », n. 5752, 16 July, **1949**, pp. 91-92.
— *Palaeolithic spear-throwers*, « Proceedings of the Prehist. Soc. », vol. XXI, **1955**, pp. 21-35.
— *Rouffignac*, « Antiquity », vol. XXXII, **1958**, pp. 231-234.

GARROD D., SAINT MATHURIN (DE) S., *The Master sculptors of 12.000 years ago revealed*, « The Illustrated London News », n. 5891, March 15, **1952**, pp. 454-457.

GEER (DE) G., *Geochronologia Suecica. Principles*, Stockholm, **1940**.

GERASIMOV M. M., *Malta, paleoliticeskaià stojanka*, Irkurtsk, **1931**.
— *Raskopki paleoliticeskoi stojanki v cele Malta*. Paleolit SSR, Moskva-Leningrad, **1935**.

GIMENEZ-REYNA S., *Memoria arqueologica de la Provincia de Malaga hasta 1946*, « Informas y memorias de la Comisaria General de Excavaciones Arqueologicas », n. 12, Madrid, **1946**, Cueva de la Pileta, pp. 11-16.

GIROD P., MASSENAT E., *Les Stations de l'âge du renne dans les Vallées de la Vézère et de la Corrèze*, Paris, **1900**.

GLORY A., *Les gravures préhistoriques de la Grotte d'Ebbou à Vallon (Ardèche)*, « La Nature », **1947**, pp. 257-262 and pp. 283-285.
— *Les gravures de la grotte du Colombier à La Bastide de Virac (Ardèche)*, « Comptes Rend. Acad. Inscrip. Belles Lettres », 28 Nov., **1947 a**.
— *La caverne ornée de Bara-Bahau (au Bugue-sur-Vézère, Dordogne)*, « Congrès préhistorique de France », C.R. XVe session, Poitiers-Angoulême, **1956** (published in 1957), pp. 529-35.
— *La grotte ornée d'Aldène ou de Fauzau (Hérault)*, « Congrès préhistorique de France », C. R. XVe session, Poitier-Angoulême, **1956 a** (published in 1957), pp. 536-41.

GLORY A., BAY R., KOBY F., *Gravures préhistoriques à l'Abri de la Sudrie (Dordogne)*, « Rivista di Scienze Preistoriche », vol. IV, **1949**, pp. 97-100.

GOLOMSHTOK E., *Trois gisements du Paléolithique supérieur russes et sibériens. I. Gagarino, II. Timonovka, III. Malta*, « L'Anthropologie », T. XLII, **1933**, pp. 333-346.
— *The Old Stone Age in European Russia*, « Transactions of the American Philosophical Society », New Series, vol. XXIX, part II, Philadelphia, March, **1938**, pp. 189-458.

GONZALES ECHEGARAY J., *Les oeuvres d'art de la grotte de « Las Chimeneas »*, « Bull. de la Soc. Préhist. de l'Ariège », T. VIII, **1953,** pp. 75-77.

GONZALES ECHEGARAY J., RIPOLL P. E., *Hallazgos en la cueva de La Pasiega (Puente Viesgo, Santander)*, « Ampurias », XV-XVI, **1953-1954,** pp. 43-65.

GOURY G., *Origine et évolution de l'homme*, 2e éd., Paris, **1948.**

GRAZIOSI P., *Su di una statuetta steatopigica preistorica rinvenuta a Savignano sul Panaro in Provincia di Modena*, « Archivio per l'Antropologia e la Etnol. », vol. LIV, **1924** (published in 1926), pp. 165-167.
— *A proposito della Venere di Savignano*, « Archivio per l'Antrop. e la Etnol. », vol. LV, **1925** (published in 1927), pp. 38-46.
— *Nuovi elementi per lo studio dei graffiti di grotta Romanelli. Le incisioni della Cova del Parpallò (Valenza)*, « Arch. per l'Antrop. e la Etnol. », vol. LXII, **1932,** pp. 142-146.
— *Les gravures de la grotte Romanelli (Puglia, Italie). Essai comparatif*, « Ipek », **1932-33,** pp. 26-36.
— *Qualche osservazione sulla nuova statuetta preistorica italiana*, « Arch. per l'Antrop. e la Etnol. », vol. LXVIII, **1938,** pp. 298-301.
— *Une nouvelle statuette préhistorique découverte en Italie*, « Bull. Soc. Préhist. Française », T. XXXVI, **1939,** pp. 159-162.
— *L'Arte rupestre della Libia*, Napoli, **1942.**
— *La Venere di Chiozza*, « Studi Etruschi », vol. XVII, **1943,** pp. 371-387.
— *La Vénus de Chiozza*, « L'Anthropologie », T. L, **1941-46,** pp. 437-440.
— *Le pietre incise della grotta di La Marche*, « Rivista di Scienze Preistoriche », vol. I, **1946,** pp. 215-222.
— *Le pitture e i graffiti preistorici dell'Isola di Levanzo nell'Arcipelago delle Egadi (Sicilia)*, « Rivista di Scienze Preistoriche », vol. V, **1950,** pp. 1-43.
— *Gravures paléolithiques de style naturaliste en Italie*, « L'Anthropologie », T. LIV, **1950 a,** pp. 455-59.
— *Nouvelles oeuvres d'art préhistorique découvertes en Sicile*, « Congrès préhist. de France », C. R. XIIIe sess., Paris, **1950 b,** pp. 322-327.
— *Les peintures et les gravures préhistoriques de la grotte de Levanzo (Archipel des Egadi, Sicile)*, « Actes du Congr. Internat. des Sciences Préhist. et Protohist. », IIIe sess., Zürich, **1950 c.**
— *Levanzo*, in : Breuil « Quatre cents siècles d'art pariétal », Montignac, **1952,** pp. 400-402.
— *Nuovi graffiti parietali della grotta di Levanzo (Egadi)*, « Rivista di Scienze Preistoriche », vol. VIII, **1953,** pp. 123-137.
— *Pietra graffita paleolitica e ciottoli dipinti nella grotta di Levanzo (Egadi)*, « Rivista di Scienze Preistoriche », vol. IX, **1954,** pp. 79-88.
— *Altamira*, in : « Grandi scoperte archeologiche », Edizioni della Radio Italiana, Torino, **1954 a,** pp. 64-75.
— *I grandi artisti dell'età della pietra*, in « Le Meraviglie del Passato », vol. I, Milano, **1954 b,** pp. 57-68.
— *Qualche osservazione sui graffiti rupestri della grotta dell'Addaura presso Palermo*, « Bullettino di Paletnologia Italiana », N.S. vol. 65, **1956,** pp. 285-296.
— *Analyses chimiques des peintures de la grotte de Rouffignac*, « La Nature », n. 3260, Déc., **1956 a,** p. 469.
— *Mostra dell'arte preistorica* (Catalogo della mostra di Palazzo Strozzi in Firenze), Firenze, **1957.**
— *La polemica di Rouffignac*, « Rivista di Scienze Preistoriche », vol. XII, **1957 a,** pp. 117-122.
— *Rouffignac again* « Antiquity » XXXIII, **1959,** pp. 135-137.

GRAZIOSI P., CADEO G. C., BRAMBILLA A., *Ciottolo con figure incise nella Grotta delle mura di Monopoli (Bari)*, « Rivista di Scienze Preistoriche », vol. XIII, **1958,** pp. 187-191.

GUERRET M., *Découverte de dessins préhistoriques dans la grotte d'Aldène*, « Bull. Soc. d'Histoire Nat. de Toulouse », **1927,** pp. 318-324.

GVOSDOVER M. D., *Skulpturnoje isobragsneje mamonta is Avdejevskoi paleoliticeskoï stoianki blis Kurska*, « Ucel. sap. Mosk. Gos. univ. vip. », 158, M., **1952,** pp. 211-214.
— *Obrabotka costi i costianie usdelia Avdeevskoi stojanki*, in : *Paleolit i Neolit SSSR*, « Materiali i issledovanija po archeologii SSSR », n. 39, Akademija Nauk, Moskva, Leningrad, **1953,** pp. 192-226. [French translation : *Le travail des os et des articles d'os a la station d'Ardeevo*, in : *Paléolithique et Néolithique de l'URSS*, published by « Annales du centre d'études et document. paléontol. », No. 18, Paris, **1956,** pp. 168-197].

HADDON A. C., *The decorative art of British New Guinea*, Dublin, **1894.**
— *Evolution in Art*, London, **1895.**

HAMAL-NANDRIN J., SERVAIS J., *La grotte dite « du coléoptère », rapport sur les fouilles 1923-1924*, « Revue Anthropologique », vol. XXXV, **1925,** pp. 120-138.

HAMY E. T., *Précis de Paléontologie humaine*, Paris, **1870.**

HANČAR F., *Die Venusstatuette von Jelisejeviči (Kreis Brjansk)*, « Ipek », **1949-53,** pp. 1-6.

HENSEL W., *Sztuka społeczeństw Paleolityczńych*, Warszawa, **1957.**

HERBERTS K., *Anfänge der Malerei. Die Fragen ihrer Maltechniken und das Rätsel der Erhaltung*, Barmen, **1941.**

HERNANDEZ-PACHECO E. (vedi PACHECO-HERNANDEZ E.).

HERVÉ G., *Le squelette de Brünn*, « Revue de l'Ecole d'Anthrop. », Année III, **1893,** pp. 20-24.

HOERNES M., *Der diluviale Mensch in Europa*, Braunschweig, **1903.**

JAMMES L., JEANNEL R., *Les peintures humaines de la grotte du Portel*, « C. R. Ass. Franç. Av. Sciences », Congrès de Lille, **1909,** pp. 811-813.

JOHNSON F., *Radiocarbon dating*, « American Antiquity », vol. XVII, n. 1, **1951,** p. 11 e pp. 50-51 (Movius H. L., « The Lascaux Cave »).

JORDÀ CERDÀ F., *Sobre la edad solutrense de algunas pinturas de la cueva de la Pileta (Malaga)*, « Zephirus », VI, **1955,** pp. 131-143.

JORDÀ CERDÀ F., BERENGUER ALONSO M., *La cueva de el Pindal (Asturias), nuevas aportaciones*, « Boletín del Instituto de Estudios Asturianos », n. 23, **1954,** pp. 1-30.

KELLEY H., *Sur quelques silex inédits des Eyzies*, « Mélanges de Préhist. ed d'Anthrop. offerts au Prof. Comte H. Begouen », Toulouse, **1939,** pp. 211-216.

KIDDER L., KIDDER H. H., *Le Puy-de-Lacan et ses gravures magdaléniennes*, « L'Anthropologie », T. XLVI, **1936,** pp. 17-31.

KLIMA B., *Vizkum palolitického sídlištĕ u Pavlova v roce 1954*, « Archeologické rozhledy », IX, **1957,** pp. 145-151.

KOBY F., *Y-a-t-il eu à Lascaux un « Bos longifrons »?*, « Bull. Soc. Préhist. Française », T. LI, **1954,** pp. 434-441.

KOPPERS W., *The « Sketch book » of an Aurignacian artist*, « Man », vol. L, **1950,** pp. 85-86.

KŘÍŽ M., *Beiträge zur Kenntnis der Quatärzeit im Mähren*, Steinitz, **1903.**

KÜHN H., *Kunst und Kultur der Vorzeit Europas (das Paläolithikum)*, Berlin und Leipzig, **1929.**
— *Neue Funde eiszeitlicher Kunst in Mähren*, « Ipek », **1934,** pp. 152-157.
— *Menschendarstellungen im Paläolithikum*, « Zeitschrift für Rassenkunde », Band IV, Heft 3, **1936,** pp. 225-246.
— *Eine Menschendarstellung der Eiszeit aus Mähren*, « Ipek », **1936-37,** p. 128.
— *Auf den Spuren des Eiszeitmenschen*, Wiesbaden, **1950.** [English translation : *On the Track of Prehistoric Man*, London, 1955].
— *Das problem des Urmonotheismus*, « Abhandlungen der geistes- und sozialwissenschaftl. Klasse. Akad. der Wissenschaften und der Literatur in Mainz », NR. 22, **1950,** pp. 1639-1672.
— *Die Felsbilder Europas*, Stuttgart, **1952.** [English translation : *Rock Pictures of Europe*, London, 1956].
— *Die Kunst Alteuropas*, Stuttgart, **1954.**

LABORIE R., *Communication sur les peintures pariétales de Lascaux*, Les Eyzies, **1948.**

LAET (de) S. J., *The Low Countries*, London, **1958.**

LALANNE J. G., *Découverte d'un bas-relief à représentation humaine dans les fouilles de Laussel*, « L'Anthropologie », T. XXII, **1911,** pp. 257-260.
— *Bas-reliefs à figuration humaine de l'abri sous roches de Laussel (Dordogne)*, « L'Anthropologie » T. XXIII, **1912,** pp. 129-149.

LALANNE J. G., BOUYSSONIE J., *Le gisement paléolithique de Laussel. Fouilles du Dr. Lalanne*, « L'Anthropologie », T. L, **1941-46,** pp. 1-65 and 117-163.

LALANNE J. G., BREUIL H., *L'abri sculpté de Cap Blanc à Laussel (Dordogne)*, « L'Anthropologie », T. XXII, **1911,** pp. 385-402.

LAMING A., *Lascaux, Paintings and Engravings*, Penguin Books, **1959.**

LAMING-EMPERAIRE, *L'Art préhistorique*, Paris, **1951.**

LANTIER R., *Las excavaciones del santuario solutrense de Roc-de-Sers (Charente) en 1951*, « Archivo Español de Arqueología », T. XXV, **1952,** pp. 321-335.

LAPLACE-JAURETSCHE G. L., *Etcheberri*, in : Breuil H., « Quatre cents siècles d'art pariétal », Montignac, **1952,** pp. 259-261.
— *Les grottes ornées des Arbailles*, « Revue d'études basques », vol. VI, **1952 a.**

LARTET L., CHAPLAIN DUPARC, *Sur une sépulture des anciens troglodytes des Pyrénées*, « Matériaux pour l'hist. primit. et nat. de l'Homme », IXᵉ vol., 2ᵉ série, **1874,** pp. 101-167.

LARTET L., CHRISTY H., *Objets gravés et sculptés des temps pré-historiques dans l'Europe Occidentale*, « Revue Archéologique », **1864,** pp. 1-37.
— *Reliquiae Aquitanicae*, London, **1875.**

LARUE M., COMBIER J., ROCHE J., *Les gisements périgordien et magdalénien du Saut-du-Perron (Loire)*, « L'Anthropologie », T. LIX, **1955,** pp. 408-413.

LAVIOSA ZAMBOTTI P., *Le più antiche culture agricole europee*, Milano, **1943.**

LECLERC J., PRADEL, *Un bâton orné du Magdalénien final de Loubressac, commune de Mazerolles (Vienne)*, « Bull. Soc. Préhist. Française », T. XLV, **1948**, pp. 402-404.

LEMOZI A., *Peintures et gravures découvertes dans les grottes des communes d'Espagnac, Sainte-Eulalie et de Cabrerets*, « Bull. Soc. Préhist. Française », T. XVII, **1920**, pp. 256-263.
— *La grotte-temple du Pech-Merle*, Paris, **1929**.
— *Quelques spécimens de l'Art Quaternaire (région de Cabrerets-Lot)*, « Congrès préhist. de France », C. R. XIIᵉ sess., Toulouse-Foix, **1936**, pp. 642-659.
— *Les figurations humaines préhistoriques dans la région de Cabrerets (Lot)*, « Congrès préhist. de France », C. R. XIIᵉ sess., Toulouse-Foix, **1936 b**, pp. 660-670.
— *La grotte du « Cantal » vallée du Célé près Cabrerets (Lot)*, « Bull. Soc. Préhist. Française », T. XXXIV, **1937**, pp. 213-223.

LEONARDI P., *Note di viaggio sulle figurazioni parietali paleolitiche franco-cantabriche*, « Rivista di Scienze Preistoriche », vol. X, **1955**, pp. 76-85.

LIBBY W. F., *Radiocarbon dating*, Chicago, second edition, **1955**.

LHOTE H., *A la découverte des fresques du Tassil*, Paris, **1958**. [English translation : *The Search for the Tassili Frescoes*, London-New York 1959].

LORIANA (DE), *Excavaciones arqueológicas realizadas en la gruta y covacho de Berroberria*, « Atlantis », XV, **1936-40**, pp. 91-112.

LOUIS M., *La Baume Latrone*, « Cahiers d'Hist. et d'Archéol. », nuov. série, n. 1, **1946**, pp. 1-8.
— *Gravures pariétales inédites de la grotte Chabot*, « L'Anthropologie », T. LI, **1947**, pp. 461-466.

LUQUET G. H., *Le réalisme dans l'art paléolithique*, « L'Anthropologie », T. XXXIII, **1923**, pp. 17-48.
— *L'Art et la religion des hommes fossiles*, Paris, **1926**.
— *Les origines de l'art figuré*, « Ipek », **1926 a**, pp. 3-28.
— *L'Art primitif*, Paris, **1930**.

LWOFF S., *La Marche. Gravures à représentations d'humains du Magdalénien III*, « Bull. Soc. Préhist. Française », T. XXXVIII, **1941**, pp. 145-161.
— *La Marche. Industrie de l'Os*, « Bull. Soc. Préhist. Française », T. XXXIX, **1942**, pp. 51-64.
— *La Marche. A, Iconographie humaine du Magdalénien III. B, Industrie de l'Os*, « Bull. Soc. Préhist. Française », T. XL, **1943**, pp. 166-180.
— *Iconographie humaine et animale du Magdalénien III, Grotte de La Marche. Commun de Lussac-les-Chateaux (Vienne)*, « Bull. Soc. Préhist. Française », T. LIV, **1957**, pp. 622-633.

MACALISTER R. A. S., *A Text-book of European Archaeology*, vol. I, *The Palaeolithic Period*, Cambridge, **1921**.

MAINAGE TH., *Les religions de la Préhistoire. L'âge paléolithique*, Paris, **1921**.

MAKOWSKY A., *Der diluviale Mensch im Löss von Brünn. Mit Funden aus der Mammuthzeit*, « Mitteilungen Anthropol. Gesell. in Wien », Band XXII, **1892**, pp. 73-84.

MALVESIN-FABRE G., *La stratigraphie de Pair-non-Pair*, « Procès Verbaux de la Soc. Linnéenne de Bordeaux », Séance du 12 janv., **1946**, pp. 1-11.

MALVESIN-FABRE G., NOUGIER L. R., ROBERT R., *Engins de chasse et de pêche du Magdalénien de la grotte de la Vache (Ariège)*, « Bulletin Soc. Préhist. de l'Ariège », T. VI, **1951**, pp. 13-30.
— *Empreintes de pieds humains préhistoriques de la caverne de Niaux (Ariège)*, « Bulletin Soc. Préhist. de l'Ariège », T. VII, **1952**, pp. 37-48.
— *L'occupation magdalénienne de la grotte de Bédeilhac (Ariège) et découverte d'un nouveau gisement dans la galérie Vidal*, « Bull. Soc. Préhist. de l'Ariège », T. VIII, **1953**, pp. 19-48.
— *Gargas*, Toulouse, **1954**.

MARCONI BOVIO J., *Incisioni rupestri dell'Addaura (Palermo)*, « Bull. di Paletnologia Italiana », N. S., VIII, parte V, **1952-53**, pp. 5-22.
— *Interpretazione dell'arte parietale dell'Addaura*, « Bull. d'Arte », Minist. P. I., n. 1, gennaio-marzo, **1953**, pp. 1-8.
— *Sui graffiti dell'Addaura (Palermo)*, « Rivista di Antropologia », vol. XL, **1953 a**, pp. 55-64.
— *Sulle forme schematizzate dei graffiti dell'Addaura (Palermo)*, « Actes du IV Congr. Intern. du Quatern. », Rome-Pise, **1953 b**, pp. 1-7.
— *Nuovi graffiti preistorici nelle grotte del Monte Pellegrino (Palermo)*, « Bull. di Paletn. Italiana », N. S. IX, vol. 64, **1954-55**, pp. 57-72.
— *Sull'esegesi del graffito dell'Addaura (Palermo)*, « Quaternaria », II, **1955**, pp. 201-207.

MARTIN H., *Manifestations artistiques solutréennes dans la vallée du Roc (Charente)*, « Ipek », **1927**, pp. 113-118.
— *La frise sculptée et l'atelier solutréen du Roc (Charente)*, « Archives de l'Inst. de Paléontologie Humaine », Mém. 5, **1928**.
— *Les sculptures du Roc*, « Préhistoire », I, fasc. T. 1, **1932**, pp. 1-8.

MASCARAUX F., *La grotte Saint-Michel d'Arudy, Basses-Pyrénées. Fouilles dans une station magdalénienne*, « Revue de l'Ecole d'Anthrop. », Année XX, **1910**, pp. 357-378.

MASKA K. J., *Der diluviale Mensch in Mähren*, Neutitschein, **1886.**

MASKA K. J., OBERMAIER H., BREUIL H., *La statuette de Mammouth de Predmost*, « L'Anthropologie », T. XXIII, **1912,** pp. 273-285.

MASSENAT E., *Les fouilles des stations des bordes de la Vézère et les oeuvres d'art de Laugerie Basse*, « Matériaux pour l'hist. prim. et nat. de l'Homme », vol. XII, **1877,** pp. 1-4.

MAUDUIT J. A., *Quarante mille ans d'art moderne*, Paris, **1954.**

MAURA M., *Los dibujos rupestres de la cueva del Reguerillo (Torrelaguna) provincia de Madrid*, « II° Congr. Nacional de Arqueologia », Madrid, **1951,** pp. 73-74.

MAURY J., *Laugerie Basse. Les fouilles de M. J.-A. Le Bel*, Le Mans, **1924.**

MAYET L., PISSOT J., *Abri-sous-roche préhistorique de la Colombière, près Poncin (Aïn)*, « Annales de l'Université de Lyon », Sér. I, vol. 39, **1915.**

MELLO M. G., *Les cavernes quaternaires de Creswell (Angleterre)*, « C. R. Assoc. Française Avanc. Sciences », Le Havre, **1877.**

MENGHIN O., *Weltgeschichte der Steinzeit*, Wien, **1931.**
— *Las pinturas rupestres de la Patagonia*, « Runa », vol. V, **1952,** pp. 5-22.

MÉROC L., MAZET J., *Les peintures de la grotte de Cougnac (Lot)*, « L'Anthropologie », T. LVII, **1953,** pp. 490-494.
— *Cougnac, grotte peinte*, avec appendice di H. BREUIL, Stuttgart, **1956.**

MÉROC L., MICHAUT L., OLLÉ M., *La grotte de Marsoulas (Haute-Garonne)*, « Bull. Soc. Méridionale de Spéléologie et Préhist. de Toulouse », **1948,** pp. 284-320.

MICHAUT L., *Nouvelles découvertes dans l'abri de Montconfort à Saint-Martory (Haute-Garonne)*, « Bulletin Soc. Préhist. de l'Ariège », T. IV, **1949,** pp. 29-31.

MILANKOVITCH M., *Astronomische Mittel zur Erforschung der Erdgeschichtlichen Klimate*, « Handb. Geophys. », 9, **1938,** pp. 593-698.

MORIN-JEAN, *Les artistes préhistoriques*, Paris, **1933.**

MORTILLET (DE) A., *Sur quelques figures peintes et gravées des grottes des environs des Eyzies*, « L'Homme Préhistorique », 1e année, **1903,** pp. 43-50.

MORTILLET (DE) G., MORTILLET (DE) A., *Musée Préhistorique*, 2e édit., Paris, **1903.**

MOVIUS H. L. JR., *Excavations at the prehistoric rock-shelter of la Colombière*, « Archaeology », vol. 2, n. 1, **1949,** pp. 22-30.
— *The Lascaux Cave*, in : Johnson F., « Radiocarbon dating », « American Antiquity », vol. XVII, n. 1, **1951,** pp. 11 e 50-51.
— *El arte mobiliar del Perigordiense Superior de la Colombière (Aïn) y su relación con el desarollo del arte contemporáneo en la región franco-cantábrica*, « Ampurias », XIV, **1952,** pp. 1-36.

NADAILLAC (DE), *Les premiers hommes et les temps préhistoriques*, Paris, **1881.**
— *Le bâton de commandement de Montgaudier*, « Bull. Mém. Soc. Anthrop. de Paris », **1887,** pp. 7-10.

NEEB E., *Eine paläolitische Freilandstation bei Mainz*, « Prähistorische Zeitschrift », XV, **1924,** pp. 1-8.

NOUGIER L., *Art et Magie*, « Pallas. Etudes sur l'Antiquité », « Annales de la Faculté des Lettres de Toulouse », I, **1953,** pp. 224-239.

NOUGIER L. R., ROBERT R., *Pech-Merle de Cabrerets*, Toulouse, **1954.**
— *Niaux*, Toulouse, **1954 a.**
— *Mas d'Azil*, Toulouse, **1954 b.**
— *Utilisation de reliefs stalagmitiques dans les peintures quaternaires d'anthropomorphes*, « Rivista di Scienze Preistoriche », vol. X, **1955,** pp. 12-18.
— *Rouffignac en Périgord : La Grotte aux Mammouths*, « La Nature », n. 3258, Octobre, **1956,** pp. 377-380.
— *Rouffignac ou la guerre des mammouths*, Paris, **1957.** [English translation: London, 1958].
— *Les figurations anthropomorphes de Rouffignac*, « La Nature », n. 3265, Mai, **1957 a,** pp. 191-194.
— *Rouffignac I Galerie Henri Breuil et grand plafond*, Florence, **1959.**

OBERMAIER H., *Institut de Paléont. Humaine. Travaux de l'année 1913. Fouilles en Bavière*, « L'Anthropologie », T. XXV, **1914,** pp. 254-262.
— *Trampas cuaternarias para espíritus malignos*, « Boletín de la Real Sociedad Española de Historia Natural », T. XVIII, **1918,** pp. 162-169.
— *Escultura cuaternaria de la cueva del Rascaño (Santander)*, « Boletín de la Associació Catalana d'Antropol., Etnol. i Prehist. », Barcelona, vol. I, **1923,** pp. 7-14.
— *El Hombre fosil*, « Comisión de investig. paleontol. y prehist. », n. 9, segunda edición, Madrid, **1925.**
— *Oeuvres d'Art du Magdalénien Final de la grotte du « Pendo » près Santander (Asturies, Espagne)*, « Préhistoire », T. I, fasc. 1, **1932,** pp. 9-18.

OBERMAIER H., VEGA DEL SELLA (DE LA), *La cueva del Buxu (Asturias)*, « Comisión de investigaciones paleontológicas y prehistóricas », Mem. n. 20, Madrid, **1918**.

OBERMAIER H., FRAUNHOLZ J., *Eine Mammutdarstellung aus Süddeutschland*, « Ipek », **1926**, pp. 29-32.
— *Der skulptierte Rengeweihstab aus der mittleren Klausenhöhle bei Essing (Niederbayern)*, « Ipek », **1927**, pp. 1-9.

OCTOBON F. C. E., *Art et magie dans la grotte de Bédeilhac (Ariège)*, « Revue Anthropol. », vol. XLVIII, **1938**, pp. 41-54.
— *Grotte de Bédeilhac. Peintures et gravures sur parois ou sol de la grotte*, « Revue Anthropol. », vol. XLIX, **1939**, pp. 222-235.
— *Une gravure inédite de la grotte de Bédeilhac (Ariège)*, « Congrès Préhist. de France », C. R. XIIIᵉ session, Paris, **1950**, pp. 522-525.
— *Contribution à l'étude des couches supérieures de la Barma-Grande*, « Cahiers de Préhistoire et d'Archéologie », 1, **1952**, pp. 3-28.

OKLADNIKOV A. P., *Novie dannie o paleoliticeskom prosclom Priboikalja*, « Kratkije soobsenija Instituta istorii materialnoi i kulturi », V, **1940**, p. 60.
— *Paleoliticeskajä statuetka ie Bureti* « Materiali i issledoovanijà po archeologhii SSR », nᵒ. 2, Moskva-Leningrad **1941 a.**
— *Istorija Jakutskoi ASSR*. T. I, Moskva-Leningrad, **1955.**
— *Paleoliticeskije jilisca v Bureti*, « Kratkije soobsenija instituta istriji materialnoi kulturi », 10, **1941**, pp. 16-32.

OVERLOOP (VAN) E., *Les origines de l'art en Belgique*, Bruxelles, **1882.**

PACE B., *Note sull'arte delle incisioni parietali di Levanzo*, « Rivista di Antropologia », XXXVIII, **1950**, pp. 56-62.

PACHECO-HERNANDEZ E., *Los grabados de la Cueva de Penches*, « Comisión de investigaciones paleontológicas y prehistóricas », Mem. 17, Madrid, **1917.**
— *La Caverna de la Peña de Candamo (Asturias)*, « Comisión de investigaciones paleontológicas y prehistóricas », Mem. 24, Madrid, **1919.**

PALMA DI CESNOLA A., *Nuova statuetta paleolitica rinvenuta in Italia*, « Archivio per l'Antrop. e l'Etnol. », vol. LXVIII, **1938**, pp. 293-297.

PARAT A., *Les grottes de la Cure et de l' Yonne. Recherches préhistoriques*, « L'Anthropologie », T. XII, **1901**, pp. 119-134.

PASQUELOT M., *Les fresques de Villars*, « Radar », nᵒ 471, Paris, 16 Fevrier, **1958.**

PASSEMARD E., *Une gravure de lièvre d'Isturitz*, « Bull. Soc. Préhist. Française », T. XVII, **1920**, pp. 79-81.
— *Un félin sculpté en bois de renne*, « Acad. Inscript. et Belles Lettres », C. R., **1920 a**, pp. 28-31.
— *La Caverne d'Isturitz (Basses Pyrénées)*, « Revue Archéologique », T. XV, **1922**, pp. 1-45.
— *Les sculptures en ronde-bosse sur pierre de la Caverne d'Isturitz*, « Ipek », **1925**, pp. 44-46.
— *Une gravure aurignacienne d'Isturitz*, « Bull. Soc. Préhist. Franç. », T. XXVII, **1930**, pp. 357-360.
— *Un Galet gravé d'un signe tectiforme de la Caverne d'Isturitz*, « Bull. Soc. Préhist. Française », T. XXXII, **1935**, pp. 299-300.
— *La Caverne d'Isturitz en Pays Basque*, « Préhistoire », T. IX, **1944**, pp. 1-95.

PASSEMARD L., *Les statuettes féminines paléolithiques dites « Vénus stéatopyges »*, Nîmes, **1938.**

PATRONATO DE LAS CUEVAS PREHISTORICAS DE LA PROV. DE SANTANDER, *La Caverna de las Monedas y sus interesantes pinturas*, Santander, **1953.**

PATRONI G., *La Preistoria*, vol. I, Milano, **1937.**

PATTE E., *Gravures inédites du Placard (Charente)*, « Mélanges de Préhist. et d'Anthrop. offerts au Prof. Comte Begouen », Toulouse, **1939**, pp. 243-247.

PÉQUART ST. J. and M., *Récente découverte de deux oeuvres d'art magdalénien au Mas d'Azil*, « La Revue scientifique », n. 3205, Février, **1942**, pp. 91-95.

PÉRICARD L., LWOFF S., *La Marche. Premier atelier Magdalénien III à dalles gravées mobiles*, « Bull. de la Soc. Préhist. Française », T. XXXVII, **1940**, pp. 155-180.

PERICOT L., *La Cueva del Parpallò*, Madrid, **1942.**
— *La España primitiva*, Barcelona, **1950.**
— *El arte rupestre español*, Barcelona-Buenos Aires, **1950 a.**

PERRET R., *Recherches archéologiques et ethnologiques au Tassili des Ajjers (Sahara Central)*, « Journal Soc. des Africanistes », T. VI, **1936**, pp. 41-64.

PETERS E., *Die altsteinzeitliche Kulturstätte Petersfels*, Augsburg, **1930.**
— *Die Kunst des Magdalenien vom Petersfels*, « Ipek », **1930 a**, pp. 1-6.

PEYRONY D., *Nouvelles fouilles aux Champs Blancs ou Jean Blancs*, « C. R. Assoc. Française pour l'Avanc. des Sciences », Congrès de Nîmes, **1921,** pp. 522-528.
— *Les peintures murales de la caverne des Merveilles à Rocamadour (Lot.)*, « L'Anthropologie », T. XXXVI, **1926,** pp. 401-407.
— *Sur quelques pièces intéressantes de la grotte de La Roche près de Lalinde (Dordogne)*, « L'Anthropologie », T. XL, **1930,** pp. 19-29.
— *Les abris Lartet et du Poisson, à Gorge d'Enfer (Dordogne)*, « L'Anthropologie », T. XLII, **1932,** pp. 241-268.
— *Les gisements préhistoriques de Bourdeilles (Dordogne)*, « Archives de l'Inst. de Paléont. Humaine », Mém. 10, **1932 a.**
— *La Ferrassie*, « Préhistoire », T. III, **1934,** pp. 1-92.
— *La station préhistorique du Pech de la Boissière*, « Bull. Soc. Préhist. Française », T. XXXI, **1934 a,** pp. 194-213.
— *L'art azilien périgourdin, ses rapports avec l'art magdalénien final et l'art capsien*, « Congrès Préhist. de France », C. R. XIe sess., Périgueux, **1934 b,** pp. 413-417.
— *Le gisement Castanet*, « Bull. Soc. Préhist. Française », T. XXXII, **1935,** pp. 418-443.
— *L'Abri de Villepin, commune de Tursac (Dordogne). Magdalénien supérieur et Azilien*, « Bull. Soc. Préhist. Française », T. XXXIII, **1936,** pp. 253-272.
— *A propos de quelques gravures du Paléolithique supérieur et du Mésolithique*, « Bull. Soc. Préhist. Française », T. XXXIX, **1942,** pp. 214-219.
— *Le Périgord préhistorique*, Périgueux, **1949.**
— *L'industrie de la grotte de Lascaux*, « Bull. Soc. Préhist. Française », T. XLVII, **1950,** pp. 135-137.
— Comunic. à la S.P.F. sur *Laugerie-Haute*, « Bull. Soc. Préhist. Française », T. XLIX, **1952,** p. 567.

PEYRONY D., PEYRONY E., *La station préhistorique des Jean-Blancs*, « Bull. Soc. Hist. et Archéol. du Périgord », T. LXI, **1934,** pp. 179-202.
— *Gravures pariétales de la galerie de droite de la grotte des Combarelles*, « Congrès Préhist. de France », C. R. XIIe sess., Toulouse-Foix, **1936,** pp. 736-739.
— *Laugerie-Haute*, « Archives de l'Instit. de Paléontol. Humaine », Mém. 19, **1938.**

PIETTE E., *L'époque eburnéenne et les races humaines de la période glyptique*, St. Quentin, **1894.**
— *La station de Brassempouy et les statuettes humaines de la période glyptique*, « L'Anthropologie », T. VI, **1895,** pp. 129-151.
— *Les galets coloriés du Mas d'Azil*, « L'Anthropologie », T. VII, **1896,** pp. 383-427.
— *Études d'Ethnographie préhistorique. Fouilles à Brassempouy, en 1896*, « L'Anthropologie », T. VIII, **1897,** pp. 165-173.
— *Gravures du Mas d'Azil et statuettes de Menton*, « Bull. et Mém. Soc. d'Anthrop. de Paris », **1902,** pp. 771-779.
— *Classification des sédiments formés dans les cavernes pendant l'Age du renne*, « L'Anthropologie », T. XV, **1904,** pp. 129-176.
— *Le chevêtre et la semi-domestication des animaux aux temps pléistocènes*, « L'Anthropologie », T. XVII, **1906,** pp. 27-53.
— *L'Art pendant l'Age du renne*, Paris, **1907,**

PIETTE E., LA PORTERIE (DE) J., *Fouilles à Brassempouy en 1896*, « L'Anthropologie », T. VIII, **1897,** pp. 165-173.
— *Fouilles à Brassempouy en 1897*, « L'Anthropologie », T. IX, **1898,** pp. 531-555.

PIJOAN J., *El arte prehistórico europeo*, in « Summa Artis » di Cossio-Pijoan, Madrid, **1934.**

PITTARD E., *Une gravure sur galet de l'époque aurignacienne*, « L'Anthropologie », T. XXIII, **1912,** pp. 307-311.

POLIKARPOVIC K. M., *Raboti po paleolitu v Sapadnoi oblasti v 1936 g.*, « Sovetskaja archeologhia », V, **1940,** p. 285.

PRADEL L., CHOLLET A., *L'Abri Périgordien de Laraux, Commune de Lussac-les-Chateaux (Vienne)*, « L'Anthropologie », T. LIV, **1950,** pp. 214-227.

RADMILLI A. M., *Esplorazioni paletnologiche nel territorio di Tivoli*, « Atti e Memorie della Società Tiburtina di Storia e d'Arte », vol. XXVI, nn. 1-4, **1954,** pp. 1-20.
— *Scavi nella grotta di Ponte Lucano*, « Atti dell'Associazione di Storia Patria di Tivoli », **1954 a.**
— *Un'opera d'arte di magia venatoria*, « Bullettino di Paletnol. Italiana », N. S., IX, vol. 64, **1954 b,** pp. 47-56.
— *La più antica arte del Lazio*, « Collezione artistica della Società Tiburtina di Storia ed Arte », vol. II, **1956.**
— *The movable art of the Grotta Polesini*, « Antiquity and Survival », n. 6, **1956,** pp. 465-473.
— *Le produzioni d'arte mobiliare nella grotta Polesini presso Roma*, « Quartär », Bd. 9, **1957,** pp. 41-59.

RAPHAEL M., *Prehistoric cave paintings*, Washington, **1946.**

RAYMOND P., *L'Arrondissement d'Uzès avant l'histoire*, Paris, **1900.**

REGALIA E., STASI P. E., *Grotta Romanelli (Castro, Terra d'Otranto). Nota preventiva*, « Archivio per l'Antropologia e la Etnologia », vol. XXXIV, **1904**, pp. 17-81.
— *Grotta Romanelli (Castro, Terra d'Otranto). Seconda nota. Due risposte ad una critica*, « Archivio per l'Antrop. e la Etnol. », vol. XXXV, **1905**, pp. 113-172.

REGNAULT F., *Empreintes de mains humaines dans la grotte de Gargas (Hautes-Pyrénées)*, « Bull. et Mém. Soc. d'Anthrop. de Paris », T. 7, 5ᵉ sér., **1906**, pp. 331-332.
— *La statuette de Sireuil et la reine de Pount ne sont pas stéatopyges*, « Bull. Soc. Préhist. Française », T. XXVIII, **1931**, pp. 262-264.

REINACH S., *Statuette de femme nue découverte dans une des grottes de Menton*, « L'Anthropologie », T. IX, **1898**, pp. 26-31.
— *Répertoire de l'Art quaternaire*, Paris, **1913**.
— *Une nouvelle statuette féminine en ivoir de mammuth*, « L'Anthropologie », T. XXXIV, **1924**, pp. 346-350.

REYGASSE M., *Gravures et peintures rupestres du Tassili des Ajjer*, « L'Anthropologie », T. XLV, **1935**, pp. 533-571.

RIEK G., *Altsteinzeitkulturen am Vogelherd bei Stetten ob Lontal (Württemberg)*, « Ipek », **1932-33**, pp. 1-26.

RIPOLL PERELLÒ E., *Una nueva cueva con pinturas en Puente Viesgo (Santander)*, « Rivista di Scienze Preistoriche », vol. VIII, **1953**, pp. 105-108.
— *Rapresentaciones de Caballos de la Cueva de las Monedas (Puente Viesgo, Santander)*, « Libro Homenaje al Conde de la Vega del Sella », Oviedo, **1956**, pp. 165-170.
— *Nota acerca de los grabados digitales de la cueva Clotilde de Santa Isabel (Santander)*, « IV Congreso Arqueologico Nacional », Saragoza, **1957**, pp. 53-58.

RIVIÈRE E., *Nouvelles recherches dans la Dordogne*, « Ass. Française pour l'Avanc. des Sciences », Congrès de Caen, T. XXIII, **1894**, II, p. 721.
— *La Grotte de La Mouthe (Dordogne)*, « Bull. et Mém. Soc. Anthrop. de Paris », T. VIII, série IV, **1897**, pp. 302-329.
— *Nouvelles recherches à Cro-Magnon*, « Bull. et Mém. Soc. Anthrop. de Paris », T. VIII, série IV, **1897 a**, pp. 503-508.
— *La lampe de grès de la grotte de La Mouthe*, « Bull. et Mém. Soc. Anthrop. de Paris », T. X, série IV, **1899**, pp. 554-563.
— *Les dessins gravés de la grotte de La Mouthe*, « Bull. et Mém. Soc. Anthrop. de Paris », T. II, série V, **1901**, pp. 509-517.
— *Les parois gravées et peintes de la grotte de La Mouthe (Dordogne)*, « L'Homme préhistorique », Année I, **1903**, pp. 65-86.

ROBERT R., *Nouvelles fouilles à Bédeilhac*, « Bull. Soc. Préhist. Française », T. XL, **1943**, pp. 276-281.
— *Une tête de propulseur sculptée de la Grotte de Bédeilhac (Ariège)*, « Ipek », 17 Band, **1943-48**, pp. 40-42.
— *Magdalénien de la Grotte de Bédeilhac (Ariège)*, « Bull. Soc. Préhist. de l'Ariège », T. IV, **1949**, pp. 17-23.
— *Une nouvelle oeuvre d'art Magdalénienne*, « L'Anthropologie », T. LV, **1951**, pp. 87-90.
— *Deux oeuvres d'art inédites de la grotte « de La Vache » (Ariège)*, « Bull. Soc. Préhist. Française », T. XLVIII, **1951 a**, pp. 185-186.
— *Une gravure inédite de la grotte de « La Vache » (Ariège)*, « Rivista di Scienze Preistoriche », vol. VI, **1951 b**, pp. 84-86.
— *« Le Faon à l'Oiseau ». Tête de propulseur sculpté du Magdalénien de Bédeilhac*, « Bull. de la Soc. Préhist. de l'Ariège », T. VIII, **1953**, pp. 11-18.
— *Une gravure inédite de la grotte de « La Vache »*, « L'Anthropologie », T. LVII, **1953 a**, pp. 101-103.

ROBERT R., KÜHN H., *Un lissoir gravé inédit de la grotte de « La Vache » (Ariège)*, « Rivista di Scienze Preistoriche », vol. VII, **1952**, pp. 235-238.

ROBERT R., MALVESIN-FABRE G., NOUGIER R., *Bisons à cupules des grottes pyrénéennes modelés et gravés sur argile*, « Bulletin archéologique », **1953** (published in 1956), pp. 195-199.
— *Sur l'existence possible d'une école d'art dans le Magdalénien pyrénéen*, « Bulletin archéologique », **1953 a** (published in 1956), pp. 187-193.

ROGHI G., *Una scoperta nella grotta di Villars*, « L'Europeo », Milano, 20 aprile **1958**.

ROSKA M., *Die erste Jungpaläolithische Plastik aus Ungarn*, « Quartär », 7/8 Band, **1956**, pp. 177-182.

ROUSSEAU L., *Le Magdalénien dans la Vienne. Découverte et fouille d'un gisement du Magdalénien à Angles-sur-l'Anglin (Vienne)*, « Bull. Soc. Préhist. Française », T. XXX, **1933**, pp. 239-256.

RUBIN M., SUESS A., *U. S. Geological Survey radiocarbon date, II*, « Science », vol. 121, febr., **1955**, pp. 481-488.

RUST A., *Kulturgeschichtlicher Teil*, in « Das Altsteinzeitliche Rentierjägerlager Meiendorf », Holstein, **1937**, pp. 73-146.

SACCASYN-DELLA SANTA E., *Les figures humaines du Paléolithique supérieur eurasiatique*, Anvers, **1947**.

SAINT-MATHURIN (DE) S., GARROD D., *Visite au gisement d'Angles-sur-Anglin*, « Congrès préhist. de France », C. R. XIIIᵉ session, Paris, **1950**, pp. 85-86.
— *Les sculptures d'Angles-sur-Anglin. Visite au Musée de l'Homme*, « Congrès préhist. de France » C. R. XIIIᵉ sess., Paris, **1950 a**, pp. 87-90.
— *La frise sculptée de l'abri du Roc aux Sorciers à Angles-sur-l'Anglin (Vienne)*, « L'Anthropologie », T. LV, **1951**, pp. 413-424.
— *Rouffignac, ses textes, ses plans*, « Bull. Soc. Préhist. Française », T. LV, **1958**, pp. 588-592.
— *Rouffignac, again*, « Antiquity », vol. XXXIII, **1959**, pp. 134-135.

SAINT-PÉRIER (DE) R., *Statuette de femme stéatopyge découverte à Lespugue (Haute-Garonne)*, « L'Anthropologie », T. XXXII, **1922**, pp. 361-381.
— *Les fouilles de 1923 dans la grotte des rideaux à Lespugue*, « L'Anthropologie », T. XXXIV, **1924**, pp. 1-15.
— *La statuette féminine de Lespugue*, « Bull. Soc. Préhist. Française », T. XXI, **1924 a**, pp. 81-84.
— *Les oeuvres d'art paléolithiques de la Vallée de la Save à Lespugue (Haute-Garonne)*, « Ipek », **1925**, pp. 33-43.
— *La Grotte des Scilles à Lespugue*, « L'Anthropologie », T. XXXVI, **1926**, pp. 15-40.
— *Les baguettes sculptées dans l'art paléolithique*, « L'Anthropologie », T. XXXIX, **1929**, pp. 43-64.
— *La Grotte d'Isturitz. I : Le Magdalénien de la Salle Saint-Martin*, « Archives de l'Inst. de Paléont. Humaine », Mém. 7, **1930**.
— *L'Art Préhistorique*, Paris, **1932**.
— *La Grotte d'Isturitz. II : Le Magdalénien de la Grande Salle*, « Archives de l'Inst. de Paléontol. Humaine », Mém. 17, **1936**.
— *Les os gravés de la Grotte de La Mairie à Teyjat*, « Bull. Soc. Préhist. Française », T. XLV, **1948**, pp. 250-252.
— *La Grotte d'Isturitz. III : Les Solutréens, les Aurignaciens et les Moustériens*, « Archives de l'Inst. de Paléontol. Humaine », Mém. 25, **1952**.

SALMONY A., *Die Kunst der Aurignacien in Malta (Sibirien)*, « Ipek », **1931**, pp. 1-6.

SAMIATNIN S. I., *Raskapki u S. Gagarino*, « Gosudarstveennja Akademija istorii materialnoï kulturi », 118, **1935**.
— *Pescternie navesi Mgvimevi blis ciaturi*, « Sovetskaja archeologhia », **1937**, n. 3, pp. 57-76.

SAUTER M. R., *Préhistoire de la Méditerranée*, Paris, **1948**.

SAUTUOLA (DE) M., *Breves apuntes sobre algunos objetos prehistóricos de la provincia de Santander*, Santander, **1880**.

SCHENK A., *La Suisse préhistorique*, Lausanne, **1912**.

SCHMIDT R. R., *Die Diluviale Vorzeit Deutschlands*, Stuttgart, **1912**.
— *Der Geist der Vorzeit*, Berlin, **1934**. [French translation by J. Nippgen : *L'aurore de l'esprit humain*, Paris, 1936].

SCHOVKOPLIAS I. G., *Nekotorie itogi issledovanija mesinskoi posdnepaleoliticeskoï stojanki v 1954-1956 g.g.*, « Sovetskaja archeologhia », **1957**, n. 4, pp. 99-115.
— *Pisniï paleolit.*, in « Narici starodavnioï istorii Ukraïncikoï R.S.R. », Akademia nauk ukrainskoï R.S.R. Institut archeologhï, Kiev, **1957 a**, pp. 16-30.

SIMONNET G., *Une nouvelle plaquette de pierre gravée Magdalénienne de la grande Grotte de Labastide, Commune de Labastide (Hautes-Pyrénées)*, « Bull. Soc. Préhist. Française », T. XLIV, **1947**, pp. 55-64.
— *Une belle parure Magdalénienne*, « Congrès Préhist. de France », C. R. XIIIᵉ session, Paris, **1950**, pp. 564-568.

STELLA L. A., *Rappresentazioni figurate paleolitiche a Grotta Romanelli*, « Rivista di Antropologia », vol. XXXI, **1935-37**, pp. 21-32.

SZOMBATHY J., *Die Aurignacienschichten im Löess von Willendorf*, « Korrespondenzblatt der Deutschen Gesellschaft für Anthrop., Ethnol. und Urgeschichte », Band XL, N. 9-12, **1909**.

TCHIKALENKO, *Etude sur l'évolution de l'ornement géometrique à l'époque paléolithique*, Praha, **1923**.

TOURNIER, GUILLON C., *Les hommes préhistoriques dans l'Aïn*, Bourg, **1895**.

TROMBE F., DUBUC G., *Le centre préhistorique de Ganties-Montespan (Haute-Garonne)*, « Archives de l'Inst. de Paléontol. Humaine », Mém. 22, **1947**.

TSCHUDI J., *Pitture rupestri del Tasili degli Azger*, Firenze, **1955**.

URIA RIU J., *La caverna prehistórica de « el Cuetu » Lledias (Asturias) y sus pinturas rupestres*, « Informas y memorias de la comis. gener. excav. arqueol. », n. 6, Madrid, **1944**.

VAUFREY R., *La statuette féminine de Savignano sur le Panaro (Province de Modène)*, « L'Anthropologie »,
T. XXXVI, **1926**, pp. 429-435.
— *Préhistoire de l'Afrique*, T. I, « Publications de l'Institut des Hautes Etudes de Tunis », vol. IV,
Paris, **1955.**

VAYSON DE PRADENNE A., *Les figurations d'oiseaux dans l'art quaternaire*, « Ipek », **1934,** pp. 3-17.

VEGA DEL SELLA (DE LA), *El Paleolítico de Cueto de la Mina*, « Comisión de Investigaciones Paleont. y
Prehist. », n. 13, **1916.**

VÉZIAN J., *La grotte du Portel*, « Bull. Soc. Préhist. du Languedoc », n. 2, **1945,** pp. 2-11.
— *Les foyers magdaléniens de la grotte du Portel (Ariège)*, « Bull. Soc. Préhist. de l'Ariège », T. IX-X,
1954-55, pp. 13-32.
— *Les utilisations de contours de la roche dans la grotte du Portel*, « Bull. Soc. Préhist. de l'Ariège »,
T. XI, **1956,** pp. 79-87.

VIDAL Y LOPEZ M., *Els insectes en l'art quaternari*, « Servei d'Investigació Prehistorica », n. 3, Valencia, **1937.**

VILASECA S., *L'estraciò taller de silex de St. Gregori*, « Memorias de la Accademia de Ciencias y Artes
de Barcelona », 3ª epoca, vol. XXIII, n. 21, **1934,** pp. 415-439.

VOLKOV TH., *Nouvelles découvertes dans la station paléolithique de Mézine (Ukraïne)*, « Congrès Internat.
d'Anthrop. et d'Archéologie Préhistoriques », XIVᵉ session, Genève, **1912,** T. I, pp. 415-428.
— *Défense de mammouth gravée du gisement paléolithique de Kiev*, « Bull. et Mém. Soc. Anthrop. de
Paris », T. I, ser. V, **1900,** pp. 478-479.

WINDELS F., *Lascaux*, Montignac-sur-Vézère, **1948.** [English translation : *The Lascaux Cave Paintings*,
London, 1949].

WOERKOM (VAN) A. J. J., *The astronomical theory of climate changes*, in : Shapley H., « Climatic change »,
Harward, **1953,** pp. 147-157.

ZOTZ L. F., *Ein altsteinzeitliches Idol des Zweigeschlechterwesens*, « Forschungen und Fortschritte », 25 Jahrg.,
N. 11-12, **1949,** pp. 121-123.
— *Idoles paléolithiques de l'Être androgyne*, « Bull. Soc. Préhist. Française », T. XLVIII, **1951,**
pp. 333-340.
— *Ewiges Europa Urheimat der Kunst*, Bonn, **1953.**
— *Das Paläolithikum in den Weinberghöhlen bei Mauern*, Quartär Bibliothek, Ludwig Röhrscheid,
Bonn, **1955.**

ZOTZ L. F., FREUND G., *Eine « paläolithische » Felszeichnung in Kleinen Schülerloch?*, « Bayerische Vor-
geschichtsblatter », **1951,** pp. 102-106.

DESCRIPTION OF THE ILLUSTRATIONS

NOTE ON THE ORDER OF ILLUSTRATIONS

The iconography for mobiliary art is presented chronologically, since mobiliary works are generally accompanied by stratigraphical data and are therefore usually datable.

On the other hand the material relating to cave-art figures, except in some rare cases where their relation to each other and to *in situ* deposits was established beyond a doubt, is not claimed to have any chronological significance but merely to present the various works according to an apparent degree of stylistic and technical evolution.

With regard both to mobiliary art and to cave art we have considered separately the two provinces — Franco-Cantabrian and Mediterranean — and classed in a different group the " schematic " art of Eastern Europe.

The examples of *mobiliary art* from the Franco-Cantabrian province are grouped according to the different processes used in their execution (sculpture, " contour découpé ", engraving on bone, engraving on stone); the geometrical, schematic and abstract figures are considered separately from the definitely representational works. Furthermore, with regard to the Magdalenian period only, human figures are grouped separately from compositions and from all attempts to achieve perspective.

The examples of *cave art* from the Franco-Cantabrian province are also grouped according to various technical processes (engraving on clay, engraving on stone, bas-relief, painting — the latter further subdivided into " painting in France " and " painting in Cantabria "); the works in each of these groups are presented in accordance with apparent stylistic evolution.

With regard to subject matter, zoomorphic figures, anthropomorphic figures and " tectiforms " or other signs are considered separately from each other.

In order to emphasize particular aspects of Franco-Cantabrian art — such as the utilization of natural accidents in the execution of figures, composition, Palaeolithic magic — some significant examples are assembled in specific groups.

For typographical reasons the captions beneath the Plates were, of necessity, reduced as far as possible; therefore, except in a few cases where the objects are more than twice enlarged, the figures are fully commented upon only in the " Description of the Illustrations ". For the same reason the names of photographers and the sources of illustrations are generally mentioned only in the " Description ".

The dimensions marked next to each work indicate maximum measurements and, unless otherwise stated, they refer to the entire object or group of figures reproduced in the illustration. In some cases such dimensions are somewhat approximate.

When various objects described successively are located in the same collection or museum, the name of the collection or museum is given only once — after the last description. The same applies to the name of the region to which two or more " locations " of prehistoric art belong.

MOBILIARY ART

THE FRANCO-CANTABRIAN PROVINCE AND ITS BRANCHES

AURIGNACIAN-PERIGORDIAN SCULPTURE.

PL. 1   La Grotte du Pape, Brassempouy (Landes) : a) ivory female head (3,5 cm.); b) ivory female torso (8 cm.). Musée des Antiquités Nationales, Saint-Germain en Laye (PIETTE, 1895, pls. I, VI).

PL. 2   a), b) La Grotte du Pape, Brassempouy (Landes) : fragmentary female and male ivory statuettes; Musée St. Germain (slightly reduced) (PIETTE, LA PORTERIE, 1897, pl. I, and *museum photograph*). c) Sireuil (Dordogne) : calcite female statuette (9,2 cm.); Musée St. Germain (*museum photograph*).

PL. 3   The " Venus " of Lespugue (Haute-Garonne), ivory (14,7 cm.) : a) viewed from the front, from the side and from the back; Musée de l'Homme, Paris (ST. PÉRIER, 1922, pl. I). b) The same, restored (*photograph of a cast*).

PL. 4   Cave of Balzi Rossi or Grimaldi (Ventimiglia). a) The steatite " Venus " of Grimaldi, viewed from the front, from the side and from the back (4,7 cm.); Musée de St. Germain (REINACH, 1898, pls. I, II). b) So-called " negroid " head and other female statuettes, all steatite with the exception of the second from last which is carved in bone; viewed from the front and from the side (the first statuette on the left measures 6 cm.); Musée St. Germain (*museum photograph*).

PL. 5   The " Venus " of Savignano (Modena), of serpentine, viewed in profile (22 cm.); Pigorini Prehistoric Museum, Rome (*museum photograph*).

PL. 6   The " Venus " of Savignano viewed from the front and from the back.

PL. 7   The " Venus " of Savignano. Detail.

PL. 8   a), b) Chiozza (Reggio Emilia) : sandstone statuette of the " Palaeolithic type " (20,5 cm.); Museum of Reggio Emilia (a = photograph of a cast; b = original viewed from three sides; DEGANI, 1940). c) The steatite statuette of Trasimeno viewed according to the first interpretation (3,7 cm.); Palma di Cesnola Collection, Florence (PALMA DI CESNOLA, 1938).

PL. 9   The " Venus " of Willendorf (Austria) sculptured in limestone, viewed in four different positions (11 cm.) (*photograph of a cast*).

PL. 10   a) Dolní Věstonice (Moravia) : small ivory human head (4,5 cm.); b) *idem* : the " Venus " of Věstonice, modelled in clayey substance mixed with powdered bone (11,4 cm.) (BAYER, 1931, pl. I); c) *idem* : female statuette, highly stylized (9 cm.). d) Brno (Moravia) : fragmentary ivory statuette (12,5 cm.); Moravské Museum, Brno (*museum photograph*).

PL. 11   Kostienki near Voronezh (Russia): a) the " Venus " of Kostienki, sculptured in mammoth ivory (8,5 cm.) (REINACH, 1924, fig. 1); b) female statuette, ivory (11 cm.); c) soft stone statuette from the same locality (15 cm.) (EPHIMENKO, reproduced by GOLOMSHTOK, 1938, fig. 45 and pl. XXI).

PL. 12   a), b), c) Gagarino near Tambov (Russia) : ivory female statuettes (GOLOMSHTOK, 1938, pls. XXIV, XXV). d), e), f) Maltà near Lake Baikal (Siberia) : ivory female statuettes (9,8; 12; 8; 13; 10; 9 cm.) (SALMONY, 1931, pl. II, with the exception of f = *photographs of casts*). g) Same locality : birds (12; 10; 10,8; 8,2; 7 cm.) (SALMONY, 1931, pl. I).

PL. 13   Cave of Vogelherd (Württemberg) : ivory statuettes : a) horse (4,8 cm.); b) mammoth (4,9 cm.); c) feline animal (6,9 cm.) (*photograph: Vor- und Frühgesch. Inst. Univ., Tübingen*).

PL. 14   Cave of Vogelherd (Württemberg): ivory statuettes: *a*) leopard (9 cm.); *b*) probable ruminant (6,7 cm.); *c*) bison (7,5 cm.); *d*) bear (6 cm.) (*photograph: Vor- und Frühgesch. Inst. Univ., Tübingen*).

PL. 15   Dolní Věstonice (Moravia): feline head and bear's head modelled in clay mixed with powdered bone (6; 7 cm.); Moravské Museum, Brno (*museum photograph*).

PL. 16   *a*), *b*), *c*), *d*) Dolní Věstonice (Moravia): rhinoceros head (4,2 cm.), owls, and indeterminable animal heads modelled in clay mixed with powdered bone (*a, c, d = museum photograph, Brno; b =* ABSOLON V, 1939, fig. 6). *e*) Předmostí (Moravia): mammoth sculptured in ivory (12,8 cm.) (MASKA, OBERMAIER, BREUIL, 1912, fig. 1). Moravské Museum, Brno.

AURIGNACIAN-PERIGORDIAN ENGRAVING.

PL. 17   *a*) Hornos de La Peña (Santander): hindquarters of a horse engraved on the frontal bone of the same animal (9 cm.); Prehistoric Museum Santander (ALCALDE DEL RIO, BREUIL, SIERRA, 1911, fig. 210). *b*), *c*), *d*) Cave of Isturitz (Basses-Pyrénées): reindeer and horses, lightly engraved on stone (*b, c*) and on bone (*d*), Upper Aurignacian (Gravettian) (10; 7; 17,5 cm.); St. Périer, Morigny Collection (ST. PÉRIER, 1952, figs. 85, 86, 87).

PL. 18   *a*) Cave of Rebières (Dordogne), Upper Aurignacian: pebble engraved with the figure of a deer (12 cm.); Institute of Anthropology of the University of Geneva (PITTARD, 1912, fig. 1). *b*) Laugerie Haute (Dordogne), Perigordian III: engravings on stone (12 cm.) (PEYRONY D., PEYRONY E., 1938, fig. 7). *c*) Laraux (Lussac-les-Chateaux, Vienne): horse engraved on stone (10,6 cm.) (PRADEL, CHOLLET, 1950, fig. 7). *d*) Gargas (Hautes-Pyrénées): engravings of Perigordian age on two schist pebbles, representing an ox, a carnivore and a bison (4; 19 cm.) (BREUIL, 1952 a, figs. 2, 6). *e*) Saut-du-Perron (Roanne, Loire) (LARUE, COMBIER, ROCHE, 1955, fig. 7).

PL. 19   *a*) Cave of Le Trilobite (Yonne): pebble engraved with superimposed figures of woolly rhinoceros (13 cm.) (CAPITAN, BREUIL, PEYRONY, 1910, pl. LXII). *b*), *c*) Abri Labatut in Sergeac (Dordogne): calcareous pebble, finely engraved on both sides with figures of horses, Perigordian (8,5 cm.) (BREUIL, 1929, fig. 1); Musée de l'Homme, Paris.

PLS. 20-21   Cave of La Colombière (Aïn): pebbles with numerous superimposed engravings of animals, from Upper Perigordian layers (the animals measure 9,5; 6,6; 7,5; 8,3 cm.); Laboratoire de Géologie de l'Université, Lyon. Mayet-Pissot excavations, 1913-14 (PIJOAN, 1934, fig. 57).

PL. 22   Cave of La Colombière (Aïn): two sides of a pebble engraved with many figures, Upper Gravettian (12 cm.). Harvard University excavations, 1948 (*photograph: Peabody Museum, Cambridge, Mass.*).

PL. 23   Cave of La Colombière (Aïn): separation of the various figures engraved on both sides of the pebble in Pl. 22, made by H. L. MOVIUS (MOVIUS, 1952, figs. 4, 5 *a*, 5 *e*, 6, 7 *a*, 7 *e*).

PL. 24   *a*) Cave of Péchialet (Dordogne): stone engraved with the figures of a bear and of two individuals, one of which is undoubtedly human (18,5 cm.); Musée St. Germain (*museum photograph*); *b*) *idem* (BREUIL, 1927, fig. 1). *c*), *d*) Laugerie Haute (Dordogne): " bâton de commandement " of reindeer antler, evolved Perigordian, with two mammoths facing each other, deeply engraved (15 cm.); Musée des Eyzies (*c* = development of the figures) (PEYRONY D., PEYRONY E., 1938, fig. 18).

PL. 25   *a*) Cave of Les Rideaux in Lespugue (Haute-Garonne): vipers engraved on bone (14 cm.); St. Périer, Morigny Collection (ST. PÉRIER, 1924, fig. 4). *b*) Cave of La Colombière (Aïn): mammoth bone with engraved figures; the figure of a man can be detected, and perhaps the incomplete outline of a female figure; also a bear and the antler of a reindeer (17 cm.); *c*) *idem*: reindeer engraved on the bone of a mammoth (20 cm.) (MAYET, PISSOT, 1915, pl. XXIV, fig. 69).

PL. 26   *a*) Solutré (Saône-et-Loire): ruminant sculptured in relief, of Solutrean age (approx. 7,5 cm.); Musée St. Germain (*photograph: Graziosi*). *b*), *c*), *d*) Cave of Isturitz (Basses-Pyrénées): horse sculptured in low relief (7,5 cm.), ibex (15,5 cm.), bison (15,5 cm.) and other animals (11 cm.) engraved on stone, Typical Solutrean; St. Périer, Morigny Collection (ST. PÉRIER, 1952, figs. 11, 12, 13). *e*), *f*), *g*) Cave of Badegoule (Dordogne): Solutrean engravings on stone: bison (10 cm.), deer (12,5 cm.), tangle of figures (9,5 cm.) among which the partial outline of a bird can be distinguished; Cheynier, Meudon Collection (CHEYNIER, 1949, figs. 13, 34, 38).

PL. 27   *a*) Obere Klause (Bavaria): mammoth engraved on ivory (9 cm.) (OBERMAIER, FRAUNHOLZ, 1926, fig. 3). *b*) Le Fourneau du Diable (Dordogne): deer engraved on a graphite pendant (11 cm.) (PEYRONY, 1932 a, fig. 38). *c*) Le Fourneau du Diable: stone engraved with Solutrean figures of ibexes (9,5 cm.) (PEYRONY, 1932 a, fig. 39) (*b, c* Musée des Eyzies). *d*) Jean-Blancs (Dordogne): Upper Solutrean figure of an ibex engraved on calcareous stone (15,5 cm.) (PEYRONY D., PEYRONY E., 1934, fig. 5).

PL. 28   Abri du Roc de Sers (Charente): *a*), *b*), *c*) horse and bison engraved on fragments of calcareous stone, from Solutrean layers (10; 9; 17 cm.); the bison in fig. *c* is of an evolved style, definitely Magdalenian; Musée St. Germain (MARTIN, 1928, figs. 13, 14, 15).

LOWER MAGDALENIAN SCULPTURE AND ENGRAVING.

PL. 29   Cave of Le Placard (Charente): head of a fox carved at the extremity of a " bâton de commandement ", Magdalenian II (35 cm.); Musée St. Germain (*photograph*: *Graziosi* and *drawings* by CAPITAN, BREUIL, PEYRONY, 1910, fig. 130).

PL. 30   *a*), *b*) Cave of Le Placard (Charente): heads of animals, Magdalenian I and II, probably a feline animal and a rabbit, carved on "bâtons de commandement" (12; 6,5 cm.) (BREUIL, 1937 a, fig. 23). *c*) Cave of Gourdan (Haute-Garonne): fish on reindeer antler (9,5 cm.) (PIETTE, 1907, pl. LXVIII). *d*) Laugerie Basse (Dordogne): probable representation of a fish on a " bâton de commandement " (22 cm.) (PIETTE, 1907, pl. VII). All, Musée St. Germain. *e*) Pech de la Boissière (Dordogne): ibex head engraved on a pebble (7,5 cm.); Early Magdalenian. Musée des Eyzies (PEYRONY, 1934 a, fig. 13). *f*), *g*) Feline animal and deer engraved on calcareous fragments, from Magdalenian III layers of the cave of La Marche (Vienne) (approx. 15-20 cm.) (PÉRICARD, LWOFF, 1940, figs. 5 b, 6 b).

PL. 31   Engravings on antler and on bone, Early Magdalenian. *a*) Cave of Le Placard (Charente); Musée St. Germain (CAPITAN, BREUIL, PEYRONY, 1910, fig. 185). *b*) Stag heads engraved on a " bâton de commandement " in Laugerie Haute (Dordogne); Musée St. Germain (CAPITAN, BREUIL, PEYRONY, 1910, fig. 169). *c*), *d*), *e*) Deer heads engraved on bone, from layers containing Solutrean industries in the cave of Altamira (BREUIL, OBERMAIER, 1935, fig. 159). *f*) Young deer engraved on bone from the cave of Castillo (Santander) (BREUIL, OBERMAIER, 1912, fig. 13). *g*) Grotte des Boeufs in Lespugue (Haute-Garonne); outline of a sole cut out of a bone (4,5 cm.); Musée St. Germain (ST. PÉRIER, 1925, fig. 3).

UPPER MAGDALENIAN SCULPTURE.

PL. 32   Ibex carved on a spear-thrower in Mas d'Azil (Ariège) viewed from the front and from the side (27 cm.); Musée St. Germain (*museum photograph* and *drawing* by PIETTE, 1907, figs. 60, 60 a).

PL. 33   Laugerie Basse (Dordogne): *a*) reindeer antler spear-thrower with horse's head and engraved figures (29,5 cm.). *b*) Reindeer carved on the end of a probable spear-thrower (38 cm.) (LARTET, CHRISTY, 1875, pls. XIX-XX, figs. 1, 5).

PL. 34   *a*), *b*) Bruniquel (Tarn-et-Garonne): reindeer sculptured in ivory (22 cm.); British Museum, London (*a* = *museum photograph*; *b* = BREUIL, 1905 a, fig. 2). *c*) Mammoth carved on a reindeer antler spear-thrower in Bruniquel (12,5 cm.); British Museum, London (*museum photograph*).

PL. 35   *a*) Fighting ibexes: sculpture on a reindeer antler spear-thrower from the cave of Les Trois Frères (Ariège) (6 cm. high). *b*) Birds carved on the extremity of a reindeer antler spear-thrower from the same cave (7,5 cm.); Begouen, Montesquieu-Avantès Collection (BEGOUEN H., 1936, p. 32). *c*) Fragment of a deer on the extremity of a spear-thrower, from the cave of Enlène (Ariège) (9 cm.) (*photograph*: *Musée St. Germain*). *d*), *e*) Fragment of sculpture on a reindeer antler spear-thrower representing a bird, Mas d'Azil (Ariège) (7 cm.); Musée St. Germain (*d* = *museum photograph*; *e* = the same, according to Breuil's reconstruction).

PL. 36   Cave of Arudy (Basses-Pyrénées): *a*), *c*) ibexes carved on the ends of reindeer antler spear-throwers (10; 7 cm.); Musée St. Germain (*museum photograph*). *b*) same subject, from the cave of Isturitz (Basses-Pyrénées) (12,5 cm.); Musée St. Germain (PASSEMARD, 1944, pl. XXIX). *d*) Fragment of spear-thrower with reindeer antler ibexes' feet, from Arudy (14,5 cm.); Musée St. Germain (*museum photograph*). *e*) Fragment of spear-thrower with horses' hoofs from Isturitz (7,3 cm.); St. Périer, Morigny collection (ST. PÉRIER, 1930, pl. XI). *f*) Ruminant's feet, probably carved on a fragment of spear-thrower, from the cave of Mas d'Azil (Ariège); Musée St. Germain (*museum photograph*).

PL. 37   *a*), *b*) Cave of Mas d'Azil (Ariège): young ibex sculptured at the end of a reindeer antler spear-thrower (29,6 cm.); Péquart collection, St. Brieuc (PÉQUART, 1942, fig. 3). *c*) Cave of Bédeilhac (Ariège): extremity of a reindeer antler spear-thrower decorated with identical subject (8 cm.); Robert collection, Tarascon s. A. (ROBERT, 1951).

PL. 38   Leaping horse on the end of a reindeer antler spear-thrower from Abri Montastruc in Bruniquel (Tarn-et-Garonne) (28 cm.); Bétirac, Montauban collection (*photograph*: *Bétirac*).

PL. 39   Cave of Laugerie Basse (Dordogne): *a*) ruminant's head sculptured on reindeer antler (9,5 cm.); Musée de l'Homme, Paris (*museum photograph*). *b*) Head, probably of a wild boar, carved on a reindeer antler " bâton de commandement " (15 cm.); Musée St. Germain (PIETTE, 1907, pl. IV). *c*) Head of a bison on a " bâton de commandement " (9 cm.); Musée de l'Homme, Paris (*museum photograph*). *d*) Cave of Arudy (Basses-Pyrénées): head of a fox carved in reindeer antler (11 cm.); Musée St. Germain (*museum photograph*).

PL. 40   Cave of Mas d'Azil (Ariège): *a*), *b*) horses' heads sculptured in reindeer antler on spear-throwers; one of them (*a*) is skinned (16,3 cm.); Musée St. Germain (*photograph*: *Graziosi*). *c*) Headless bison sculptured in reindeer antler, probably on a spear-thrower (10,7 cm.); Musée St. Germain (*museum photograph*).

PL. 41   Cave of La Madeleine (Dordogne): *a*) bison turning its head sculptured in reindeer antler, probably on the end of a spear-thrower (10,2 cm.). *b*) Sculpture, on a spear-thrower, possibly representing a hyena. *c*) Fragmentary bison, reindeer antler. All, Musée St. Germain (*museum photograph*).

PL. 42   *a*) Cave of Mas d'Azil (Ariège): probable ivory pendant sculptured on both sides with figures of ibexes (13 cm.) (*photograph of a cast*). *b*) Cave of Les Espéluges in Lourdes (Hautes-Pyrénées): horse sculptured in ivory (7,5 cm.) (PIETTE, 1907, pl. XII). All, Musée St. Germain.

PL. 43   Cave of Mas d'Azil (Ariège): *a*), horse's head, reindeer antler (5,5 cm.); Musée St. Germain (*a* = *photograph*: *Graziosi*; and PIETTE, 1907, fig. 55). *b*), *c*) Skinned horses' heads (9; 8 cm.); Musée St. Germain (*photograph*: *Graziosi*).

PL. 44   *a*) Kesslerloch (Thayngen-Switzerland): ruminant, on a spear-thrower; Musée de Tous les Saints, Schaffhausen (BANDI) 1947, pl. XII). *b*) Cave of Bédeilhac (Ariège): fragmentary horse's head, stone (4 cm.) (*photograph*: *Musée St. Germain*). *c*) Laugerie Basse (Dordogne): probable representation of a feline animal (8 cm.) (*photograph*: *Musée St. Germain*). *d*) Laugerie Basse: head, probably of a reindeer (7 cm.) (*photograph*: *Musée St. Germain*). *e*), *f*) Cave of Les Espélugues in Lourdes (Hautes-Pyrénées): ruminants' heads, reindeer antler, sculptured on the extremities of " bâtons de commandement " (5 cm.) (PIETTE, 1907, pls. XIX, XXVI). Musée St. Germain.

PL. 45   *a*) Laugerie Basse (Dordogne): bison heads sculptured on a " bâton de commandement " (13,2 cm.); *b*) same origin: ruminant's head on a " bâton de commandement " (9 cm.). *c*) Mas d'Azil (Ariège): fragmentary bison, probably on the extremity of a " bâton de commandement "; Musée St. Germain (*photograph*: *Graziosi*). *d*) Laugerie Basse: head of a reindeer carved in reindeer antler (5,8 cm.); Musée de l'Homme, Paris (*museum photograph*). *e*) Head of indeterminate animal, reindeer antler, from Mas d'Azil (4 cm.); Musée St. Germain (PIETTE, 1907, pl. LXI). *f*) Horse sculptured on bone from the cave of Isturitz (Basses-Pyrénées) (12 cm.); St. Périer, Morigny collection (ST. PÉRIER, 1930, fig. 92).

PL. 46   Cave of Isturitz (Basses-Pyrénées): *a*) feline animal sculptured in reindeer antler, peppered with holes, with two harpoons engraved on its body; probably a magical object (9,5 cm.); Musée St. Germain (PASSEMARD, 1944, pl. XXVI). *b*) Sandstone horse's head (8 cm.); St. Périer, Morigny collection (ST. PÉRIER, 1930, pl. XII).

PL. 47   Sculptures from the cave of Isturitz (Basses-Pyrénées): *a*) Body of a quadruped, probably a bear (8,6 cm.). *b*) Head of a bear (4 cm.). *c*) Hindquarters of a ruminant (6,5 cm.). *d*) Horse's head (7,5 cm.). All sculptures in stone. Musée St. Germain (PASSEMARD, 1944, pl. XXVI). *e*) Horse's head, amber, from the same cave (4 cm.); St. Périer, Morigny collection (ST. PÉRIER, 1939, fig. 72).

PL. 48   Head of a ruminant sculptured on the end of a " bâton de commandement " in the cave of La Vache (Ariège) (7 cm.); Robert collection, Tarascon s. A. (MALVESIN, NOUGIER, ROBERT, 1951). *b*) Cave of El Rascaño (Santander): head of a deer sculptured on a reindeer antler " bâton de commandement " (9,5 cm.); Duke of Alba collection (OBERMAIER, 1923, pl. I, fig. 1). *c*) Fish sculptured on a reindeer antler " bâton de commandement " in the cave of El Pendo (Santander) (10,5 cm.); Prehistoric Museum, Santander (*photograph*: *Graziosi*).

PL. 49   *a*) Laugerie Basse (Dordogne): probable representation of a salamander sculptured in reindeer antler (10,5 cm.); Musée de l'Homme, Paris (*photograph of a cast* and *drawing* by BREUIL, ST. PÉRIER, 1927, fig. 67). *b*) Mas d'Azil (Ariège): spear-thrower sculptured in the shape of an eel (20 cm); close to the animal's head is the tail of a fish. Musée St. Germain (PIETTE, 1907, pl. LI). *c*) Cave of Les Espélugues in Lourdes (Hautes-Pyrénées): trout, sculptured in bone (14,5 cm.); Musée St. Germain (*photograph*: *Graziosi*).

UPPER MAGDALENIAN " CONTOURS DÉCOUPÉS ".

PL. 50
a) Tail of a fish from Gourdan (Haute-Garonne) (4,5 cm.); Musée St. Germain (*photograph*: *Graziosi*). *b*) Fish-tails cut out of the extremities of bone spatulas in the caves of Rey and Bout-du-Monde in Les Eyzies (Dordogne) (11,5; 12 cm.). *c*) *Idem*, from the cave of Mas d'Azil (Ariège) (12,5 cm.) (BREUIL, ST. PÉRIER, 1927, fig. 8). *d*) Cave of Rey in Les Eyzies : spatula with fish-shaped handle (the animal is 9,2 cm. high) (*photograph*: *Graziosi* and *drawing* by BREUIL, ST. PÉRIER, 1927, fig. 8). *e*) Lorthet (Hautes-Pyrénées) : front part of a fish; the internal organs are seen in " transparency " (8,5 cm.) (*photograph*: *Graziosi*). *f*) Laugerie Basse (Dordogne) : horse's head (6 cm.); Musée de l'Homme (*museum photograph*).

PL. 51
" Contours découpés ". *a*) Cave of Isturitz (Basses-Pyrénées) : bison cut out of bone (21,5 cm.) (PASSEMARD, 1944, pl. XXIV). *b*) Feline animal, probably lynx, from the cave of Arudy (Basses-Pyrénées) (5,5 cm.). *c*) Mas d'Azil (Ariège) : ibex head (5,5 cm.). *d*) Lorthet (Hautes-Pyrénées) : horse (6 cm.). All, Musée St. Germain (*museum photograph*). *e*) Cave of Isturitz: ibex head (5,5 cm.); St. Périer, Morigny collection (ST. PÉRIER, 1930, pl. IX). *f*), *g*) Arudy : horse's head (4,5 cm.); Musée St. Germain (*f*= *museum photograph*; *g*, enlarged= by PIETTE, 1907, pl. XCIII).

PL. 52
Horses' heads cut out of hyoid bones, from the cave of Mas d'Azil (Ariège), with the exception of the second and third in the third row (bottom) which were found, respectively, in Arudy (Basses-Pyrénées) and Gourdan (Haute-Garonne), and of the third in the fourth row found in Lorthet (Hautes-Pyrénées) (all between 5,2 and 7,3 cm.); Musée St. Germain (*museum photograph*).

PL. 53
a) Ibexes' heads with suspension hole, from the cave of Labastide (Hautes-Pyrénées); at the centre is a probable bison's head (between 5 and 6 cm.) (SIMONNET, 1950, fig. 1). *b*), *c*) Snakes from the cave of Lorthet (Hautes-Pyrénées) (15; 13,5 cm.); Musée St. Germain (*museum photograph* and *drawing* by PIETTE, 1896, fig. 51). *d*) Fish from the cave of El Pendo (Santander) (17,5 cm.); Prehistoric Museum, Santander (*photograph*: *Graziosi*).

UPPER MAGDALENIAN BAS-RELIEF.

PL. 54
Cave of Arudy (Basses-Pyrénées) : " bâton de commandement " with ruminants' heads sculptured in low relief, seen from two sides (22 cm.); Musée St. Germain (*museum photograph* and *drawings* by PIETTE, 1906, figs. 29, 29 a).

PL. 55
a) Caves of Arudy (Basses-Pyrénées) : horse's head in bas-relief (16,5 cm.); Musée St. Germain (*museum photograph* and PIETTE, 1907, pl. LXXXVIII). *b*) Bird carved on a " bâton de commandement " from Chancelade in Raymonden (Dordogne) (16,5 cm.); Musée du Périgord, Périgueux (*museum photograph* and CAPITAN, BREUIL, BOURRINET, PEYRONY, 1909, fig. 10).

PL. 56
a) Mas d'Azil (Ariège) : horse's head sculptured on a " bâton de commandement " (21 cm.); Musée St. Germain, *photograph of a cast*). *b*), *c*) Laugerie Basse (Dordogne) : reindeer and reindeer's head sculptured on a " bâton de commandement " (30 cm.); Musée de l'Homme, Paris (*museum photograph* and *drawings* by CAPITAN, BREUIL, PEYRONY, 1910, fig. 152).

PL. 57
a) Mas d'Azil (Ariège) : reindeer sculptured in shallow low relief on bone; Musée St. Germain (*museum photograph*). *b*) Isturitz (Basses-Pyrénées) : bison's head sculptured on reindeer antler (15,5 cm.); St. Périer, Morigny collection (ST. PÉRIER, 1930, pl. II). *c*) Laugerie Basse (Dordogne) : reindeer sculptured on bone (the animal measures 10,5 cm.) (cast from Musée St. Germain). *d*) Laugerie Basse : ibex; British Museum, London (LARTET and CHRISTY, 1875, B, pl. II). *e*) horse from the same cave (10 cm.); on the opposite side is the figure in Pl. 85, *c* (PIETTE, 1907, pl. XXIX); Musée St. Germain.

PL. 58
Cave of Isturitz (Basses-Pyrénées) : fragmentary reindeer, sculptured in low relief on stone (*a* = 15 cm.; *b* = 15,5 cm.; *c* = 11,5 cm.); Musée St. Germain (PASSEMARD, 1944, pls. XXX, XXXI).

PL. 59
Cave of Isturitz (Basses-Pyrénées) : *a*), *b*) reindeer and bison sculptured on stone (15,5; 10 cm.); Musée St. Germain (PASSEMARD, 1944, pls. XXX, XXXI). *c*) Laugerie Basse (Dordogne) : bison sculptured in stone (7,5 cm.) (BOURLON, 1916, fig. 16).

UPPER MAGDALENIAN ENGRAVING ON BONE AND IVORY.

PL. 60
a) La Madeleine (Dordogne) : mammoth engraved on a mammoth's tusk (24,5 cm.) (*photograph of a cast*). *b*) Cave of Les Trois Frères (Ariège) : birds, grasshopper and other figures engraved on bone (10 cm.); Begouen, Montesquieu-Avantès collection (BEGOUEN, 1928, pl. 3 c; 1936, p. 29). *c*) Cave of Les Harpons in Lespugues (Haute-Garonne) : horses en-

graved on bone (St. Périer, 1925, fig. 6). *d*) Mas d'Azil (Ariège) : horse engraved on bone; Musée St. Germain (*museum photograph*). *e*) Horse engraved on bone from the cave of Creswell Crags (Derbyshire); British Museum, London (from Guide to the British Museum, 1902, fig. 75).

Pl. 61   *a*) Isturitz (Basses-Pyrénées) : horse engraved on bone (18,5 cm.); Musée St. Germain (*museum photograph*). *b*), *c*) Mas d'Azil (Ariège) : oxen engraved on bone; Musée St. Germain (*museum photograph*).

Pl. 62   *a*) Laugerie Basse (Dordogne) : bison engraved on bone; Musée de l'Homme, Paris (*museum photograph*). *b*) Mas d'Azil (Ariège) : ibexes engraved on bone (13,3 cm.); Musée St. Germain (Breuil, 1902). *c*) Cave of Isturitz (Basses-Pyrénées) : bison and ibexes engraved on bone (8,5; 13 cm.); St. Périer, Morigny collection (St. Périer, 1936, pl. IX). *d*) Bird engraved on a reindeer antler, from the cave of Isturitz (dimensions : 6 cm.); Musée St. Germain (*museum photograph* and Passemard, 1922, fig. 38).

Pl. 63   *a*) Laugerie Basse (Dordogne) : bone disk with engraved young deer (3 cm.); Musée du Périgord, Périgueux (*museum photograph*). *b*) Same origin : pierced bone disk with the figure of an ox; Musée St. Germain (*museum photograph*). *c*) Cave of Duruthy in Sordes (Landes) : pendants made with a bear's tooth and bearing the figures of a fish and a seal (8,5; 9,5 cm.); Musée d'Histoire Naturelle, Toulouse, and Museum of Le Mans (Sarthe) (Lartet, Chaplain-Duparc, 1874, figs. 37, 38). *d*) Mas d'Azil (Ariège) : deer engraved on a reindeer antler (the animal measures 15 cm.) (Piette, 1907, pl. LVII). *e*) Brassempouy (Landes) : horses engraved on bone (9 cm.) (Piette, 1907, pl. LXXVIII).

Pl. 64   *a*), *b*) Cave of Lorthet (Hautes-Pyrénées) : deer and salmon engraved on reindeer antler; original (24,5 cm.) and restored cast (the figures measure 14 cm. altogether); Musée St. Germain (*museum photograph*). *c*) Massat (Ariège) : head of a bear engraved on a " bâton de commandement " (the object measures 14,5 cm.); Musée St. Germain (*museum photograph*).

Pl. 65   *a*) Les Hoteaux (Aïn) : deer engraved on a " bâton de commandement " (22,5 cm.); Musée St. Germain (*museum photograph* and *drawing* by Capitan, Breuil, Peyrony, 1910, fig. 170). *b*) Montgaudier (Charente) : " bâton de commandement " engraved with eels or snakes, two seals and a fish (37,5 cm.); Musée St. Germain (*museum photograph* and *drawings from a cast by A. Micheli and Isola*).

Pl. 66   *a*) Abri Mège in Teyjat (Dordogne) : reindeer antler "bâton de commandement" engraved with two horses, a young deer, birds, snakes and masked human beings (30 cm.) (see also Pl. 87, *f*); Musée St. Germain (*museum photograph*). *b*) Cast of same and drawing of the two horses (Capitan, Breuil, Bourrinet, Peyrony, 1919, fig. 5). *c*) Gourdan (Haute-Garonne) : reindeer antler " bâton de commandement " engraved on both sides with a series of chamois' heads as well as the head of a deer and, probably, the head of a skunk or a beaver (13,5 cm.); Musée St. Germain (*museum photograph*). *d*) The same according to Piette's tracing (Piette, 1907, pl. LXXXIV).

Pl. 67   *a*) Kesslerloch (Thayngen = Switzerland): "bâton de commandement" engraved with a reindeer (20 cm.); Rosgarten Museum, Konstanz. *b*) Schweizersbild : horse; Schweiz. Landesmuseum, Zürich (*museum photograph*).

Pl. 68   *a*) Kesslerloch (Thayngen = Switzerland) : horse engraved on a " bâton de commandement " (Bandi, 1947, pl. IX). *b*) Petersfels (Baden) : reindeer engraved on a " bâton de commandement " (the complete animal measures 8 cm.) (Peters, 1930, pl. XXIII).

Pl. 69   Pekarna (Moravia) : *a*) ruminant's head engraved on a reindeer bone (12 cm.). *b*) Animal engraved on a " bâton de commandement " (17 cm.). *c*), *d*) Large spatulas fashioned out of horses' lower jawbones engraved with the figures of a bison, a saiga antelope (*c*), a horse (*d*), and ornamental patterns (35,6; 28,5 cm.). Moravské Museum, Brno (*museum photograph*). *e*) Bison facing each other, engraved on bone (30 cm.) (Absolon K., 1939, pl. XXII).

Pl. 70   *a*) " La Grotte du Pape " in Brassempouy (Landes) : figures of animals, probably ruminants, engraved on bone (10 cm.); Musée St. Germain (*museum photograph* and *drawing* Piette, 1898, fig. 14). *b*) Cave of La Vache (Ariège) : wolves facing each other, engraved on bone (9 cm.); Robert collection, Tarascon s. A. (Malvesin, Nougier, Robert, 1951). *c*) Cave of Mas d'Azil (Ariège) : oxen engraved on bone (8 cm.) (*museum photograph, St. Germain*, and *drawing* by Piette 1907, Pl. LXIX).

Pl. 71   *a*) Cave of La Vache (Ariège) : engravings on bone polisher representing the heads of a young deer, a bison, another ruminant viewed from the front, tree-shaped signs, etc. (12,5 cm.); Robert collection, Tarascon s. A. (Robert, Kühn, 1952, fig. 1). *b*) Cave of Massat (Ariège) : reindeer engraved on bone; Magdalenian V; Musée St. Germain (*museum photograph*). *c*) Cave of Chaffaud (Vienne) : young deer engraved on bone; Magdalenian V-VI. This and the engraved bone of Le Veyrier (Pl. 91, *b*) were the first works of Palaeolithic art to be discovered; Musée St. Germain (*museum photograph*). *d*) Couple of reindeer engraved on reindeer antler in La Madeleine (Dordogne) (15,5 cm.) (LARTET, CHRISTY, 1875, B, pl. II). *e*) Reindeer engraved on bone from La Madeleine (Dordogne); Magdalenian VI; Musée St. Germain (*museum photograph* and *drawing* by CAPITAN, PEYRONY, 1928, fig. 55).

PL. 72
a) Cave of El Pendo (Santander) : horse and snake engraved on two sides of a bone; Magdalenian VI; Museo Prehistorico, Santander (*photograph*: *Graziosi*). *b*) Cave of El Valle (Santander) : series of horses engraved on a bird's bone (10 cm.); Magdalenian VI; Museo Prehistorico, Santander (*photograph of a restored cast*). *d*) Cave of Castillo (Santander): deer engraved on a reindeer antler " bâton de commandement " (the animal measures 15 cm.); Museo Prehistorico, Santander (*photograph*: *Graziosi*). *c*), *e*) Cave of La Madeleine (Dordogne) : series of horses engraved in shallow relief on " bâtons de commandement " (*c* = 31,5 cm.; *e* = 30,5 cm.); British Museum, London (LARTET, CHRISTY, 1875, B, pl. XXX, XXXI). *f*) Loubressac (Vienne) : bison engraved on a " bâton de commandement " (20 cm.); final Magdalenian VI. Note the evident stylistic decadence of the figure (LECLERC, PRADEL, 1948, figs. 1, 2).

PL. 73
a), *b*) Cave of El Pendo (Santander): " bâton de commandement " roughly carved in the shape of a horse's head and engraved on both sides with five deer heads (16,5 cm.), final Magdalenian; Museo Prehistorico, Santander (*photograph*: *Graziosi* and *drawing* by CARBALLO, LARIN 1932, figs. 107, 108). *c*) Cave of El Valle (Santander) : head of a deer and stylized human figures engraved on a reindeer antler " bâton de commandement " (13 cm.); Sierra collection (ALMAGRO, 1947, fig. 256).

UPPER MAGDALENIAN ENGRAVING ON STONE.

PL. 74
Cave of Isturitz (Basses-Pyrénées) : hare (13,5 cm.); Musée St. Germain (PASSEMARD, 1944, p. XXXIX).

PL. 75
a) Cave of Isturitz (Basses-Pyrénées) : horse's head (9 cm.); St. Périer, Morigny collection (ST. PÉRIER, 1930, pl. VIII). *b*) Cave of Labastide (Hautes-Pyrénées) : storks, or perhaps herons (18 cm.) (SIMONNET, 1947, fig. 2).

PL. 76
Laugerie Basse (Dordogne). Figures engraved on pebbles : *a*) deer (7 cm.); Burkitt collection, Cambridge, England. *b*) Bison (10 cm.). *c*) young deer and deer (9,5 cm.). *d*) Bear (opposite side of previous pebble). (BOURLON, 1916, figs. 17, 15, 13, 19). *e*), *f*), *g*) Horses and reindeer (9; 6; 9,5 cm.); Musée de l'Homme, Paris (BREUIL, 1936, figs. 6, 7).

PL. 77
a) Cave of Petersfels (Baden) : horse engraved on a piece of lignite (the animal measures 8,5 cm.) (PETERS, 1930, pl. XXIV). *b*) Klause (Bavaria) : horse engraved on a fragment of calcareous substance (8,5 cm.) drawing by Breuil (OBERMAIER, 1914, fig. 25). *c*) Cave of Massat (Ariège) : bear engraved on a pebble (the animal measures 9 cm.); Musée de Foix (*photograph*: *Robert*).

PL. 78
a), *b*) Bison and bird engraved on sandstone from Puy-de-Lacan (Corrèze) (*a* = 20 cm.; *b* = 15 cm. high); Magdalenian V (KIDDER, 1936, pls. I, II, figs. 5, 6). *c*) Le Bout-du-Monde (Les Eyzies, Dordogne) : young deer engraved on stone (6,5 cm. high); Magdalenian V (ALCALDE DEL RIO, BREUIL, SIERRA, 1911, fig. 222). *d*) Bison engraved on a stone from Mas d'Azil (Ariège) (9 cm.); Musée St. Germain (PIETTE, 1907, pl. XLVI).

PL. 79
a), *b*) Reindeer and horse engraved on stone from La Madeleine (Dordogne); Musée St. GERMAIN (CAPITAN, PEYRONY, 1928, pls. 2, 10). *c*), *d*), *e*) Oxen, reindeer and horse engraved on stone from Limeuil (Dordogne) Magdalenian VI (*c* = 20 cm.; *d* = 25 cm.; *e* = horse's head, 7,5 cm.); Musée St. Germain (CAPITAN, BOUYSSONIE, 1924, pls. XLII, XXXII, XLIV).

PL. 80
Engravings on stone from Limeuil (Dordogne). Magdalenian VI : *a*) ibex (19 cm. high). *b*) Horse (11,5 cm.). *c*) Indeterminable animal, perhaps a horse or a young ibex (12 cm. high). *d*) Horse. *e*) Reindeer (25 cm.). *f*) Bear (23 cm.). Musée St. Germain (CAPITAN, BOUYSSONIE, 1924, pls. XL, XXV, XX, IV, XXIV).

THE HUMAN FORM IN MAGDALENIAN MOBILIARY ART.

PL. 81
a) Gourdan (Haute-Garonne) : head, probably anthropomorphic or of an ibex, on the extremity of a spear-thrower (27,6 cm.); Musée St. Germain (*museum photograph*). *b*) Detail of same (CAPITAN, BREUIL, PEYRONY, 1924, fig. 93). *c*) Cave of Placard (Charente) : grotesque head, probably human, on a " bâton de commandement " (14 cm.); Musée St. Germain (*museum photograph* and BREUIL, 1937 a, fig. 23). *d*) Placard : human mask (10 cm.); Magdalenian III (BREUIL, 1937 a, fig. 23). *e*) Schematized human face from " Grotte des Fées " in Marcamps (Gironde) (11 cm.) (BREUIL, 1937 a, fig. 23).

PL. 82   *a*) Laugerie Basse (Dordogne) : ivory female statuette (8 cm.); Musée de l'Homme, Paris (*photograph of a cast*). *b*) Laugerie Basse : anthropomorphic figure, reindeer antler (5 cm.); Musée St. Germain (*museum photograph*). *c*) Bédeilhac (Ariège) : human head with a sort of hood, sculptured on the root of a horse's tooth (4,5 cm.) (BEGOUEN, 1929, pl. 3). *d*) Mas d'Azil (Ariège) : human figure sculptured on a horse's tooth (5,5 cm.) (PIETTE, 1895, pl. IV). *e*), *f*) Petersfels (Baden): schematic female figures carved in lignite (4; 3 cm.) (PETERS, 1930 a, pl. 3). *g*) Schematic female figure, bone, from Pekarna (Moravia), according to Absolon of Aurignacian age (4 cm.) (ABSOLON, CZYŻEK, 1932, p. XXII). *h*) Mauern (Bavaria) : calcite human statuette (7,2 cm.) (*photograph*: Zotz). *i*), *j*), *k*) Cave of La Marche (Vienne) : obese female figures engraved on stone (8; 8; 6 cm.) (LWOFF, 1943, figs. 8, 11; *Idem*, 1941, fig. 12).

PL. 83   *a*)-*d*) Cave of La Marche (Vienne) : human heads and individual shown in the act of dancing or of handling a weapon, engraved on stone (12; 3,5; 14; 30 cm.) (PÉRICARD, LWOFF, 1940, figs. 4, 4 bis; LWOFF, 1943, fig. 5; *Idem*, 1941, figs. 4, 7). *e*) Cave of Les Trois Frères (Ariège) : anthropomorphic figure engraved on stone (11 cm.); Begouen, Montesquieu-Avantès collection (BEGOUEN L., 1939, p. 292). *f*) Cave of Bédeilhac (Ariège) : engraved human figures (9 cm. high) (*drawing by E. Octobon*).

PL. 84   *a*), *b*) *c*) Cave of Isturitz (Basses-Pyrénées) : human figures engraved on stone (*a* = 7 cm.; *b* = 4,5 cm.; *c* = 5 cm.) (ST. PÉRIER, 1930, pl. VIII, fig. 76). *d*) Same locality : figure of a woman pursued by a man and struck in the flank by a harpoon, engraved on bone (10,5 cm.) (ST. PÉRIER, 1936, pl. IX, fig. 66). St. Périer, Morigny collection. *e*) Gourdan (Haute-Garonne) : male figure engraved on a "bâton de commandement" (11,5 cm.); Musée St. Germain (*photograph of a cast* and *drawing* by CAPITAN, BREUIL, PEYRONY, 1924, fig. 98). *f*) Cave of Isturitz : anthropomorphic figures engraved on bone (10,5 cm.); St. Périer, Morigny collection (ST. PÉRIER, 1936, fig. 65). *g*) Limeuil (Dordogne) : anthropomorphic figures engraved on stone (12 cm.) (CAPITAN, BOUYSSONIE, 1924, pl. XXX).

PL. 85   *a*) Mas d'Azil (Ariège) : anthropomorphic figures engraved on bone disks (7,5 cm.); Musée St. Germain (*photograph*: *Graziosi*). *b*) Lourdes (Hautes-Pyrénées) : bearded man engraved on schist (12 cm.); Musée St. Germain (CAPITAN, BREUIL, PEYRONY, 1924, fig. 98). *c*) Laugerie Basse (Dordogne) : pregnant woman and forelegs of a reindeer; engraving on bone fragment, on the opposite side of which is the figure of a horse shown in Pl. 57, *e* (10 cm.) (PIETTE, 1904, pl. I). *d*) Mas d'Azil : human being, probably a youth, engraved on bone; Musée St. Germain (CAPITAN, BREUIL, PEYRONY, 1924, fig. 92). *e*) Anthropomorphic figures engraved on stone from Gourdan (Haute-Garonne) (the figures measure 5,5 cm.); Musée St. Germain (CAPITAN, BREUIL, PEYRONY, 1924, fig. 99).

PL. 86   *a*) Laugerie Basse (Dordogne): man following a bison; engraving on reindeer antler (the figures measure 19 cm.); Musée St. Germain (*photograph of a cast*). *b*) La Madeleine (Dordogne) : pebble engraved with the figures of a masked man and woman (the figures measure 7,5 cm.); Musée St. Germain (*photograph*: *Musée des Eyzies* and *drawing*: CAPITAN, BREUIL, PEYRONY, 1924, fig. 99). *c*) La Madeleine: anthropomorphic figure engraved on bone; Musée des Eyzies (*museum photograph*). *d*) Human figures engraved on bone in La Madeleine (CAPITAN, PEYRONY, 1928, fig. 42). *e*) Gourdan (Haute-Garonne) : line of individuals engraved on bone (the object measures 6,5 cm.); Musée St. Germain (PIETTE, 1907, pl. LXXXIII).

PL. 87   *a*), *b*) Cave of Les Eyzies (Dordogne) : men parading in front of a bison; engraving on bone (the figures are 9,5 cm. high). Musée des Eyzies (*museum photograph* and *drawing* by CAPITAN, BREUIL, PEYRONY, 1924, fig. 102). *c*), *d*) Chancelade in Raymonden (Dordogne) : men in double file; head, backbone and forelegs of a bison; engraving on bone (8,5 cm.). Musée du Périgord, Périgueux (*museum photograph* and *drawing* by CAPITAN, BREUIL, PEYRONY, 1924, fig. 102). *e*) La Madeleine (Dordogne) : man, horses and snake engraved on a reindeer antler (15,5 cm.); Musée St. Germain (LARTET, CHRISTY, 1875, pl. II). *f*) Abri Mège à Teyjat (Dordogne) : masked personages with chamois hides, dancing, engraved on a stag antler "bâton de commandement", shown in Pl. 66, *a*, *b* (maximum height 5 cm.) (CAPITAN, BREUIL, BOURRINET, PEYRONY, 1909, fig. 11).

PERSPECTIVE AND COMPOSITION IN MAGDALENIAN MOBILIARY ART.

PL. 88   Animal figures viewed in frontal perspective. *a*) Gourdan (Haute-Garonne) : probable representation of an elk engraved on reindeer antler (12 cm.); Musée St. Germain (PIETTE, 1904, fig. 52). *b*) Heads of deer from Abri Mège à Teyjat (Dordogne) (12 cm.); Musée St. Germain (ST. PÉRIER, 1932, pl. XXXV). *c*) "Bâton de commandement" from Gourdan, with various decorative patterns, one of which is derived from the rope wound around the centre of the stick itself. Note the representation of an ox in dorsal perspective, of a ruminant with head viewed from the back, of another animal's head, probably a horse, viewed from the front, and of a fish (22 cm.); Musée St. Germain (PIETTE, 1907, pl. LXXXII). *d*) Stylized ibex viewed from the front, from Laugerie Basse (Dordogne) (6 cm.);

Musée St. Germain (GIROD, MASSENAT, 1888). *e*) Horse's head viewed from the front, from Gourdan (6 cm.); Musée St. Germain (BREUIL, 1937 a, fig. 29). *f*) Head of a bear viewed from the front, from Massat (Ariège) (5 cm.); Musée d'Histoire Naturelle, Toulouse (CAPITAN, BREUIL, PEYRONY, 1924, fig. 114). *g*) Ox with head viewed from above, engraving on stone in Limeuil (Dordogne) (11 cm.); Musée St. Germain (CAPITAN, BOUYSSONIE, 1924, pl. XIX). *h*) Gourdan : stylized horned animals, viewed from the front, engraved on deer antler; Magdalenian VI (11,5; 9 cm.) (BREUIL, 1937 a, fig. 38).

PL. 89   *a*) Isturitz (Basses-Pyrénées) : series of horses; engraving on bone (9,5 cm.). St. Périer, Morigny collection (ST. PÉRIER, 1936, fig. 43). *b*) Cave of Chaffaud (Vienne) : herds of horses; engraving on bone (12 cm.) (CARTAILHAC, 1903, p. 180). *c*) Cave of La Mairie à Teyjat (Dordogne) : engravings on an eagle's bone, very much deteriorated, barely perceptible, interpreted by Breuil as the synthetic representation of a herd of reindeer (20 cm.) (CAPITAN, BREUIL, BOURRINET, PEYRONY, 1908, fig. 97). *d*) La Vache (Ariège) : group of bears (BREUIL, NOUGIER, ROBERT, 1956, p. 18).

PL. 90   *a*)-*c*) Representation of an identical scene (an animal, probably carnivorous, pursuing a deer whose head is viewed from the back) found in three different deposits : *a*) Mas d'Azil (Ariège) : engraving on deer antler (11 cm.); Musée St. Germain (PIETTE, 1907, pl. XCVI). *b*) Cave of Lorthet (Hautes-Pyrénées) : engravings on a bone spatula (5,5 cm.); Musée St. Germain (*museum photograph*). *c*) Cave of El Pendo (Santander): engravings on a deer antler pendant; Museo Prehistorico, Santander (*photograph: Graziosi*). *d*) Couple of ruminants in La Madeleine (Dordogne), engraved on bone (7 cm.) (LARTET, CHRISTY, 1875, B. pl. II). *e*), *f*), *g*) Cave of Limeuil (Dordogne) : herds of horses and deer engraved on stone (16,5; 16; 23 cm.) (CAPITAN, BOUYSSONIE, 1924, pls. XX, XV).

VEGETABLE FORMS AND WEAPONS IN FRANCO-CANTABRIAN MOBILIARY ART.

PL. 91   Twigs and plants : *a*) engraved bone (Perigordian) from the cave of Le Trilobite (Arcy-sur-Cure, Yonne) (11 cm.); Musée St. Germain (*museum photograph*). *b*) Le Veyrier (Haute-Savoie) : " bâton de commandement (28 cm.); Musée d'art et d'Histoire, Geneva (*museum photograph* and *drawing* by BREUIL, 1937 a, fig. 41). *c*, *d*) Engraved bones from Mas d'Azil (Ariège) (14 cm.) and Laugerie Basse (Dordogne) (11 cm.); Musée St. Germain (*museum photograph*). *e*) Engraved bone from Mas d'Azil (9,5 cm.); Musée St. Germain (PIETTE, 1907, pl. XLVIII). Representations of harpoons : *f*) from Isturitz (Basses-Pyrénées), engraved on bone (9 cm.); St. Périer, Morigny collection (ST. PÉRIER, 1930, fig. 53); *g*) from Duruthy (Landes), engraved on a tooth (10,5 cm.); Musée de Le Mans (LARTET, CHAPLAIN-DUPARC, 1874, fig. 34). *h*) Harpoon with single row of barbs engraved on bone, from the cave of La Vache (Ariège); Robert collection, Tarascon s. A. (MALVESIN-FABRE, NOUGIER, ROBERT, 1951, fig. 3).

GEOMETRICAL ORNAMENTAL DESIGNS, SCHEMATIZATIONS, STYLIZATIONS, ETC., IN FRANCO-CANTABRIAN MOBILIARY ART.

PL. 92   Various ornamental designs on bone and on ivory. *a*)-*c*) On ivory objects from Brassempouy (Landes), of Aurignacian age (9,5; 4; 8 cm.); Musée St. Germain (*museum photograph*). *d*), *e*) Maltà (Siberia) (14 cm.) (SALMONY, 1931, pl. I). *f*) On bone, from Isturitz (Basses-Pyrénées), of Solutrean age (5 cm.); St. Périer, Morigny collection (ST. PÉRIER, 1952, fig. 11). *g*)-*j*) On bone, from Placard (Charente) Magdalenian I and II (15; 12; 16; 10 cm.); Musée St. Germain (BREUIL, 1937 a, fig. 21). *k*) On horses' teeth from the cave of La Marche (Vienne), Magdalenian III (PÉRICARD, LWOFF, 1940, figs. 7, 8).

PL. 93   Various ornamental designs on bone. *a*), *b*), *c*) Marsoulas (Haute-Garonne) (11,2; 10,5; 11,2 cm.); Musée St. Germain (BREUIL, 1937 a, fig. 27); *d*) *Idem*, Musée d'Histoire Naturelle, Toulouse (8,5 cm.) (CAUDURBAN, 1885, fig. 98). *e*) Le Placard (Charente) (15 cm.) (CHAUVET, 1910, fig. 75). *f*) Saint Marcel (Indre) (10,5 cm.); Musée St. Germain (BREUIL, 1902 a, fig. 5). *g*) On bone, from Lespugue (Haute-Garonne) (ST. PÉRIER, 1932, pl. LIII). *h*)-*j*) Isturitz (Basses-Pyrénées) (*h* = 8 cm.) (ST. PÉRIER, 1936, fig. 50, and PASSEMARD, 1922, figs. 32, 33). *k*) On ivory, from Laugerie Basse (Dordogne) (8 cm.); Musée St. Germain (BREUIL, 1937 a, fig. 27).

PL. 94   Reindeer antler rods with spiral ornaments from Late Magdalenian : *a*) Arudy (Basses-Pyrénées) (8; 11 cm.); Musée St. Germain (*museum photograph*); *b*) Lespugue (Haute-Garonne) photograph and tracing (19 cm.) (ST. PÉRIER, 1929, fig. 1); *c*), *d*) Lespugue (actual size) (ST. PÉRIER, 1929, figs. 6,7). *e*) *Idem* (ST. PÉRIER, 1929, fig. 2). St. Périer, Morigny collection. *f*) Lourdes (Hautes-Pyrénées) (15 cm.); Musée St. Germain (*museum photograph*).

PL. 95   Rods with spiral ornaments from Isturitz (Basses-Pyrénées) (all actual size); St. Périer, Morigny collection (ST. PÉRIER, 1936, fig. 51 and pl. VIII).

PL. 96   Geometrical decorations on objects and various signs. *a*) Lalinde (Dordogne) : large ivory pendant with geometrical decorations which has been compared to Australian "churingas" or humming tablets (18 cm.); Chicago Natural History Museum (*Musée St. Germain photograph*). *b*) St. Marcel Indre) : bone pendant (5,5 cm.); Musée St. Germain (*museum photograph* and *drawing* by BREUIL, 1902 a, fig. 4). *c*) Mas d'Azil (Ariège) bone disk with simple decoration of parallel lines; Musée St. Germain (*museum photograph*). *d*) Petersfels (Baden) : ivory button (8 cm.) (PETERS, 1930, pl. XXV). *e*) Cave of Isturitz (Basses-Pyrénées) : probable "tectiform" engraved on stone; Musée St. Germain (PASSEMARD, 1935). *f*) Mas d'Azil : ivory phallic sculpture (9,5 cm.); Musée St. Germain (*photograph : Graziosi*). *g*) Gorge d'Enfer (Dordogne) : extremity of a "bâton de commandement » with phallic sculptures (9,5 cm.); Musée St. Germain (*photograph of a cast*). *h*) Signs believed to be alphabetical from Gourdan (Haute-Garonne); *i*), *j*), *k*) *Idem*, from Placard (Charente), Lorthet (Hautes-Pyrénées), La Madeleine (Dordogne). (DÉCHELETTE, 1908, fig. 95). *l*) Cave of Le Trilobite (Yonne) : stylized coleopteron carved in lignite (approx. 4 cm.) (VIDAL Y LOPEZ, 1937, fig. 4). *m*) Laugerie Basse (Dordogne) : ivory lady-bird (1,5 cm.); Musée St. Germain (MORTILLET G. and A., 1903, fig. 238). *n*) Klause (Bavaria) : schematic paintings on stone (14,5 cm.) (OBERMAIER, 1941, fig. 24).

PL. 97   Derivations of spiral-shaped figures similar to sculptured rods from Isturitz (Basses-Pyrénées), Lourdes (Hautes-Pyrénées), Lespugue (Haute-Garonne) (see Pls. 94, 95) from the synthetic representation of the eye and the horn of the bison : *a*) Puy-de-Lacan (Corrèze) (KIDDER, 1936, fig. 5); *b*) Maszycka near Oikow (Poland) (HOERNES, 1903, fig. 77). *c*) Le Placard (Charente) (BREUIL, 1937 a, fig. 19). *d*) La Madeleine (Dordogne) (CAPITAN, PEYRONY, 1928, fig. 40). *e*) Lourdes (BREUIL, 1937, fig. 26). Derivation of oval figures from the eye of the reindeer or horse. *f*) Brassempouy (Landes). *g*) Bruniquel (Tarn-et-Garonne). *h*) Gourdan (Haute-Garonne). *i*) Laugerie Basse (Dordogne) (BREUIL, 1937 a, figs. 26, 27). Derivation of festooned figures from the stylized representation of a horse's coat. *j*) Horse from Lourdes (see Pl. 42). *k*) Isturitz (ST. PÉRIER, 1936, fig. 46). *l*) Lourdes (ST. PÉRIER, 1937, pl. LIII). *n*) Progressive stylizations, on the same object, of an ibex head, from Massat (Ariège) (ST. PÉRIER, 1937, pl. LVIII).

PL. 98   *a*), *b*) Derivation of shuttle-shaped figures, filled in with parallel lines, from the representation of a fish : *a*) La Madeleine (Dordogne) (CAPITAN, PEYRONY, 1928, fig. 57); *b*) Lorthet (Hautes-Pyrénées) (11 cm.) (PIETTE, 1907, pl. XLVII). *c*), *d*) Oval figures, deeply engraved, also derived from fish, from La Madeleine (12; 19 cm.) (ST. PÉRIER, 1932, pl. LI and *photograph of a cast*).

PL. 99   *a*) Petersfels (Baden) : progressive stylization of the figure of a fish on the same object (19 cm.) (PETERS, 1930 a, pl. 5). *b*) Fish tails forming a seriated ornamental pattern in La Madeleine (CAPITAN, PEYRONY, 1928, fig. 40). *c*) "Bâton de commandement" from Laugerie Basse (Dordogne) with ornaments probably derived from the tail of a fish (approx. 25 cm.); Musée de l'Homme, Paris (*museum photograph*). Progressive derivation of V-shaped patterns from the figure of an ibex viewed from the front, on objects found in the same deposit. *d*) Ibex, already synthetized, engraved on the antler of a deer in the cave of El Pendo (Santander); Museo Prehistorico, Santander (*photograph : Graziosi*). *e-g*) Successive schematizations of the same subject engraved on the antler of a deer in the same cave; Museo Prehistorico, Santander (CARBALLO, LARIN, 1932, figs. 76, 78, 77).

SCHEMATIC ART IN EASTERN EUROPE

PL. 100   Predmosti (Moravia) : *a*) highly stylized female figure engraved on a mammoth tusk (the figure is 15,5 cm. high); Moravské Museum, Brno (*museum photograph*). *b*) Ivory pendant with engraved digital designs (10 cm.) (KŘÍŽ, 1903, p. 215). *c*)-*e*) Geometrical patterns engraved on bone (13; 24; 12 cm.); Moravské Museum, Brno (KŘÍŽ, 1903, p. 216, and BREUIL, 1924, fig. 21).

PL. 101   Mézine (Ukraine) : *a*)-*j*) ivory sculptures believed to be stylizations of the female form (maximum dimension 12,5 cm.) (*photographs of casts* and *drawings* by GOLOMSHTOK, 1938, fig. 60). *k*) Greek key designs on ivory (15 cm.) (GOLOMSHTOK, 1938, fig. 59). *l*) Kiev (Ukraine) : indecipherable signs on a mammoth tusk (GOLOMSHTOK, 1938, pl. XXXI).

THE MEDITERRANEAN PROVINCE

PL. 102   Cave of Parpallò (Valencia) : animals engraved and painted on stone, from Aurignacian and Solutrean layers. *a*), *b*) Horse and ox, engraved; Late Aurignacian (20; 16 cm.). *c*) Engraved deer, Early Solutrean (32 cm.). *d*), *e*) Painted horse and painted and engraved deer, Early Solutrean (23; 19 cm.). *f*) Deer nursing its young, Early Solutrean engraving (39 cm.). *g*) Engraved deer, Middle Solutrean (9,5 cm.). *h*) Painted deer and " pectiforms ", Middle Solutrean (15,5 cm.). *i*) Painted ibex, Middle Solutrean (18 cm.). Museo Prehistorico, Valencia (*a-g* = PÉRICOT, 1942, figs. 80, 85, 97, pls. XXVIII, XXIX; fig. 125, pl. XII; *h, i* = *photograph*: *Museum of Valencia*).

PL. 103 Cave of Parpalló (Valencia) : figures painted and engraved on pebbles from Solutrean and Final Solutrean-Aurignacian layers. *a*), *b*) Engraved geometrical designs, Middle Solutrean (20; 24 cm.). *c*) Late Solutrean deer (16 cm.). *d*) Late Solutrean engraved deer (12,5 cm.). *e*), *f*) Painted horse and deer, Final Solutrean-Aurignacian (38; 21 cm.). *g*), *h*) Engraved horse and oxen, from indeterminate layers (8; 13; 5 cm.). Museo Prehistorico, Valencia (PÉRICOT, 1942, figs. 175, 176, 195, 191, pls. XXX, XXXI, XXVII, XXVI).

PL. 104 Cave of Parpalló (Valencia) : Engravings and paintings on stone from Magdalenian layers. *a*) Ox, Magdalenian III (8 cm.). *b*)-*i*) Engraved geometrical patterns, Magdalenian III (5; 9; 4,5; 8; 13,5; 7; 16,5; 5,5 cm.). *j*), *k*) Tree-shaped figure and ibex head, painted; Magdalenian IV (13; 12 cm.) Museo Prehistorico, Valencia (*drawings* by PÉRICOT, 1942, figs. 314, 401, 315, 402, 313, 339, 398, 369, 370, 371, 372, 373 and *museum photograph*).

PL. 105 Cave of Parpalló (Valencia) : Engravings on stone. *a*), *b*), *d*), *e*), *g*)-*i*) animals and geometrical patterns from Magdalenian III layers (5,5; 5,5; 7; 3,5; 6; 9,5; 8; 6 cm.); *c*), *f*) Magdalenian II (8; 4,5 cm.). *j*) Magdalenian IV (5,8 cm.); *k*)-*n*) from undetermined layers (5,3; 6; 5; 6,5 cm.). Museo Prehistorico, Valencia (drawings by PÉRICOT, 1942, figs. 353, 352, 289, 334, 362, 295, 390, 397, 420, 441, 573, 554, 540, 497).

PL. 106 *a*) Cave of Arene Candide (Finale Ligure) : elk antler " bâton de commandement " decorated with groups of parallel lines; Museo di Pegli (*photograph* : *Cardini*). *b*) Cave of Barma Grande (Grimaldi) : geometrical designs engraved on a pebble; Musée St. Germain (*museum photograph* and *drawing by Octobon*). *c*) *Idem*, network design on a fragment of steatite; Musée St. Germain (*museum photograph* and *drawing by A. Micheli*). *d*) Cave of Monopoli (Apulia) : head of an ox lightly engraved on a pebble (*photograph* : *Anelli*).

PL. 107 Grotta Polesini (Tivoli). *a*) Carnivore, probably a wolf, engraved on a pebble from Upper Palaeolithic strata (5 cm.) (*drawings by Micheli*) (RADMILLI, 1954 b, figs. 1, 2). *b*) Horse's head engraved on stone (7 cm.). *c*) Deer heads on bone (7,5 cm.). *d*) Hindquarters of a deer in stone (28,5 cm.). *e*), *f*) Ox heads lightly engraved on pebbles (6,5 cm.). Museo Preistorico " L. Pigorini ", Rome (*drawings by Micheli*). (See also RADMILLI, 1954; *Idem*, 1956 a, figs. 8, 4, 5; *Idem*, 1957, fig. 11).

PL. 108 Grotta Polesini (Tivoli): *a*) figure shaped like a fish tail engraved on a pebble; *b*), *c*) uninterpretable figures, perhaps schematic fish, engraved on stone; *d*), *e*), *f*), *g*), *h*), *i*), *k*), *l*) zigzag, fret and other geometrical figures engraved on bone; *j*) leaf-shaped figures engraved on bone. All in natural size. Museo Preistorico " L. Pigorini " (*drawings by Micheli*). (See also RADMILLI, 1956 a, fig. 2; *Idem*, 1957, figs. 8, 9).

PL. 109 Grotta Romanelli (Otranto) : figures lightly engraved on pebbles from Upper Palaeolithic strata. *a*) Hindquarters of an animal, probably feline, covered with intersecting parallel lines (19 cm.). *b*), *c*), *d*) Probable representation of a wild boar and of deer (10; 14; 17 cm.). *e*) Ribbon-shaped figures on both sides of a pebble, widening to a bow or noose engraved on one end, and knot half way up one side. *f*) Development of preceding figures. *g*), *h*), *i*) Strips of lines. Blanc collection, Rome (*a-c* = BLANC A. C., 1940, pls. I, II; *d* = STELLA, 1935, figs. 2, 3; *e-i* = BLANC G. A., 1928, pls. XLII, XLIV).

PL. 110 Grotta Romanelli (Otranto) : *a*)-*d*) ribbon-shaped and tree-shaped figures, lightly engraved (10,5; 12; 7,5; 8 cm.). *e*) Strips of interwoven parallel lines, vigorously engraved (19 cm.). *f*) " Pectiforms " painted in red ochre (36 cm.). Blanc collection, Rome (BLANC G. A., 1928, pls. XLIII, XLIV; BLANC A. C., 1940, pls. I, II; 1938, fig. 2).

PL. 111 Cave of Levanzo (Egadi) : *a*) engraved stone found in Upper Palaeolithic layers (the animal measures 17,5 cm.) (*photograph* : *Graziosi*). *b*) Drawing of same showing (to the right, inside the figure) the head of a ruminant finely engraved (GRAZIOSI, 1953, figs. 1, 2).

CAVE ART

PL. 122   Cave of Le Gabillou (Dordogne): *a*) head of an ox (22 cm.). *b*) Bison with horns viewed in frontal perspective (60 cm.). *c*) Reindeer (40 cm.). *d*) Hare (25 cm.). (*Photograph*: *Malvesin-Fabre*, *drawings*: *Isola*).

PL. 123   Cave of La Mouthe (Dordogne): bison and ox deeply engraved (85; 120 cm.) (*photograph*: *Laborie*).

PL. 124   Cave of La Mouthe (Dordogne): galloping bull, engraved and partly painted (1,53 m.) (*photograph*: *Laborie*).

PL. 125   Cave of Barabao near Le Bugue (Dordogne): ox, horse, feline animal (*photograph*: *Laborie*).

PL. 126   Hornos de la Peña (Santander): *a*) horse engraved near the entrance of the cave (40 cm.) (*photograph*: *Robert*). *b*), *c*) Other horses engraved in the interior of the cave (34; 70 cm.) (ALCALDE DEL RIO, BREUIL, SIERRA, 1911, pls. LVII, LVIII).

PL. 127   Cave of Los Casares (Guadalajara): *a*) woolly rhinoceros (35 cm.). *b*) Great stag (1,70 m.) and other animals. *c*) Wolverine (45 cm.). *d*) Feline animal (?). *e*) Horse (15cm.) (CABRÉ AGUILÓ, 1935).

PL. 128   Cave of Castillo (Santander): *a*) deer (38 cm.) (*photograph*: *Graziosi*). *b*) Ibex (30 cm.) (*photograph*: *Laborie*). *c*) Horse (50 cm.) (*photograph*: *Graziosi*).

PL. 129   Engravings in the cave of Gargas (Hautes-Pyrénées): *a*) horse (*photograph*: *Robert*). *b*), *c*) Various animal figures (the two groups measure 3,60 and 1,90 m. respectively) (BREUIL, 1952, figs. 288 and 284).

PL. 130   Calcareous blocks engraved with oxen from the Magdalenian III layers of Laugerie Haute (Dordogne); Musée des Eyzies (*a*, 38 cm. = PEYRONY, 1938, pl. V; *b*, *c*, the block measures 55 cm. (*photograph*: *Musée des Eyzies*).

PL. 131   Cave of El Buxu: *a*), *b*) engraved horses (50; 54 cm.); *c*) engraved and painted deer (the animal at the bottom is 39 cm. high) (OBERMAIER, VEGA DEL SELLA, 1918, pls. XII, XIII, V, XVI).

PL. 132   Engravings in the cave of Lascaux (Dordogne): *a*) deer (1 m.); *b*) horse's head (*photograph*: *Laborie*).

PL. 133   *a*) Engraved deer in the cave of Altamira (Santander) (62 cm.) (ALMAGRO, 1947, fig. 29). *b*) Deer heads lightly engraved in the cave of Altamira (32 cm.) (BREUIL, OBERMAIER, 1935, fig. 58). *c*) *Idem* in the cave of Castillo (Santander) (21; 20 cm.) (ALCALDE DEL RIO, BREUIL, SIERRA, 1911, fig. 169). *d*) Ibex engraved in the cave of Castillo (40 cm.) (ALMAGRO, 1947, fig. 29).

PL. 134   Cave of Pindal (Oviedo): fish and horse lightly engraved (43; 60 cm.) (see also Pl. 235) (*a* = ALCALDE DEL RIO, BREUIL, SIERRA, 1911, pl. XLIII; *b* = ALMAGRO, 1947 a, fig. 32).

PL. 135   Cave of La Peña de Candamo (Oviedo): wounded deer and bison (1,50; 0,90 m.) (HERNANDEZ PACHECO, 1919, figs. 14, 37).

PL. 136   Cave of La Peña de Candamo (Oviedo): bulls (1,75; 1,12 m.) (FERNANDEZ PACHECO, 1919, figs. 22, 23).

PL. 137   *a*) Cave of La Peña de Candamo (Oviedo): deer's head with extravagantly shaped antlers (47 cm.). *b*) Group of finely engraved figures, some of them also painted, in the same cave: deer, bison, chamois, and one anthropomorphic figure (the figure at bottom right, 28 cm.). (HERNANDEZ PACHECO, 1910, fig. 41, pl. 23). *c*) Cave of La Loja (Oviedo): engraved oxen (1,70 m.) (ALCALDE DEL RIO, BREUIL, SIERRA, 1911, fig. 53).

PL. 138   Engravings on clay. *a*) Fish in the cave of Niaux (Ariège) (30 cm.) (SCHMIDT, 1936, pl. 38). *b*), *d*) Bison and horse's head in the cave of Bédeilhac (Ariège) (25; 11 cm.) (BEGOUEN, 1929, pl. I). *c*) Horse's head in the cave of Montespan (Haute-Garonne) (15 cm.) (TROMBE, DUBUC, 1947, fig. 36).

PL. 139   Cave of Les Combarelles (Dordogne): engravings of reindeer, an ox, a donkey, a horse (42; 100; 31; 36; 114) (CAPITAN, BREUIL, PEYRONY, 1924: *a* = pl. LIII; *c*, *d*, *e* = figs. 51, 79, 78, 69). See also the engravings from Les Combarelles reproduced in Pl. 284, *b*.

PL. 140   Cave of Les Combarelles (Dordogne): *b*) horse (the entire animal measures 84 cm.) (*photograph*: *Laborie*); *a*) deer (60 cm.); *c*), *d*) mammoths (72; 100 cm.); *e*) woolly rhinoceros (CAPITAN, BREUIL, PEYRONY, 1924, fig. 89, pl. XIX, figs. 121, 52, pl. XXV).

PL. 141   Cave of Les Combarelles (Dordogne): cave lion (68 cm.) (CAPITAN, BREUIL, PEYRONY, 1924, pl. XV, fig. 43).

PL. 142   Cave of Les Combarelles (Dordogne): cave bear (45 cm.) (CAPITAN, BREUIL, PEYRONY, 1924, pl. XVII, fig. 39).

PL. 163   Cave of La Magdeleine (Tarn): *a*), *b*) bas-reliefs of two reclining women; (BÉTIRAC, 1954, pls. I, II). *c*) Horse sculptured in light relief (*photograph*: *Vergnes*).

PL. 164   *a*) Cave of Isturitz (Basses-Pyrénées): bas-relief of a reindeer and some deer covered by Magdalenian layers (m. 1,20) (*photograph*: *Passemard*). *b*) Cave of Bédeilhac (Ariège): clay bas-relief of a bison (29 cm.) (*photograph*: *Robert*). *c*), *d*) La Chaire à Calvin (Charente): horses, probably Solutrean, in low relief (DAVID, 1947, fig. 1).

CLAY STATUES.

PL. 165   Tuc d'Audoubert (Ariège): *a*) entrance to the cave (*photograph*: *Graziosi*); *b*) the clay bison (the animal on the right measures 61 cm.) (BEGOUEN H., 1936).

PL. 166   Tuc d'Audoubert (Ariège). The clay bison viewed *a*) from the side, *b*) from the front (*photograph*: *Graziosi*).

PL. 167   Tuc d'Audoubert (Ariège). *a*), *b*) The male bison viewed from the back and from above: note in photograph *b*), the stones that were used to prop up the statue. *c*) Human heel-prints on the clayey floor of the cave, and the holes from which the clay for the statues was extracted. (*photograph*: *Graziosi*).

PL. 168   Cave of Montespan (Haute-Garonne). Clay statue of a headless bear: *a*) viewed from the side (CASTERET, 1937, fig. 51); *b*), *c*) viewed from the front and from the back (1 m.) (*photograph*: *Graziosi*). *d*) Incomplete clay statue of a headless feline animal, viewed from the front (*photograph*: *Graziosi*); *e*) the same, viewed from the side (1,60 m.) (TROMBE, DUBUC, 1947, fig. 59).

CAVE PAINTING IN FRANCE.

PL. 169   *a*) Painting on a large block of stone found in the Aurignacian deposit of Abri Blanchard in Sergeac (Dordogne) (BREUIL, 1952, fig. 315). *b*) Stag painted in black on a block of stone from the Perigordian layers of Abri Labatut in Sergeac (Dordogne) (40 cm.) (BREUIL, 1927, fig. 2). *c*) Cave of Marcenac (Lot): wall painting of a bison with horns viewed from the front (LAMING-EMPERAIRE, 1951, fig. 40).

PL. 170   Cave of Pech-Merle (Lot): ox and deer with horns viewed from the front, painted in red (30; 28 cm.) (*photograph*: *Laborie*).

PL. 171   Cave of Cougnac (Lot): paintings in red and in black. *a*) Large elephant (centre) (73 cm. high) and partial outline of another elephant (right), ibex antlers (right), human figure struck by darts (level with the head of the central elephant) and another human figure struck by darts (further right). *b*) Ibexes (the animal on the left measures 30 cm.) (*photograph*: *Geb*). *c*) Great deer with large palmate antlers (1,50 m.), smaller, incomplete deer, ibex, and incomplete human figure struck by darts (MÉROC, MAZET, 1953, fig. 1).

PL. 172   Cave of Le Portel (Ariège): paintings of the archaic type. *a*), *b*) Deer antlers viewed from the front (24 cm. high). *c*) owl (35 cm.). *d*) Horse with elongated nose (1,40 m.). *e*) Ibex (35 cm.). *f*) Probable horse (*photograph*: *Robert*).

PL. 173   Cave of Le Portel (Ariège): horses of the archaic type: *a*) red, outlined in black; *b*) black (110; 60 cm.) (*photograph*: *Robert*).

PL. 174   Cave of Lascaux (Dordogne): deer (each one measures approx. 80 cm.) (*photograph*: *Laborie*).

PL. 175   Cave of Lascaux (Dordogne): great bull and running horses (the bichromatic horse measures 2,80 m.) (*photograph*: *Laborie*).

PL. 176   Cave of Lascaux (Dordogne): great black bull superimposed upon figures of red oxen, (cf. Pl. 181) very much distorted by the photograph (5,50 m.) (*photograph*: *Malvesin-Fabre*).

PL. 177   Cave of Lascaux (Dordogne): great black bulls superimposed upon red oxen, considerably distorted by the photograph (the central bull measures approx. 4 m.) (*photograph*: *Malvesin-Fabre*).

PL. 178   Cave of Lascaux (Dordogne): "hall of bulls" and entrance to the axial corridor (*photograph*: *Malvesin-Fabre*).

PL. 179   Cave of Lascaux (Dordogne): large red cows painted on the ceiling of the axial corridor (*photograph*: *Laborie*).

PL. 180   Cave of Lascaux (Dordogne): *a*) overall view of the frieze on the left wall of the great "hall of bulls"; *b*) fantastic animal, known as "the unicorn" (1,65 m.) (*photograph*: *Laborie*).

PL. 181   Cave of Lascaux (Dordogne) : detail of the great bull in Pl. 176; the entire animal measures 5,50 m. (WINDELS, 1948, p. 22).

PL. 182   Cave of Lascaux (Dordogne) : a) cow painted in red with black head (2,80 m.); b) great black bull superimposed upon red oxen (3 m.) (WINDELS, pp. 74 and 89).

PL. 183   Cave of Lascaux (Dordogne) : detail of the great bull in Pl. 182, b (photograph : Windels).

PL. 184   Cave of Lascaux (Dordogne) : view of the corridor that continues the " hall of bulls " in an axial direction; photograph taken from the end of the corridor, looking towards the hall (photograph : Laborie).

PL. 185   Cave of Lascaux (Dordogne) : a) painted ceiling of the axial corridor; b) upside-down horse (the total length of the horse is 2 m.) (photograph : Laborie).

PL. 186   Cave of Lascaux (Dordogne) : " Chinese " horse surrounded by probable representations of darts (1,40 m.) (photograph : Laborie).

PL. 187   Cave of Lascaux (Dordogne) : horse and probable representations of darts or missiles (1,30 m.) (photograph: Laborie).

PL. 188   Cave of Lascaux (Dordogne) : cow, horse and dots (the cow measures 2 m.) (photograph : Laborie).

PL. 189   Cave of Lascaux (Dordogne) : jumping cow, small horses and reticulate figure; the red colour showing through the black belongs to an earlier figure underlying the cow (the cow measures 1,70 m.) (photograph : Malvesin-Fabre).

PL. 190   Cave of Lascaux (Dordogne) : horses, ibexes and rectangular figures (the horse at lower right measures approx. 80 cm.) (photograph : Laborie).

PL. 191   Cave of Lascaux (Dordogne) : detail of a horse and hindquarters of a bison (photograph : Laborie).

PL. 192   Cave of Lascaux (Dordogne) : running horse and probable representation of a javelin (3 m.) (photograph : Malvesin-Fabre).

PL. 193   Cave of Lascaux (Dordogne) : bison (the entire group measures 2,40 m.) (photograph : Laborie).

PL. 194   Cave of Lascaux (Dordogne) : a) series of deer heads painted in black (5 m.); b) series of ibex heads, painted and engraved: the colour has mostly disappeared (40 cm. high) (photograph : Windels). c) Bear covered by the stomach of one of the bulls on the right wall of the great hall (1 m.) (photograph : Laborie).

PL. 195   Cave of Lascaux (Dordogne) : a) deer with extravagantly shaped antlers (1,40 m. high) (photograph : Windels). b) Woolly rhinoceros painted in black in " blown technique "; close to the scene of the bison and the man (see Pl. 283, b) (1,50 m.) (photograph : Windels).

PL. 196   Cave of Pech-Merle (Lot) : the great panel with horses painted in black, covered with dots and with the negative impressions of human hands (3,40 m.) (photograph : Laborie).

PL. 197   Cave of Pech-Merle (Lot) : mammoths painted in black (60; 65 cm.) (photograph: Laborie).

PL. 198   Cave of Pech-Merle (Lot) : great frieze of the " mammoth chapel ". a) Left side, b) right side : mammoths, oxen, horses, bison painted in black (the largest mammoth measures 1,40 m.) (photograph : Laborie).

PL. 199   Cave of Pech-Merle (Lot) : a), b) oxen in the " mammoth chapel ", left side. Compare the animal with lowered head with analogous figure in La Pasiega (Santander) (P. 228, b). c) Figures recently discovered in a narrow chamber of the cave, painted in black, not clearly identifiable; among them are some goat-like figures, whose small heads can be detected at upper left (photograph : Laborie).

PL. 200   Cave of Le Portel (Ariège) : a) bison painted in black with engraved outline (63 cm.). b), c) Bison painted in black (63; 44 cm.). d) Reindeer painted in black on the ceiling of a low, narrow corridor, considerably distorted by the photograph (30 cm.). e) Incomplete horse, outlined in black (25 cm.) (photograph : Robert). See also paintings in the same cave in PL. 284, c.

PL. 201   Cave of Le Portel (Ariège) : horses of an evolved style, painted in black; the first is considerably distorted by the photograph (45; 70; 70 cm.) (photograph : Robert).

PL. 202   Cave of Rouffignac (Dordogne) : a) herd of rhinoceros painted in black; b) detail of same c), d) ibex and horse head painted in black. (NOUGIER, ROBERT, 1957, figs. 17, 18, 28, 21).

PL. 203   Cave of Rouffignac (Dordogne) : a) herd of mammoths painted in black; b) mammoths opposite each other painted in black; c) mammoth painted in black; d) bison opposite each other painted in black : one also engraved. Above, partial view of a mammoth. (NOUGIER, ROBERT, 1956, fig 4; Idem, 1957, figs. 13, 24, 29).

PL. 204   Cave of Niaux (Ariège): *a*) the great group of bison in the " Black Hall " (*photograph*: *Yan*). *b*) Ibex painted in black (27 cm.) (*photograph*: *Robert*).

PL. 205   Cave of Niaux (Ariège): " Black Hall ". *a*) Ibex (52 cm.). *b*) Bison struck with darts (1,50 m.): at bottom is an ibex, partly covered by stalagmite; at top the head of an ibex. (*Photograph*: *Yan*).

PL. 206   Cave of Niaux (Ariège): more bison in the " Black Hall " (the bison at the top measures 95 cm.) (*photograph*: *Yan*).

PL. 207   Cave of Niaux (Ariège): " Black Hall ". Bison painted in black, one of which is struck by darts, and small ibex, also struck by darts (the bison at the bottom measures 1 m.) (*photograph*: *Yan*).

PL. 208   Cave of Niaux (Ariège): " Black Hall ". Bison struck by dart (90 cm.); below, the little ibex in Pl. 201 (*photograph*: *Yan*).

PL. 209   Cave of Niaux (Ariège): " Black Hall ". Bison struck by darts, two of which are painted in red, incomplete horse and, at bottom, another small horse, the same as in Pl. 211 (the bison on the right measures 1,27 m.) (*photograph*: *Yan*).

PL. 210   Cave of Niaux (Ariège): *a*) detail of group in Pl. 209 (*photograph*: *Yan*). *b*) Horse in " Black Hall " (70 cm.) (*photograph*: *Robert*).

PL. 211   Cave of Niaux (Ariège): " Black Hall ". *a*) Horse: detail of figure *b*) (the entire animal measures 1,70 m.). Above is another small horse (the same as in Pl. 209). *c*) Horse (80 cm. high). (*Photograph*: *Yan*).

PL. 212   Cave of Niaux (Ariège): deer in " Black Hall " (1 m.) (*photograph*: *Yan*).

PL. 213   Cave of Bédeilhac (Ariège): sepia-coloured bison of the polychromatic phase, rather deteriorated (2 m.) (*photograph*: *Robert*). *b*) Cave of Marsoulas (Haute-Garonne): bison painted with dotted lines (87 cm.) (*photograph*: *Yan* and *drawing* by BREUIL, 1952, fig. 261).

PL. 214   The cliff of Font-de-Gaume in the Vézère valley (Dordogne) and the entrance to the cave (*photograph*: *Graziosi*).

PL. 215   Cave of Font-de-Gaume (Dordogne): *a*) painted and engraved bison (*photograph*: *Laborie*); *b*) the same according to Breuil's tracing (1,35 m.) (see also fig. 33 in text) (CAPITAN, BREUIL, PEYRONY, 1910, pl. XXXI).

PL. 216   Cave of Font-de-Gaume (Dordogne): *a*) horse pursuing a mare; only the hindquarters of this figure are visible. Stalagmitic formations were made use of in its execution (see also Pl. 276, *a*, *b*) (*photograph*: *Laborie*). *b*) The same according to Breuil's tracing (1,15 m.) (CAPITAN, BREUIL, PEYRONY, 1910, pl. VII).

PL. 217   Cave of Font-de-Gaume (Dordogne): *a*) male and female reindeer facing each other, painted and engraved (*photograph*: *Laborie*); *b*) the same according to Breuil's tracing (2,45 m.) (CAPITAN, BREUIL, PEYRONY, 1910, pl. XXVIII).

PL. 218   Cave of Font-de-Gaume (Dordogne): *a*) rhinoceros painted in red (70 cm.). *b*) ox painted in black (65 cm.). *c*), *d*) Polychromatic wolf and reindeer (1,20 m.). *e*) Series of mammoths, bison and horses, painted and engraved (5 m.) (see also fig. 34 in text). All according to Breuil's tracings (CAPITAN, BREUIL, PEYRONY, 1910, pls. IV, XII, XXXVII, XXV, XIV).

CAVE PAINTING IN SPAIN.

PL. 219   Cave of La Peña de Candamo (Oviedo): bulls painted in red with horns viewed in frontal perspective, covered with dots at a later period (the animal on the right measures 57 cm.) (*a = photograph*: *Graziosi*; *b =* the same according to H. Pacheco's tracing) (HERNANDEZ PACHECO, 1919, fig. 25).

PL. 220   *a*) Cave of Pindal (Oviedo): elephant, probably a mammoth, painted in red (44 cm.). *b*) Cave of Castillo (Santander): another elephant painted in red (36 cm.) (*photograph*: *Graziosi*).

PL. 221   *a*) Entrance to the cave of Castillo (Santander). The photograph was taken in September, 1951: on the steps, top to bottom; Burkitt (England), Movius (U.S.A.), Graziosi (Italy), Althin (Sweden) (*photograph*: *Robert*). *b*) Head of an ox painted in black with horns viewed from the front, from the same cave (32 cm.). *c*) Bison painted in black (1 m.) (*photograph*: *Graziosi*).

PL. 222   Cave of Castillo (Santander): *a*) horse, painted in red (70 cm.) (*photograph*: *Laborie*). *b*) Ox painted in black (65 cm.) (*photograph*: *Graziosi*). *c*) Great bison painted in red, head downwards (1,20 m.) (*photograph*: *Graziosi*).

PL. 223 Cave of La Pasiega (Santander) : a) deer with horns viewed from the front (45 cm. high) and horse of the archaic type, painted in red; b) the same as a); c) horse (55 cm.) (photograph : Graziosi). d) Deer and horses, in different parts of the cave, among which are the specimens shown in photographs a and e of this plate, according to tracings by Breuil and Obermaier (BREUIL, OBERMAIER, ALCALDE DEL RIO, 1913, pl. VIII). e) Horses of the archaic type painted in red (the smallest one measures 30 cm.). f) Idem (32 cm.) (photograph : Graziosi).

PL. 224 Cave of La Pasiega (Santander) : a) horse painted in red with linear outline and some touches of chiaroscuro (45 cm.); this is one of the finest works of Franco-Cantabrian cave art (photograph : Graziosi). b) The same according to Breuil's tracing (BREUIL, OBERMAIER, ALCALDE DEL RIO, 1913, pl. XIV). c) Linear figure in red, of young deer, and incomplete stag (young deer 65 cm.) (photograph : Graziosi). d) The same, after Breuil (BREUIL, OBERMAIER, ALCALDE DEL RIO, 1913, pl. VI).

PL. 225 Cave of La Pasiega (Santander) : deer and horse (the horse measures 47,5 cm.) (photograph : Robert).

PL. 226 Cave of La Pasiega (Santander) : horse (77,5 cm.) (photograph : Robert).

PL. 227 Cave of La Pasiega (Santander) : ox (80 cm.) (photograph : Robert).

PL. 228 Cave of La Pasiega (Santander) : figures traced partly with lines and partly with dots, painted in red. a), e), f) Horses (1,15; 0,40; 0,40 m.) : compare them with the figures of Covalanas (Pl. 230 and foll.). b) Ox with head downwards (52 cm.) see similar figure in Pech-Merle (Pl. 199, b, c). d) Young deer placed one before the other on the same rock wall (30; 24 cm.) (photograph : Graziosi).

PL. 229 a), c) Cave of Las Chimeneas (Santander) : inside view and paintings of deer. d, e) Cave of Las Monedas (Santander) : wild goat, and horse (30; 64 cm.). (Photograph : Patronato de las Cuevas Prehistoricas de la prov. de Santander).

PL. 230 View of the cave of Covalanas near Ramales (Santander) and figures of a horse and a young deer painted in red (see Pl. 231, b) (photograph : Graziosi).

PL. 231 Cave of Covalanas (Santander) : a) group of young deer painted in red (detail); d, e) young deer painted in red with continuous or dotted line (80; 85 cm.) (photograph : Graziosi). b), c) The figures of the preceding plate and those of photograph a according to Breuil's tracings (the groups measure 1,67 and 2,50 m.) (ALCALDE DEL RIO, BREUIL, SIERRA, 1911, pls. XII, IX).

PL. 232 Cave of Covalanas (Santander) : a), c), d), e) young deer painted in red with continuous or dotted outlines (70 ; 75; 97; 83 cm.). b) Ox painted in red : the outline of the back is marked by the margin of the rock (1,38 cm.) (see also Pl. 274). (Photograph : Graziosi).

PL. 233 Cave of La Peña de Candamo (Oviedo). a) Superimposed horses, painted in black and in sienna; at top is the incomplete figure of an ox, in a reddish colour; to their right is the head of a horse bent down, painted in black (the horse at the bottom measures 75 cm.) (photograph : Graziosi). b) The same group according to tracings by J. Cabré. See also, in same cave, the paintings in Pls. 238, d, 257, d.

PL. 234 Cave of La Peña de Candamo (Oviedo) : deer painted in black (66 cm.) and horse, engraved and painted in brown (68 cm.) (HERNANDEZ PACHECO, 1919, fig. 19, pl. XVII).

PL. 235 Cave of Pindal (Oviedo). a) Group of paintings and engravings : engraved horse, bison partly painted and partly lightly engraved, horse's head and bison painted in red, dotted and club-shaped signs (the animal at the extreme right measures 52 cm.) (ALMAGRO, 1947 a, fig. 32). b) Detail of the preceding group (photograph : Graziosi).

PL. 236 Cave of Santimamiñe (Biscay). a) View of the side of the valley in which the cave opens (centre). b) Inside the recess containing the main groups of paintings (on left wall). c) Detail of the principal pictorial group : outline of the backs of two bison placed vertically, bison and horse (the horse measure 45 cm.). (Photograph : Graziosi).

PL. 237 Cave of Santimamiñe (Biscay) : b) principal pictorial group (ARANZADI, BARANDIARAN, EGUREN, 1925, fig. 21). a), c), d) Details of the same group (60; 38, 70 cm.) (photograph : Graziosi).

PL. 238 a) Cave of Santimamiñe (Biscay) : head of a deer and bear, painted in black (the bear measures 32 cm.) (photograph : Graziosi and drawing by ARANZADI, BARANDIARAN, EGUREN, 1925, fig. 19). b) Bison facing each other, in a vertical position on a wall of the same cave (80 cm.) (photograph : Graziosi). c) Cave of La Pasiega (Santander) : bison painted in brown and outlined in black in the lower part, of an advanced style (66 cm.) (photograph : Graziosi). d) Cave of La Peña de Candamo (Oviedo) : bison's head in black, in the same style as the preceding figure (40 cm.) (photograph : Graziosi).

PL. 239   Cave of Altamira (Santander): *a*) the spectacular group of polychromatic figures on the ceiling of the great hall (*photograph: Laborie*). *b*) Overall view of the paintings on the ceiling of the great hall (BREUIL, OBERMAIER, 1935, fig. 3).

PL. 240   Cave of Altamira (Santander): *a*), *b*) ibex and horse in a more archaic style than the figures that follow them (the horse measures 1,65 m.); *c*), *d*) head of an ox in black, and polychromatic bison (the bison measures 1,25 m.) (*photograph: Robert*); *e*) engraved parts of figure *d* (BREUIL, OBERMAIER, 1935, fig. 21).

PL. 241   Cave of Altamira (Santander): *a*) polychromatic bison (1,95 m.) (*photograph: Robert*). *b*) Engraved parts of same (BREUIL, OBERMAIER, 1935, fig. 14).

PL. 242   Cave of Altamira (Santander): *a*) lowing bison, polychromatic (1,25 m.) (*photograph: Robert*). *b*) Engraved parts of same (BREUIL, OBERMAIER, 1935, fig. 12).

PL. 243   Cave of Altamira (Santander): *a*) polychromatic bison (2,5 m.) (*photograph: Robert*). *b*) Partly engraved outline of same (BREUIL, OBERMAIER, 1935, fig. 19).

PL. 244   Cave of Altamira (Santander): *a*) bison and head of a horse or wild boar, superimposed (the bison measures 1,80 m.) (*photograph: Robert*). *b*) Engraved parts of same (BREUIL, OBERMAIER, 1935, fig. 16).

PL. 245   Cave of Altamira (Santander): *a*) polychromatic bison (*photograph: Robert*). *b*) Engraved parts of same (BREUIL, OBERMAIER, 1935, fig. 8).

PL. 246   Cave of Altamira (Santander): *a*) crouching polychromatic bison (1,60 m.) (*photograph: Laborie*). *b*) The same: BREUIL, OBERMAIER, 1935, fig. 13).

PL. 247   Cave of Altamira (Santander): *a*) polychromatic crouching bison (1,85 m.) (*photograph: Laborie*). *b*) Engraved parts of same (BREUIL, OBERMAIER, 1935, fig. 9).

PL. 248   Cave of Altamira (Santander): *a*) polychromatic crouching bison (1,55 m.) (*photograph: Robert*). *b*) Engraved parts of same (BREUIL, OBERMAIER, 1935, fig. 10).

PL. 249   Cave of Altamira (Santander): *a*) crouching female bison, polychromatic (*photograph: Laborie*). *b*) Engraved parts of same (BREUIL, OBERMAIER, 1935, fig. 11).

PL. 250   Cave of Altamira (Santander): bison, black and polychromatic (*photograph: Robert*).

PL. 251   Cave of Altamira (Santander): *a*) polychromatic horse superimposed upon a young deer (1,60 m.) (*photograph: Robert*). *b*) Engraved parts of same (BREUIL, OBERMAIER, 1935, fig. 18).

PL. 252   Cave of Altamira (Santander): *a*) polychromatic young deer and small black bison (the young deer measures 2,25 m.) (*photograph: Robert*). *b*) Engraved parts of the young deer (BREUIL, OBERMAIER, 1935, fig. 22).

PL. 253   Cave of Altamira (Santander): detail of the young deer in Pl. 252 (*photograph: Robert*).

PL. 254   Cave of Altamira (Santander): *a*) polychromatic wild boar (*photograph: Robert*). *b*) Engraved parts of same (BREUIL, OBERMAIER, 1935, fig. 5).

PL. 255   Cave of Altamira (Santander): head of an ox in black in the great hall (see also Pl. 240, *c*) (*photograph: Laborie*).

PL. 256   Cave of Altamira (Santander): *a*) bison in black (*photograph: Graziosi*). *b*) Incomplete deer's head (48 cm.) (*photograph: Laborie*).

THE HUMAN FORM.

PL. 257   *a*), *b*) Female figures engraved on clay in the cave of Pech-Merle (Lot) (see also Pl. 116) (BREUIL, 1924, figs. 2, 3). *c*) Ithyphallic human figure painted in the cave of Portel (Ariège), only partly visible in the photograph (the entire figure measures 38 cm.) (*photograph: Robert*). *d*) Human figure in La Peña de Candamo (Oviedo) (42 cm.) (*photograph: Robert*). *e*) Man, apparently armed with a bow; painted in the cave of Pech-Merle (51 cm.) (LAMING-EMPERAIRE, 1951, fig. 37). *f*), *g*) Anthropomorphic figures engraved in the cave of Los Casares (Guadalajara) (50; 80 cm.) (CABRÉ AGUILÓ, 1940, figs. 2, 9).

PL. 258   Engraved anthropomorphic figures. *a*) Cave of Los Casares (Guadalajara) (33 cm.) (CABRÉ AGUILÓ, 1940, fig. 3). *b*) Cave of Le Gabillou (Dordogne): female figure wearing a sort of hood (*photograph: Malvesin-Fabre, drawing: Isola*). *c*), *e*) Human heads in the cave of Marsoulas (Haute-Garonne) (CARTAILHAC, BREUIL, 1905, figs. 5, 7). *d*) Probable schematic female figures, Magdalenian III, from the cave of La Roche (Dordogne); Musée des Eyzies (*museum photograph*). *f*), *g*) Cave of Les Combarelles (Dordogne) *f*) 38 cm.; *g*), 72 cm. high) (CAPITAN, BREUIL, PEYRONY, 1924, figs. 21, 68).

PL. 259   Engraved anthropomorphic figures : *a*) Les Combarelles (50 cm.) (CAPITAN, BREUIL, PEYRONY, 1924, pl. IX); *b*) Altamira (the largest figure measures 60 cm.) (*tracings by Benitez*). *c*) Hornos de la Peña (Santander) (70 cm.) (ALCALDE DEL RIO, BREUIL, SIERRA, 1911, pl. LV).

HANDS.

PL. 260   *a*) Negative impression of a hand in red and dots in the cave of Pech-Merle (Lot) (*photograph* : *Laborie*). *b*), *d*) Negative impressions of hands in the cave of Gargas (Hautes-Pyrénées) some with mutilations (*photograph* : *Robert*). *c*) Positive impressions of hands in the cave of Bédeilhac (Ariège) (*photograph* : *Robert*).

PL. 261   Engraved hands : *a*) in the cave of Barabao (Dordogne) (*photograph* : *Laborie*). *b*) In Abri du Cap Blanc (Dordogne) (*photograph* : *Graziosi*). *c*) Probable representation of a fist engraved in clay in the cave of Niaux (Ariège) (*photograph* : *Robert*).

PL. 262   Cave of Castillo (Santander) : negative impression of a hand (*photograph* : *Robert*).

PL. 263   Cave of Gargas (Hautes-Pyrénées): negative impressions of hands, in red and black (*photograph* : *Robert*).

VARIOUS SIGNS.

PL. 264   Red dots : *a*) in the cave of Les Trois Frères (Ariège) (BEGOUEN J., 1939, pl. I). *b*), *c*) In the cave of Castillo (Santander) (*photograph* : *Graziosi*).

PL. 265   Cave of Castillo (Santander) : various signs painted in red : *a*) "tree-shaped" figure, dotted (58 cm.). *b*), *c*) "Club-shaped" figures, and dotted "tectiforms" (the largest measures 63 cm. [fig. *c*]). *d*) "boat-shaped" figure (92 cm.) (*photograph* : *Graziosi* and *tracing*).

PL. 266   *a*), *b*) "Tectiforms" and "shield-shaped" figures painted in red; "branch-shaped" figure, painted in black, from the cave of Castillo (Santander) (*a*, 48 cm.; *b*, the "branch-shaped" figure, 80 cm.) (*photograph* : *Graziosi*). *c*) "Tectiforms" painted in red inside a narrow cleft of the cave of Pasiega (Santander) (the longest is 40 cm.) (*photograph* : *Graziosi*). *d*) The same, according to Breuil's tracing (BREUIL, OBERMAIER, ALCALDE DEL RIO, 1913, pl. X). *e*), *f*) uninterpretable symbolic figures painted in red, from the same cave (56 cm.) (BREUIL, OBERMAIER, ALCALDE DEL RIO, 1913, pl. XXIV, fig. 20).

PL. 267   Cave of Castillo (Santander) : "Tectiform" (55 cm.) (*photograph* : *Robert*).

PL. 268   Cave of Altamira (Santander) : "shield-shaped" figure and "ribbon-shaped" figure (*photograph* : *Robert*).

PL. 269   Cave of Lascaux (Dordogne) : "checkerboards", painted and engraved; known as "blazons" (22 × 24 cm.) (*photograph* : *Laborie*).

PL. 270   "Tectiforms" and similar figures : *a*) painted in the cave of Portel (Ariège) (45 cm.) (*photograph* : *Robert*). *b*), *c*), Painted in the cave of Font-de-Gaume (Dordogne) (*b*, the group measures 75 cm.; *c*, the figure on the left measures 23 cm.) (CAPITAN, BREUIL, PEYRONY, 1910, fig. 223). *d*) Engraved in the same cave (the figure on the right measures 26 cm.) (CAPITAN, BREUIL, PEYRONY, 1910, fig. 216). *e*) Engraved in the cave of Les Combarelles (Dordogne) (the figure on the right measures 22 cm.) (CAPITAN, BREUIL, PEYRONY, 1924, fig. 91). *f*) "Hut" painted in red and black, in the cave of La Mouthe (Dordogne) (80 cm. high) (*photograph* : *Laborie*).

PL. 271   *a*) "Tectiform" engraved in the cave of Buxu (Oviedo) (30 cm.) (*photograph* : *Robert* and *drawing* by OBERMAIER, VEGA DEL SELLA, 1918, pl. VI). *b*) Cave of Santian (Santander) : signs in the shape of stylized feet and hands painted in red (*photograph* : *Graziosi*). *c*) The same according to Breuil's tracing (maximum length : 45 cm.) (ALCALDE DEL RIO, BREUIL, SIERRA, 1912, fig. 32). *d*) "Club-shaped" signs painted in red in the cave of Pindal (Oviedo) (maximum length : 33 cm.) (*photograph* : *Graziosi*). *e*) "Club-shaped" signs painted in red in the cave of La Pasiega (Santander) (the largest measures 64 cm.) (BREUIL, OBERMAIER, ALCALDE DEL RIO, 1913, fig. 19).

PL. 272   *a*) Cave of Altamira (Santander) : "tectiforms" painted in red (CARTAILHAC, BREUIL, 1906, pl. 5). *b*) Cave of Niaux (Ariège) : dots and "club-shaped" figures painted in red (the "club-shaped" figure is 20 cm. high) (CARTAILHAC, BREUIL, 1908, fig. 19). *c*) "Club-shaped" figure painted in red in the cave of Les Trois Frères (Ariège) (BEGOUEN J., 1939, p. 284). *d*), *e*) Dots and various signs in the cave of Niaux (Ariège) (*photograph*: *Robert*). *f*) "Tree-shaped" figures in red and modern inscriptions in the same cave (*photograph* : *Robert*). *g*), *h*) Barbed lines painted in red, probably Mesolithic, in the cave of Marsoulas (Haute-Garonne) (*photograph* : *Yan*).

33. — P. GRAZIOSI, *Palaeolithic Art.*

UTILIZATION OF NATURAL ACCIDENTS.

PL. 273   Cave of Altamira (Santander): rocky protuberances on the ceiling of the great hall, which were made use of in the execution of the polychromatic paintings of bison. The paintings thus acquire particular relief (*photograph*: *Robert*).

PL. 274   Cave of Covalanas (Santander): painted ox; a natural spur of rock forms the outline of the back and thigh (1,38 m.) (*photograph*: *Robert*).

PL. 275   Utilization of natural features in the creation of animal figures. *a*) A stalagmitic formation in the cave of Castillo (Santander) transformed, by the addition of black signs, into a bison rearing up on its hindquarters (80 cm.) (*photograph*: *Graziosi*). *b*) Cave of Niaux (Ariège): head of an ox obtained by making use of some clefts in the rock and completing the missing parts with black strokes (BEGOUEN H., 1934, pl. I).

PL. 276   *a*), *b*) Cave of Font-de-Gaume (Dordogne): utilization of stalagmitic formations in the figure of a probable mare (1,80 m.) (photograph and drawing). *c*), *d*) Utilization of a swelling on the rock surface of the same cave in the execution of a painted and engraved bison (1,35 m.) (photograph and drawing). (CAPITAN, BREUIL, PEYRONY, 1910, pl. XLVIII, fig. 78, pl. XLI, fig. 42 a). *e*) Cave of Mas d'Azil (Ariège): head of an animal, probably feline, obtained by making use of a natural irregularity of the rock surface (*photograph*: *Robert*). *f*) Cave of Portel (Ariège): horse painted in red, in which the eye is formed by a calcite concretion (17 cm.) (*photograph*: *Robert*).

PL. 277   Cave of Niaux (Ariège): bison engraved on clay; some small pre-existing cavities made by dripping water were used to represent the eye and the wounds (58 cm.) (*photograph*: *Robert*).

PL. 278   Cave of Pech-Merle (Lot): large natural stalagmitic formations that resemble mammoths; they may have inspired the Palaeolithic artists in the execution of the many mammoths painted in the same cave (see Pls. 197 and 198) (*photograph*: *Laborie*).

PL. 279   Cave of Pech-Merle (Lot): *a*) utilization of stalagmite in the picture, barely sketched, of a mammoth; *b*) mammoth painted in black, complete, in the same cave, shown here for comparison with the preceding figure (*photograph*: *Laborie*).

PALAEOLITHIC MAGIC.

PL. 280   Hunting magic: wounded animals. *a*) Horse struck by darts or missiles in the cave of Lascaux (Dordogne) (1,05 m.). *b*) Horse struck by a dart in the same cave (1,10 m.); next to the animal is a rectangular object, perhaps a trap. (WINDELS, 1948, p. 79, 50). *c*) Cave of Montespan (Haute-Garonne): outline of a horse engraved on clay, pierced with javelin wounds (30 cm.) (*photograph*: *Trombe-Dubuc*). *d*) Bear engraved in the cave of Les Trois Frères (Ariège), covered with wounds and vomiting blood (60 cm.) (BREUIL, BEGOUEN, 1930).

PL. 281   *a*) The "Sorcerer" of the cave of Les Trois Frères (*photograph*: *Yan*). *b*) The same according to Breuil's reproduction, in which the engraved part of the figure can be seen (75 cm.) (BEGOUEN H., 1936, p. 20).

MAGIC AND COMPOSITION.

PL. 282   *a*) Feline animal and horses; composition engraved in the cave of Font-de-Gaume (Dordogne) (the largest horse measures 65 cm.) (CAPITAN, BREUIL, PEYRONY, 1910, fig. 94). *b*) Cave of Lascaux (Dordogne): pregnant mare (WINDELS, 1948, p. 85). *c*) Engraving in the cave of Les Trois Frères (Ariège): hybrid animals: reindeer with webbed fore-feet followed by an animal that is part bison and part reindeer, and by a human figure camouflaged as a bison. *d*) Fantastic being with the body of a bison and the legs of a man, from the same cave (30 cm.). (BEGOUEN, BREUIL, 1934, figs. 1, 2).

PL. 283   *a*) Cave of Les Trois Frères (Ariège). Hybrid animals: bears, one with a wolf's head, the other with a bison's tail (the composition measures 38 cm.) (BREUIL, BEGOUEN, 1930, fig. 2). *b*) Painting in black in the cave of Lascaux (Dordogne), the most complex of the rare scenographic compositions in Franco-Cantabrian art: wounded bison charging a man with a bird's head (WINDELS, 1948, p. 57).

PL. 284   *a*) Cave of La Mairie à Teyjat (Dordogne): bull pursuing a cow, engraved (1,05 cm.) (CAPITAN, BREUIL, PEYRONY, BOURRINET, 1912, fig. 3). *b*) Reindeer facing each other, engraved in the cave of Les Combarelles (Dordogne) (1,70 m.) (CAPITAN, BREUIL, PEYRONY, 1924, fig. 48). *c*) Cave of Portel (Ariège): bison facing each other, painted in black (1,20 m.) (*photograph*: *Robert*).

THE MEDITERRANEAN PROVINCE

PL. 285   Cave of La Pileta (Malaga) : a), b), c) serpentine signs (BREUIL, OBERMAIER, VERNER, 1915, pl. IV) (1,20; 1; 1,30 m.). d), e) Oxen and horse painted in black (55; 55 cm.) (GIMENEZ-REYNA, 1946, pls. V, IV). f) Pictorial group in the " Sanctuary ", of which figs. d and e are a part (2,88 m.) (BREUIL, OBERMAIER, VERNER, 1915, pl. XIII).

PL. 286   La Pileta (Malaga) : a), b) radiating figures of obscure significance and horse of Pl. 285, e; c), d) oxen and ibexes (c, 2,50 m.; d, 5,50 m.) (BREUIL, OBERMAIER, VERNER, 1915, pls. XVI, VII, XI). e), f) Fish and ibex in the same cave (the fish measures 1,50 m., the ibex 0,50 m.) (GIMENEZ-REYNA, 1946, pl. VI).

PL. 287   La Baume Latrone (Gard) : figures traced with figures dipped in the red clay of the cave. a) Principal group with elephants and a fantastic animal with a carnivore's head and a serpentine body (2 m.). b), d), e) Elephants traced with several fingers. c) Rhinoceros with linear outline (photograph : Louis).

PL. 288   Cave of Ebbou (Ardèche) : a) horse (62 cm.); b) ibex (40 cm.); c), d) oxen (35; 110 cm.) (GLORY, 1947, figs. 13, 8, 11, 12).

PL. 289   Grotta Romanelli (Otranto): a) view of the cave from the sea. b) The cave's entrance seen from the interior. c) Partial view of the interior of the cave with deposit containing human artifacts, and of the ceiling upon which part of the figures are engraved (photograph : Graziosi).

PL. 290   Grotta Romanelli (Otranto) : a) ox engraved on the northern wall (50 cm.) (photograph : Graziosi). b) Geometrical pattern engraved near the preceding figure (47 cm.) (photograph : Guido).

PL. 291   Grotta Romanelli (Otranto) : a) oval figure, probably a vulvar representation (40 cm.), and shuttle-shaped figures engraved on the cornice of the ceiling of the cave. b) More oval figures on the south wall (photograph : Graziosi). c) Shuttle-shaped and oval figures, mostly the same as in the photographs (BLANC G. A., 1928, pls. L, LII). d) Shuttle-shaped figure, probably anthropomorphic, engraved on the south wall (50 cm.); e) other shuttle-shaped figures on the same wall (the longest measures 47 cm.) (photograph : Graziosi).

PL. 292   Cave of Levanzo (Egadi) : a) view from the sea. b), c) The rear of the cave in which the Palaeolithic engravings were found. Paintings of a later period can be seen on the wall (photograph : Graziosi).

PL. 293   Cave of Levanzo (Egadi) : young deer turning its head (20 cm. long) (photograph : Graziosi).

PL. 294   Cave of Levanzo (Egadi) : deer; photographs and tracings of the same engravings (37; 53 cm.) (photograph : Graziosi).

PL. 295   Cave of Levanzo (Egadi) : a), b) young deer (30; 18 cm.); c) horse, or perhaps Equus hydruntinus (21 cm.) (photograph : Graziosi).

PL. 296   Cave of Levanzo (Egadi) : a) photograph and tracing of an engraved Equus hydruntinus (18 cm.). b) Another equine figure (21 cm.). c) Couple of equines (36 cm.) : tracing and photograph (photograph : Graziosi).

PL. 297   Cave of Levanzo (Egadi) : a) large ox head underneath which two small running human legs are discernible; b) tracing of same, showing also the entire figure of an equine animal, only partly visible in the photograph (the group measures 65 cm.). c) Incomplete bull following a cow (62 cm.) : photograph and tracing (photograph : Graziosi).

PL. 298   Cave of Levanzo (Egadi) : a) group consisting of a large bull facing another bull, incomplete and viewed from the front, and a grazing horse (photograph : Graziosi); b), c) tracing of the bulls. The large bull c measures 50 cm.

PL. 299   Cave of Levanzo (Egadi) : a) tracing of the horse of the photograph in Pl. 298, a (35 cm.). b) Hindquarters of an incomplete horse; a schematic painting, of late Neolithic or later date, can be seen superimposed upon one of the legs (32 cm.). c) Ox (49 cm.). d) Probable representation of a deer or an ox (15 cm.) (photograph : Graziosi).

PL. 300   Cave of Levanzo (Egadi) : masked human figures, apparently in the act of dancing; above is a band of parallel lines of obscure significance (the largest figure is 31 cm. high) (photograph : Graziosi).

PL. 301   Cave of Addaura on Monte Pellegrino (Palermo) : human figures, engraved in various postures, some of them masked, with thick hair; at the centre are two individuals, perhaps wearing phallic sheaths, with sharply bent knees and feet apparently tied to the neck by a rope (the figure at top centre measures 24 cm.) (photograph : Superintendency of Antiquities, Palermo).

PL. 302   Cave of Addaura (Palermo) : *a*) engraved human figures, one of which, a female, is carrying a sort of pack on her shoulders; underneath them are equine figures very similar to those engraved in the cave of Levanzo (Egadi) (sse Pl. 296) (the group measures 68 cm.) (MARCONI, 1953, figs. 2-53). *b*) Detail of preceding figure. *c*) Another human figure (15 cm.) (*photograph*: *Superintendency of Antiquities, Palermo*).

PL. 303   Cave of Addaura (Palermo) : figures included in the same groups shown in Pls. 301, 302; at centre, a man bearing a long pole; to the left, female figure carrying a sort of bulky pack on her shoulders; to the right, a fallow deer (the deer measures 31 cm.) (*photograph*: *Superintendency of Antiquities, Palermo*).

PL. 304   Cave of Addaura (Palermo) : equine figures and oxen of a rather schematic order (*b*, 44 cm.; *c*, 44 cm.) (MARCONI, 1952-53, figs. 3, 10 and *photograph*: *Superintendency of Antiquities, Palermo*).

PL. 305   Cave of Addaura (Palermo) : *a*) head of a fallow deer finely engraved, underlying the legs of the individual in Pl. 301, upper right (13 cm.). *b*), *c*) Addaura B : animals tending to the schematic, probably oxen (*photographs of casts, Superintendency of Antiquities, Palermo*).

PL. 306   Cave of Niscemi on Monte Pellegrino (Palermo) : oxen and small horses (*photograph*: *Superintendency of Antiquities, Palermo* and *drawings* by MARCONI, 1954-55, fig. 3).

INDEX OF NAMES OF PEOPLE

Numbers refer to text pages when in Roman type;

to Plates when in Italics.

INDEX OF NAMES OF PLACES

Numbers refer to text pages when in Roman type;
to Plates when in Italics.

PLATES

MOBILIARY ART

THE FRANCO-CANTABRIAN PROVINCE

AND ITS BRANCHES

Pl. 1

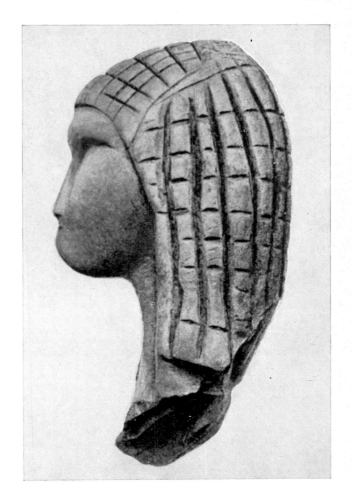

a

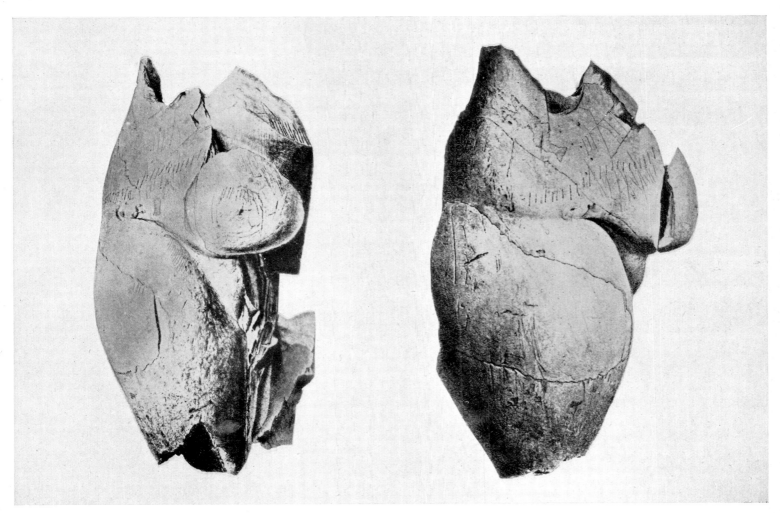

b

AURIGNACIAN-PERIGORDIAN SCULPTURE: - Brassempouy (*Landes*): *a*) small head (enlarged almost 4 times); *b*) ivory female torso.

Pl. 2

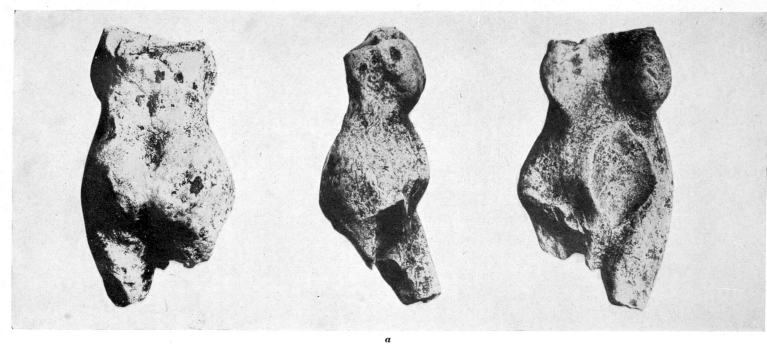

a

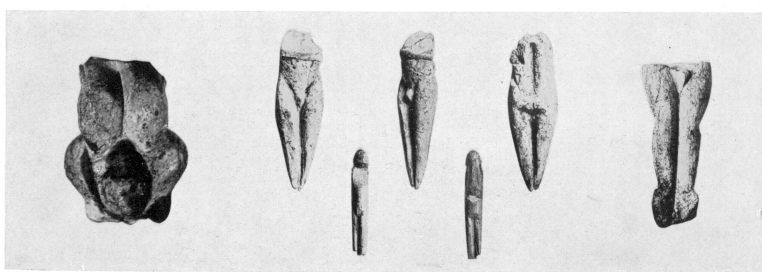

b

c

AURIGNACIAN-PERIGORDIAN SCULPTURE: - *a*), *b*) Brassempouy (*Landes*): anthropomorphic ivory statuettes; *c*) Sireuil (*Dordogne*): calcite statuette.

Pl. 3

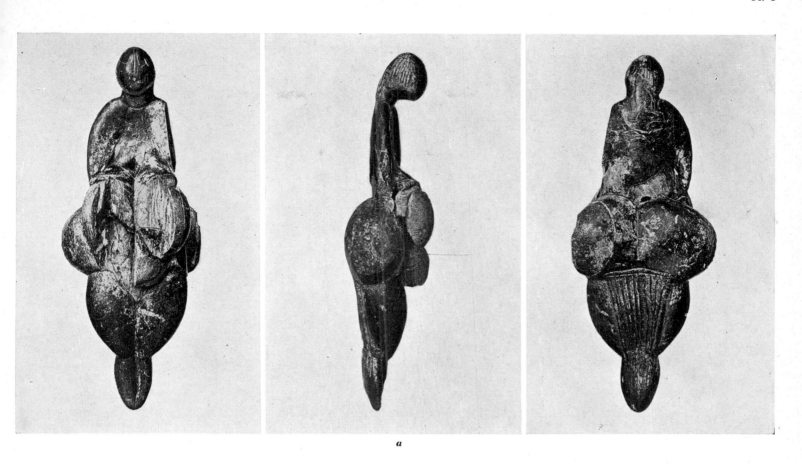

a

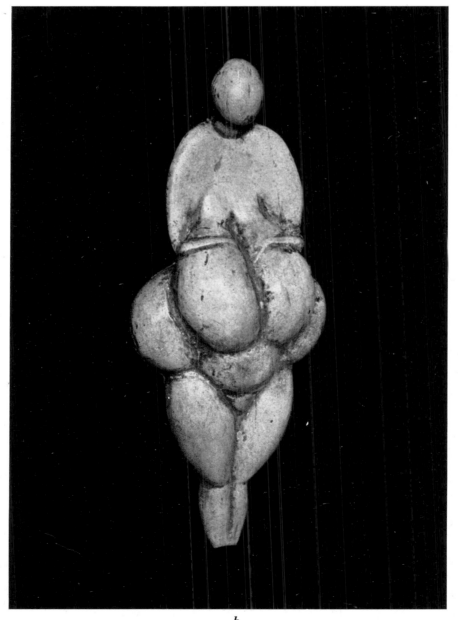

b

AURIGNACIAN-PERIGORDIAN SCULPTURE: - Ivory « Venus » of Lespugue (*Haute-Garonne*): *a*) original piece viewed from three sides, *b*) restored cast.

Pl. 4

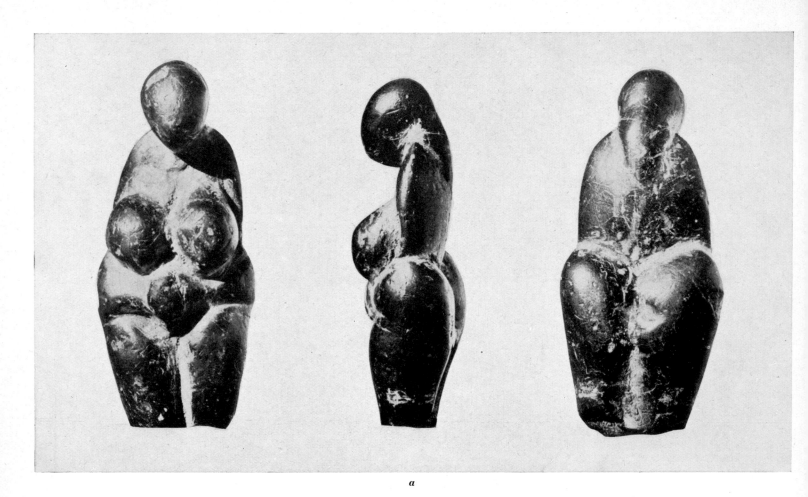

a

b

SCULPTURE OF THE AURIGNACIAN-PERIGORDIAN TYPE FOUND IN ITALY: - Balzi Rossi (*Ventimiglia*): *a*) steatite « Venus » (twice enlarged); *b*) small « negroid » head and other female statuettes.

Pl. 5

SCULPTURE OF THE AURIGNACIAN-PERIGORDIAN TYPE FOUND IN ITALY: - The « Venus » of Savignano (*Modena*), carved in serpentine stone, viewed in profile.

Pl. 6

The « Venus » of Savignano (*Modena*), viewed from the front and from the back.

Pl. 7

The Savignano « Venus » (detail).

Pl. 8

a

b

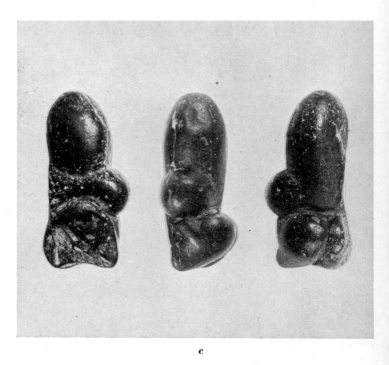

c

SCULPTURE OF THE AURIGNACIAN-PERIGORDIAN TYPE FOUND IN ITALY: - *a*), *b*) The sandstone statuette of Chiozza (*Reggio-Emilia*): cast and original piece; *c*) the steatite statuette of Trasimeno, viewed according to the first interpretation.

Pl. 9

AURIGNACIAN-PERIGORDIAN SCULPTURE: - The calcareous « Venus » of Willendorf (*Austria*): cast.

Pl. 10

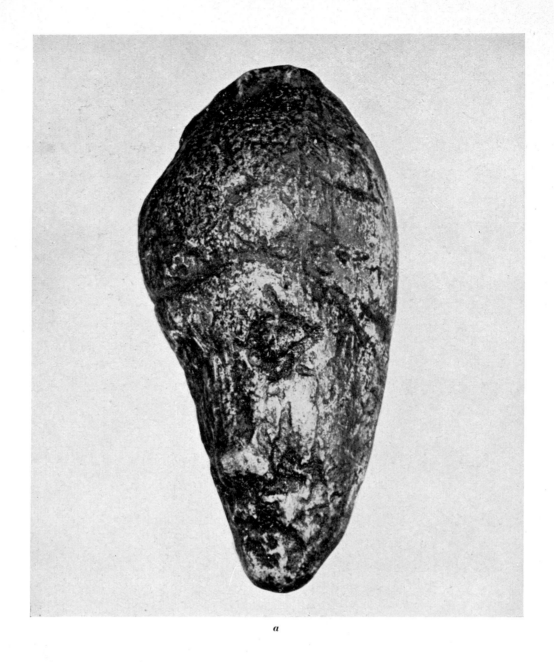

a

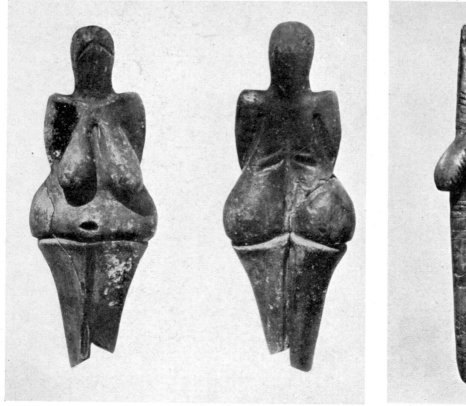

b   *c*   *d*

AURIGNACIAN-PERIGORDIAN SCULPTURE: - *a*)-*c*) Dolní Vestonice (*Moravia*): small ivory head (enlarged about 3 times) and statuettes modelled in clayey substance; *d*) Brno (*Moravia*): ivory statuette.

Pl. 11

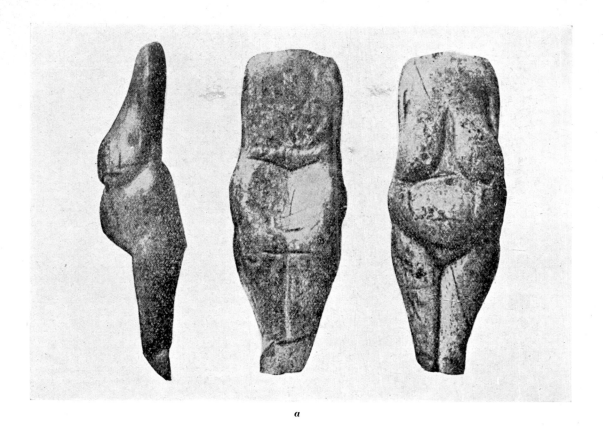

a

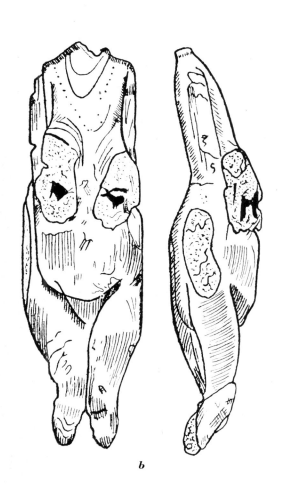

b

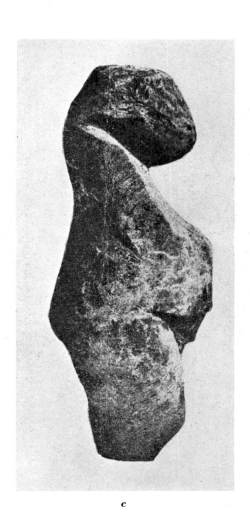

c

AURIGNACIAN-PERIGORDIAN SCULPTURE: - Kostienki, near Voronezh (*Russia*): *a*), *b*) ivory statuettes; *c*) stone statuette.

Pl. 12

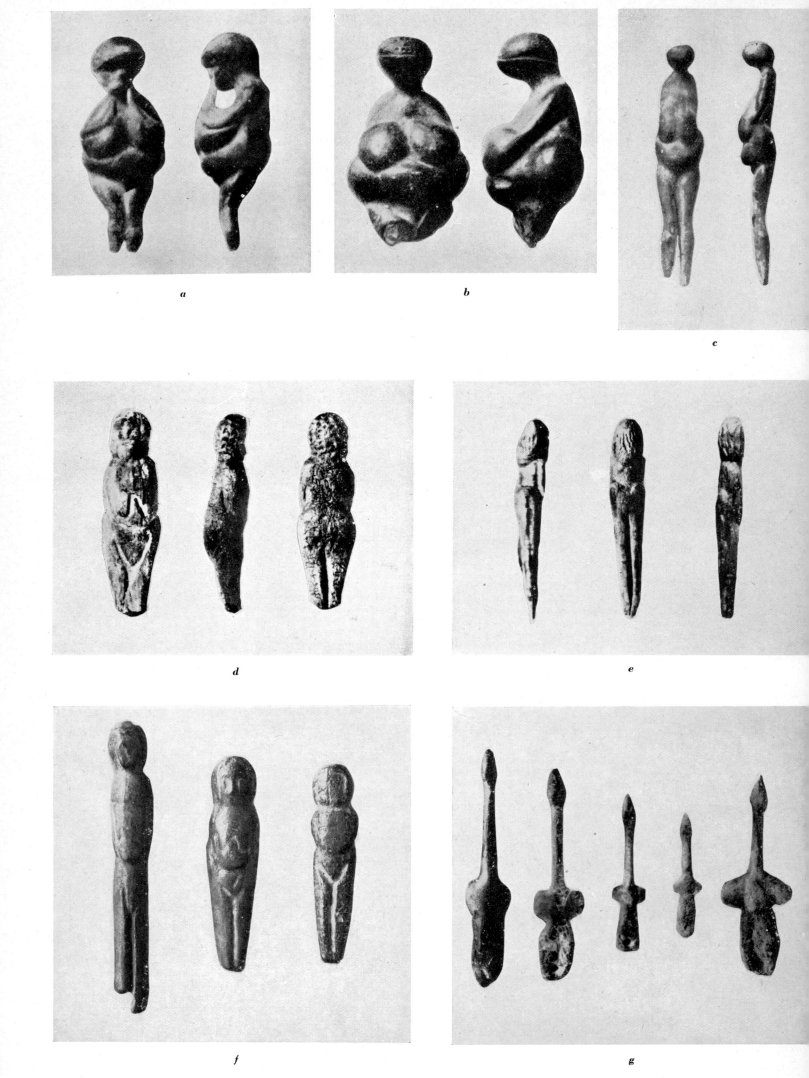

AURIGNACIAN-PERIGORDIAN SCULPTURE: - Ivory statuettes: *a*)-*c*) Gagarino, near Tambov (*Russia*): *d*)-*g*) Maltà, near Lake Baikal (*Siberia*).

Pl. 13

a

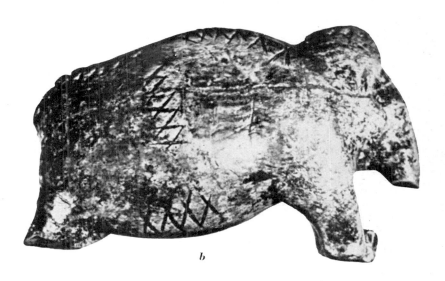

b

c

AURIGNACIAN-PERIGORDIAN SCULPTURE: - Vogelherd (*Würtemberg*): ivory horse, mammoth and feline animal (approx. twice enlarged).

Pl. 14

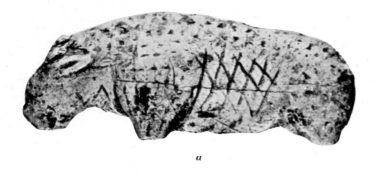

a

b

c

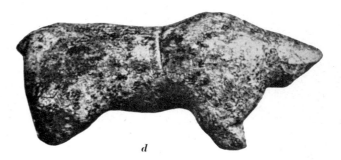

d

AURIGNACIAN-PERIGORDIAN SCULPTURE: - Vogelherd (*Würtemberg*): Leopard and other ivory animals.

Pl. 15

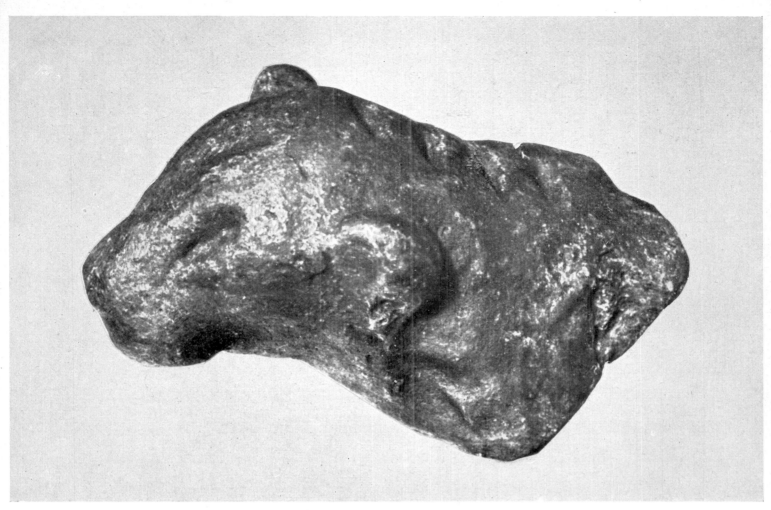

a

b

AURIGNACIAN-PERIGORDIAN SCULPTURE: - Dolní Vestonice (*Moravia*) feline head and bear modelled in clay mixed with pulverized bone (approx. twice enlarged).

Pl. 16

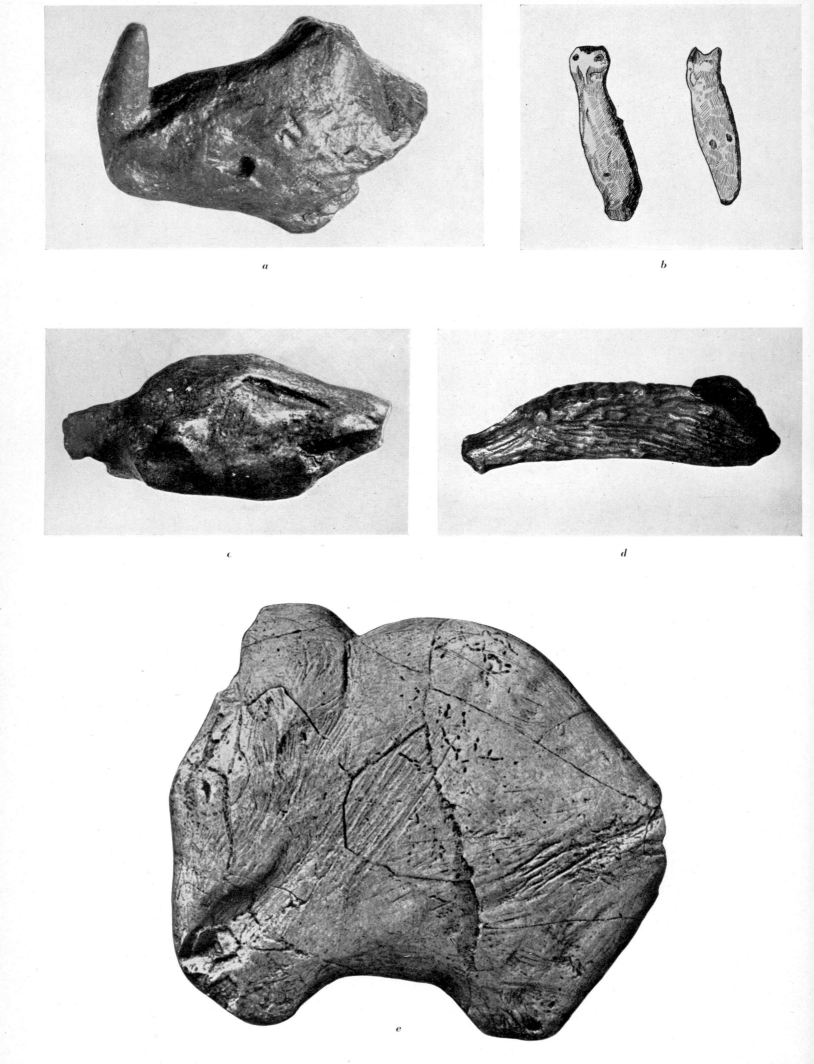

AURIGNACIAN-PERIGORDIAN SCULPTURE: - *a*), *b*) Dolní Vestonice (*Moravia*): rhinoceros head (approx. twice enlarged), owls and *c*), *d*) other clay animal heads; *e*) Predmosti (*Moravia*): ivory mammoth.

Pl. 17

a

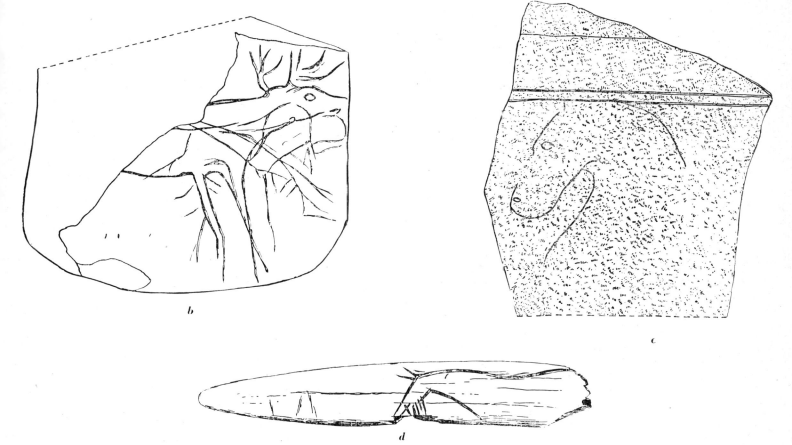

b

c

d

AURIGNACIAN-PERIGORDIAN ENGRAVINGS: - *a*) Hornos de la Peña (*Santander*), on bone; *b*), *c*) Isturitz (*Basses-Pyrénées*), on stone; *d*) Isturitz, on bone (*b, c, d*, drawn by Rilly).

Pl. 18

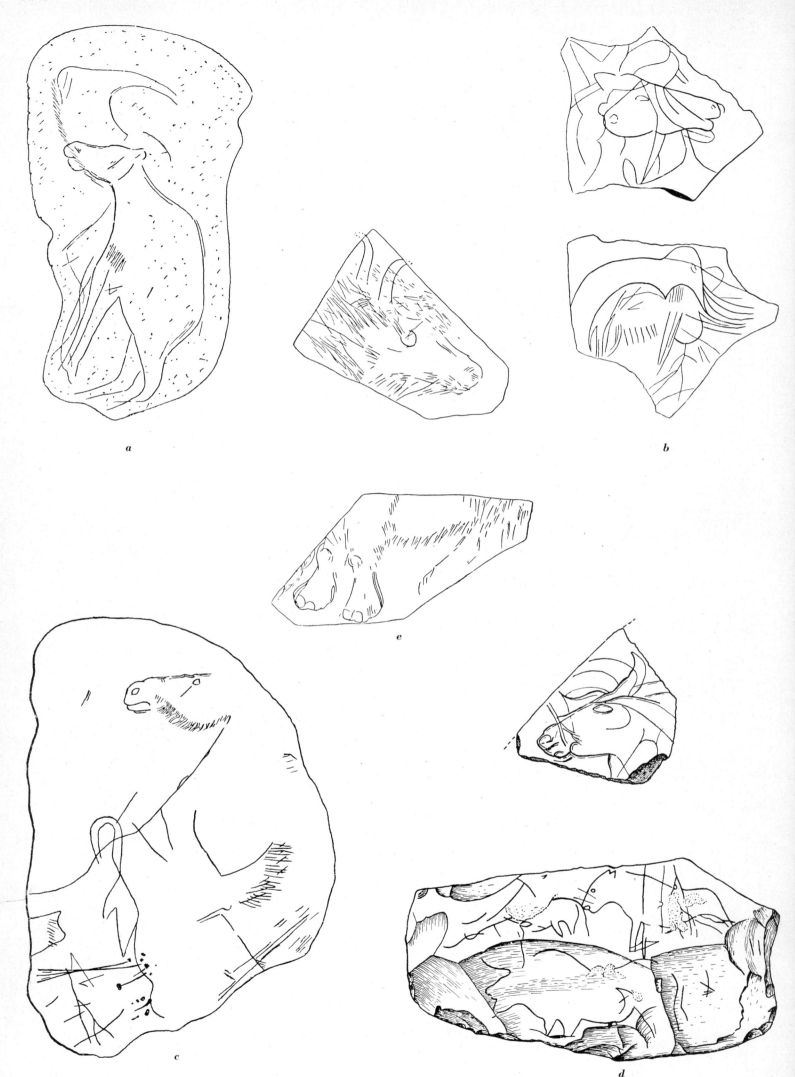

AURIGNACIAN-PERIGORDIAN ENGRAVINGS: - Engravings on stone: *a*) Rebières, drawn by Montandon *b*) Laugerie Haute (*Dordogne*) drawn by Peyrony; *c*) Laraux (*Vienne*); *d*) Gargas (*Hautes-Pyrénées*), drawn by Breuil; *e*) Saut-du-Perron (*Loire*), drawn by Combier.

Pl. 19

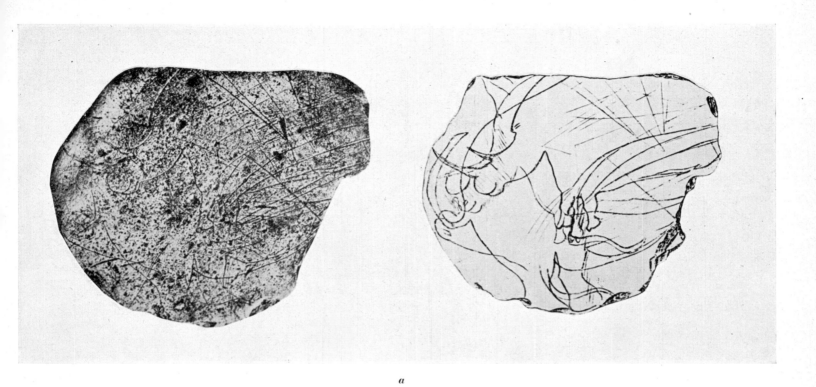

a

b

c

AURIGNACIAN-PERIGORDIAN ENGRAVINGS: - Engravings on pebbles: *a*) Le Trilobite (*Yonne*); *b*), *c*) Abri Labatut (*Dordogne*), two sides of the same pebble, drawings by Breuil.

Pl. 20

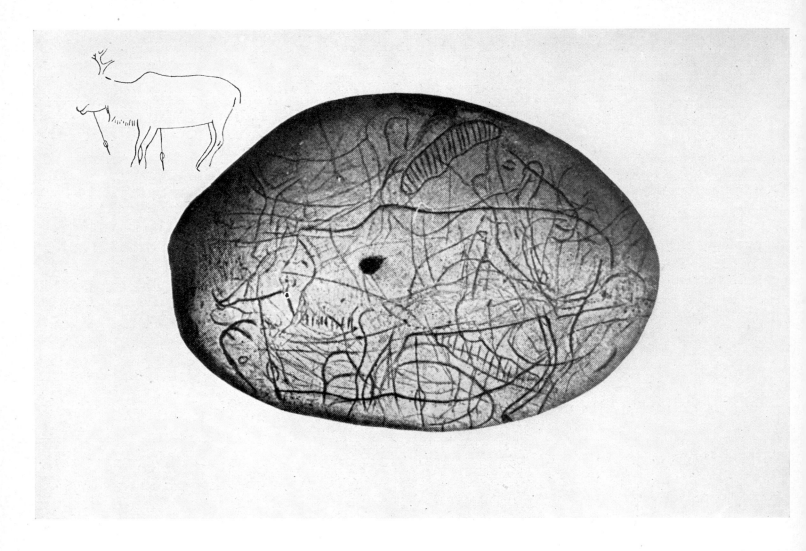

AURIGNACIAN-PERIGORDIAN ENGRAVINGS: - La Colombière (Aïn): pebbles engraved with superimposed animals. Mayet-Pissot excavations.

Pl. 21

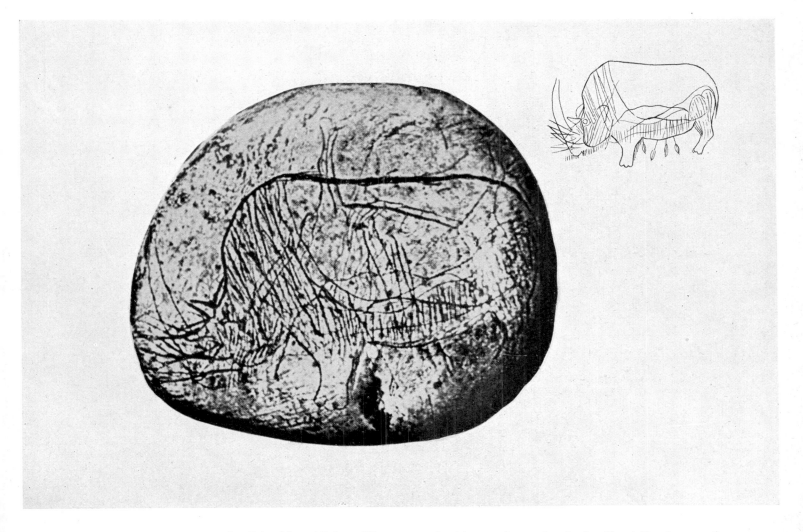

AURIGNACIAN-PERIGORDIAN ENGRAVINGS: - La Colombière (*Aïn*): pebbles engraved with superimposed animals. Mayet-Pissot excavations.

Pl. 22

AURIGNACIAN-PERIGORDIAN ENGRAVINGS: - La Colombière (*Aïn*): pebbles engraved with superimposed figures. Harvard University excavations.

Pl. 23

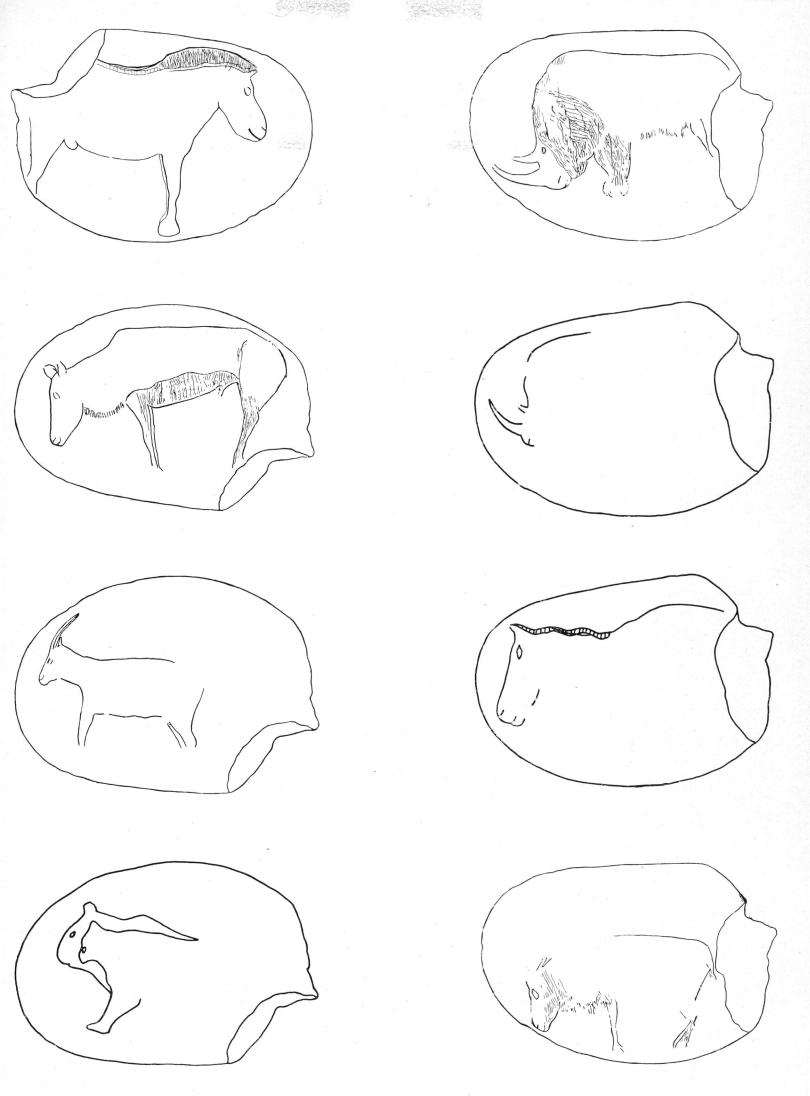

AURIGNACIAN-PERIGORDIAN ENGRAVINGS: - La Colombière (*Aïn*): separate outlines of figures engraved on the pebble in Pl. 22, traced by H. L. Movius.

Pl. 24

a

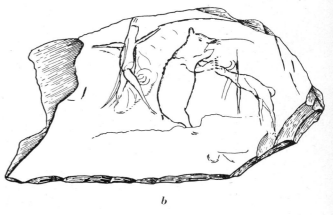

b

c

d

AURIGNACIAN-PERIGORDIAN ENGRAVINGS: - *a*), Péchialet (*Dordogne*): bear and men engraved on stone; *b*) same traced by Breuil *c*), *d*) Laugerie Haute (*Dordogne*): mammoths engraved on antler.

Pl. 25

a

b

c

AURIGNACIAN-PERIGORDIAN ENGRAVINGS: - Engravings on bone. *a*) Les Rideaux, Lespugue (*Haute-Garonne*): vipers; *b*), *c*) La Colombière (*Aïn*): man, reindeer and other figures.

Pl. 26

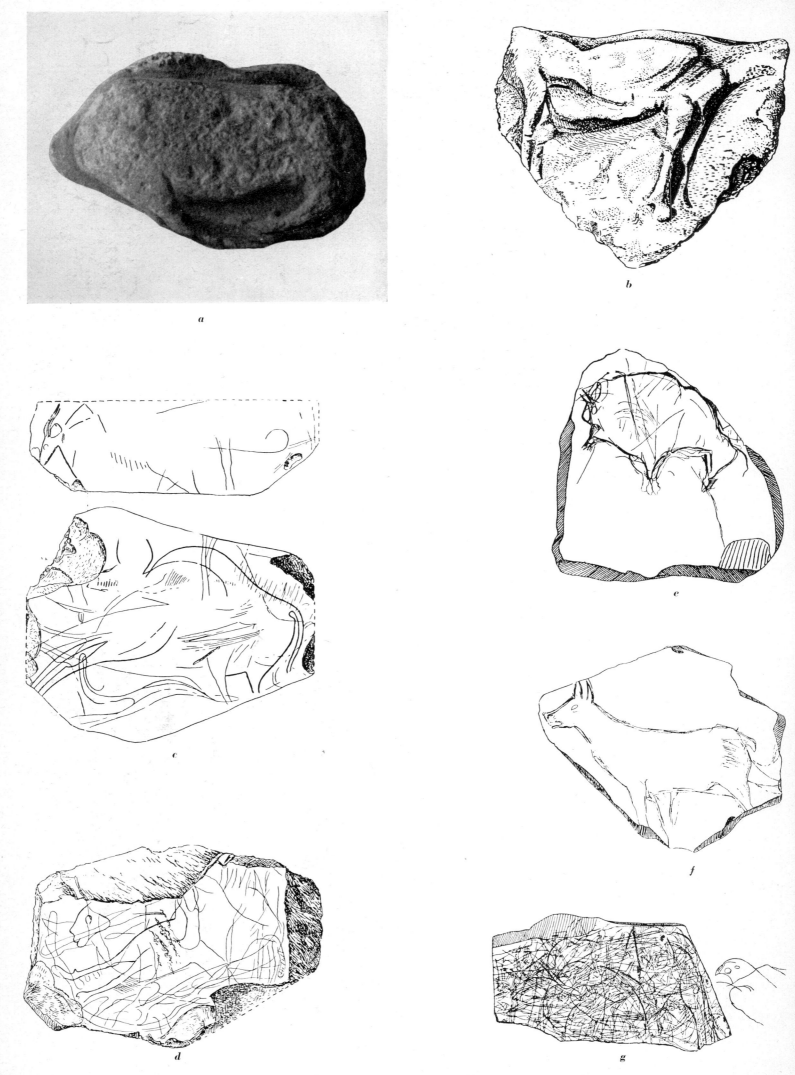

SOLUTREAN ENGRAVINGS AND RELIEF SCULPTURE: - On stone: *a*) Solutré (*Saône-et-Loire*); *b*)-*d*) Isturitz (*Basses-Pyrénées*), drawings by Rilly; *e*)-*g*) Badégoule (*Dordogne*), drawn by Cheynier.

Pl. 27

a

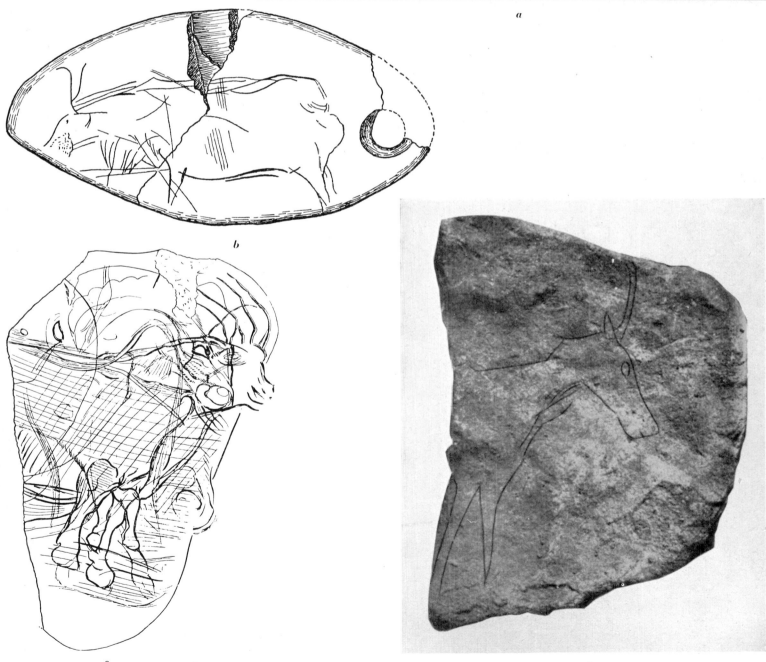

b

c

d

SOLUTREAN ENGRAVINGS: - *a*) Obere Klause (*Bavaria*): mammoth on ivory; *b*), *c*) Le Fourneau du Diable, drawn by Breuil; *d*) Jean-Blancs (*Dordogne*): engravings on stone.

Pl. 28

a

b

c

SOLUTREAN ENGRAVINGS: - Le Roc de Sers (*Charente*): horse and bison engraved on stone.

Pl. 29

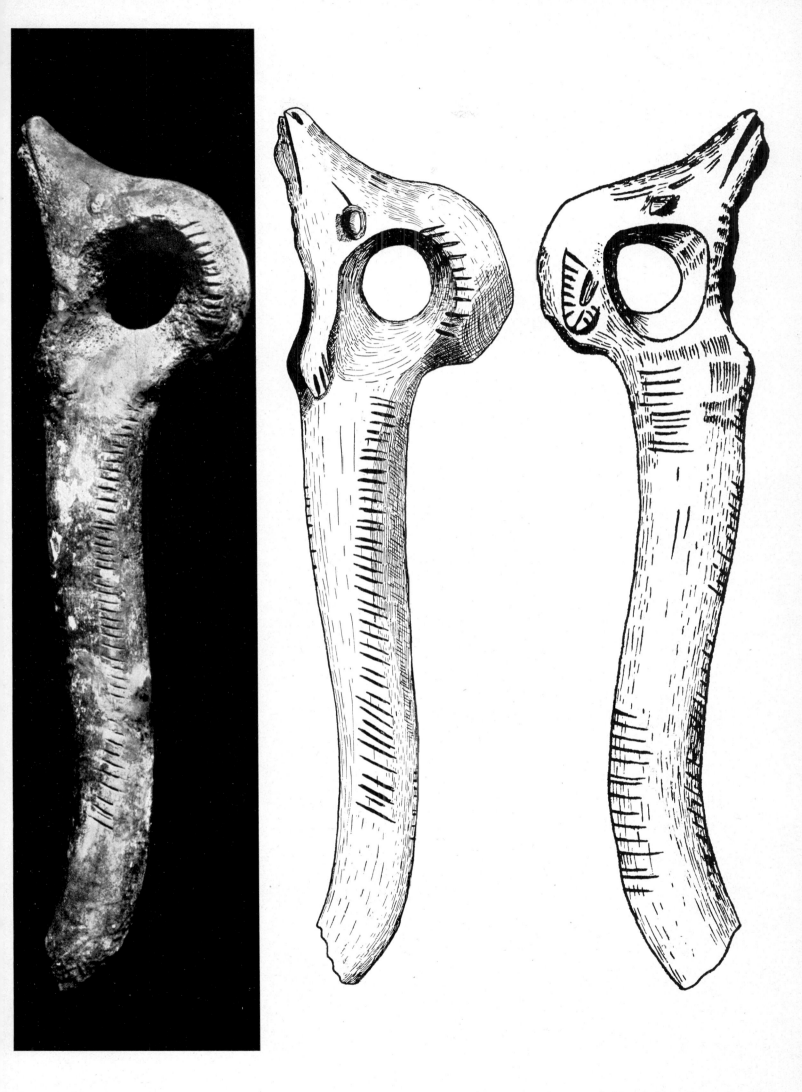

LOWER MAGDALENIAN SCULPTURE: - Le Placard (*Charente*): fox head carved on a « bâton de commandement » fashioned from the antler of a reindeer, drawings by Breuil.

Pl. 30

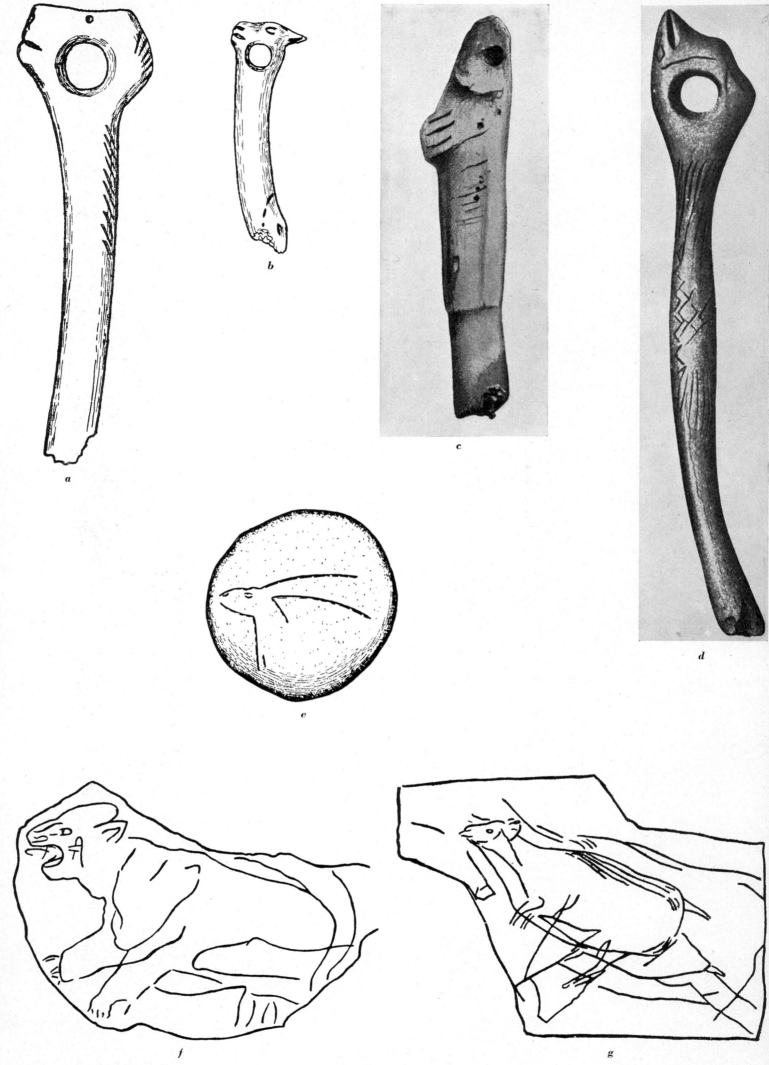

LOWER MAGDALENIAN SCULPTURE AND ENGRAVINGS: - Carvings on antler and engravings on stone: *a*), *b*) Le Placard (*Charente*), drawn by Breuil; *c*) Gourdan (*Haute-Garonne*); *d*) Laugerie Basse; *e*) Pech de la Boissière (*Dordogne*); *f*), *g*) La Marche (*Vienne*), drawn by Lwoff.

Pl. 31

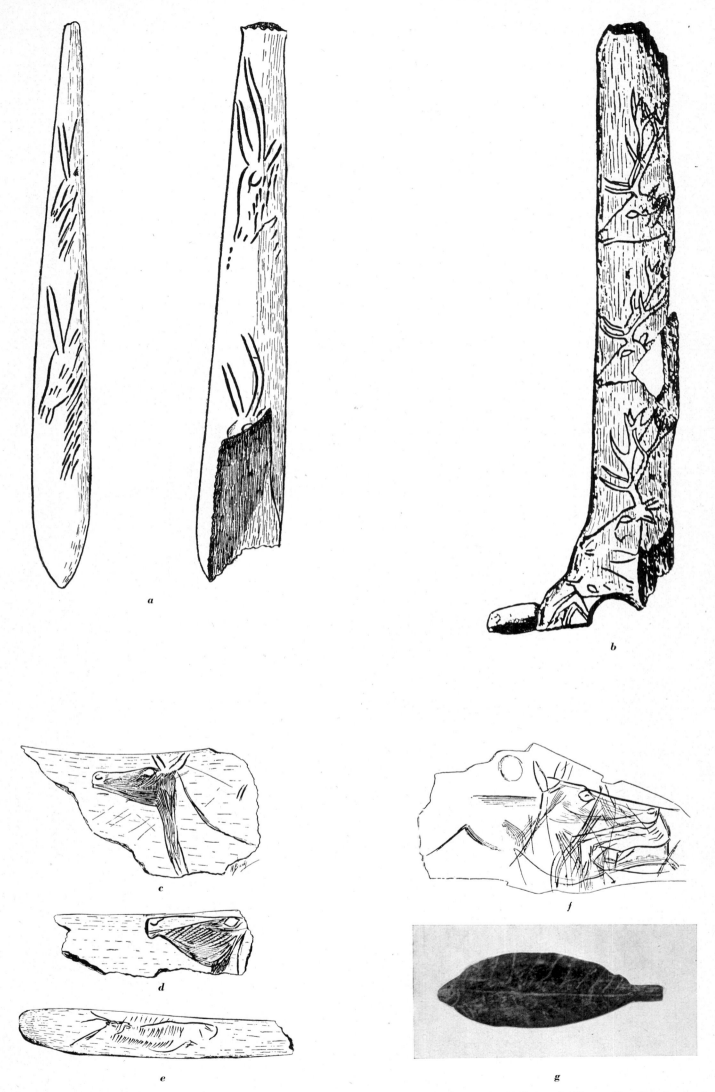

LOWER MAGDALENIAN ENGRAVINGS: - Ibexes and deer on antler and bone: *a*) Le Placard (*Charente*); *b*) Laugerie Haute (*Dordogne*); *c*) - *e*) Altamira (from layer still containing Solutrean implements); *f*) Castillo (*Santander*); *g*) Lespugue (*Haute-Garonne*): cut-out profile of a sole, drawings by Breuil.

Pl. 32

 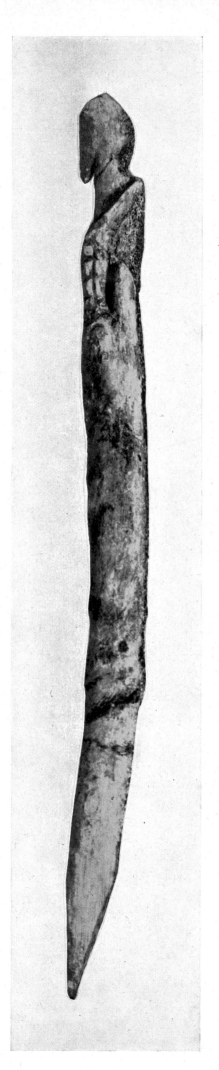 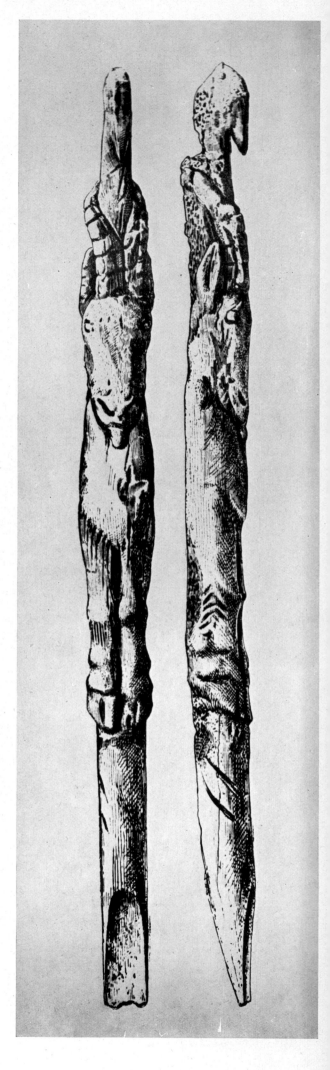

UPPER MAGDALENIAN SCULPTURE: - Mas d'Azil (*Ariège*): ibex carved on a spear-thrower, drawings by Breuil.

Pl. 33

b

a

UPPER MAGDALENIAN SCULPTURE: - Laugerie Basse (*Dordogne*): *a*) horses on a spear-thrower; *b*) reindeer.

Pl. 34

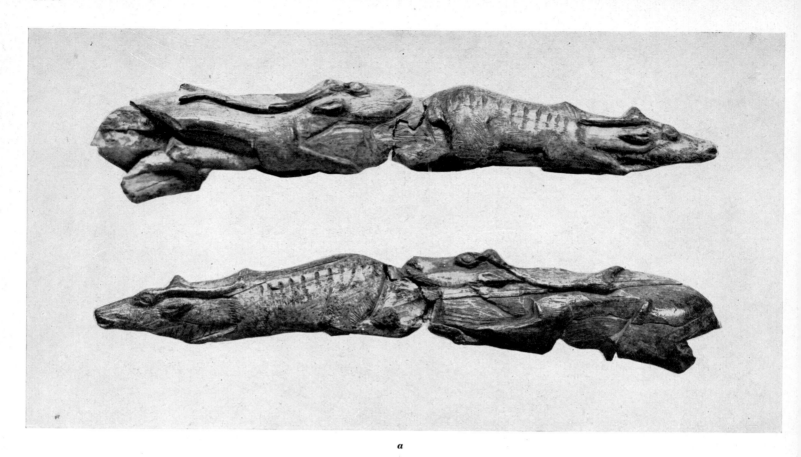

a

b

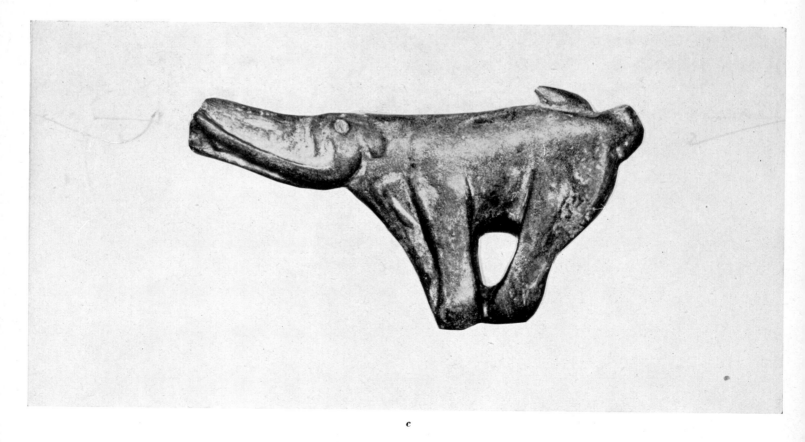

c

UPPER MAGDALENIAN SCULPTURE: - Bruniquel (*Tarn-et-Garonne*): *a*), reindeer carved on ivory; *b*) same drawn by Breuil; *c*) mammoth carved on antler.

Pl. 35

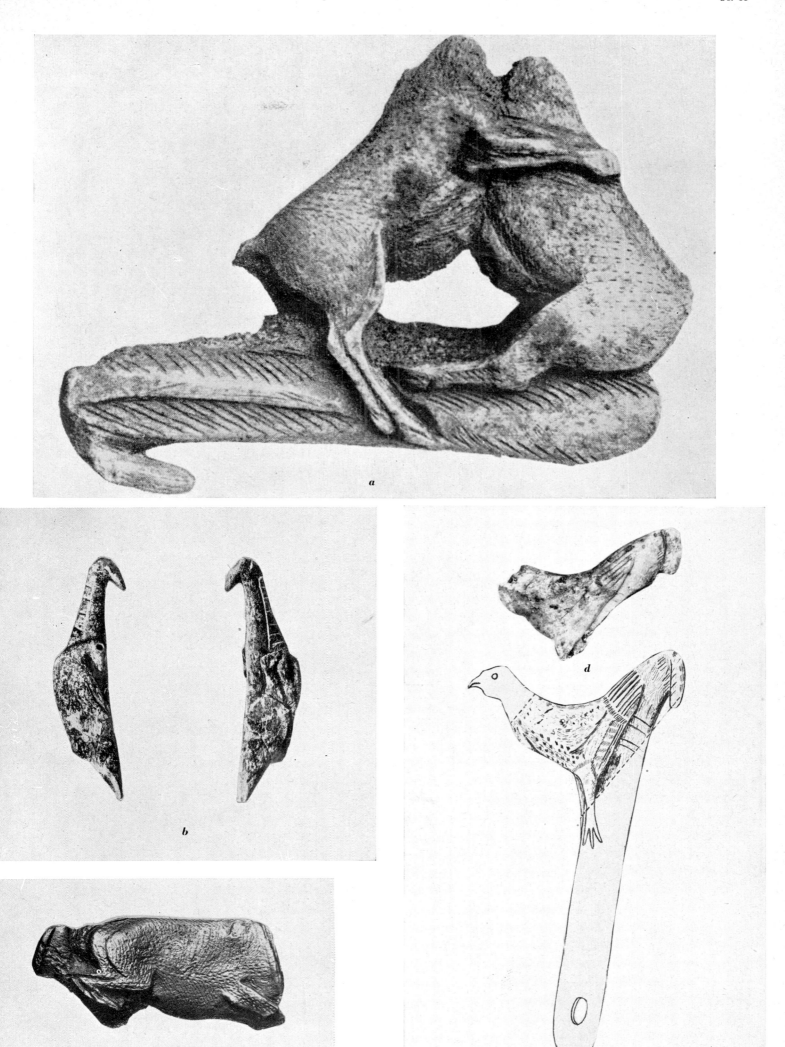

UPPER MAGDALENIAN SCULPTURE: - Animals carved on antler: *a*), *b*) Les Trois Frères (*a* approx. twice enlarged); *c*) Enlène, *d*), *e*) Mas d'Azil (*Ariège*) (*d* = original piece, *e* = Breuil's reconstruction).

Pl. 36

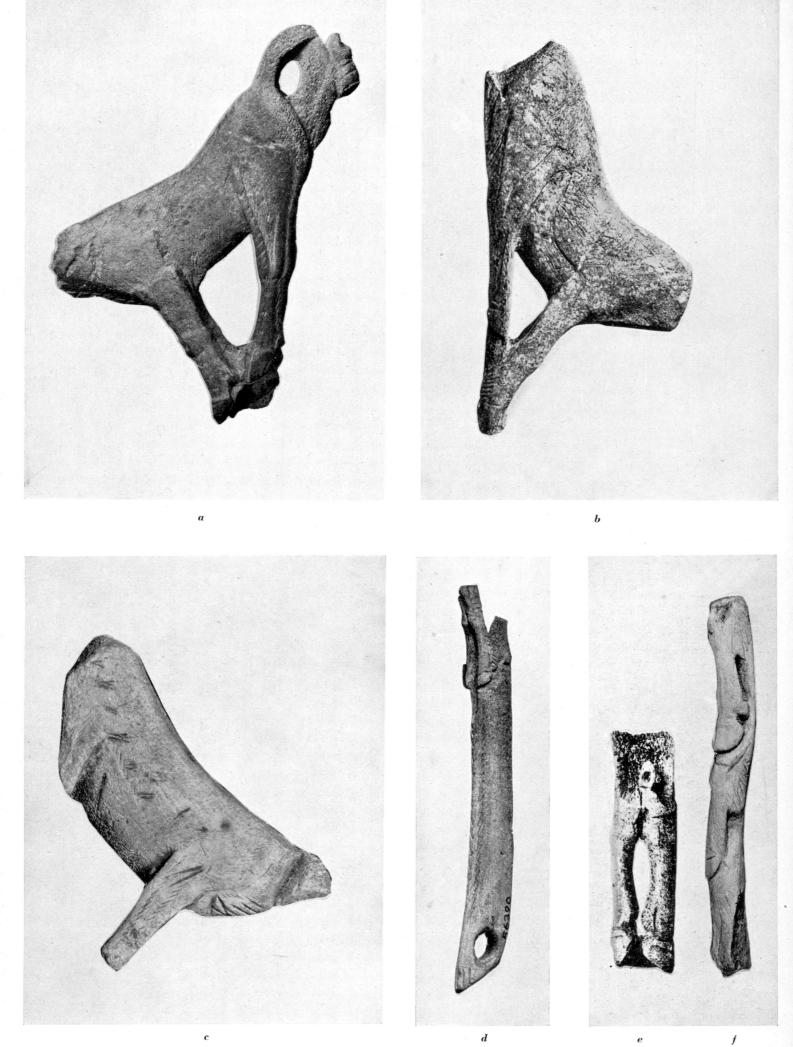

a

b

c

d

e

f

UPPER MAGDALENIAN SCULPTURE: - Animals carved on antler: *a)*, *c)*, *d)* Arudy, *b)*, *e)* Isturitz (*Basses-Pyrénées*); *f)* Mas d'Azil (*Ariège*).

Pl. 37

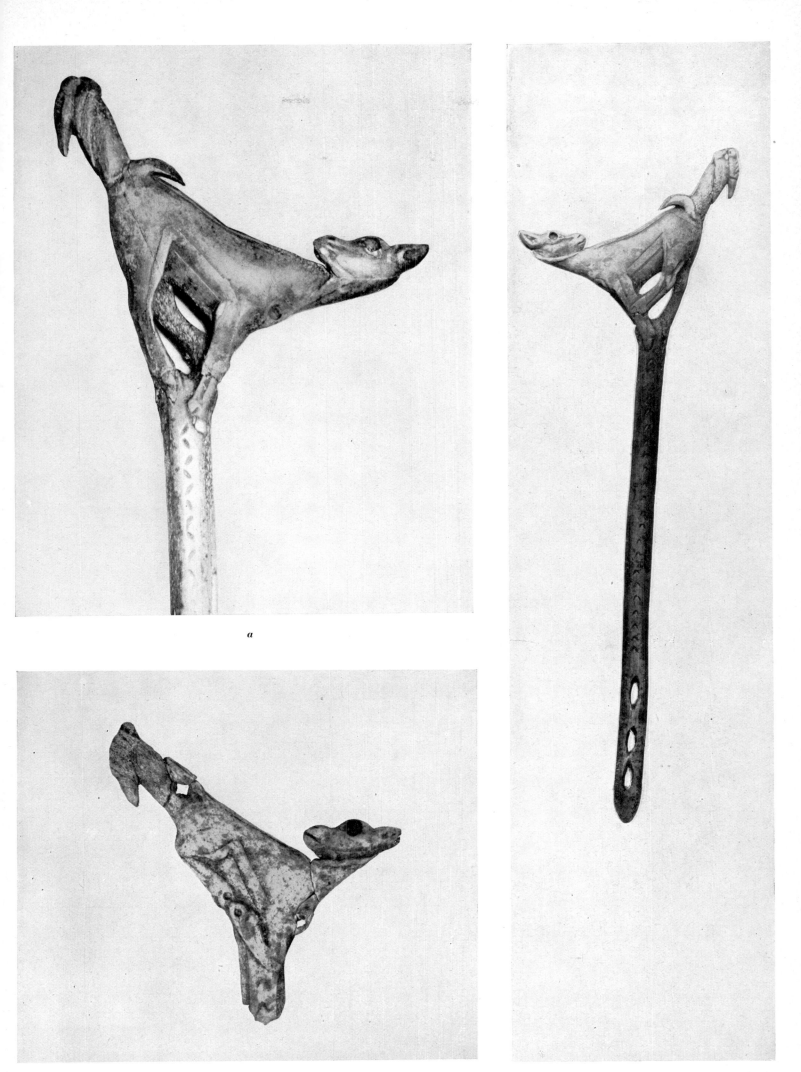

a

c

b

UPPER MAGDALENIAN SCULPTURE: - Young ibexes carved on antler spear-thrower: *a*), *b*) Mas d'Azil, *c*) Bédeilhac (*Ariège*).

Pl 38

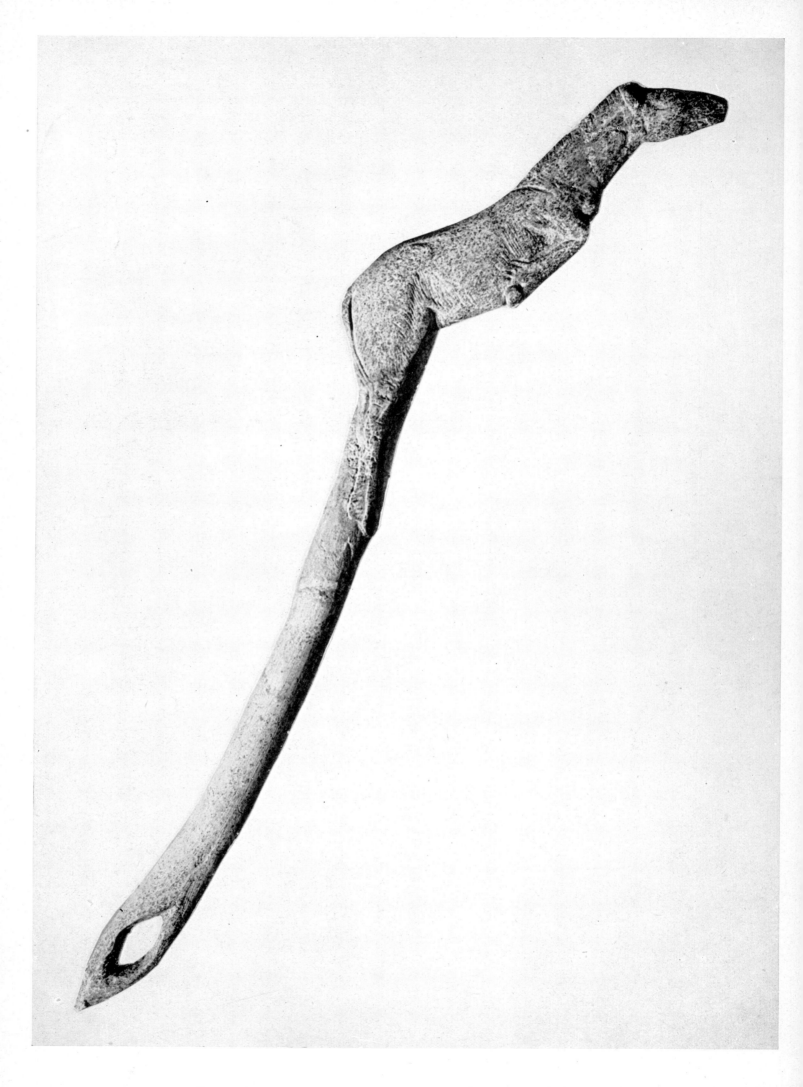

UPPER MAGDALENIAN SCULPTURE: - Bruniquel (*Tarn-et-Garonne*): leaping horse on antler spear-thrower.

Pl. 39

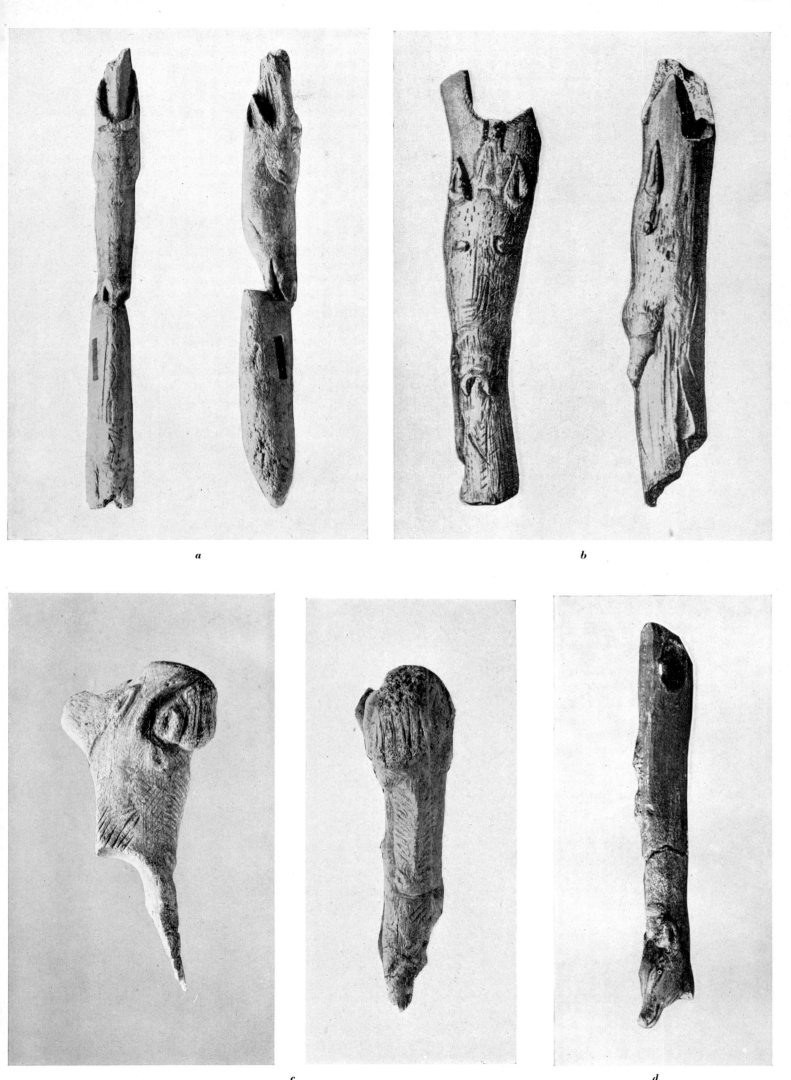

a   *b*

c   *d*

UPPER MAGDALENIAN SCULPTURE: - Heads of animals on antler: *a)-c*) Laugerie Basse (*Dordogne*); *d*) Arudy (*Basses-Pyrénées*).

Pl. 40

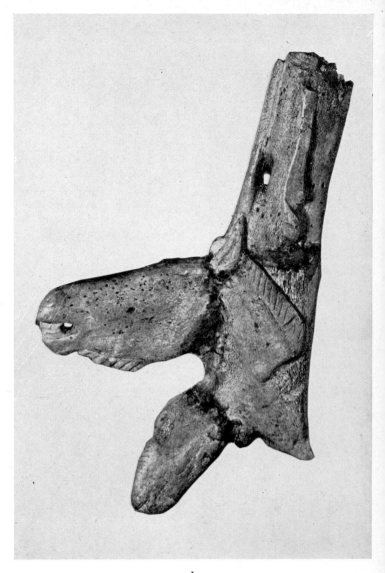

a

b

c

UPPER MAGDALENIAN SCULPTURE: - Mas d'Azil (*Ariège*): *a*), *b*) horses' heads, one of them skinned; *c*) bison on antler.

Pl. 41

a

b

c

UPPER MAGDALENIAN SCULPTURE: - La Madeleine (*Dordogne*): *a*), *c*) bison, on antler; *b*) probably a hyena, on ivory.

Pl. 42

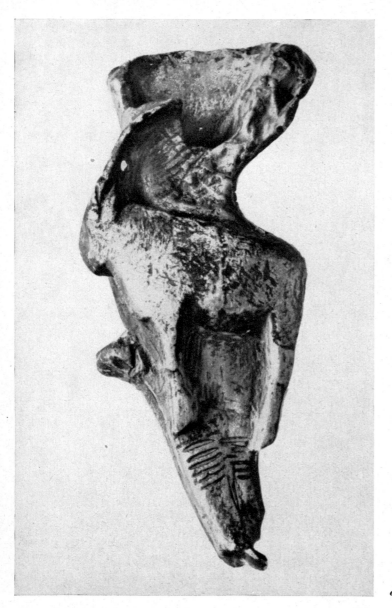

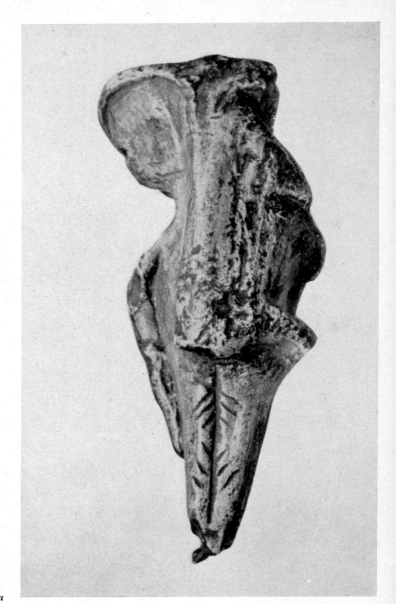

a

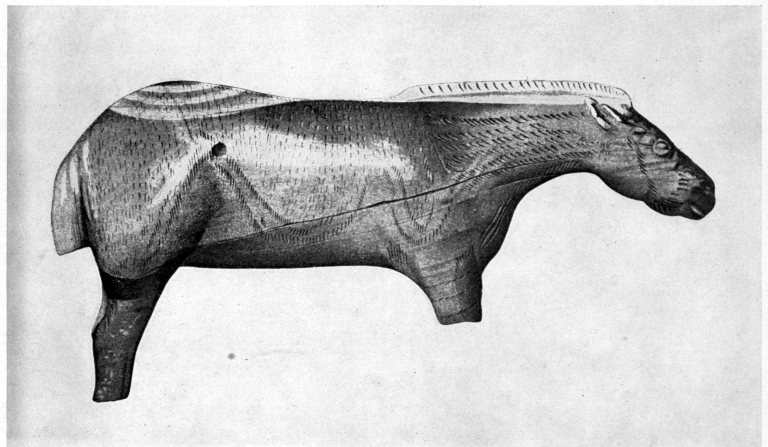

b

UPPER MAGDALENIAN SCULPTURE: - *a*) Mas d'Azil (*Ariège*): ivory ibex. *b*) Les Espélugues, Lourdes (*Hautes-Pyrénées*): ivory horse (more than twice enlarged).

Pl. 43

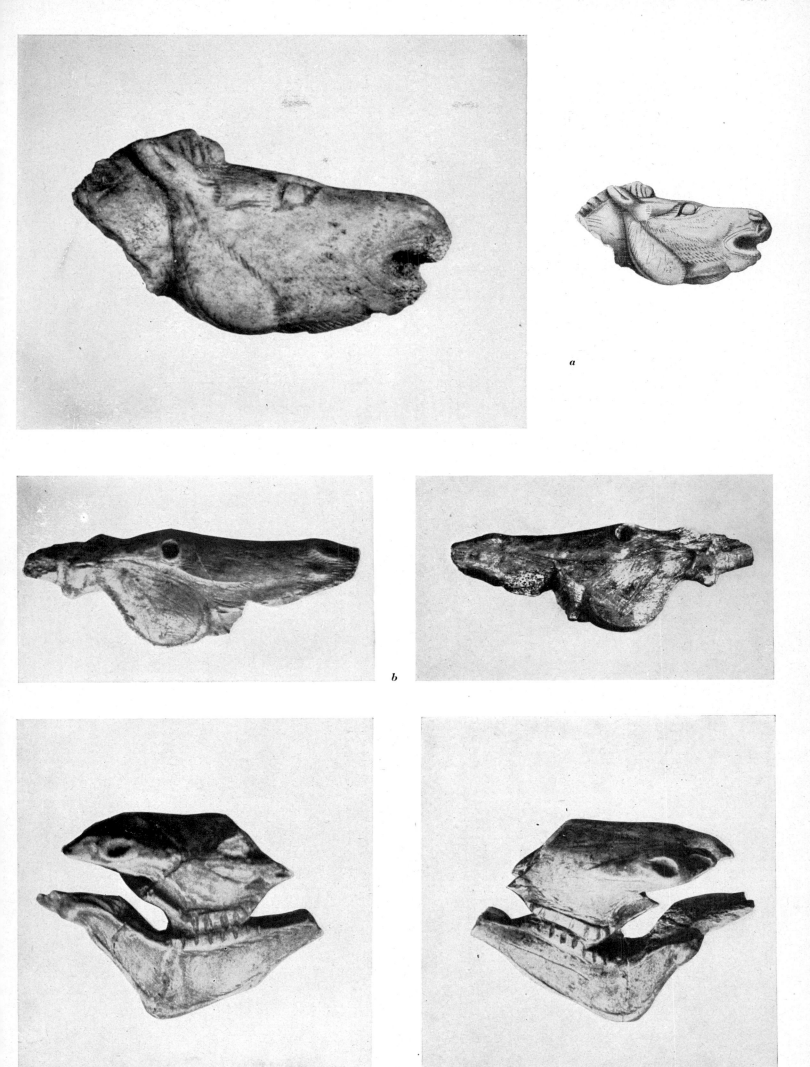

a

b

c

UPPER MAGDALENIAN SCULPTURE: - Mas d'Azil (*Ariège*): horses' heads on antler, drawn by Breuil; *b* and *c* are skinned.

Pl. 44

a

b

c

d

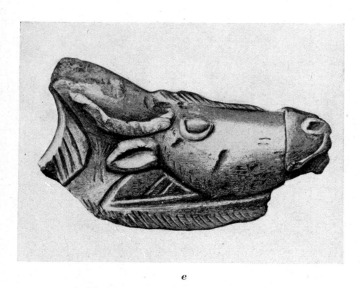

e

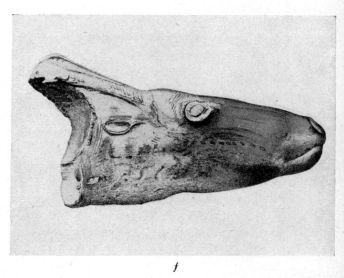

f

UPPER MAGDALENIAN SCULPTURE: - Animals on antler and stone: *a*) Kesslerloch (*Thayngen-Switzerland*); *b*) Bédeilhac (*Ariège*) (stone, twice enlarged); *c*), *d*) Laugerie Basse (*Dordogne*); *e*), *f*) Les Espélugues, Lourdes (*Hautes-Pyrénées*).

Pl. 45

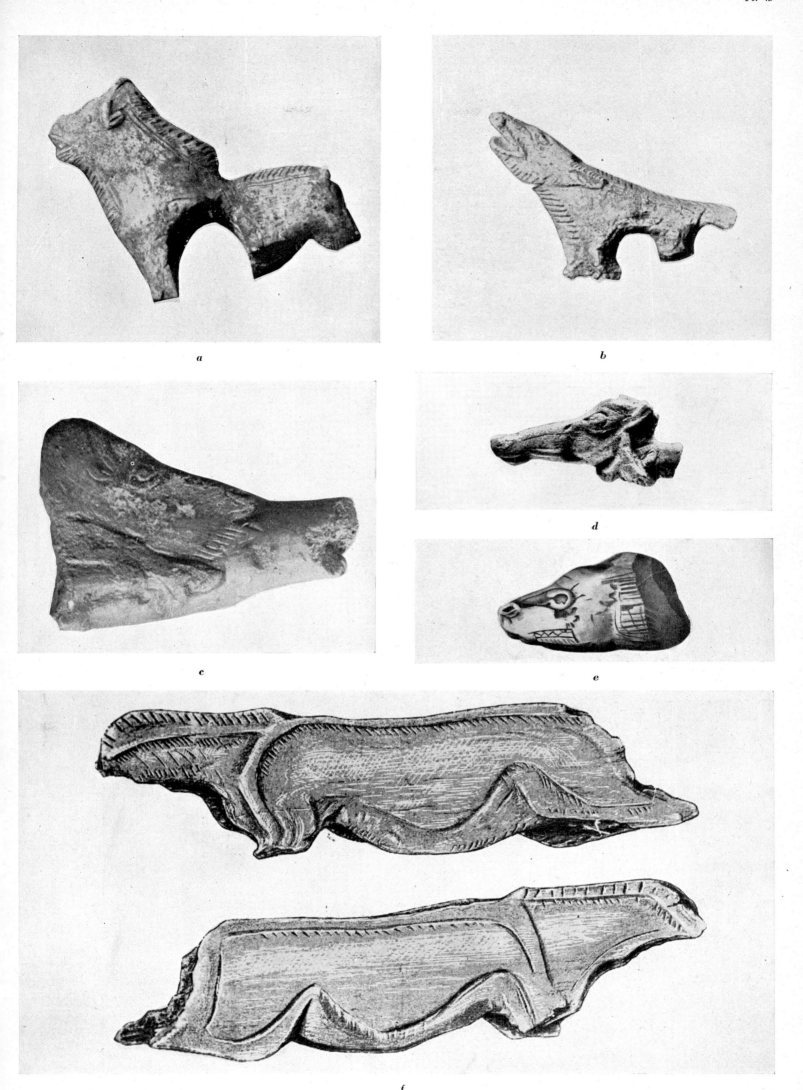

a   *b*

c   *d*

e

f

UPPER MAGDALENIAN SCULPTURE: - Animals, on antler and bone: *a*), *b*), *d*) Laugerie Basse (*Dordogne*); *c*), *e*) Mas d'Azil (*Ariège*); *f*) Isturitz (*Basses-Pyrénées*).

Pl. 46

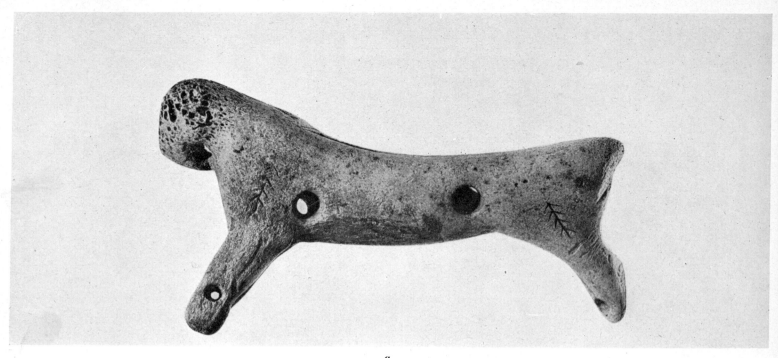

a

b

UPPER MAGDALENIAN SCULPTURE: - Isturitz (*Basses-Pyrénées*): *a*) feline animal on antler; *b*) horse's head on sandstone.

Pl. 47

a

b

c

d

e

UPPER MAGDALENIAN SCULPTURE: - Isturitz (*Basses-Pyrénées*): *a*)-*d*) fragments of stone animals; *e*) amber horse's head.

Pl. 48

a

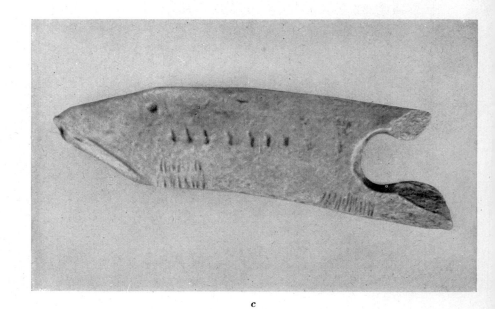

b

c

UPPER MAGDALENIAN SCULPTURE: - Animals on antler: *a*) La Vache (*Ariège*); *b*) El Rascaño (*Santander*); *c*) El Pendo (*Santander*), fish.

Pl. 49

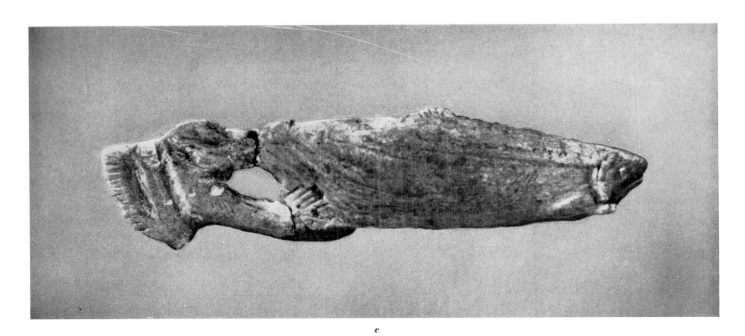

UPPER MAGDALENIAN SCULPTURE: - Animals on antler and bone: *a*) Laugerie Basse (*Dordogne*), salamander, drawn by Breuil; *b*) Mas d'Azil (*Ariège*) and *c*) Les Espélugues, Lourdes (*Hautes-Pyrénées*), fish.

Pl. 50

UPPER MAGDALENIAN CUT-OUT PROFILES: - Fish and horse's head on bone: *a*) Gourdan (*Haute-Garonne*); *b*) Rey and Bout-du-Monde at Les Eyzies (*Dordogne*); *c*) Mas d'Azil (*Ariège*); *d*) Rey at Les Eyzies; *e*) Lorthet (*Hautes-Pyrénées*); *f*) Laugerie Basse (*Dordogne*), drawings by Breuil.

Pl. 51

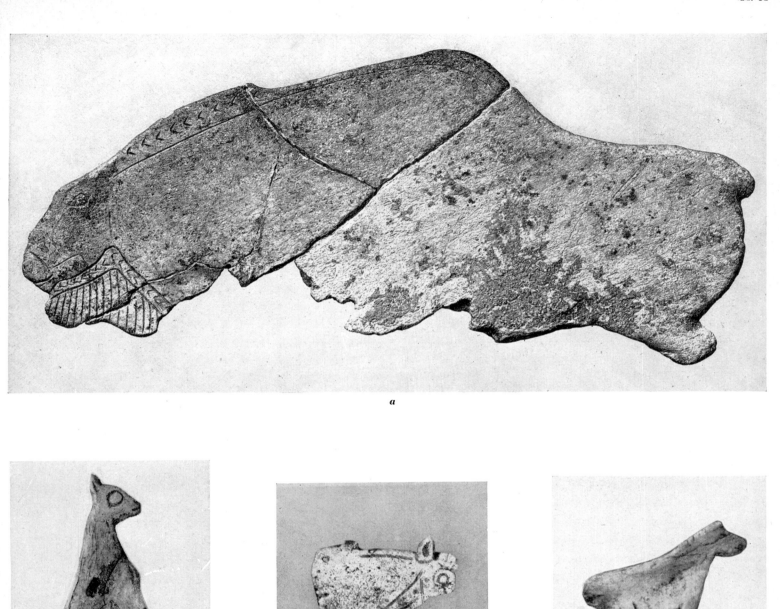

a

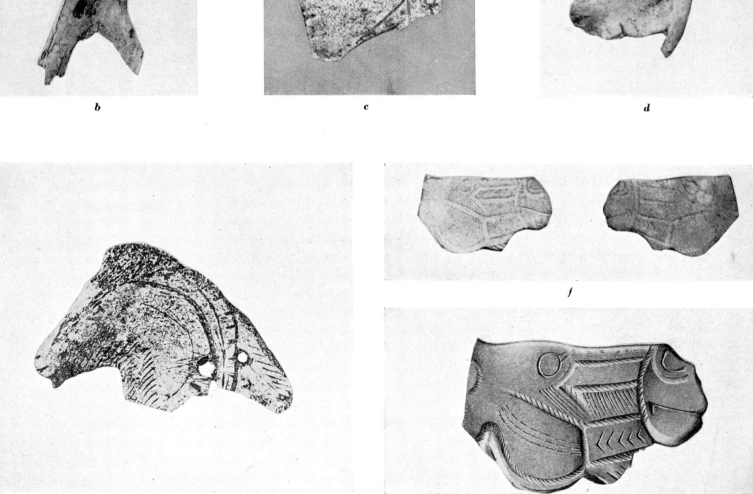

b   *c*   *d*

e   *f*

g

UPPER MAGDALENIAN CUT-OUT PROFILES: - *a*) Isturitz (*Basses-Pyrénées*), bison; *b*), *f*), *g*. Arudy (*Basses-Pyrénées*), lynx and horse's head; *c*) Mas d'Azil (*Ariège*), ibex; *d*) Lorthet (*Hautes-Pyrénées*); horse; *e*) Isturitz, ibex.

Pl. 52

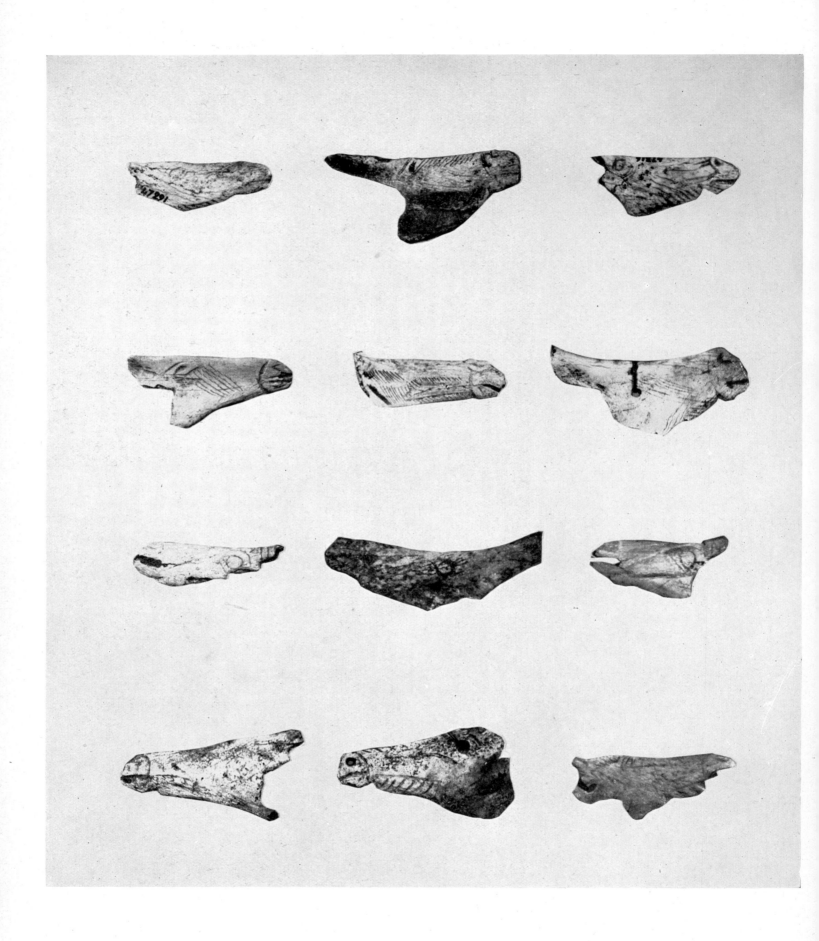

UPPER MAGDALENIAN CUT-OUT PROFILES: - Horses' heads on bone, Mas d'Azil (*Ariège*), Arudy (*Basses-Pyrénées*), Gourdan (*Haute-Garonne*), Lorthet (*Hautes-Pyrénées*).

Pl. 53

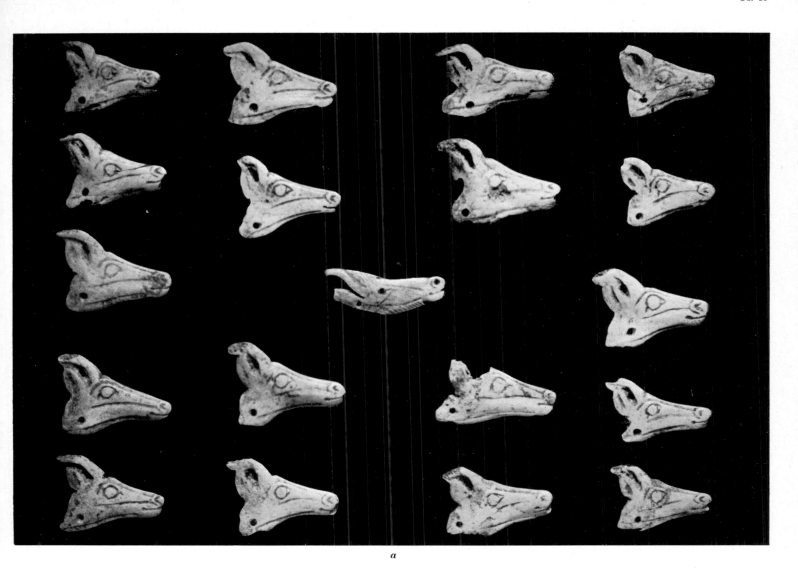

a

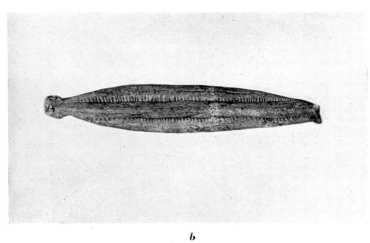

b

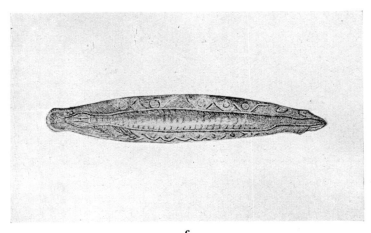

c

d

UPPER MAGDALENIAN CUT-OUT PROFILES: - *a*) Labastide (*Hautes-Pyrénées*), ibexes' heads; *b*), *c*) Lorthet (*Hautes-Pyrénées*), snakes; *d*) El Pendo (*Santander*), fish.

Pl. 54

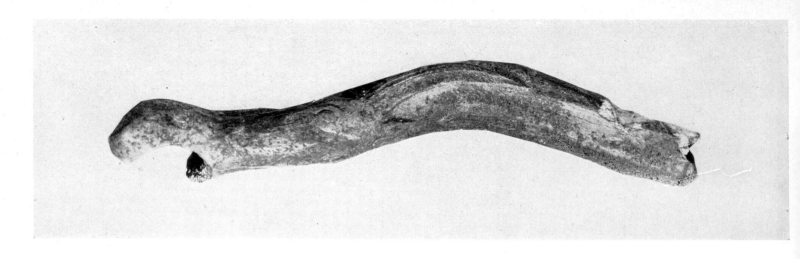

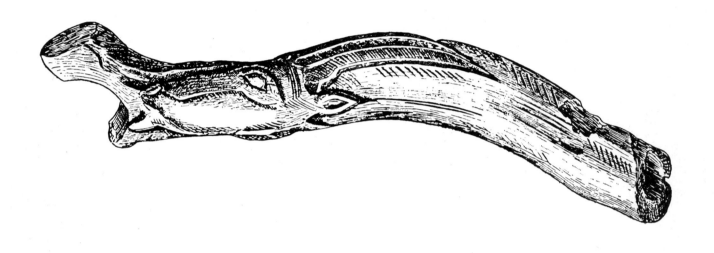

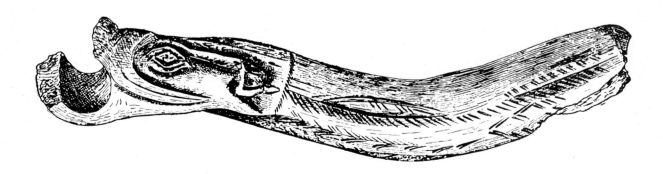

UPPER MAGDALENIAN BAS-RELIEFS: - Arudy (*Basses-Pyrénées*): ruminants on a « bâton de commandement » carved on antler, viewed from both sides, drawings by Breuil.

Pl. 55

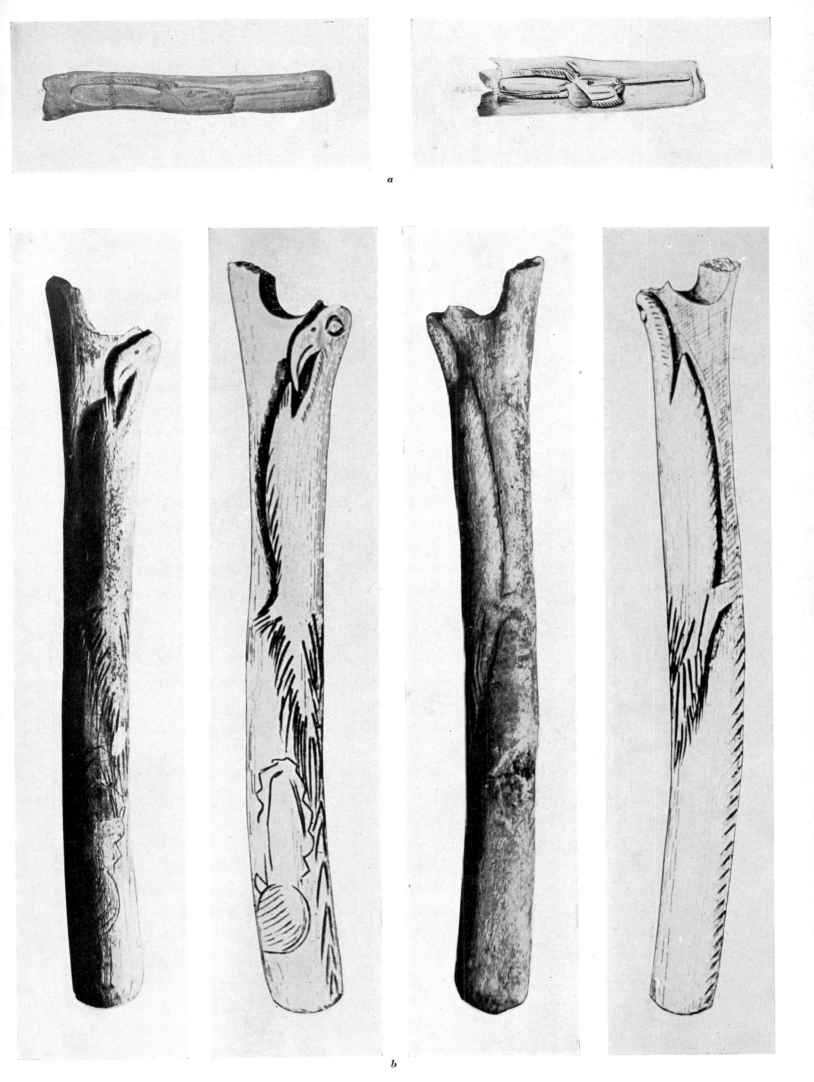

a

b

UPPER MAGDALENIAN BAS-RELIEFS: - On antler: *a*) Arudy (*Basses-Pyrénées*), horse, *b*) Raymonden (*Dordogne*) bird, drawing by Breuil.

Pl. 56

a

b

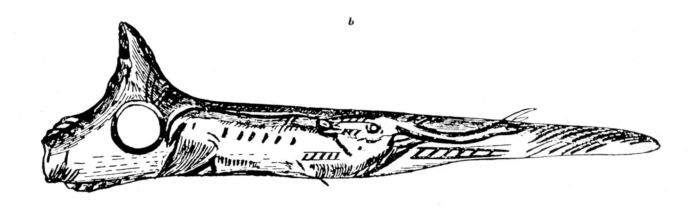

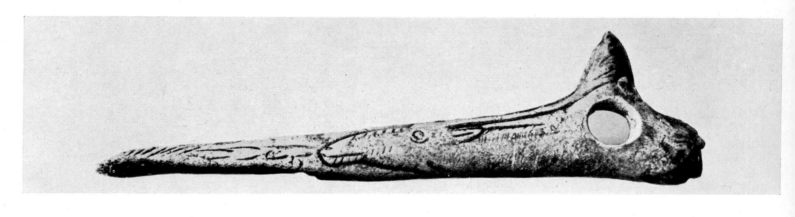

c

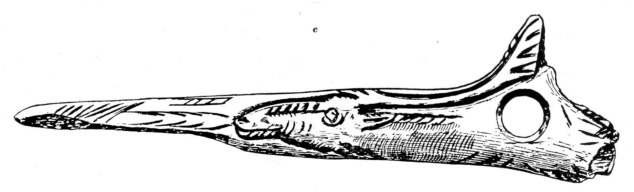

UPPER MAGDALENIAN BAS-RELIEFS: - Horse and reindeer on antler: *a*) Mas d'Azil (*Ariège*); *b*), *c*) Laugerie Basse (*Dordogne*), « bâton de commandement » viewed from both sides, drawings by Breuil.

Pl. 57

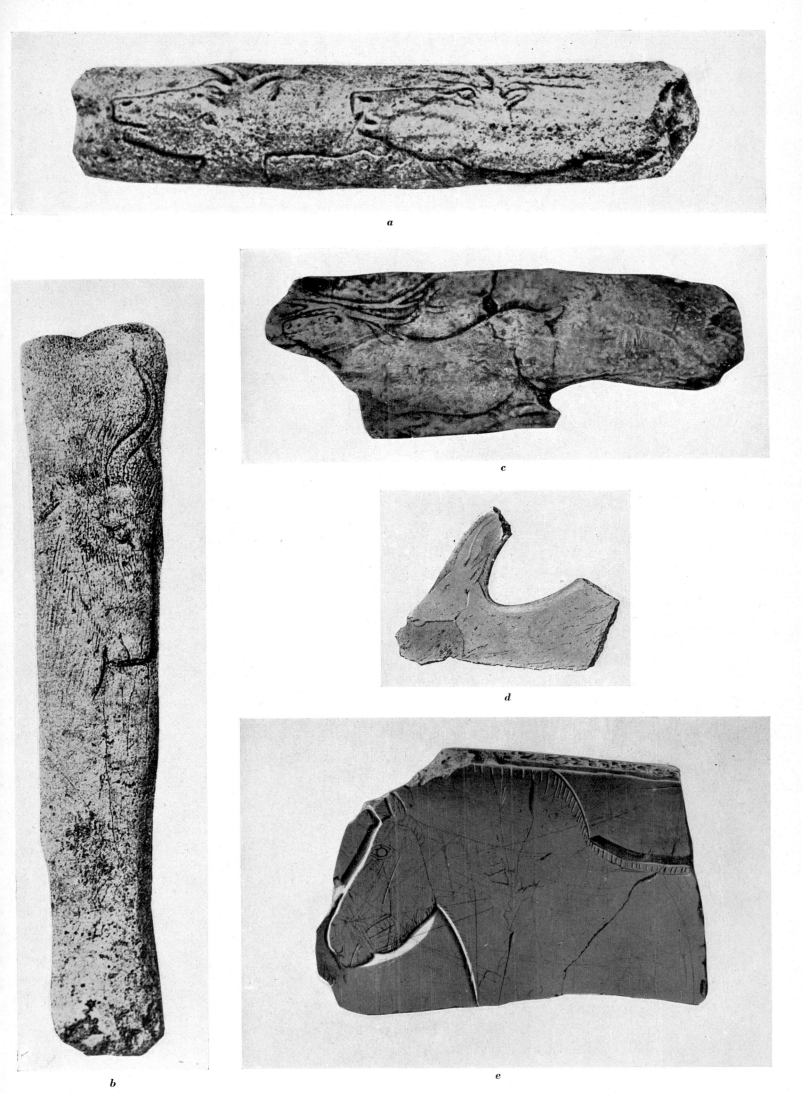

a

c

d

b

e

UPPER MAGDALENIAN BAS-RELIEFS: - Animals on antler and bone: *a*) Mas d'Azil (*Ariège*); *b*) Isturitz (*Basses-Pyrénées*); *c*)-*e*) Laugerie Basse (*Dordogne*).

Pl. 58

a

b

c

UPPER MAGDALENIAN BAS-RELIEFS: - Isturitz (*Basses-Pyrénées*): reindeer carved on stone.

Pl. 59

a

b

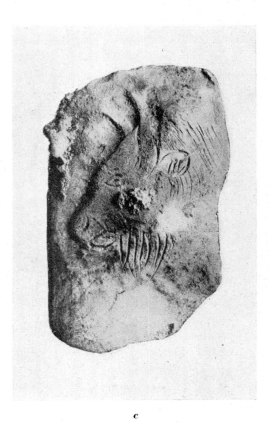

c

UPPER MAGDALENIAN BAS-RELIEFS: - Carvings on stone: *a*), *b*) Isturitz (*Basses-Pyrénées*), reindeer and bison; *c*) Laugerie Basse (*Dordogne*), bison.

Pl. 60

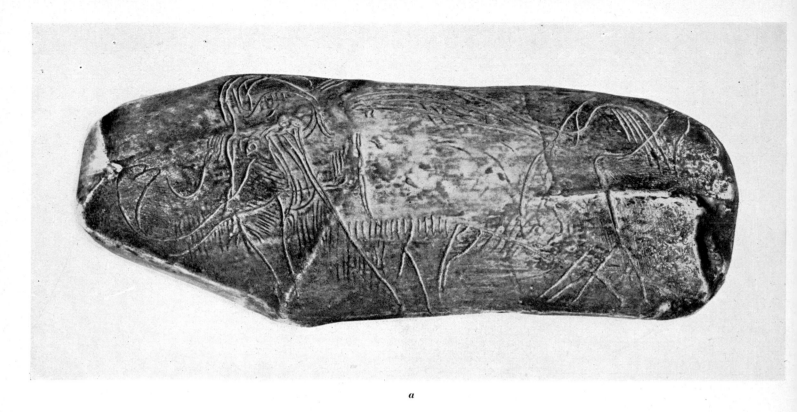

a

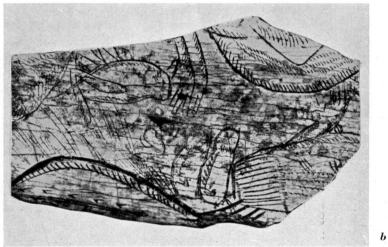

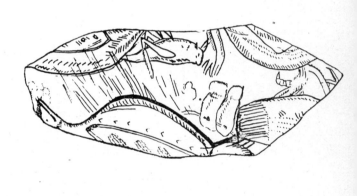

b

d

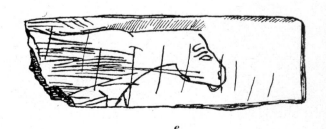

e

c

UPPER MAGDALENIAN ENGRAVINGS ON BONE AND IVORY: - *a*) La Madeleine (*Dordogne*), mammoth on ivory; *b*) Les Trois Frères (*Ariège*), birds, grasshopper and other figures, drawing by Bégouën. Horses; *c*) Lespugue (*Haute-Garonne*), *d*) Mas d'Azil (*Ariège*), *e*) Creswell Crags (*Derbyshire*).

Pl. 61

a

b

c

UPPER MAGDALENIAN ENGRAVINGS ON BONE: - *a*) Isturitz (*Basses-Pyrénées*), horse; *b*), *c*) Mas d'Azil (*Ariège*), oxen.

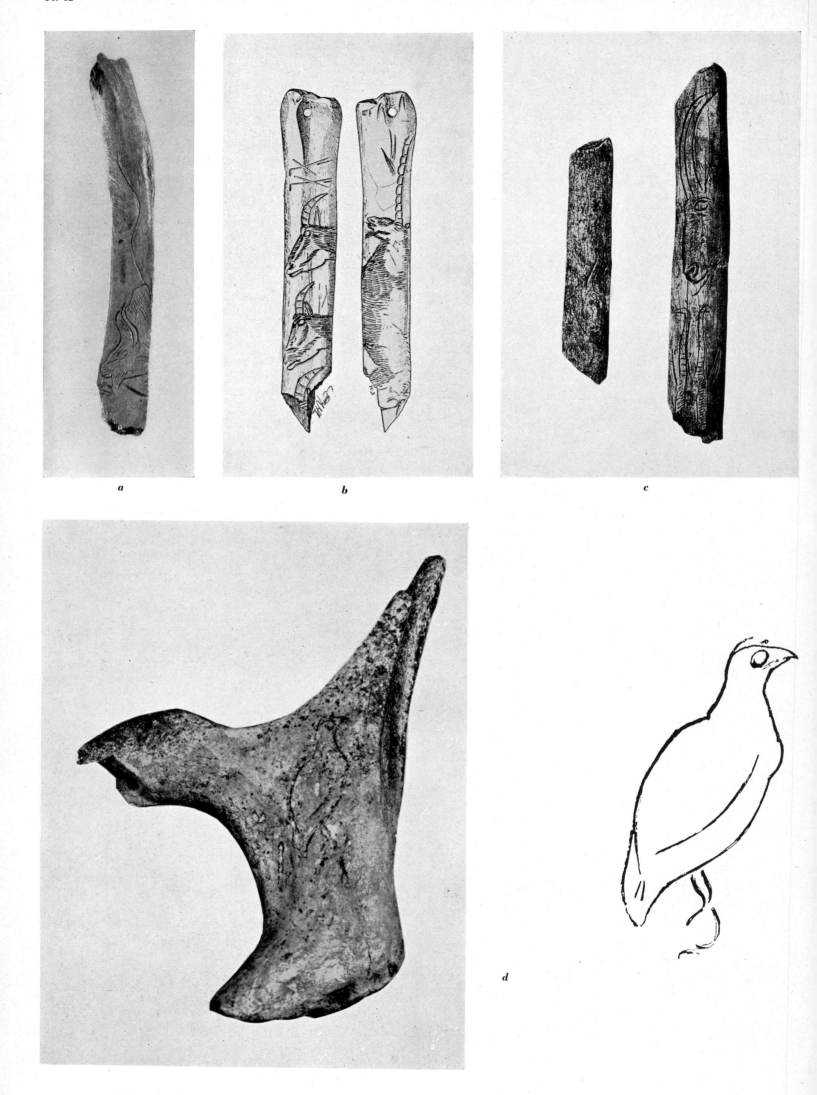

Pl. 62

a   *b*   *c*

d

UPPER MAGDALENIAN ENGRAVINGS ON BONE AND ANTLER: - *a*) Laugerie Basse (*Dordogne*); *b*) Mas d'Azil (*Ariège*) drawn by Breuil; *c*), *d*) Isturitz (*Basses-Pyrénées*) drawn by Passemard.

Pl. 63

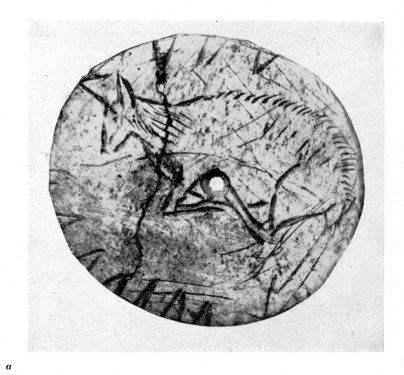

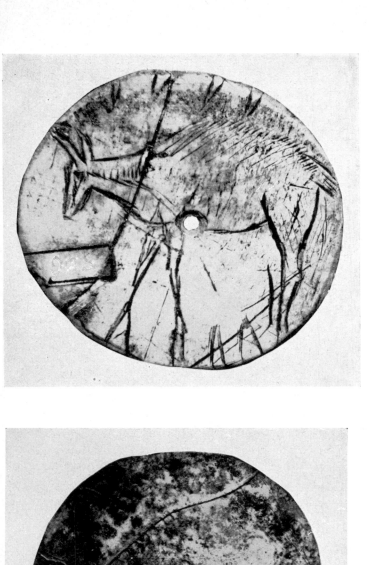

a

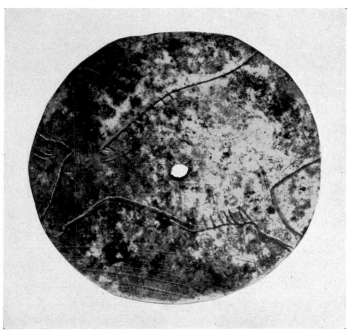

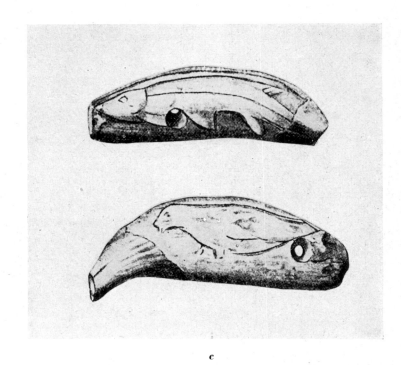

b

c

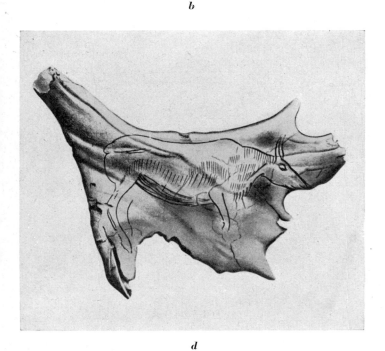

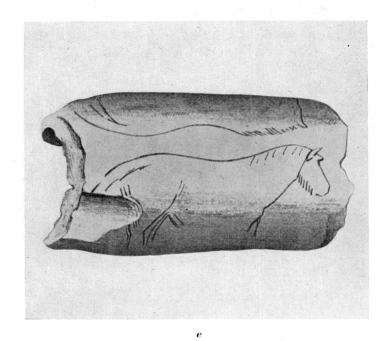

d

e

UPPER MAGDALENIAN ENGRAVINGS ON BONE, TEETH AND ANTLER: - *a*), *b*) Laugerie Basse (*Dordogne*): animals engraved on bone disks (*a* = enlarged almost 3 times); *c*) Duruthy (*Landes*): on bears' teeth; *d*) Mas d'Azil (*Ariège*); *e*) Brassempouy (*Landes*).

Pl. 64

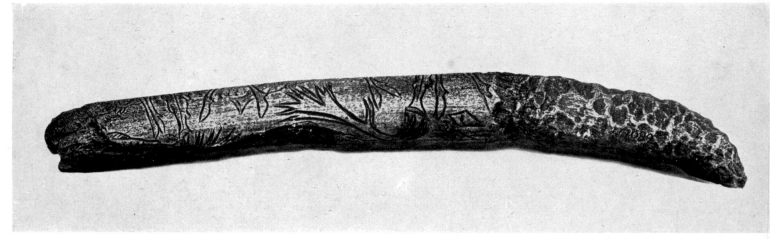

a

b

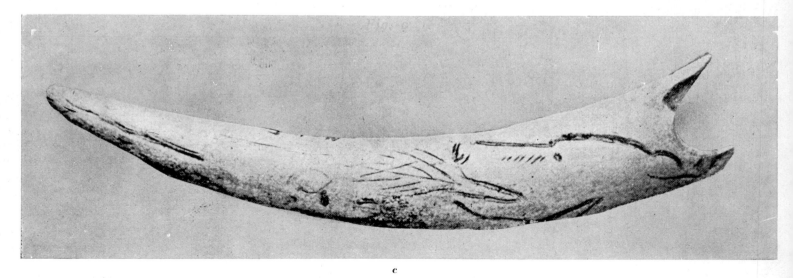

c

UPPER MAGDALENIAN ENGRAVINGS ON ANTLER: - *a*), *b*) Lorthet (*Hautes-Pyrénées*), deer and salmon; *c*) Massat (*Ariège*), bear.

Pl. 65

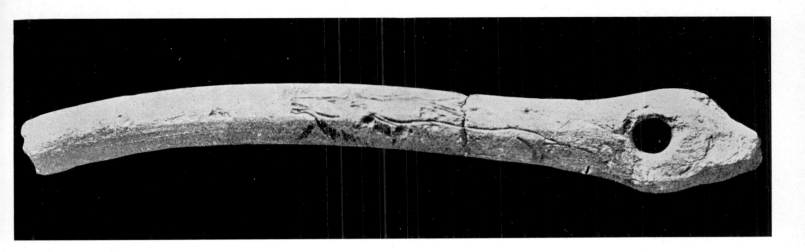

a

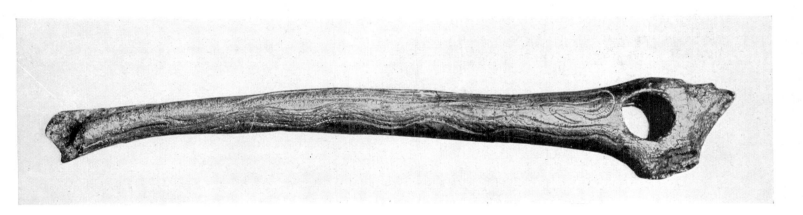

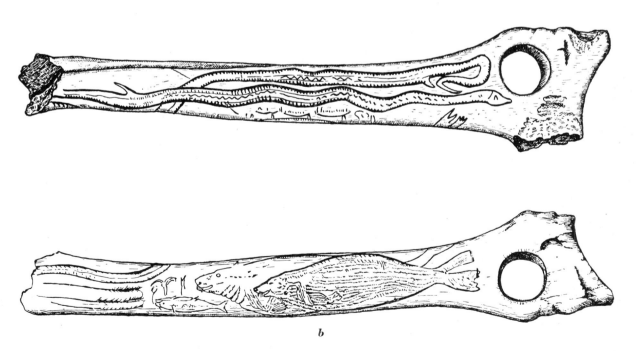

b

UPPER MAGDALENIAN ENGRAVINGS ON ANTLER: - *a*) Les Hoteaux (*Aïn*), deer, drawing by Breuil; *b*) Montgaudier (*Charente*), seals and snakes or eels, drawings by Micheli and Isola.

Pl. 66

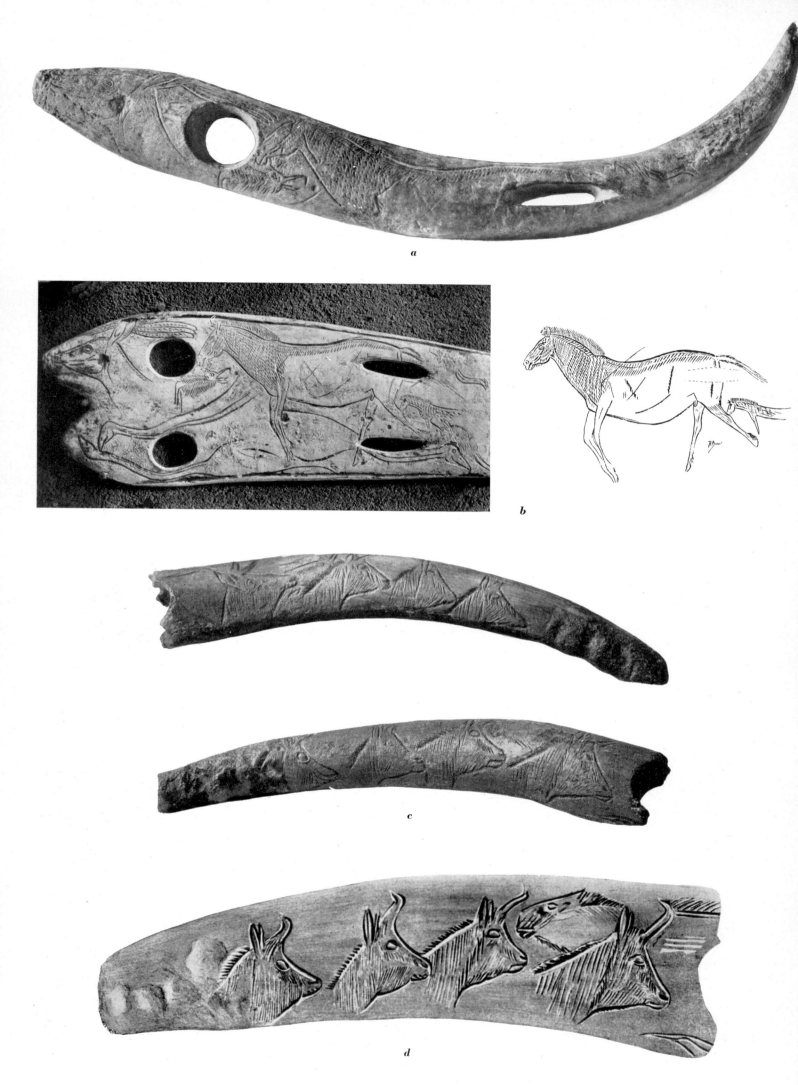

UPPER MAGDALENIAN ENGRAVINGS ON ANTLER: - a), b) Abri Mège à Teyjat (*Dordogne*): horses, snakes, etc., drawing by Breuil; c), d) Gourdan (*Haute-Garonne*): chamois.

Pl. 67

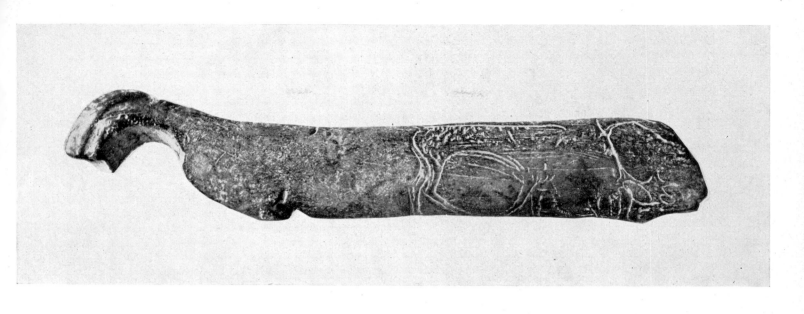

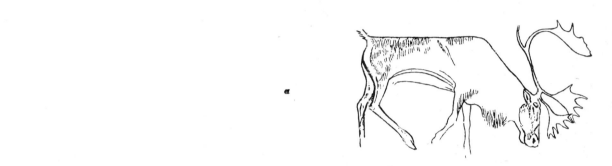

UPPER MAGDALENIAN ENGRAVINGS ON ANTLER: - *a*) Kesslerloch (*Thayngen-Switzerland*): reindeer; *b*) Schweizersbild (*Schaffhausen-Switzerland*): horse.

Pl. 68

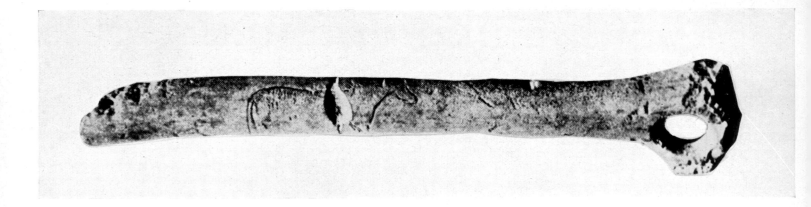

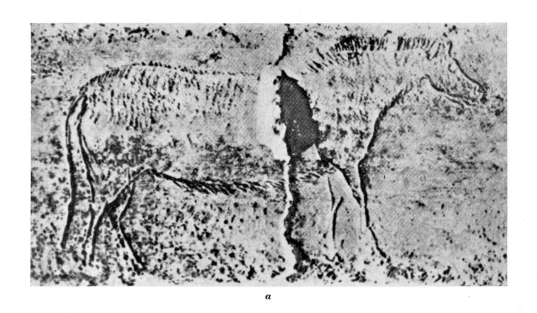

a

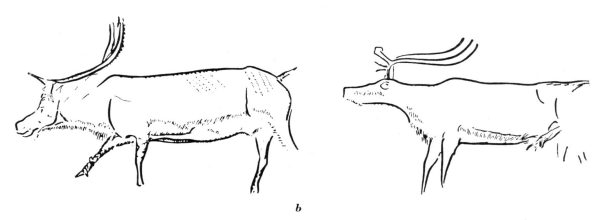

b

UPPER MAGDALENIAN ENGRAVINGS ON ANTLER: - Horse and reindeer: *a*) Kesslerloch (*Thayngen-Switzerland*), *b*) Petersfels (*Baden*), drawn by Peters.

Pl. 69

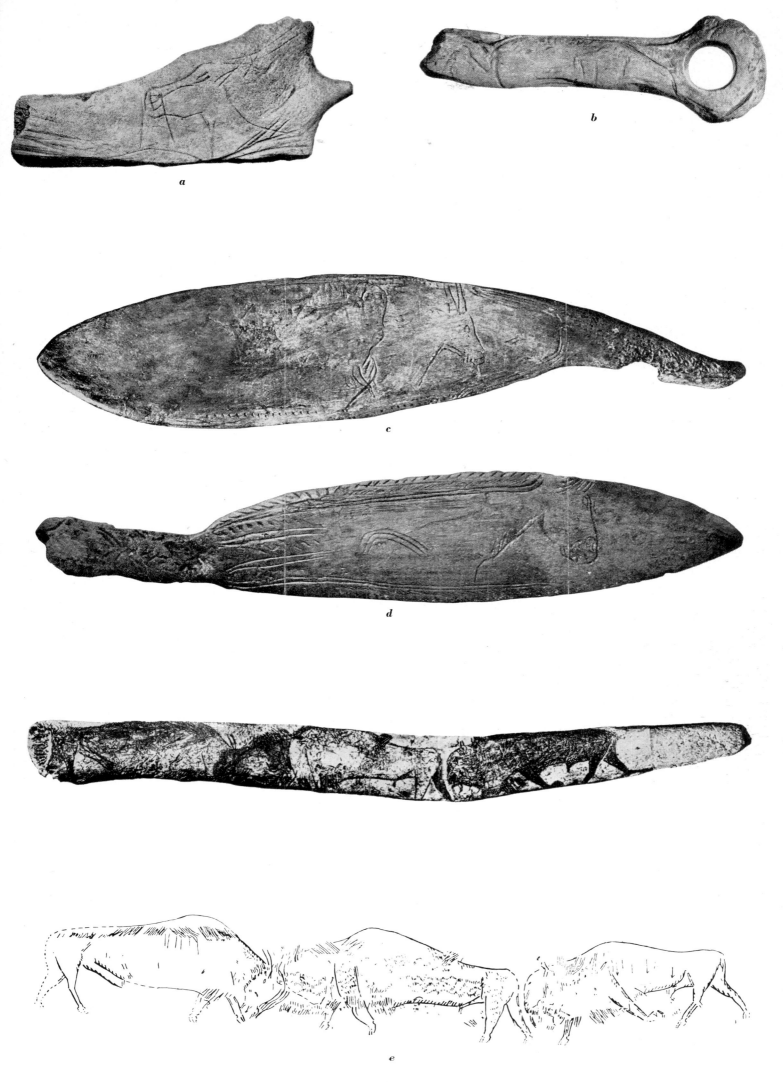

UPPER MAGDALENIAN ENGRAVINGS ON ANTLER AND BONE: - Pekarna (*Moravia*): *a*), *b*) animals on antler; *c*), *d*) spatulas fashioned from horses' jawbones with animal figures; *e*) bison on bone, drawing by Absolon.

Pl. 70

a

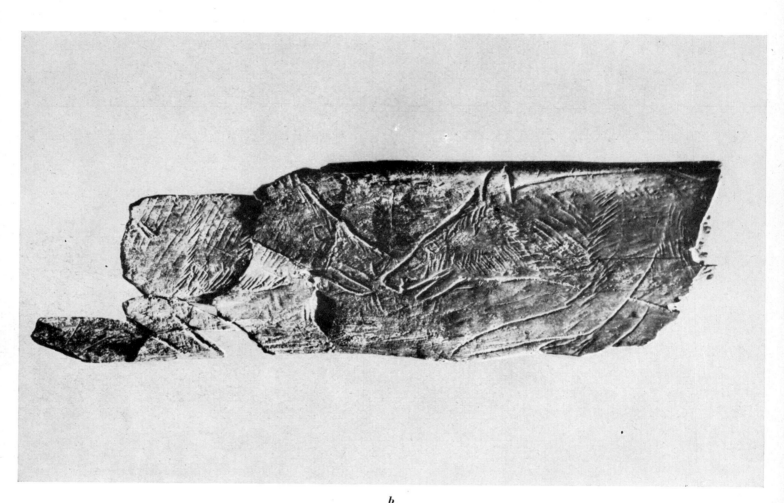

b

c

UPPER MAGDALENIAN ENGRAVINGS ON BONE: - Ruminants and wolves: *a*) Brassempouy (*Landes*); *b*) La vache (twice enlarged), *c*) Mas d'Azil (*Ariège*).

Pl. 71

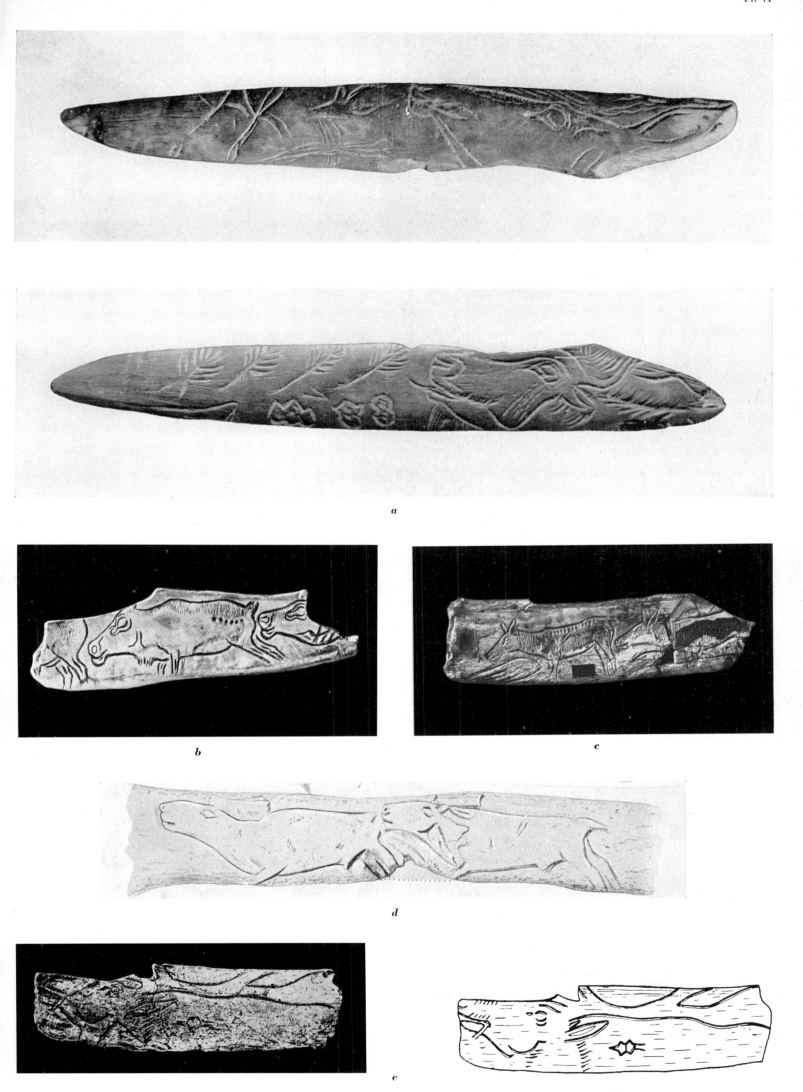

UPPER MAGDALENIAN ENGRAVINGS ON BONE AND ANTLER: - *a*) La Vache *b*) Massat (*Ariège*); *c*) Chaffaud (*Vienne*); *d*), *e*) La Madeleine (*Dordogne*), (*e*, drawing by Breuil).

Pl. 72

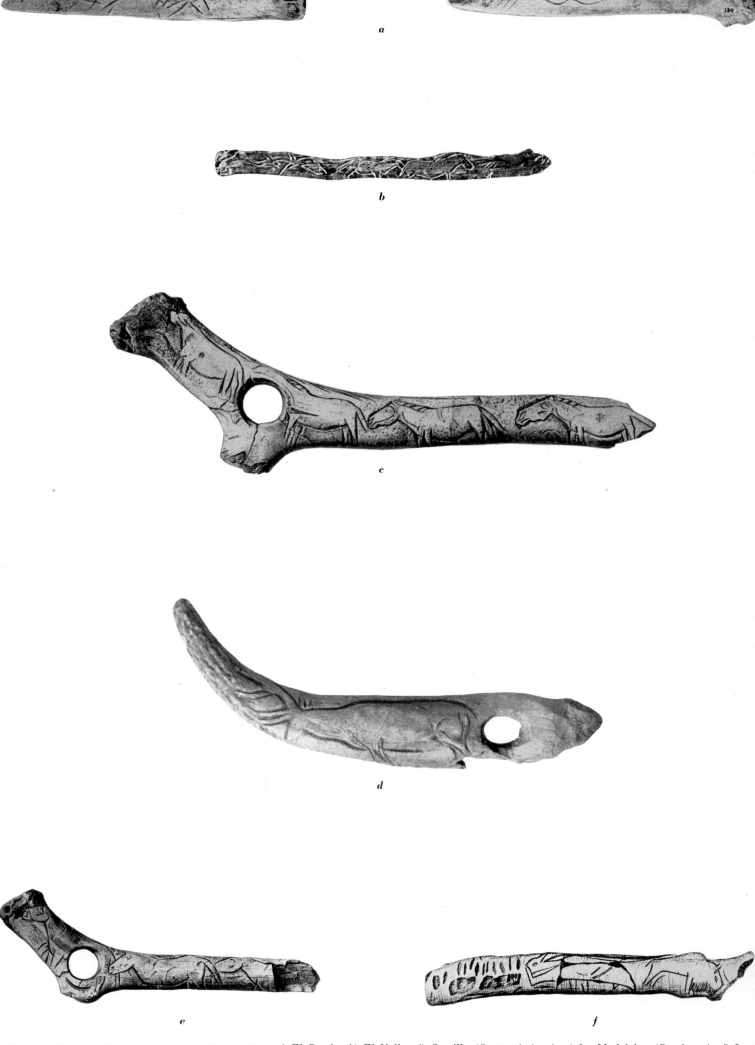

UPPER MAGDALENIAN ENGRAVINGS ON BONE AND ANTLER: - *a*) El Pendo, *b*) El Valle, *d*) Castillo (*Santander*); *c*), *e*) La Madeleine (*Dordogne*); *f*) Loubressac (*Vienne*), drawn by Leclerc and Pradel.

Pl. 73

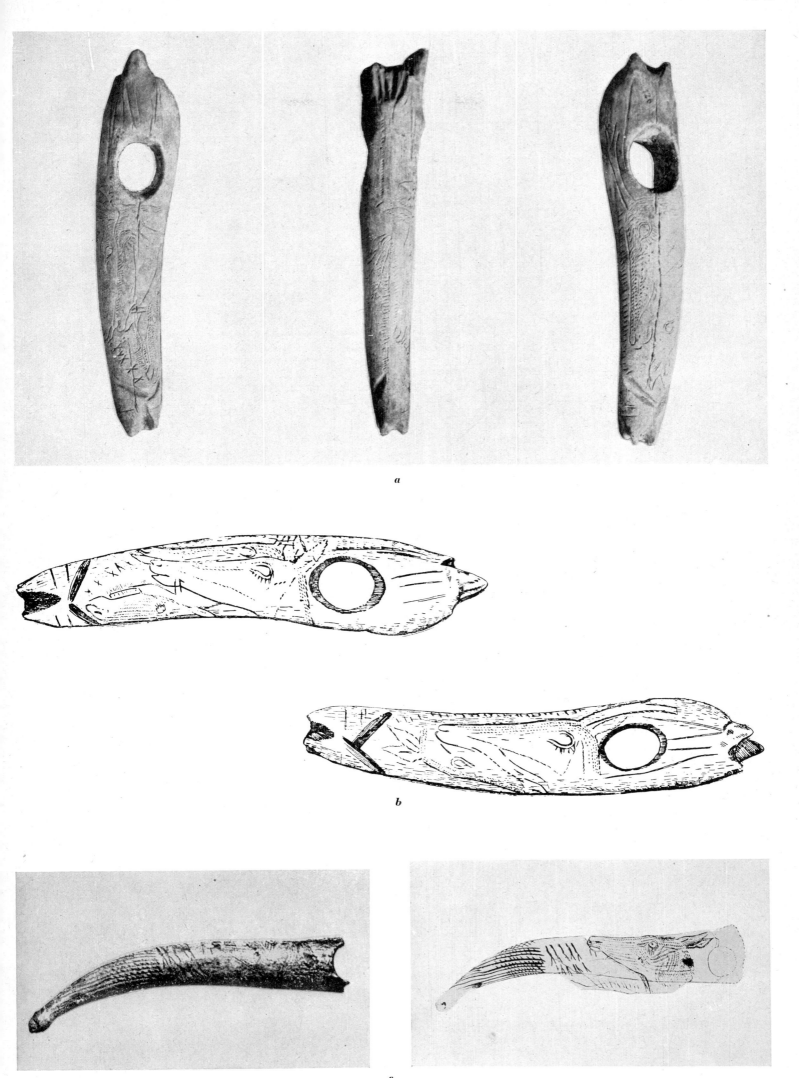

a

b

c

UPPER MAGDALENIAN ENGRAVINGS ON ANTLER: - *a*), *b*) El Pendo (*Santander*), « bâton de commandement » carved in the shape of a horse's head and engraved; drawings by Carballo and Larin; *c*) El Valle (*Santander*).

Pl. 74

UPPER MAGDALENIAN ENGRAVINGS ON STONE: - Isturitz (*Basses-Pyrénées*): hare, drawn by Passemard.

Pl. 75

a

b

UPPER MAGDALENIAN ENGRAVINGS ON STONE: - *a*) Isturitz (*Basses-Pyrénées*), horse's head; *b*) Labastide (*Hautes-Pyrénées*), birds, drawn by Simonnet.

Pl. 76

a

b

c

d

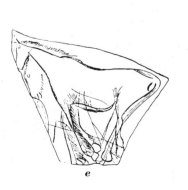

e

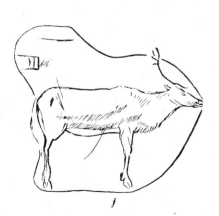

f

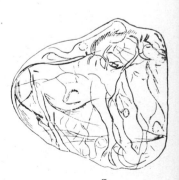

g

UPPER MAGDALENIAN ENGRAVINGS ON STONE: - Laugerie Basse (*Dordogne*): deer, bison, bear, horses and reindeer, drawings by Breuil.

Pl. 77

UPPER MAGDALENIAN ENGRAVINGS ON STONE: - *a*) Petersfels (*Baden*): horse engraved on lignite, drawing by Peters; *b*) Klause (*Bavaria*), on stone, drawn by Breuil; *c*) Massat (*Ariège*): bear engraved on a pebble.

Pl. 78

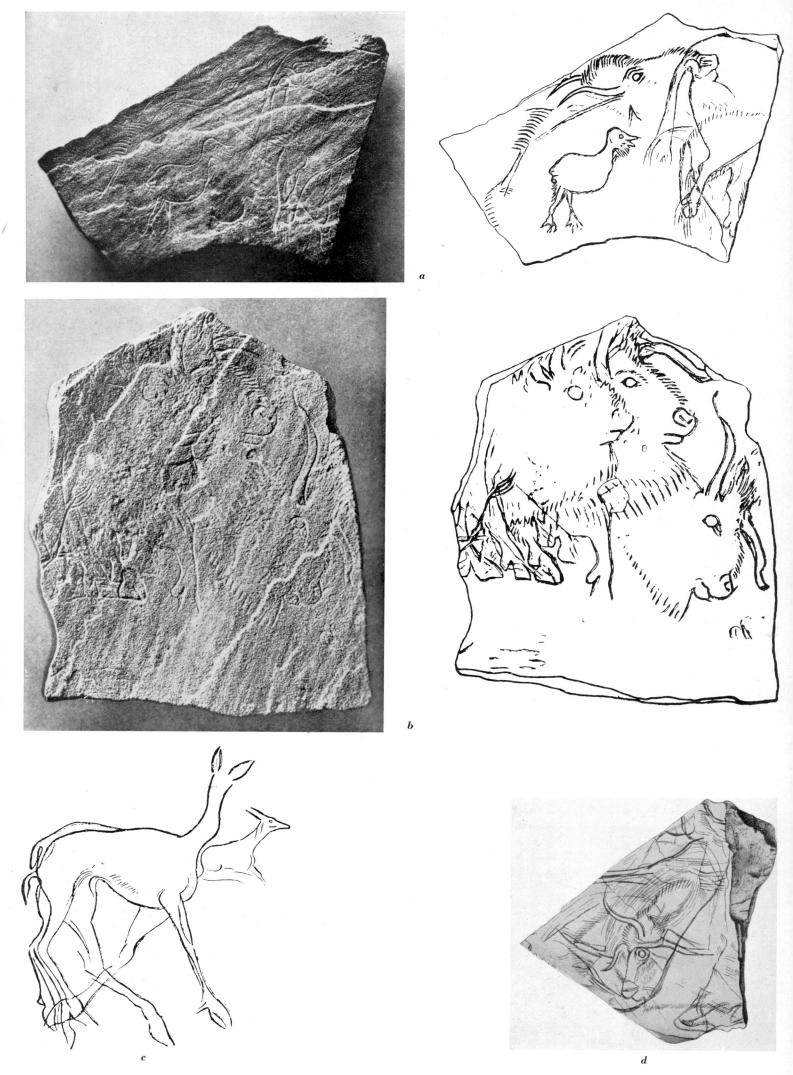

UPPER MAGDALENIAN ENGRAVINGS ON STONE: - a), b) Puy de Lacan (*Corrèze*); c) Le Bout du Monde (*Dordogne*), drawn by Breuil; d) Mas d'Azil (*Ariège*).

Pl. 79

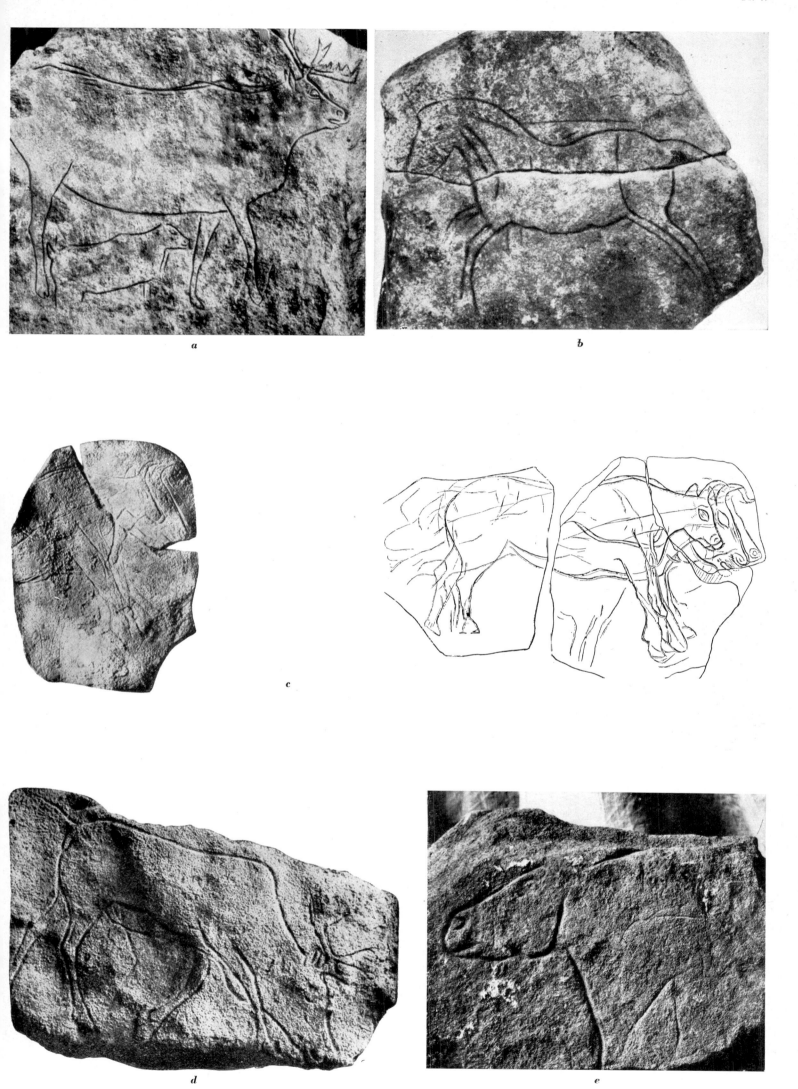

a

b

c

d

e

UPPER MAGDALENIAN ENGRAVINGS ON STONE: - Reindeer, horses and oxen: *a*), *b*) La Madeleine, *c*)-*e*) Limeuil (*Dordogne*), drawing by Bouyssonie.

Pl. 80

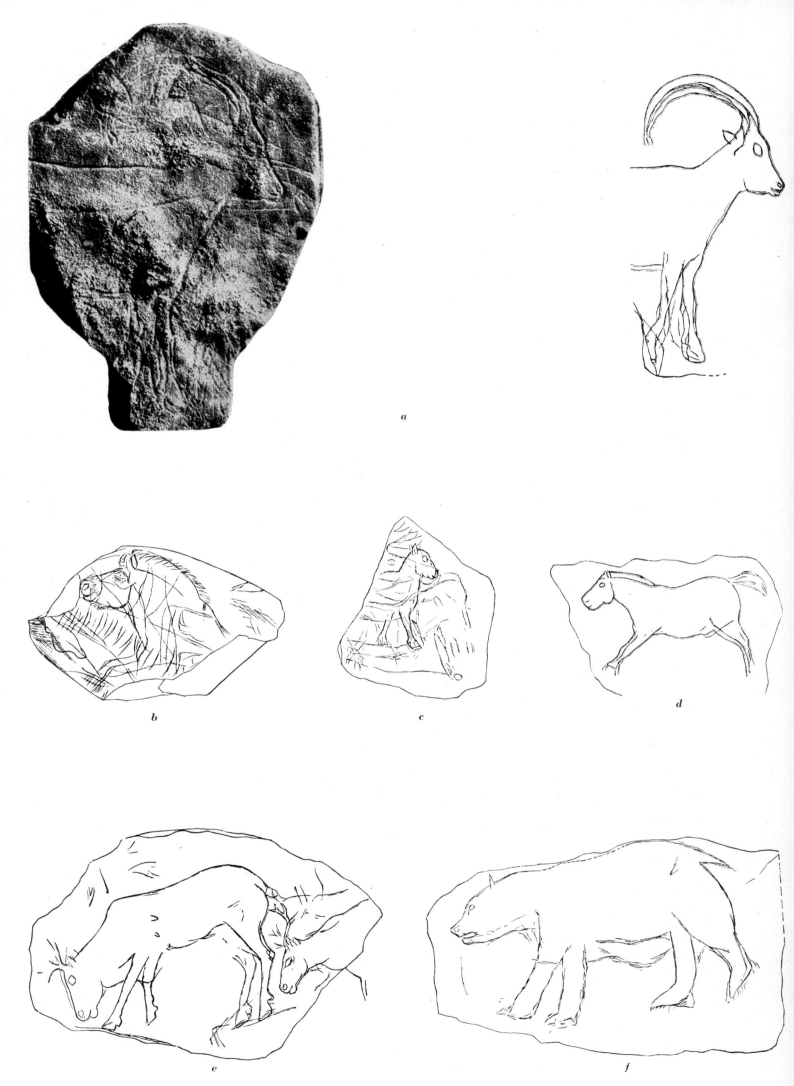

UPPER MAGDALENIAN ENGRAVINGS ON STONE: - Limeuil (*Dordogne*): Ibex, horses, reindeer, bear; drawings by Bouyssonie.

Pl. 81

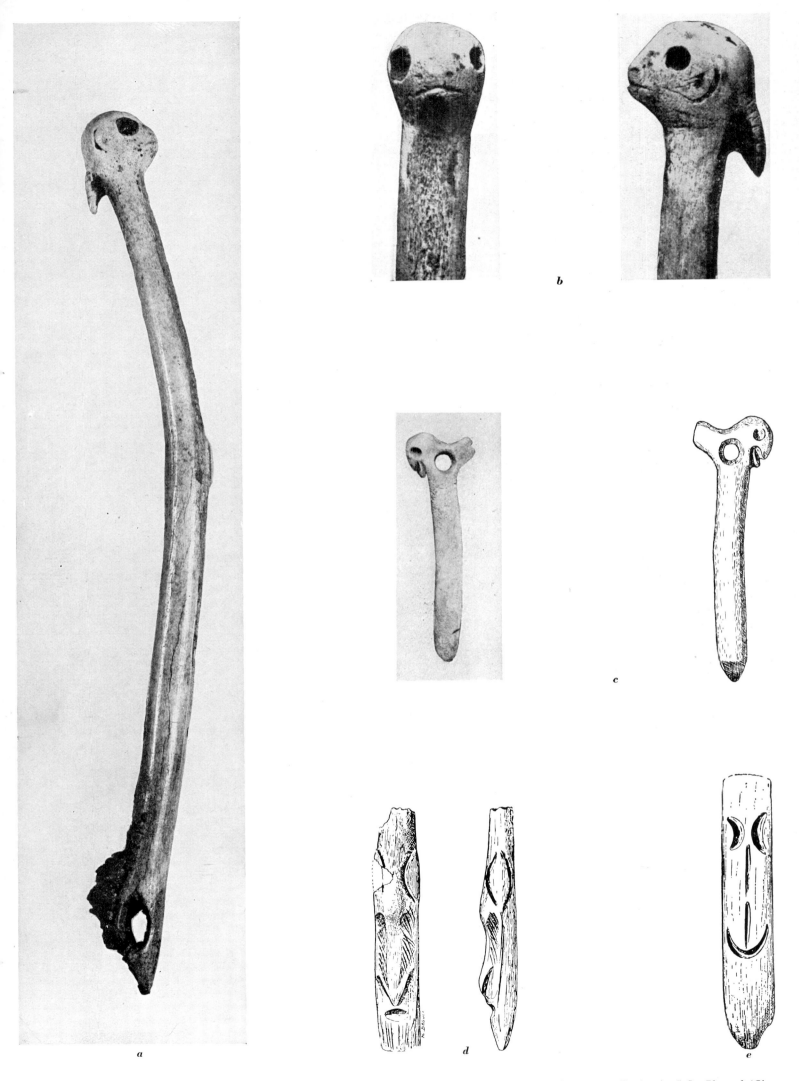

THE HUMAN FORM IN MAGDALENIAN ART: - Sculpture on antler: a), b) Gourdan (*Haute-Garonne*): (probably man or ibex); c), d) Le Placard (*Charente*); e) Les Fées (*Gironde*), drawings by Breuil.

Pl. 82

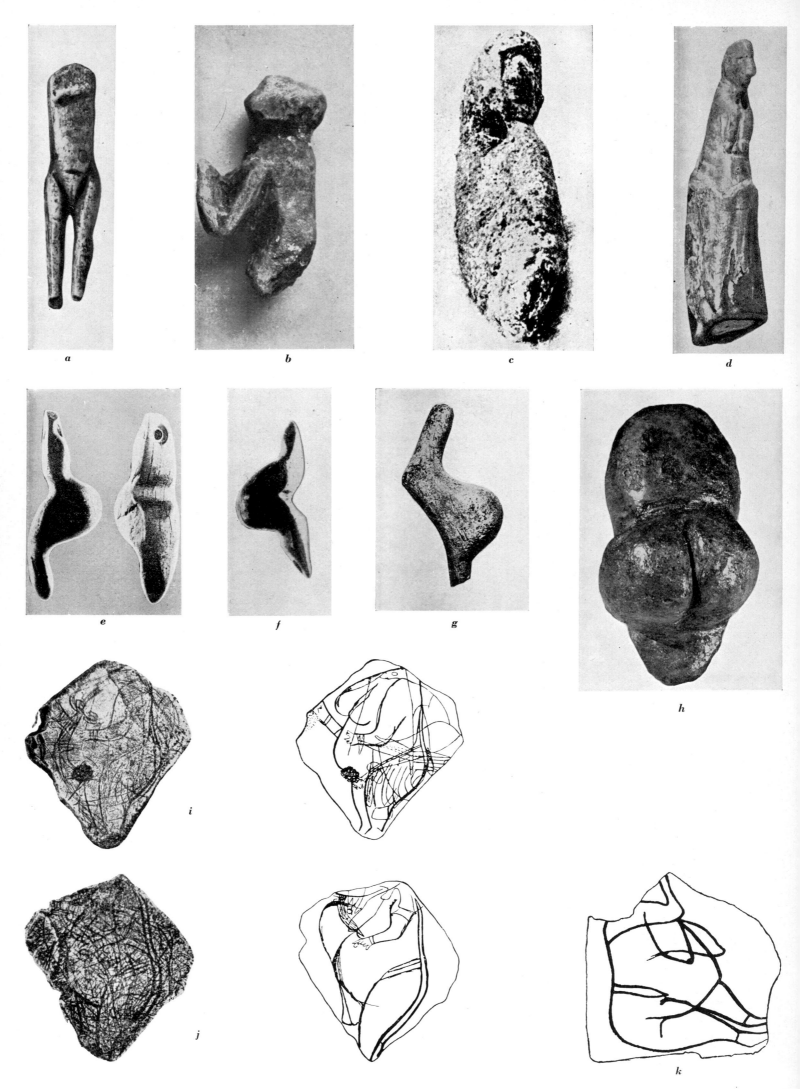

THE HUMAN FORM IN MAGDALENIAN ART: - Sculpture and engravings on ivory, bone and stone: *a*), *b*) Laugerie Basse (*Dordogne*); *c*) Bédeilhac, *d*) Mas d'Azil (*Ariège*); *e*), *f*) Petersfels (*Baden*); *g*) Pekarna (*Moravia*); *h*) Mauern (*Bavaria*); *i*) - *k*) La Marche (*Vienne*), drawings by Lwoff.

Pl. 83

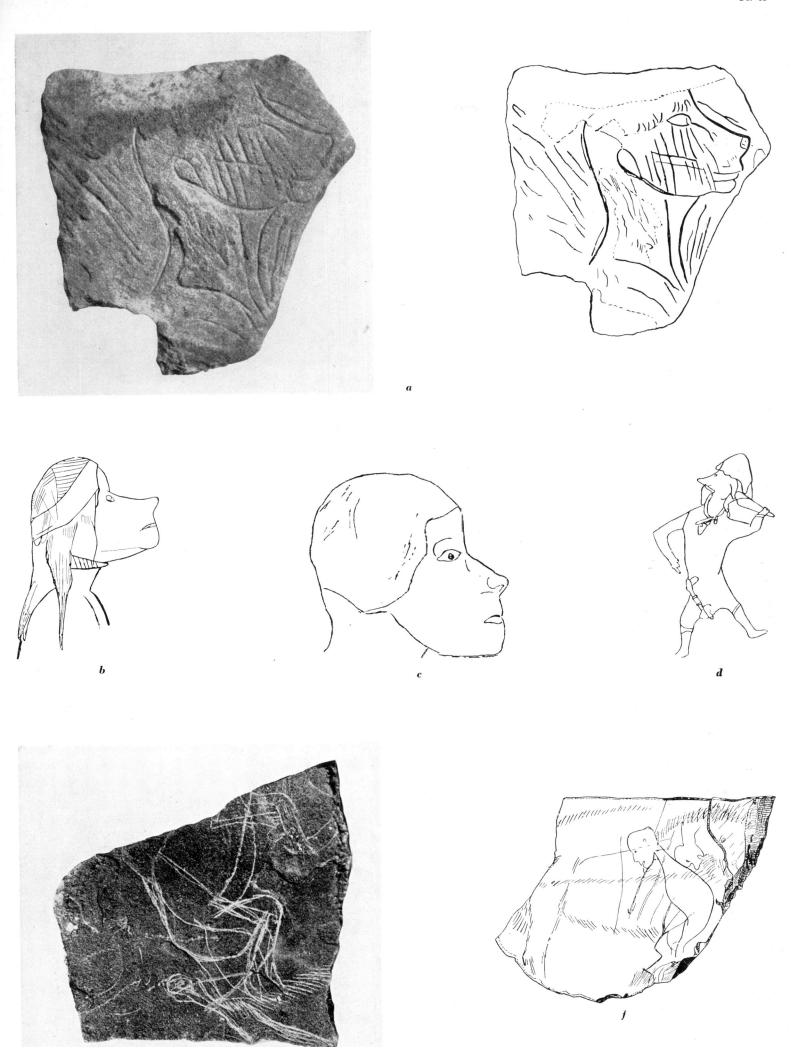

THE HUMAN FORM IN MAGDALENIAN ART: - Engravings on stone; *a*)-*d*) La Marche (*Vienne*), drawings by Lwoff. (*d*, very doubtful), *e*) Les Trois Frères, *f*) Bédeilhac (*Ariège*), drawn by Octobon.

Pl. 84

THE HUMAN FORM IN MAGDALENIAN ART: - Engravings on stone and bone: *a)-d)*, *f)* Isturitz (*Basses-Pyrénées*); *e)* Gourdan (*Haute-Garonne*); *g)* Limeuil (*Dordogne*), drawn by Bouyssonie.

Pl. 85

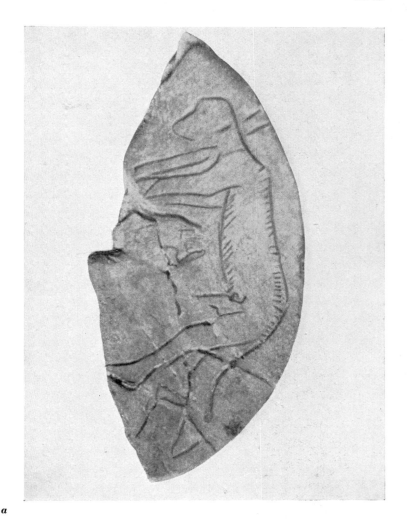

a

c

b

d

e

THE HUMAN FORM IN MAGDALENIAN ART: - Engravings on bone and stone: *a*) Mas d'Azil (*Ariège*); *b*) Lourdes (*Hautes-Pyrénées*); *c*) Laugerie Basse (*Dordogne*), pregnant woman and reindeer; *d*) Mas d'Azil (*Ariège*); *e*) Gourdan (*Haute-Garonne*) (*b, e,* drawn by Breuil).

Pl. 86

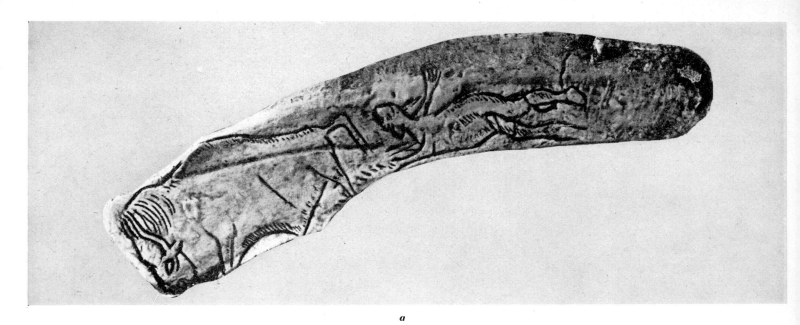

a

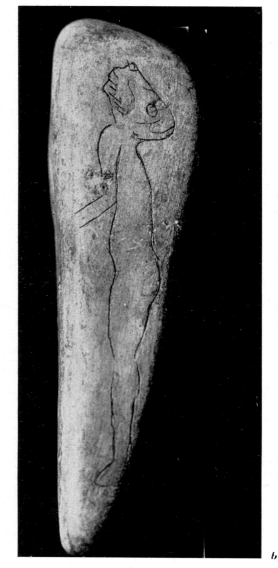

b

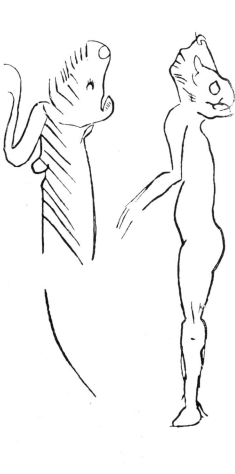

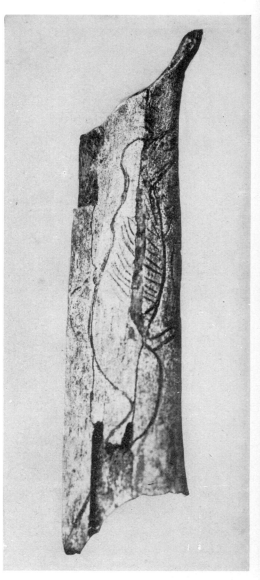

c

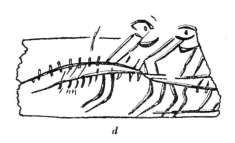

d

e

THE HUMAN FORM IN MAGDALENIAN ART: - Engravings on bone and stone: *a*) Laugerie Basse (*Dordogne*), man pursuing a bison; *b*) La Madeleine (*Dordogne*), woman and man on two sides of pebble; *c*), *d*) La Madeleine (*b*, *d*, drawn by Breuil); *e*) Gourdan (*Haute-Garonne*) (approx. twice enlarged).

Pl. 87

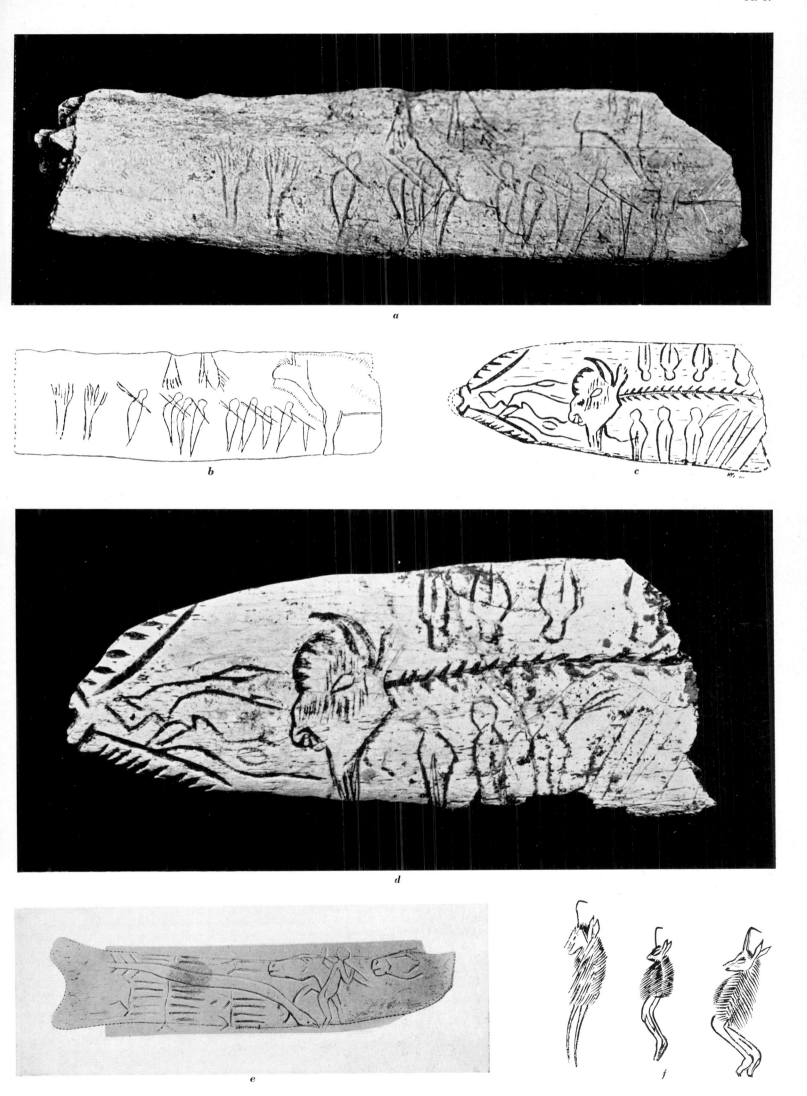

THE HUMAN FORM IN MAGDALENIAN ART: - Human figures and animals in groups of obscure significance engraved on bone: *a*), *b*) Les Eyzies, *c*), *d*) Raymonden, *e*) La Madeleine, *f*) Abri Mège à Teyjat (*Dordogne*) (see Pl. 66, *a*, *b*) (*b, c, f*, drawn by Breuil).

Pl. 88

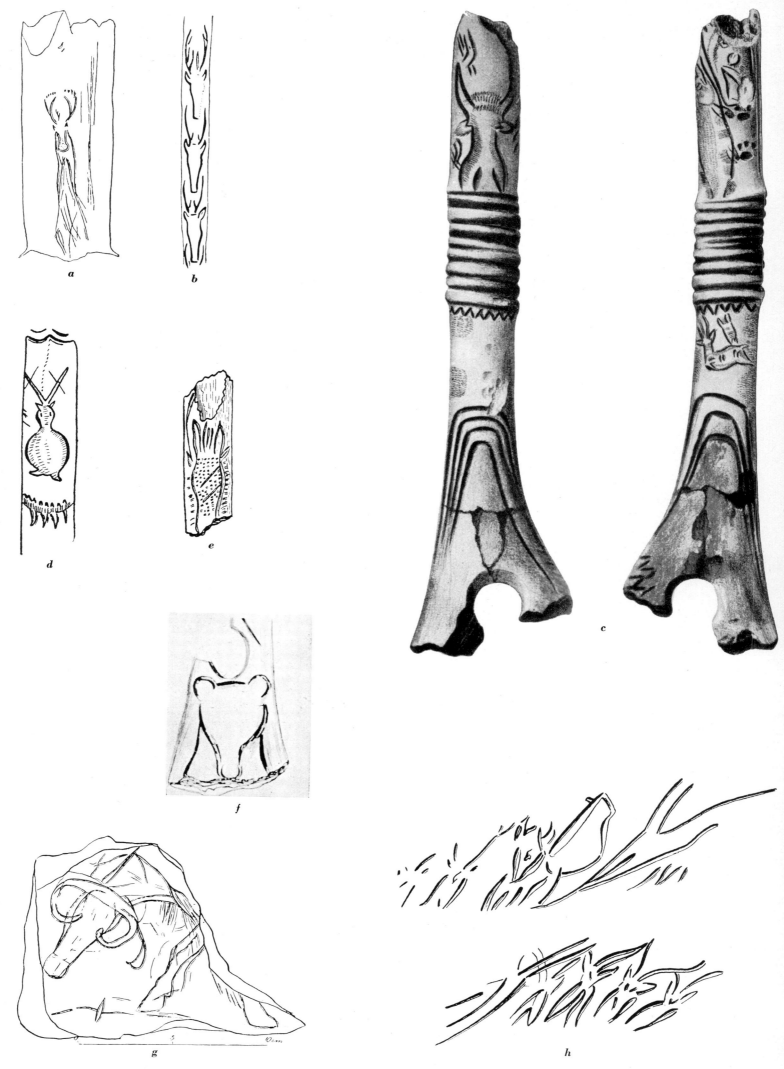

PERSPECTIVE AND COMPOSITION IN MAGDALENIAN ART: - Animals viewed in frontal perspective: *a*), *c*), *e*), *h*) Gourdan (*Haute-Garonne*); *b*) Abri Mège à Teyjat, *d*) Laugerie Basse (*Dordogne*); *f*) Massat (*Ariège*); *g*) Limeuil (*Dordogne*). (Drawings by Breuil (*e*, *b*, *h*) and Bouyssonie, *g*).

Pl. 89

a

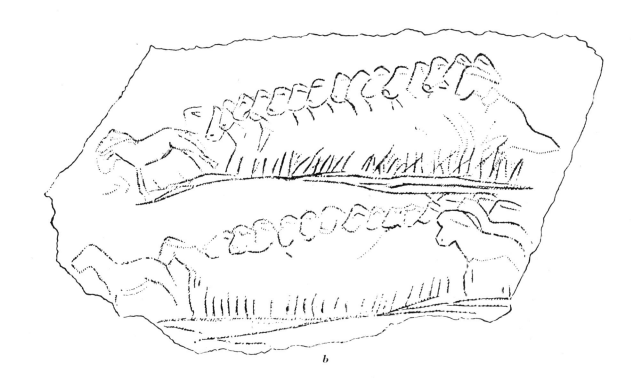

b

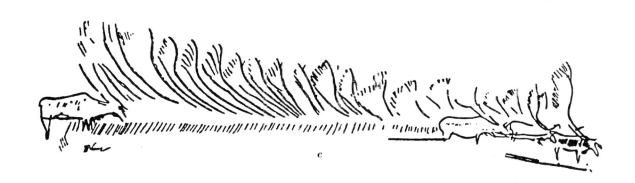

c

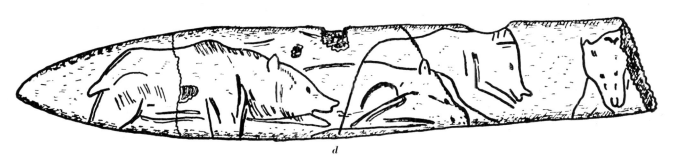

d

PERSPECTIVE AND COMPOSITION IN MAGDALENIAN ART: - *a*) Isturitz (*Basses-Pyrénées*): procession of horses; *b*) Chaffaud (*Vienne*): herds of horses, drawn by Cartailhac; *c*) La Mairie à Teyjat (*Dordogne*): herd of reindeer, drawn by Breuil; *d*) La Vache (*Ariège*): bears, drawn by Robert.

Pl. 90

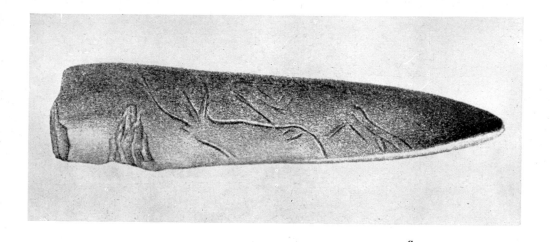

a

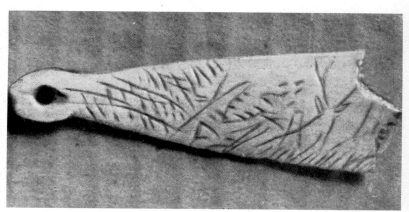

b

c

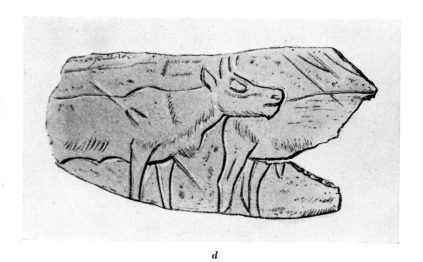

d

e

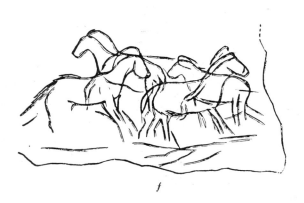

f

g

PERSPECTIVE AND COMPOSITION IN MAGDALENIAN ART: - *a*), *c*) identical subject engraved on bone in Mas d'Azil (*Ariège*), Lorthet (*Hautes-Pyrénées*), El Pendo (*Santander*); *d*) La Madeleine: ruminants; *e*)-*g*) Limeuil (*Dordogne*) herds of horses and deer, drawn by Bouyssonie.

Pl. 91

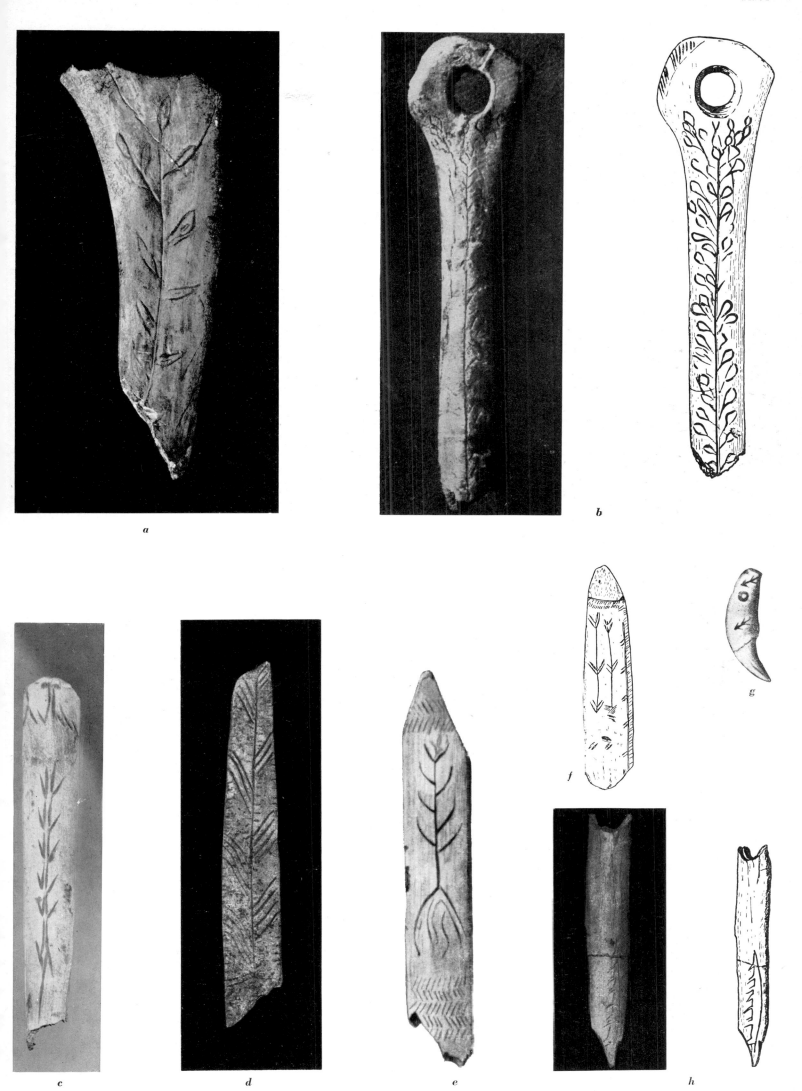

VEGETABLE FORMS AND WEAPONS IN FRANCO-CANTABRIAN ART: - Engravings on bone. Figures of twigs and plants: *a*) Le Trilobite (*Yonne*); *b*) Le Veyrier (*Haute-Savoie*), drawing by Breuil; *c*), *e*) Mas d'Azil (*Ariège*); *d*) Laugerie Basse (*Dordogne*). Engravings of barbed harpoons; *f*) Isturitz (*Basses-Pyrénées*); *g*) Duruthy (*Landes*); *h*) La Vache (*Ariège*), drawn by Robert.

Pl. 92

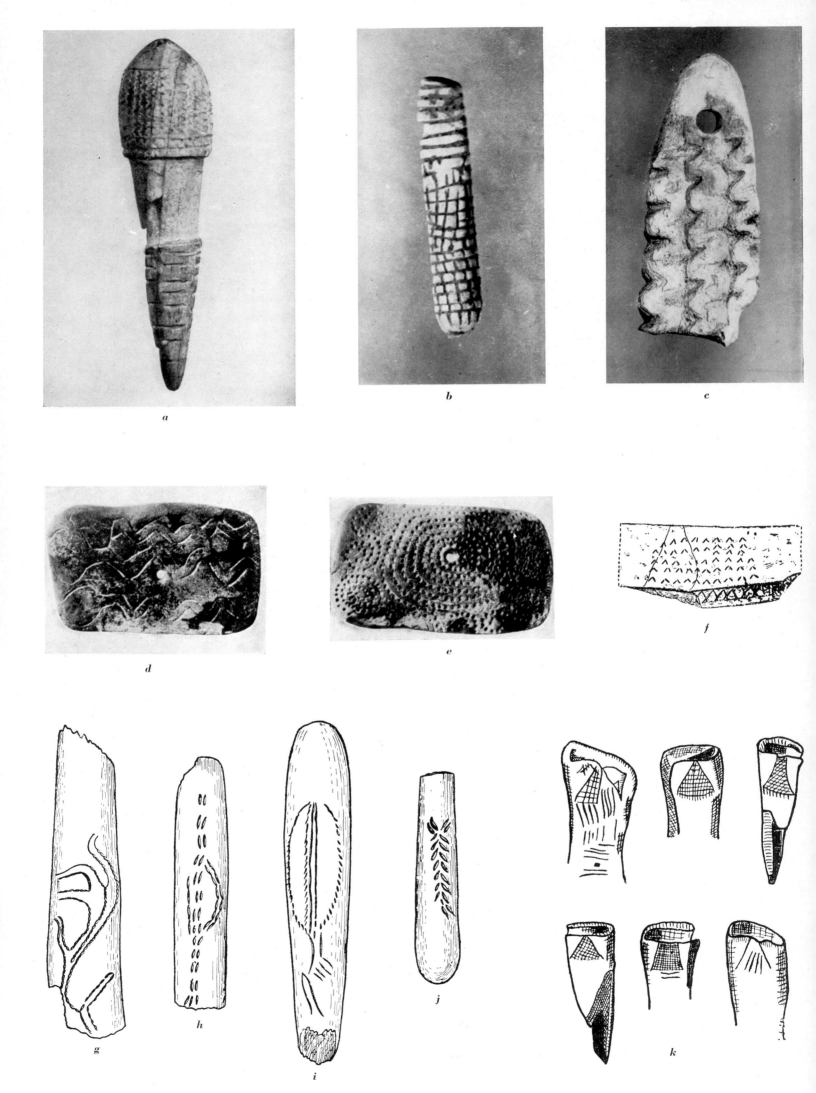

GEOMETRICAL ORNAMENTAL DESIGNS, SCHEMATIZATIONS, ETC., IN FRANCO-CANTABRIAN ART: - Engravings on bone and ivory: *a*), *c*) Brassempouy (*Landes*); *d*), *e*) Maltà (*Siberia*); *f*) Isturitz (*Basses-Pyrénées*), drawn by Rilly; *g*)-*j*) Le Placard (*Charente*), drawn by Breuil; *k*) La Marche (*Vienne*), drawn by Lwoff.

Pl. 93

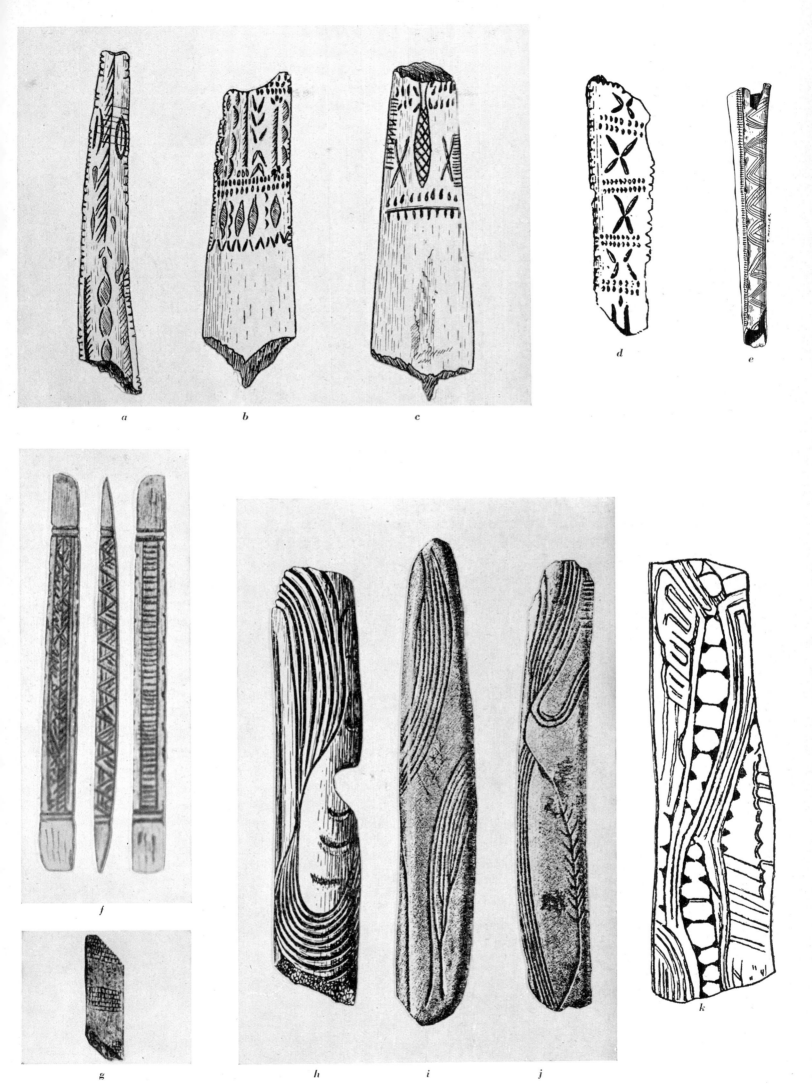

GEOMETRICAL ORNAMENTAL DESIGNS, SCHEMATIZATIONS, ETC., IN FRANCO-CANTABRIAN ART: - Engravings on bone: *a)-d)*, drawn by Breuil, Marsoulas (*Haute-Garonne*); *e*) Le Placard (*Charente*), drawn by Mourier; *f*) Saint Marcel (*Indre*), drawn by Breuil, g) Lespugue (*Haute-Garonne*); *h)-j*) Isturitz (*Basses-Pyrénées*); *k*) Laugerie Basse (*Dordogne*), drawn by Breuil.

Pl. 94

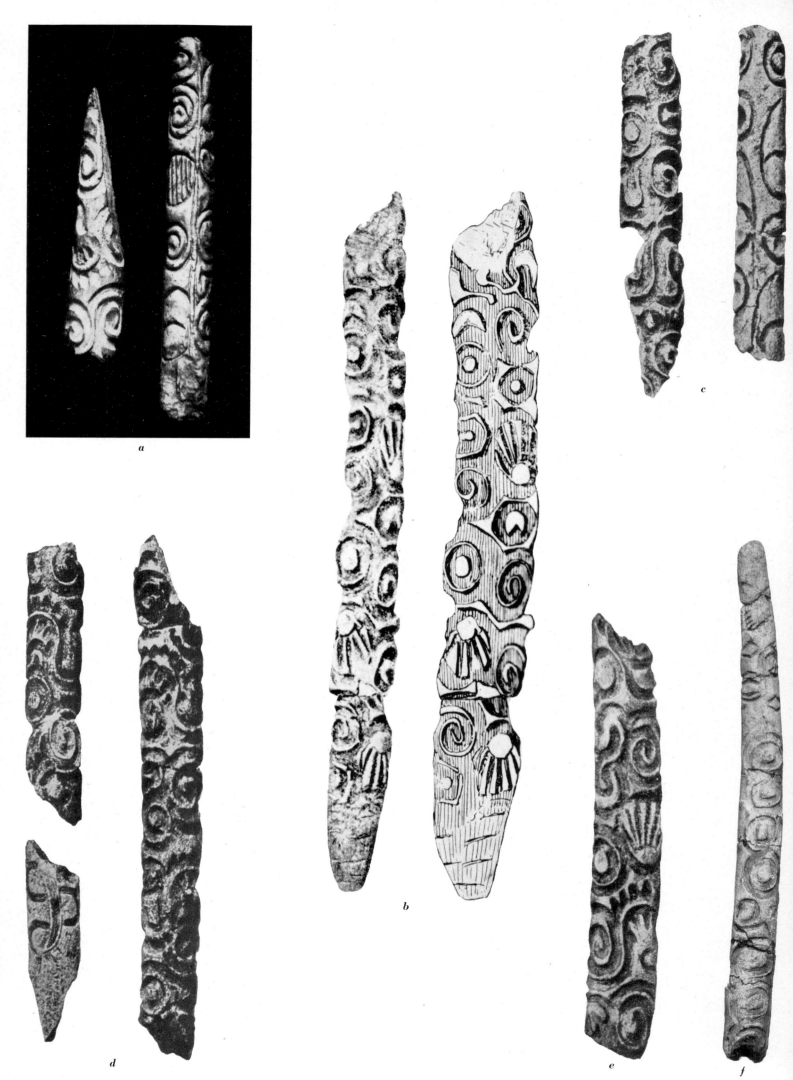

SPIRAL ORNAMENTS ON BONE STAFFS, UPPER MAGDALENIAN: - *a*) Arudy (*Basses-Pyrénées*); *b*)-*e*) Lespugue (*Haute-Garonne*); *f*) Lourdes (*Hautes-Pyrénées*).

Pl. 95

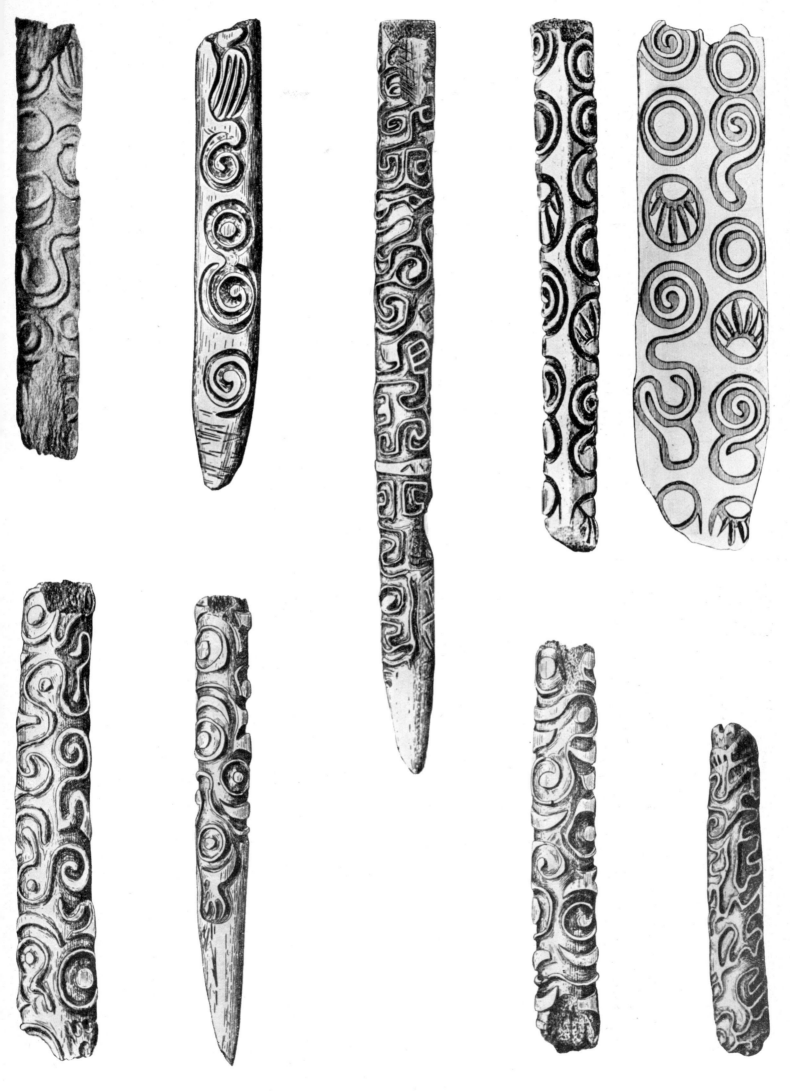

SPIRAL ORNAMENTS ON BONE STAFFS, UPPER MAGDALENIAN: - Isturitz (*Basses-Pyrénées*).

Pl. 96

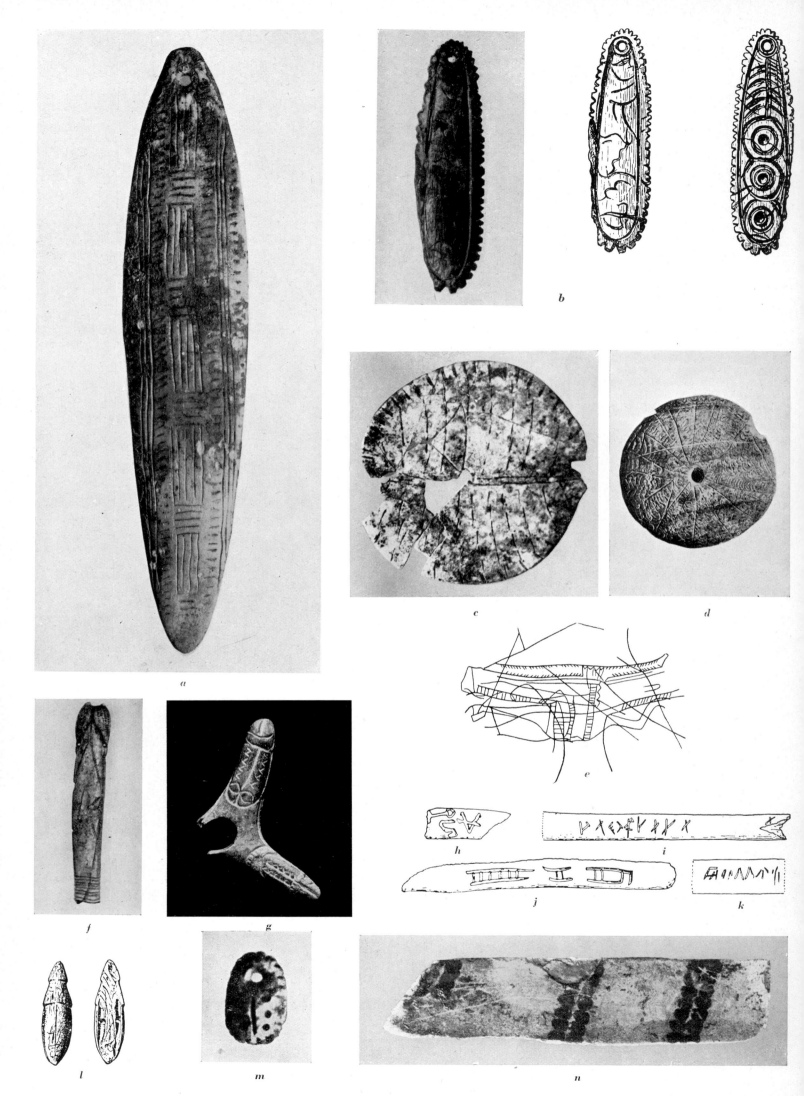

GEOMETRICAL ORNAMENTAL DESIGNS, SCHEMATIC FIGURES, ABSTRACT DESIGNS, ETC., IN MAGDALENIAN ART: - *a*) Lalinde (*Dordogne*); *b*) Saint Marcel (*Indre*), drawings by Breuil; *c*), *f*) Mas d'Azil (*Ariège*); *d*) Petersfels (*Baden*); *e*) Isturitz (*Basses-Pyrénées*), drawing by Passemard; *g*) Gorge d'Enfer (*Dordogne*); *h*) Gourdan (*Haute-Garonne*); *i*) Le Placard (*Charente*); *j*) Lorthet (*Hautes-Pyrénées*); *k*) La Madeleine (*Dordogne*); *l*), *m* stylized coleoptera from Le Trilobite (*Yonne*) and Laugerie Basse (*Dordogne*); *n*) Klause (*Bavaria*).

Pl. 97

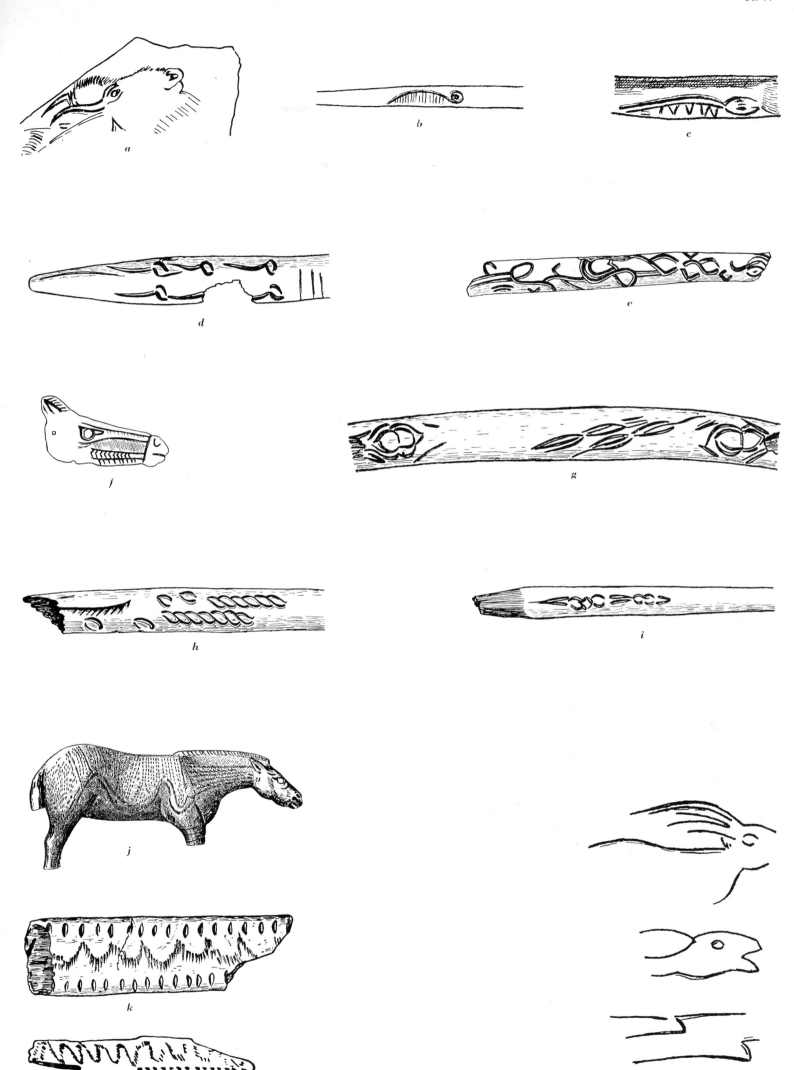

STYLIZATION IN MAGDALENIAN ART: - Derivative ornamental designs (various localities); *a*)-*e*) from the eye and the horn of the bison; *f*)-*i*) from the eye of the reindeer or horse; *j*)-*l*) from the hide of the horse; *m*) stylizations, on the same object, of an ibex head; *c*)-*m*) drawn by Breuil.

Pl. 98

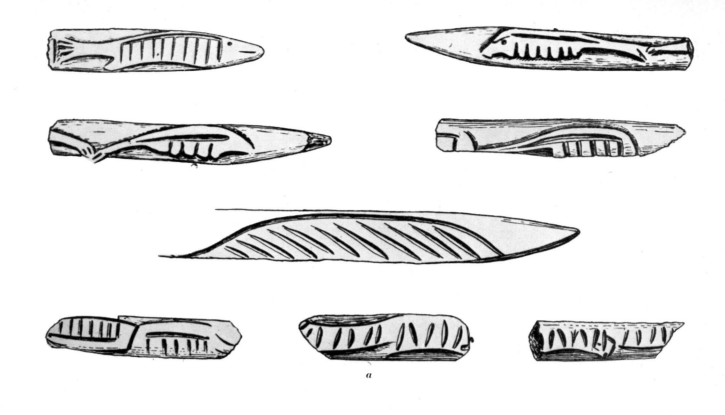

a

b

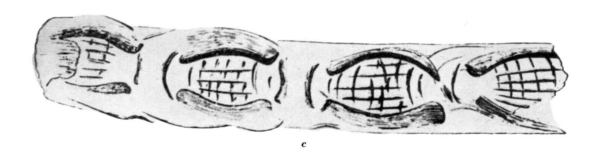

c

d

STYLIZATION IN MAGDALENIAN ART: - Designs derived from fish in: *a*), *c*), *d*) La Madeleine (*Dordogne*), drawings by Breuil; *b*) Lorthet (*Hautes-Pyrénées*).

Pl. 99

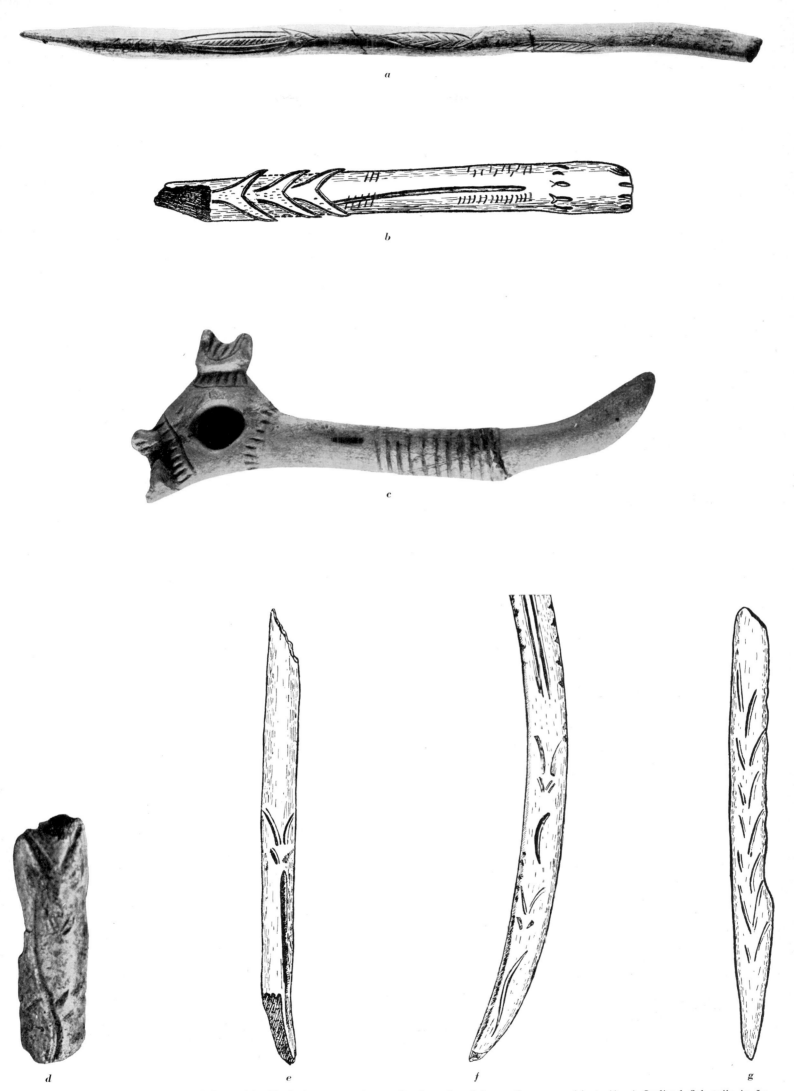

STYLIZATION IN MAGDALENIAN ART: - *a*) Petersfels (*Baden*): progressive stylization of a fish on the same object. *b*), *c*) Stylized fish-tails in La Madeleine and Laugerie Basse (*Dordogne*). *d*) - *g*) El Pendo (*Santander*): progressive stylization of an ibex; (drawings by Breuil (*b*) and Carballo and Larin (*e* - *g*).

Pl. 100

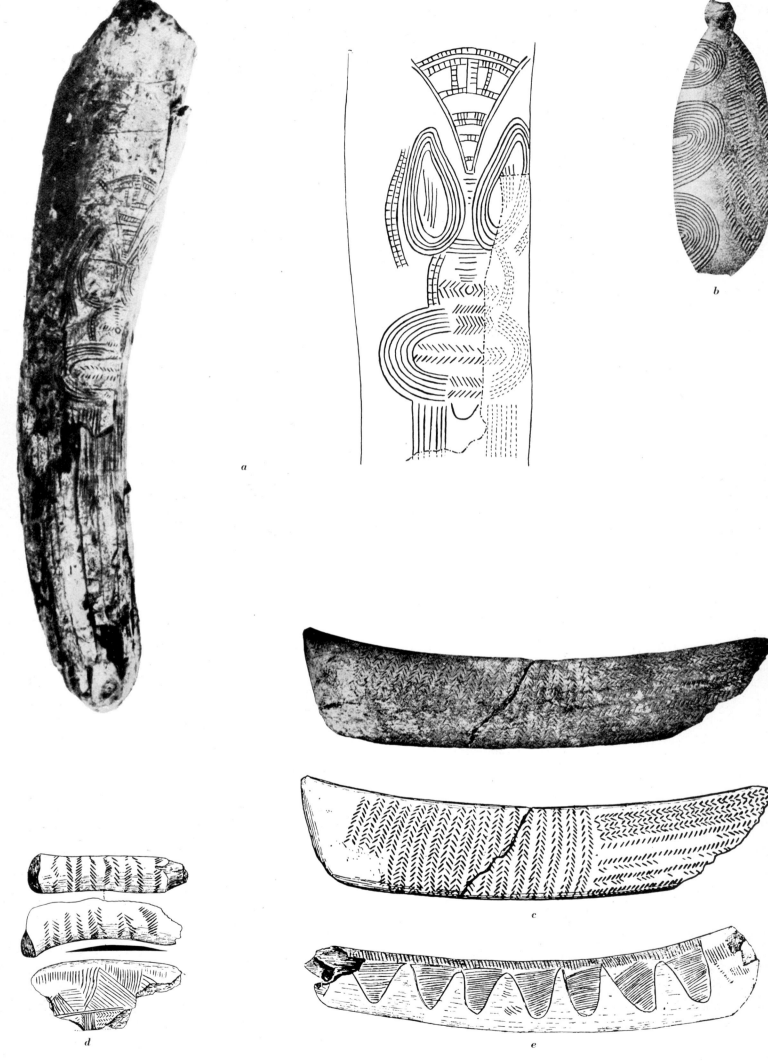

SCHEMATIC ART IN EASTERN EUROPE: - Predmosti (*Moravia*): *a*) stylized woman; *b*) - *e*) geometrical designs, drawings by Breuil.

Pl. 101

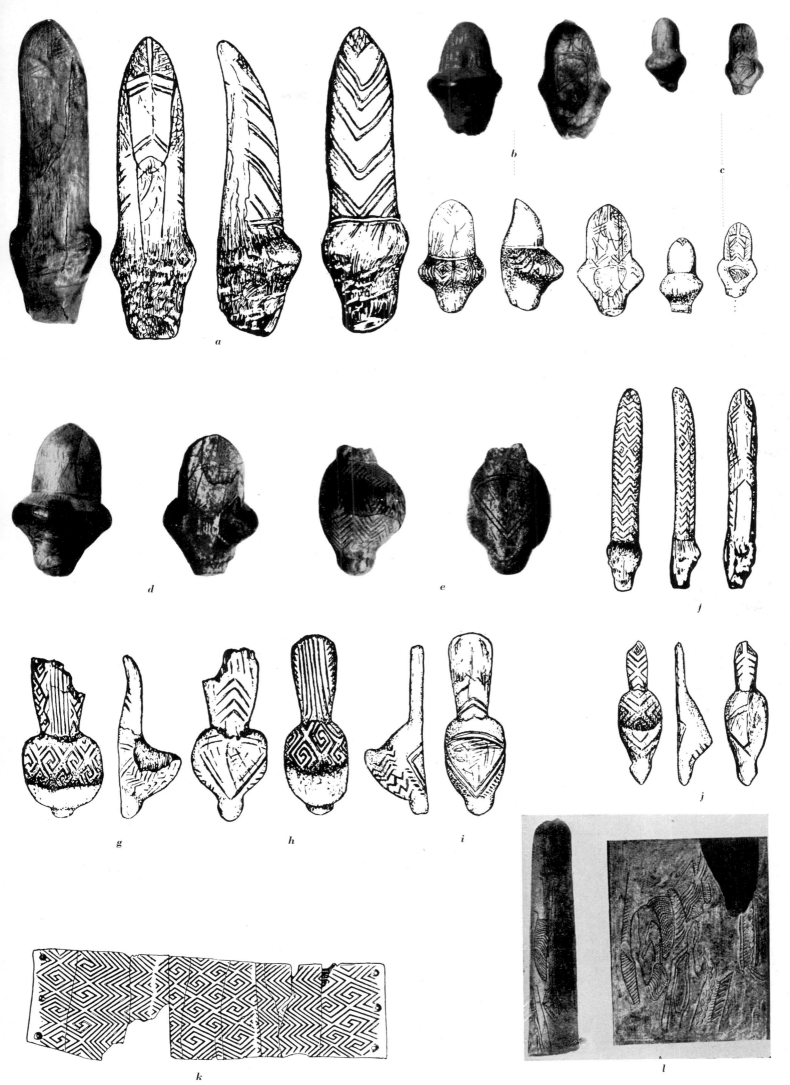

SCHEMATIC ART IN EASTERN EUROPE: - a) - k) Mésine (Ukraine): anthropomorphic ivory carvings and geometrical designs: l) Kiev (Ukraine): undecipherable signs.

THE MEDITERRANEAN PROVINCE

Pl. 102

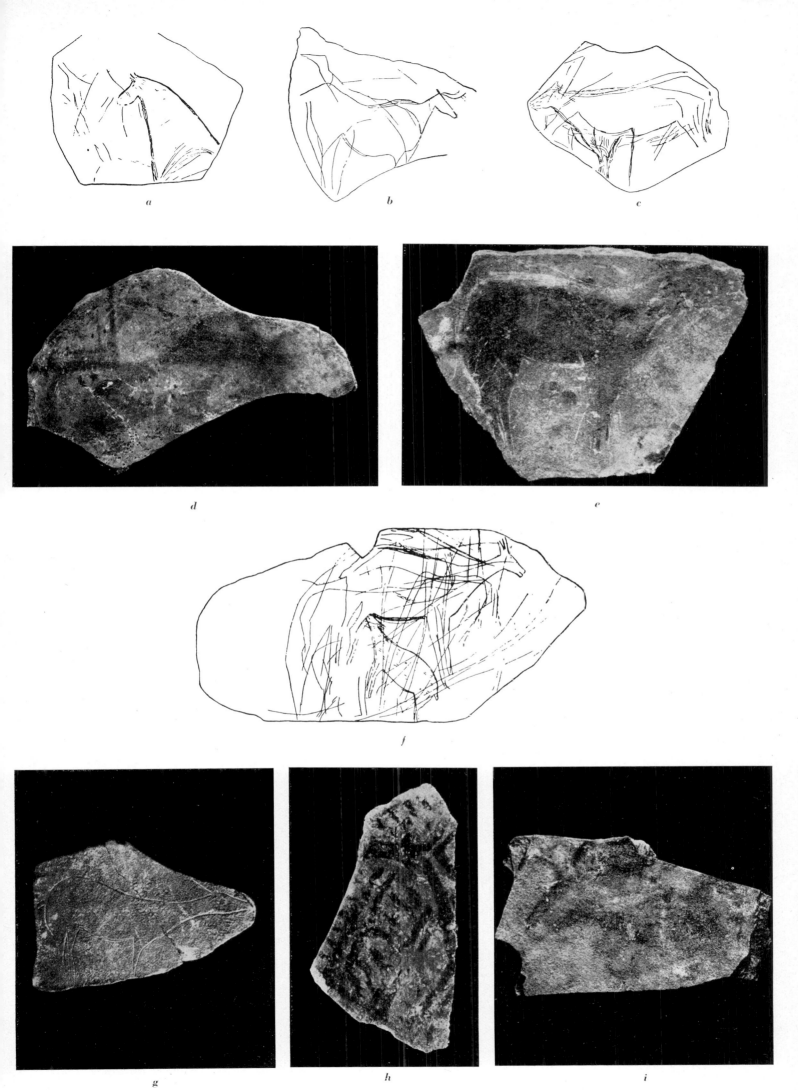

Parpalló (*Valencia*), animals engraved and painted on stone; *a*), *b*) from Upper Aurignacian layers; *c*)-*i*) from Solutrean layers, drawings by Pericot.

Pl. 103

Parpalló (*Valencia*), engravings and paintings on stone; *a*)-*f*) from Solutrean layers; *g*), *h*) from undetermined layers, drawings by Pericot.

Pl. 104

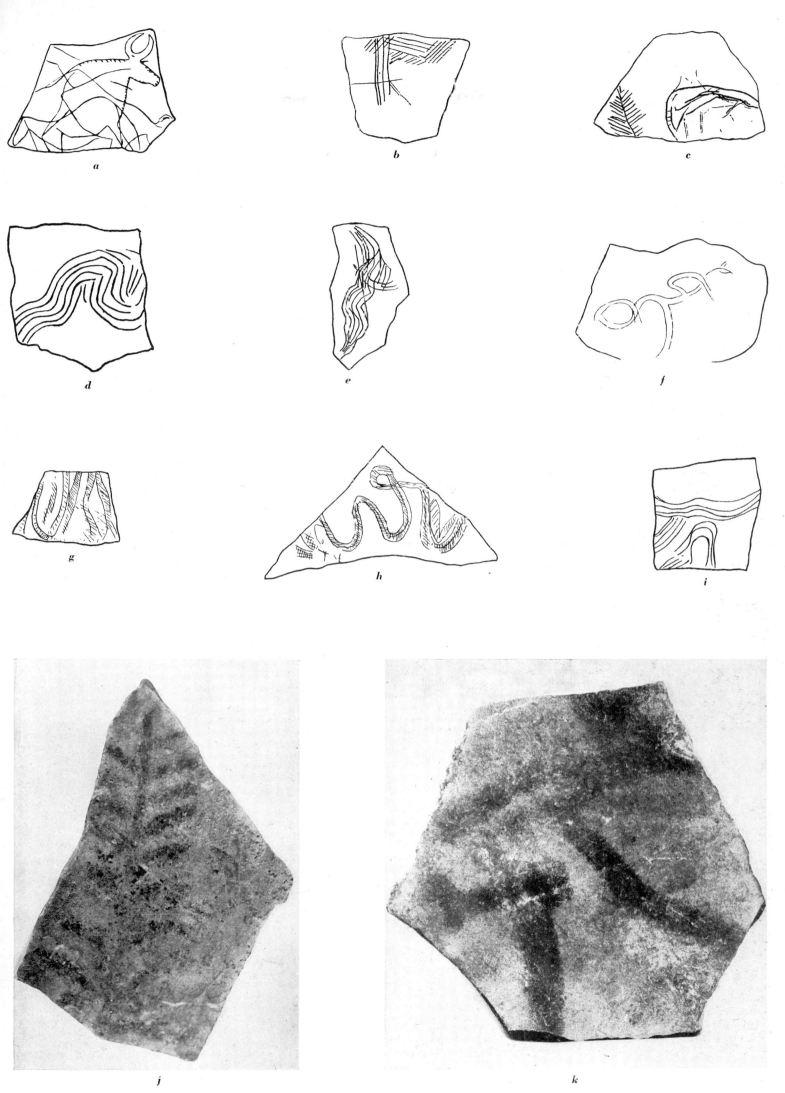

Parpalló (*Valencia*), Magdalenian engravings and paintings on stone, drawings by Pericot.

Pl. 105

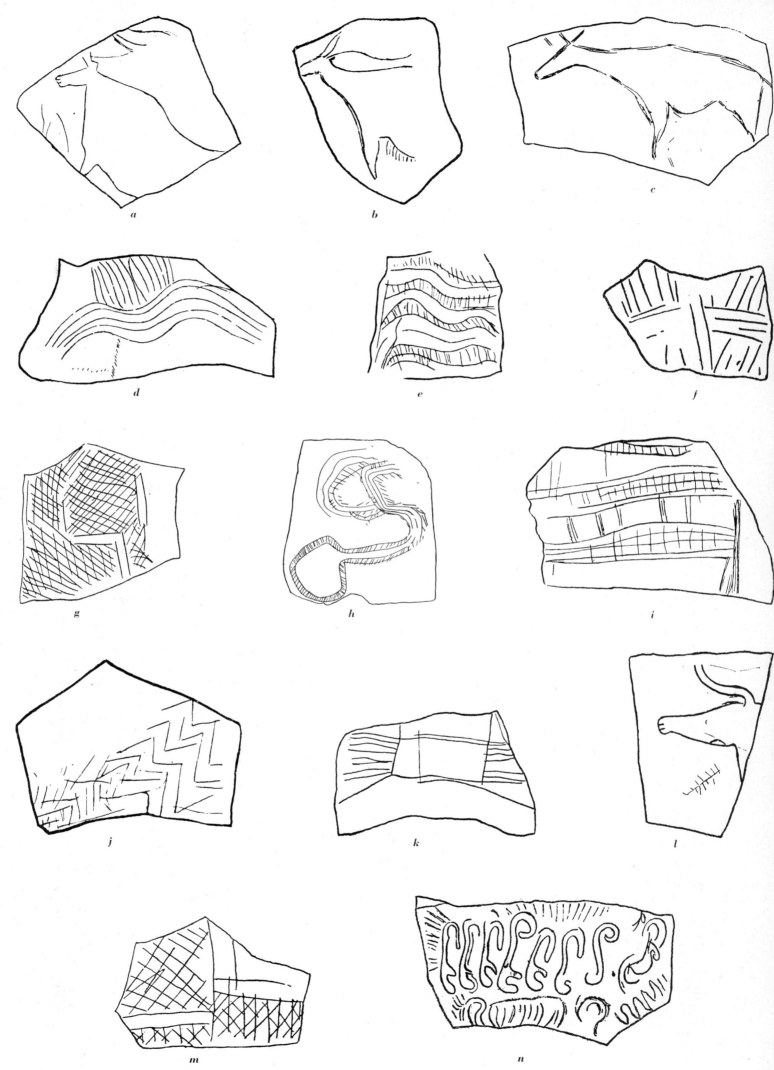

Parpalló (*Valencia*), engravings on stone; *a*)-*j*) from Magdalenian layers; *k*)-*n*) from undetermined layers, drawings by Pericot.

Pl. 106

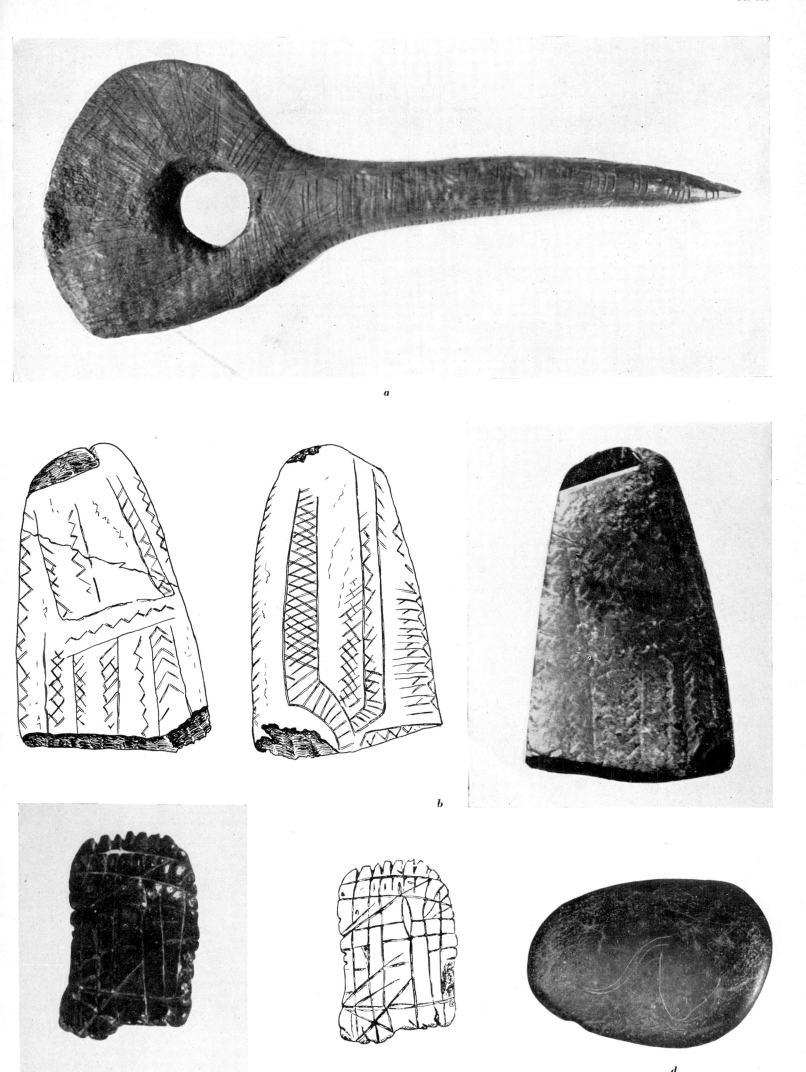

Geometrical designs engraved on stag-horn, pebbles and bone: *a*) Arene Candide (*Firale Ligure*); *b*), *c*) Barma Grande (*Grimaldi*); *d*) Grotta Mura di Monopoli (*Apulia*): ox head engraved on a pebble.

Pl. 107

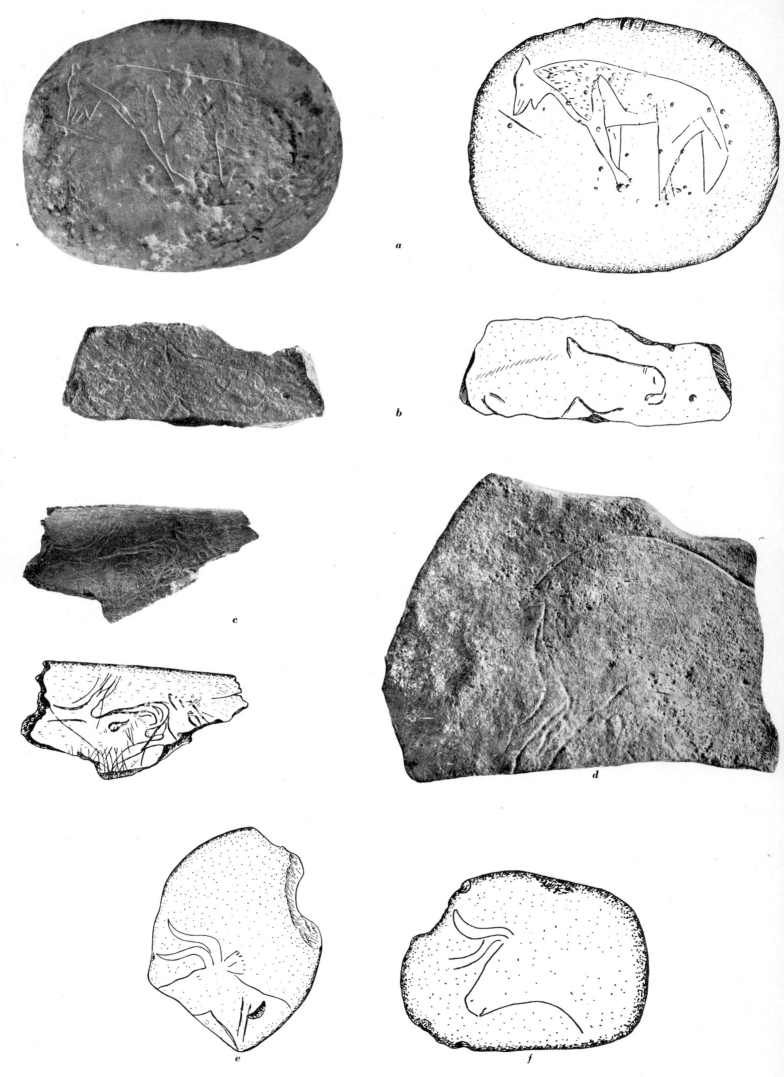

Polesini (*Tivoli*): engravings on stone and on bone (*c*) representing a carnivore, a horse, deer and oxen, drawings by Micheli.

Pl. 108

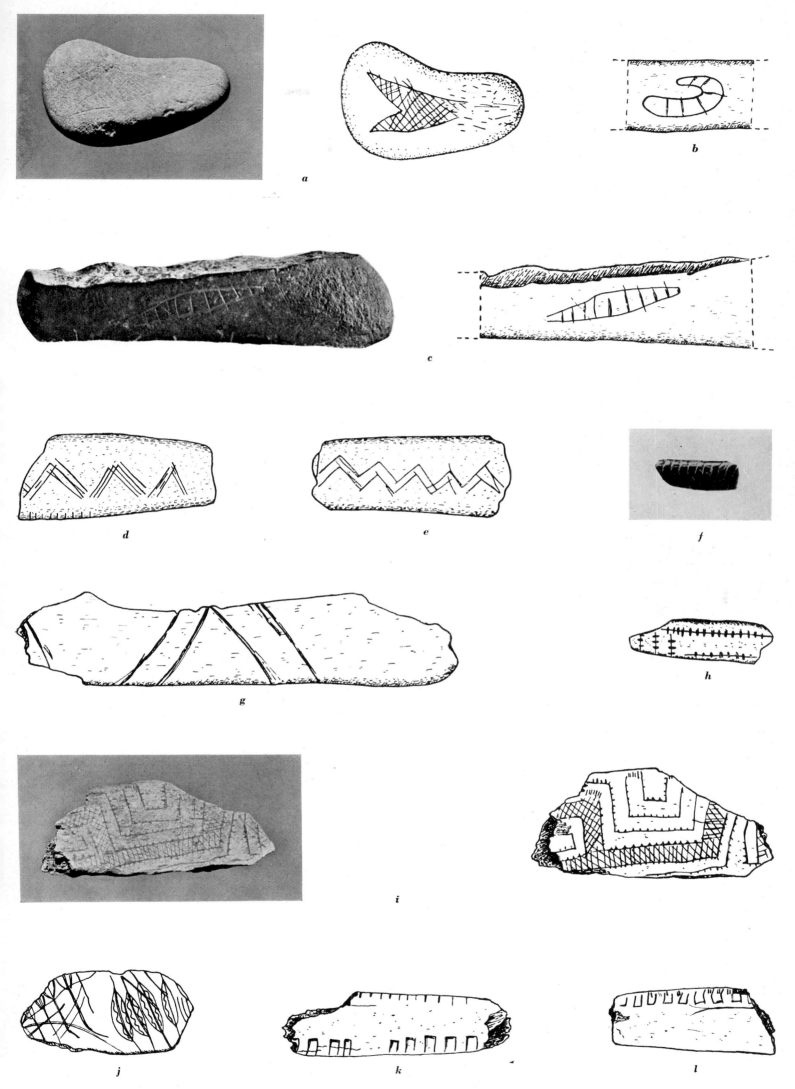

Polesini (*Tivoli*): geometrical designs engraved on stone and on bone, drawings by Micheli.

Pl. 109

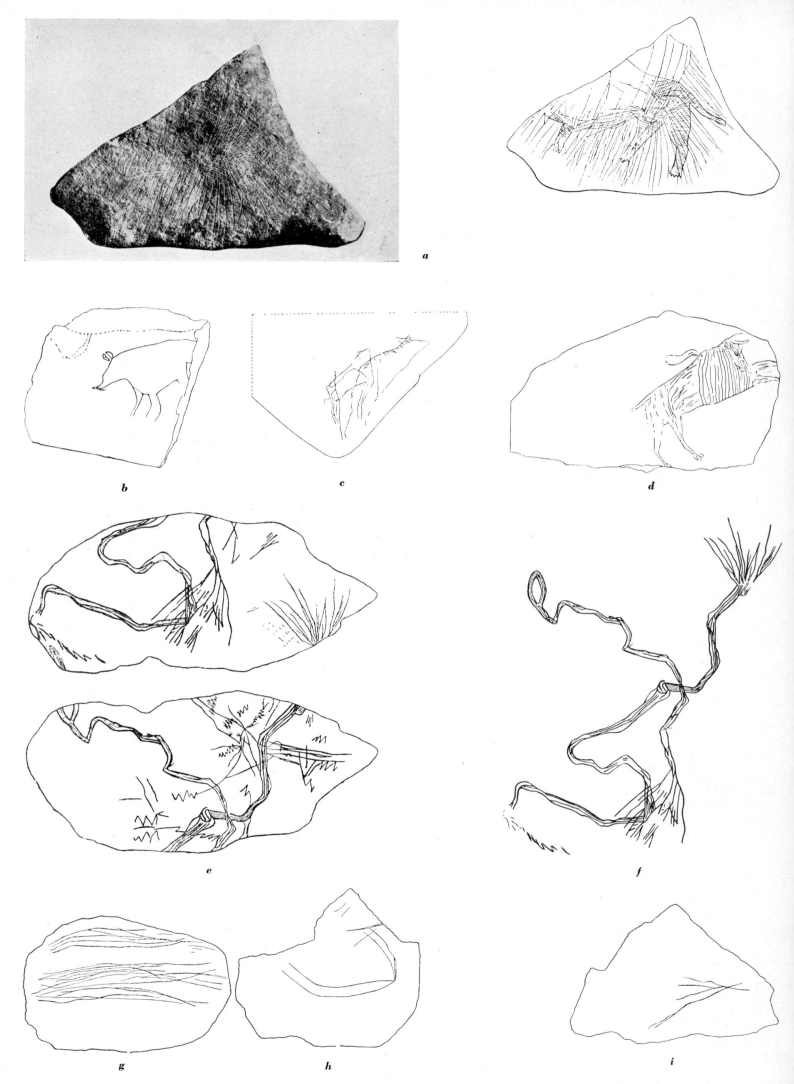

Romanelli (*Otranto*): animal figures and abstract designs engraved on stone (*f* = development of the figures on both sides of the pebble shown in *e*); drawing by Blanc (*a - c*), Di Pasquale (*d*) and Cardini (*e - i*).

Pl. 110

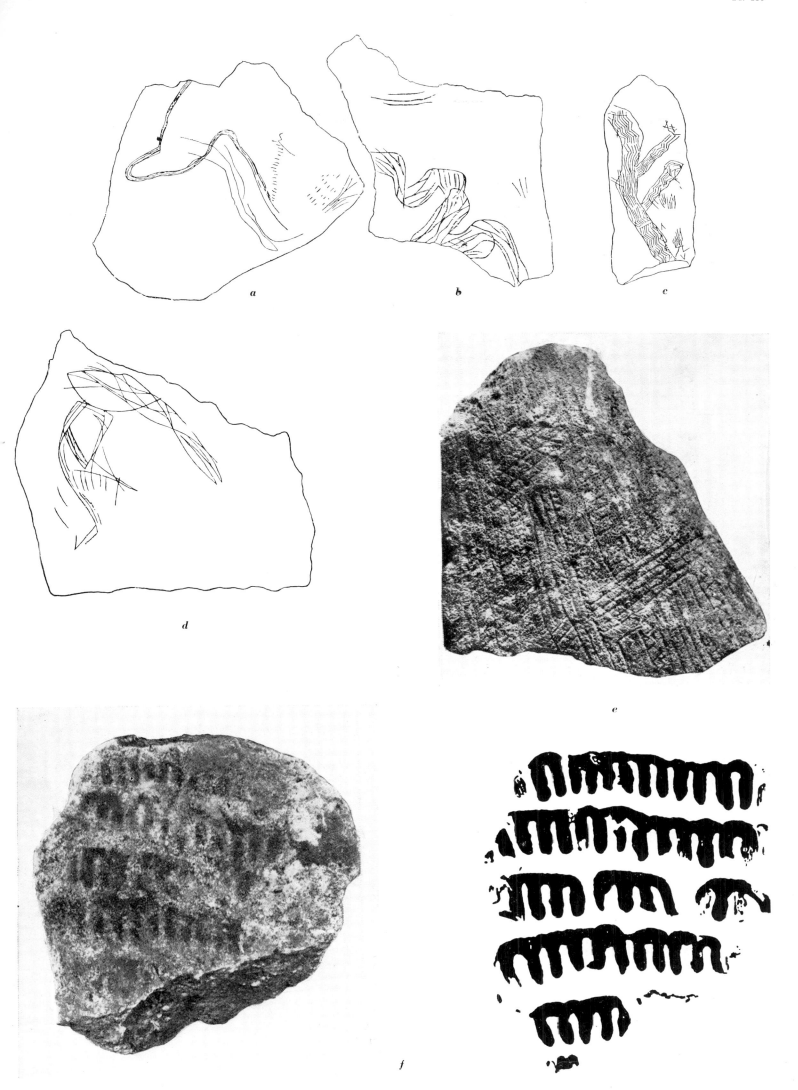

Romanelli (*Otranto*): various engraved designs (*a - e*) and «pectiforms» painted on stone (*f*), drawings by Cardini (*a - d*), and Blanc (*f*).

Pl. 111

Levanzo (*Egadi*): ox engraved on stone, drawing by Micheli.

CAVE ART

Pl. 112

a

b

c

Footprints of Palaeolithic man on clay in caves: *a*) Niaux (*Ariege*), *b*) Pech-Merle (*Lot*), *c*) Aldène (*Hérault*).

Pl. 113

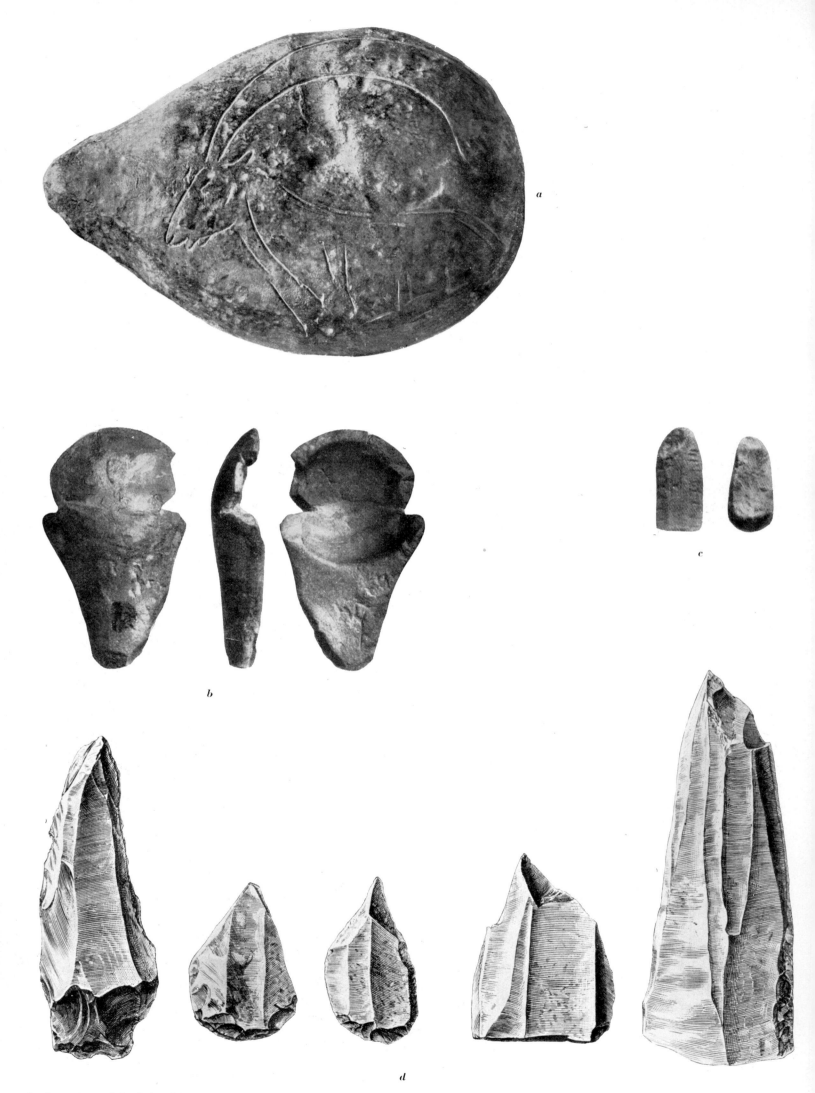

Implements used by Palaeolithic man in the execution of figures in caves: *a*), *b*) stone lamps of La Mouthe (*Dordogne*) and Lespugue (*Haute-Garonne*); *c*) ochre crayons found in Abri Blanchard (*Dordogne*); *d*) gravers probably used to carve the rock in Le Roc (*Charente*).

Pl. 114

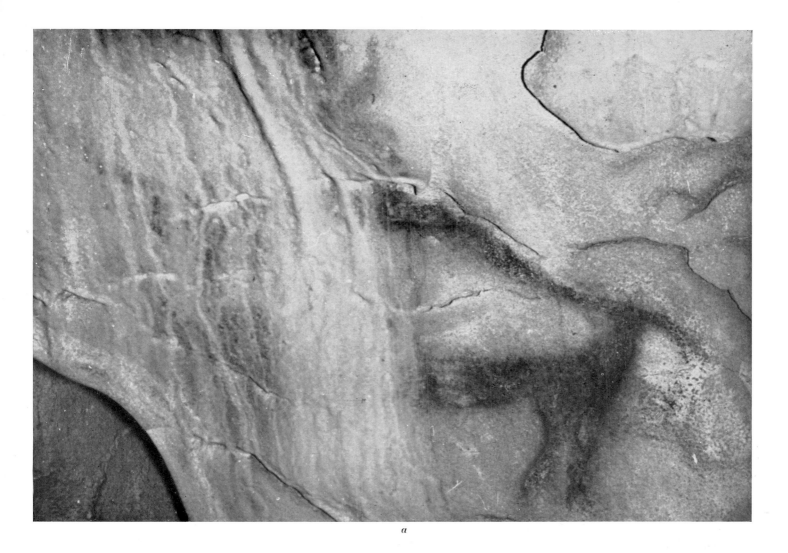

a

b

PROOF OF AUTHENTICITY OF CAVE FIGURES: - Painting and engraving in the Portel Cave (*Ariège*) and in Levanzo (*Egadi*), covered by stalagmitic concretions.

THE FRANCO-CANTABRIAN PROVINCE

Pl. 115

a

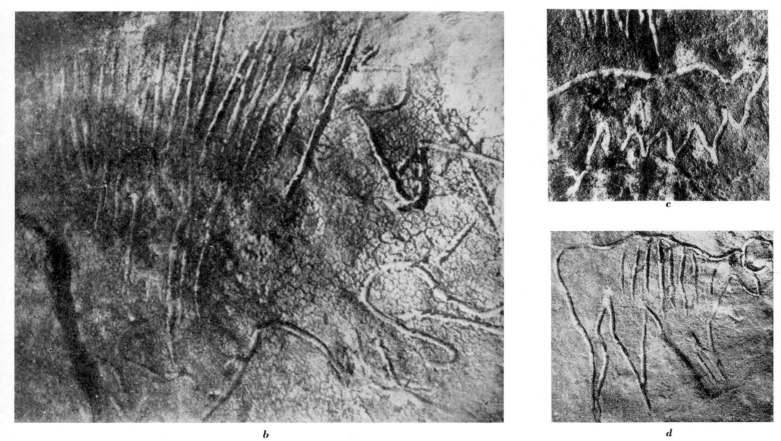

b　　　　　　　　　　　　　*d*

ENGRAVINGS ON CLAY: - *a*) Meanders of Altamira (*Santander*); *b*), *c*), *d*) animals, La Clotilde de Santa Isabel (*Santander*).

Pl. 116

a

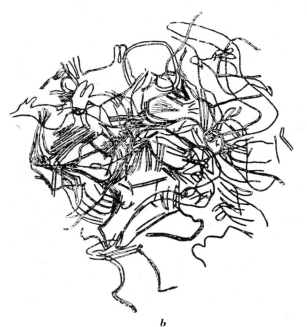

b

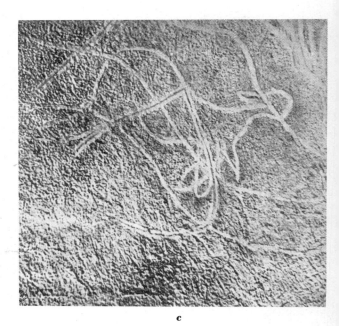

c

ENGRAVINGS ON CLAY: - Pech-Merle (*Lot*): mammoth head and female figures; drawing by Lemozi.

Pl. 117

a

b

c

ENGRAVINGS ON CLAY: - *a*) elk (*cervus megaceros*), Pech-Merle (*Lot*), drawing by Lemozi; *b*) horse, Gargas (*Hautes-Pyrénées*); *c*) young deer, Niaux (*Ariège*).

Pl. 118

ENGRAVINGS ON ROCK: - *a*), *b*) Vulviform figures in La Ferrassie and Abri Blanchard (*Dordogne*); *c*), *d*) animals and various signs, La Ferrassie; *e*) ibex, Belcayre (*Dordogne*); engravings on blocks from Aurignacian layers.

Pl. 119

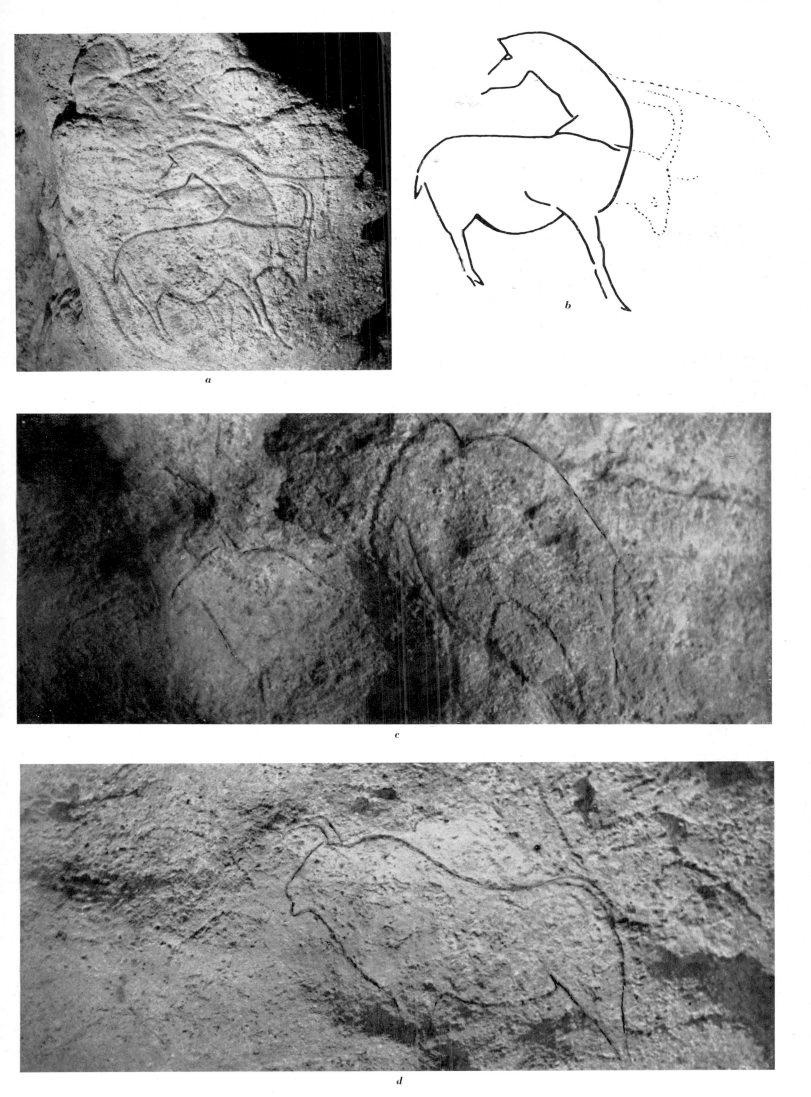

ENGRAVINGS ON ROCK: - Pair-non-Pair (*Gironde*): ibex, horse, mammoth, ox. They were covered by Perigordian layers. *b*) Early interpretation of the so-called « Agnus-Dei »; *a*) David and Malvesin-Fabre's new interpretation of same.

Pl. 120

a

b

ENGRAVINGS ON ROCK: - Pair-non-Pair (*Gironde*): horses and ibexes.

Pl. 121

<small>ENGRAVINGS ON ROCK:</small> - Bison in the small cave of La Grèze (*Dordogne*).

Pl. 122

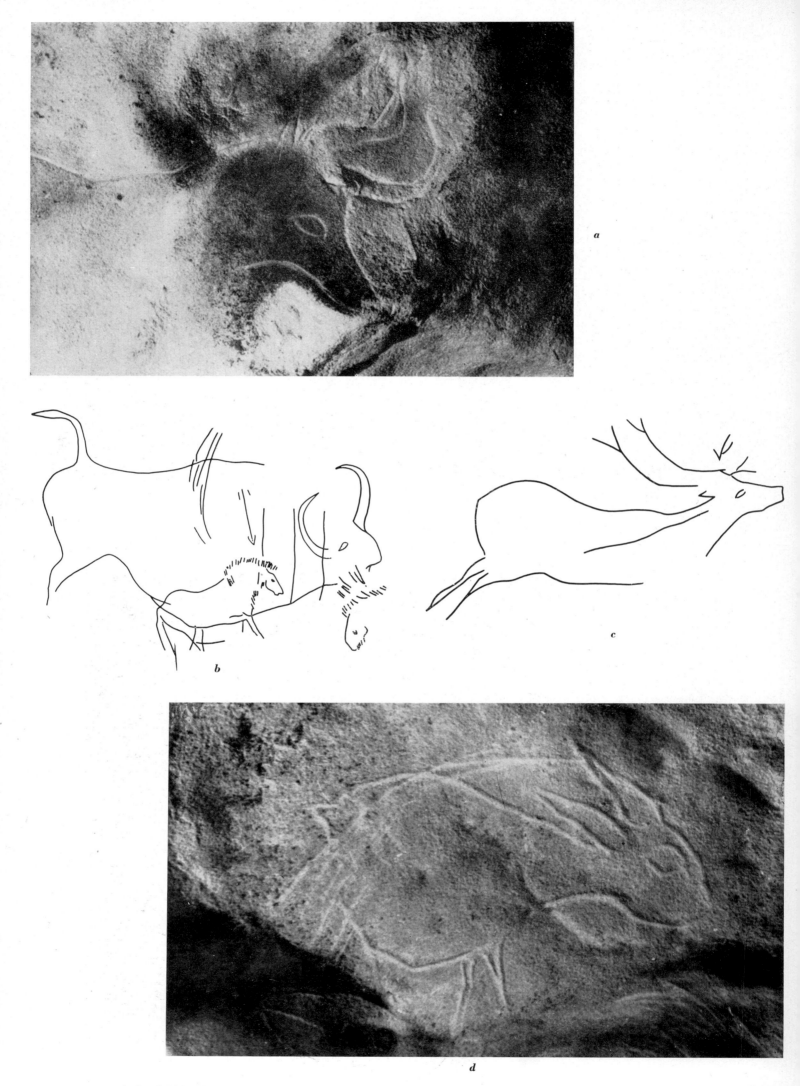

ENGRAVINGS ON ROCK: - Le Gabillou (*Dordogne*): *a*) head of an ox; *b*) bison with horns seen in frontal perspective; *c*) reindeer, drawings by Isola; *d*) hare.

Pl. 123

a

b

ENGRAVINGS ON ROCK: - La Mouthe (*Dordogne*): bison, with horns seen in frontal perspective, and ox.

Pl. 124

ENGRAVINGS ON ROCK: - La Mouthe (*Dordogne*): galloping bull, partially painted.

Pl. 125

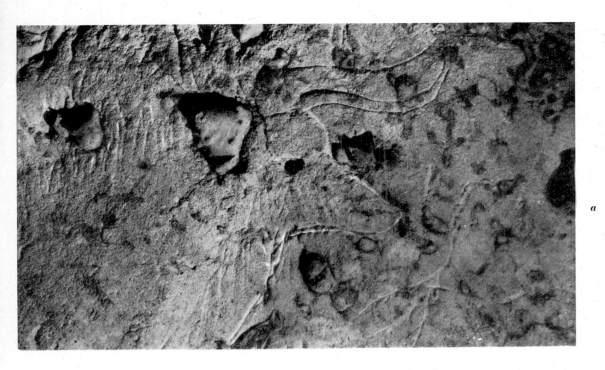

ENGRAVINGS ON ROCK: - Barabao near Le Bugue (*Dordogne*): ox, horse, feline animal.

Pl. 126

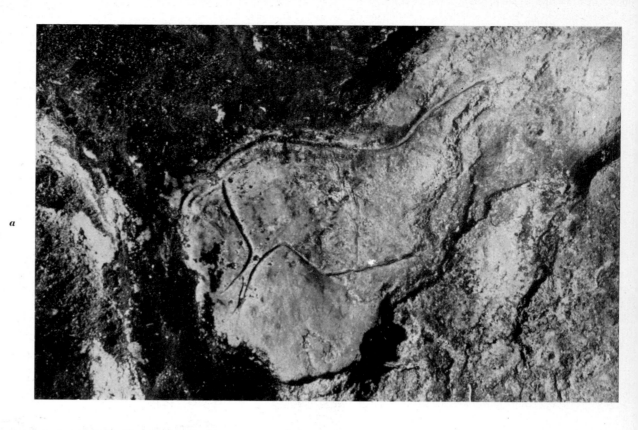

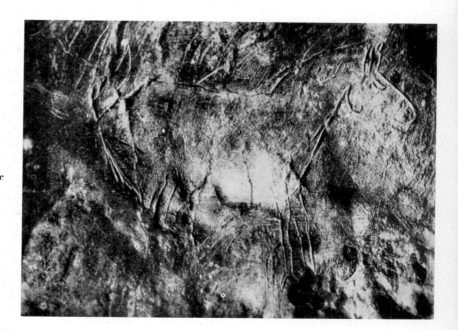

ENGRAVINGS ON ROCK: - Hornos de la Peña (*Santander*), engraved horses: *a*) near the entrance, *b*), *c*) inside the cave.

Pl. 127

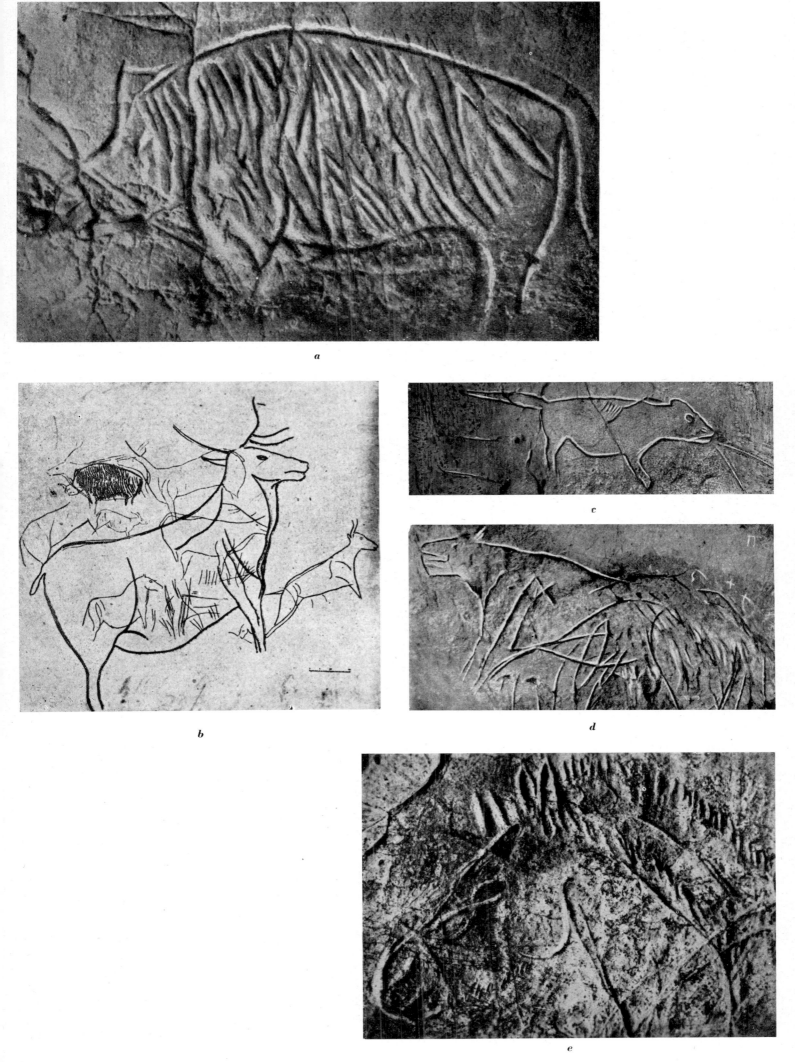

ENGRAVINGS ON ROCK: - Los Casares (*Guadalajara*): *a*) rhinoceros; *b*) deer and other animals, according to Cabré's tracing; *c*) wolverine; *d*) feline animal; *e*) horse.

Pl. 128

a

b

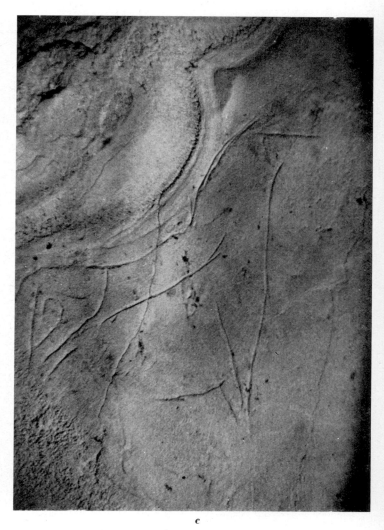

c

ENGRAVINGS ON ROCK: - Castillo (*Santander*): *a*) deer; *b*) ibex; *c*) horse.

Pl. 129

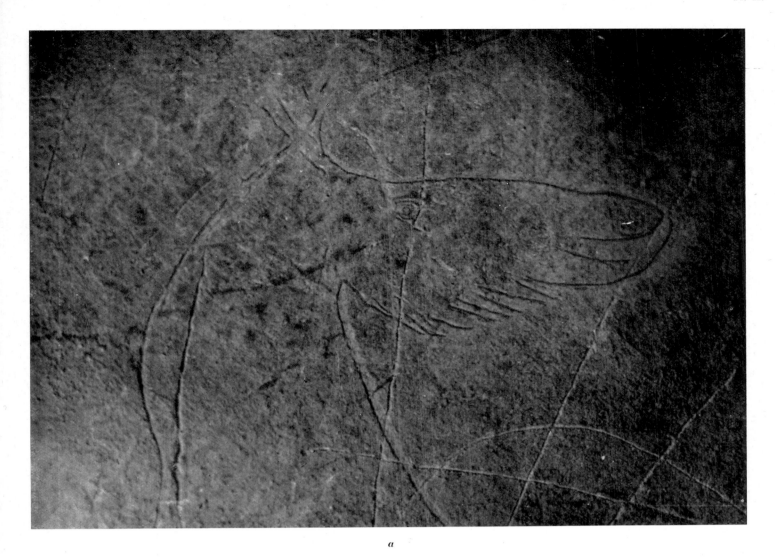

a

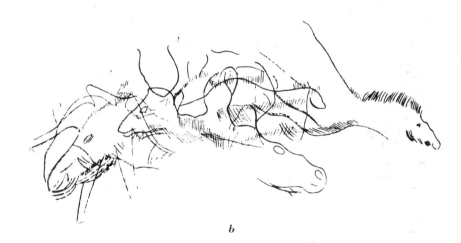

b

c

ENGRAVINGS ON ROCK: - Gargas (*Hautes-Pyrénées*): *a*) horse; *b*), *c*) various animal figures, drawings by Breuil.

Pl. 130

a

b

c

ENGRAVINGS ON ROCK: - Laugerie Haute (*Dordogne*): oxen engraved on blocks from Magdalenian III layers.

Pl. 131

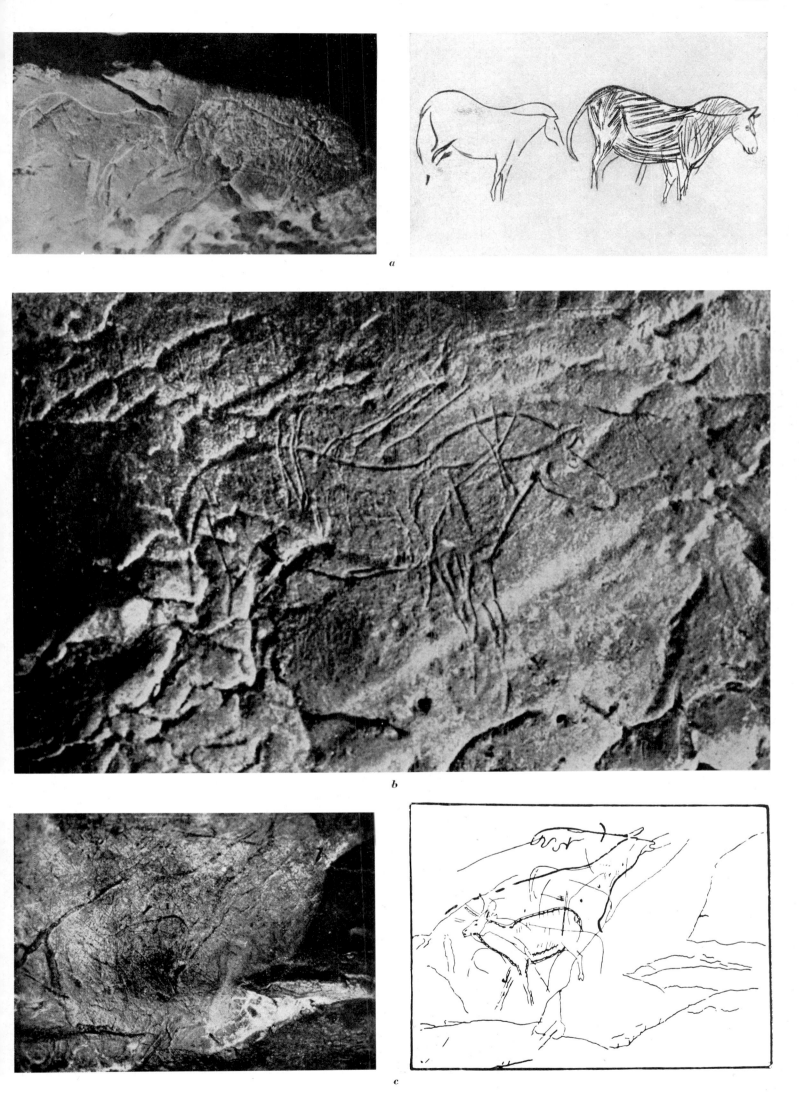

ENGRAVINGS ON ROCK: - El Buxu (*Oviedo*): *a*), *b*) horses; *c*) deer, engraved and painted, drawings by Benitez.

Pl. 132

a

b

ENGRAVINGS ON ROCK: - Lascaux (*Dordogne*): deer and horse's head.

Pl. 133

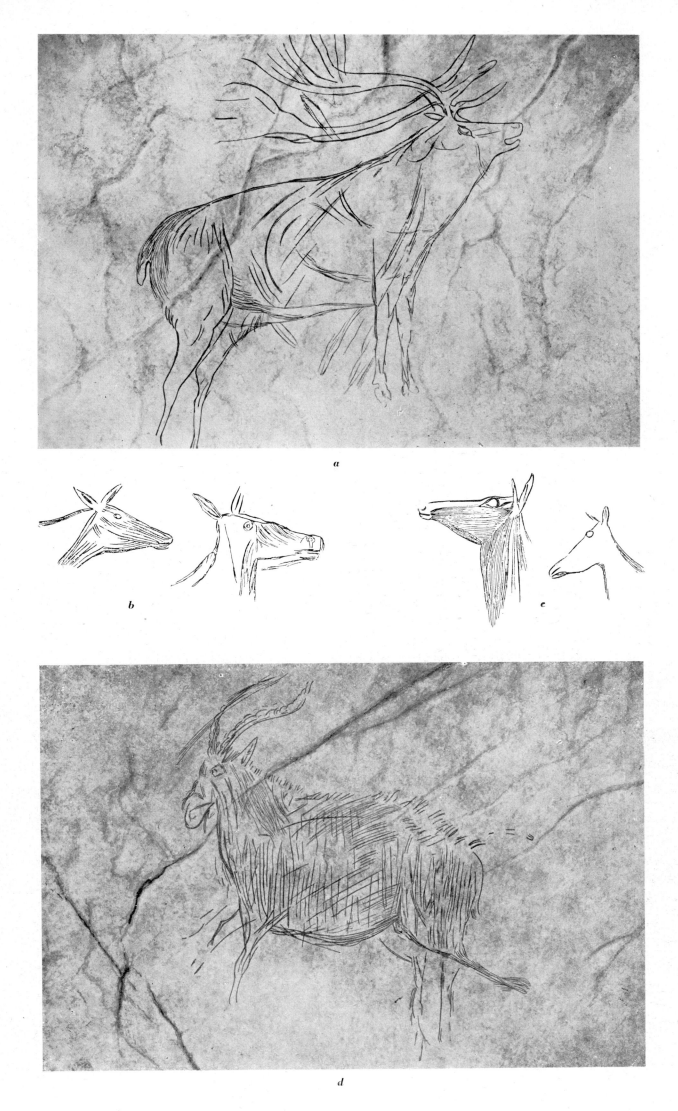

a

b

c

d

ENGRAVINGS ON ROCK: - *a*), *b*) engraved deer, Altamira (*Santander*); *c*), *d*) deer and ibex, Castillo (*Santander*). Drawings by Breuil (*b, c*) and Benitez (*a, d*).

Pl. 134

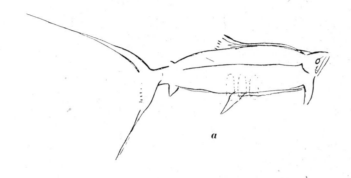

a

b

ENGRAVINGS ON ROCK: - Pindal (*Oviedo*): fish and horse, lightly engraved, (*a* drawn by Breuil, *b* by Benitez).

Pl. 135

a

b

ENGRAVINGS ON ROCK: - La Peña de Candamo (*Oviedo*): wounded deer and bison, according to Cabré's tracings.

Pl. 136

a

b

ENGRAVINGS ON ROCK: - La Peña de Candamo (*Oviedo*): bulls, according to Cabre's tracings.

Pl. 137

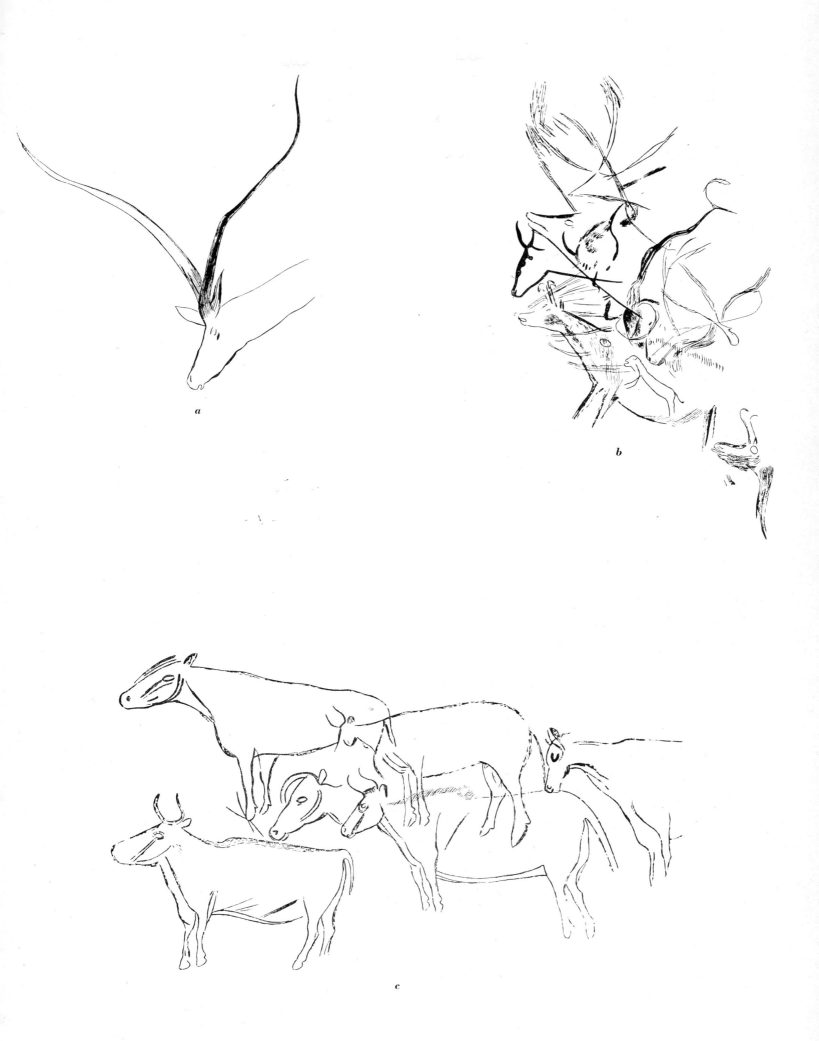

ENGRAVINGS ON ROCK: - a), b) La Peña de Candamo (*Oviedo*): lightly engraved animals, according to Cabré's tracing; c) La Loja (*Oviedo*): oxen, according to Breuil's tracing.

Pl. 138

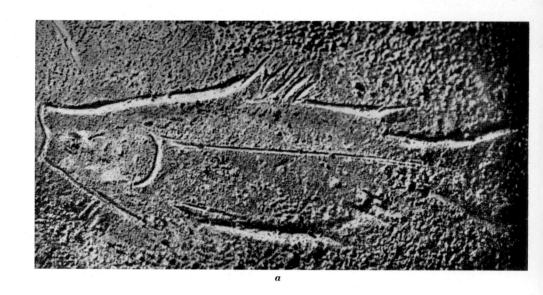

ENGRAVINGS ON CLAY: - *a*) fish, Niaux (*Ariège*); *b*), *d*) bison and horse's head, Bédeilhac (*Ariège*) *c*) horse, Montespan (*Haute-Garonne*).

Pl. 139

ENGRAVINGS ON ROCK: - Les Combarelles (*Dordogne*): reindeer, ox, donkey, horse, (see also Pl. 284 *b*), drawings by Breuil.

Pl. 140

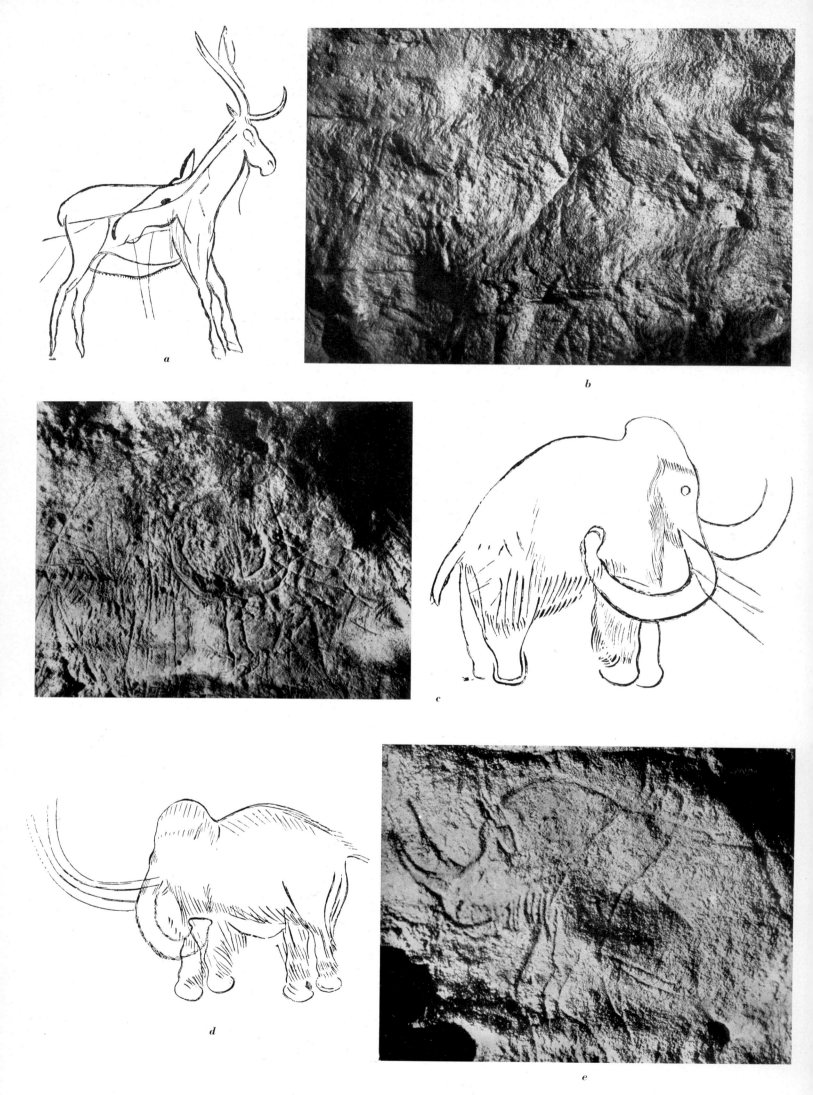

ENGRAVINGS ON ROCK: - Les Combarelles (*Dordogne*): deer, horse, mammoth, rhinoceros; drawings by Breuil.

Pl. 141

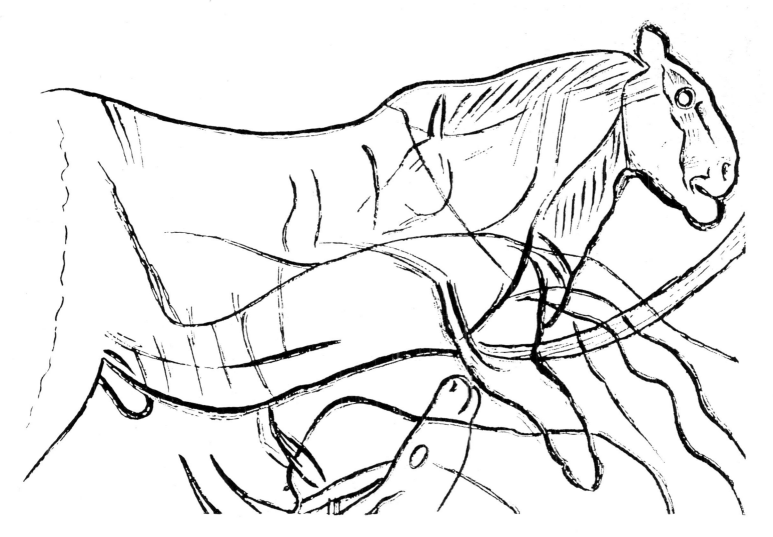

ENGRAVINGS ON ROCK: - Les Combarelles (*Dordogne*): cave lion, drawing by Breuil.

Pl. 142

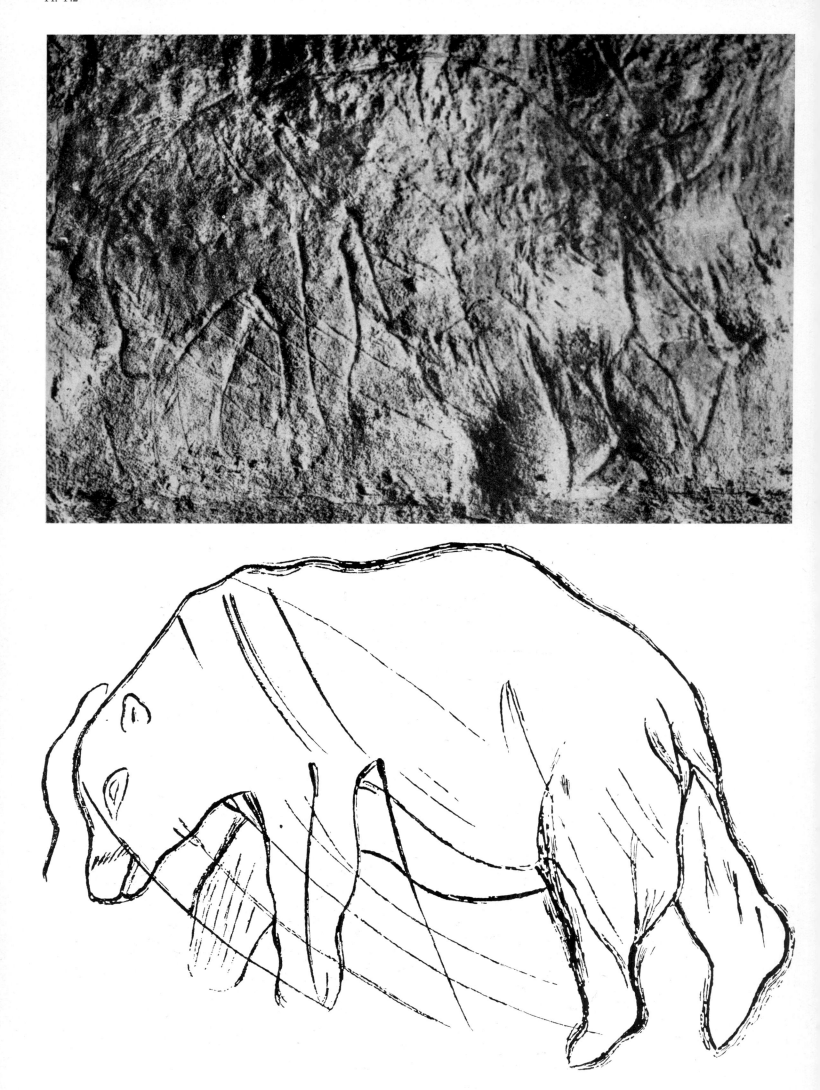

ENGRAVINGS ON ROCK: - Les Combarelles (*Dordogne*): cave bear, drawing by Breuil.

Pl. 143

a

b

c

ENGRAVINGS ON ROCK: - Tuc d'Audoubert (*Ariège*): reindeer head and horses.

Pl. 144

a

b

ENGRAVINGS ON ROCK: - Les Trois Frères (*Ariège*): bison and lion, drawing by Breuil.

Pl. 145

a

b

c

ENGRAVINGS ON ROCK: - Les Trois Frères (*Ariège*): *a*) « cameo »-engraved bison; *b*), *c*) tangles of lightly engraved figures, drawings by Breuil.

Pl. 146

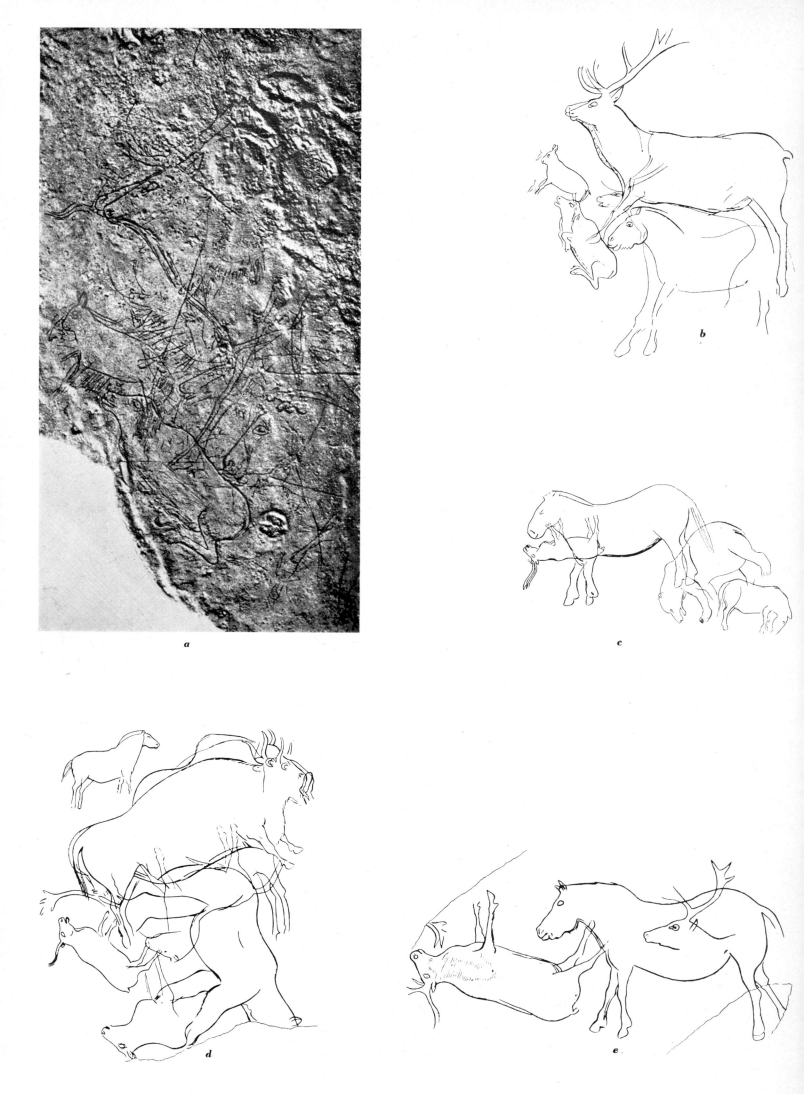

ENGRAVINGS ON ROCK: - La Mairie à Teyjat (*Dordogne*): deer, reindeer, bears, bison and horses lightly engraved on stalagmites, drawings by Breuil, (see also Pl. 284 *a*).

Pl. 147

a

b

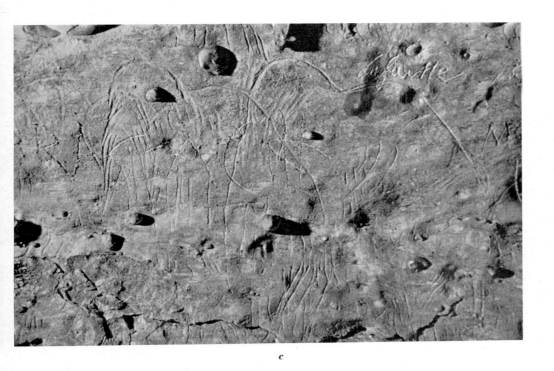

c

ENGRAVINGS ON ROCK: - Rouffignac (*Dordogne*): rhinoceros (*a*) and mammoths engraved on the altered plastic surface of the rock.

Pl. 148

a

b

c

ENGRAVINGS ON ROCK: - Rouffignac (*Dordogne*): mammoths engraved on the altered plastic surface of the rock.

Pl. 149

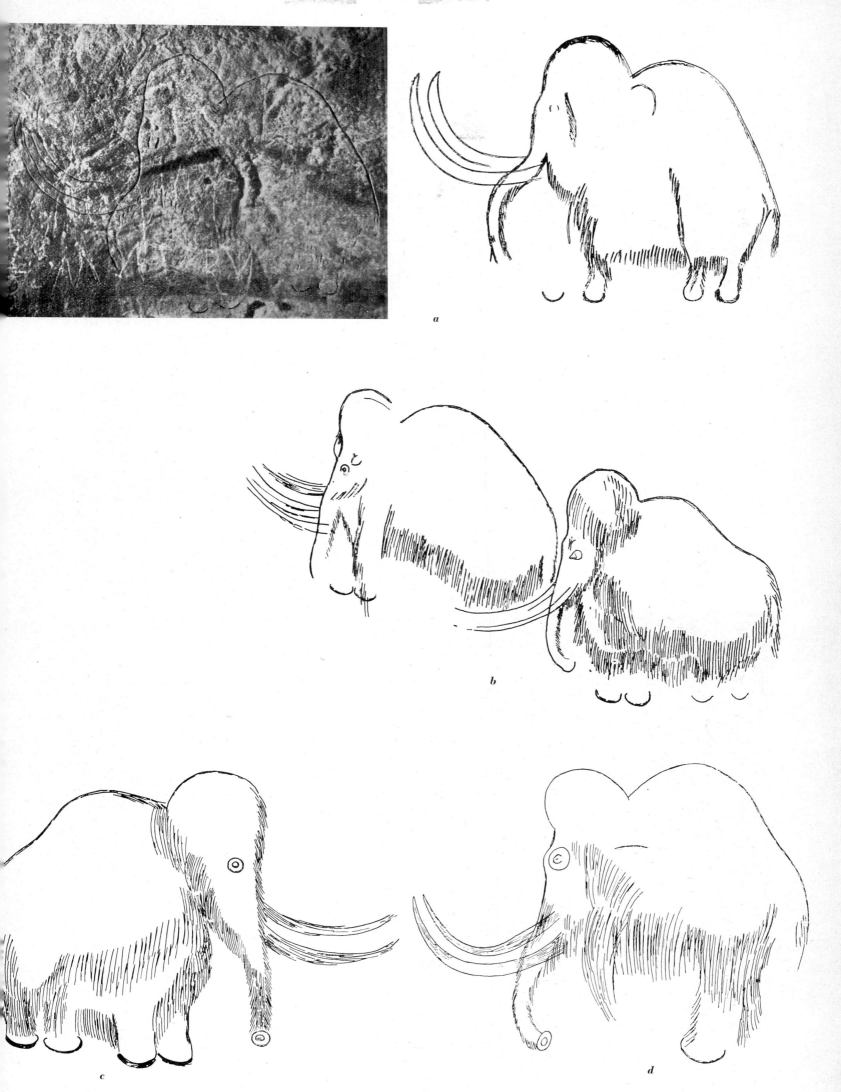

ENGRAVINGS ON ROCK: - Font-de-Gaume (*Dordogne*): lightly engraved mammoths superimposed on polychromatic paintings in the cave, drawings by Breuil.

Pl. 150

BAS-RELIEFS: - Laussel Shelter (*Dordogne*): « Venus » (from Perigordian layers).

Pl. 151

a

b

c

BAS-RELIEFS: - Laussel Shelter (*Dordogne*): *a*), *b*) female figures; *c*) double human figure (from Perigordian layers).

Pl. 152

BAS-RELIEFS: - Laussel Shelter (*Dordogne*): male figure (from Perigordian layers).

Pl. 153

a

b

c

BAS-RELIEFS: - *a*) Terme Pialat (*Dordogne*): human figures; *b*) Abri Labatut (*Dordogne*): horse (from Perigordian layers); *c*) Abri du Poisson (*Dordogne*): salmon.

Pl. 154

a

b

BAS-RELIEFS: - Le Roc (*Charente*): *a*) situation of bas-reliefs in the cave according to H. Martin's reconstruction; *b*) pregnant mare and bison transformed into a wild boar (from Solutrean layers).

Pl. 155

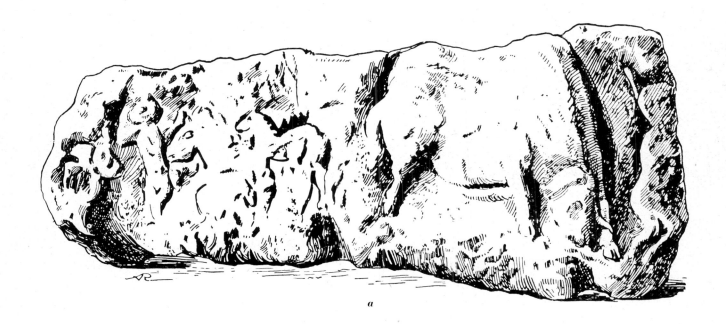

a

b

c

BAS-RELIEFS: - Le Roc (*Charente*): *a*) bull pursuing a man, drawing by Riolet; *b*), *c*) pregnant mares (from Solutrean layers).

Pl. 156

a

b

BAS-RELIEFS: - Le Roc (*Charente*): *a*) ibex from the Lantier excavations; *b*) fighting ibexes (from Solutrean layers).

Pl. 157

a

b

c

BAS-RELIEFS: - Le Fourneau du Diable (*Dordogne*): *a*) sculptured block; *b*) the same, in the deposit (from Solutrean layers); *c*) Laugerie Haute (*Dordogne*): head of a musk ox (probably from Magdalenian layers).

Pl. 158

a

b

c

BAS-RELIEFS: - Le Cap Blanc (*Dordogne*): large sculptured frieze with horses (related to Magdalenian layers).

Pl. 159

a

b

BAS-RELIEFS: - Le Cap Blanc (*Dordogne*): details of sculptured frieze.

Pl. 160

BAS-RELIEFS: - Angles-sur-Anglin (*Vienne*): human head, carved and painted.

Pl. 161

BAS-RELIEFS: - Angles-sur-Anglin (*Vienne*): ibex head (from Magdalenian III layers).

Pl. 162

a

b

c

BAS-RELIEFS: - Angles-sur-Anglin (*Vienne*): *a*) female figures; *b*), *c*) horse's head and bison (covered by Magdalenian layers).

Pl. 163

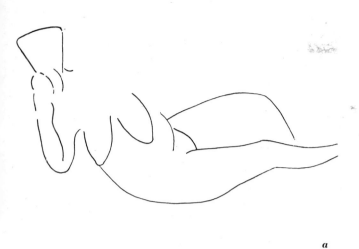

a

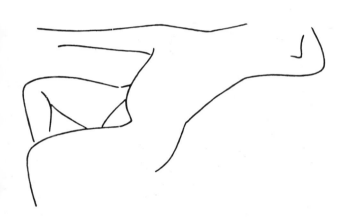

b

c

BAS-RELIEFS: - La Magdeleine (*Tarn*): women and horse.

Pl. 164

a

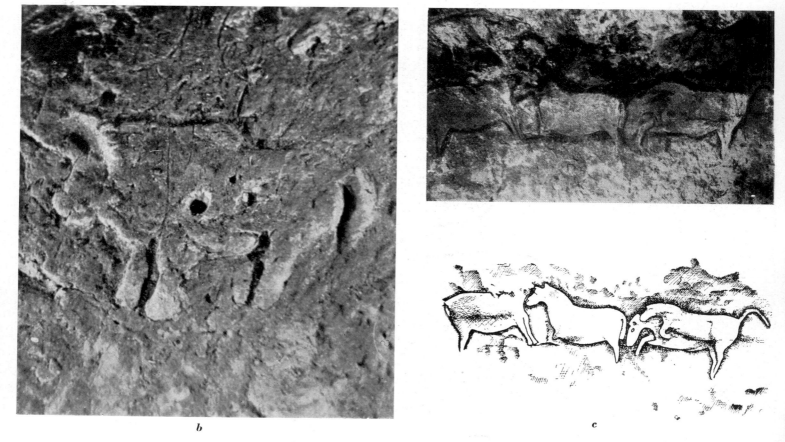

b   *c*

BAS-RELIEFS: - Isturitz (*Basses-Pyrénées*): deer (covered by Magdalenian layers); *b*) Bédeilhac (*Ariège*): clay bison; *c*) La Chaire à Calvin (*Charente*): horses (probably Solutrean).

Pl. 165

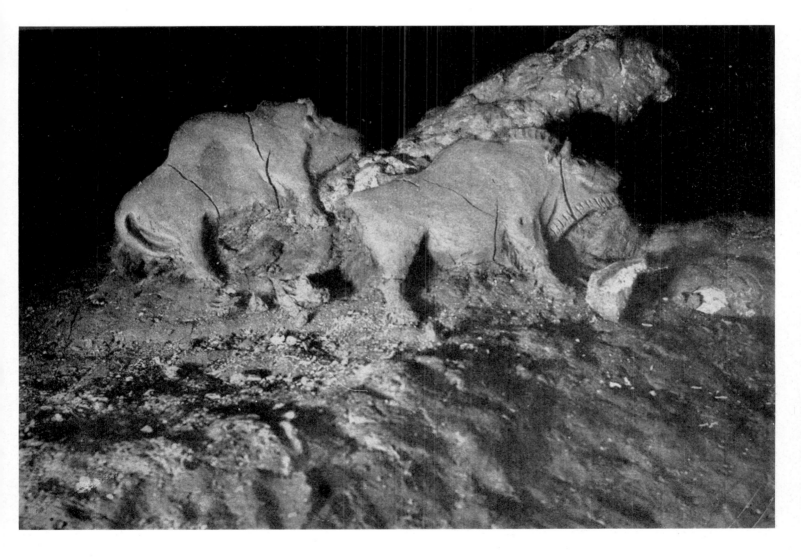

CLAY STATUES: - Tuc d'Audoubert (*Ariège*): entrance to the cave and bison.

Pl. 166

a

b

CLAY STATUES: - Tuc d'Audoubert (*Ariège*): bison viewed from the side and from the front.

Pl. 167

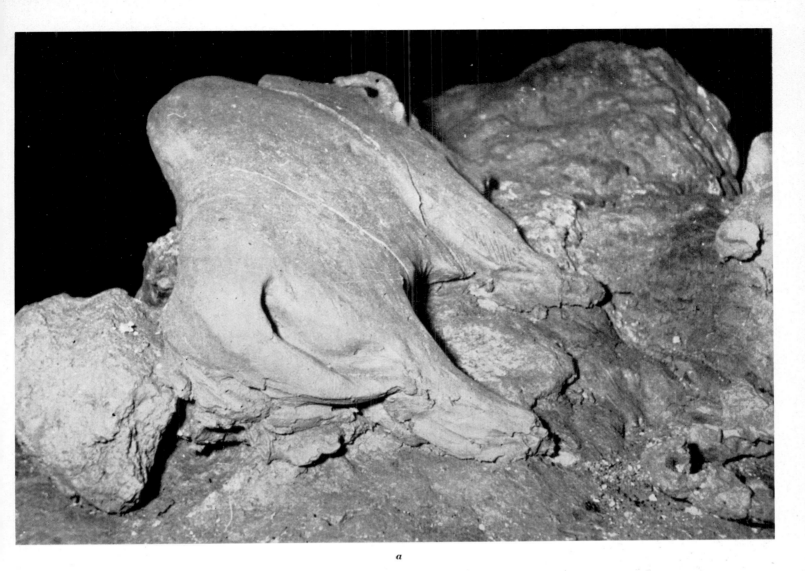

a

b   *c*

CLAY STATUES: - Tuc d'Audoubert (*Ariège*): *a*), *b*) bison viewed from the back and from above; *c*) human heelprints and holes in the clay floor of the cave.

Pl. 168

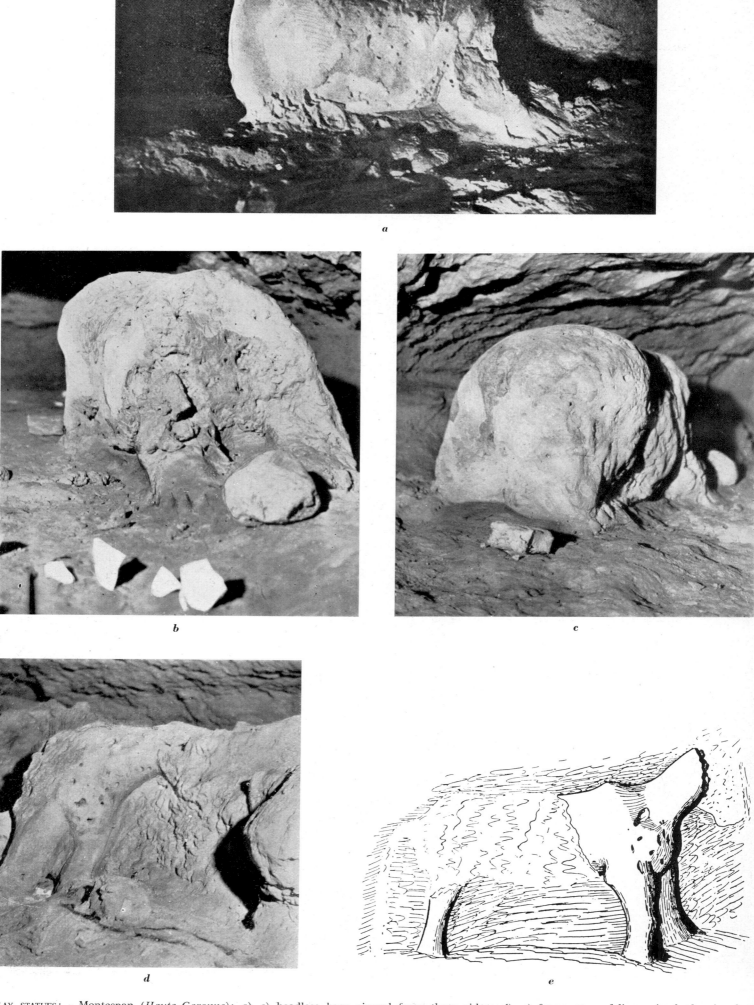

CLAY STATUES: - Montespan (*Haute-Garonne*): *a*)-*c*) headless bear viewed from three sides; *d*), *e*) fragmentary feline animal, drawing by Breuil.

Pl. 169

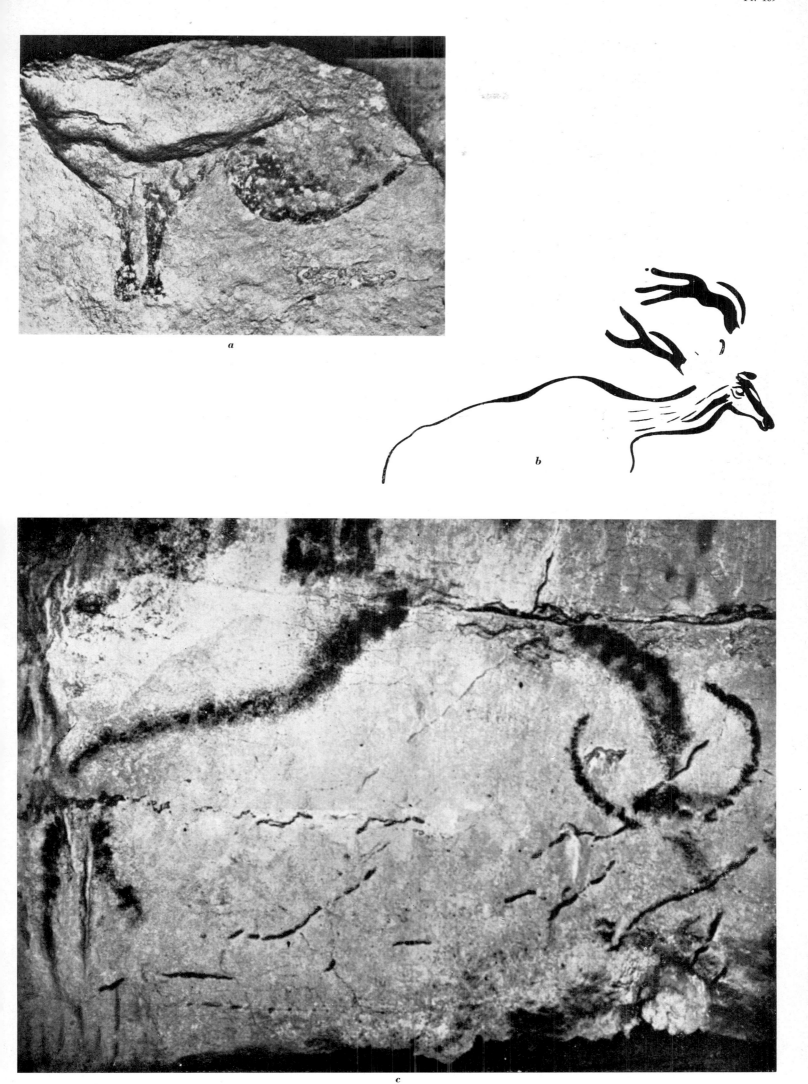

CAVE PAINTINGS IN FRANCE: - *a*), *b*) figures on blocks in Abri Blanchard (*Dordogne*) (from Aurignacian layers) and Abri Labatut (*Dordogne*) (from Perigordian layers), drawing by Breuil; *c*) rock painting in Marcenac (*Lot*).

Pl. 170

a

b

CAVE PAINTINGS IN FRANCE: - Pech-Merle (*Lot*): ox and deer with horns seen from the front.

Pl. 171

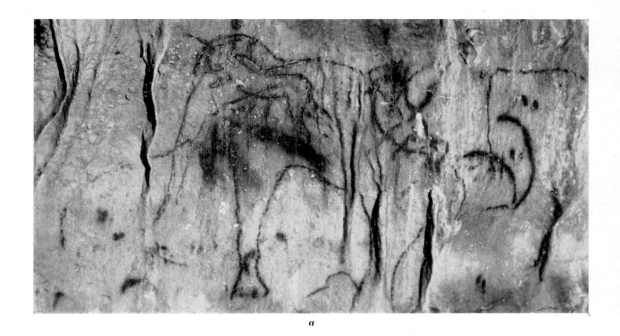

a

b

c

CAVE PAINTINGS IN FRANCE: - Cougnac (*Lot*): elephants, ibexes, deer and human figures struck by arrows.

Pl. 172

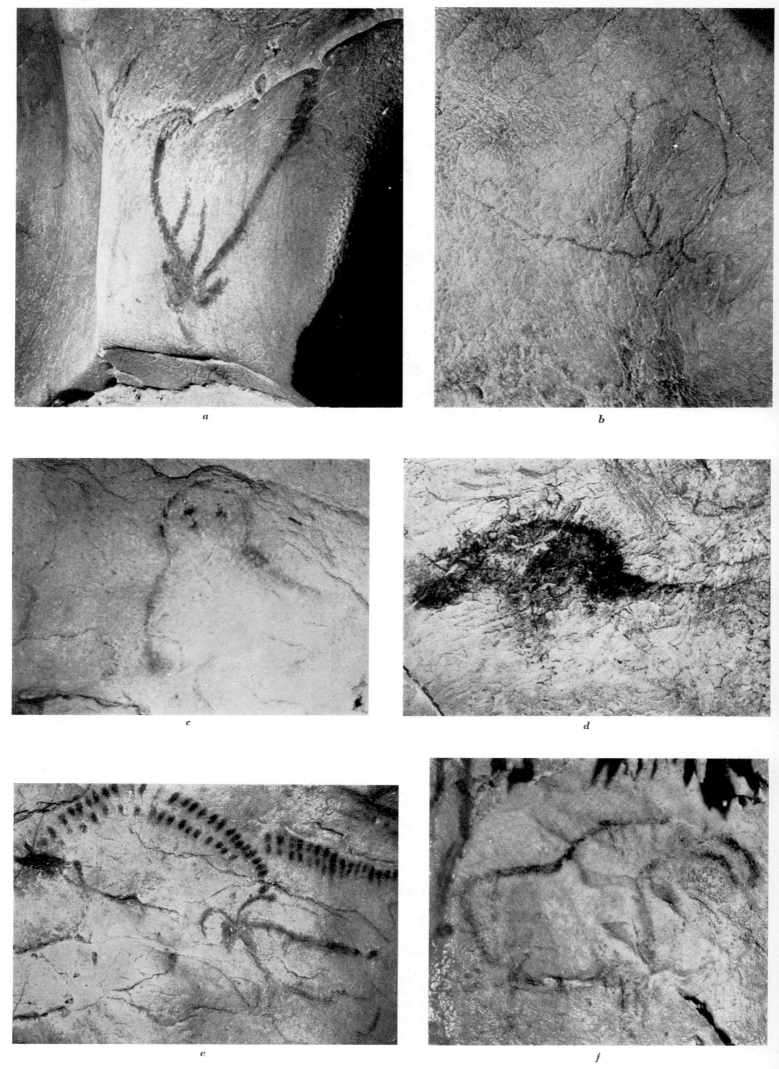

CAVE PAINTINGS IN FRANCE: - Le Portel (*Ariège*): figures of archaic style: *a*), *b*) antlers; *c*) owl; *d*), *f*) horses; *e*) ibex.

Pl. 173

a

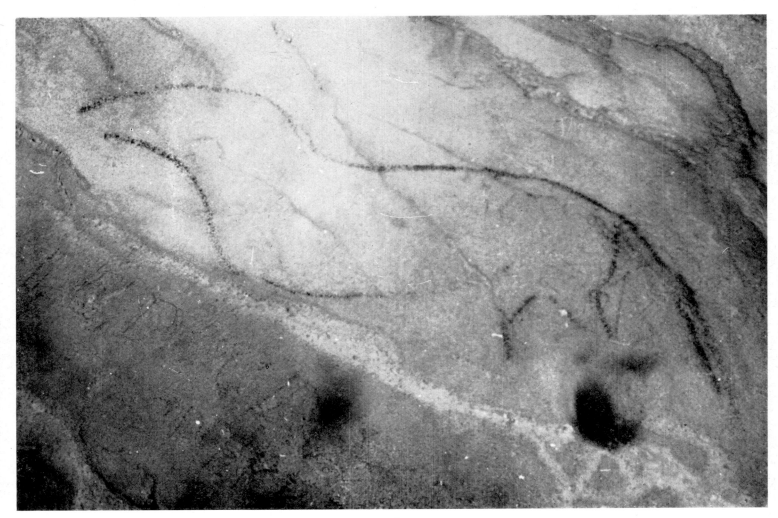

b

CAVE PAINTINGS IN FRANCE: - Le Portel (*Ariège*): horses of archaic style.

Pl. 174

CAVE PAINTINGS IN FRANCE: - Lascaux Cave (*Dordogne*): deer.

Pl. 175

CAVE PAINTINGS IN FRANCE: - Lascaux Cave (*Dordogne*): large bull and running horses.

Pl. 176

CAVE PAINTINGS IN FRANCE: - Lascaux Cave (*Dordogne*): large black bull superimposed upon red cow, the same as in Pl. 181 (5,50 metres long).

Pl. 177

<small>CAVE PAINTINGS IN FRANCE:</small> - Lascaux Cave (*Dordogne*): large black bull superimposed upon red cows.

Pl. 178

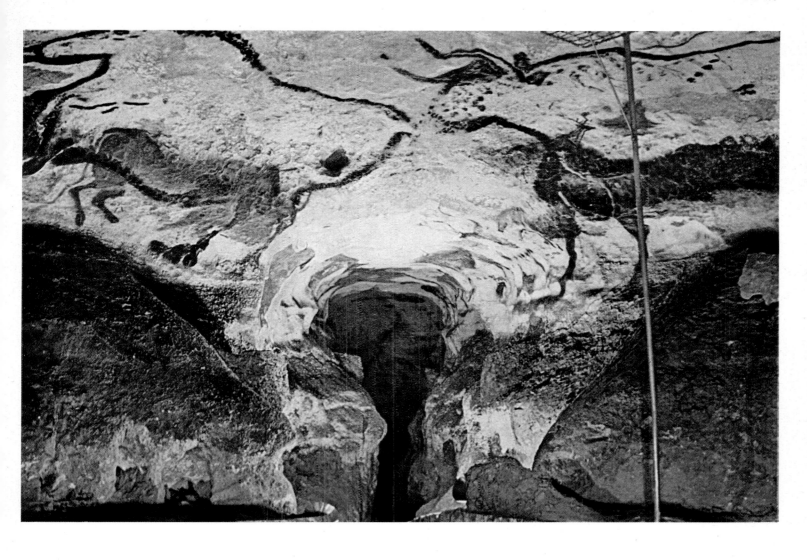

CAVE PAINTINGS IN FRANCE: - Lascaux Cave (*Dordogne*): « Hall of Bulls » and entrance to axial corridor.

Pl. 179

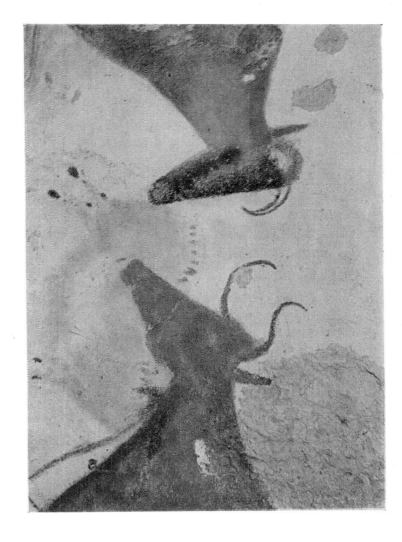

CAVE PAINTINGS IN FRANCE: - Lascaux Cave (*Dordogne*): large red cows painted on ceiling of axial corridor.

Pl. 180

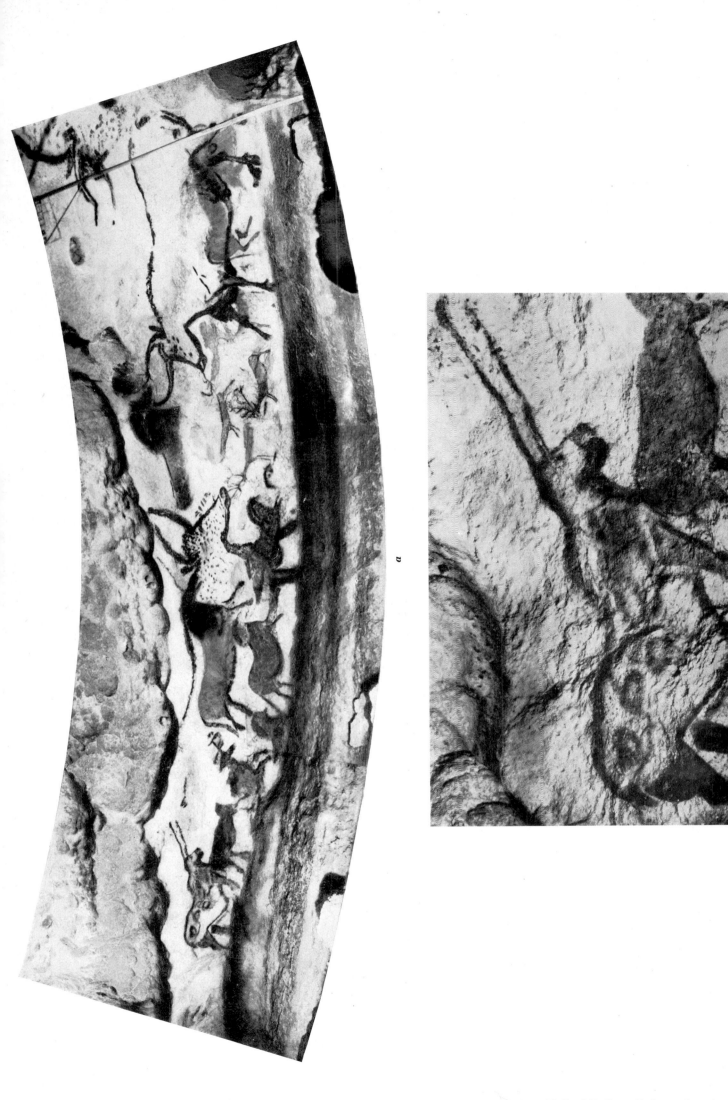

CAVE PAINTINGS IN FRANCE: - Lascaux Cave (*Dordogne*): *a*) the great frieze on the left wall of the « Hall of Bulls »; *b*) fantastic animal known as « the unicorn ».

Pl. 181

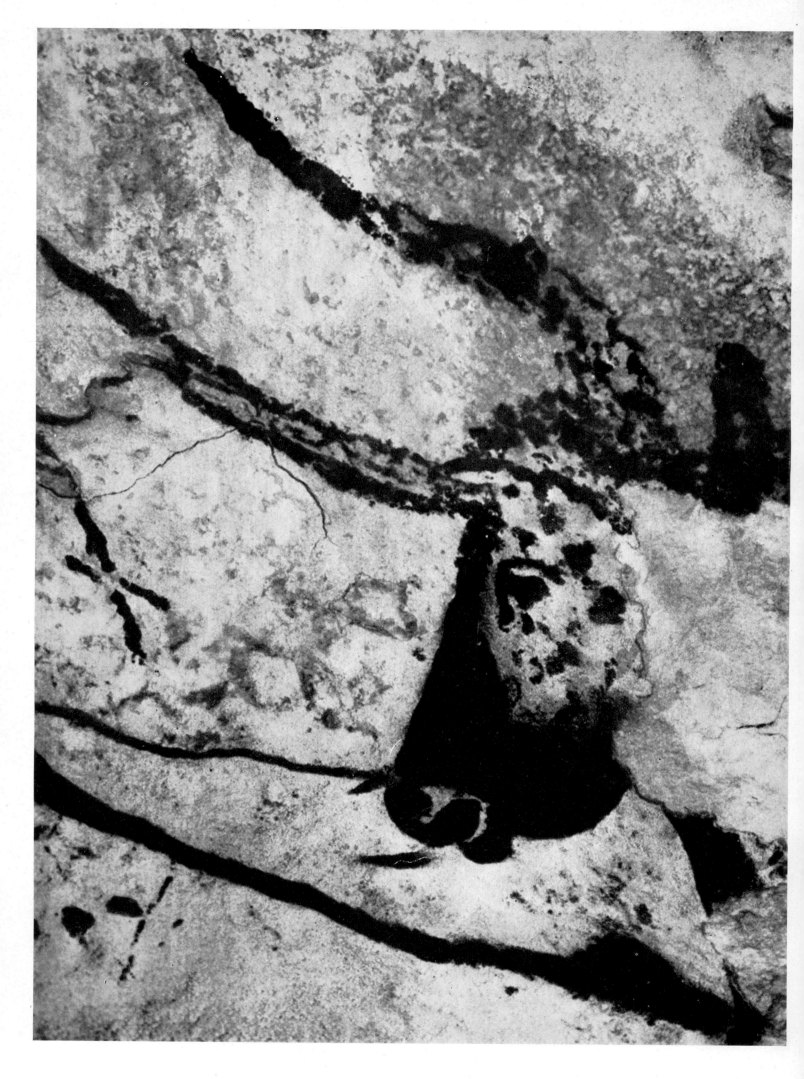

CAVE PAINTINGS IN FRANCE: - Lascaux (*Dordogne*): detail of the large bull in Pl. 176.

Pl. 182

a

b

CAVE PAINTINGS IN FRANCE: - Lascaux (*Dordogne*): *a*) cow painted red with black head; *b*) large black bull superimposed upon red cows.

Pl. 183

CAVE PAINTINGS IN FRANCE: - Lascaux (*Dordogne*): detail of bull in Pl. 182 *b*.

Pl. 184

CAVE PAINTINGS IN FRANCE: - Lascaux (*Dordogne*): corridor leading from « Hall of Bulls » in axial direction.

Pl. 185

a

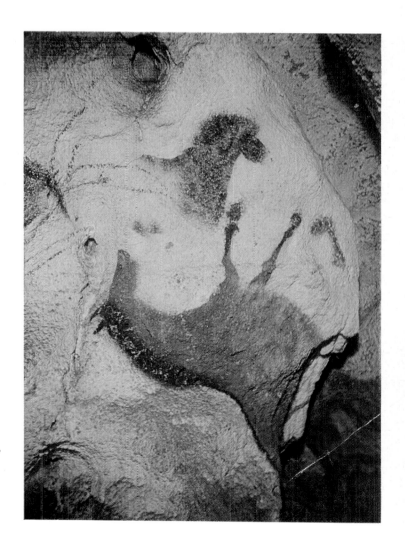

b

CAVE PAINTINGS IN FRANCE: - Lascaux Cave (*Dordogne*): *a*) painted ceiling of axial corridor; *b*) upside-down horse.

Pl. 186

CAVE PAINTINGS IN FRANCE: - Lascaux Cave (*Dordogne*): « Chinese » horse surrounded by probable representations of arrows.

Pl. 187

CAVE PAINTINGS IN FRANCE: - Lascaux Cave (*Dordogne*): horse and probable representations of arrows.

Pl. 188

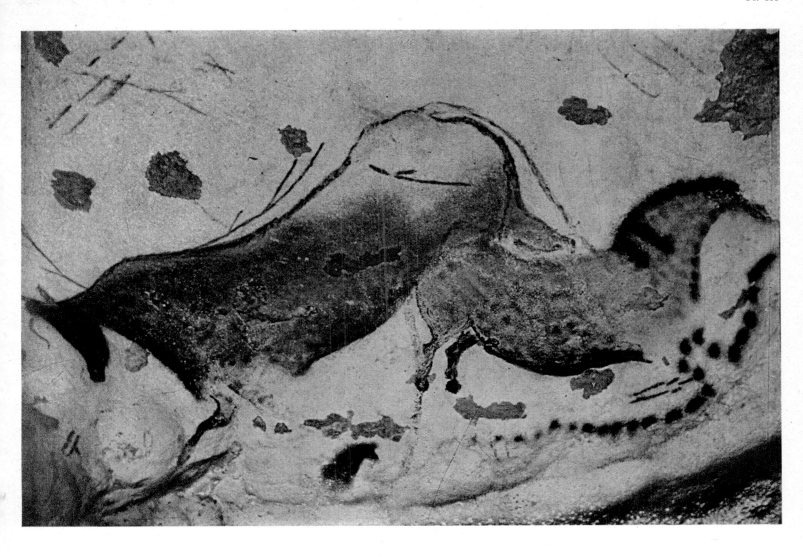

CAVE PAINTINGS IN FRANCE: - Lascaux Cave (*Dordogne*): cow, horse and dotted line.

Pl. 189

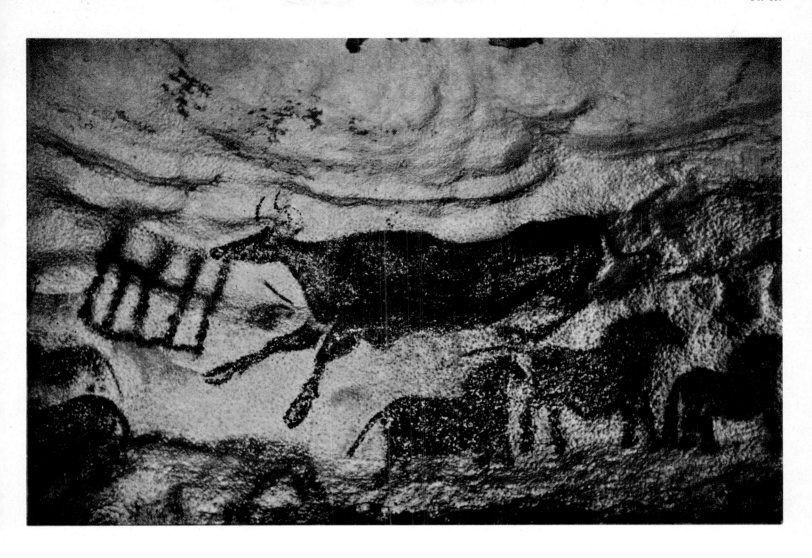

CAVE PAINTINGS IN FRANCE: - Lascaux Cave (*Dordogne*): jumping cow, small horses and « blazon »; the red showing through belongs to an earlier painting which underlies the cow.

Pl. 190

CAVE PAINTINGS IN FRANCE: - Lascaux Cave (*Dordogne*): horses, ibexes and rectangular figures.

Pl. 191

CAVE PAINTINGS IN FRANCE: - Lascaux Cave (*Dordogne*): horse and hindquarters of a bison.

Pl. 192

CAVE PAINTINGS IN FRANCE: - Lascaux Cave (*Dordogne*): running horse and probable representation of a javelin.

Pl. 193

CAVE PAINTINGS IN FRANCE: - Lascaux Cave (*Dordogne*): bison.

Pl. 194

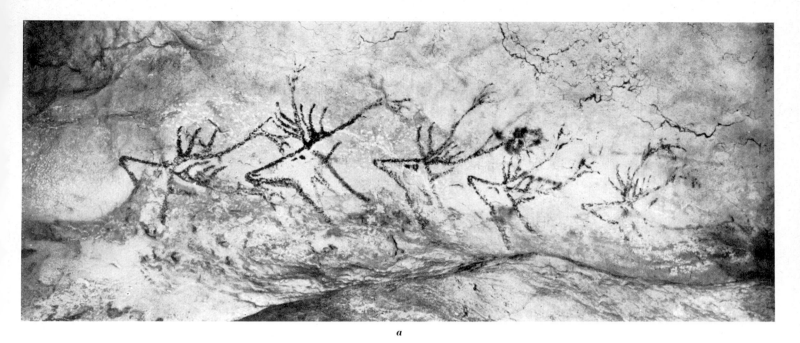

a

b

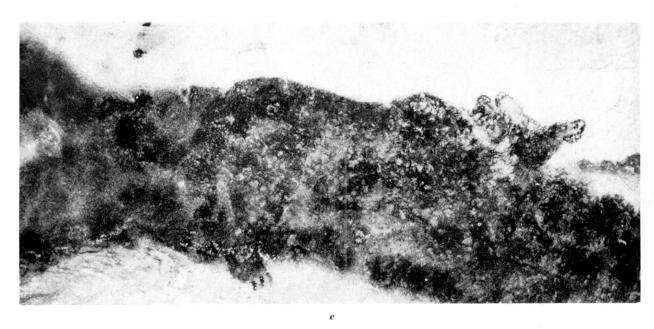

c

CAVE PAINTINGS IN FRANCE: - Lascaux (*Dordogne*): *a*) heads of deer, painted in black; *b*) heads of ibexes painted and engraved; *c*) bear.

Pl. 195

a

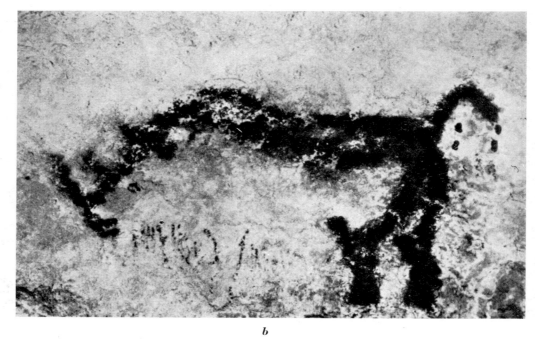

b

CAVE PAINTINGS IN FRANCE: - Lascaux (*Dordogne*): *a*) deer with extravagantly shaped antlers; *b*) rhinoceros painted in « blown technique ».

Pl. 196

CAVE PAINTINGS IN FRANCE: - Pech-Merle (*Lot*): horses covered with dots and negative impressions of hands (see also Fig. 22).

Pl. 197

a

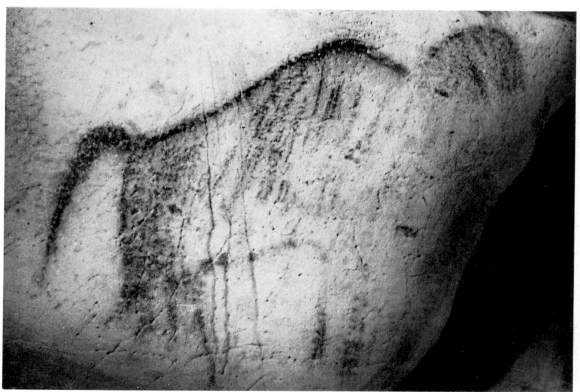

b

CAVE PAINTINGS IN FRANCE: - Pech-Merle (*Lot*): mammoths painted in black.

Pl. 198

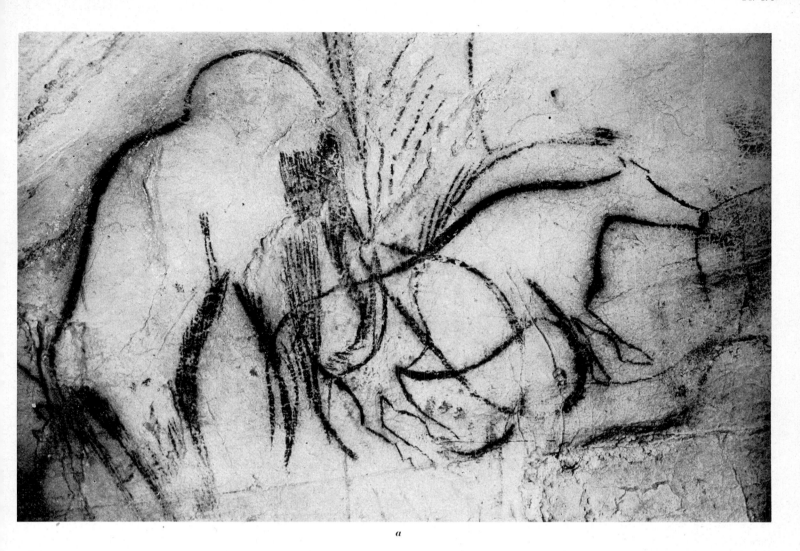

a

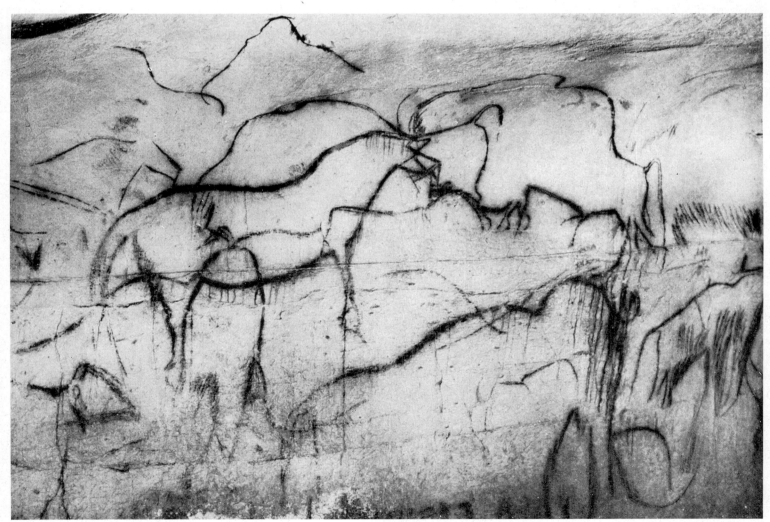

b

CAVE PAINTINGS IN FRANCE: - Pech-Merle (*Lot*): details of the great frieze in the « Mammoth Chapel ».

Pl. 199

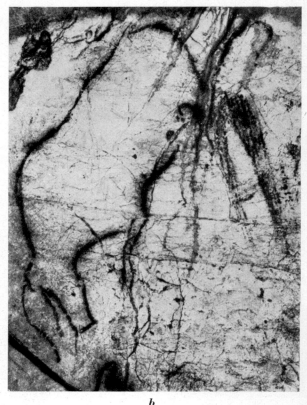

a

b

c

CAVE PAINTINGS IN FRANCE: - Pech-Merle (*Lot*): *a*), *b*) oxen painted in the « Mammoth Chapel » and *c*) figures in other parts of the cave.

Pl. 200

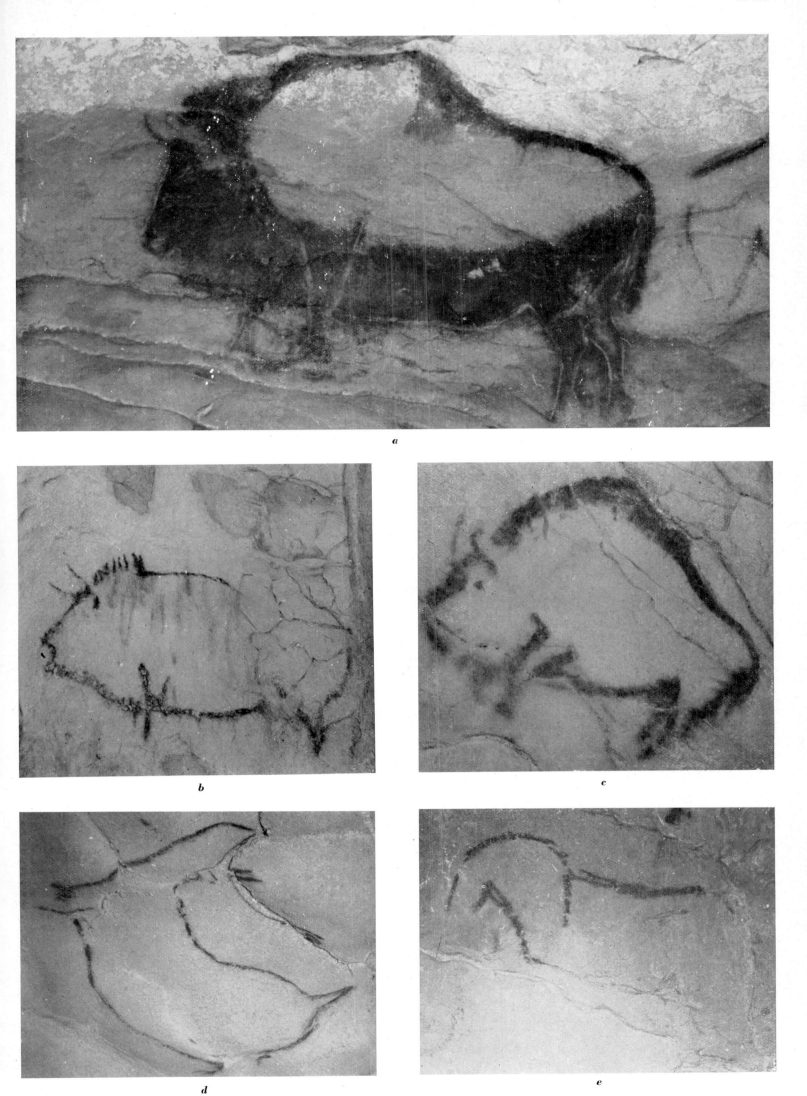

CAVE PAINTINGS IN FRANCE: - Le Portel (*Ariège*): *a*) bison, painted and engraved; *b*)-*e*) bison, reindeer (distorted by photograph) and horse. (See also paintings in same cave in Pl. 284, *c*).

Pl. 201

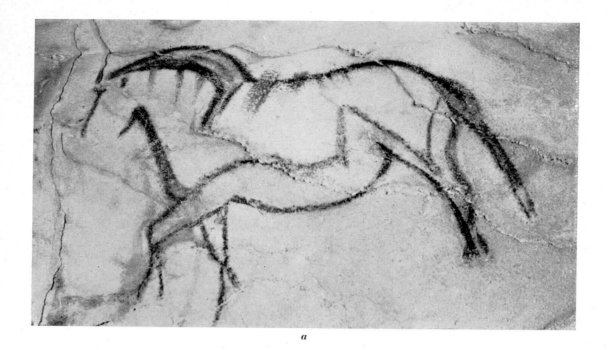

a

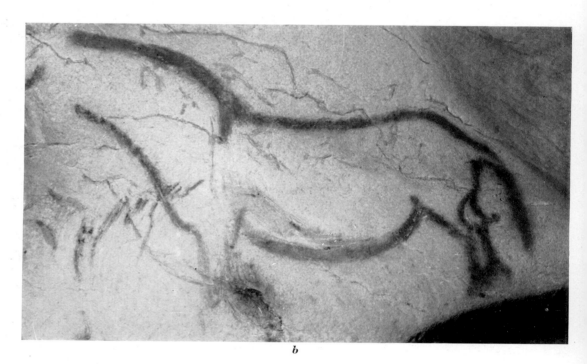

b

c

CAVE PAINTINGS IN FRANCE: - Le Portel (*Ariège*): horses painted in black in an evolved style.

Pl. 202

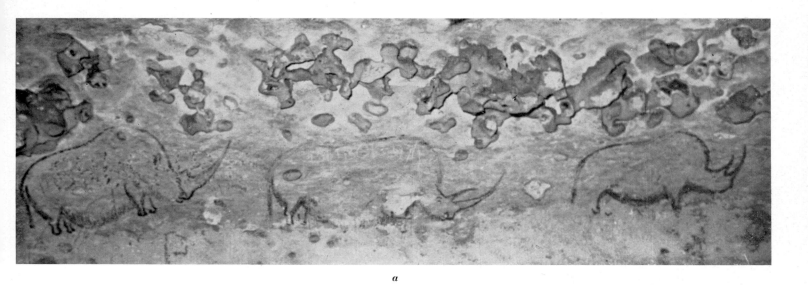

a

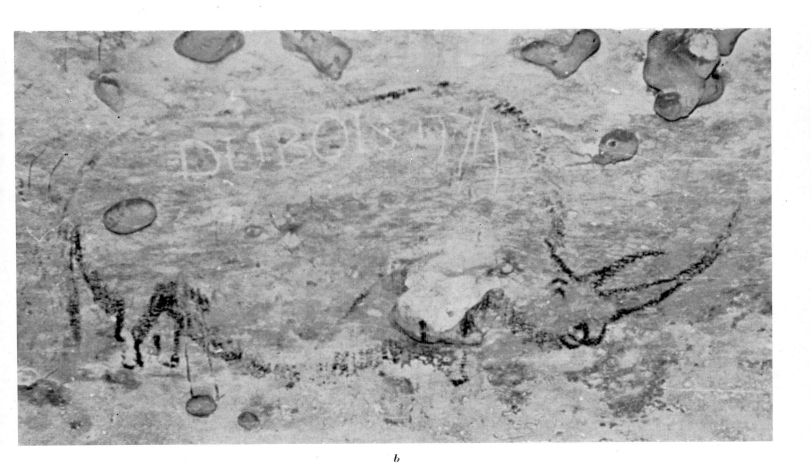

b

c

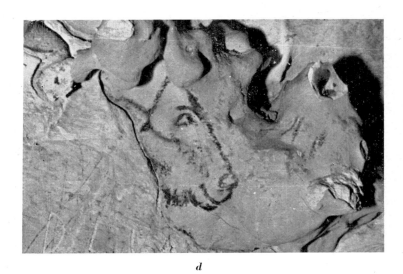

d

CAVE PAINTINGS IN FRANCE: - Rouffignac (*Dordogne*): rhinoceros, ibex and horse painted in black.

Pl. 203

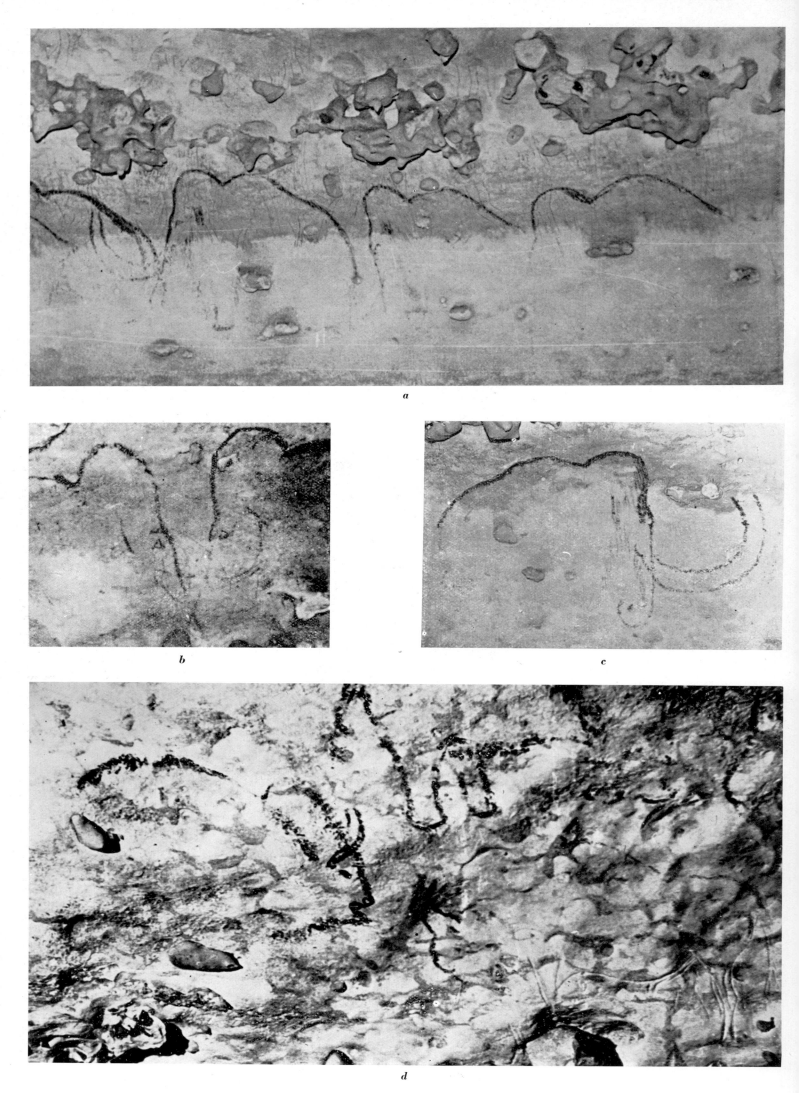

CAVE PAINTINGS IN FRANCE: - Rouffignac (*Dordogne*): *a)-c*) mammoths painted in black; *d*) bison painted and engraved.

Pl. 204

a

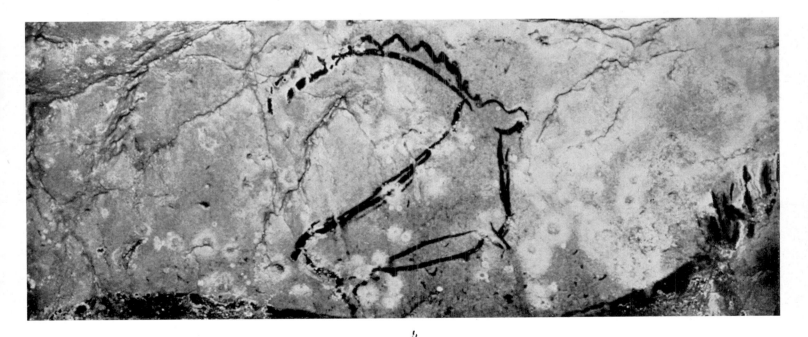

b

CAVE PAINTINGS IN FRANCE: - Niaux (*Ariège*): *a*) the great pictorial composition of bison in the « Black Hall »; *b*) ibex.

Pl. 205

a

b

CAVE PAINTINGS IN FRANCE: - Niaux (*Ariège*): *a*) ibex; *b*) bison struck by arrows, and ibex.

Pl. 206

CAVE PAINTINGS IN FRANCE: - Niaux (*Ariège*): more bison in the « Black Hall ».

Pl. 207

Pl. 207

CAVE PAINTINGS IN FRANCE: - Niaux (*Ariège*): bison, one of which is struck by arrows.

Pl. 208

CAVE PAINTINGS IN FRANCE: - Niaux (*Ariège*): bison struck by arrow; below, the small ibex shown in Pl. 207.

Pl. 209

CAVE PAINTINGS IN FRANCE: - Niaux (*Ariège*): bison struck by arrows, incomplete horse and another small horse.

Pl. 210

a

b

CAVE PAINTINGS IN FRANCE: - Niaux (*Ariège*): *a*) detail of composition in Pl. 209; *b*) horse.

Pl. 211

a

b

c

CAVE PAINTINGS IN FRANCE: - Niaux (*Ariège*): horses, one of which is incomplete (*c*); *b*) drawn by Breuil.

Pl. 212

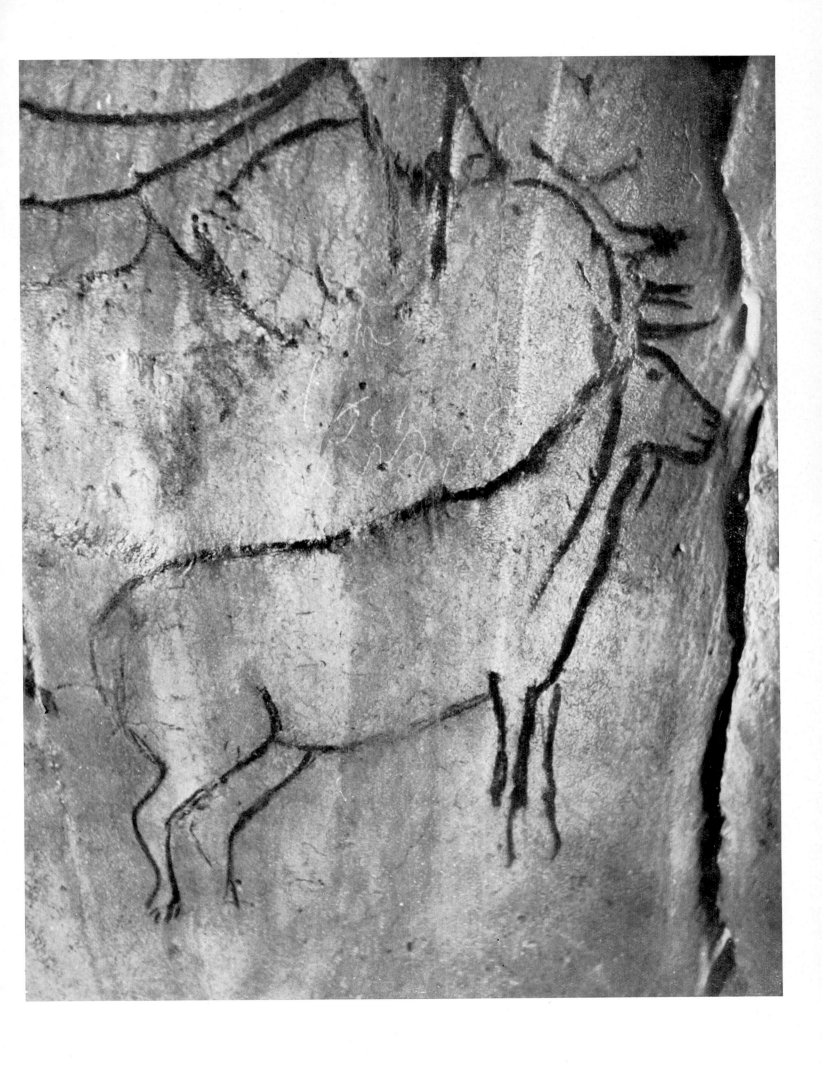

CAVE PAINTINGS IN FRANCE: - Niaux (*Ariège*): deer in the « Black Hall ».

Pl. 213

a

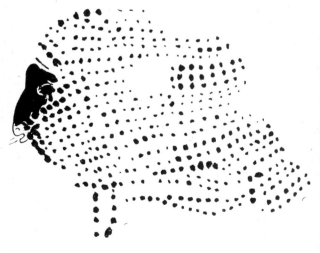

b

CAVE PAINTINGS IN FRANCE: - *a*) Bédeilhac (*Ariège*): sepia-coloured bison of the polychromatic phase; *b*) Marsoulas (*Haute-Garonne*): dotted bison, drawn by Breuil.

Pl. 214

a

b

CAVE PAINTINGS IN FRANCE: - The cliff of Font-de-Gaume in the Vézère valley (*Dordogne*) and the entrance to the cave.

Pl. 215

a

b

CAVE PAINTINGS IN FRANCE: - Font-de-Gaume Cave (*Dordogne*): *a*) bison; *b*) same, according to Breuil.

Pl. 216

a

b

CAVE PAINTINGS IN FRANCE: - Font-de-Gaume Cave (*Dordogne*): *a*) horse pursuing a mare; stalactitic formations were used in the execution of the mare, whose hindquarters alone are visible (see also Pl. 276 *a*, *b*); *b*) same, according to Breuil.

Pl. 217

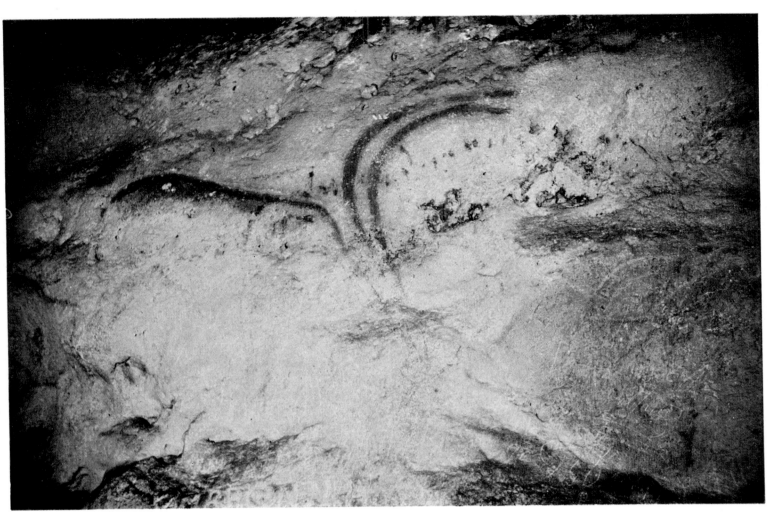

a

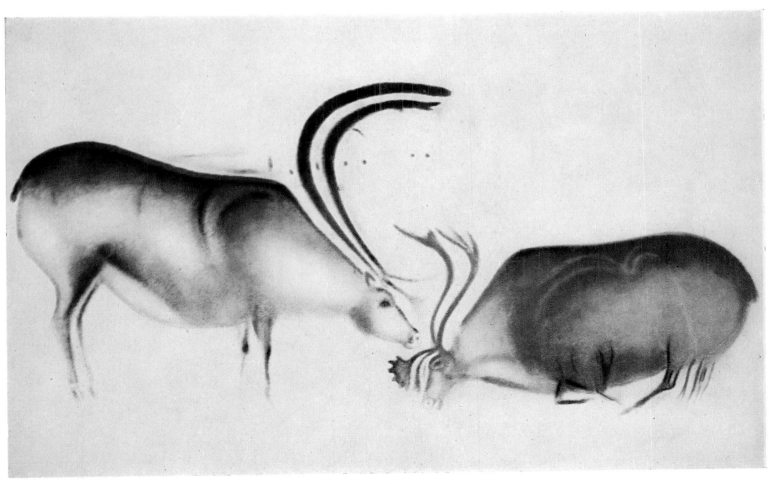

b

CAVE PAINTINGS IN FRANCE: - Font-de-Gaume Cave (*Dordogne*): *a*) male and female reindeer opposite each other; *b*) same, according to Breuil.

Pl. 218

a

b

c

d

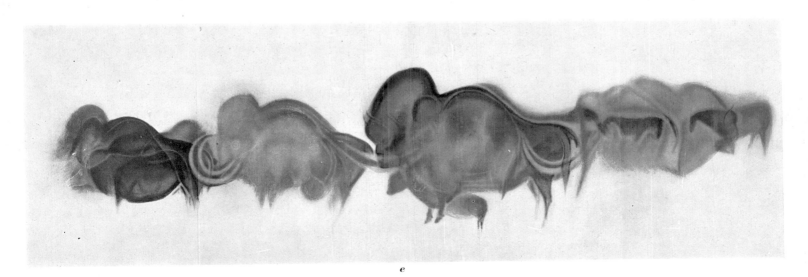

e

CAVE PAINTINGS IN FRANCE: - Font-de-Gaume (*Dordogne*): *a*) rhinoceros painted in red; *b*) ox painted in black; *c*)-*e*) polychromatic animals, according to Breuil.

Pl. 219

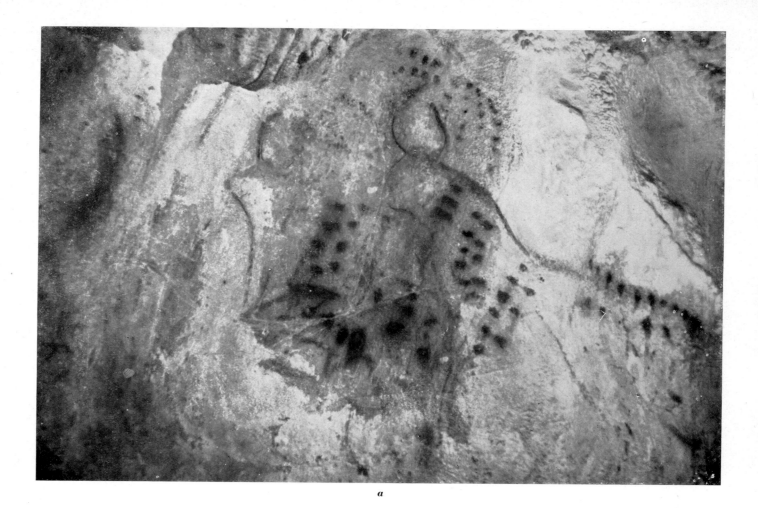

a

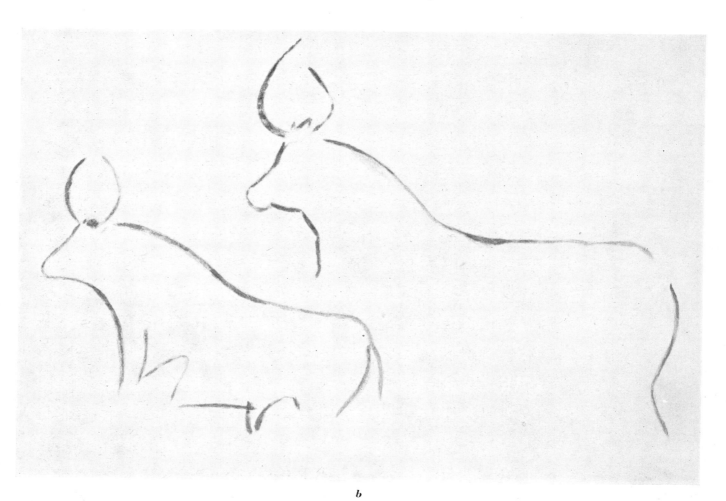

b

CAVE PAINTINGS IN SPAIN: - La Peña de Candamo (*Oviedo*): bulls with horns seen from the front, according to Cabré's tracings.

Pl. 220

a

b

CAVE PAINTINGS IN SPAIN: - *a*) Pindal (*Oviedo*): mammoth painted in red; *b*) Castillo (*Santander*): elephant, probably a mammoth, painted in red.

Pl. 221

a

b

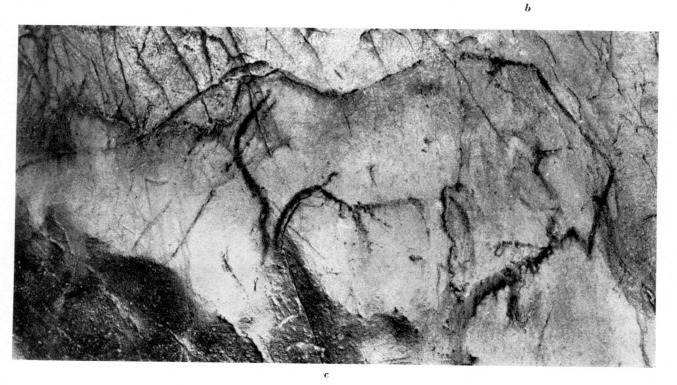

c

CAVE PAINTINGS IN SPAIN: - Castillo (*Santander*): *a*) entrance to cave; *b*), *c*) ox head and bison painted in black.

Pl. 222

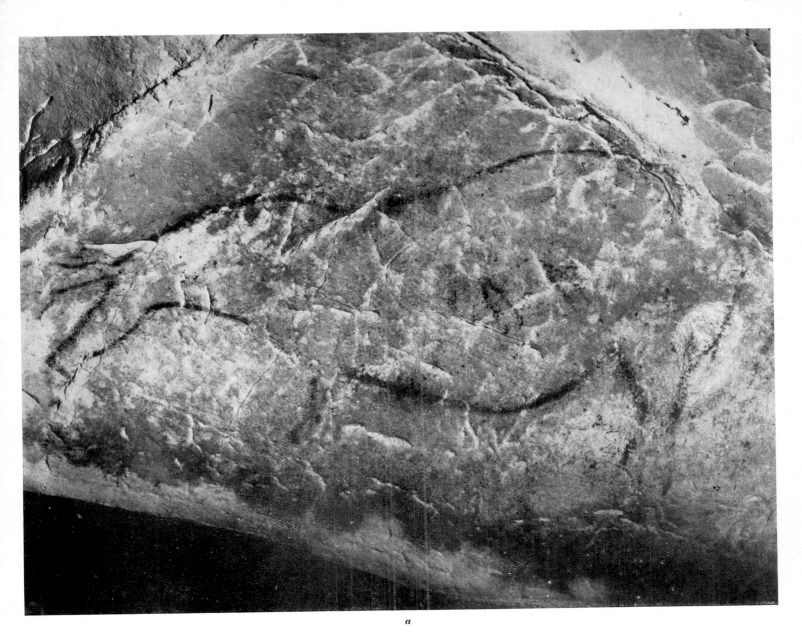

a

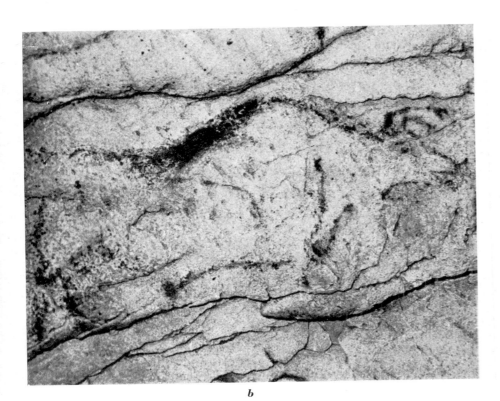

b

c

CAVE PAINTINGS IN SPAIN: - Castillo (*Santander*): horse, ox and large bison head downward.

Pl. 223

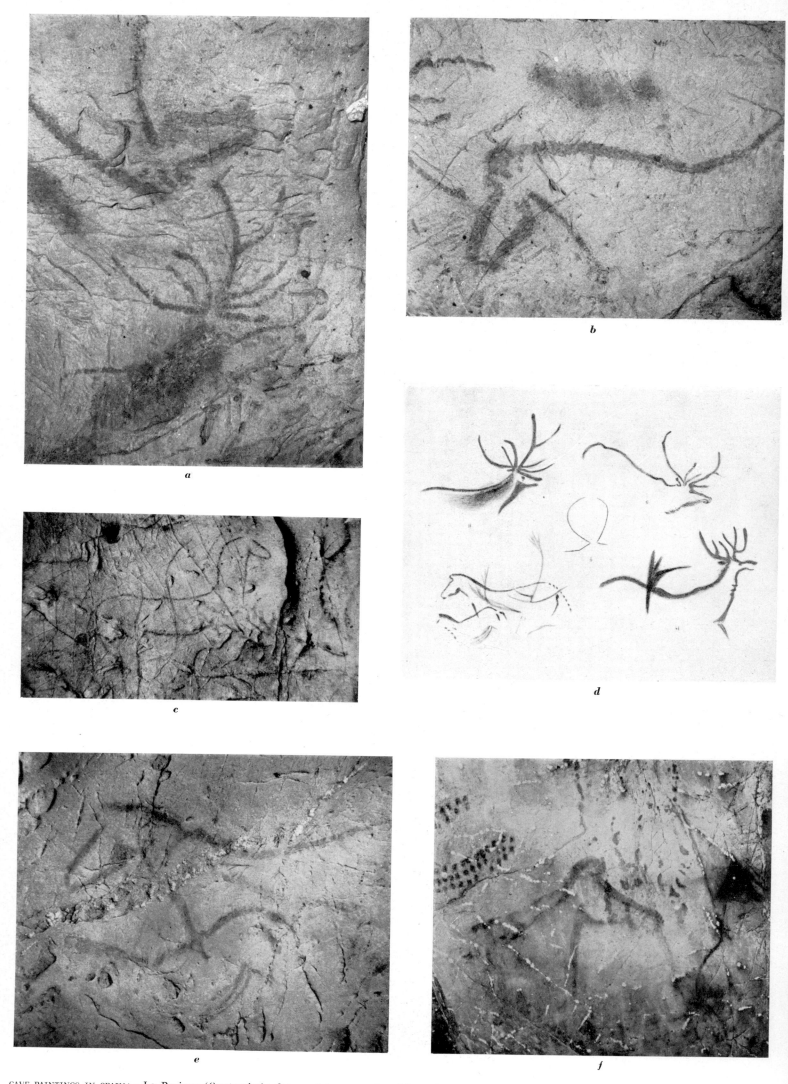

a

b

c

d

e

f

CAVE PAINTINGS IN SPAIN: - La Pasiega (*Santander*): deer and horses painted in red, archaic style; *d*) according to Breuil's tracings.

Pl. 224

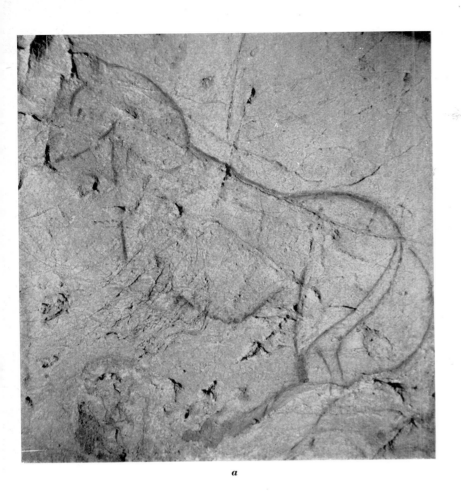

a

b

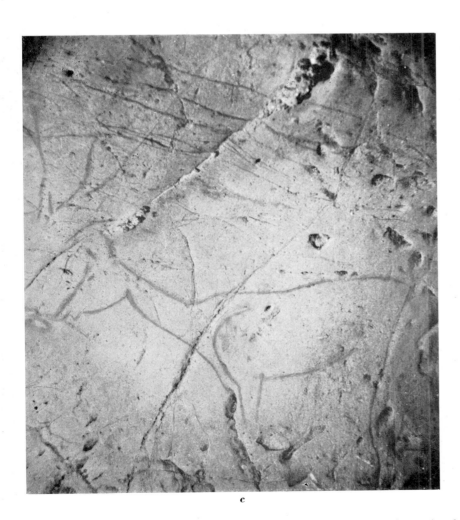

c

d

CAVE PAINTINGS IN SPAIN: - La Pasiega (*Santander*): horse and young deer painted in red; *b*, *d*) according to Breuil's tracings.

Pl. 225

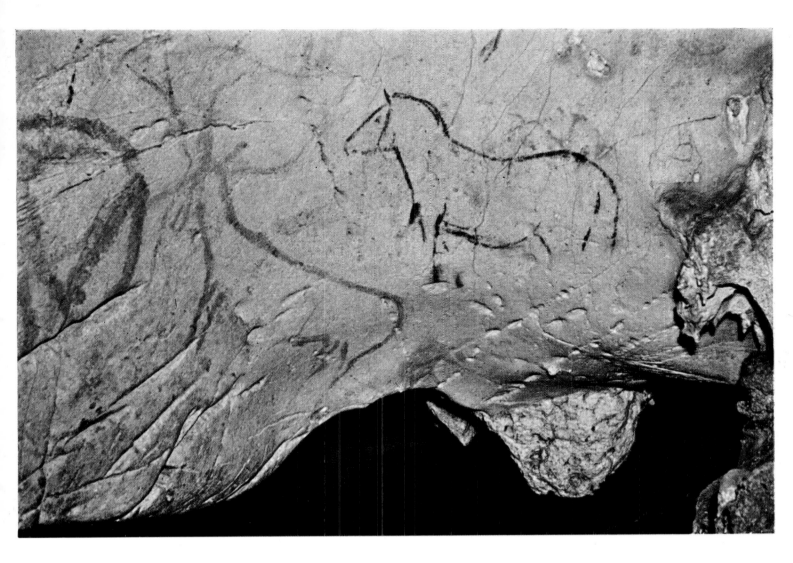

CAVE PAINTINGS IN SPAIN: - La Pasiega Cave (*Santander*): deer and horse.

Pl. 226

Pl. 227

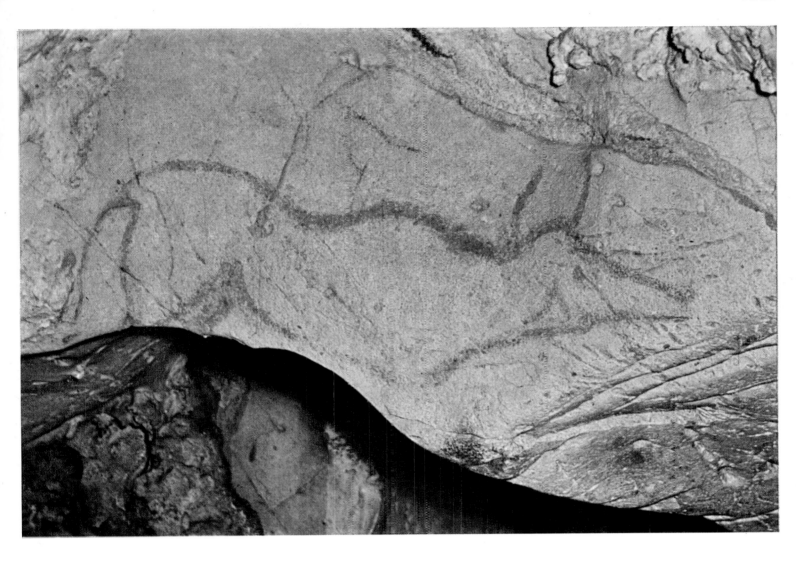

CAVE PAINTINGS IN SPAIN: - La Pasiega Cave (*Santander*): OX.

Pl. 228

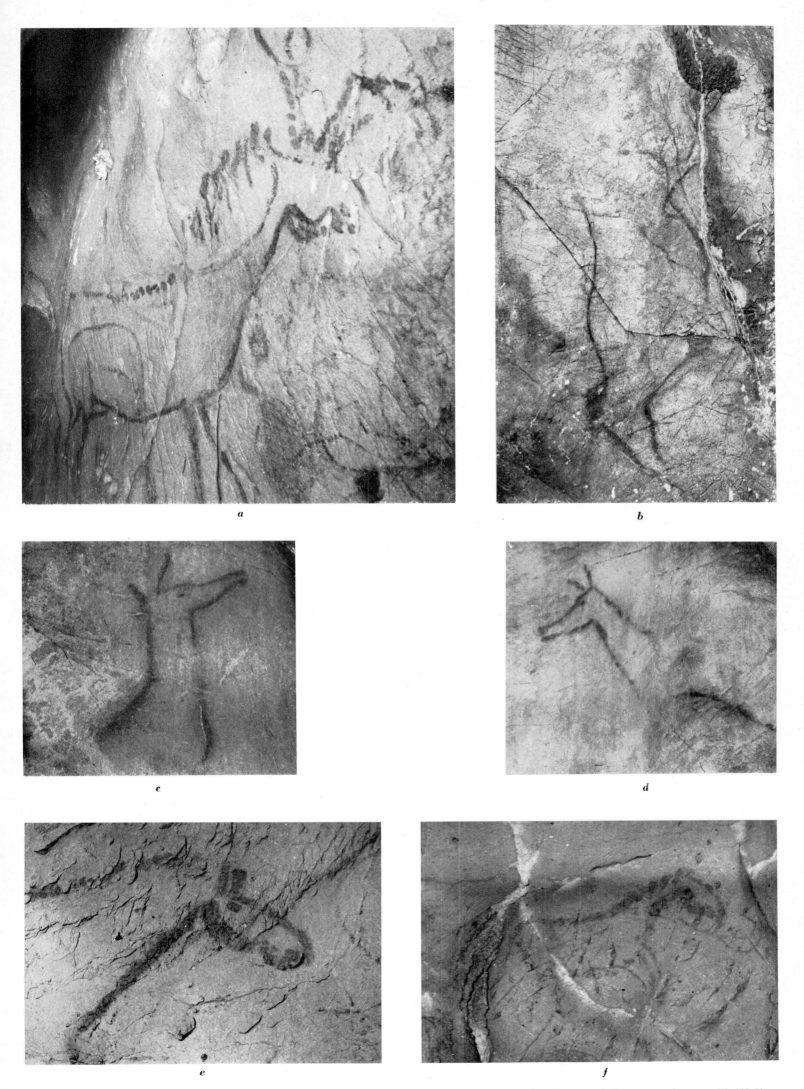

CAVE PAINTINGS IN SPAIN: - La Pasiega (*Santander*): *a*), *e*), *f*) horses; *c*), *d*) young deer; *b*) ox, head downward (for comparison see Pl. 199 *b*).

Pl. 229

a

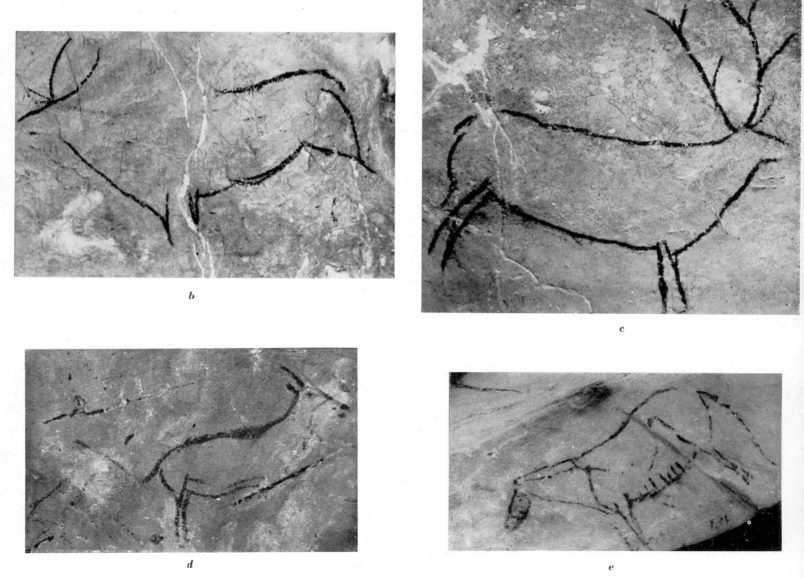

b

c

d

e

CAVE PAINTINGS IN SPAIN: - *a*) Las Chimeneas (*Santander*): inside view of cave and *b*), *c*) figures of deer; *d*), *e*) Las Monedas (*Santander*): wild goat, horse.

Pl. 230

a

b

CAVE PAINTINGS IN SPAIN: - Covalanas Cave (*Santander*): *a*) overall view; *b*) horse and young deer painted in red.

Pl. 231

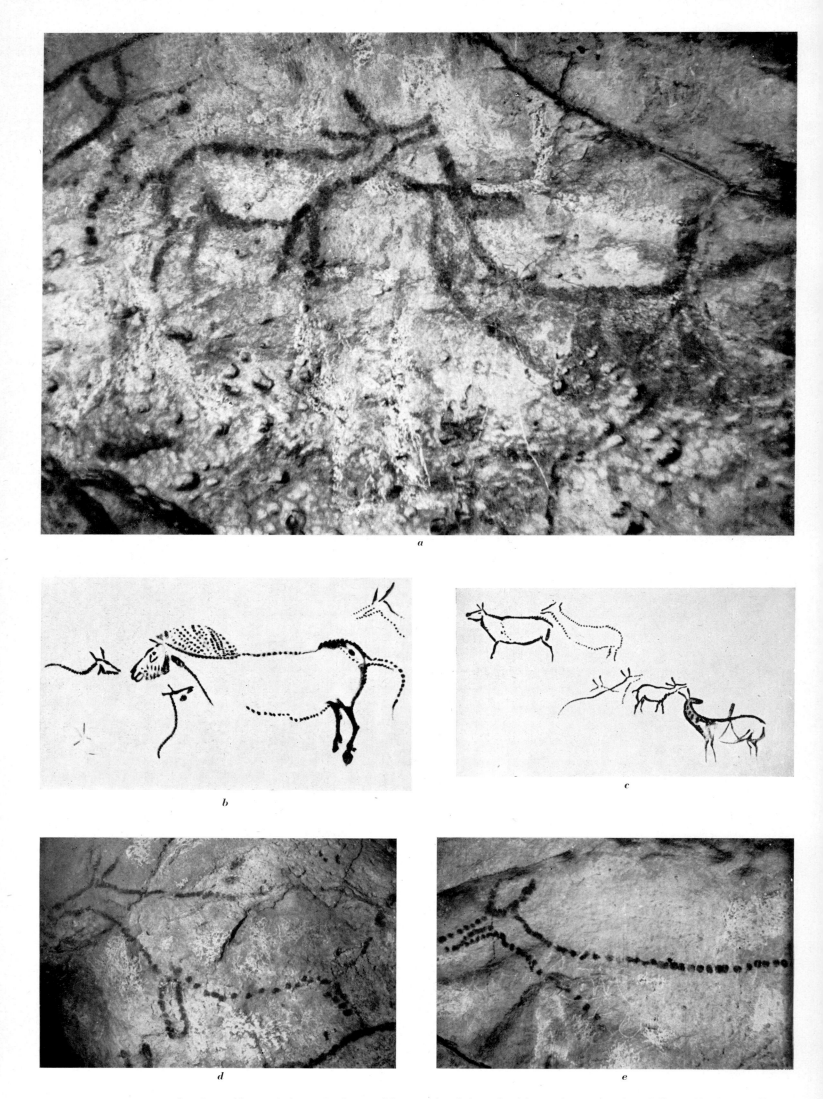

a

b

c

d

e

CAVE PAINTINGS IN SPAIN: - Covalanas (*Santander*): young deer and horse painted in red with continuous or dotted lines; *b*), *c*) according to Breuil's tracings.

Pl. 232

a

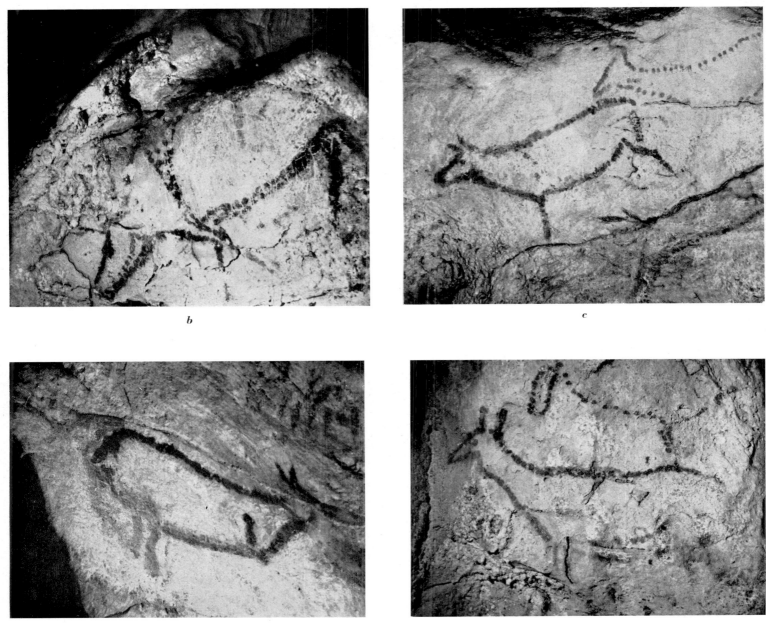

b

c

d

e

CAVE PAINTINGS IN SPAIN: - Covalanas (*Santander*): *a*), *c*) - *e*) young deer painted in red, *b*) ox painted in red (see also Pl. 274).

Pl. 233

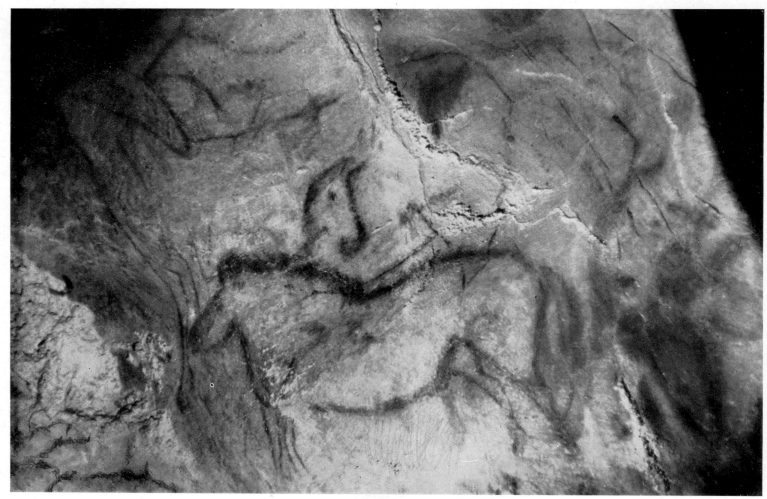

a

b

CAVE PAINTINGS IN SPAIN: - La Peña de Candamo (*Oviedo*): horses, and, above, incomplete figure of an ox; painted in black and brown; *b*) according to Cabré's tracings.

Pl. 234

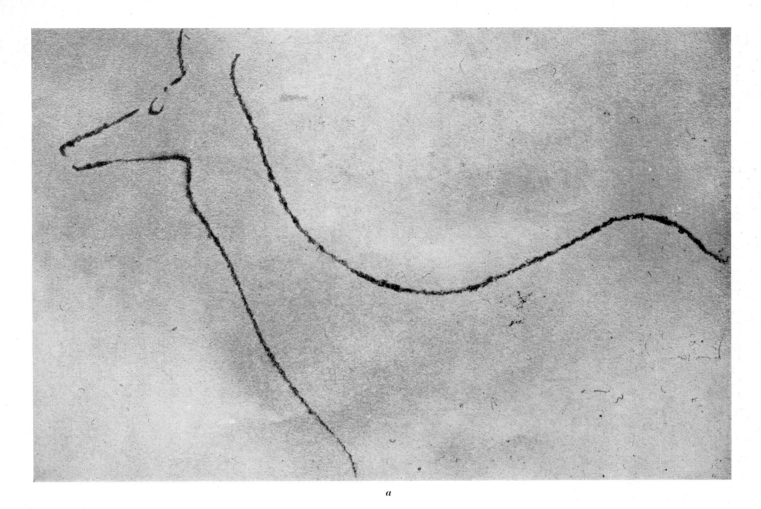

a

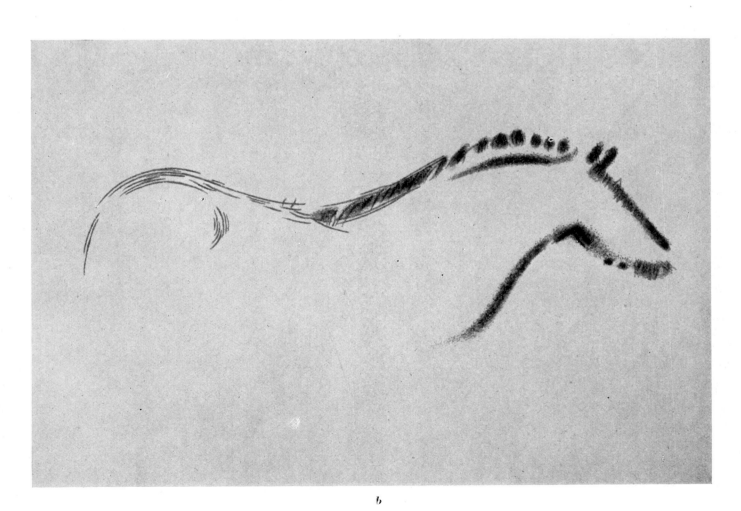

b

CAVE PAINTINGS IN SPAIN: - La Peña de Candamo (*Oviedo*): deer painted in black and horse engraved and painted in brown (see also paintings in same cave, Pls 238 *d* and 257 *d*), according to Cabré's tracings.

Pl. 235

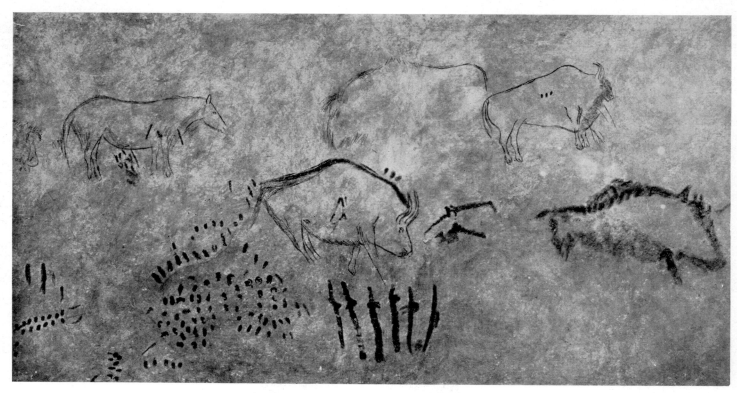

a

b

CAVE PAINTINGS IN SPAIN: - Pindal (*Oviedo*): bison, horses and various signs, painted and lightly engraved. Overall view and detail. *a*) drawn by Benitez.

Pl. 236

a

b

c

CAVE PAINTINGS IN SPAIN: - Santimamiñe (*Biscay*): *a*), *b*) panoramic view and inside of cave; *c*) horse and bison.

Pl. 237

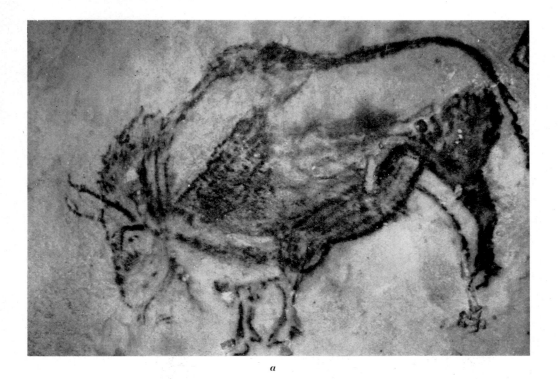

a

b

c

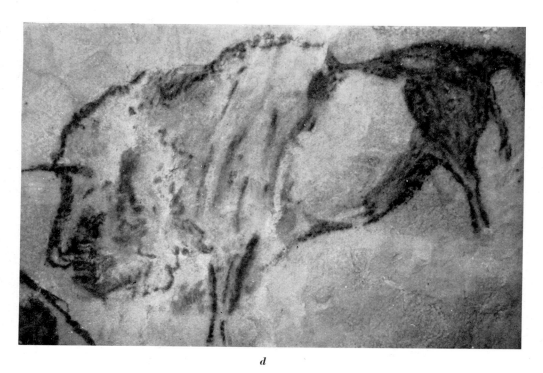

d

CAVE PAINTINGS IN SPAIN: - Santimamiñe (*Biscay*): *b*) principal pictorial composition; *a*), *c*), *d*) details.

Pl 238

a

b

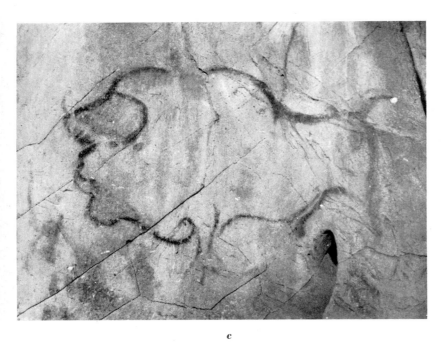

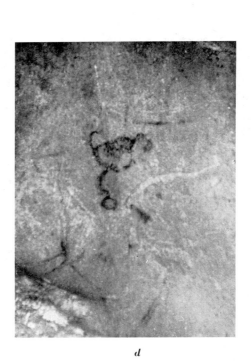

c

d

CAVE PAINTINGS IN SPAIN: - Santimamiñe (*Biscay*): deer, bear and bison in vertical formation; *c*) La Pasiega (*Santander*) *d*) Candamo (*Oviedo*), bison.

Pl. 239

a

b

CAVE PAINTINGS IN SPAIN: - Altamira Cave (*Santander*): *a*) the impressive composition of polychromatic figures on the ceiling of the great hall.
b) The paintings on the ceiling of the great hall according to Breuil's tracing.

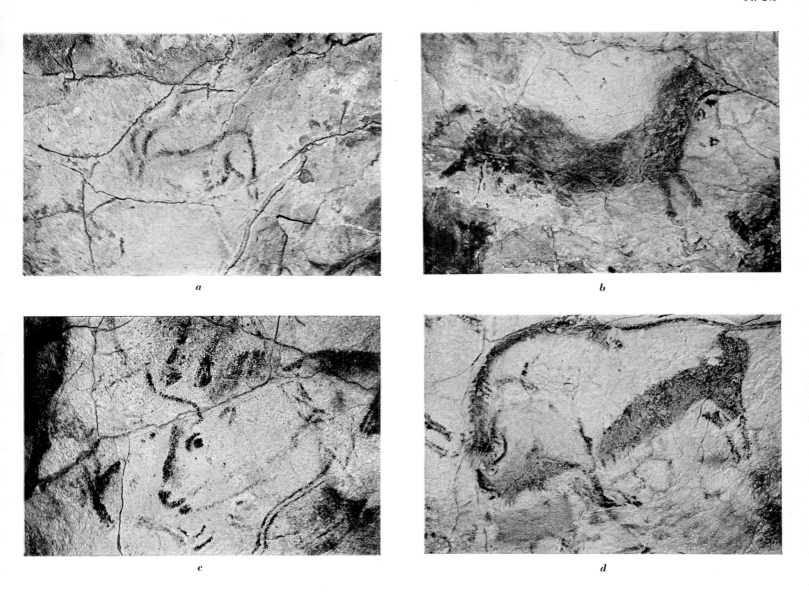

Pl. 240

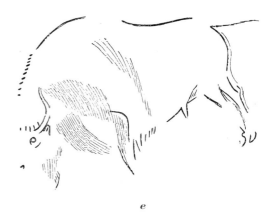

CAVE PAINTINGS IN SPAIN: - Altamira Cave (*Santander*): *a*), *b*) ibex and horse executed in a more archaic style than the following figures; *c*), *d*) bison head and bison painted in black; *e*) engraved outline of figure *d*), according to Breuil's tracings.

Pl. 241

a

b

CAVE PAINTINGS IN SPAIN: - Altamira Cave (*Santander*): *a*) polychromatic bison; *b*) engraved outline of same, according to Breuil's tracing.

Pl. 242

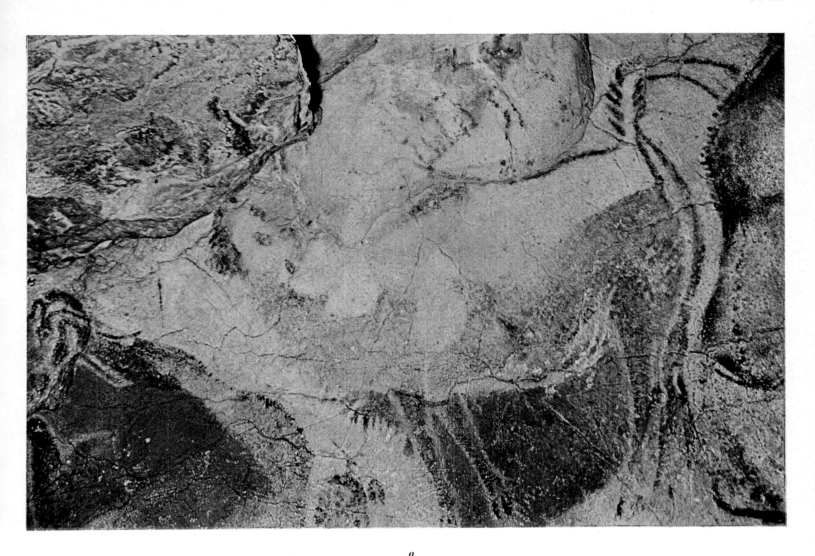

a

b

CAVE PAINTINGS IN SPAIN: - Altamira Cave (*Santander*): *a*) lowing bison, polychromatic; *b*) engraved parts of same, according to Breuil's tracings.

Pl. 243

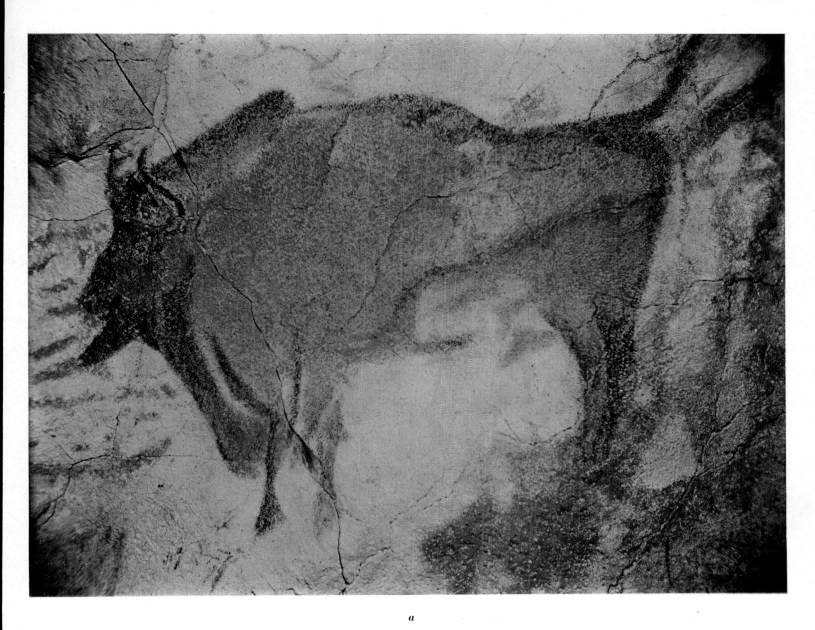

a

b

CAVE PAINTINGS IN SPAIN: - Altamira Cave (*Santander*): *a*) polychromatic bison; *b*) engraved outline of same, according to Breuil's tracings.

Pl. 244

a

b

CAVE PAINTINGS IN SPAIN: - Altamira Cave (*Santander*): *a*) bison and head of horse or boar, superimposed; *b*) engraved outlines of same, according to Breuil's tracings.

Pl. 245

a

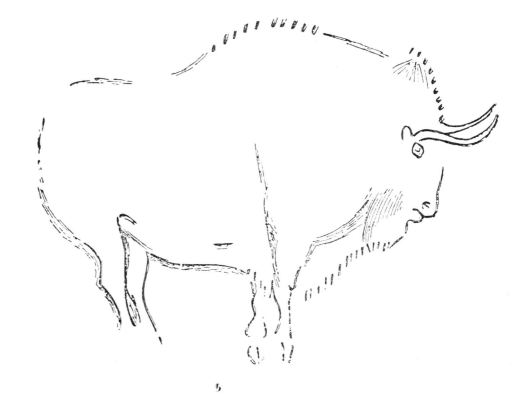

b

CAVE PAINTINGS IN SPAIN: - Altamira Cave (*Santander*): *a*) Polychromatic bison; *b*) engraved outline of same, according to Breuil's tracing.

Pl. 246

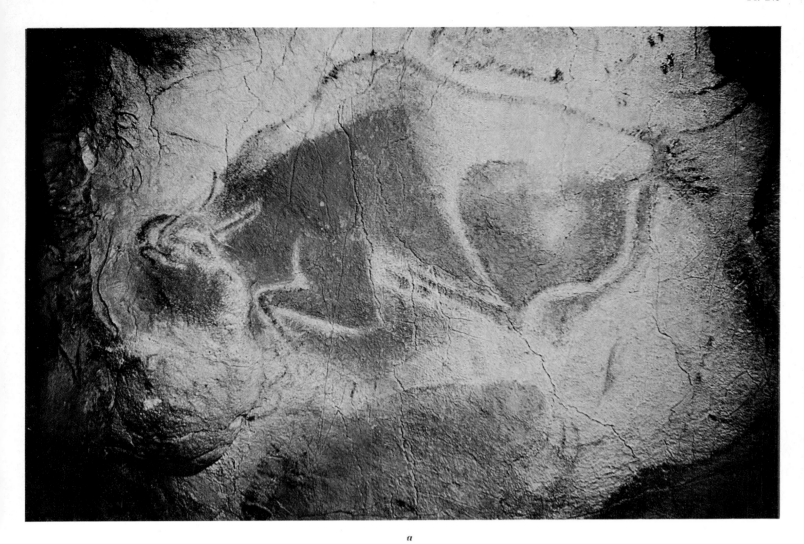

a

b

CAVE PAINTINGS IN SPAIN: - Altamira Cave (*Santander*): *a*) crouching bison, polychromatic; *b*) engraved outline of same, according to Breuil's tracing.

Pl. 247

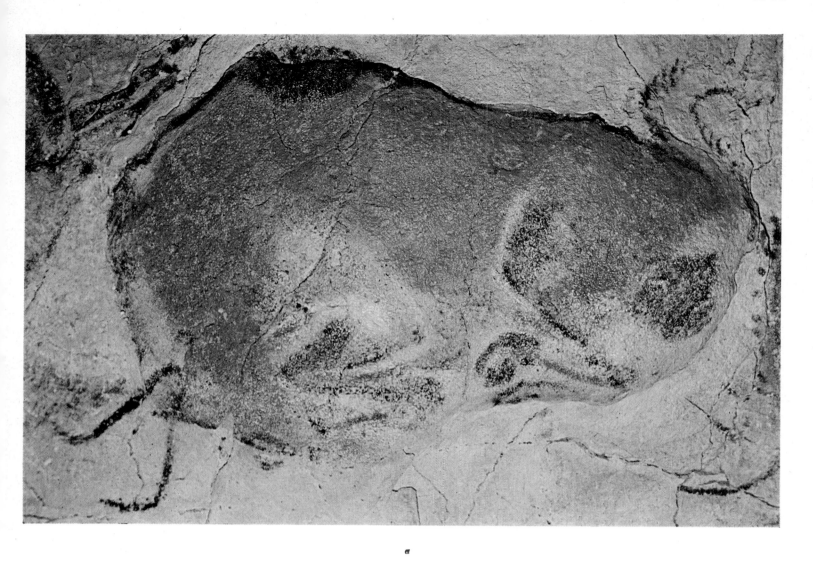

a

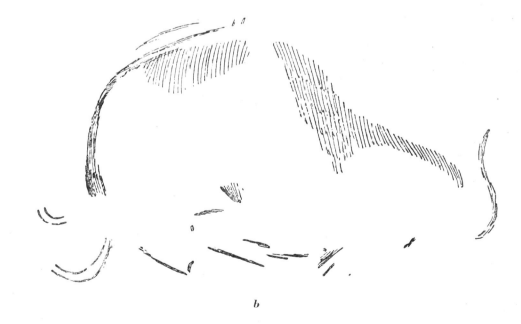

b

CAVE PAINTINGS IN SPAIN: - Altamira Cave (*Santander*): *a*) crouching bison, polychromatic; *b*) engraved parts of same, according to Breuil's tracing.

Pl. 248

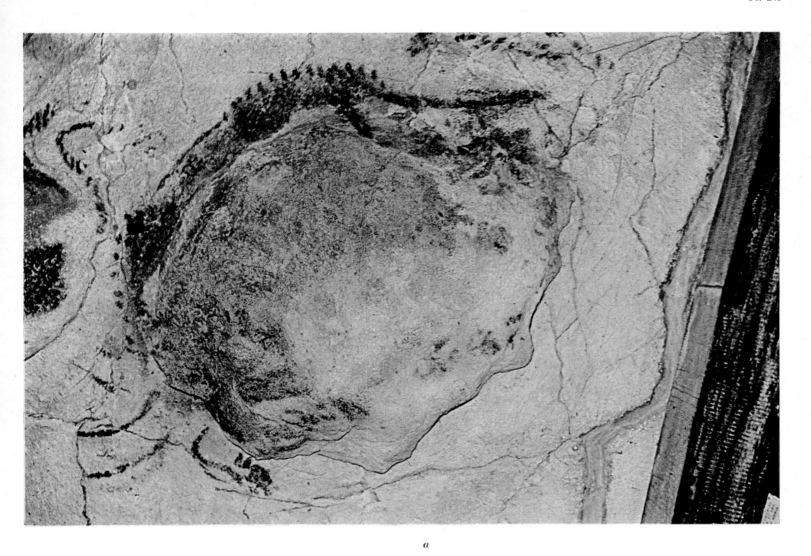

a

b

CAVE PAINTINGS IN SPAIN: - Altamira Cave (*Santander*): polychromatic bison; *b*) engraved parts of same, according to Breuil's tracings.

Pl. 249

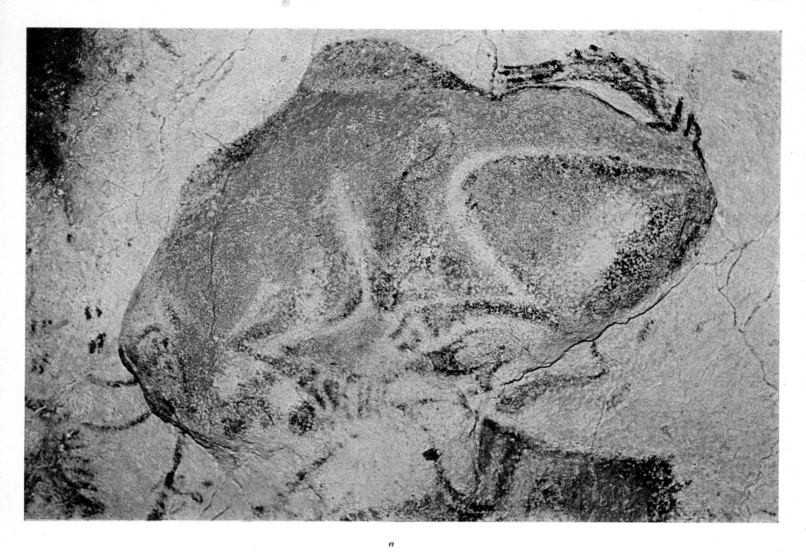

a

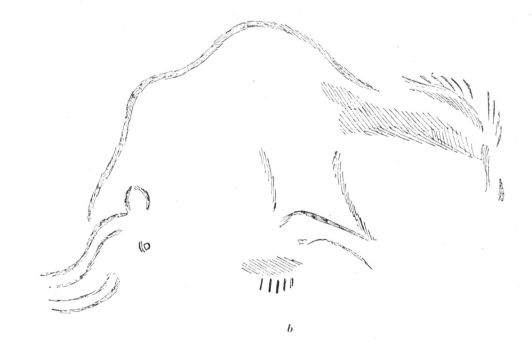

b

CAVE PAINTINGS IN SPAIN: - Altamira Cave (*Santander*): *a*) polychromatic bison; *b*) engraved parts of same, according to Breuil's tracing.

Pl. 250

a

b

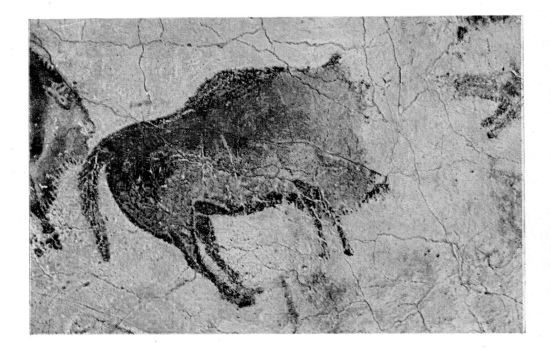

c

CAVE PAINTINGS IN SPAIN: - Altamira Cave (*Santander*): bison, black and polychromatic.

Pl. 251

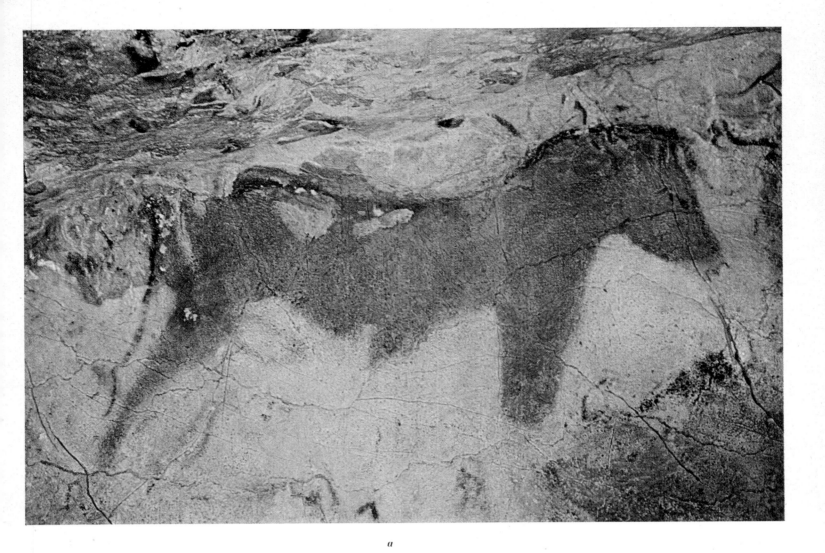

a

b

CAVE PAINTINGS IN SPAIN: - Altamira Cave (*Santander*): *a*) horse and young deer, superimposed; *b*) engraved parts of same, according to Breuil's tracings.

Pl. 252

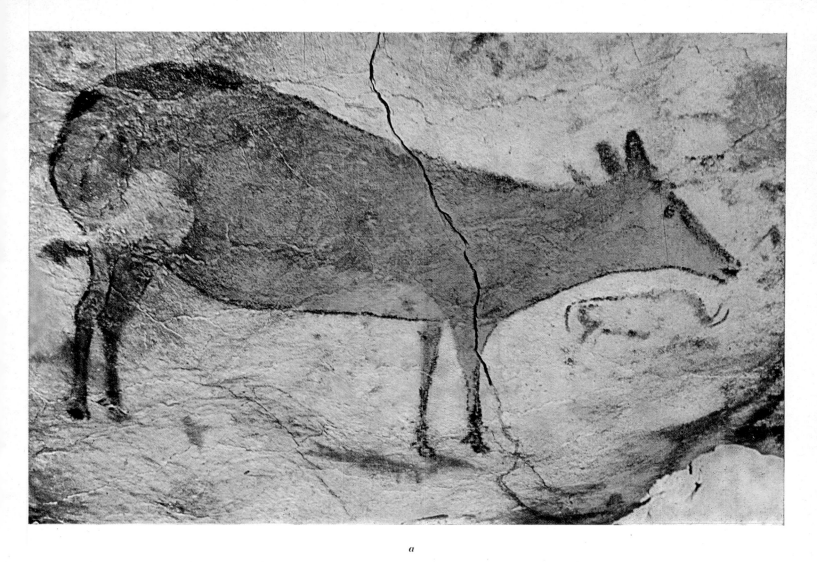

a

b

CAVE PAINTINGS IN SPAIN: - Altamira Cave (*Santander*): *a*) polychromatic deer and small black bison; *b*) engraved outline of former, according to Breuil's tracing.

Pl. 253

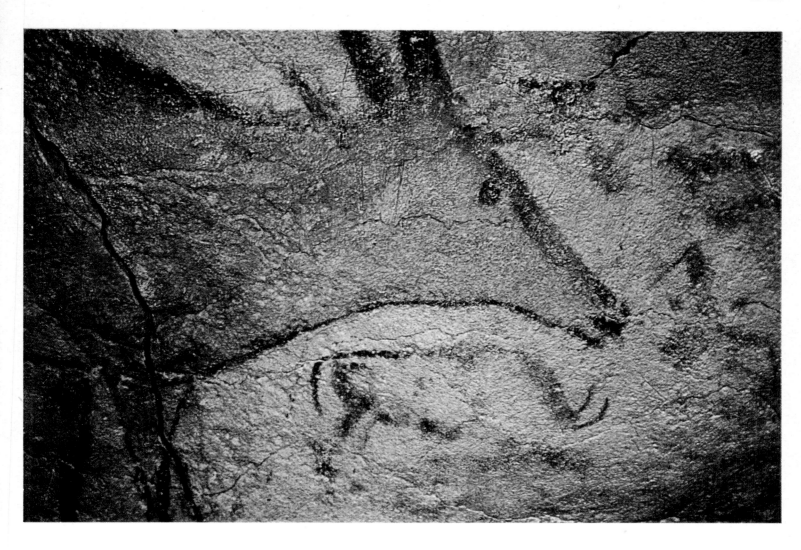

Pl. 254

a

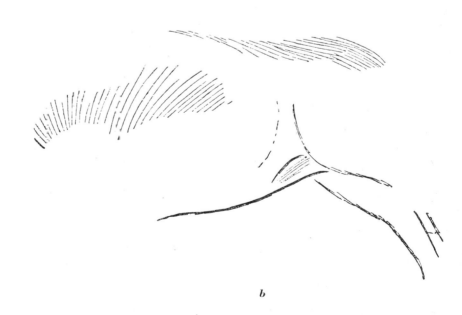

b

CAVE PAINTINGS IN SPAIN: - Altamira Cave (*Santander*): *a*) polychromatic boar; *b*) engraved parts of same, according to Breuil's tracing.

Pl. 255

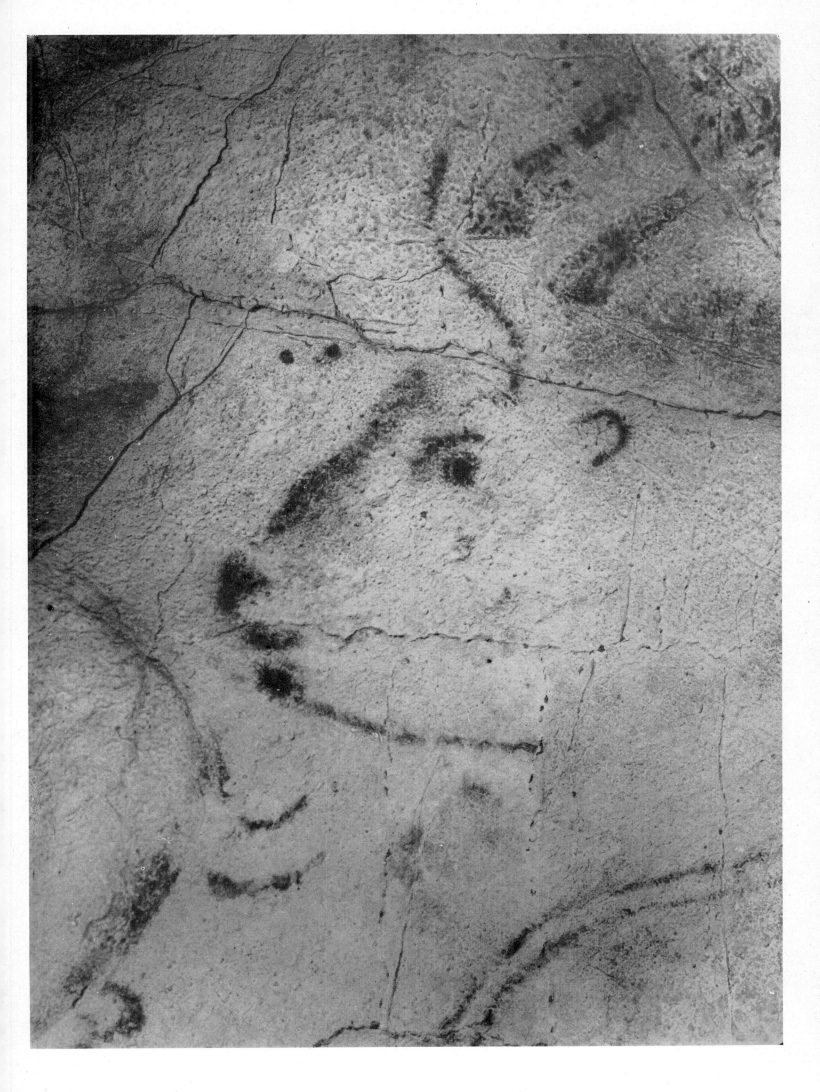

CAVE PAINTINGS IN SPAIN: - Altamira (*Santander*): ox head painted in black (see also Pl. 240 *c*).

Pl. 256

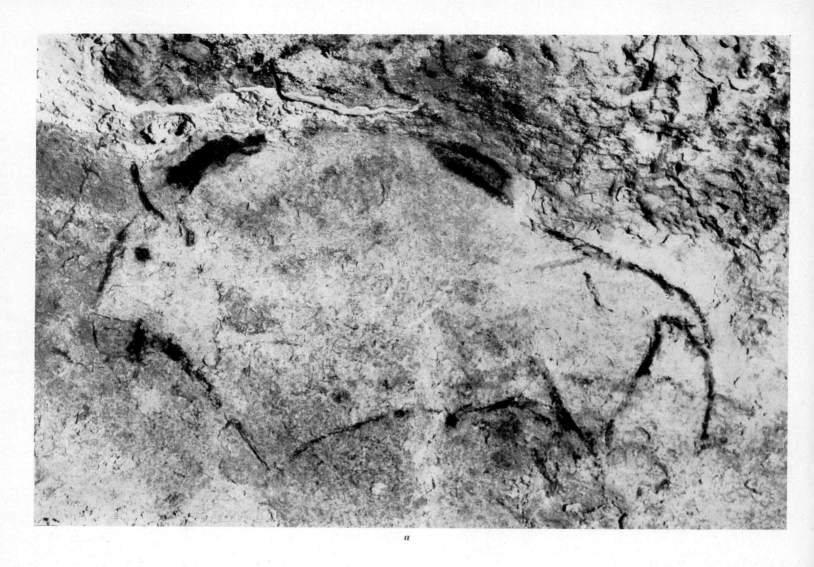

a

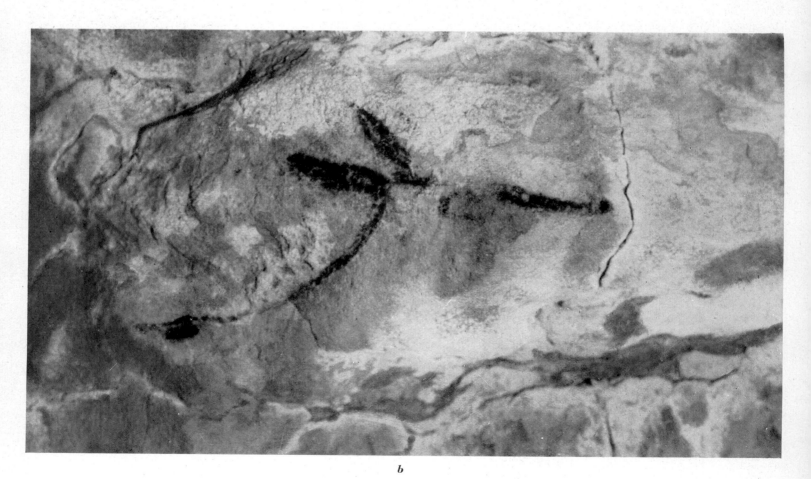

b

CAVE PAINTINGS IN SPAIN: - Altamira (*Santander*): bison painted in black; *b*) deer's head.

Pl. 257

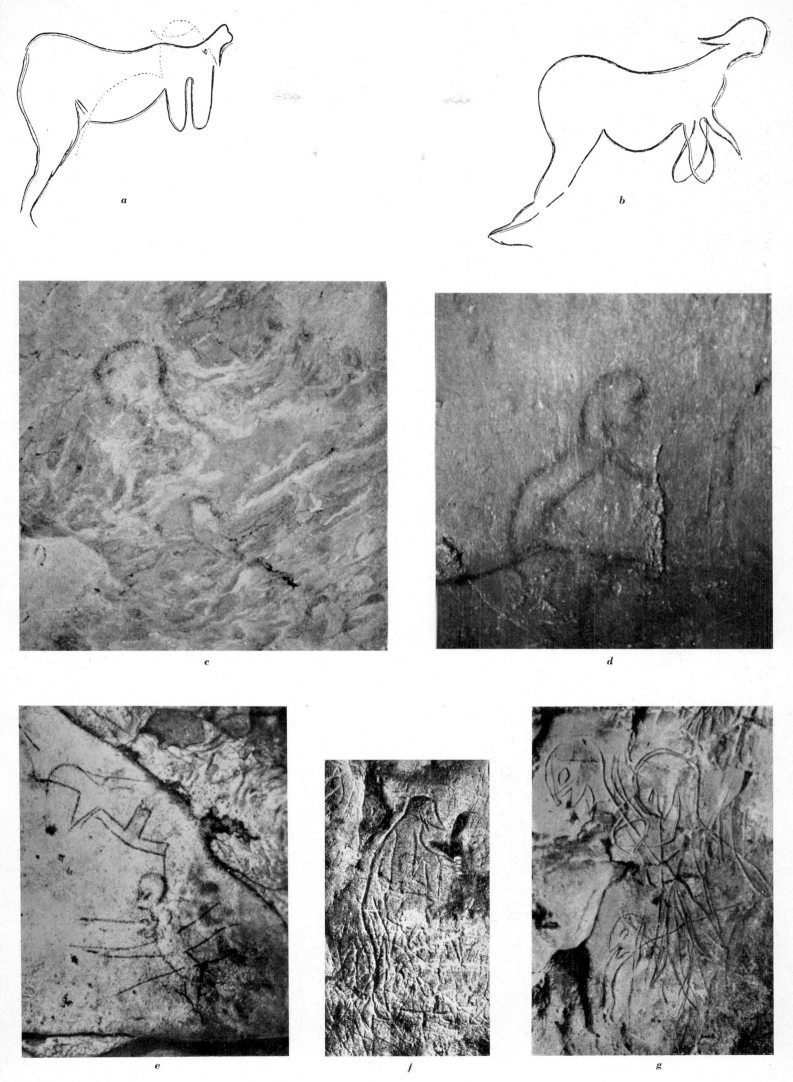

THE HUMAN FORM: - *a*), *b*) Female figures engraved on clay in Pech-Merle (*Lot*), according to Breuil's tracings (see also Pl. 116). Anthropomorphic figures, painted and engraved: *c*) in Le Portel (*Ariège*), *d*) in Candamo (*Oviedo*), *e*) in Pech-Merle, *f*), *g*) in Los Casares (*Guadalajara*).

Pl. 258

THE HUMAN FORM: - Engravings in: *a*) Los Casares (*Guadalajara*); *b*) Le Gabillou, according to Malvesin's tracing, *d*) La Roche (*Dordogne*); schematic anthropomorphic figures from Magdalenian layers: *c*), *e*) Marsoulas (*Haute-Garonne*); *f*), *g*) Les Combarelles (*Dordogne*), according to Breuil's tracings.

Pl. 259

a

b

c

THE HUMAN FORM: - Engravings in: *a*) Les Combarelles (*Dordogne*); *b*) Altamira, according to Breuil's tracings, *c*) Hornos de la Peña (*Santander*).

Pl. 260

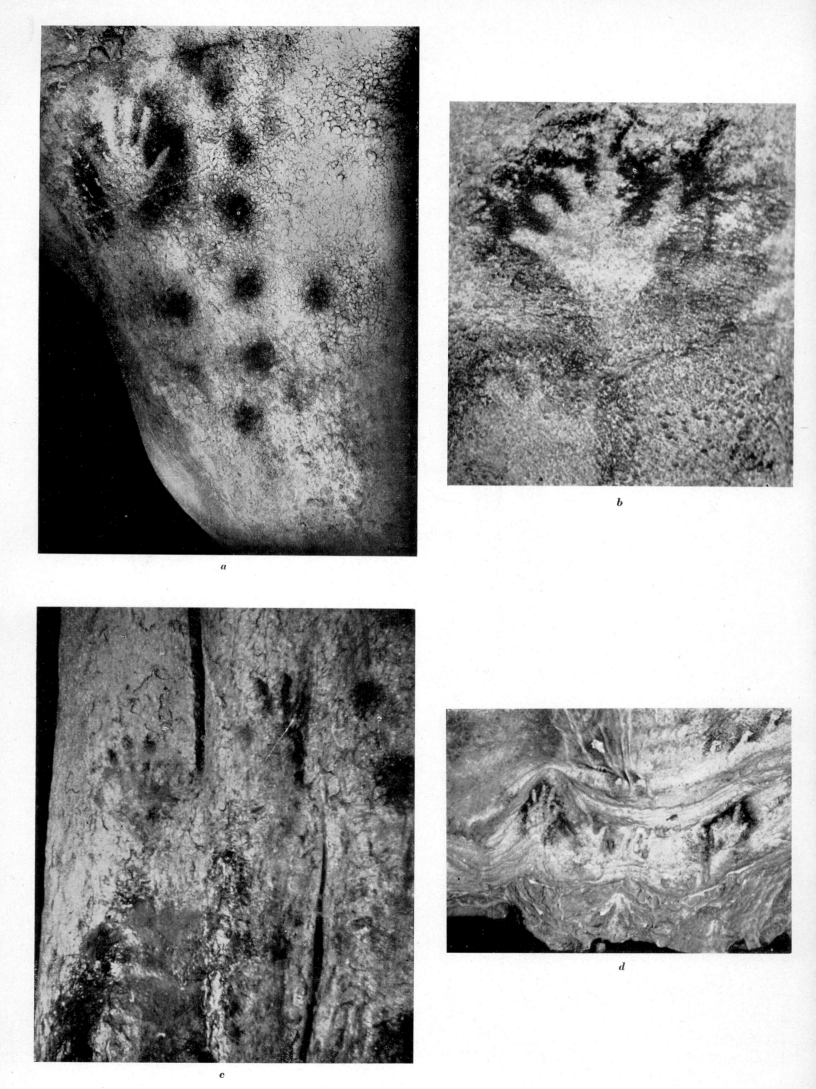

HANDS: - *a*) Pech-Merle (*Lot*), *b*), *d*) Gargas (*Hautes-Pyrénées*), negative impressions; *c*) Bédeilhac (*Ariège*), positive impressions.

Pl. 261

a

b

c

HANDS: - Engraved hands: *a*) Barabao (*Dordogne*), *b*) Cap Blanc (*Dordogne*); *c*) on clay, Niaux (*Ariège*).

Pl. 262

HANDS: - Castillo Cave (*Santander*): negative impression of hand.

Pl. 263

HANDS: - Gargas Cave (*Hautes-Pyrénées*): negative impressions of hands in red and in black.

Pl. 264

a

b

c

VARIOUS SIGNS: - Dotted lines, red: *a*) Les Trois Frères (*Ariège*); *b*), *c*) Castillo (*Santander*).

Pl. 265

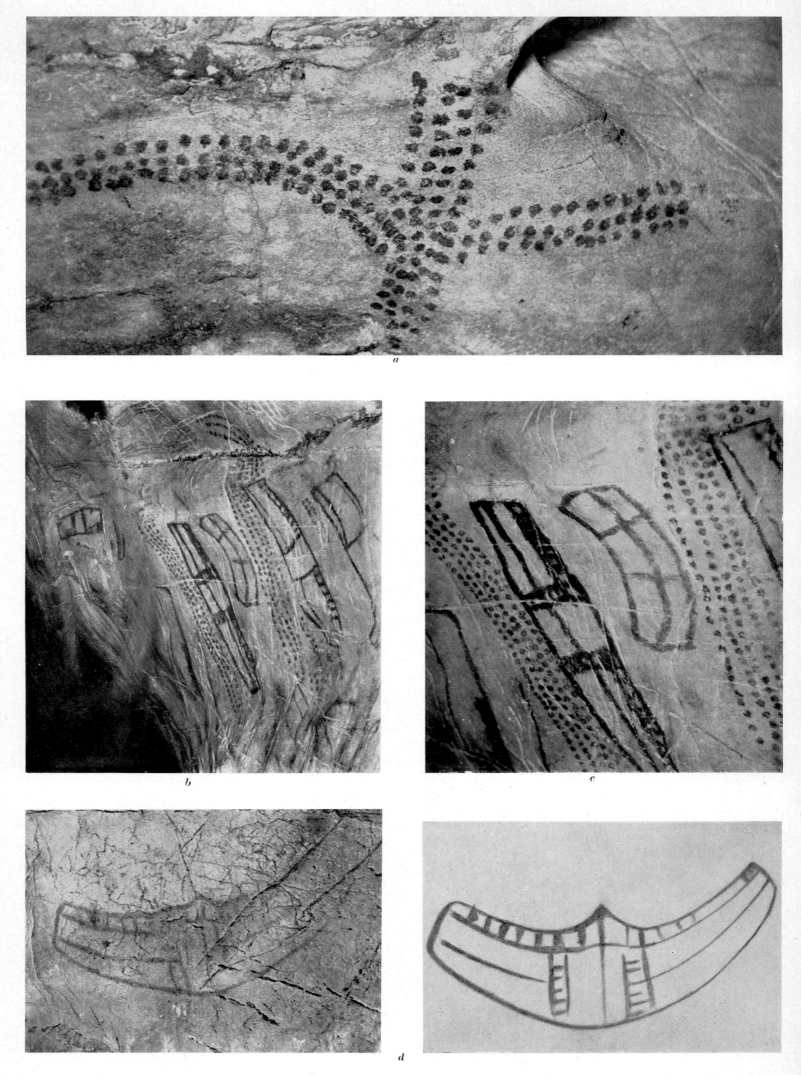

VARIOUS SIGNS: - Castillo (*Santander*): tree-shaped figures, shield-shaped figures, « tectiforms », etc.

Pl. 266

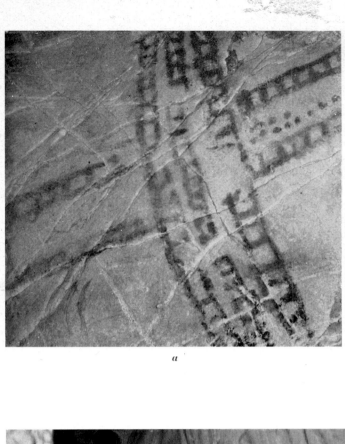

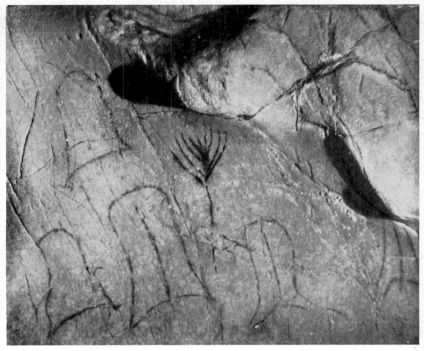

a

b

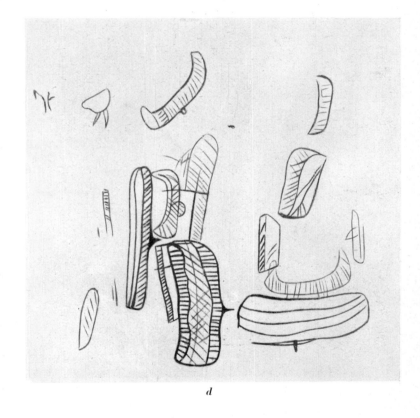

c

d

e

f

VARIOUS SIGNS: - « Tectiforms », shield-shaped figures, tree-shaped figures, etc.: *a*), *b*) Castillo (*Santander*); *c*) - *f*) La Pasiega (*Santander*), *d*), *f*) according to Breuil's tracings.

Pl. 267

VARIOUS SIGNS: - Castillo Cave (*Santander*): « tectiform » figure.

Pl. 268

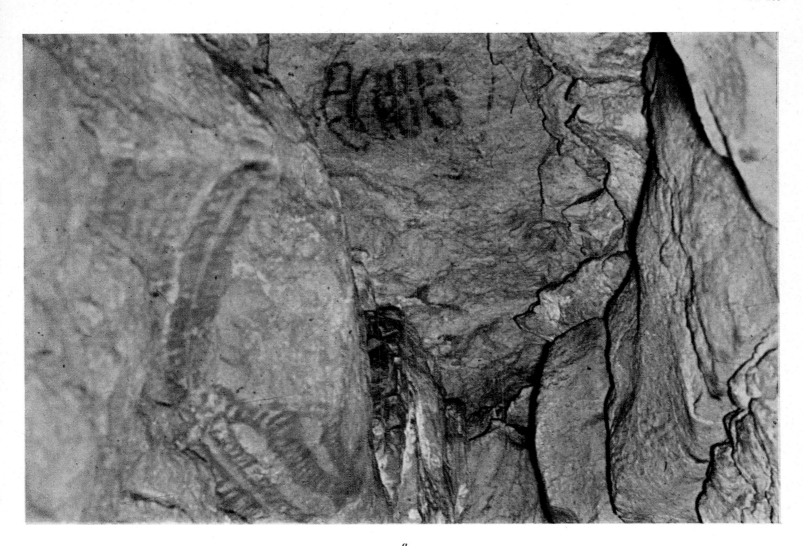

a

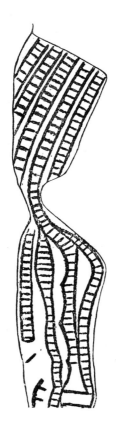

b

VARIOUS SIGNS: - Altamira Cave (*Santander*): *a*) shield-shaped and ribbon-shaped figures; *b*) the same according to Breuil's tracings.

Pl. 269

VARIOUS SIGNS: - Lascaux Cave (*Dordogne*): painted and engraved « blazons ».

Pl. 270

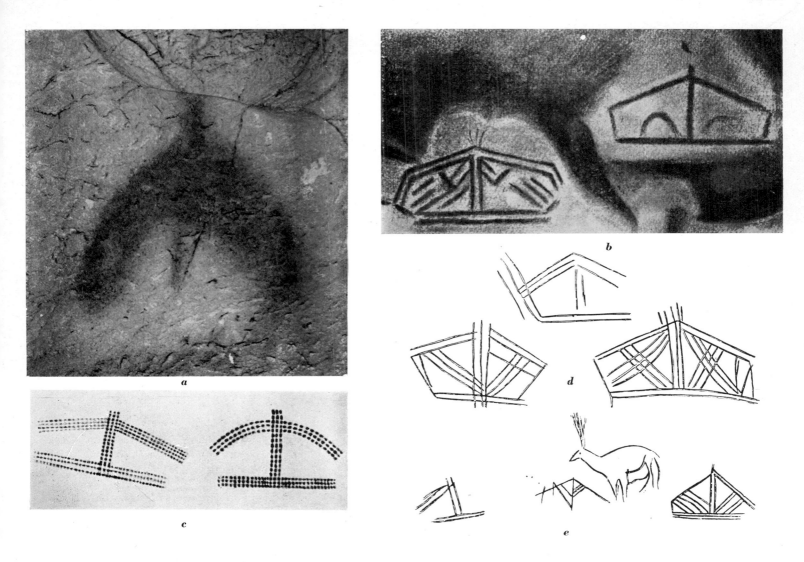

VARIOUS SIGNS: - « Tectiform » and other figures painted and engraved: *a*) Le Portel (*Ariège*); *b*)-*d*) Font-de-Gaume, *e*) Les Combarelles, *f*) La Mouthe (*Dordogne*); *b*)-*e*) according to Breuil's tracings.

Pl. 271

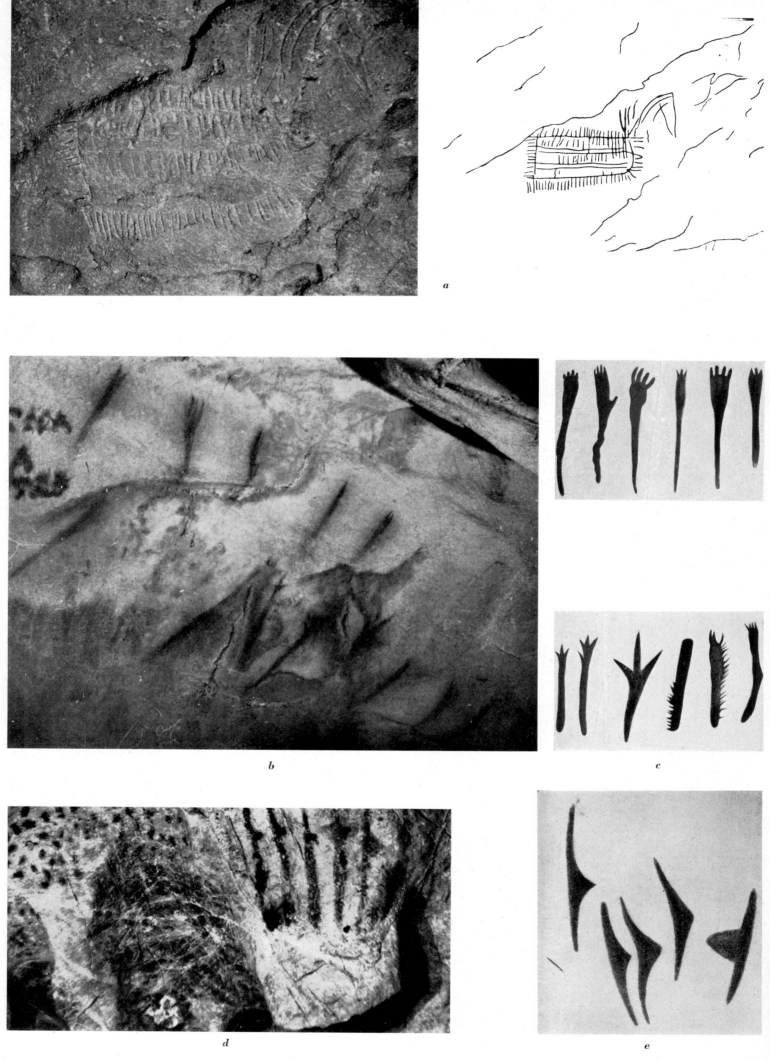

VARIOUS SIGNS: - « Tectiforms », club-shaped figures, etc., engraved and painted in: *a*) Buxu (*Oviedo*); *b*), *c*) Santian (*Santander*); *d*) Pindal (*Oviedo*); *e*) La Pasiega (*Santander*), drawings by Benitez (*a*), and by Breuil (*c*, *e*).

Pl. 272

VARIOUS SIGNS: - « Tectiforms », club-shaped figures, etc., in: *a*) Altamira (*Santander*); *b*), *d*), *e*), *f*) Niaux, *c*) Les Trois Frères (*Ariège*); *g*), *h*) Marsoulas (*Haute-Garonne*), probably Mesolithic; *a*), *b*) according to Breuil's tracings.

Pl. 273

UTILIZATION OF NATURAL ACCIDENTS: - Altamira Cave (*Santander*): rocky protuberances on the ceiling of the great hall used in the execution of polychromatic paintings of bison, to each of which they give an extra dimension.

Pl. 274

UTILIZATION OF NATURAL ACCIDENTS: - Covalanas Cave (*Santander*): painted ox. A natural spur of rock forms the outline of the back and of the hindquarters.

Pl. 275

a

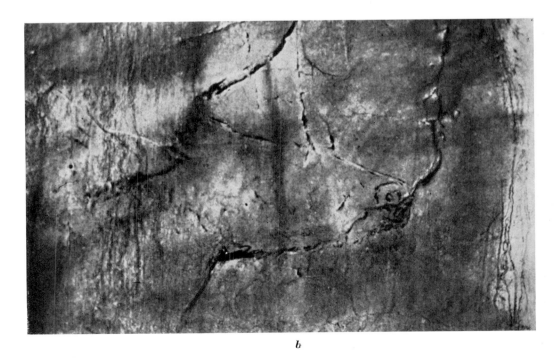

b

UTILIZATION OF NATURAL ACCIDENTS: - *a*) Castillo (*Santander*): bison; *b*) Niaux (*Ariège*): ox.

Pl. 276

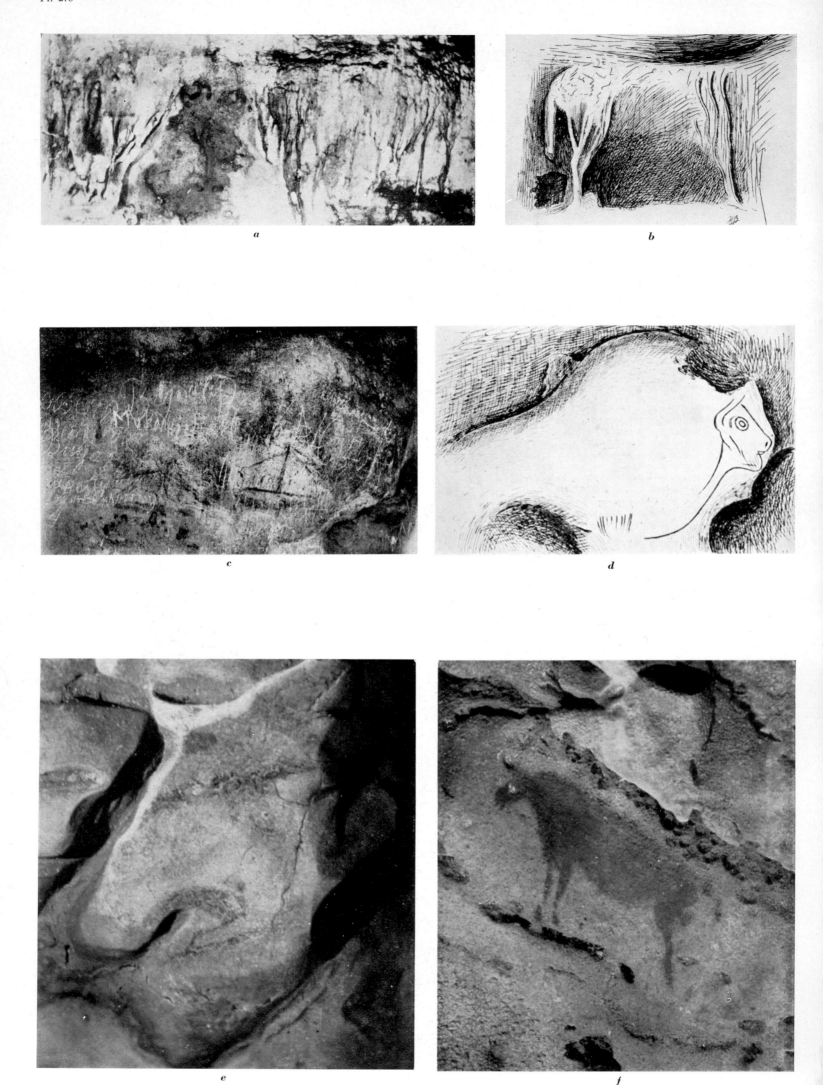

UTILIZATION OF NATURAL ACCIDENTS: - *a*)-*d*) Font-de-Gaume (*Dordogne*), mare and bison, (*b, d,* drawings by Breuil); *e*) Mas d'Azil, head of a feline animal; *f*) Le Portel (*Ariège*), horse.

Pl. 277

UTILIZATION OF NATURAL ACCIDENTS: - Niaux (*Ariège*): impressions made by water dropping on clay, used to represent the eye and the wounds of a bison.

Pl. 278

Pech-Merle (*Lot*): stalagmites resembling mammoths, which may have inspired Palaeolithic artists in the execution of the mammoth figures painted in the cave.

Pl. 281

a

b

PALAEOLITHIC MAGIC: - *a*) The « sorcerer » of Les Trois Frères (*Ariège*), *b*) Same according to Breuil's tracing.

Pl. 282

a

b

c　　　　　　　　*d*

MAGIC AND COMPOSITION: - *a*) Font-de-Gaume (*Dordogne*), lion and horses; *b*) Lascaux (*Dordogne*), pregnant mare; *c*), *d*) Les Trois Frères (*Ariège*), composite animals and hybrid anthropomorphic beings, (*a, c, d* according to Breuil's tracings).

Pl. 283

a

b

MAGIC AND COMPOSITION: - *a*) Les Trois Frères (*Ariège*), hybrid animals, according to Breuil's tracings; *b*) Lascaux (*Dordogne*), wounded bison charging a man.

Pl. 284

a

b

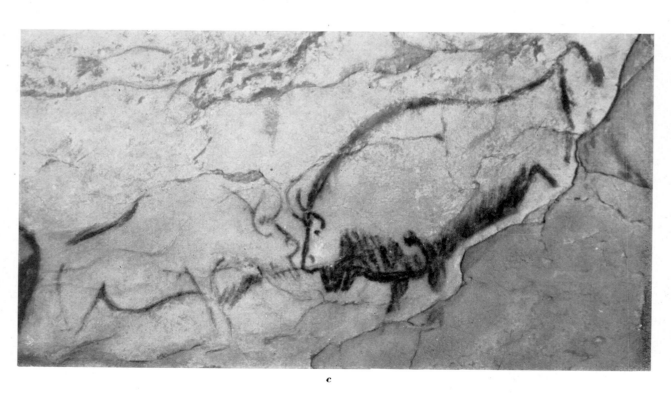

c

MAGIC AND COMPOSITION: - The magic of reproduction. Couples of animals: *a*) La Mairie, *b*) Les Combarelles (*Dordogne*), according to Breuil's tracings; *c*) Le Portel (*Ariège*).

THE MEDITERRANEAN PROVINCE

Pl. 285

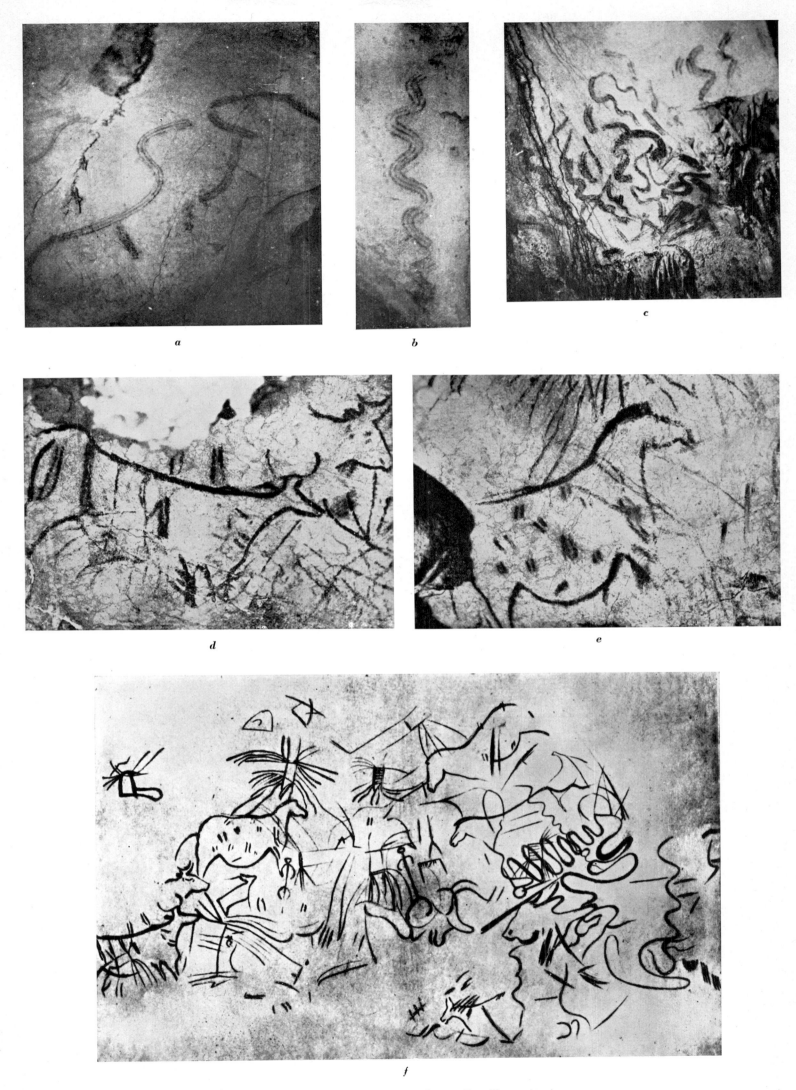

La Pileta (*Malaga*): serpentine painted figures, oxen and horses, (*f*, according to Breuil's tracings).

Pl. 286

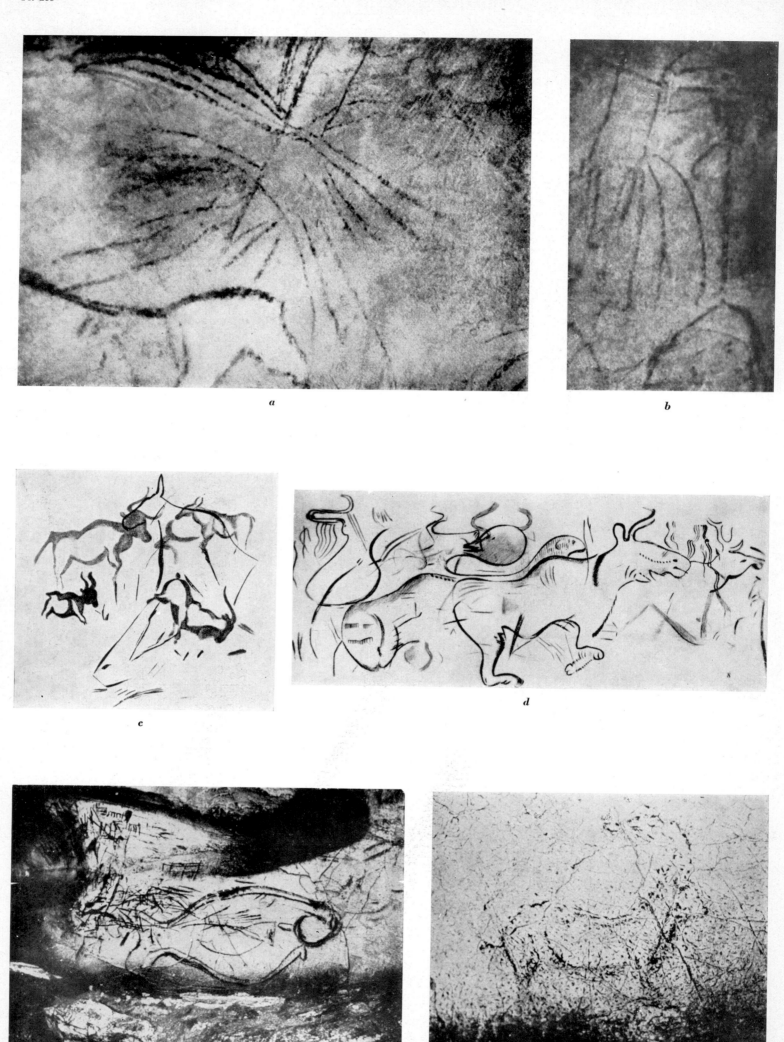

a

b

c

d

e

f

La Pileta (*Malaga*): patterns of radiating lines, and animals, (*c*, *d* according to Breuil's tracings).

Pl. 287

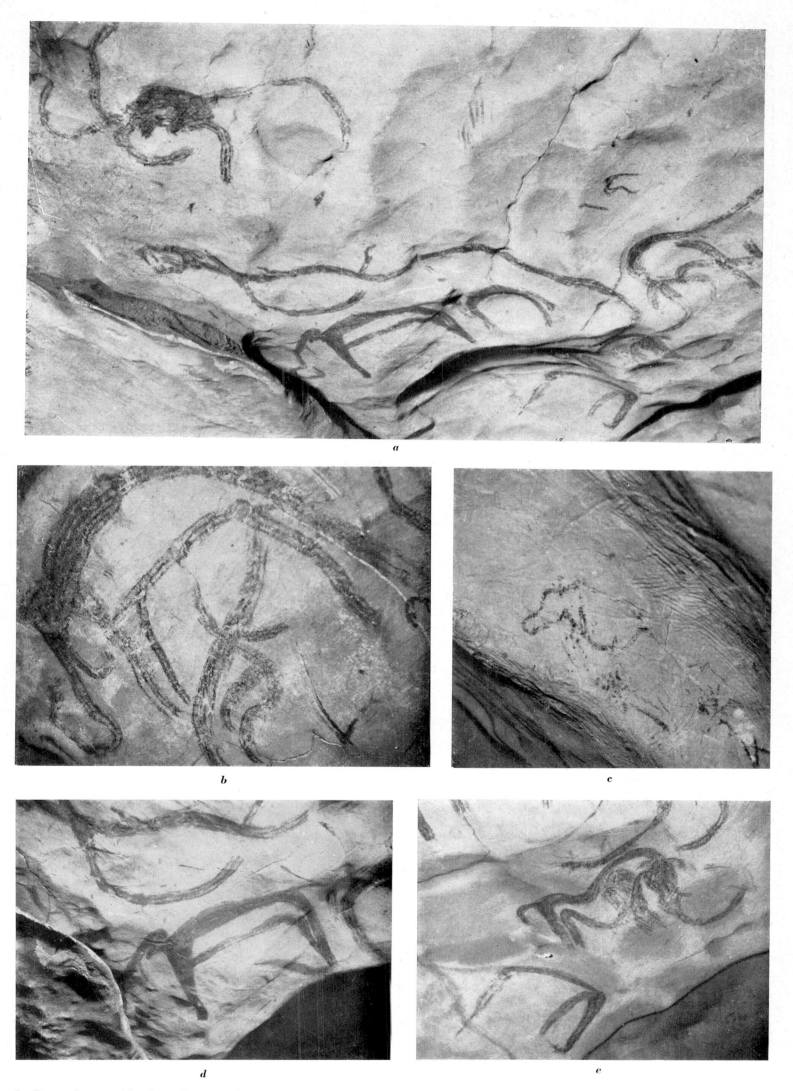

La Baume Latrone (*Gard*): outlines of animal figures traced with the red clay found in the cave; highly stylized elephants (*b, d, e*); fantastic serpentine figure (*a*); rhinoceros (*c*).

Pl. 288

a

b

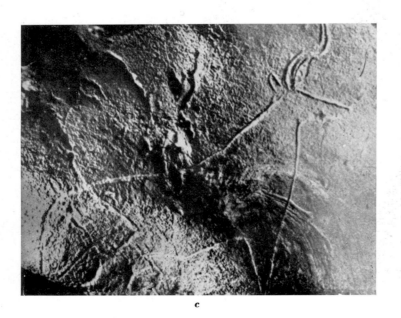

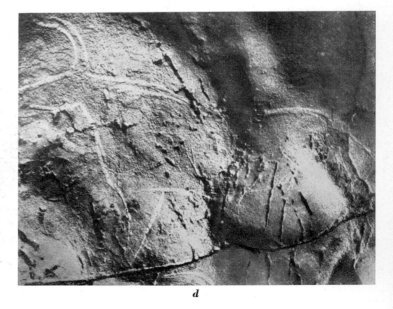

c

d

Ebbou (*Ardèche*): engraved horse, ibex and oxen.

Pl. 289

a

b

c

Romanelli (*Otranto*): *a*) the cave seen from the exterior; *b*), *c*) inside views, with cave deposit.

Pl. 290

a

b

Romanelli (*Otranto*): ox and geometrical design, engraved.

Pl. 291

Romanelli (*Otranto*): oval and shuttle-shaped designs, engraved, (*c*, according to Blanc's tracings).

Pl. 292

a

b

c

Levanzo (*Egadi*): *a*) the cave viewed from the sea; *b*), *c*) the back of the cave, with paintings of a late prehistoric period.

Pl. 293

Levanzo (*Egadi*) young deer turning its head.

Pl. 294

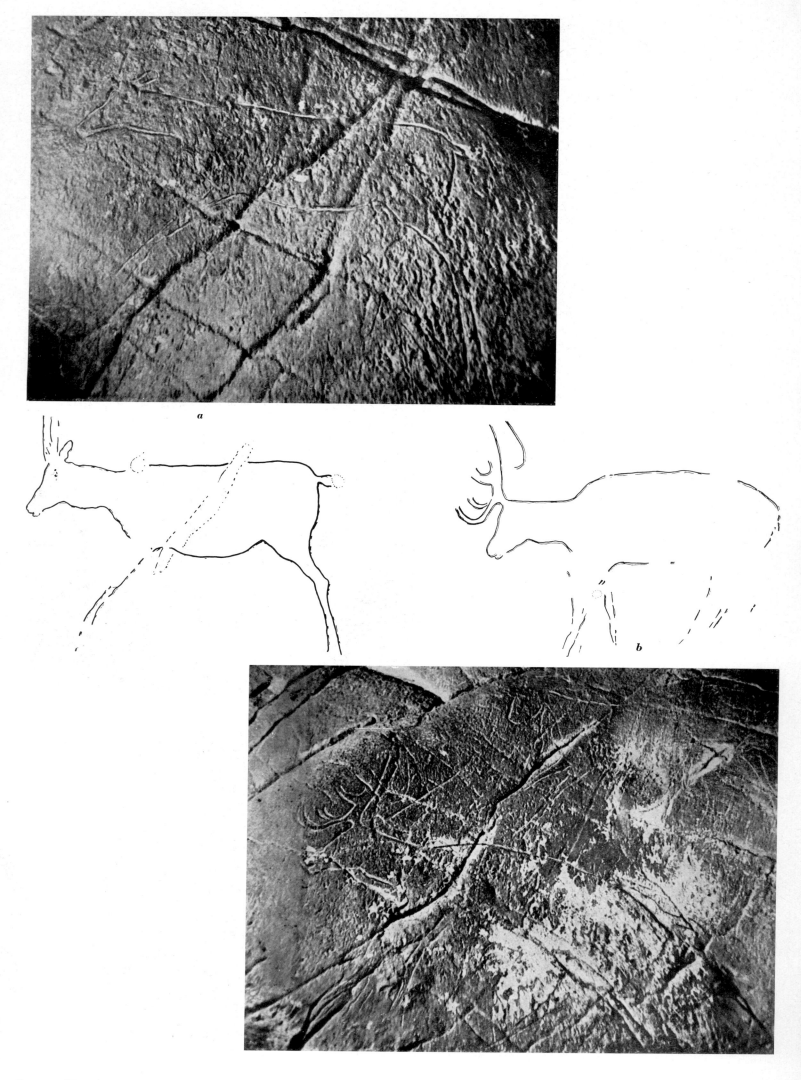

a

b

Levanzo (*Egadi*): engraved deer.

Pl. 295

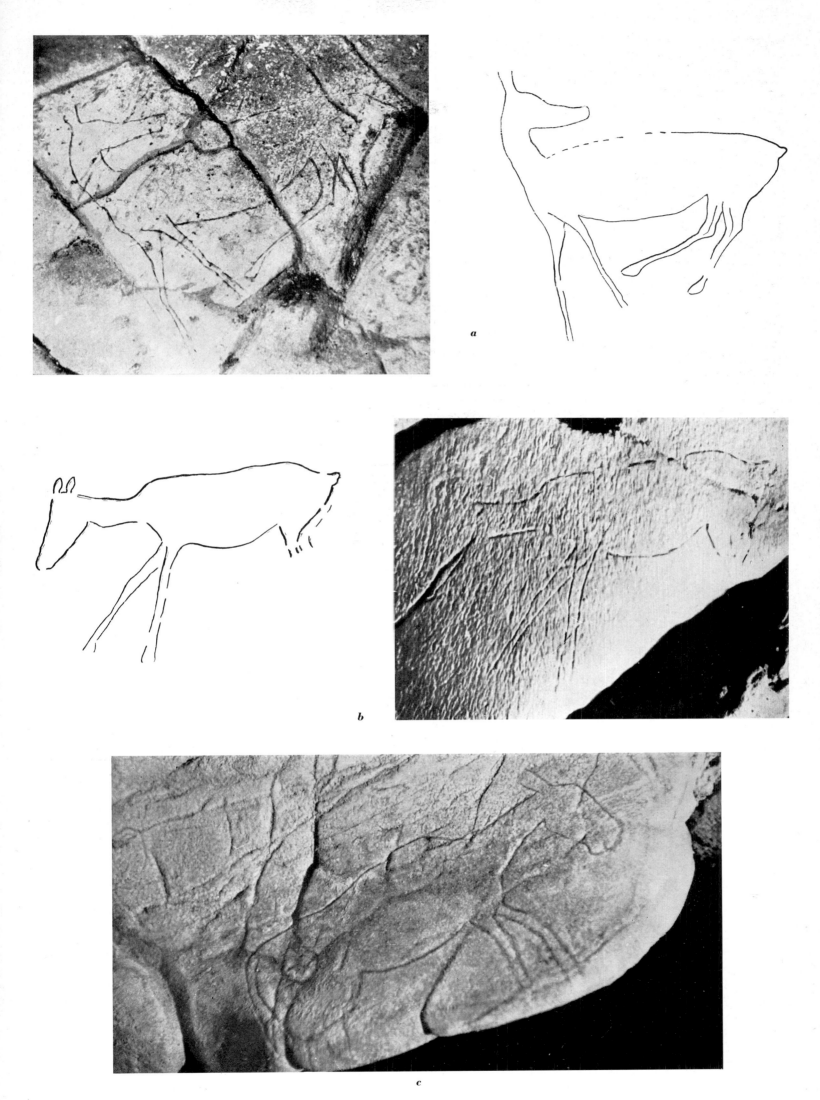

Levanzo (*Egadi*): *a*), *b*) young deer; *c*) horse, perhaps *Equus hydrvntinus*.

Pl. 296

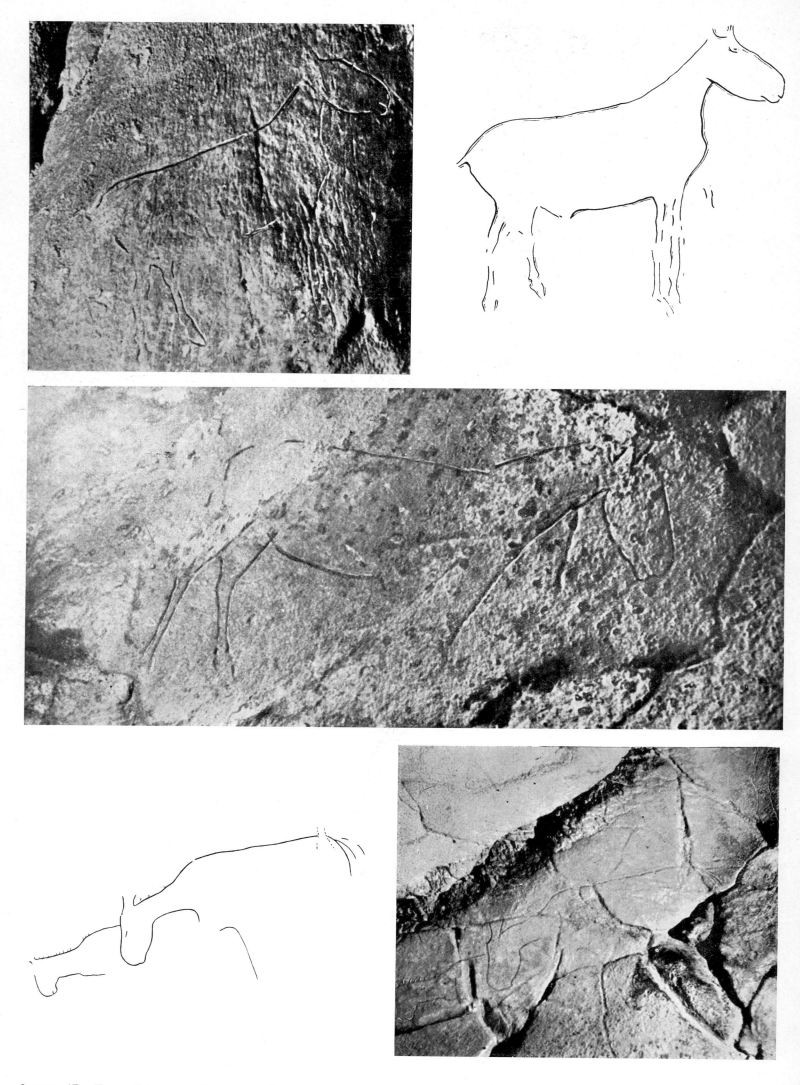

Levanzo (*Egadi*): small horses, perhaps *Equus hydruntinus*.

Pl. 297

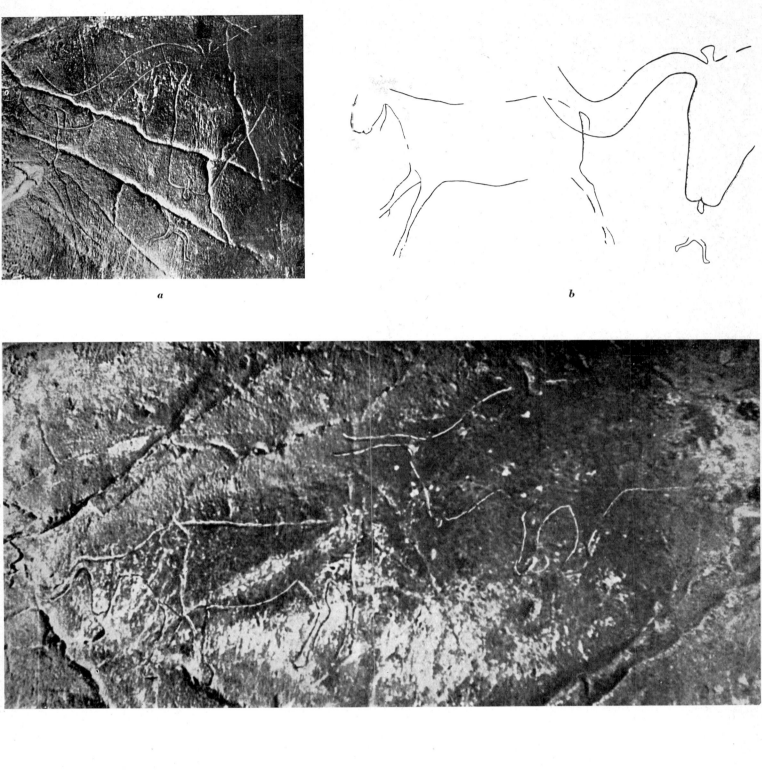

Levanzo (*Egadi*): *a*), *b*) ox head, horse and small human legs; *c*) bull pursuing a cow.

Pl. 298

a

b

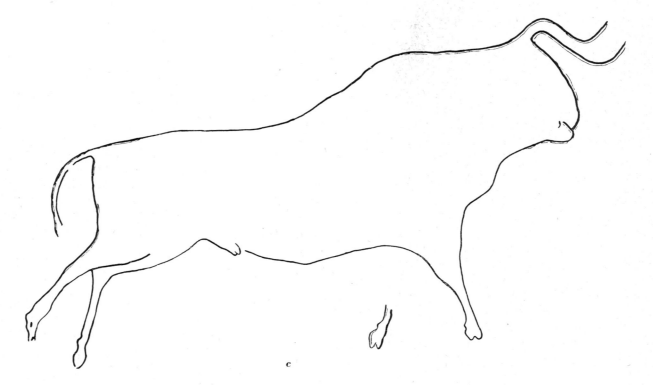

c

Levanzo (*Egadi*): bull, cow and horse.

Pl. 299

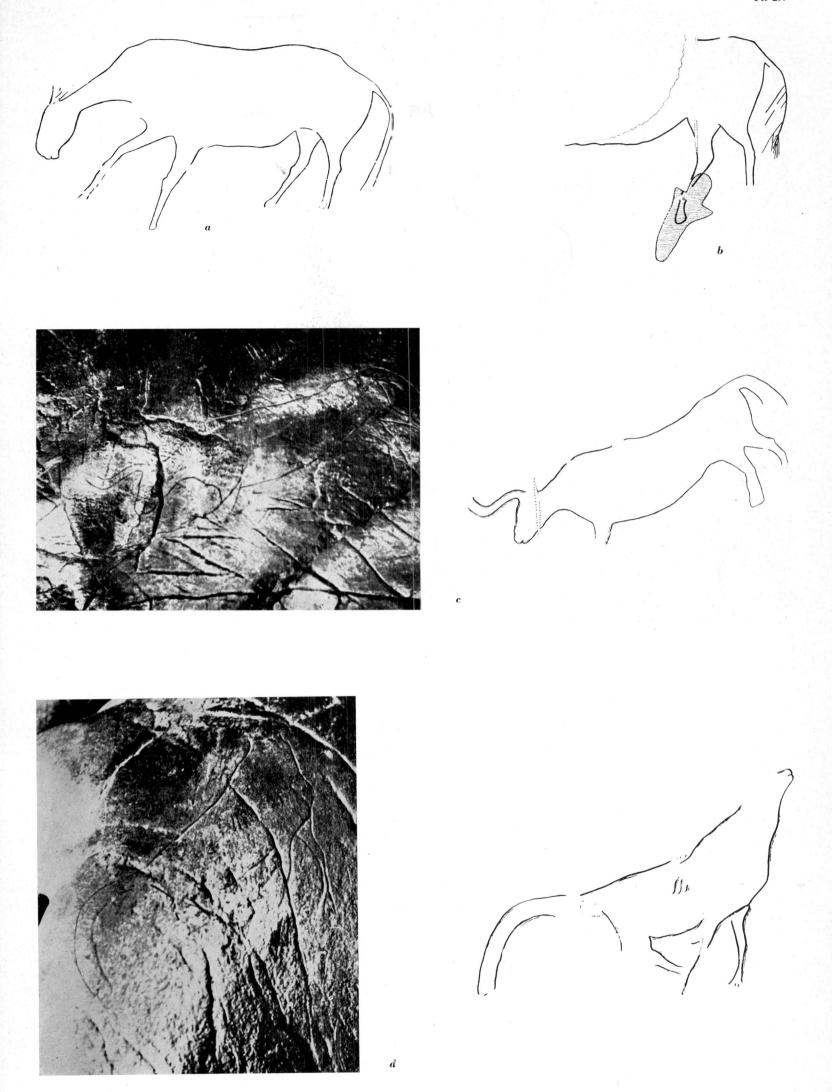

Levanzo (*Egadi*): *a*) horse, the same as in Pl. 298 *a*; *b*) horse with superimposed painting of late period; *c*) ox; *d*) probably a deer.

Pl. 300

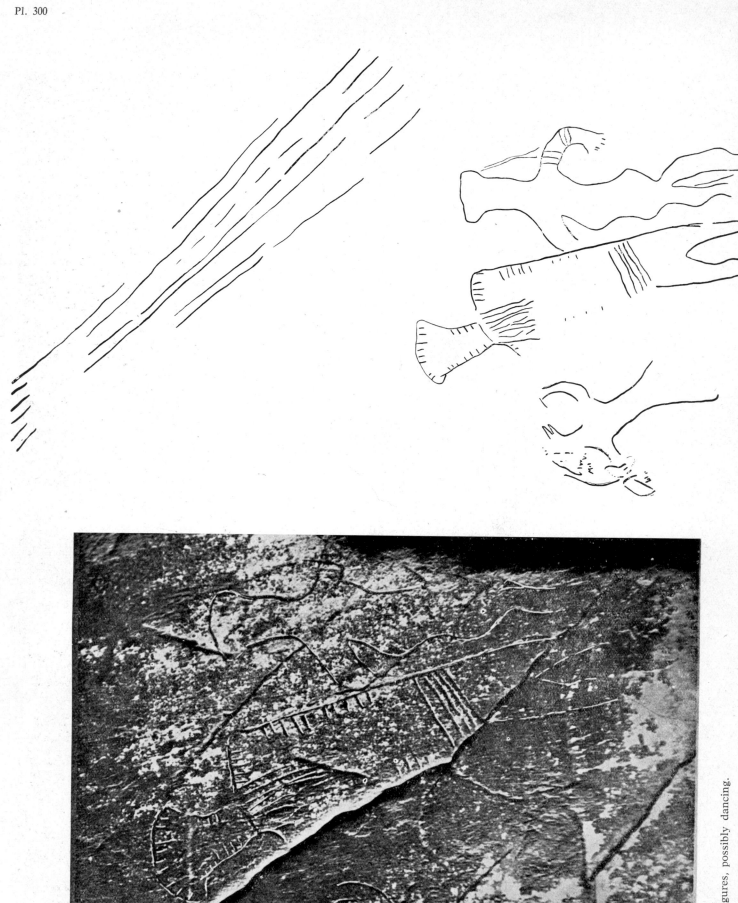

Levanzo (*Egadi*): masked human figures, possibly dancing.

Pl. 303

Monte Pellegrino (*Palermo*), Addaura Cave: men, woman carrying a pack on her shoulders (the same as in Pl. 302) and fallow-deer.

Pl. 304

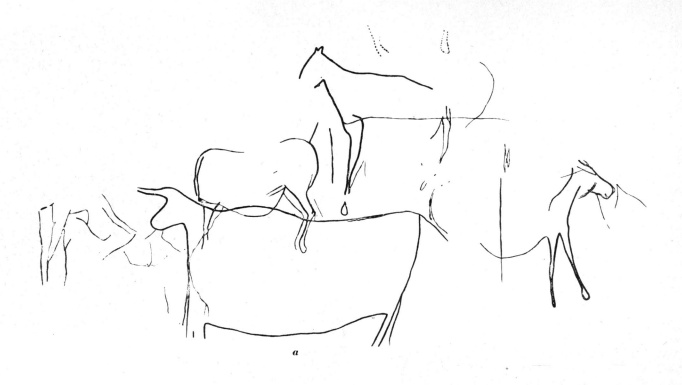

a

b

c

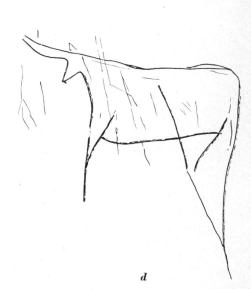

d

Monte Pellegrino (*Palermo*), Addaura Cave: horses and oxen, considerably schematized, (*a, d* according to Bovio Marconi's tracings).

Pl. 305

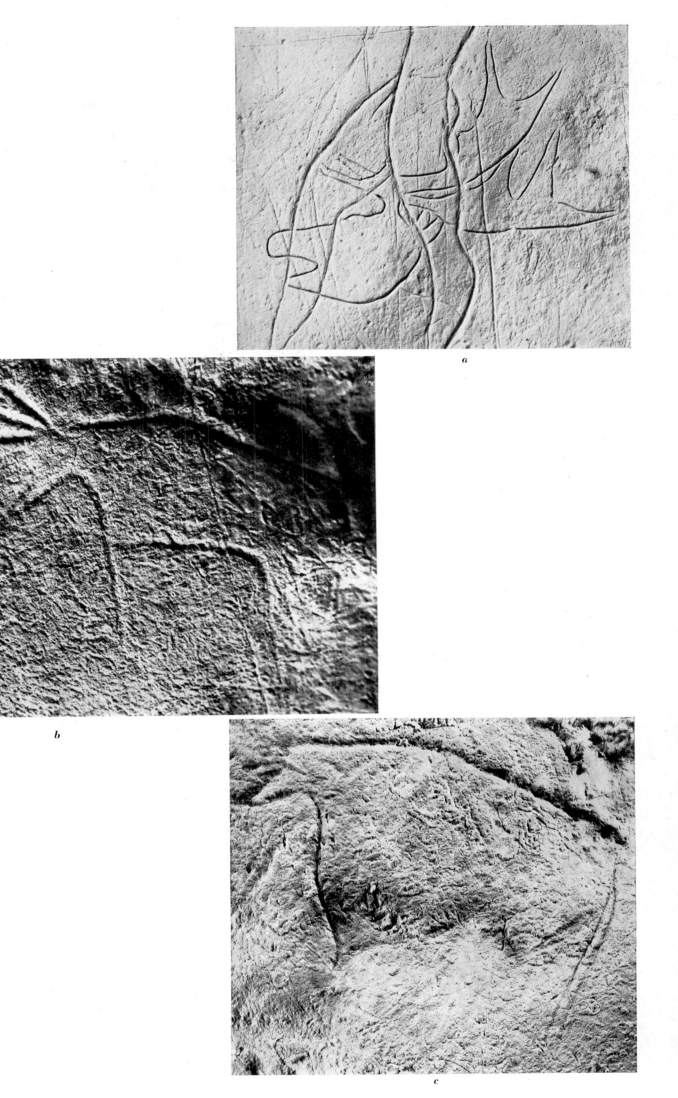

Monte Pellegrino (*Palermo*): *a*) Addaura Cave, fallow-deer head; *b*), *c*) Addaura B, more or less schematized animals, probably oxen.

Pl. 306

a

b

a) Monte Pellegrino (*Palermo*), Niscemi Cave: oxen and horses, *b*) same according to Bovio Marconi's tracings.

Black-and-white plates and color plates printed by Tipocolor, Florence
Text printed by « L'Impronta », Florence
Binding by Stabilimento Stianti, Sancasciano Val di Pesa, Florence.

3831